Cisco CCNA/CCENT Exam 640-802, 640-822, 640-816 Preparation Kit

Contributors

Naomi J. Alpern

David Andersson

Kimarie Hazelbaker

C. Eric Irvin

Steve Long

Johan Loos

Renato Martins

Kevin Miller

Derrick Rountree

Robert J. Shimonski

Scott Sweitzer

Cisco CCNA/CCENT Exam 640-802, 640-822, 640-816 Preparation Kit

Dale Liu
Lead Author and Technical Editor

Brian Barber
Contributing Technical Editor

Luigi DiGrande
Contributing Technical Editor

ELSEVIER

AMSTERDAM • BOSTON • HEIDELBERG • LONDON
NEW YORK • OXFORD • PARIS • SAN DIEGO
SAN FRANCISCO • SINGAPORE • SYDNEY • TOKYO
Syngress is an imprint of Elsevier

SYNGRESS

PUBLISHED BY
Syngress Publishing, Inc.
Elsevier, Inc.
30 Corporate Drive
Burlington, MA 01803

Cisco CCNA/CCENT Exam 640-802, 640-822, 640-816 Preparation Kit

ISBN 13: 978-1-59749-306-2

Publisher: Laura Colantoni
Acquisitions Editor: Rachel Roumeliotis
Developmental Editor: Matthew Cater
Lead Author and Technical Editor: Dale Liu
Project Manager: Andre Cuello

Page Layout and Art: diacriTech
Copy Editors: Audrey Doyle, Charles Roumeliotis
Indexer: diacriTech
Cover Designer: Michael Kavish

For information on rights, translations, and bulk sales, contact Matt Pedersen, Director of Corporate Sales, Elsevier; e-mail: m.pedersen@elsevier.com.

Library of Congress Cataloging-in-Publication Data
Liu, Dale.
   Cisco CCNA/CCENT exam 640-802, 640-822, 640-816 preparation kit / Dale Liu.
      p. cm.
   Includes index.
   ISBN 978-1-59749-306-2
1. Computer networks—Examinations—Study guides. 2. Telecommunications engineers—Certification. I. Title.
   TK5105.5.L567 2009
   004.6076—dc22
                                                                          2009016847

Printed in the United States of America
1 2 3 4 5 6 7 8 9 0

Contents

v

ACKNOWLEDGEMENTS

I would like to dedicate this book first to the staff, publisher, and editors at Syngress:

- Laura Colantoni, Publisher

- Matt Cater, Developmental Editor

- Rachel Roumeliotis, Senior Acquisitions Editor

I thank all of the other contributing authors, editors, and copy editors, without whom this project could not have succeeded!

I thank Tommy and the entire staff of the ***Bull and the Bear Tavern and Eatery,*** in Houston, Texas, especially Table no. 1, where a lot of the book was created and edited; you really have a great place to work!

And finally and most importantly, I dedicate this book to Amy Mitamura, my muse, inspiration, support, and in-house editor, whose continued support and understanding were vital for this process to come to completion!

I thank you all!

—Dale Liu

About the Authors

LEAD AUTHOR AND TECHNICAL EDITOR

Dale Liu (MCSE Security, CISSP, MCT, IAM/IEM, CCNA) has been working in the computer and networking field for more than 20 years. Dale's experience ranges from programming to networking to information security and project management. He currently teaches networking, routing, and security classes, while working in the field performing security audits and infrastructure design for medium to large companies.

Dale was the lead author and technical editor for *Next Generation SSH2 Implementation: Securing Data in Motion* (ISBN: 978-1-59749-283-6, Syngress), lead author and technical editor for *Cisco Router and Switch Forensics: Investigating and Analyzing Malicious Network Activity*, (ISBN: 978-1-59749-418-2, Syngress), technical editor for *The IT Regulatory and Standards Compliance Handbook: How to Survive an Information Systems Audit and Assessments* (ISBN: 978-1-59749-266-9, Syngress), and a contributing author to *Securing Windows Server 2008: Prevent Attacks from Outside and Inside your Organization* (ISBN: 978-1-59749-280-5, Syngress).

He currently resides in Houston, Texas, with two cats. He enjoys cooking and beer brewing with his girlfriend and live-in editor Amy.

CONTRIBUTING TECHNICAL EDITORS

Brian Barber (Linux+, MCSE, MCSA, MCP+I, MCNE, CNE, CNA-GW) works for the Canada Deposit Insurance Corporation (CDIC) as a project manager and architect for CDIC's IT service management program. His primary areas of interest are operating systems, infrastructure design, multiplatform integration, directory services, and enterprise messaging. He is also an experienced instructor and courseware developer. In the past he has held the positions of Principal Consultant with Sierra Systems Group Inc., Senior Technical Coordinator at the LGS Group Inc. (now a part of IBM Global Services), and Senior Technical Analyst at MetLife Canada. He has been co-author, technical editor, or lead author for more than 15 books and certification guides. Recently, he was a Contributing Technical Editor for *Cisco Router and Switch Forensics: Investigating and Analyzing Malicious Network Activity* (ISBN: 978-1-59749-418-2, Syngress).

Luigi DiGrande is a Senior Systems Administrator with Ingres Corporation. In his role at Ingres, Luigi supports the global IT infrastructure. Luigi specializes in working with Microsoft and Cisco-based systems. Luigi has designed and deployed Windows-based systems for over 10 years and has in-depth practical knowledge of how the client and server-based systems operate, Windows network and security, Exchange 2003/2007.

CONTRIBUTING AUTHORS

Naomi J. Alpern currently works for Microsoft as a consultant specializing in Unified Communications. She holds many Microsoft certifications, including an MCSE and MCT, as well as additional industry certifications such as Citrix-Certified Enterprise Administrator, CCNA, Security+, Network+, and A+. Since the start of her technical career she has worked in many facets of the technology world, including IT administration, technical training, and, most recently, full-time consulting. She likes to spend her time reading cheesy horror and mystery novels, when she isn't browsing the Web. She is also the mother of two fabulous boys, Darien and Justin, who mostly keep her running around like a headless chicken.

David Andersson (CCNA, MCT, MCSE, CIW Instructor, CIW Security Analyst, Master CIW Administrator, CNA, A+) is a CIS faculty member at the American Public University System. David instructs in the Information Technology degree and certificate curriculum, acts as the SME for the security, Cisco, and Microsoft-centric classes and is a key contributor to the classroom and online curriculum development of the Information Technology Program.

David holds a bachelor's degree from Indiana University, a master's degree from Western Kentucky University, a master's degree from ISIM University, an Ed.S. degree from Nova Southeastern University, his doctorate from Northcentral University, and is a member of the ACM and the IEEE. David currently resides in the Chicago metro area with his family, Nataliya, Elizabeth, Charles, and Lucy.

Kimarie Hazelbaker is a technical consultant and trainer specializing in designing, implementing, and troubleshooting local- and wide-area networks, using mostly Cisco devices. She has been working in the information technology industry for more than 20 years and has considerable experience with a variety of hardware, operating systems, and client and server applications. Kimarie currently operates her consulting and training business out of northwestern Colorado.

C. Eric Irvin (CISSP, MCITP: Enterprise Admin, MCSE, MCSA, CCNA) is a Security Engineering Analyst for Blue Cross and Blue Shield of Alabama, and consultant for IrvTech, LLC. He specializes in security project management, as well as end-user security awareness, and security compliance assurance. He specializes in Cisco routers, switches, and VPN solutions. His focus is in providing business-enablement solutions that provide functionality and security to the customers of his organization.

Eric holds a bachelor's degree from Amridge University, and is a member of Infragard and the Information Systems Security Association. He volunteers his security background with local municipal government organizations. Eric currently resides in Birmingham, Alabama.

Steve Long is a senior software engineer/systems analyst with Wilmington Trust. Steve has more than 14 years of database and application design and development experience. He currently provides database and application support to trading applications and processes using Microsoft technologies. He also serves as technical lead on significant projects in addition to lending his infrastructure, project management, and business process expertise to all initiatives. Before making a full-time switch to the information technology field, Steve spent a number of years working in the accounting field.

Steve holds a bachelor's degree from Goldey-Beacom College in Wilmington, Delaware, and a Client/Server Technology certification from Pennsylvania State University. He is currently working toward his graduate degree at Goldey-Beacom.

Johan Loos (Network+, Security+, MCT, MCITP, MCSE 2003 Security, CCNA, SCNA, GCWN, CEH) is an independent trainer/consultant at Access Denied, a company based in Belgium. He has several years of experience as a trainer and consultant. His specialization is security and he is involved in security projects for medium and enterprise-sized companies. He lives with his wife Anja and their son Stef.

Renato Martins (PMP, SCJP, SCWCD, ITIL Foundation MCSE, MCSA, MCPD, MCDBA, MCITP, MCTS, MCSD, MCAD, IBM Soa Designer, IBM DB2 DBA + Developer, IBM Portal Admin) has extensive teaching and information technology industry experience. Renato has created training material for programming (Delphi, ASP), database (SQL Server), and operating system (Windows Server) courses. He has been teaching at official training centers and universities since 1998.

Renato has worked as a developer/architect for Griaule Biometrics, creating image processing and fingerprint recognition solutions. In 2004, he joined IBM and worked on its services division in Brazil for more than 3 years. He moved to IBM's software group in Ireland, in mid-2008, where he currently provides level 2 support for Lotus and Websphere products.

Kevin Miller (CCNP, CCSP, CCDP, JNCIA-SSL, MCSE) is a Network Architect with Herman Miller Inc., an international office furniture manufacturer. From his home office in Huntsville, Alabama, he provides network management, design, and support services throughout Herman Miller's network. His primary areas of expertise include Cisco routing and switching, firewalls, wireless and web content services, as well as Juniper's SSL concentrators. Kevin's background includes significant experience with both VPN and Quality of Service technology. He was a contributing author to *Juniper(r) Networks Secure Access SSL VPN Configuration Guide* (ISBN: 978-1-59749-200-3, Syngress).

Derrick Rountree (CCNP, MCSE, MCT, CCEA, SSCP) has been in the IT industry for more than 15 years. He has a Bachelors of Science in Electrical Engineering degree. Derrick has held positions as a network administrator, IT consultant, and QA engineer. He has contributed to multiple Syngress publications in the areas of computer hardware and Citrix certification.

Robert J. Shimonski (MCSE, etc) is an entrepreneur, a technology consultant, and a published author with more than 20 years of experience in business and technology. Robert's specialties include designing, deploying, and managing networks, systems, virtualization, storage-based technologies, and security analysis. Robert also has many years of diverse experience deploying and engineering mainframes and Linux- and Unix-based systems such as Red Hat and Sun Solaris. Robert has in-depth work-related experience with and deep practical knowledge of globally deployed Microsoft- and Cisco-based systems and stays current on the latest industry trends. Robert consults with business clients to help forge their designs, as well as to optimize their networks and keep them highly available, secure, and disaster free.

Robert was the technical editor for and a contributing author to *Sniffer Pro Network Optimization & Troubleshooting Handbook* (ISBN: 978-1-931836-57-9, Syngress), the technical editor for *Security+ Study Guide and DVD Training System* (ISBN: 978-1-931836-72-2, Syngress), lead author and technical editor for *Network+ Study Guide & Practice Exams: Exam N10-003* (ISBN: 978-1-931836-42-5, Syngress), and technical editor for and a contributing author to *Building DMZs for Enterprise Networks* (ISBN: 978-1-931836-88-3, Syngress). Robert was most recently a contributing author to *Microsoft Vista for IT Security Professionals* (ISBN: 978-1-59749-139-6), a contributing author to *The Real MCTS/MCITP Configuring Microsoft Windows Vista Client Exam 70-620 Prep Kit* (ISBN: 978-1-59749-233-1, Syngress), and technical reviewer for *The Real MCTS/MCITP Windows Server 2008 Configuring Active Directory Exam 70-640 Prep Kit*, (ISBN: 978-1-59749-235-5, Syngress). Robert can be found online at www.shimonski.com.

Scott Sweitzer (CCNA, CCAI, MCSE, MCSA, MCITP, MCTS, MCP+I, MCT, A+, Network+, Server+, INet+, HTI+, DHTI+) is a senior analyst at Ricoh. He currently works with career changing students providing Microsoft training in Indianapolis, Indiana. His specialties include Cisco routers and LAN switches, Microsoft Windows NT4-2008, Virtualization, and Update services. He also works with home technology integration projects.

In addition Scott is the owner of consulting companies MicrosoftITPros.com and TrainingMicrosoft.net, where he works with the small and medium business market. Scott's background also includes positions as a Department Chair Technology Programs at Indiana Business College and systems engineer at the Systems House.

Scott and his family live in a suburb of Indianapolis.

Introduction to Networking

INTRODUCTION

To have a successful career as a Cisco Certified Network Associate (CCNA), it is imperative that you understand the terminology used by individuals in the field of networking. To communicate effectively with peers and staff, you need to have a firm grasp on concepts and jargon you will be exposed to as a CCNA. Understanding basic terms and concepts will be essential for any individual trying to become successful in the field of networking. An in-depth understanding of basic networking concepts is critical for any individual trying to pass the CCNA certification exam.

Successful CCNAs will need to be able to identify hardware associated with common networks, such as switches and routers. CCNAs also need to have a firm grasp of concepts such as Ethernet networks, Network Topologies and Protocols. The field of networking is constantly being revised and updated with newer, more efficient technologies. For this reason, it is also imperative that CCNAs keep abreast of the latest trends in the field, such as 802.11n, Voice over Internet Protocol (VoIP), and IPv6.

Cisco tends to be a leader in implementing new technologies in their hardware and software products. Cisco will therefore expect that individuals who pass their CCNA examination will have a grasp on the latest technology. This is one of the many reasons that the CCNA certification is widely respected and coveted by many people within the industry. To pass the certification exam and become a successful CCNA, it is essential to have a solid understanding of networking vocabulary and concepts.

NETWORKING HARDWARE

A number of different devices are available to run a network. In this section, we will take a look at the different types of devices, cabling, and new wireless technologies to assist you in understanding what devices accomplish what connectivity in the network. To understand the technology, we need a brief understanding of the seven-layer Open System Interconnect (OSI) model that helps us to understand where each device is, see Chapter 2 for more detail on the OSI model. The seven layers of the OSI model are shown in Table 1.1.

Each networking item will work at one or more of the OSI layers, and we will define them.

Exam Warning

Cisco places a lot of emphasis on the matching of devices to their OSI layer. Some devices will be described in an obscure manner, and you will have to identify the device. Pay close attention to the multiple ways some devices will be defined in this chapter.

Table 1.1 OSI Model Layers

Layer	Function
7 Application	Protocols that affect data like FTP, HTTP, SMTP, and so forth
6 Presentation	Compression of data, code conversion, and encryption
5 Session	Handshaking and virtual circuit setup
4 Transport	TCP and UDP ports and segmenting of data
3 Network	IP, routing, and creation of packets
2 Data link	MAC/physical address and creation of Frames
1 Physical	Cable, NIC, and breaking of frames into the bits that get transferred over the media

One more important item with the OSI model is that the different protocol data units created in Layers 4, 3, 2, and 1 will be important in what devices do what functions!

To have a network you will need five things:

- Sender
- Receiver
- Message
- Media
- Protocol

The *sender* prepares the *message* to send to the *receiver* over the *media* using the agreed upon set of rules called the *protocol*. The OSI model will help you to define and troubleshoot problems with your network and defines the different ways data are transmitted. There are three types of transmissions on your network. *Unicast traffic* is from one sender to one receiver. *Multicast traffic* is from one sender to a known group of receivers. *Broadcast traffic* is from one sender to an unknown number of receivers. Each of these traffic types will be referenced in the definitions and standards further in this chapter.

Cabling

There are two common methods of connectivity in networking today, the use of cables or the use of wireless. Cables come in many types of materials and methods of moving data; as we look at these types all cable media is at Layer 1 of the OSI model. The physical layer defines the media type, specifications, and the methods for transmitting bits across the media. All of these are important for the CCNA, and as we look at some legacy and current cable standards remember that on the test any of these can still be used for test questions.

Ethernet

Ethernet, originally developed by Robert Metcalf, Chuck Thacker, Butler Lampson, and David Boggs in 1972 to 1975 at the Xerox Palo Alto Research Center (PARC) in California, has become the most widely used standard for transmitting data inside a local area network (LAN). Over time it has defined standards using coaxial cable, twisted pair cable, and fiber optical cables.

Robert Metcalf left Xerox, he took the base of the protocol to Digital Equipment Corporation (DEC) and Intel and they worked on the proposed

Digital/Intel/Xerox (DIX) Standard of Ethernet. The first draft of the standard submitted to the Institute of Electrical and Electronic Engineers (IEEE) was the 802.3 Experimental Ethernet submitted by Xerox in 1972 and progressed to the DIX standard Ethernet II in 1982, and the first full IEEE Ethernet was 10BASE5 in 1983 (also called *ThickNet* as it used a thick piece of coax). The standard has progressed as technology has advanced in the areas of cable quality and speeds capable of being achieved.

All of the Ethernet standards use a transmission scheme known as carrier sense multiple access with (/) collision detection (CSMA/CD). All the devices on the shared media listen to the media, cable, for a break in transmission so that the listening device can transmit their message, if multiple messages are placed on the wire there will be a collision of the data messages. The system will detect the collision report to the transmitting stations and they will repeat their messages at a randomly determined amount of time later. The other method for transmission is CSMA/CA (used by the AppleTalk Protocol). It uses the same CSMA but instead of collision detection it uses collision avoidance; this technique sends a warning packet out to clear the line for the real message.

The Ethernet (802.3) standards that will be covered for the test are as follows:

- 10Base5

- 10Base2

- 10BaseT

- 100BaseTX

- 100BaseFX

- 1000BaseSX

- 1000BaseLX

- 1000BaseT

The way to read the aforementioned standards are to look at the left most number that is the speed of the protocol 10, 100, and 1,000 MBps, then the BASE is short for Baseband, meaning that each wire used carries a single signal. Neither multiplexing like frequency-division multiplexing (FDX) is being done nor is any other frequency shifting algorithm are being used. The last portion of the naming convention relates to some part of the wiring standards, for example, 5 designates thick coax cable specially designated for Thicknet standards with a 50 Ω characteristic. This inflexible coax cable could have a maximum run from endpoint to endpoint of 500 m.

Serial

In the CCNA level of information the serial lines are either WIC-1T or WIC-CSUDSU. The WIC1T has a V.32 serial connection that can support the following serial standards, V.35, X.21, RS-232, RS-449, RS-530, and the WIC-xx CSU DSU is an internal channel service unit/data service unit (CSU/DSU), with either one channel (56K) or full T1 (24 56K Channels). On the serial interfaces there are two sides to the circuit, the data terminal equipment (DTE) and the data circuit-terminating equipment (DCE).

On the DTE/DCE circuit there needs to be a signal that synchronizes the link. The signal is called *clock rate* in the Cisco IOS, without clock rate these devices would not be able to communicate. In this circuit the DCE provides the clock rate—remember C for DCE and C for clock rate and you will have no problems.

The IOS command to see what side of the DTE/DCE link you are is **show controllers sX**, where X is the interface number. For example, on a Cisco 1721 router with a link to another router upstream, the output of the command on the DTE and DCE side is displayed in Figures 1.1 and 1.2.

The V.35 connector on the serial WIC-1T is a d-shaped connector with 60 PINs. It can connect, with the appropriate cable from Cisco, to CSU/DSU's, modems, and other Layer 2 devices. The serial interface operates at the physical layer of the OSI model.

FIGURE 1.1

DTE Output of Show Controllers Command

```
CCNA_Router 2#sh controllers s0
Interface Serial0
Hardware is PowerQUICC MPC860
DTE V.35 TX and RX clocks detected.
idb at 0x83714200, driver data structure at 0x8371B90C
SCC Registers:
General [GSMR] = 0x2:0×00000030, Protocol-specific [PSMR] = 0x8
Events [SCCE] = 0x0000, Mask [SCCM] = 0x001F, Status [SCCS] = 0x06
Transmit on Demand [TODR] = 0x0, Data Sync [DSR] = 0x7E7E
Interrupt Registers:
Config [CICR] = 0x00365F80, Pending [CIPR] = 0x00008000
Mask   [CIMR] = 0x40204000, In-srv [CISR] = 0x00000000
Command register [CR] = 0x600
```

FIGURE 1.2

*DCE Output of Show
Controllers Command*

```
CCNA_Router 1#sh controllers s0
Interface Serial0
Hardware is PowerQUICC MPC860
DCE V.35, clock rate 64000
idb at 0x81DCF630, driver data structure at 0x81DD7444
SCC Registers:
General [GSMR] = 0x2:0x00000030, Protocol-specific [PSMR] = 0x8
Events [SCCE] = 0x0300, Mask [SCCM] = 0x001F, Status [SCCS] = 0x03
Transmit on Demand [TODR] = 0x0, Data Sync [DSR] = 0x7E7E
Interrupt Registers:
Config [CICR] = 0x00365F80, Pending [CIPR] = 0x00000000
Mask   [CIMR] = 0x40204000, In-srv [CISR] = 0x00000000
Command register [CR] = 0x600
```

RTS/CTS

On serial lines there is a signal called *Ready To Send/Clear To Send*. When working with CSU/DSUs and modems this signal is used to tell the device that it is ready to transmit. On each type of connector there is a wire that is designated for this signal, also this has been defined in the 802.11 wireless standards by the IEEE.

Exam Warning

Some of the Cisco test questions will have only minor differences in the way the answer is displayed. For example if Cisco was to ask the question; how do you set the clock rate on a serial interface to 64,000 bits per second?

   A. router > clock rate 64,000

   B. router# clock rate 64,000

   C. router(config)# clock rate 64,000

   D. router(config-line)# clock rate 64,000

   E. router(config-if)# clock rate 64,000

The correct answer would be **E**, the prompt of router(config-if)# would be displayed if you were working on serial interface 0. In this example the only difference in the answers are the prompt.

Next we will lay out the important things to know about Ethernet in Table 1.2.

Standard	Speed (MBps)	Cable Type	Distance
10Base5	10	Think coax	500 m endpoint to endpoint
10Base2	10	Thin coax	About 285 m from endpoint to endpoint
10BaseT	10	Cat 5 twisted pair	100 m from endpoint to hub or switch
100BaseTX	100	Cat 5 twisted pair	100 m from endpoint to hub or switch
100BaseFX	100	Fiber-optic cable	400 m half duplex 2 km full duplex
1000BaseSX	1,000	Fiber-optic cable	Multimode fiber 500 m
1000BaseLX	1,000	Fiber-optic cable	Single-mode fiber 5 km
1000BaseT	1,000	Cat 6 twisted pair	100 m from endpoint to hug or switch

Table 1.2 Ethernet Standards

Fiber

Fiber-optic cable is made of tiny glass strands and data is passed over the glass using light pulses. The first documented installation of fiber optics was in Chicago, IL, in 1976. There are two encoding methods for transmissions over the fiber: they are single-mode fiber (SMF) and multimode fiber (MMF). In SMF the optic cable carries only one stream of light, known as a mode, this one mode may vary in wavelength but carries only one stream. In MMF the glass core is larger and can handle multiple data streams. MMF is used more in local or campus area networks (CANs), supports data rates from 10 MBps to 10 GBps, and can sustain high speeds at distances up to 2 km. SMF is higher in cost and is generally used for high precision scientific applications.

The cable is constructed in the following manner; a core glass rod is surrounded by a coating called *cladding* that contains the light inside the glass core. The cladding is then surrounded by a shield called the *coating*. The coating is then surrounded by fibers to strengthen the cable so the glass core is not broken. Then finally the coating of polyvinyl chloride (PVC) surrounds all the other components. Each fiber-optic cable has to be terminated with some form of connector; each connector has different properties, connectivity type, and function. The most common connectors you will encounter in computer networking are straight tip/bayonet fiber-optic connector (ST/BFOC) and the SC could mean subscriber connector, standard connector, or Siemon connector depending on which standard you read. The ST/BFOC connector is more commonly used today.

To install a fiber you will need special tools and training. The cost of the tools is prohibitive and the training is expensive. Where you can buy a basic termination kit for twisted pair cables for under $40, the basic fiber tool kit runs near $700. This investment is unnecessary at the CCNA level as you will not be expected to terminate fiber at the entry level. The training for the 5-day basic *certified fiber-optic technician* (CFOT) is about $2,000.

NEW & NOTEWORTHY...

The Dollars and Sense of Fiber-Optic Training

There is a growing need for fiber-optic installers. If you invest in this training and you can become proficient in fiber installation and termination your job prospects will increase. The CFOT certification is a good add-on to the CCNA. For more information see the official fiber-optic association Web site www.thefoa.org/

Coax

An abbreviation of coaxial cable, coax is a type of cable with a central conductor surrounded by plastic coating, followed by a metal shield, and covered with PVC outer coating. There are two primary types of coax used in networking—Thicknet (10Base5) and Thinnet (10Base2). The components of a coax network are terminators, resistors that stop the signal from bouncing back and forth on the wire, adapters that connect the computers to the line, and the coax cable.

For 10Base5, the cable is a thick (about ½ an inch in diameter) coaxial cable that can carry signal from endpoint terminator to endpoint terminator 500 feet maximum. The adapter that is used is called a *vampire tap*, which has a sharp "tooth" that bites into the wire. The vampire tap uses a db-15 connection called an *attachment unit interface* (AUI) or *Digital Intel Xerox* (DIX) connector to connect the vampire tap to the network interface card (NIC). The cable type is RG-11 coaxial cable.

For 10Base2, the cable is thinner and it appears similar to the coax cable used for cable television. It can support signals from endpoint terminator to endpoint terminator of 185 m (nearly 200 m). It uses T style connectors to connect the personal computers (PCs) to the network. The cable type is RG-54 coaxial cable.

Both networks employ a bus topology (explained in detail later). When one computer on the network goes down you have to test each connection individually to determine which device caused the loss of connectivity. This is comparable to testing a set of Christmas tree lights one at a time to see which one is dead. The bus topology is a serial style network.

NICs

Network interface cards (NICs) come in many types, styles, connectivity types and speeds, and bus types. Let us start with bus types. Since the advent of the PC there have been many ways to add new features by way of add-on cards. They connect to the computer through a connector called a *Bus adapter*. These connectors allow you to add things like MODEMs (MODulator/DEModulator), serial adapters, parallel adapters, or NICs. The different bus types are as follows: 8 bit, 16 bit, 32 bit, and 64 bit. The chart mentioned later will cover the different bus types, and the features are shown in Table 1.3.

Once you determine that your computer supports the bus type, then you have to determine the type of network you are on; twisted pair, coax, or fiber. Once you have done all of this you need to determine the speed of your network 10/100/1,000 MBps. Once you have done all of this you can purchase an NIC. Today, the two most common network cards are PCI 32- or 64-bit running 10/100/1,000 twisted pair (RJ-45 connector) and PCI 32- or 64-bit running 1000 MBps over fiber-optic cable.

The purpose of the NIC is to join the media (Layer 1 of the OSI model) and the data link layer (OSI Layer 2) to the rest of the computer (Layers 3 to 7). This is the junction point where your computer meets the rest of the network. The network card is responsible also for the signaling of data onto the media and for receiving the signal from the media and making it useable for the computer. The data link layer functions of the network card include the Media Access Control (MAC) address of the card. This address, also known as the physical address, the Ethernet address, or if you are working with Cisco, the *Burned In Address* (BIA). This address is used to identify data destined for your computer as well as, when working with bridges or switches, in which collision domain you are located.

Table 1.3 PC Card Bus Types

Bus Name	Bit Rate	Connection Type	PC Platform
PC-XT	8 bit	Card edge	PC-XT
ISA (industry standard architecture)	16 bit	Card edge	PC-AT
EISA (enhanced ISA)	32 bit	Card edge	PC Pentium-based
Microchannel	32 bit	Card edge	IBM proprietary
PC card	16 bit	ISA in PCMCIA card	Early laptops
Cardbus	32 bit	PCI in a PCMCIA card	Laptops
PCI	32/64 bit	Card edge	Modern PCs

The MAC address is a 48-bit address that uses hexadecimal numbers (base 16 0-F). It can be displayed in a standard notation or Cisco notation. It has a total of six 8-bit bytes and the first three are the organization and the last three are the id of the network card. In Figure 1.3, the MAC address is displayed in standard notation; in Figure 1.4, the MAC address is displayed in Cisco notation. In the first image the MAC address is referred to the physical address and is 00-0E-35-0B-28-3E, the 00-0E-35 is the identifier for the manufacturer of the network card (Intel in this case), and the 0B-28-3E

FIGURE 1.3

Display of MAC Address

```
Ethernet adapter Wireless Network Connection:

        Connection-specific DNS Suffix .:
        Description...................: Intel(R) PRO/Wireless 2200BG Network
Connection
        Physical Address...........: 00-0E-35-0B-28-3E
        Dhcp Enabled..............: Yes
        Autoconfiguration Enabled.....: Yes
        IP Address...................: 192.168.3.102
        Subnet Mask...................: 255.255.255.0
        IP Address...................: fe80::20e:35ff:fe0b:283e%7
        Default Gateway.................: 192.168.3.1
        DHCP Server...................: 192.168.3.1
        DNS Servers...................: 192.168.3.1
                        fec0:0:0:ffff::1%2
                        fec0:0:0:ffff::2%2
                        fec0:0:0:ffff::3%2
        Lease Obtained.................: Thursday, September 18, 2008 1:47:04
PM
        Lease Expires.................: Saturday, September 20, 2008 1:47:04
PM
```

FIGURE 1.4

Cisco Format of MAC Address

```
CCNA_Router 1#sh int
FastEthernet0 is up, line protocol is up
  Hardware is PQUICC_FEC, address is 0014.a875.8f39 (bia 0014.a875.8f39)
Internet address is 192.168.2.241/24
MTU 1500 bytes, BW 100000 Kbit, DLY 100 usec,
  reliability 255/255, txload 1/255, rxload 1/255
Encapsulation ARPA, loopback not set
Keepalive set (10 sec)
Full-duplex, 100Mb/s, 100BaseTX/FX
ARP type: ARPA, ARP Time out 04:00:00
```

is the unique card identifier. If you have two cards on the network with the same MAC address there will be a conflict and neither will receive any data. All network devices on your network must have a unique MAC address.

Test Day Tip

Remember the format of the MAC address, the first three bytes identify the manufacturer and the last three bytes identify the host.

The MAC/physical address is known as the BIA in Cisco Speak. Anytime on the exam you are asked for the BIA of the network adapter of a PC, they are asking for the MAC/physical address.

Wired

We discussed coax and fiber-optic cable types earlier; here we will focus on twisted pair and the standards and uses of this cable type.

Twisted pair cable is rated by the category. Each category is measured by twists per inch. The most common twisted pair cable in use is still Category 5 twisted pair and it has three twists per inch using 24-gauge copper cable.

In Table 1.4, we will outline the different categories of twisted pair cable and their common uses.

In view of the increasing speeds of networking, categories 5e and 6 are being installed in most new networks. There are two common twisted pair types, unshielded twisted pair (UTP) and shielded twisted pair (STP). UTP can be purchased in each category and this type of cable does not have a metal shielding that protects the cable from electromagnetic interference (EMI). If you run UTP cable near motors or other devices that generate EMI,

Table 1.4 Twisted Pair Standards

Category	Number of Pairs	Maximum Data Speed (MBps)	Common Usage
Category 1	2	1	Voice/modem
Category 2	2	4	IBM cabling and Token Ring
Category 3	4	16	High-speed Token Ring
Category 4	4	20	High-speed Token Ring
Category 5	4	100	100BaseTX Ethernet
Category 5e	4	1,000	1000BaseT short run
Category 6	4	1,000	1000BaseT 100 m run

like older microwaves and photocopiers, the network will not work reliably as their signals will overshadow the signal carried over the cable. STP has a metal shielding that protects the cable from this interference. If EMI is a high concern, fiber optic is the best cable type as it uses light instead of electronic signals to represent the data.

The other measure for twisted pair is the coating.

HEAD OF THE CLASS...

Cable coating, law, and safety
If you chose the wrong coating for the cable type and run them in your building you may not only be violating building code, you could be putting lives in danger.

The two types of coating are plenum and nonplenum. The term plenum refers to the space between a drop ceiling and the real roof. To be plenum grade cable your cables should not contain PVC as this cable is in the "air space" between the two ceilings and if the PVC burns it gives off a toxic gas that is highly poisonous. If you use nonplenum grade cable they must be run in pipes in the walls and ceilings called *conduits*. These conduits will contain the toxic gas and protect the people. Most cables today are plenum grade, but be sure to check.

Now that you are familiar with the common wired cable types of twisted pairs, it is time to talk about the connector. The most commonly used connector with twisted pair cabling is called the *RJ-45 connector*. It is a four pair modular connector available in two types, *straight through* and *cross over*. The straight through cable connects devices that are different in nature; you would use a straight through cable to connect a computer to a switch, hub, or bridge. A cross over cable is for connecting similar device types, such as bridge to bridge, switch to switch, computer to computer, and so forth. The differences between the two types of cables are in the Telecommunications Industry Association/Electronics Industry Alliance (TIA/EIA) Cable Definitions for the type of wiring in each end of the cable. The two standards are defined in the TIA/EIA 568-A and TIA/EIA 568-B. If the 568-A standard is used on both ends of the cable it is a straight through cable, both sides have the pins in the same place. If one side is 568-A and the other side is 568-B then this is a crossover cable. The cable standards for both cable end types are given in Tables 1.5 and 1.6.

Finally, you can make your own twisted pair cables with just a couple of simple tools. With a few tools called a crimp tool and wire stripper and a supply of cable and ends, also known as bullets, you can build your own TIA/EIA twisted pair cables. Some companies sell complete tool kits that will

Table 1.5	TIA/EIA 568-A Cable End
Pin	**Color**
1	White green stripe
2	Green solid
3	White orange stripe
4	Blue solid
5	White blue stripe
6	Orange solid
7	White brown stripe
8	Brown solid

Table 1.6	TIA/EIA 568-B Cable End
Pin	**Color**
1	White orange stripe
2	Orange solid
3	White green stripe
4	Blue solid
5	White blue stripe
6	Green solid
7	White brown stripe
8	Brown solid

also do phone and coax cables. The wire stripper gets rid of the protective shell of the cable and also the protective shield of each strand. Once the cables are stripped place the correct strand into the correct place in the cable end. Once all strands are in the correct place you would use the crimp tool to close the cable end and create the cable.

Once you have the cables you will also need to test the connectivity of the tools. There are many types of cable testers available to test the tools. One important thing to remember with twisted pair is that the maximum length from endpoint to endpoint is only 100 m. If you have a cable between the computer and the wall jack and then from the wall jack to the switch and/or the hub and they are more than 100 m total—your cables may be correctly built but you have exceeded the maximum distance!

CONFIGURING & IMPLEMENTING...

Cable Kits

Tool kits for all types of cable making and testing can be purchased from Tecra Tools, which is located at www.tecratools.com

The two most common test tool types are *tone and probe* and *cable integrity testing*. With the tone and probe you would plug a device into the jack that would provide an audible tone across the cable, and you would use the probe to follow the wire through the walls until you found the other end where it terminated. The cable integrity testing tool tells you if the cable is pined out correctly and that there are no shorts or flaws in the cable. Both these tools will aid you in the network diagnostics.

Wireless

As users want more freedom of movement while using computer equipment and as networks grow in flexibility, wireless technology is increasing in use. There are a few standards you need to know to prepare for the CCNA exam. Table 1.7 covers the basics of wireless Ethernet today.

Just like with NIC defined earlier, you will need a card or an imbedded card to access wireless network systems. The same rules apply to computer bus type; however, you will need to know what standards are supported. Most wireless adapters today support either A only or B and G only, or B and G and N only. There were a few manufacturers that made cards that would support A and B, but they were very expensive and very rare. There are many problems with deploying a wireless network. The construction of the building is very important to the range you can get as well as other devices that are between the wireless card and the access point (wireless connector) that you are trying to reach. If you have a lot of steel or brick, you will find it difficult to achieve the maximum range. Also, if you have devices that operate

Table 1.7 Wireless Standards

Standard	Maximum Speed	Frequency (GHz)	Range (m)
802.11a	54	5	>30
802.11b	11	2	~30
802.11g	54	2	~30
802.11n	200	2	~30

at the same frequency (for example in the 2 GHz range certain appliances like microwave ovens will interfere with your wireless access) and may keep your entire wireless network from working.

The other major component with wireless networking is called the *wireless access point* (WAP). This device connects the wireless network to the wired network and you will normally find it connected to the switch or router. This device allows anyone who knows the Service Set IDentifier (SSID), this is the name of the wireless network and can be set via the WAPs control software, to connect to that wireless network.

CONFIGURING & IMPLEMENTING...

SSID and Security

Once you setup a wireless network take a few moments to change all the default security settings. Change the default SSID, password, and admin username. More than 70 percent of the WAPs on the Internet still have all the default settings making you vulnerable to attackers.

Once you have configured the basic attributes, like the Internetwork Protocol (IP) address and SSID, of a wireless network you then should select an encryption protocol. There are a few encryption protocols that will be described later in this chapter; however, even if you enable an encryption protocol you may want to set up a firewall between the WAP and the wired network to give another layer of protection. Most encryption protocols for wireless have been breached by attackers and the methods are well documented. With a firewall between the wireless and wired network, part of the defense in depth methodology (DID), you can implement a virtual private network (VPN) connection between the wireless client and the firewall and create a higher encrypted tunnel between the weak wireless and the secure wired network (Figure 1.5).

Test Day Tip

Make sure that you know the frequency and standard for each wireless type. Cisco expects all CCNAs to be familiar with these key facts.

The keys to the wireless portion of the Cisco exam is to remember the standards defined earlier and that security of wireless should conform to the DID methodology.

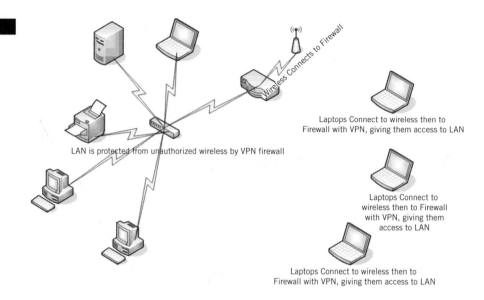

FIGURE 1.5

Wireless LAN to VPN Firewall for Access to Wired LAN

Laptops Connect to wireless then to Firewall with VPN, giving them access to LAN

LAN is protected from unauthorized wireless by VPN firewall

Laptops Connect to wireless then to Firewall with VPN, giving them access to LAN

Laptops Connect to wireless then to Firewall with VPN, giving them access to LAN

Security

The problem with wireless networks is that they can be difficult to secure. In the aforementioned illustration, we talked about a way to allow wireless users to attach to the wireless network then make a VPN connection to the wired secure network. There are protocols that will give you some protection on the wireless network. Later, we will give you an overview of the wireless secure encryption protocols. These protocols will help to protect your wireless network but due to the limitations of each protocol, you will face some exposure to hackers.

WEP

Wired Equivalency Protocol (WEP), established in 1999, was intended to provide the same level of protection across the wireless network that you would have over the wired (or twisted pair Category 5 cable) network. The problem was that the level of encryption was not strong enough to provide the level of protection available. Today WEP can be broken in minutes, with common software tools available over the Internet. It uses the RC4 (Rivest Cipher 4) encryption algorithm and the CRC-32 Check Sum (CRC means cyclical redundancy check) hashing algorithm. The RC4 encryptions the traffic and the CRC-32 ensures that the data is received without errors. WEP was the first attempt to secure the wireless networks from abuse by hackers and other attackers.

WPA

Wi-Fi Protected Access (WPA) was developed as a solution to the WEP protocols shortcomings. There are actually two protocols in the WPA specification,

WPA and WPA2. WPA was the introductory encryption protocol; it was a stopgap between WEP and WPA2, which is the full WPA standard implementation. In each protocol there are also two implementations, personal and enterprise. The major difference between personal and enterprise is that in personal mode the preshared key is available to all devices, and in enterprise the key is contained on a server with authentication. WPA2 is compliant with the complete specifications of the WPA standards.

NEW & NOTEWORTHY...

WPA and WPA2 Specifications

To view the complete standards for WPA and WPA2 go to www.wi-fi.org/knowledge_center/wpa/. This will help you to understand the encryption protocols strengths and weaknesses.

LEAP

Lightweight Extensible Authentication Protocol (LEAP) is a new protocol that, while being a proprietary wireless access authentication method, is not widely used today and is something on the horizon. This protocol requires you to authenticate (log in) to the wireless network before actually connecting to the LAN with your wireless (802.11) devices. This protocol gives you not only an encryption standard but also an authentication requirement. The LEAP Protocol uses a modified version of the Microsoft Challenge Authentication Protocols (MS-CHAP) combined with the Extensible Authentication Protocols (EAP). By combining the encryption with the authentication you add a layer of security to the wireless network. Even with the added security, you must remember the layered defensive tactics, which allows you to protect your key business data from exposure. Figure 1.5 shows a VPN connection device between a wireless user and the wired network is still the best method of protection.

Repeaters

A repeater is a Layer 1 device that takes voltage from the line, amplifies the voltage, and sends it down the line. This device cannot translate, analyze, manipulate, or do any processing of the voltage. It is a simple amplifier that will increase the signal strength of the signal. If there is any "noise" caused by EMI on the wire it will also amplify the noise and send it on. The general rule of thumb is to have no more than three repeaters in a row. Once you get past the third repeater you will be sending only noise.

These devices work with only one media type. If you have Thinnet coming in, you must have Thinnet going out; it cannot do any media conversion.

This is the most basic device and has no processor or programming to make it any more robust.

These devices are not in common use anymore; they have been replaced by hubs, bridges, and switches.

Hubs

A hub is nothing more than a multiport repeater. Electrical signal comes through one port of the hub and gets amplified and sent out through all ports of the hub. Like the repeater you cannot mix and match media. Hubs and repeaters create what is called a collision domain. You can only have one signal on the wire at any one time. As described earlier, Ethernet uses CSMA/CD, which means that if two signals are on the wires at the same time they will collide and cause a collision. This collision means that no data is delivered to the remote receiver. The more ports you have on the hubs (and the more hubs connected together), the more likely you are to have collisions. If you look at the front of the hub you will see an indicator called the *collision light*, the more often it blinks the more often your data is not getting to its destination.

Bridges

Bridges area is a Layer 2 device that separates collision domains by determining what MAC addresses are on each side of the bridge and only passing traffic if the destination address is on the other side of the bridge. The bridge will also handle the placing of the data on the collision domain to try and reduce the collisions. It also uses CSMA/CD and will check the frame for errors and collisions on each side of the bridge. Bridges create broadcast domains. Frames with a MAC address of FF:FF:FF:FF:FF:FF are called *broadcast frames* and every network device must look at the data; therefore, any frame that is a broadcast must cross all bridges.

Switches

A switch is a multiport bridge. This device creates a new collision domain on each port, the original intent of switches was to connect a hub to each port and connect departmental devices to the hub. For example, you would have a hub that contained the sales-people's computers and a file and print server so that if the sales Person was working on their own files it would not affect the rest of the network. The same would go for the marketing department, the finance department, and so forth. This would reduce the traffic that had to be processed by the switch and would speed up the overall network. This would ensure that the switch had tables of MAC addresses on each port and that would be contained in its own collision domain and the switch would only forward traffic when resources were outside its own collision domain. More and more each device has been plugged into its own port on the switch creating a single device collision domain. This means that each frame created on the network must be looked at on the switch and checked for errors and forwarded by the switch. Each frame must be processed by the switch thus negating the collision domains. This causes collisions on the backbone of the switch and buffer overflows on the ports where corporate resources are located. In Figure 1.6 we see a switch with devices on each port; this has become less than the standard in today's networking. Notice Destination Port FastEthernet0/8 has three MAC addresses assigned to it. So if the devices of 0011.50ff.971c, 0011.d918.e6fe, and 001c.b3333.428e were communicating together the data would not enter the switch. If 0011.50ff.971c and 007.e974.8217 were communicating the switch would send the frame to FastEthernet0/3 to reach that destination MAC address. Use the **show mac-address-table** command (sh mac-add in the Figure 1.6) on the switch to display this table.

Two questions I hear a lot are "What is a Layer 3 switch?," and "What is the difference between a Layer 2 switch and a Layer 3 switch?" First, there is no such thing as a Layer 3 switch. All switching is done at the data link layer of the OSI model. It uses the MAC address to move frames from one collision

```
Switch#sh mac-add
Dynamic Address Count:            12
Secure Address Count              0
Static Address {User-defined} Count   0
System Self Address Count:        35
Total MAC addresses:              47
Maximum MAC addresses:            2048
Non-static Address Table:
Destination Address     Address Type     VLAN     Destination Port
----------------------   -----------------   -------   ----------------------
0007.e974.8217          Dynamic          1        FastEthernet0/3
000e.832a.f4b2          Dynamic          1        FastEthernet0/1
0011.50ff.971c          Dynamic          1        FastEthernet0/8
0011.d918.e6fe          Dynamic          1        FastEthernet0/8
0014.a875.8f39          Dynamic          1        FastEthernet0/2
0019.0725.1355          Dynamic          1        FastEthernet0/3
001c.b333.428e          Dynamic          1        FastEthernet0/8
001d.60b5.4a6b          Dynamic          1        FastEthernet0/3
001d.726e.e4d8          Dynamic          1        FastEthernet0/9
0030.6ec4.e566          Dynamic          1        FastEthernet0/5
00c0.9f0e.b917          Dynamic          1        FastEthernet0/7
00c0.9f0e.b993          Dynamic          1        FastEthernet0/6
Switch#
```

FIGURE 1.6

Display of MAC Table on Cisco Catalyst Router

domain to the other. The Router (described later) handles the movement from one logical network to the other. A Layer 3 switch is a Layer 2 switch that has an embedded router to route between virtual local area network (VLANs).

Routers

At the network layer we find Routers. Routers handle IP addresses. These addresses are 32-bit addresses divided into 8-bit octets. Each octet can support a number from 0 to 255 (256 combinations). There are five classes of addresses A, B, and C are used to address publicly accessible devices on the Internet. To determine the class of address you will look at the first octet of the address. In later chapters you will see more on this but for now we will look at the basics. If the first octet is 1 through 126 you are a Class A address that means the first octet, by default, is the network portion of the address and the remaining three octets are the host. This supports 16,777,214 addresses per Class A network. Class B networks are 128 through 191 and the first two octets are the network portion of the address, meaning that for each Class B network there are 65,534 hosts per network. The final class of network for addressing workstations is Class C and that uses 192 through 223 in the first octet. The Class C uses the first three octets for network and the last octet for host, allowing 254 addresses per network. The network 127 is reserved for testing and the address 127.0.0.1 is called either as *loopback* or *local host address*. Each computer uses this to test that the IP stack is configured and functional on the device. Routers work at this layer and the key to routers is that they join IP networks. They are the intersections of two, or more, networks. Routers pass packets from one logical network to another logical network. They use the Internet Protocol address and network mask to determine which interface to pass the packet. In the aforementioned examples, each device had a different name from two ports to multiple ports, a multiport repeater was a hub and a multiport bridge was a switch. In this case a multiport router is a router. There is another device called a *Brouter*, this device is a Layer 3 router that can bridge Layer 2 protocols over a wide area network (WAN). A brouter will move nonroutable protocols over the WANs. Historically there are two major groups of protocols, routable (they have a network portion and a host portion of the address) and nonroutable (no network portion, only host portion of the address). Before brouters were created only routable protocols could be moved over the WAN. Routable protocols include IP, IPX, AppleTalk, SNA. Nonroutable protocols include data link control (DLC), NetBUI, LAT, DRP, and MOP. Back in the minicomputer days there was a computer called the *HP 3000*. It ran the DLC protocol and there was no network address, only a host address to move data from one HP 3000 to another over a WAN you needed a router that could also act as a Layer 2 bridge. Cisco routers today all support bridging.

Exam Warning

One of the things to remember is that a multiport repeater is a hub, a multiport bridge is called a switch, and a multiport router is called a router. These may show up as a few test questions on the exam.

One question about routers that I hear a lot is "Is there such a thing as a single port router? If you only have one port on the router, how can you route to two or more logical IP networks?" The answer is yes, you can have a single port router, if you plug the router into a switch on a port that is setup to be a port that will allow you to route between VLAN's, then this one port can move traffic between these networks. It can also be called a *router on a stick*.

Wireless Access Point

A WAP is a device that allows different types of wireless network cards connect without cables, hence wireless, to connect to LANs and access resources, including the Internet. A WAP plugs into a hub or switch and is the device that joins the unwired network to the wired network. As shown earlier, you can put a router or firewall between the wireless network and the wired network providing a secure barrier between the unsecure wireless network and the secure wired network. WAPs support the standards we defined earlier; if you are using an 802.11b WAP then most 802.11b/g/n cards should be able to access them as they all operate on the same 2 GHz frequency. If you have an 802.11a access point you will need an 802.11a card as this is not in the same frequency as the other standards. There are a few access points that support both the 2 GHz and the 5 GHz range. They are rare and expensive. There are also routers that support wireless connections as well. They range from home use to commercial/business use. For home use, you will find Linksys (a Cisco company) routers that will support both wired and wireless access to digital subscriber line (DSL) or cable Internet connections, all the way up to the Cisco 1800 line that are commercial level routers that include a wireless feature set as well as wired connections. The price range runs from $80 to $5,000 depending on the features and level of router you purchase.

NETWORK TYPES

The various network types you will have to deal with on the CCNA exam are LAN, CAN, metropolitan area network (MAN), and WAN. These types of networks define the technology you use to build them out. Later we will define them and discuss what makes each one different.

Local Area Networks

A LAN is a logical grouping of computers, servers, workstations, printers, and other devices that are connected by a common media; copper and fiber are the most common, and wireless is increasing. It supports speeds from 10 up to 1,000 MBps (Gigabit per second). It can span one floor of a building up to the entire building. The company that uses the LAN generally owns and manages the LAN. Some companies may outsource management of the LAN, but in general it remains the property of the company that owns it. Ethernet is used as the method of transmitting the data over the LAN and the speeds tend to be high.

Private IP Address Ranges

On the LAN there are three ranges of addresses reserved for internal, private usage. Earlier we talked about the three classes of IP address, there is one Class A network, the 10.0.0.0/8. In the Class B range we have 16 Class B networks, the 172.16.0.0/16 to the 172.31.0.0/16 networks and finally in the Class C range we have the 192.168.0.0/24 to the 192.168.255.0/24 networks. If you are using one of these networks you are conforming to the Internet standards. If you are using any other range of addresses and your Router/Firewall is using network address translation (NAT) you are still working within the guidelines of the Internet (using a NAT protocol called NAT overlapping where your inside addresses appear to be public and you are being translated to the true public Internet); however, if your Router/Firewall stops performing, the NAT function you will be changing the routing tables of the Internet and redirecting traffic to your network from the original network. This may cause other problems of a routing and a legal nature. You should always use a private range of network addresses while supporting an IPv4 Network, later you will be introduced to the new IPv6 (or IPng Internet Protocol Next Generation Protocol). For even more information refer to *Configuring IPv6 for Cisco IOS*, Syngress, ISBN: 978-1-928994-84-8. Once you have chosen your private IP range you can then subnet it (refer section "Subnetting" in Chapter 3).

APIPA

Automatic Private Internet Protocol Addressing (APIPA) assigns an address in the range of 169.254.0.1 through 169.254.255.254. It does not assign an address for the gateway router so no Internet access is permitted; see RFC 3972 for complete detail. It was introduced in Windows 98 Second Edition and other operating systems near the end of the 90s. APIPA was intended to allow access to local resources when the Dynamic Host Configuration

Protocol (DHCP) server was not available. Even though this uses what is apparently a public IP address range, it is not a risk due to the fact that it does not route traffic to the Internet, as there is not gateway address set.

Wide Area Networks

WANs connect networks from city to city or state to state or country to country (or even earth to the international space station). They employ technologies like Frame Relay, which uses connectivity like T1s or T3s. A T1 Frame Relay moves data at 1.544 MBps and a T3 is 28 T1s and will carry data at the rate of approximately 43 MBps. As the name implies Frame Relay operates at the data link layer (Layer 2 of the OSI model). You will notice that the data rates drop dramatically from the LAN to the WAN. Thus, the bottleneck of the connection is the point between the LAN and the WAN. Cable Internet and DSL have become more common over the last couple of years. There are other technologies like X.25 that can carry data over long distances; however, these legacy protocols are not in common usage.

Public IP Address Ranges

If the ranges of addresses are not in the 10.0.0.0/8 or the 172.16.0.0/16 through 172.31.0.0/16 or the 192.168.0.0/24 through 192.168.255.0/24/24, you are on the "public" Internet. Let us first deal with the concept of the "public" Internet. Every access device, router, server, database, Web page is owned by someone. There is not one device on the Internet that is freely available and on the public domain. Every resource is owned by some company, agency of a government, or individual. The Internet was initially designed for the military to allow for teletype printers to receive orders and launch codes from the military in the event of a global nuclear war. In 1990 the initial Internet, then called the Advanced Research Projects Agency (ARPA) network, that was designed to allow connectivity with the government and university research networks to share data, was passed off to the National Science Foundation. This network not only allowed the government and research facilities to share data, but also allowed high technology companies to participate in this information sharing. In 1993, researchers at the University of Illinois Urbana, Champaign developed the first graphical browser for the Hypertext Transfer Protocol (HTTP) developed by Tim Berners-Lee in 1989. Before 1995 when the "Internet" was opened up to the public, companies that were allowed to (government, university and high tech companies), had to purchase a block of addresses that allowed access to the resources available over these interconnected networks of private networks.

Metropolitan Area Networks

MANs are networks where one local telecommunications provider connects your building in a single area code. These networks were very popular in the 70s and 80s as it allowed you to connect multiple buildings that could not be connected privately due to distance. Most of these have been replaced with newer connectivity to the Internet and then the buildings are connected via point to point VPNs. The keys to this part of the exam is to understand that while not in common use today, MANs employ many of the same features and structures of WANs. The same Frame Relay Networking is used (see WAN mentioned earlier) to connect the different LANs over the common telecommunications frame works.

Campus Area Networks

CANs are defined as a network that is owned by the organization and uses either fiber-optic cable or wireless bridges to connect buildings together that are in one contained area, like a college campus (hence the name). Companies use CANs to share local area resources between separate buildings (see Figure 1.7).

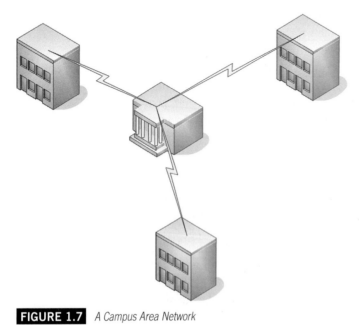

FIGURE 1.7 *A Campus Area Network*

Virtual Private Networks

VPNs are encrypted communications between one endpoint and another, and they come in two varieties, point to point VPNs or remote access VPNs. In a point to point VPN you are connecting one building to another over the Internet; you will either use a VPN concentrator (dedicated VPN device), a firewall, or a router on each end. This allows users on each side of the point to point connection to access resources on the other side of the connection. This also makes it possible to create a LAN over multiple locations and share resources like active directory and DHCP servers, thus reducing the cost of resources needed in a company. The remote access VPNs allow individual people from any location that has connectivity to the Internet to connect to the corporate office and the resources contained therein. With a remote access VPN you have your PC or laptop computer with a wired, wireless, or modem connection to the Internet and you use client software (either native to the device, or provided by the VPN provider, like Cisco VPN client). You configure the client with the Internet Protocol (IP) address of the VPN connector at the companies' location. You then authenticate using a username and password, once connected you have whatever rights you have to resources as allowed by the VPN policy (See *Firewall Policies and VPN Configurations*, Syngress, ISBN: 978-1-59749-088-7) Some of the encryption technologies used in VPN connections are Data Encryption Standard (DES), Triple Data Encryption Standard (3DES), and Advanced Encryption Standard (AES).

Storage Area Networks

Storage area networks (SANs) are used to increase the speed of data retrieval between servers and data storage devices. The data storage devices are separated from the servers and connected by some high-speed (like fiber) media. The storage, even though separated, appears local. SANs allow servers to access more types of storage and in larger capacities than they could handle locally.

NETWORKING TOPOLOGIES

A network topology describes how devices on a network communicate over the shared access media. There are many different topologies; however, for the Cisco CCNA Exam the ones you need to focus on are listed and described later. The two most common topologies in use today are the Star and the Star-Bus. These work with the 802.3 Ethernet standards as we defined earlier.

Star

This topology employs a central connectivity device, either a hub or a switch, and each device connects to it (Figure 1.8). This ensures that the connections are point to point and the loss of a single node (computer, server, printer, and so forth) does not bring the entire network down. In the 802.3 standard using twisted pair cable your maximum cable length from endpoint to central point is 100 m (approximately 300 feet); if using fiber optic it can be between 400 m and 5 km depending on the cable and encoding type (defined earlier).

FIGURE 1.8
Star Network Topology

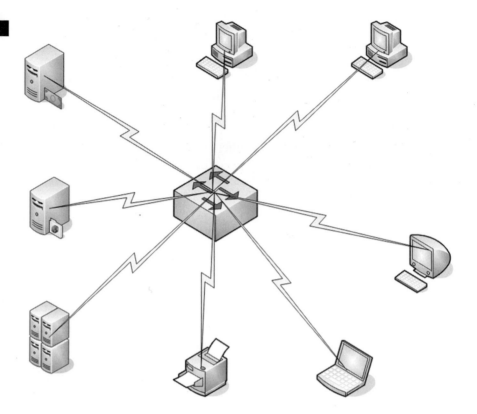

Bus

On the bus network topology, each computer is connected to each one on each side; this is a serial type of topology (Figure1.9), where the cable runs from one end to the other and the computers are connected one at a time, on ethernet. They are connected to either thick or thin coax cable with either a vampire tap (defined earlier) or a BNC connector. At each end of the bus is a terminator (resistor) that absorbs the signal so it does not continue to bounce back and forth from endpoint to endpoint. If any computer in the series goes down the entire network goes down and you have to take each one offline one at a time until you find the one that has the problem; it is like checking Christmas tree lights for the burnt out bulb.

Star-Bus

In the Star-Bus topology (Figure 1.10), you have multiple central connectivity devices (like hubs or switches) connected together with cable making the backbone between the connectivity devices on a bus network. The failure of

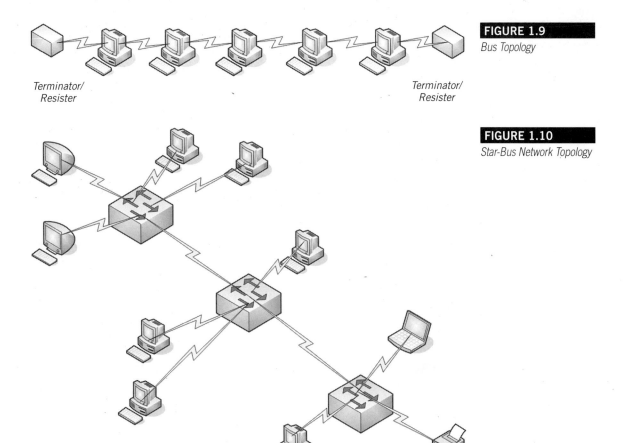

FIGURE 1.9
Bus Topology

*Terminator/
Resister*

*Terminator/
Resister*

FIGURE 1.10
Star-Bus Network Topology

one central connectivity device does not bring down the whole network; it only affects the devices on that hub or switch. The star bus network increases the number of devices that can be used on one LAN.

Test Day Tip
It is important to remember that hubs joined together in the Star-Bus create one large collision domain, and switches joined together create a large broadcast domain.

Ring

The ring topology (Figure 1.11), not to be confused with the Token Ring Protocol (defined later), is a topology where all the devices are connected either in a physical or logical circle. Traffic passes from computer to computer

FIGURE 1.11

Ring Topology

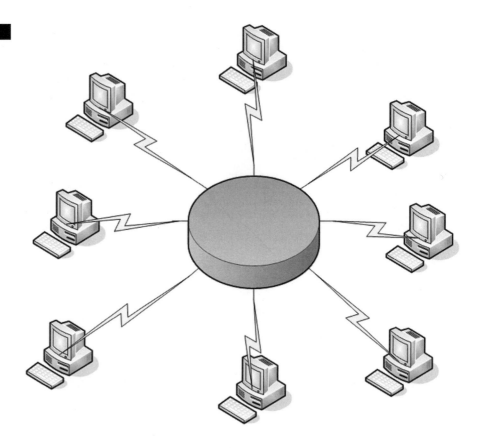

Test Day Tip

Remember not to confuse the Ring Topology with the Token Ring Protocol (802.5). The ring topology supports different protocols, whereas the 802.5 Token Ring Standard is a protocol.

around the circle until it reaches the destination workstation. There are different ways to determine how computers send data over the ring. Defined below in the 802.5 Token Ring Protocol you will see one method. Another protocol that uses a ring topology is fiber distributed data interface (FDDI).

Mesh

In the mesh topology each computer is connected to each of the other computers. If you have six computers you would need five network cards in each computer to connect to all the other computers in the LAN. This

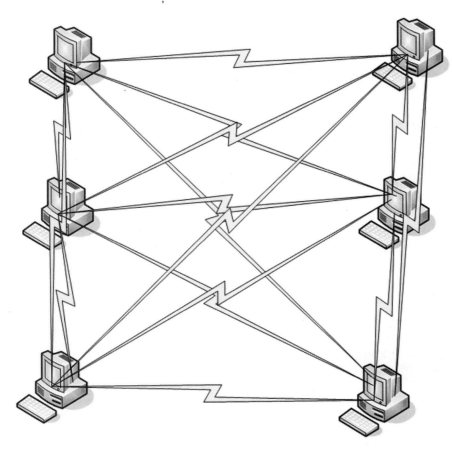

FIGURE 1.12
Mesh Topology

topology is very expensive as you need a cable run to all the other computers in the building and a network connection for each. To add computers to the network you would have to add a cable run and a network card to each computer. This topology (Figure 1.12) requires the most cable and hardware to keep the network running. On the plus side, at least if links or computers go down there are always multiple paths to get the data through. The Internet is considered a partial mesh topology as there are multiple paths through the backbone.

The formula to determine the number of connections is as follows:

$$N(N-1)/2$$

where N is the number of hosts on the network. Let's try this with the above six hosts. You would take $6 \times (6 - 1)$ which would be 5, then divide by 2. So the answer would be $6 \times 5 = 30/2 = 15$. Is that correct? Count the number of links above and see!

Exam Warning

Remember this formula for the exam. In the Cisco CCNA you will have many formulas to calculate and you will not have the advantage of using the Windows calculator, like you can on the Microsoft Certified System Engineer (MCSE) Exams.

IEEE

The IEEE is the standards organization that embodies the technology standards for the physical and data link layers of the OSI model. Originally founded in 1884 by the American Institute of Electrical Engineers, their motto is *The world's leading professional association for the advancement of technology*. All of the 802.x standards have been founded and developed under the watch of the IEEE. We have talked about the 802.3 standards for Ethernet and the 802.11 standards for wireless earlier. Subsequently, we will look at the 802.5 Token Ring Protocol and how it differs from the Ethernet and Ethernet Wireless Protocols (802.3 and 802.11, respectively).

NEW & NOTEWORTHY...

IEEE Membership

Membership in the IEEE at the time of this writing is $169 for standard membership. You can be a nonvoting associate member, or a student member for different prices. Membership in the IEEE will give you access to materials and references that will help you in your technical career. Once you become a member, you can also become a senior member if you have over 10 years in the industry. To access the IEEE go to www.ieee.org.

For a complete download of the 802 standards go to the following Web site, http://grouper.ieee.org/groups/802/index.html. Here you will find the detailed standards (these are like the Request for Comments (RFC) of the Internet).

802.5

In the material aforementioned we covered the 802.3 (Ethernet) and the 802.11 (Wireless) Protocols. Here we will talk about the 802.5 Token Ring Protocols. These protocols dictate the 4 and 16 MBps Token Ring Protocols. The devices are in a logical ring topology (see earlier) and each device can only communicate when it is in possession of the "token," a specific data frame that dictates who can communicate. This token as defined in the 802.5 IEEE standard, is a 24-bit package; the first 8 bits are the *starting delimiter* (SD), the next 8 bits are the *access control* (AC), and the last 8 bits are the *ending delimiter* (ED). This token tells the holding station they have permission to send one data stream (this would be a Network Layer Packet).

Token Ring (802.5) is preferred over the CSMA/CD Ethernet network when large images and files need to be transmitted.

Devices used on an 802.5 Token Ring network include MAU, MSAU, NIC, and cables. This protocol was originally developed by International Business Machines (IBM) in 1985. Later, we will explain these devices.

MAU/MSAU

The media access unit (MAU), also known as the multistation access unit (MSAU), is the Token Ring equivalent of a hub or switch on the Ethernet networks. All stations connect to the MAU/MSAU in a physical star topology but inside the MAU/MSAU it is a logical ring topology.

NIC

As described earlier, the NIC is used to connect the computer and media together with the network. There are two types of network cards available for 802.5 Token Ring networks. The first is a 4 MBps card and the other supports both 4 MBps and 16 MBps. A lot of people think that Token Ring is not in common use today, as Ethernet (IEEE 802.3) is installed in most office LANs, but in hospitals and other medical facilities 802.5 (Token Ring) is preferred when large images (like X-rays) have to be moved from the diagnostic network to the physician network.

Cable

The cable used for 802.5 Token Ring is a twisted pair cable with a special hermaphroditic type of connector. This connector is unique and is considered genderless (not a male plug with pins or a female plug with receptacles for the pins). The cable is shielded against EMI and can extend to lengths of 100 meters.

> **Exam Warning**
>
> Although Token Ring is rare in networks today, don't dismiss this as something you don't need to know as there are still places this will show up. Watch the Switching Chapter (Chapter 11) of this book for what kind of switches supports both Ethernet and Token Ring networks on the same switch!

BASIC NETWORKING CONCEPTS

In the aforementioned sections, we have addressed a lot of networking terms; in this section we will define other terms that are important to you as a network technician. Some of the topics are important as a technician and some are important to you as a security professional.

MAC Address

The MAC address, or as defined earlier the Cisco BIA, is the Layer 2 address in the OSI Model. It is a 48-bit address that is "burned" into the network interface of the Ethernet card (or the CSU/DSU device). This address is used to identify the device on the Layer 2 (data link) network. This address (source and destination) is in the header of the Layer 2 "frame" to move data from one computing device to another over the frame relay cloud. As displayed above there are two ways to display the address of the device.

Vendor OUI

The first half of the MAC address is the Vendor Organizationally Unique Identifier; this part of the address identifies the company that makes the NIC. This address is a permanent part of the network card and cannot be changed.

Spoofing

Although the MAC address cannot be changed, some devices will let you present a different address to the LAN. This is called *spoofing*. There are legitimate reasons to "spoof" your MAC address on the Internet and there are also reasons to spoof your address for ill gain. Most Cisco devices give you a way to spoof your address on the network. Some of the reasons to spoof your address are for things like getting DHCP information from your Internet server provider (ISP), or to "poison" the Address Resolution Protocol (ARP) table. By poisoning this table you can make yourself the "Default Gateway" and all data destined to the Internet comes to your station first, so you can capture it first, then you send the data to the correct gateway. Once the data comes back to the network from the gateway it is forwarded to you so you can capture the data before sending it back to the device that should receive the data. This type of attack is called a *Man in the Middle Attack*. A common reason to "spoof" your MAC address is when you have a cable or DSL high speed connection, and you have connected to this link with a single computer and you want to connect multiple computers to this network. You need a router or other device to connect multiple devices on your LAN to the Internet. This device not only has to handle the NAT address, but also has to receive information from the service provider, like IP address, network mask, and default gateway, so that all traffic from the LAN can access the Internet and data on this network. So the first device from which you access the Internet gives its MAC address to the ISP and only a device that has that MAC address can obtain the automatic configuration information from the ISP (Internet) provider.

Protocols

A protocol is an agreed-upon set of rules that tells the sender and the receiver how to send the message over the media. Later we will look at some of the protocols you will have to know for the CCNA Exam. Of the protocols listed, the IP is the most important to know. The Novell Internetwork Packet Exchange/Sequenced Packet Exchange (IPX/SPX) and the AppleTalk Protocol are of lesser importance for the exam.

TCP/IP

In 1971, the Department of Defense Advanced Research Projects Agency (DAPRA) set out to construct an interconnected series of devices that would push data to teletype printers in the event of a global nuclear war. The devices were called Internet Message Processors, and the original protocol, called 1822, did not have the ability to send files or remotely log on to other devices as the teletype was a receive-only printer. In 1974, Bob Kahn and Vint Cerf suggested changes to the 1822 to make it more robust and flexible. They called this new suite of protocols Transmission Control Protocol over an Internet Protocol (TCP/IP). This suite of protocols will support up to 65,536 TCP, up to 65,536 UDP (User Datagram Protocols), and 256 IP. The TCP and UDP protocols ride over the IP, allowing many different types of transmissions to occur in a flexible stack. TCP/IP uses a 32-bit binary addressing scheme that is translated into four decimal fields (called octets, as each field represents 8 bits); this notation is called *dotted decimal*.

The original TCP/IP ARPA network was to connect universities and government research agencies together to share research and other nonsecret information. The TCP/IP protocols have undergone many standard updates and changes throughout the years; the governing body of the Internet standards is the Internet Engineering Task Force (IETF). They maintain the database of RFC that are the defining documents of the protocols supported currently in TCP/IP protocol suit.

IPX/SPX

Internetwork Packet Exchange/Sequenced Packet Exchange (IPX/SPX) was developed by Novell™ as an alternative to the TCP/IP Protocol suite, this protocol was introduced in Novell's networking software called Netware in early 1980s. IPX is comparable to the IP layer of the TCP/IP Protocol where both of them work at the network layer or Layer 3 of the OSI model. The addressing in IPX uses a network number and then uses the MAC address for the host identifier of the workstation. Two devices on the same network can share data without the use of a router, whereas addresses on two different networks would require a router. Although it was a very popular protocol in the 1980s and early 90s, Novell soon replaced their IPX/SPX with TCP/IP in Netware version 5.

AppleTalk

AppleTalk was introduced in 1984 when the first Apple Macintosh computers were released. This Legacy Protocol was proprietary to the Macintosh line of computers and has been replaced with the more popular TCP/IP. Apple designed this protocol to be "self" configuring, so that it did not take an administrator to maintain the network. The two major protocols that defined AppleTalk are described in the following section.

The AppleTalk Address Resolution Protocol (AARP) generated the 4 byte address and published it into the Name Binding Protocol (NBP). NBP was a database where all the addresses and their associated names were stored. The NBP database is similar to what we use in TCP/IP with the Domain name service (DNS). AppleTalk has been compared to Xerox's XNS (Xerox Network Services) and the Banyan Vines Protocols.

IP Address

In 1974, Vint Cerf and Bob Kahn proposed a new suite of protocols as we discussed earlier. The first addressing scheme they developed was in the Version 4 Standard of TCP/IP and the second scheme was introduced in the Version 6 standard. When referring to the address scheme you will refer to them by version number, so IPv4 is the version 4 standard and IPv6 is the version 6 standard.

IPv4

IPv4 addresses are 32-bit binary (base 2) addresses or 2^{32} power, with four fields of 8 bits. Each field is called an octet (represents 8 bits). While the computer uses the binary it is displayed to the computer in decimal (base 10) and each octet is separated by a period; this is called *dotted decimal notation*. Each field can contain a number from 0 to 255 (256 combinations or 2^8 power). Each position in the binary octet represents a value, the eight positional values are 128 64 32 16 8 4 2 1 (from left to right). To convert a decimal value to binary you would attempt to subtract the position value from the decimal number. For example if you had an IP address of 192.168.31.2 you would perform the following calculations:

	128	64	32	16	8	4	2	1
192	1	1	0	0	0	0	0	0

Can you subtract 128 from 192? If the answer is yes, put a one in the 128 position; that leaves a remainder of 64. Can you subtract 64 from 64? Yes, so put a one in the 64 position and the remainder is 0, so put 0s in all the rest of the value positions. Next we move on to the 168 field

$$
\begin{array}{ccccccccc}
& 128 & 64 & 32 & 16 & 8 & 4 & 2 & 1 \\
168 & 1 & 0 & 1 & 0 & 1 & 0 & 0 & 0
\end{array}
$$

Again we start with Can you subtract 128 from 168, yes or no? Yes we can with a reminder of 40, so we put a 1 in the 128 value position and ask the next question. Can we subtract 64 from 40? The answer to that is no, so we put a 0 in the 64 value position and go on to the next question. Can we subtract 32 from 40? Yes, so we put a 1 in the 32 value position with a reminder of 8. So we then try and subtract 16 from 8 and that is a no; 8 is the next value and we can subtract 8 from 8 with a reminder of 0, so we can put 0s in the rest of the positions.

We do this for all four values and we then get our solution:

11000000.10101000.00011111.00000010—This is our IPv4 address and this gets compared with the subnet mask (see later) and from here we can determine the network portion and host portion of our address. There are five classes of IP addresses used in IPv4 and three are for workstations, servers, hosts, and routers. The three classes used for device addresses are given in Table 1.8.

The first number of the IP address determines the class of address and the default mask. If you change the mask from the default, you are creating "sub" nets, or splitting up the larger single network to create many smaller ones. An analogy of this would be purchasing a large piece of land and subdividing it into smaller parcels. For example if you had the address of 10.20.50.2 with a subnet mask of 255.255.0.0, you have taken the Class A network of 10.0.0.0 and made 254 subnets with 65,534 hosts on each network and this device is on the 10.20.0.0 subnet. You would read this as a Class A network subnetted 8 bits.

Table 1.8 Class A, B, and C Address Ranges

Class	Range	Default Mask	No. of Hosts
A	1 to 126	255.0.0.0	16,777,214
B	128 to 191	255.255.0.0	65,534
C	192 to 223	255.255.255.0	254

On each network there are two addresses you cannot use for host devices. The address binary host bits all zero and binary host bits all ones. Using the aforementioned example, 10.20.50.2 is my address and 255.255.0.0 is my subnet mask, so the all zeros host address would be 10.20.0.0 and my all ones address would be 10.20.255.255, meaning I could use all the addresses from 10.20.0.1 to 10.20.255.254 for workstations, servers, printers, and so forth. The remaining addresses (above 223) are reserved for different functions; the range from 224 to 239 is reserved for multicast and 240 to 254 are reserved for government testing.

IPv6

The new address scheme for IPv6 support approximately 340,000,000,000, 000,000,000,000,000,000,000,000 addresses, it is a 128 bit binary address or 2^{128} power. Instead of being displayed in decimal like the IPv4 address this one is displayed in hexadecimal format (base 16) and separated by colons instead of commas. Like the IPv4 address there is a network portion and a host portion to the address and can be determined by comparing the binary address to the subnet mask.

In IPv6 the address space available allows for newer "smart" technology as the pressure for publicly available addresses are being alleviated, as well as defining more security into the IP standards. Under IPv6 every device will have a globally routable unique IP address. During the initial discussion phases about IPv6, many network administrators were unhappy that all their devices would be using global/public addresses, the fear being that anyone would be able to get into their networks. Once people realized that the firewall would still prevent unauthorized traffic from outside to inside, this concern was overcome. The main benefits with IPv6 are that the addresses will be automatically assigned by the perimeter router, and NAT will no longer be needed. An administrator can open up a port on the firewall allowing external traffic to go to the "public"/global address without first creating a translation from a "public" address to a reserved private inside address, thus putting less overhead on the firewall.

IPv6 addresses are laid out in the following manner:

XXXX:XXXX:XXXX:XXXX:XXXX:XXXX:XXXX:XXXX

where each block represents 16 bits and the first 64 bits are by default the network portion and the last 64 bits are host.

Subnet Mask

The subnet mask is used in IPv4 and IPv6 to show what part of the address is the network portion and what part of the address is the host portion. In IPv4 there are three default subnet masks corresponding to the three classes of IP addresses (as illustrated earlier). There are currently three ways of showing the subnet masks for IPv4 addresses; you can show them in dotted decimal, binary, or classless interdomain routing (CIDR). Dotted decimal is shown in Table 1.8, the binary notation for a Class A default mask would look like 11111111.0000 0000.00000000.00000000 and finally the CIDR notation uses a slash/then the number of bits that need to be turned on in the mask. So for a Class A it would be /8, for a Class B it would be /16, and finally for a Class C it would be /24.

For IPv6 the default subnet mask is /64 (the first 64 bits are the network portion). You could subnet this to make a few smaller networks as with the default mask you have 18,446,744,073,709,551,616 possible addresses on one IPv6 network.

Gateway

The "default" gateway or the gateway of last resort in Cisco speak is the router that connects you to the Internet. This router is where you send network requests for networks not in the current routing table. On your computer you have a routing table that shows all the known networks (Figure 1.13) that your computer can access, there are two addresses in the table to handle destination networks you don't know. The first one is 0.0.0.0 with a mask of 0.0.0.0, it points to the gateway router and it is used when the destination network is not in the list.

The other address is 255.255.255.255 with a mask of 255.255.255.255. This address is the "universal" broadcast, and it literally means send this Layer 3 packet to every device on every network in the world. If this actually worked that way you could bring down the entire Internet by pinging that address; however, this does not happen because routers do not pass broadcast traffic.

If the gateway is not defined, you can only get to networks you know; you will see a router with a gateway set and a router without the gateway in Figures 1.14 and 1.15. The gateway entry in the routing table is a "static route." Static routes normally take precedence over routes learned via a routing protocol; however, in this case the static route has an * next to the S (static) designator making this the "candidate" default. This designation makes it the last possible choice in the routing table. In the other figure if the route is not in the list, you have no option to get to other networks as there is no candidate default.

DHCP

Dynamic Host Configuration Protocol (DHCP) is a protocol that will automatically assign TCP/IP addressing information to workstations over the

FIGURE 1.13

*Routing Table from a
Personal Computer*

```
route print
===============================================================================
Interface List
0x1 .......................... MS TCP Loopback interface
0x2 ...00 50 56 c0 00 08 ...... UMware Virtual Ethernet Adapter for UMnet8
0x3 ...00 50 56 c0 00 01 ...... UMware Virtual Ethernet Adapter for UMnet1
0x4 ...00 08 0d 4f ca f2 ...... Intel(R) PRO/100 UE Network Connection - Packet
Scheduler Miniport
0x5 ...00 0e 35 0b 28 3e ...... Intel(R) PRO/Wireless 2200BG Network Connection
- Packet Scheduler Miniport
===============================================================================
===============================================================================
Active Routes:
Network Destination        Netmask          Gateway       Interface  Metric
          0.0.0.0          0.0.0.0      192.168.3.1   192.168.3.118      30
        127.0.0.0        255.0.0.0        127.0.0.1       127.0.0.1       1
      192.168.3.0    255.255.255.0    192.168.3.118   192.168.3.118      30
    192.168.3.118  255.255.255.255        127.0.0.1       127.0.0.1      30
    192.168.3.255  255.255.255.255    192.168.3.118   192.168.3.118      30
     192.168.13.0    255.255.255.0    192.168.13.1    192.168.13.1       20
     192.168.13.1  255.255.255.255        127.0.0.1       127.0.0.1      20
   192.168.13.255  255.255.255.255    192.168.13.1    192.168.13.1       20
    192.168.195.0    255.255.255.0   192.168.195.1   192.168.195.1       20
    192.168.195.1  255.255.255.255        127.0.0.1       127.0.0.1      20
  192.168.195.255  255.255.255.255   192.168.195.1   192.168.195.1       20
        224.0.0.0        240.0.0.0    192.168.3.118   192.168.3.118      30
        224.0.0.0        240.0.0.0    192.168.13.1    192.168.13.1       20
        224.0.0.0        240.0.0.0   192.168.195.1   192.168.195.1       20
  255.255.255.255  255.255.255.255    192.168.3.118   192.168.3.118       1
  255.255.255.255  255.255.255.255    192.168.3.118               4       1
  255.255.255.255  255.255.255.255    192.168.13.1    192.168.13.1       1
  255.255.255.255  255.255.255.255   192.168.195.1   192.168.195.1       1
Default Gateway:       192.168.3.1
===============================================================================
Persistent Routes:
  None
```

network (see IETF draft standard RFC 2131, 2132, and 3397). The most common options set by DHCP are the network address, subnet mask, gateway, and DNS server address. There are many other options you can set with DHCP in including time server, domain name, and many others. One thing people often overlook is that DHCP is not just for Windows networks, there is a compatible protocol called Bootstrap Protocol (BOOTP) that does many of the same features as DHCP. When setting up DHCP on your network you should consider that DHCP uses broadcast packets and if you have any routers separating subnets, the DHCP server will only be accessible to the computers on that subnets as routers, as described earlier, do not pass broadcasts. If you need to pass DHCP information over networks separated by routers you can either setup a DHCP relay server or you can use the helper address feature on the Cisco routers. The helper address feature tells the router to "listen" for DHCP packets, and then the router repackages the packet into a unicast packet and sends it to the DHCP server on the other network and waits for the reply. It then repackages the packet to a broadcast

```
Codes: C - connected, S - static, R - RIP, M - mobile, B - BGP
       D - EIGRP, EX - EIGRP external, O - OSPF, IA - OSPF inter area
       N1 - OSPF NSSA external type 1, N2 - OSPF NSSA external type 2
       E1 - OSPF external type 1, E2 - OSPF external type 2, E - EGP
       i - IS-IS, su - IS-IS summary, L1 - IS-IS level-1, L2 - IS-IS level-
       ia - IS-IS inter area, * - candidate default, U - per-user static ro
       o - ODR, P - periodic downloaded static route

Gateway of last resort is 10.1.1.1 to network 0.0.0.0

     10.0.0.0/8 is variably subnetted, 2 subnets, 2 masks
C       10.1.1.0/24 is directly connected, Vlan1
C       10.200.1.1/32 is directly connected, Loopback1
S*   0.0.0.0/0 [1/0] via 10.1.1.1
```

FIGURE 1.14

Cisco Router Routing Table with Gateway Set

```
Mayberry#show ip route
Codes: C - connected, S - static, I - IGRP, R - RIP, M - mobile, B - BGP
       D - EIGRP, EX - EIGRP external, O - OSPF, IA - OSPF inter area
       E1 - OSPF external type 1, E2 - OSPF external type 2, E - EGP
       i - IS-IS, L1 - IS-IS level-1, L2 - IS-IS level-2, * - candidate default

Gateway of last resort is not set

     10.0.0.0 255.255.0.0 is subnetted, 4 subnets
C       10.2.0.0 is directly connected, Serial0
R       10.3.0.0 255.255.0.0 is possibly down,
          routing via 10.1.1.1, Ethernet0
C       10.1.0.0 is directly connected, Ethernet0
R       10.4.0.0 [120/1] via 10.2.2.2, 00:00:00, Serial0
Mayberry#
```

FIGURE 1.15

Cisco Router Routing Table without Gateway Set

and puts it back on the network for the client. If you are in an environment that has routers separating buildings DHCP packets would not cross the router as routers block broadcast traffic and DHCP is a broadcast protocol. To pass this traffic you would need a special service called a DHCP Relay server. This server listens for DHCP broadcasts and makes them a dedicated unicast packet and sends it to the DHCP server on the other side of the router and waits for the answer packet and turns it back into a broadcast.

Domain Name System

After the Internet and the IP were developed, there was a need to map IP addresses to names. The early adopters of the ARPAnet/Internet used a file called a HOSTS file to map the addresses to names. This file was updated regularly and maintained on a computer at the Stanford Research Institute (SRI), and during the first 10 years of the ARPA/Internet one computer was added every 20 days so this file only needed to be downloaded about every

2 weeks. As the network of connected networks expanded we needed a new and more automatically enabled way to resolve names into IP addresses.

The concept behind the DNS process is to distribute the services of name resolution from top level (called *root servers*) servers that point to servers (*top level domain servers*) that contain the addresses of servers controlled by companies that have DNS servers that actually contain the name to address resolution data. In the beginning there were only three top level domains, they were GOV for government, MIL for military, and EDU for education. In 1990, when the ARPA net was given over to the National Science Foundation (NSFnet) the COM top level domain was added as companies like Microsoft, Intel, and Xerox were added to the network.

The root servers (currently 13 of them) are currently owned by the U.S. Commerce Department. The United Nations (UN) has been trying to put pressure on the U.S. government to turn over the root servers to an international agency.

VoIP

The Voice over Internet Protocol (VoIP) allows you to use phones to talk to people all over the world over the Internet. The phones on the receiving side can be either VoIP or traditional wired phones. VoIP was initially developed as the Network Voice Protocol in 1973. The NVP protocol was not a widely used standard and as standards in moving voice over the network advanced and technology advanced, the TIA (Telecommunications Industry Association) proposed a standard for connecting PBX (Private Branch eXchange) equipment, the equipment that each company owns that connects the phones on the desktop to the telephone companies backbone so that each desktop can make calls. The TIA standards (TR41 and TIA-470-C) define how to connect companies' telecommunications equipment to the Internet instead of dedicated voice technology circuits.

There are many companies that offer VoIP technology, including Cisco, that can provide wide scale access to voice technology over the Internet data network. There are different levels of access to the VoIP network; they include personal/home, small business, and large corporate WAN access. In the home category, you will connect your phones to a VoIP access router that will convert the analog voice phones to the digital Internet. In small and large access the PBX is connected to the LAN and the phones are treated like personal computers or other access devices on the network; they have not just a telephone extension (controlled by the PBX) and they also have IP addresses. These devices pass voice traffic encapsulated in IP data packets.

HEAD OF THE CLASS...

VoIP and Packet Capture

If your VoIP provider did not enable encryption on the phones, you may be vulnerable to packet capture attacks. Programs like Wireshark can capture IP packets on the LAN and then display them on the screen. In the case of voice packets they can also play the data stream out your sound card.

On your personal network, companies like Time Warner, Comcast, and AT&T DSL can connect your home phones to the Internet so you can make voice calls. In the home environment, VoIP companies (like Time Warner, Comcast, and Vonage) are replacing traditional analog phone lines provided by the local bell system company in almost 75 percent of the market. Most homeowners that live in gated communities have VoIP for the sole reason for allowing for takeout restaurants to access the VoIP phone instead of the primary phone of cellular, which most people use to communicate. The classic example is, one spouse wants to order pizza and the gate is keyed to the other spouse's cellular phone. So when the driver gets to the gate and keys in the entry to contact the homeowner, it goes to the cell phone of the spouse not at home, so the spouse has to enter the code so the other spouse can have their pizza! In the VoIP world I can have a phone at home and have my gate code keyed to that phone so that neither spouse has to be disturbed on their cellular phone to open the gate.

NEW & NOTEWORTHY...

911 Emergency Service

One thing you need to do when looking at a VoIP service is the 911 emergency call service provisions. If you implement a VoIP solution and cannot identify your location with a 911 local service you will have problems getting response from the emergency services. For governmental information on VoIP and 911 go to www.fcc.gov/cgb/consumerfacts/voip911.html. The Federal Communications Commission (FCC) has a recommended standard and a procedure in place for complaints.

SUMMARY OF EXAM OBJECTIVES

In this section you need to know the devices that make up both the LANs and WANS, like repeaters, hubs, switches, bridges, and routers. The basics of IP are important foundations to your learning and testing process. As you build your knowledge with the use of this book, keep the following in mind:

- You must score 740 of 1,000 to pass this exam and you cannot use a calculator in the math and subnetting processes.

- The exam contains multiple choice, drag and drop, fill in the command, and simulations.

- The exam can be taken in either a one- or two-test format.

If you take the one test you will have to answer questions both on networking and subnetting, and router and switch devices.

In the two-test format, the first test is networking and subnetting while the second test is switching and routing devices.

EXAM OBJECTIVES FAST TRACK

Networking Hardware

- Cabling

- NICs

- Repeaters/Hubs

- Bridges Switches

- Routers

- Wireless Access Points

Network Types

- LAN

- WAN

- MAN

- CAN

- VPN

- SAN

Networking Topologies

- Star

- Bus

- Star Bus

- Ring

- Mesh

IEEE

- IEEE

- 802 Protocols

- 802.5 Token Ring

Basic Networking Concepts

- MAC Address

- Protocols

- IP Address

- Subnet Mask

- Gateway

- DHCP

- DNS

VoIP

- Commercial

- Residential

- Bandwidth

EXAM OBJECTIVES FREQUENTLY ASKED QUESTIONS

Q: Why do we study the OSI model when none of the protocols we study align with the model?

A: The OSI model allows us to break down other protocols and compare the functions at each layer. This allows us to troubleshoot problems with each protocol.

Q: Is there such a thing as a Single Port Router?

A: Yes, a router with only one interface can be used to route between VLAN. This is also called router on a stick.

Q: Why do they call multiport repeaters hubs and multiport bridges switches, yet they call a multiport router a router?

A: This is because routers were designed to join multiple ports initially, whereas repeaters and hubs were designed to connect two sides first. Then the technology was expanded to be multiport.

Q: Why do we have different standards organizations like the IETF, TIA, IANA, and IEEE?

A: Each organization is responsible for different parts of the Information Technology industry and founded to control parts of the growth of technology. The IETF was created to maintain controls of the RFC for the protocols of the Internet, while the Telecommunications Industry Association (TIA) is responsible for the standards for telephones, modems, and cable standards for most voice and data applications. The Internet Assigned Numbers Authority (IANA) is responsible for the TCP and UDP port associations with the application (Layer 1) protocols. The IEEE is an old organization that has been around for many decades that handles the standards for not only networks but many engineering standards in use today.

SELF TEST

1. A Cisco router at your location is no longer connecting your company to the Internet; you have noticed that users can no longer access resources on the VPN and the public Internet. You have a T1 connection to the Internet and you are the data terminal interface (DTE) side of the serial (Frame Relay) link. You have issued the show IP interface brief command and see that your CSU/DSU interface has the status of up and the protocol down. What command will tell you if the clock from the DCE is set?

   A. Router1# show controllers s0

   B. Router1(config#) show controllers s0

   C. Router1# show clock setting

   D. Router1# show clock rate

   E. Router(config-if)# show clock rate

2. A workstation in building A of an office campus network needs to obtain IP configuration information from a DHCP server in building B

of the same campus. Do you need a DHCP relay server in building A to accomplish this?

A. Yes

B. No

3. You have computers deployed into every cubicle in the office. One computer cannot access network resources on an Ethernet twisted pair network. No other users are having problems connecting to the network resources. You have tested the physical cable and there are no shorted wires or other physical problems; you have tested the NIC and also found no problems. What other factor could prohibit you from accessing the network? Pick two answers.

A. Patch panel not wired correctly

B. Server not online

C. Length of wire from end point to end point

D. Electromagnetic interference

4. You are given the number 229 in decimal notation and are asked to convert it to binary, what would the correct binary notation be?

A. 11011110

B. 11100101

C. 00100111

D. 10101010

E. 11001111

5. What is the maximum number of combinations that you can combine in an 8-bit number?

A. 1,024

B. 2,048

C. 254

D. 256

E. 100

6. You are the administrator of a small business network. You notice that as you add workstations to the network, over time the speed of the network decreases. What devices would you replace in your network with what other device to resolve this problem?

A. Replace repeaters with hubs.

B. Replace routers with hubs.

C. Replace routers with switches.

D. Replace hubs with switches.

E. Replace switches with hubs.

7. What are the five items required to have a network?

   A. Data, segment packet frame, and bits

   B. Supercomputer, mainframe computer, desktop, laptop, handheld

   C. Sender, receiver, message, media, and protocol

   D. Video, audio, broadcast, multicast, unicast

8. As the administrator of a network you have one user that cannot see the network. Everyone else can see all of the network resources. In what order of the OSI model layers would you try and troubleshoot this problem?

   A. Application, physical, data link, session

   B. Physical, data link, session, network

   C. Physical, network, application

   D. Physical, data link, application, network

   E. None of the above as the OSI model does not pertain to troubleshooting.

SELF TEST QUICK ANSWER KEY

1.	A	**5.**	D
2.	B	**6.**	D
3.	A and C	**7.**	C
4.	B	**8.**	C

The Open Systems Interconnect Model

INTRODUCTION

To prepare for the Cisco Certified Network Associate (CCNA) exam, you should begin by reviewing the foundations of networking. Among these, you must understand the logical models on which networks are designed and created, the protocols they use to communicate, the addressing schemes by which they identify individual devices on the network, and the technologies they use to ensure that data reaches its destination. In this chapter, we will cover the Open Systems Interconnect (OSI) model in depth and then begin the discussion on Transmission Control Protocol/Internet Protocol (TCP/IP). Both are covered in great detail on the exam and need to be completely understood before sitting the exam if you want success.

The vast majority of networks today (including the Internet) use TCP/IP to transmit information among computers and networks in a wide area network (WAN). Together, TCP and IP are referred to as a *protocol stack* or as *network/transport* protocols because they work together at two different levels (called the network and transport layers) to enable computers to communicate with each other. This is important because TCP/IP, like other protocol suites (groupings) such as Internetwork Packet Exchange/Sequenced Packet Exchange (IPX/SPX), is arranged as a suite of protocols that provide different functionality. If you want to send an e-mail to someone today, you will most likely need IP communications to establish communication and complete the transmission of the message. The models and the protocols (as you will see) tie very closely together, and that is why it's hard to discuss one without the other. As a matter of fact, no matter how long you are in networking, you will find the OSI model is referenced on a daily basis all the way from the beginning student to a networking master.

In this chapter, we'll look at the networking models that provide guidelines for vendors of networking products, including the early Department of Defense (DoD) model as well as the International Organization for Standardization (ISO) OSI model.

AN OVERVIEW OF THE OSI MODEL

The OSI model was developed by the ISO in 1979 and updated again in 1984. It is useful for guiding network development, troubleshooting, and instruction efforts. The OSI model is a seven-layer approach to data networking, with each layer encompassing a specific set of tasks or standards that must be met in order for the network to function.

This model consists of seven layers that separate the tasks, services, and protocols into various layers of the stack. The word *stack* is used to define the layers that are set upon each other. The higher you go in the stack, the closer you are to the application. The opposite also is true; as you travel down the stack, you're getting closer to the layers that deal with specific network functionality. The layers are usually stated from top down due to how applications communicate: application, presentation, session, transport, network, data link, and physical.

OSI is nothing more than a reference model to help guide the development of new protocols and applications. You will not find it running on the network such as TCP/IP or IPX/SPX. Originally, it was developed as a protocol stack with the intentions that it would become widely used. It was designed to be vendor neutral and cross-compatible among operating systems (OS). OSI never did take off as a protocol, but in time, it became a model used to help describe what should occur at each layer. The model allows programmers to focus on how their respective programs will talk to the network portion of the stack. This saves the programmer work, and it keeps the industry from having a whole bunch of proprietary network protocols that are based strictly on a certain application. As long as vendors base their applications on the OSI model, existing protocol stacks can be used and software integration will be possible with other vendors.

The OSI model is broken down using more layers than other protocols such as TCP/IP or IPX/SPX. The OSI model has more layers, which allows for a better definition of what should happen at each level. Each of the protocol stacks has some similarities in each of the layers. Some protocol stacks have layers that are combined differently than others, but overall, they can be mapped back to the OSI model. For instance, the upper three layers of the OSI model are equally comparable to the first application layer in the TCP/IP stack. (The use of the words *protocol stack* and *protocol suite* will be used interchangeably throughout the chapter. Both are referring to the alignment of protocols in a vertical manner.) There will be many references to the TCP/IP protocol stack compared with the OSI model so that real world examples of how it's used today can be shown. The TCP/IP protocol suite provides the purpose of allowing one networked system to talk to another. Each layer in the stack receives help from the layer below it and provides help to the layer above it. The Internet layer would receive the segment from the transport layer and then place a header onto it to include the source and destination IP address along with source and destination port numbers. Once the header is combined with the existing segment, it sends the combined information off as a packet to the network interface layer, which then adds another header to create a frame. The process of encapsulation is repeated throughout most of the transition from Layer 7 to Layer 1. When the remote side receives the frame, the reverse process is done to strip away the layers until only the data is left.

Test Day Tip

Each layer in the stack has many protocols that operate at each of the levels. TCP/IP would use different protocols at various levels of the stack than the IPX/SPX protocol would, so don't be confused when you see that each level has many protocols that can operate there. Not all of them operate at the same time nor do they belong to the same protocol stack. It really depends on what protocol stack is being used at the time.

The word *encapsulation* is a term we need to discuss before walking through the layers of the OSI model. Encapsulation provides the capability to package extra information with the original data to tell the network where to send it. For instance, you cannot place data from the application layer onto the network and expect it to get to the destination. You have to tell the OS to send the data to the computer that contains an IP address of X and a Media Access Control (MAC) address of Y. Encapsulations (as shown in Figure 2.1) allow you to add

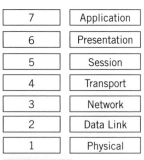

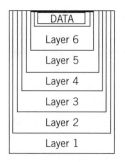

Encapsulation Process at Each Layer of the Protocol Stack

this additional information to guide the data. The computer sending the data will take the data and encapsulate it at each of the layers as it travels down the stack. When the destination host receives the information, it will do the reverse process by stripping away each of encapsulated layers until only the data is left. Each of the layers in the stack knows only how to strip away the encapsulated header and footer that relates to the sending host's protocol stack. An example would be that the network layer on the sending host side encapsulates the information while only the network layer on the receiving host can reverse the process of that same layer.

Physical Layer

The bottom layer in the protocol stack is the physical layer, which converts the binary information presented from the data link into electrical signaling. This layer also takes into consideration the network interface card (NIC) for the reason that it needs to know what kind of signaling to send through the media. An example would be the difference between a network card using a fiber interface and one using an unshielded twisted pair (UTP) interface. Each presents the information differently to the media. Network cards with fiber interfaces require the binary information to be converted to light patterns, whereas UTP cabling uses voltage and frequency variations to communicate. The physical layer also provides features to determine the speed (that is, 10, 100, or 1000 Mbps) at which to transmit the data, along with what to do in case line noise or cross-talk occurs.

Devices

The devices that are associated with this layer are

- NIC
- Cables
- Repeaters
- Multiport repeaters (hubs)

Data Link Layer

The data link layer takes the packet from the network layer and breaks it into frames. The header in this layer provides the source and destination

MAC addresses. It is the data link layer that will convert the data into binary digits such as 1 and 0 and then prepare them for the physical layer. It has to be aware of what type of NIC is being used to prepare the packet in a certain way. A frame prepared for Ethernet format would not be understood by a network setup with Token Ring. Thus, this layer takes the network interface into consideration before converting the packet. Cyclic redundancy checking (CRC) is another feature found in the data link layer that provides the capability to detect if a received frame was damaged. This checking feature is normally done by the local area network (LAN) switch or WAN frame relay switch.

Layer 2 devices that operate at this level are switches and bridges. They work by guiding the traffic to a destination based on the MAC address. The *MAC address* is a unique series of numbers and letters used to identify a certain network card. They are sometimes referred to as the physical address because this address is hard coded into the network card. A switch can direct traffic to the correct computer only if it's aware of to what port the computer's network card is attached. This is done by the computer presenting the MAC address from its network card to the switch when it first comes online.

There are a variety of protocols that work at this layer. Some are used by hosts and others by network devices such as switches. Spanning Tree Protocol (STP) and Rapid Spanning Tree Protocol (RSTP) are examples of protocols used by switches in this layer. They provide the capability to make sure there is only one Layer 2 path to get to a destination. Point-to-Point Protocol (PPP) and Layer 2 Tunneling Protocol (L2TP) are used by hosts. PPP provides the capability for a host to connect to a remote side using a modem. L2TP allows a host to connect to a remote side using a secure connection.

Devices

Devices that operate at this layer are

- NIC
- Bridges
- Multiport bridges (switches)

MAC

The MAC sublayer provides control for accessing the transmission medium. It is responsible for moving data packets from one NIC to another across a shared transmission medium such as an Ethernet or fiber-optic transmission medium.

Physical addressing is addressed at the MAC sublayer. Every NIC has a unique MAC address, also called the *physical address*, which identifies that specific NIC on the network. The MAC address of an NIC is usually burned into a read-only memory (ROM) chip on the NIC. Each manufacturer of network cards is provided a unique set of MAC addresses so that (theoretically, at least) every NIC that is manufactured has a unique MAC address. Obviously, it would be confusing if there were two or more NICs with the same MAC address. A packet intended for NIC #35 (a simplification of the MAC address) would not know to which NIC #35 it was destined. To avoid this confusion, MAC addresses, in most cases, are permanently burned into the NIC's memory. This is sometimes referred to as the Burned-In Address (BIA).

Exam Warning

A MAC address consists of six hexadecimal numbers. The highest possible hexadecimal number is FF:FF:FF:FF:FF:FF, which is a broadcast address. The first 3 bytes contain a manufacturer code, and the last 3 bytes contain a unique station ID. You must understand the functionality of an NIC card, and what a MAC address is for the CCNA exam. On Ethernet NICs, the physical or MAC address (also called the *hardware address*) is expressed as 12 hexadecimal digits, arranged in pairs with colons between each pair, for example, 12:3A:4D:66:3A:1C. In binary notation, this translates to a 48-bit (or 6-byte) number, with the initial 3 bytes representing the manufacturer and the last 3 bytes representing a unique NIC made by that manufacturer. On Token Ring NICs, the MAC address is 6 bytes long, too, but the bits of each byte are reversed. That is, Ethernet transmits in canonical or least significant bit (LSB) mode, with the LSB first, whereas Token Ring transmits with the most significant bit first (MSB or noncanonical mode). Although duplicate MAC addresses are rare, they do show up because some manufacturers have started to use their numbers over again. This usually is not a problem because the duplicates almost never show up on the same network. Some cards allow you to change the MAC address by using special software to "flash" the card's chip.

Another important issue that's handled at the MAC sublayer is media access control. This refers to the method used to allocate network access to computers and prevent them from transmitting at the same time, causing data collisions. Common MAC methods include carrier sense multiple access/collision detection (CSMA/CD) used by Ethernet networks, CSMA/collision avoidance (CA) used by AppleTalk networks, and token passing used by Token Ring and Fiber Distributed Data Interface (FDDI) networks.

Logical Link Control

The Logical Link Control (LLC) sublayer provides the logic for the data link; thus it controls the synchronization, flow control, and error-checking functions of the data link layer. This layer can handle connection-oriented transmissions (unlike the MAC sublayer below it), although connection-less service can also be provided by this layer. Connectionless operations are known as *Class I LLC*, whereas Class II can handle either connectionless or connection-oriented operations. With connection-oriented communication, each LLC frame that is sent is acknowledged. The LLC sublayer at the receiving end keeps up with the LLC frames it receives (these are also called *protocol data units* (PDUs)), and if it detects that a frame has been lost during the transmission, it can send back a request to the sending computer to start the transmission over again, beginning with the PDU that never arrived.

The LLC sublayer sits above the MAC sublayer and acts as a liaison between the upper layers and the protocols that operate at the MAC sublayer such as Ethernet, Token Ring, and so on (IEEE (Institute of Electrical and Electronics Engineers, Inc.) standards). The LLC sublayer itself is defined by IEEE 802.2. Link addressing, sequencing, and definition of service access points (SAPs) also take place at this layer.

Network Layer

The responsibility of network layer is to discover the layout of the network. This layer determines if communication will stay on the same network or will be routed. It does not guarantee that data will get to the destination and relies on the transport layer for that functionality. It is able to determine whether the source and destination hosts are on the same network by inspecting the IP address and subnet mask set to each. If the hosts happen to be on different networks, then routing is needed for them to communicate, and this layer can perform that function. Thus, to generalize this statement, the network layer allows one logical address to communicate with another logical address, whether they are on the same or different networks. The term *logical address* is referring to an IP address that you would assign to a computer or network connection device. Each host on the network must have a unique IP address. A few of the more commonly known protocols that operate at this layer are IP, Internet Control Message Protocol (ICMP), and IPX. Protocols in this layer work in conjunction with protocols in the transport layer. For instance, TCP at the transport layer works with IP at the network layer, thereby creating TCP/IP.

Figure 2.2 is an example of communication between two network hosts on different networks, and it shows how the data will travel to get from

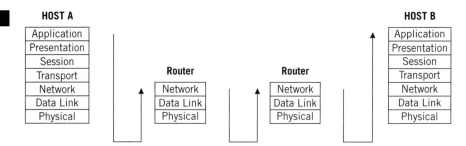

one host to another. On Host A, the data is encapsulated as it's passed down the protocol stack. At the physical layer, it's converted into voltage, frequency, or light so that it can be sent across the network. It may need to pass through several networks before arriving at a router that contains an interface in the same network as the destination host. Notice that not all network devices will use the entire protocol stack to communicate. A router operates at the network layer and is able to guide the traffic to the correct location based on the IP addresses. It doesn't care about the application itself; it cares only to get the packet to the end host. Once the data gets to the router that has an interface located in the same network as the destination host, it will cross the IP address to the MAC address and forward it to the switch. From there, the switch directs the traffic based on MAC address to the correct network port where the device is connected. Host B receives the information and performs the opposite procedure of Host A. It strips each of the encapsulated layers off as it goes up the stack until it has only the data left.

Note

To understand the difference between physical and logical addresses, consider this analogy: If you buy a house, it has a physical address that identifies exactly where it is located on the earth, at a specific latitude and longitude. This never changes (unless you have a mobile home that can be moved from one plot of land to another). This is like the MAC address on an NIC. Your house also has a logical address assigned to it by the post office, consisting of a street number and street name. The city can (and occasionally does) change the names of streets or renumber the houses located on them. This is like the IP address assigned to a network interface.

Devices

- The devices at this layer are routers.

Routing

Routing refers to forwarding packets from one network or subnet to another. Without routing, computers can communicate only with other computers that are on the same network via Address Resolution Protocol (ARP) broadcasts. Routing makes it possible for computers to send data through many networks to other computers that are on the other side of the world. Routing is the key to the global Internet and is one of the most important duties of the network layer. Easy to remember, routing is simple to understand. If you start with an LAN that has the 10.1.1.0 255.255.255.0 network and you want to get to the 10.1.2.0 255.255.255.0 network (which has a different network number in the third octet), you would need a router with a routing table (so it knows where to send the packet) to get it there.

Some of the protocols you will see in this book are Open Shortest Path First (OSPF), Routing Information Protocol (RIP), and Enhanced Interior Gateway Routing Protocol (EIGRP).

Transport Layer

The transport layer takes the data from the session layer and splits it up into smaller pieces of information that are the right size for network transmission. Before sending the data out, this layer makes a checklist of how to ensure that the other side has received all the data and that it is not damaged in any way. It does this by doing a handshaking process prior to sending the data. That handshaking process determines the amount of data to be sent, how to judge if some of the data was lost in the transmission, and how to verify the data was not corrupted. The process that's performed in this layer is often confused with the session layer. The difference between them is that the transport layer is building sessions between the end devices, whereas the session layer is building sessions between the applications.

There are three protocols that work at this layer: TCP, User Datagram Protocol (UDP), and SPX.

TCP is a connection-oriented protocol, which means it will set up a reliable connection between hosts before sending any data. There are actually three phases used by TCP: connection setup, data transfer, and connection tear-down. In the connection setup phase, transmission parameters are negotiated among the endpoints. TCP uses the SYN, SYN/ACK, and ACK flags to let both sides participate in the negotiation of how much data should be sent at a time, along with flow control, and how to detect errors while recovering from them. Once the agreement is made between the hosts, the data can be sent. If one of the hosts detects a problem with the received traffic, it will request the segment to be retransmitted. This ensures that the data is error free and completely received by the destination. TCP uses acknowledgements (ACKs) to tell the sending computer that it has received the expected amount of data and that the integrity of it is good. Any data not acknowledged is re-sent to the destination, as it is assumed lost. Finally, when the conversation is done, the transport layer closes the conversation between hosts by sending an acknowledged finish (ACK/FIN) packet. The opposite end responds back with an ACK that it received the ACK/FIN. Once both sides agree to end the session through the use of ACK, the conversation can close.

A connectionless protocol such as UDP doesn't have the three-phase approach like TCP. It just sends the data as soon as it's ready and assumes the endpoint receives it all. UDP expects the application to put the data back together instead of the protocol used in this layer.

HEAD OF THE CLASS...

Connection-Oriented versus Connectionless

What's the difference between a connection-oriented protocol and a connectionless protocol? A connection-oriented protocol such as TCP creates a connection between the two computers before actually sending the data, and then it verifies that the data has reached its destination by using ACK (messages sent back to the sending computer from the receiving computer that acknowledge receipt). Connectionless protocols send the data and trust that it will reach the proper destination.

Consider an analogy: you need to send a very important letter to a business associate, containing valuable papers that must not get lost along the way. You call him before mailing the letter, to let him know he should expect it (establishing the connection). You might even insure it or send it via certified mail. After a few days have passed, your friend calls you back to let you know that he did receive the letter or you get back the return receipt that you requested (acknowledgement). This is the way a connection-oriented communication works. It's different from mailing a relatively unimportant item, such as a postcard to a friend when you're on vacation. In that case, you just drop it in the mailbox and hope it gets to the addressee. You don't expect or require any ACK. This is like a connectionless communication.

Session Layer

The session layer is responsible for managing the conversations between the local and remote applications from start to end. This includes starting the session, making sure it stays established, and then closing the connection when finished. There can be one or more sessions occurring at the same time between two network-connected hosts. The session layer is the layer responsible for keeping track of each of these sessions so that there is no confusion between the various conversations that may be occurring at the same time. A Web server may have thousands of sessions occurring due to people browsing its Web site. It's up to this layer to manage every one of those sessions. This layer may be better understood if we describe the communication modes that can occur here:

1. Simplex: communications flow in one direction

2. Half-duplex: communication in both directions but only one side can speak at a time

3. Full-duplex: communication in both directions and both sides can speak at the same time.

After the transport layer has established the virtual connection, a communication session can be established. A communication session occurs between two processes on two different computers. The session layer is responsible for establishing, monitoring, and terminating sessions, using the virtual circuits established by the transport layer.

The session layer is also responsible for putting header information into data packets to indicate where the message begins and ends. Once header information is attached to the data packets, the session layer performs synchronization between the sender's session layer and the receiver's session layer. The use of ACK messages helps coordinate transfer of data at the session layer.

A very important function of the session layer is controlling whether the communications within a session are sent as full-duplex or half-duplex, half-duplex messages. Half-duplex, half-duplex communication goes in both directions between the communicating computers, but information can travel in only one direction at a time (as with walkie-talkie radio communications, in which you have to hold down the **microphone** button to transmit and cannot hear the person on the other end when you do). With full-duplex communication, information can be sent in both directions at the same time (as in a regular telephone conversation, in which both parties can talk and hear one another at the same time).

Two very important terms to be familiar with as a CCNA are permanent virtual circuit (PVC) and switched virtual circuit (SVC). When you have a technology like a Frame Relay or T1 Circuit, it is always connected and you would have to establish a circuit. This circuit would be called a *PVC*, and you would have a PVC ID. If you were using technologies such as Digital Subscriber Line (DSL) and cable, they establish the connection when there is data to send or receive and their ID is called a *SVC*, which is provided as the link is established.

The session layer, then, is responsible for setting up the connection between an application process on one computer and an application process on another computer, after the transport layer has established the connection between the two machines.

Test Day Tip

Earlier in this chapter we mentioned multiplexing. Computer communications can be in half-duplex or full-duplex mode. *Simplex* or unidirectional (one-way) communication generally is not used in computer networking. It is the type of communication used for radio and over-the-air TV broadcasts (many CATV transmissions now use two-way signaling to allow for interactive TV).

There are a number of important protocols that operate at the session layer, including Windows Sockets (the WinSock interface) and the Network Basic Input/Output interface (NetBIOS).

Presentation Layer

The presentation layer receives the data from the application layer and translates it into a format and syntax that's readable by other computers. In order for the other systems to recognize this data, it's converted into a generic format that is not application specific. This layer doesn't care what the actual data is. It's merely a translation stage for data formats. Thus, as the application passes the data down the stack, it's translated from what the application understands to a generic format. The system that ends up receiving this data does the reverse process by translating the generic data format into a format understood by that computer. Various OS and applications may expect the data to be presented a certain way. The presentation layer provides the capability to translate the data to suit the applications needs. Some of the format types found in this layer are as follows: ASCII, EBCDIC, JPEG, MPEG, TIFF, Binary, and so on. This layer is also able to provide encryption and compression if the application layer asks it to do so.

When data is sent from sender to receiver, the data is translated at the presentation layer. The sender's application passes data down to the presentation layer, where it is put into a common format. When the data is received on the other end, the presentation layer changes the data from the common format back into a format that is useable by the application. Protocol translation, the conversion of data from one protocol to another so that it can be exchanged between computers that use different platforms or OS, takes place here.

This is the layer at which many gateway services operate. *Gateways* are connection points between networks that use different platforms or applications. Examples include e-mail gateways (which allow for communications between two different e-mail programs using a common protocol such as Simple Mail Transfer Protocol (SMTP)), Systems Network Architecture (SNA) gateways (which allow PCs to communicate with mainframe computers), and gateways that cross-platforms or file systems (for example, allowing Microsoft clients that use the Server Message Block (SMB) protocol for file sharing to access files on NetWare servers that use NetWare Core Protocol). Gateways are usually implemented via software, such as the Gateway Services for NetWare (GSNW). Software redirectors also operate at this layer.

This layer is also where data compression can take place, to minimize the actual number of bits that must be transmitted on the network media to the receiver. Data encryption and decryption take place in the presentation layer as well.

Application Layer

Communication between two networked devices starts at the application layer. This layer is sometimes confused by people who think that the "application layer" refers to the applications with which the user interfaces. This is actually not true. The application layer refers to the protocols that operate at this layer. Thus, if a program needs to send data

LAYER	
7	Application
6	Presentation
5	Session
4	Transport
3	Network
2	Data Link
1	Physical

FIGURE 2.3   *How the User Interfaces with the Protocol Stack*

across the network to another computer, it will pass the data down to the application layer with instructions on what to do with it. A Web browser, for instance, does not operate at the application layer but the Hypertext Transfer Protocol (HTTP) does. The Web browser uses the HTTP protocol to communicate. An application program interface (API) (as shown in Figure 2.3) is found between the Web browser and the HTTP protocol. The API is responsible for talking to the application layer protocols.

The following is a small list of protocols that operate at the application layer. The easiest way to think of this is to picture what you type into the URL string for your Web browser. For instance, if you want to go to Google, you would type **http://www.google.com**, which would use the HTTP protocol to access the Web server at Google. Whatever URL you choose, it's going to start with HTTP, File Transfer Protocol (FTP), or something of that nature. These references are telling the Web browser with which protocol to communicate.

- HTTP: Hypertext Transfer Protocol

- SMTP: Simple Mail Transfer Protocol

- POP3: Post Office Protocol version 3

- IMAP: Internet Message Access Protocol

- FTP: File Transfer Protocol

- TFTP: Trivial File Transfer Protocol

Application (FTP, Telnet, SMTP)
Transport (Provides error-free connections (TCP))
Network (Provides a logical address (IP))
Network Interface (The physical connection components)

FIGURE 2.4 *TCP/IP (DoD) Model*

Layer Seven—Application Layer	Application
Layer Six—Presentation Layer	
Layer Five—Session Layer	
Layer Four—Transport Layer	Transport
Layer Three—Network Layer	Network
Layer Two—Data Link Layer	Network Interface
Layer One—Physical Layer	

FIGURE 2.5 *Comparison of the OSI Model with the TCP Model*

AN OVERVIEW OF THE TCP/IP MODEL

The TCP/IP model was developed by Vint Cerf and Bob Kahn in 1974 to enhance the Department of Defense Advance Research Project Agency (DARPA) network. It uses a four-layer architecture as apposed to the OSI model's seven layers. Figure 2.4 shows the TCP/IP model and its four layers.

To help identify the functions of the TCP/IP model, we can compare it with the OSI model (Figure 2.5).

In this model, the upper three layers of the OSI model (application, presentation, and session) are represented by the application layer in the TCP/IP model. The transport layer (where the TCP and UDP ports live) is the same in both models as is in the network layer where the IP address lives. Finally, the data link and physical layer are combined into the network interface layer of the TCP/IP model. Many CCNA students ask why the two models are different; the reason is that the DoD model was developed before the OSI model and the OSI model was developed so we can talk about any protocol in a structured manner.

Network Interface Layer

The TCP/IP protocol suite provides networking protocols that work at all layers of the DoD model. TCP/IP generally follows the DoD model since they were developed at roughly the same time. There is not a clean mapping to the OSI model for TCP/IP, so we will use the DoD model and make reference to what OSI model layers it maps to, which you should already know as all these layers were discussed earlier in the chapter. In this section, we're going to look at the TCP/IP protocols that work at each of the four layers defined in the DoD model (DARPA). Also known as the physical and data link layers in the OSI model, the network interface layer combines both under one layer.

As you recall, the network interface layer maps to the physical and data link layer in the OSI model. At the network interface layer, we're working with 0s and 1s being transmitted back and forth across the network medium (in many offices, the medium is twisted-pair Category 5 Ethernet cable). The network interface layer is responsible for controlling the movement of bits across the medium. As such, it must use some organized method of managing the sending and receiving of data. In Ethernet networks, the most common method is CSMA/CD. However, there are other less common methods of managing data on the network, including CSMA/CA and token passing. Each is discussed in turn in the next sections.

CSMA/CD

Ethernet, a common network architecture used in PC networking, uses CSMA/CD to manage media access. CSMA/CD is used on multiple access networks as defined in the IEEE 802.3 specification. Using this method, devices that have data to transmit listen for an opening on the line before transmitting (Carrier Sense). That is, they wait for a time when there are no signals traveling on the cable. When a device detects an opening, it transmits its data. The problem is that several devices may sense simultaneously that the line is clear and they may all transmit at the same time. When this happens, the data packets collide and the data is lost; this is called a *collision*.

Using the CSMA/CD protocol, the devices will detect that a collision has occurred (CD), and each of the devices that transmitted at the same time will wait a random amount of time and then retransmit. The likelihood of one or more devices *randomly* selecting the same delay is almost zero, so the retransmission is likely to be successful. Higher network traffic, larger numbers of computers on a network segment, and longer cables all contribute to an increased number of collisions, which in turn lowers the efficiency of the network because even more traffic is generated by larger number of retransmissions. A *collision domain* is a segment of cable on which two stations can't transmit at the same time without causing a collision. For example, all computers attached to the same hub in a star topology network, or all the computers on the same bus (linear segment) in a bus topology network, comprise a single collision domain. By using a switch, you can create separate collision domains and reduce network traffic.

With CSMA/CD, unlike with some access control protocols (such as demand priority), all stations or nodes are equal in their capability to send data when there is an opening; no station gets higher priority than any other.

A number of IEEE working groups continue to develop new standards for CSMA/CD, such as those pertaining to Gigabit Ethernet and Ethernet over fiber (100BaseFX).

CSMA/CA

A media access protocol that is related to CSMA/CD is CSMA/CA, which is also used on multiple access networks such as token passing or wireless topologies. With CSMA/CA, a device listens for an opportunity to transmit its data just as devices do on CSMA/CD networks. However, when the device senses an opening, it does not immediately transmit the data; instead it transmits a signal notifying other devices that it is transmitting (a sort of warning message) before actually sending the data. This means data packets will never collide (although warning packets may).

Traditionally, CSMA/CA was most commonly used by AppleTalk networks. However, today most Apple computers can use Ethernet hardware, and this access method has fallen out of favor because it creates significant overhead—it adds unnecessary traffic to the network, slowing everything down. The preferred method of dealing with collisions is the CD method, which is the method now used in Ethernet networking technologies.

CSMA/CA solves the problem of potential collisions on the wireless network by taking a more active approach than CSMA/CD, which kicks in only after a collision has been detected. Using CSMA/CA, a wireless workstation first tries to detect if any other device is communicating on the network. If it senses it is clear to send, it initiates communication. The receiving device sends an ACK packet to the transmitting device indicating successful reception. If the transmitting device does not receive an ACK, it assumes a collision has occurred and retransmits the data. However, it should be noted that many collisions can occur and that these collisions can be used to compromise the confidentiality of Wired Equivalent Privacy (WEP) encrypted data.

CSMA/CA is only one way in which wireless networks differ from wired networks in their implementation at the MAC layer. For example, the IEEE standard for 802.11 at the MAC layer defines additional functionality, such as virtual collision detection (VCD), roaming, power saving, asynchronous data transfer, and encryption.

The fact that the WEP protocol is defined at the MAC layer is particularly noteworthy and has significant consequences for the security of wireless networks. This means that data at the higher levels of the OSI model, particularly TCP/IP data, is also encrypted. Because much of the TCP/IP communications that occur between hosts contain a large amount of frequently repeating and well-known patterns, WEP may be vulnerable to known plaintext attacks, although it does include safeguards against this kind of attack.

Test Day Tip

Make sure you understand the fundamentals of CSMA/CA and wireless for the CCNA exam. The current standards include the IEEE 802.11g and the security protocols WEP, Wi-Fi Protected Access (WPA), and WPA2.

Internet Layer

The TCP/IP suite has four core protocols that work at the Internet layer, which maps to the network layer of the OSI model. The Internet layer is responsible for packaging, addressing, and routing the data. The four core protocols used in the TCP/IP suite are

- The Internet Protocol

- The ICMP

- The Internet Group Management Protocol (IGMP)

- The ARP

IPv4

The IP is probably the best known of the TCP/IP protocols. Many people, especially those who have even a passing familiarity with computer technology, have heard or used the term IP address. Later in this chapter, we'll take an in-depth look at how the IP protocol works and you'll learn the intricacies of IP addressing.

With regard to the TCP/IP architecture, IP is a routable protocol (meaning it can be sent across networks) that handles addressing, routing, and the process of putting data into or taking data out of packets. IP is considered to be connectionless because it does not establish a session with a remote computer before sending data. Data sent via connectionless methods are called *datagrams*. An IP packet can be lost, delayed, duplicated, or delivered out of sequence, and there is no attempt to recover from these errors. Recovery is the responsibility of higher layer protocols including transport layer protocols such as TCP.

IP packets contain data that include

- **Source IP address** The IP address of the source of the datagram

- **Destination IP address** The IP address of the destination for the datagram

- **Identification** Identifies a specific IP datagram as well as all fragments of a specific IP datagram if the datagram becomes fragmented

- **Protocol** Indicates to which protocols the receiving IP should pass the packets

- **Checksum** A simple method of error control that performs a mathematical calculation to verify the integrity of the IP header.

- **Time-to-Live (TTL)** Designates the number of networks the datagram can travel before it is discarded. This prevents datagrams from circling endlessly on the network.

ICMP

The ICMP is not as well-known as its famous cousin, IP, but is used so often that it would seem that you hear about this protocol more than IP. Many programs that you use as a network engineer rely on ICMP, such as Ping and Traceroute. ICMP is responsible for handling errors related to IP packets that cannot be delivered. For instance, if a packet cannot be delivered, a message called *Destination Unreachable* is sent back to the sending device, so it will know that there was an undelivered message. The Destination Unreachable message has several subtypes of messages that can be sent back to the host to help pinpoint the problem. For instance, Network Unreachable and Port Unreachable are two examples of Destination Unreachable messages that may be returned to help the host determine the nature of the problem.

If you have ever used the Ping utility (discussed at the end of this chapter) and received an error, it was ICMP that was responsible for returning the error. In addition to announcing errors, ICMP also announces network congestion (source quench messages) and timeouts (which occur when the TTL field on a packet reaches zero).

IGMP

The IGMP manages host membership in multicast groups. IP multicast groups are groups of devices (typically called hosts) that listen for and receive traffic addressed to a specific, shared multicast IP address. Essentially, IP multicast traffic is sent to a specific MAC address but processed by multiple IP hosts. As you'll recall from our earlier discussion, each NIC has a unique MAC address, but multicast MAC addresses use a special 24-bit prefix to identify them as such. IGMP runs on the router, which handles the distribution of multicast packets (often, multicast routing is not enabled on the router by default and must be configured).

Multicasting makes it easy for a server to send the same content to multiple computers simultaneously. IP addresses in a specific range (called Class D addresses) are reserved for multicast assignment. The IGMP protocol allows for different types of messages, used to join multicast groups and to send multicast messages.

A unicast message is sent directly to a single host, whereas a multicast is sent to all members of a particular group. Both use connectionless datagrams and are transported via UDP, which we'll discuss in the next section. A multicast is sent to a group of hosts known as an *IP multicast group* or *host group*. The hosts in this group listen for IP traffic sent to a specific IP multicast address. IP multicasts are more efficient than broadcasts because the data is received only by computers listening to a specific address. A range of IP addresses, known as Class D addresses, is reserved for multicast addresses. Windows Server 2003 supports multicast addresses and, by default, is configured to support both the sending and receiving of IP multicast traffic.

Exam Warning

Although their acronyms are very similar and they function at the same layer of the networking models, ICMP and IGMP perform very different functions, so be sure you don't get them confused on the test.

ARP

The ARP is the last of the four core TCP/IP protocols that work at the Internet layer. As we've discussed, each NIC has a unique MAC address and is also assigned an IP address that is unique to the network on which it resides. When a packet is sent on a TCP/IP network, the packet headers include a destination IP address (along with other information). The IP address must be translated into a specific MAC address for the data to reach its intended recipient. Without ARP, computers must send broadcast messages each time an IP address has to be matched to a MAC address.

ARP is responsible for maintaining the mappings of IP addresses to MAC addresses. These mappings are stored in the ARP cache, so if the same IP address needs to be matched to a MAC address again, the mapping can be found in the cache; it's not necessary to repeat the discovery process.

The protocol includes four different types of messages: ARP request, ARP reply, Reverse Address Resolution Protocol (RARP) request, and RARP reply, where RARP resolves addresses in the opposite direction (MAC address to IP address). These messages are used to discover the MAC addresses that correspond to specific IP addresses (and vice versa). When the MAC address is correlated to the specific IP address, the data can be sent to the proper host.

ARP was originally designed for DEC/Intel/Xerox (DIX) 10 Mbps Ethernet networks, but it is now used with other types of IP-based networks as well.

These are the four primary protocols involved in TCP/IP at the Internet layer, which is responsible for addressing, packaging, and routing packets of data. As we move up the protocol stack, we will examine the transport layer.

> **Exam Warning**
>
> The ARP is used to resolve the IP address to the MAC address that is unique to each NIC manufactured. This concept is very important to understand. All network communication to a destination host requires knowledge of the MAC address to complete the transmission of data in the collision domain where that host is connected. ARP performs the function of resolving the IP (logical) address to the MAC (hardware) address so that the data can be delivered.

Transport Layer

Layer 3 in TCP/IP is the host-to-host transport layer, sometimes called the transport layer. It maps to the transport layer (Layer 4) in the OSI model. As the name implies, this layer is responsible for transporting the data. It sets up communications between the application layer and the lower layers.

Because this layer establishes a connection, it can also take on some of the responsibilities of the session layer of the OSI model. In TCP/IP, the two core protocols used at the host-to-host layer are TCP and UDP. As we discussed earlier, one of the key distinguishing features of these two protocols is that TCP is considered connection-oriented and UDP is connectionless.

TCP

The TCP provides reliable one-to-one communications because it establishes a connection with the receiving host prior to transmitting and because it provides a number of control features to ensure reliable communications. TCP is connection-oriented because it establishes a TCP connection prior to sending data. This is similar to the way a modem works when the modem dials another computer and establishes a connection before data is transmitted. This ensures that someone is on the other end before data is sent. TCP sequences the packets, acknowledges sent packets, and helps recover lost packets. Data is transmitted in segments, and each segment is numbered sequentially. When the receiving host receives data, it sends an ACK message to the sender. If the sender does not receive this ACK within a specified amount of time, the data segment is re-sent, based on the assumption that the data was not received.

Data from the transport layer's TCP is organized into segments. These are sent down through the protocol stack and headers are added. Each network technology (Ethernet, Token Ring, and so forth) has a particular way it encapsulates data. This particular encapsulation is called the *frame format*. Each technology uses its own frame format. In Ethernet technologies, the frame of data is a fixed-length and is generally referred to as a packet. The Ethernet IP packet contains a preamble, destination and source address, data, and an error-checking sequence, among other things. The frame format describes the required data and the order in which it appears inside the data packet, which is the unit of data sent across the network medium.

Each TCP segment has a header that contains, among other things, the following important fields:

- TCP port to send the data

- TCP port to receive the data

- Sequence number for the segment

- ACK number

- Window size (not to be confused with the Microsoft Windows OS), which indicates the current size of the TCP buffer on the sending host's end. The TCP buffer is used to hold incoming segments and must have room to accept additional segments when received.

To establish a connection, TCP uses a three-part handshake, which works as follows:

1. The client computer sends a SYN (synchronization request) message with a sequence number that is generated by the client.

2. The server computer responds with an ACK message. This consists of the original sequence number plus 1. The server also sends a SYN number that it generates.

3. The client adds a 1 to the SYN number that was sent by the server, and returns it as an ACK.

This process, with each computer acknowledging the other, results in the establishment of a connection. A similar process is used to terminate the connection. TCP establishes this one-to-one (host-to-host) connection and also adds header information to ensure reliable communications. The downside to this reliability is that it adds both time and data in the transmission, which slows down communication somewhat.

There are three distinct steps used to establish a reliable connection. These same steps are used to end a connection. This handshake process is what creates a reliable connection because both hosts must indicate that they are ready to send/receive and that they have finished sending/receiving. The first step is to establish the connection. The sending host (we'll call it Host A for clarity) sends a TCP segment to the receiving host (Host B) with an initial sequence number for the connection and the TCP window size, which indicates the sender's receiving buffer size. The receiving computer, Host B, replies with a TCP segment that contains its chosen sequence number and its initial TCP window size. Host A sends a segment back to Host B acknowledging Host B's chosen sequence number.

UDP

In some cases, it's appropriate to send a quick message without needing to sequence the data or to get an ACK that it's been received. In these cases, an application developer might choose to use the UDP instead of TCP. Remember that protocols are agreed-upon rules that developers use to ensure their applications work within the TCP/IP framework. UDP is often described as connectionless or "best-effort delivery" because it does not establish a connection before sending, it does not sequence packets before sending, and it does not provide error control through retransmission. In short, it's a one-shot deal that is fast but not always reliable.

The UDP header contains three important fields:

- The source port

- The destination port

- The UDP checksum

Both TCP and UDP use port numbers, as we discussed previously. Port numbers are assigned by the Internet Assigned Numbers Authority (IANA). It is important to have a centralized body to assign these numbers so that everyone will use the same ports for the same functions. There are many well-known TCP and UDP ports, as well as many obscure ports. When you secure a network server, it is usually advisable to disable all TCP and UDP ports that are not in use, so they cannot be used by hackers looking for a back door.

TCP and UDP may use the same port numbers, but they are not the same ports. Each uses its own distinct set of ports. TCP port 20 is different from UDP port 20. A few of the common TCP and UDP ports are shown in Table 2.1.

For a list of commonly hacked (or probed) ports, see www.linux-firewall-tools.com/linux/ports.html. Although the site is a Linux site, the TCP and UDP ports used by TCP/IP services (and by hackers) are the same regardless of the OS.

Table 2.1 Common TCP and UDP Ports

Common TCP Ports	Common UDP Ports
Port 20 – FTP (data channel) queries	Port 53 – Domain name system (DNS) name
Port 21 – FTP (control channel)	Port 137 – NetBIOS name service
Port 23 – Telnet	Port 138 – NetBIOS datagram service
Port 80 – HTTP	Port 161 – SNMP

Test Day Tip

TCP versus UDP; you are very likely to run into some questions on the exam that are related to TCP and UDP. It's critical to understand the difference between these two transport protocols. UDP is an unreliable, connectionless, fast transport protocol used for sending short messages or messages that do not require ACK of receipt. An easy way to remember the difference is **TCP** is *Trustworthy* and **UDP** is *Unreliable*.

What's important to remember about TCP and UDP is that although one is considered reliable and the other unreliable, it does not mean that one is inherently better than the other. TCP establishes a connection before information is sent to the receiver; UDP does not. Many applications do not require ACK that sent data was received because it sends the data in small amounts. In these scenarios, using a connectionless UDP datagram is far more efficient. Therefore, UDP datagrams are used in a variety of applications including NetBIOS name service, NetBIOS datagram service, Simple Network Management Protocol (SNMP), and Domain Name System (DNS).

Application Layer

The application layer protocols of the TCP/IP protocol suite operate at the session, presentation, and application layers of the OSI model. In the DoD model, this layer enables applications to communicate with one another, and it provides access to the services of the other underlying layers (DoD Layers 1 through 3). There is a wide variety of application layer protocols, and more are being developed because they can rely on all the TCP/IP services beneath them in the protocol stack.

We briefly mentioned some of the application layer protocols in our discussion of the OSI application layer. In the following sections, we will describe some of these in more detail. We won't cover every single application layer protocol in use today (we couldn't, without turning this book into an encyclopedia set), but we will cover some of the protocols and services that you're not only likely to work with on the job as a network technician, but that you're also likely to encounter on the CCNA certification exam.

SMB/CIFS

The SMB protocol was originally developed by International Business Machines (IBM) in the 1980s and was later expanded by IBM, Microsoft, Intel, and 3Com. SMB was primarily used for file and print sharing, but it is also used for sharing serial ports and abstract communications technologies such as named pipes and mail slots. SMB is also now known as *Common Internet File System* (CIFS); both names are used interchangeably.

CIFS is a protocol that, like many application layer protocols, is operating-system-independent. It evolved from SMB and NetBIOS file and print sharing methods in earlier versions of the Windows OS. It can be used by different platforms and OS and across different network/transport protocols; it is not TCP/IP-dependent. The connection from client to server can be made via NetBEUI or IPX/SPX. After the network connection from client to server is established, then SMB commands can be sent to the server so that the client can open, read and write files, and so on.

CIFS is being jointly developed by Microsoft and other vendors, but no published specification currently exists. UNIX and Linux clients can connect to SMB shares using *smbclient* from SAMBA or *smbfs* for Linux. Server implementations of SMB for non-Microsoft OS include SAMBA and LAN Manager for OS/2 and SCO.

Telnet

Telnet is a terminal emulation protocol that allows you to log onto a remote computer. The remote computer must be using TCP/IP and have the Telnet server service running. To connect to a remote host, you must start the Telnet client and must possess a username and password for the remote host computer. In Windows Server 2003, the Telnet server service is present, but it must be started to service Telnet clients.

If you have never used the *command prompt* in Windows, here's how: click **Start | Run** and type **cmd** in the dialog box (in Windows OS prior to Windows 98, the 16-bit command was **command**. In Windows 98 and beyond, the 32-bit command, **cmd**, is supported). This will open a command window. Type **telnet** at the prompt. Type **help** for a list of commands and **quit** to close Telnet. Use **exit** to close the *command prompt window*.

Exam Warning

Remember that Telnet uses port 23 (both TCP and UDP) for communication, SSH (which stands for Secure Shell and is essentially encrypted Telnet) runs on port 22 (also TCP and UDP). Telnet information is sent in plaintext, so it's very easy to capture packets and read the contents such as usernames and passwords.

It is also important to note that while Telnet is a protocol, it is also an application that can be used to connect to other protocols by changing what destination port you attempt to attach to (for example, 25 for SMTP, 80 for HTTP, and 110 for POP3).

SMTP

The SMTP is a protocol used to transfer e-mail messages and attachments. SMTP is used to transmit e-mail between e-mail servers and from e-mail clients (such as Microsoft Outlook or UNIX and Linux's sendmail) to e-mail servers (such as Microsoft Exchange). Most e-mail clients, however, use other protocols, such as POP3 or IMAP4, to *retrieve* e-mail from the server. These two server applications (SMTP and POP or IMAP) may exist on the same physical server machine.

As with the other protocols and services discussed in this section, SMTP operates at the application layer and relies on the services of the underlying layers of the TCP/IP suite to provide the actual data transfer services.

POP

Post Office Protocol is a widely used e-mail application protocol that can be used to retrieve e-mail from an e-mail server for the client application, such as Microsoft Outlook. The current version of POP is POP3.

POP servers set up mailboxes (actually directories or folders) for each e-mail account name. The server receives the mail for a domain and sorts it into these individual folders. Then, a user uses a POP client program (such as Outlook or Eudora) to connect to the POP server and download all the mail in that user's folder to the user's computer. Usually, when the mail messages are transferred to the client machine, they are deleted from the server.

IMAP

IMAP, like POP, is used to retrieve e-mail from a server and creates a mailbox for each user account. It differs from POP in that the client program can access the mail and allow the user to read, reply to, and delete it while it is still on the server. Microsoft Exchange functions as an IMAP server. This is convenient for users because they never have to download the mail to their client computers (saving space on their hard disks), but especially because they can connect to the server and have all their mail available to them from any computer, anywhere. When you use POP to retrieve your mail, old mail that you've already downloaded is on the computer you were using when you retrieved it, so if you're using a different computer, you won't be able to see it. IMAP is preferred for users who use different computers (for example, a home computer, an office computer, and a laptop) to access their e-mail at different times.

HTTP

Hypertext Transfer Protocol is the protocol used to transfer files used on the Internet to display Web pages. When you type an Internet address (a URL) into your browser's **Address** field, it uses the HTTP protocol to retrieve and display the files located at that address.

A URL typically contains a server name, a second-level domain name, and a top-level domain name, with the parts of the address separated by dots. Individual folder and filenames may follow, separated by slashes. For example, www.rsnetworks.net/index.htm indicates an Hypertext Markup Language (HTML) document (Web page) on a Web server named www in the rsnetworks.net domain. The first part of the URL may also be entered as an IP address if it is known.

HTTP was defined and used as early as 1990. However, there were no published specifications for HTTP in the beginning, and different vendors modified HTTP as they saw fit. As the World Wide Web continued to evolve and grow to be the enormous resource that it is today, additional functionality was needed in HTTP. The first formal definition was labeled HTTP/1, and it was later replaced by HTTP/1.1.

FTP

The FTP is used to transfer files from one host to another, regardless of the hosts' physical locations. It is one of the oldest application layer protocols and was used on Advanced Research Projects (ARPANET) to transfer files from one mainframe to another. Still in use today, FTP is widely used on the Internet to transfer files. One of the problems with FTP is that it transmits users' passwords in clear text, so it is not a secure protocol.

In contrast to the single connections used by Network News Transfer Protocol (NNTP), HTTP, and SMTP, two separate connections are established for an FTP session. One transmits commands and replies, and the other transmits the actual data. The command and control information is sent, by default, via TCP port 21. The data, by default, is sent via TCP port 20.

DNS

The Domain Naming System is used to resolve a hostname to an IP address to facilitate the delivery of network data packets. As mentioned previously, DNS is now the primary method used in Microsoft Windows Server 2003 to resolve hostnames to IP addresses. DNS is also the protocol used on the Internet to resolve hostnames (such as those in URLs) to IP addresses.

Prior to DNS, hostname-to-IP resolution was accomplished via a text file called *hosts*. In the days of ARPANET, this file was compiled and managed by the Network Information Center at the Stanford Research Institute. This plain text file contained the name and address of every single computer, but there were only a handful of computers on the network at the time. When a new computer was added, or a computer changed its IP address, the file had to be edited manually and distributed to all the other computers. As computers and networks proliferated, another more automated solution had to be devised and the specifications for a distributed naming system, called the *Domain Naming System*, were developed.

DNS servers on the Internet store copies of the DNS database. Because of the explosive growth of the Internet in the past decade, DNS databases are specialized. For instance, a set of databases is responsible for top-level domain information only. Examples of top-level domains are .com, .gov, .edu, .net, .org, and so on. All requests for an address ending with .com will be forwarded to a particular set of DNS servers. These servers will query their databases to find the specific .com domain requested (for example, microsoft .com). DNS databases are replicated periodically to refresh the data.

Network Time Protocol

Network Time Protocol (NTP) is a protocol that provides a very reliable way of transmitting and receiving an accurate time source over TCP/IP-based networks. NTP, defined in Request for Comments (RFC) 1305 (www.ietf.org/rfc/rfc1305.txt), is useful for synchronizing the internal clock of the computers to a common time source. Some systems, such as Novell NetWare's Novell Directory Services (NDS, or now known simply as e-Directory) as well as Microsoft Windows Server 2003 and 2000, rely on a time source to keep things running right. For system maintenance, troubleshooting of issues, and documentation, it is important that all systems be time synchronized. In addition, for prosecution of security breaches or attacks, security logs need to be accurate and so on. NTP, when used properly, can have a hierarchical disaster recovery system designed into it, with primary sources of time as well as secondaries. Having the correct time on your system(s) is very important. Many problems can surface if networked machines are not synchronized.

SNMP

The SNMP is used for communications between a network management console and the network's devices, such as bridges, routers, and hubs. This protocol facilitates the sharing of network control information with the management console. SNMP uses a management system/agent framework to share relevant network management information. This information is stored in a *Management Information Base* (MIB) and contains a set of objects, each of which represents a particular type of network information such as an event, an error, or an active session. SNMP uses UDP datagrams to send messages between the management console and the agents.

Now that we have covered the OSI model (as well as the DoD model) in depth, you should now have a good idea of its importance and why it's so important to know for the CCNA exam. This modular approach to network communications makes development less time-consuming and more consistent across vendors, networks, and systems. As a result, new application layer protocols are constantly being developed. This section is not meant to serve as an exhaustive look at the wide array of application protocols available today, but it is to give you a better idea of the more common protocols and services that operate at this layer and provide an understanding of how the layered approach works.

We've reviewed the seven layers of the OSI model (starting from the lowest level, physical, data link, network, transport, session, presentation, and application) and the four layers of the DARPA (TCP/IP) model (network interface, Internet, host-to-host, and application), and we've learned how these layers map to one another.

PDU

One very important area for the CCNA student is to know the PDUs (the way TCP/IP breaks down the data as it goes down the protocol stack). We compare this to the OSI model instead of the DoD model as that is the way it will appear on the CCNA exams.

Your data will be broken down four times, as it travels down the stack and will be put together in its whole only on the destination system, but it will exist in the other forms depending on what device it crosses. Figure 2.6 shows the OSI layer and what PDUs are at each layer. There are two primary reasons that the data is broken down. The first is for data contention. If we don't break the data down into smaller units, one device could take over the entire network thus preventing any other devices to send data. The other reason is error correction. If we send one stream of data from sender to receiver and any data is lost in the transmission, there would first be no indication of data loss until the entire message was received, and second, we would have to send the data all over again. By using the PDUs, data can be checked as it is sent across the network and across the Internet and can be resent closer to the source, so the receiver only has to check large blocks that have been tested in smaller units across the way.

Layer Seven—Application Layer	
Layer Six—Presentation Layer	
Layer Five—Session Layer	
Layer Four—Transport Layer	Segment
Layer Three—Network Layer	Packet
Layer Two—Data Link Layer	Frame
Layer One—Physical Layer	Bit

FIGURE 2.6   *OSI Model and PDUs*

Each PDU has what is called a *checksum* (also known as a CRC) in the footer of each unit. This is simply an algorithm that is run on the data being encapsulated into the unit and stored in the footer. So each time the unit crosses the device that checks that unit, they can run the same algorithm across the data received; if this checksum matches, the data is unharmed and can pass onto the next step. If the checksum does not match, it can request a retransmission from the device that sent it.

Exam Warning

The CCNA exam places a lot of emphasis on these PDUs. You will have various types of questions including drag and drop, layer matching, and device matching. You need to really know all the devices that operate at each layer, and what is in the header of each unit.

One easy way to remember the order of the PDUs is to use this little sentence:

Some People Fry Bacon = Segment Packet Frame Bit

Segment

At the transport layer, the data is broken down for the first time; this breakdown occurs at the OS level. If you were sending or receiving a file using FTP on a Microsoft Windows-based system, the sending server would break the file into segments and would put a segment number and other information about the segment into the header; it would then run the checksum and place that in the footer. If you were having segment problems, you would have to look at the sending and receiving systems event log for the problems.

Packet

At the network layer, the segments are broken down into packets. Remember that the network layer is responsible for the routing of packets from one logical network to another.

The header of the packet is like the manifest of a truck; it tells you where the data is coming from, where it is going to, and what kind of data it is carrying. So the header would consist of Source IP address, Source TCP or UDP port, Destination IP address, and Destination TCP or UDP port. The Source IP address tells where the data is coming from, and the Source TCP/UDP port is used by network address translation (NAT) to identify which computer on the LAN. The Destination IP address is where the traffic is headed, and the Destination TCP/UDP port is the type of traffic the packet is carrying. Again, the checksum is in the footer.

Routers handle the packets, and each time a packet crosses a router, it is checked first for errors. Then, the Destination IP address is looked at and the next routers are determined and the packet is forwarded. So if you are having packet errors, packet problems, or dropped packets, look at the routers.

Exam Warning

On the CCNA exam, you may have a question on how to tell what router in the path may be causing packet loss between a source and destination, and the command is traceroute on a Cisco router.

Frame

The next PDU is called a *frame*, and frames exist both on the LAN and the WAN. The header of a frame contains the Source MAC address and the Destination MAC address (also known as the BIA in Cisco Speak), and the footer contains a checksum. Every time your frame crosses a network switch on the LAN or a "Frame" switch (remember Frame Relay for T1) on the WAN, the frame will be checked for errors and the destination BIA will be looked at to determine the next device to receive the data. Switches, Frame Relay Devices, and any other devices that work at Layer 2, handle frames and that is where your diagnostics and trouble shooting should start.

Exam Warning

One protocol that often is used for troubleshooting frames is the ARP, and the command to look at the ARP table on a Cisco router is show arp. It is important to know this for the exam.

Bit

The final PDU is the bit, the 1s and 0s that go out over the media. There is no header, no footer, and no checksum. This is the raw data on the wire. If the signal crossed the network, you are having bit errors in the NIC card, the media (copper, fiber, wireless, and so forth), or the hubs or other connectivity devices.

SUMMARY OF EXAM OBJECTIVES

In this chapter, we covered the OSI model in depth. For those of you unfamiliar with working with network models, it should be clear now that working with them can bring many benefits, such as ease of development and troubleshooting. Networking models can be very helpful to you. In this chapter, we covered two of them in particular: the OSI model and the DoD model, both of which are similar and share common core elements, but have differences as well.

From the DARPA experiment came the understanding that networking would become increasingly common—and increasingly complex. The OSI model was developed, based on the original DoD DARPA model, and approved by the Open Systems Interconnection (OSI) subcommittee of the ISO. The OSI model defined seven layers for standard, reliable network communications: physical, data link, network, transport, session, presentation, and application. The acronym commonly used to remember this is (in reverse order) **A**ll **P**eople **S**eem **T**o **N**eed **D**ata **P**rocessing.

If you were to follow each layer and map to it a protocol and a device, then by reading this chapter you would remember that the physical layer is responsible for signaling, transmission medium, and ones and zeros traversing the wire. As we move up the model, things get increasingly more complex. The next layer, the data link layer, is where your MAC address is located. We discussed the functionality of a NIC card and what a MAC address is. On Ethernet NICs, the physical or MAC address (also called the hardware address) is expressed as 12 hexadecimal digits, arranged in pairs with colons between each pair, for example, 12:3A:4D:66:3A:1C. In binary notation, this translates to a 48-bit (or 6-byte) number, with the initial 3 bytes representing the manufacturer and the last 3 bytes representing a unique NIC made by that manufacturer. The data link layer is subdivided into two sublayers known as the LLC and MAC layers. The LLC sublayer is responsible for providing the logic for the data link, and thus it controls the synchronization, flow control, and error-checking functions of the data link layer.

The TCP/IP protocol suite provides the functionality specified in the OSI model using the four related layers of the DoD model: network interface, Internet, host-to-host, and application. The network interface maps to the physical and data link layers, and the Internet layer maps to the OSI network layer. The host-to-host layer maps to the transport layer, and DoD's application layer maps to the session, presentation, and application layers of the OSI model. Some of the more commonly known application layer protocols are FTP, HTTP, POP3, Windows Internet Name Service (WINS), DNS, and Dynamic Host Configuration Protocol (DHCP). Understanding the details of the TCP/IP protocol suite is fundamental to managing computers in today's networked environment. Being able to subnet, assign IP addresses, create subnet masks, and set up routing are essential skills you'll need on the job and to successfully master the material on the CCNA exam.

Remember also the PDU; there will be a number of questions on segments, packets, frames, and bits.

EXAM OBJECTIVES FAST TRACK

An Overview of the OSI Model

- Seven layers used to describe the methodology of how data is transferred from source to destination.

- Application layer handles top level protocols such as FTP, SMTP, HTTP, and so forth.

- Presentation layer handles compression, encryption, and data formatting.

- Session layer handles the virtual circuits PVCs and SVCs.

- Transport layer is where TCP and UDP ports are and the PDU is called a *segment*.

- Network layer is where IP lives, and the IP address is used. Routers operate at this layer. The PDU is called a *packet*.

- Data link layer is where the MAC (or BIA) lives, as well as switches and bridges. The frame is the PDU at this layer.

- Physical layer is where the bits flow; bits are the PDU at this layer. Hubs, repeaters, and cables live here.

- NICs operate at both the physical and data link layer.

An Overview of the TCP/IP Model

- The DoD DARPA model was developed by Vint Cerf and Bob Khan.

- Foundation of the Internet

- Four layers

- The application layer maps to the application, presentation, and session layers of the OSI.

- The transport layer maps to the transport layer of the OSI.

- The network layer maps to the network layer of the OSI.

- The network interface layer maps to the data link and physical layers of the OSI.

- Public domain protocol is used by millions of devices all over the world.

ACKNOWLEDGEMENT

We fully acknowledge use of Chapter 2, "OSI model and Then Some," from *Next Generation SSH2 Implementation: Securing Data in Motion*, ISBN: 978-1-59749-283-6 and Chapter 5, "OSI model," from *Network+ Study Guide & Practice Exams: Exam N10-003*, ISBN: 978-1-931836-42-5.

EXAM OBJECTIVES FREQUENTLY ASKED QUESTIONS

Q: How likely am I to see a question related to the DoD DARPA model or ARPANET on the exam?

A: It's unusual to see a question directly related to these topics, but you will see questions that rely upon your understanding of both the OSI model and the TCP/IP suite. Understanding the origins of these models will help you answer questions related to the networking models.

Q: Isn't ARPANET the same thing as the Internet? Why do I need to know this anyway?

A: ARPANET was the first working implementation of internetworking. The structures devised in the experiment as well as the knowledge gained during that project form the foundation of the Internet. The ARPANET was a network of a few mainframe computers and was not universally available, as the Internet is today, nor was it a commercial network (all nodes were located at universities or government agencies). It is possible that you'll see an exam question that uses ARPANET as an answer. Understanding the origins of the Internet can help you answer other questions on the exam, sometimes by simply helping you eliminate wrong answers.

Q: How exactly does the network interface layer of the DoD model map to the physical and data link layers of the OSI model?

A: The DoD's network interface layer maps directly to the physical and data link layers of the OSI model, with one notable exception. There are two parts to the data link layer—the LLC and the MAC sublayers. TCP/IP does not implement the LLC element at the network interface layer. This function is handled further up the protocol stack at the host-to-host (transport) layer.

Q: There are a lot of application layer protocols in the TCP/IP suite. Am I expected to memorize them all?

A: There is an ever-expanding set of application layer protocols in use today. It's important to get a firm understanding of the most common protocols and to have at least a familiarity with the less common protocols. At the very least, you should be very familiar with NetBIOS over TCP, Windows Sockets, DNS, DHCP, WINS, Telnet, SMTP, HTTP, FTP, RIP, and SNMP.

SELF TEST

1. What is the unique physical address (BIA) that is found on all NICs called?
   A. DNS Address
   B. NAT Address
   C. IP address
   D. MAC Address

2. Which of the following is a valid MAC address?
   A. 00:05:J6:0D:91:K1
   B. 10.0.0.1 - 255.255.255.0
   C. 00:05:J6:0D:91:B1
   D. 00:D0:A0:5C:C1:B5

3. When working with MAC addresses, which layer of the OSI model do MAC addresses, frames, and switches associate to?
   - **A.** Data link
   - **B.** Host-to-Host
   - **C.** Presentation
   - **D.** Application

4. From the list of choices, which of the following media access methods is used for an IEEE 802.5 network?
   - **A.** Direct sequence
   - **B.** Token passing
   - **C.** CSMA/CD
   - **D.** CSMA/CA

5. Which OSI model layer is responsible for frame sequencing?
   - **A.** The physical layer
   - **B.** The transport layer
   - **C.** The data link layer
   - **D.** The application layer

6. POP3 is identified by which TCP/IP port number?
   - **A.** UDP Port 21
   - **B.** TCP Port 23
   - **C.** UDP Port 25
   - **D.** TCP Port 110

7. Standards for CSMA/CD are specified by which IEEE 802 sublayer?
   - **A.** 802.1
   - **B.** 802.2
   - **C.** 802.3
   - **D.** 802.5

8. From the choices listed, which of the following protocols represents e-mail protocols? Please choose two from the list below.
   - **A.** POP3
   - **B.** SNMP
   - **C.** IMAP4
   - **D.** Telnet

9. From the following protocols listed, select the protocol that network management applications used to monitor network devices remotely.
   - **A.** SNMP
   - **B.** DNS
   - **C.** SMTP
   - **D.** DHCP

10. When discussing the OSI model and the DoD model, which layers of the OSI model handle what you would find in the application layer of the DoD model? Choose all that apply.
    - **A.** Application
    - **B.** Presentation
    - **C.** Transport
    - **D.** Session

11. You are a network technician assigned to install a new network hub. Which layer of the OSI model does a standard hub operate at? Select only one answer.

    A. Physical layer
    B. Data link layer
    C. Network layer
    D. Transport layer

12. You are a network technician assigned to install a new network switch. Which layer of the OSI model does a standard switch (or bridge) operate at? Select only one answer.

    A. Physical layer
    B. Data link layer
    C. Network layer
    D. Transport layer

13. You are a network technician assigned to install a new network router. Which layer of the OSI model does a standard router operate at? Choose all that apply.

    A. Physical layer
    B. Data link layer
    C. Network layer
    D. Transport layer

14. You are a network technician assigned to install a new NIC in a PC. Which layer of the OSI model does a NIC operate at? Select only two answers.

    A. Physical layer
    B. Data link layer
    C. Network layer
    D. Transport layer

15. What is a multiport repeater called?

    A. Hub
    B. Switch
    C. Router
    D. Brouter
    E. Modem

SELF TEST QUICK ANSWER KEY

1. D	**9.** A
2. D	**10.** A, B, and D
3. A	**11.** A
4. B	**12.** B
5. C	**13.** C
6. D	**14.** A and B
7. C	**15.** A
8. A and C	

CHAPTER 3

Subnetting, CIDR, and Variable Length Subnet Masking

INTRODUCTION

If you want to pass the Cisco Certified Network Associate (CCNA) certification exam and have a successful career in the field of networking, you need to understand how to divide and combine networks through the process of subnetting and classless interdomain routing (CIDR). It is imperative to understand what devices on a network are able to communicate with one another. Network configurations such as an incorrect subnet mask can result in two devices not being able to communicate.

CCNAs are not the only individuals who need to understand CIDR notation. Computer forensic investigators, intrusions investigators, penetration testers, and even hackers need to be aware of CIDR notation and its implications related to the devices on the network. Anyone who works with or configures network settings on a frequent basis needs to understand what impact different CIDR notations will have on a network.

Understanding the bits behind the scene will help CCNA students to have a better grasp on how CIDR and subnetting settings will affect devices on the network. A student needs to enter a CCNA exam prepared to analyze what devices will be able to communicate with one another on a network based on their CIDR notation. Being able to understand how networks can be divided and Internet Protocol (IP) addresses can be allocated efficiently is important to pass the CCNA exam as well as having a successful career within the field of networking.

IP ADDRESSES

Once computers are networked, and you wish to send data from one computer to another, there needs to be a way to find the computer that is going to receive the data. When the receiving computer gets the data you have sent, it must know where the data came from.

There are two useful analogies here. The first is to compare the data traffic over the Internet, between two PCs (for instance, exchanging messages through instant messaging) with letters posted in the mail. The second analogy is to compare that same data traffic with the placement of telephone calls. But, as telephone calls most of the time take place over data networks, let's elaborate on the mail example.

When you wish to send a letter to a friend, you would write your friend's address as the recipient, and your address as the sender. Imagine the problems the postman would have if one of the addresses was not unique, one of the addresses was incomplete, or one of the addresses was not valid.

Obviously, there will be problems in delivering the letter on each of those situations. To avoid those problems, ways to guarantee uniqueness, verify completeness, and accuracy of the addresses needed to be in place. And, just in case something went wrong after all, there would always be a return address to send the undeliverable message.

On computer networks, it's exactly the same. The main difference being that computers don't understand names too well, as they are number machines. So, the addresses are numbers, instead of street names. On the prevailing "type of network" in existence today, which uses the Transmission Control Protocol/Internet Protocol (TCP/IP) suite of protocols (detailed in Chapter 1), the addressing scheme is provided by IP addresses.

Test Day Tip
IP addresses are nothing more than big numbers, ranging from 0 to 4294967296. What? Doesn't this look like a typo, as you've probably seen IP addresses as numbers separated by dots? Yes, it's simply another way of representing them.

The IP addresses are thus used to target a specific machine in the world. Getting back to the comparison with the postal service, when you write the address of the letter's recipient, you break apart the address in number, street, district, city, and country. A similar approach is used in the IP addresses, where the address is split in blocks. Each block is separated from the other with dots. IP addresses are composed of four blocks. Each of the four blocks is called an *octet* (the name octet comes from the fact that each block is composed of eight bits—more on that when we talk about number systems). Each octet's allowed value ranges from 0 to 255.

Exam Warning

An IP address is often written in a format called *dotted decimal*. This splits the address in four octets, separated by dots. Each octet is named according to the position in which it appears: first octet, second octet, third octet, and fourth octet.

    The allowable range of values for each octet is from 0 to 255. This comes from the fact that an octet is actually the decimal representation of a binary number composed of eight digits. The smallest possible number with eight binary digits is 0, and the biggest is 255. There are a couple of other restrictions in the allowable values for IP addresses, which will be detailed later.

IP addresses were designed in a hierarchical way. Thus, each octet will identify a part of the recipient's location. Instead of having all the constituent parts of a postal address, IP addresses have only network and host subdivisions. These are called network ID and host ID.

The creation of the IP protocol dates back to 1974 when, on a paper authored by Vint Cerf and Bob Kahn entitled *A Protocol for Packet Network Interconnection*, a protocol for data communication to be later called TCP/IP, was described. The IP version discussed in this chapter is called *IPv4*, and is currently the dominant protocol used for Internetworking. IPv4 is defined on the Request for Comments-791 (RFC) (http://rfc.net/rfc791.txt), which was published in 1981.

Having been created so long ago, one of the reasons the IPv4 protocol remains the most used protocol nowadays is its flexibility. It's suitable for large or small networks. One of the cornerstones of its flexible nature is that you are able to divide the addresses (in network and hosts) in the way that best suit your needs. This is achieved by having an additional number with the IP address, to indicate how it should be split into network ID and host ID.

This additional number is called the subnet mask.

Subnet Mask

Given the hierarchical nature guiding the creation of the IP addressing scheme, we can refer back to the postal service's example. A postal address is usually composed of (at least) the following:

- Country
- City
- District
- Street
- Number

It would be useful to represent that hierarchical nature in IP addresses too, so that based only on the address, the data packet should be delivered to the right network, and once on that network, be sent to the host that's expecting for it. The division made in the IP address is then made to have a part of the address representing the network (called network ID), and another part of the address representing the host on that network (host ID). On a given network (specific network ID), no host should have the same number. It's the same as that on a given street (network ID), no two houses (host ID) should have the same number, or the postman would have no clue to which house the letter should be delivered.

The prevalent way of achieving this subdivision is by having the IP address accompanied by another number, also having 32 bits split in four octets, called the subnet mask. This mask, once applied over the IP address, will reveal which part of it is the network ID, and which part is the host ID.

Abiding to the same rules governing an IP address, a network mask is composed of four octets. There are restrictions on the values these octets can have.

Refer to Exercise 3.1 to identify valid and invalid subnet mask values.

Test Day Tip

Seen in the binary format (only 0s and 1s), a subnet mask can have only an uninterrupted chain of 1s, followed by 0s. This limits the allowable values a subnet mask can have.

The allowable values in a subnet mask are 255, 254, 252, 248, 240, 224, 192, 128, and 0. The rule is that, after the first non-255 value appears, all remaining octets must be 0.

Table 3.1 shows the allowed values in a subnet mask and their representation in binary notation (observe they're all 1s, followed by all 0s).

EXERCISE 3.1   Identifying Valid Subnet Masks

Which of the following values are invalid for a subnet mask?

1. 255.255.192.0
2. 255.255.0.0
3. 255.254.0.0
4. 255.255.255.224
5. 255.254.255.0
6. 225.0.0.0
7. 255.224.0.0
8. 248.255.0.0

The invalid subnet masks are (5), (6), and (8). Let's transform all subnet masks in their binary representation to identify why are they valid or invalid. The final answer can be seen in Table 3.4.

Step 1—convert each mask from dotted decimal to "dotted binary" (refer to Table 3.1). Place your conversions in Table 3.2.

Step 2—after conversion, you need to identify if you have, after the first zero, any number one. If this happens, that's an invalid subnet mask. Fill Table 3.3 with your answers.

Your answers should look similar to the ones in Table 3.4.

Table 3.1	Valid Values on Subnet Masks
Decimal Value	**Binary Value**
255	11111111
254	11111110
252	11111100
248	11111000
240	11110000
224	11100000
192	11000000
128	10000000
0	00000000

Table 3.2 Converting Subnet Masks to Binary

Subnet Mask in Dotted Decimal	Subnet Mask in "Dotted Binary"
255.255.192.0	
255.255.0.0	
255.254.0.0	
255.255.255.224	
255.254.255.0	
225.0.0.0	
255.224.0.0	
248.255.0.0	

Table 3.3 Looking for 1s After the First Zero

Subnet Mask in Dotted Decimal	Subnet Mask in "Dotted Binary"	Reason for Being Valid or Invalid
255.255.192.0	11111111.11111111.11000000.00000000	
255.255.0.0	11111111.11111111.00000000.00000000	
255.254.0.0	11111111.11111110.00000000.00000000	
255.255.255.224	11111111.11111111.11111111.11100000	
255.254.255.0	11111111.11111110.11111111.00000000	
225.0.0.0	11100001.00000000.00000000.00000000	
255.224.0.0	11111111.11100000.00000000.00000000	
248.255.0.0	11111000.11111111.00000000.00000000	

Table 3.4 Identifying Invalid or Valid Subnet Masks—Answer

Subnet Mask in Dotted Decimal	Subnet Mask in "Dotted Binary"	Reason for Being Valid or Invalid
255.255.192.0	11111111.11111111.11000000.00000000	Valid. All 1s, followed by all 0s.
255.255.0.0	11111111.11111111.00000000.00000000	Valid. All 1s, followed by all 0s.
255.254.0.0	11111111.11111110.00000000.00000000	Valid. All 1s, followed by all 0s.

Continued

Subnet Mask in Dotted Decimal	Subnet Mask in "Dotted Binary"	Reason for Being Valid or Invalid

Table 3.4 Identifying Invalid or Valid Subnet Masks—Answer *continued*

Subnet Mask in Dotted Decimal	Subnet Mask in "Dotted Binary"	Reason for Being Valid or Invalid
255.255.255.224	11111111.11111111.11111111.11100000	Valid. All 1s, followed by all 0s.
255.254.255.0	11111111.11111110.11111111.00000000	Invalid. All 1s, followed by one zero, which is not followed by all 0s.
225.0.0.0	11100001.00000000.00000000.00000000	Invalid. There is a 1, after the zeroes begin.
255.224.0.0	11111111.11100000.00000000.00000000	Valid. All 1s, followed by all 0s.
248.255.0.0	11111000.11111111.00000000.00000000	Invalid. All 1s, followed by zeroes, which are not followed by all 0s.

BINARY DECIMAL CONVERSIONS

Daily, when we think about numbers, we usually think on 0, 1, 2, 3, 4, 5, 6, 7, 8, 9. And using these "building blocks," we are able to write whichever number we'd like, because the principle is really simple. You start at 0, go incrementing up until 9. When you reach 9 and want to get the next number (obviously 10), what you actually do is increase the number on the left by one, and cycle the current number to the first one. But wait! What number on the left? There was a single digit! Well, sort of... Let's take a closer look at it.

When you have the number 1, it's exactly the same as 01, which in turn is the same as 001, which is the same as 0001, and so on. We simply decide not to write the zeroes on the left. So, when you have reached 9, you were actually writing 09 (only omitting the zero on the left). To get to 10, you have actually done the following:

- 0 9 → last number for the second digit

- 1 0 → increase the digit to the left by one, and cycle the digit that was on its last number

The principle is the same no matter how big the number is. That's why we know that after 39299 comes 39300. Breaking it down into steps, we have

- 39299 + 1 → increase the rightmost digit by 1 (as it's on the last number, we cycle it to 0, and increase by 1 the next one to the right). But it's at the last number too... Then we must cycle it to 0, and increase by one the next one to the right, getting to 39300.

Sounds easy and even stupid, as you know this since you learned how to talk, right? But this number system that goes from 0 to 9 (thus having

10 possible numbers) is simply one of the several number systems in existence. It's called "the decimal system," or in computer terms, the base-10 numbering system. Probably this is the one used by humans because we have 10 fingers on both hands, and it's thus simple to learn. Any other number system can be created. For instance, in a base-8 (called octal) number system, eight possible numbers are available (from 0 to 7), thus making $7 + 1 = 10$, and $17 + 1 = 20$, due to the same principle explained earlier.

Computers, internally, use yet another number system. It's called the *binary system*, which has only two numbers, 0 and 1. One of the reasons for this number system is that computers are electronic machines, and in this sense, the numbers mean

- $0 \rightarrow$ off, no current, no tension, false

- $1 \rightarrow$ on, current, tension, true

In the binary system, we would have $1 + 1 = 10$ and $11 + 1 = 100$. Let's detail the first sum:

$1 + 1 = 10$

- $01 + 1 \rightarrow$ just another way of representing 1, showing the zero to the left.

If we want to add 1, we add to the rightmost number, which is already on the highest number it can represent. Then, we cycle it to 0, and increase the next to the right by 1. Thus $1 + 1 = 10$.

As we're studying IP addresses, we will focus only on binary (0, 1) and decimal (0, 1, 2, 3, 4, 5, 6, 7, 8, 9) systems, which are basically the only ones used. But keep in mind that computers (mainly on programming tasks) also use a lot of hexadecimal, or base-16 number system (having 0..9, A, B, C, D, E, F as the numbers).

An important task to be performed on the binary numbers is to convert them to decimal and back. On the decimal system (base-10) we know that the rightmost digit represents units, the next to the right represents tens, the next hundreds, the next thousands, and so forth. So, we could say that 13,456 (thirteen thousand four hundred and fifty-six) is actually the following:

- 10,000 (ten thousand) +

- 3,000 (three thousand) +

- 400 (four hundred) +

- 50 (fifty) +

- 6 (six)

And this is exactly the same as mentioned above and it is as follows:

- 1 × 10,000 (one times ten thousand)

- 3 × 1,000 (three times one thousand)

- 4 × 100 (four times one hundred)

- 5 × 10 (five times ten)

- 6 × 1 (six times one)

The general behavior when writing the numbers is that whenever you move to the left, you are actually multiplying the number by its base, starting at 1. So, the rightmost position multiplies the number by 1. The next to the left multiplies it by 1 × base (on base-10, 1 × 10 = 10). The next multiplies it by 1 × base × base (on base-10, that's 1 × 10 × 10 = 100). And this goes on and on. Formally speaking, given a base-n, each position is (from right to left) multiplied by n0, n1, n2, n3, and so on. An example detailing this can be seen on Table 3.5, for the number 21335.

To work on base-2, it's exactly the same idea, but instead of 1, 10, 100, 1,000, you will have 1, 2, 4, 8, ..., as shown in Table 3.6.

Thus, given the number 10110 in base 2, its equivalent in base-10 would be obtained by doing the same breakdown made for a base-10 number, where we'll have the results shown in Table 3.7.

We have the decimal (base-10) equivalent of the binary (base-2) number 10110 being 1 × 16 + 0 × 8 + 1 + 4 + 1 × 2 + 0 × 1= 22.

To convert a decimal number to its binary representation, there are two general approaches. It's up to you to decide which one you like most. We will show the two approaches through Exercises 3.2 (first approach) and 3.3 (second approach).

Table 3.5 Breaking Down 21335, Base 10

"Broken Down" Number	Powers of 10	Relative Position (Power of 10, "Solved")	"Broken Down" Numbers Multiplied by their Relative Position
2	10^4	10,000	2 × 10,000
1	10^3	1,000	1 × 1,000
3	10^2	100	3 × 100
3	10^1	10	3 × 10
5	10^0	1	5 × 1

Table 3.6 Powers of 2

Powers of 2 (from 0 to 7)	Calculated Value
2^0	1
2^1	2
2^2	4
2^3	8
2^4	16
2^5	32
2^6	64
2^7	128

Table 3.7 10110 in Base 2, Converted to Base 10

"Broken Down" Number	Powers of 2	Relative Position (Power of 2, "Solved")	"Broken Down" Numbers Multiplied by their Relative Position
1	2^4	16	1×16
0	2^3	8	0×8
1	2^2	4	1×4
1	2^1	2	1×2
0	2^0	1	0×1

EXERCISE 3.2   Converting Decimals to Binaries

Let's convert the number 2, from decimal to binary. We already know, from the text (Table 3.7), or by using a calculator, that its value in binary format is 10110.

1. Create a table with the powers of 2.

You need to create a two-row table, with eight columns (it could be more columns for bigger numbers, but specifically for IP addressing, where the biggest number is 8 bits long, eight columns is enough).

The first row should be filled with the powers of 2. We will then use the second row for "fitting" the decimal number. The idea here is to compare the number to each power of 2, from left to right. If the number is less than the power of 2 in the current cell, place a 0 in that position. If the number is greater than or equal to the power of 2 in the current cell, place a 1 there, and subtract that power of 2 from the number. Use the result for the remaining cells. Table 3.8 shows how it should look.

Table 3.8 Empty Table with Powers of 2

$128 = 2^7$	$64 = 2^6$	$32 = 2^5$	$16 = 2^4$	$8 = 2^3$	$4 = 2^2$	$2 = 2^1$	$1 = 2^0$

The basic principle is to ask the question: Is the number greater than (or equal) the number in the current cell? If it is, place a 1 there, and subtract the value on that cell from the number. If it isn't, place a zero there, and go to the next cell.

2. Is the number greater than or equal to 128? It isn't, place a 0 there, as seen in Table 3.9.

Table 3.9 Table with Powers of 2, First Column Filled

$128 = 2^7$	$64 = 2^6$	$32 = 2^5$	$16 = 2^4$	$8 = 2^3$	$4 = 2^2$	$2 = 2^1$	$1 = 2^0$
0							

3. Is the number greater than or equal to 64? It isn't, place a 0 there, as seen in Table 3.10.

Table 3.10 Table with Powers of 2, First and Second Columns Filled

$128 = 2^7$	$64 = 2^6$	$32 = 2^5$	$16 = 2^4$	$8 = 2^3$	$4 = 2^2$	$2 = 2^1$	$1 = 2^0$
0	0						

4. Is the number greater than or equal to 32? It isn't, place a 0 there, as seen in Table 3.11.

Table 3.11 Table with Powers of 2, Filled to the Third Column

$128 = 2^7$	$64 = 2^6$	$32 = 2^5$	$16 = 2^4$	$8 = 2^3$	$4 = 2^2$	$2 = 2^1$	$1 = 2^0$
0	0	0					

5. Is the number greater than or equal to 16? It is, then place a 1 there, and subtract 16 from the number, leaving you with 6, as seen in Table 3.12.

Table 3.12	Table with Powers of 2, Filled to the Fourth Column						
$128 = 2^7$	$64 = 2^6$	$32 = 2^5$	$16 = 2^4$	$8 = 2^3$	$4 = 2^2$	$2 = 2^1$	$1 = 2^0$
0	0	0	1				

6. Is the number (**now 6, not 22 anymore!**) greater than or equal to 8? It isn't, place a 0 there, as you can see in Table 3.13.

Table 3.13	Table with Powers of 2, Filled to the Fifth Column						
$128 = 2^7$	$64 = 2^6$	$32 = 2^5$	$16 = 2^4$	$8 = 2^3$	$4 = 2^2$	$2 = 2^1$	$1 = 2^0$
0	0	0	1	0			

7. Is the number greater than or equal to 4? It is, then, place a 1 there, and subtract 4 from the number, with 2 remaining now, as you see in Table 3.14.

Table 3.14	Table with Powers of 2, Filled to the Sixth Column						
$128 = 2^7$	$64 = 2^6$	$32 = 2^5$	$16 = 2^4$	$8 = 2^3$	$4 = 2^2$	$2 = 2^1$	$1 = 2^0$
0	0	0	1	0	1		

8. Is the number greater than or equal to 2? It is, place a 1 there, and subtract 2 from the number, leaving you with 0, as you see in Table 3.15.

Table 3.15	Table with Powers of 2, Filled to the Seventh Column						
$128 = 2^7$	$64 = 2^6$	$32 = 2^5$	$16 = 2^4$	$8 = 2^3$	$4 = 2^2$	$2 = 2^1$	$1 = 2^0$
0	0	0	1	0	1	1	

9. Is the number (now 0) greater than or equal to 1? It isn't, place a 0 there, as you can see in Table 3.16.

Table 3.16	Table with Powers of 2, Completely Filled						
$128 = 2^7$	$64 = 2^6$	$32 = 2^5$	$16 = 2^4$	$8 = 2^3$	$4 = 2^2$	$2 = 2^1$	$1 = 2^0$
0	0	0	1	0	1	1	0

That's it. The number is 00010110. Just remember that we can ignore zeroes on the left, which makes the number equal to 10110, as stated in the beginning of the exercise.

Now we will see another method of converting from decimals to binaries. This method is called the *successive divisions* method. It works by repeatedly dividing the original number by 2, and using the result of the latest division, as the input to the next one.

EXERCISE 3.3   Converting Decimals to Binaries—Successive Divisions

The second approach consists of making successive integer divisions by 2 with the original number. A table with a column for each of the terms will be used (dividend, divisor, quotient, and remainder), using the number 22 as the example, you would have. Table 3.17 gives the names for the division terms.

The divisor will be always 2, as this is the destination base of the conversion.

The resulting number is the last quotient, followed by all the remainders, read from the bottom up. For the example used in Table 3.18, I have placed letters beside the numbers that will be used. This will give you the letters:

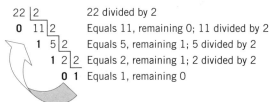

- edcba, which are the numbers 10110

In Figure 3.1, you can see the same exercise, represented in a more concise manner.

FIGURE 3.1 *Alternative Representation for a Successive Division*

Table 3.17	Terms of a Division	
Dividend		Divisor
Remainder		Quotient

Table 3.18	Using the Successive Divisions Method to Convert 22 from Decimal to Binary			
Dividend	**Divisor**	**Quotient**	**Remainder**	**Explanation**
22	2	11	0 (a)	Simply divide the original number by 2. The quotient is then used as the dividend for the next step.
11	2	5	1 (b)	Once again, the quotient is the dividend for the next step.
5	2	2	1 (c)	Once again, the quotient is the dividend for the next step.
2	2	1 (e)	0 (d)	This is the last step, as the quotient is smaller than the divisor.

Network ID

The network ID, as its name implies, is the part of an IP address that identifies the network where it belongs. To obtain the network ID from an IP address, you need to combine, through a special operation, the IP address and the network mask. It's useful to look at each of the octets in its binary representation. Conversions from binary to decimal and decimal to binary were just explained. If you wish, you can perform the same conversions using your operating system calculator. Assuming you're on Windows, just run *calc*. Go to the menu **View | Scientific**. You will see it as Figure 3.2 shows. The two highlighted radio buttons are the ones which you will use to convert between binary and decimal. Just type a number in decimal, click on the "Bin" radio button, and it will be shown in binary format, and vice versa.

FIGURE 3.2

Using the Windows Calculator to Convert from Decimal to Binary and Vice Versa

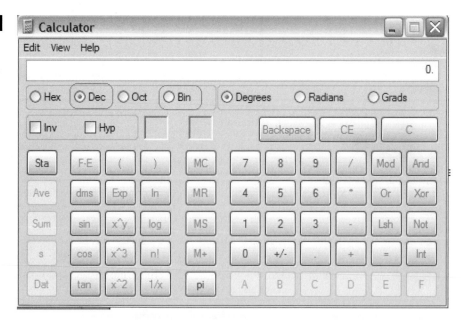

The subnet mask, once applied to an IP address, will then split it into the network ID and the host ID. To perform the split, you will look at the two addresses (subnet mask and IP address) represented in their binary format. Remember that a subnet mask is a contiguous sequence of 1s, followed by 0s. All bits, on the IP address, which have, in the same position on the subnet mask, a 1, make up the network ID. The remaining bits (which have a 0 in the corresponding position of the subnet mask) make up the host ID. The remaining bits are zeroes in the subnet mask. This will be better illustrated by Exercises 3.4 and 3.5.

Exam Warning

Pay special attention in the exam to "nonstandard" subnet masks. These come in two varieties:

1. The masks that do not contain only 255s and 0s. These are specially tricky when obtaining the network and host ID, because you will have part of the octet as the network ID.

2. Subnet masks that are standard (255s and 0s), but used on a different class that the one they were originally intended for (refer to Table 3.28 for all the default masks).

Practice the conversion from binary to decimal and use it on the exam day.

The network ID is then used by routers to find the destination network in its routing tables. They will either have a direct link, or a neighboring router to send the packet, so it goes closer to its destination.

Going back to the analogy with the postal service here, the postal service in Los Angeles, USA does not need to know in detail about the address for a letter whose recipient is in Berlin, Germany. It only needs to know that it's for Europe, and send it to a partner who deals with letters in Europe.

In the same way, a computer in the network 192.168.0.0 does not have to know how to reach the network 223.124.96.0. It just needs to send the packet to its neighboring router, who will either have a direct connection to the destination, or send it through another router, until it eventually gets to its destination.

Host ID

The first part of the IP address (network ID) is used to find the network where the packet needs to be sent. Once the packet arrives to its destination network, it needs to be delivered to a given host (computer, PDA, videogame, mobile phone) in that network. The address of that host is the host ID.

The process for extracting the host ID out of an IP address is almost the same as the process used to extract the network ID. The only difference is that, whereas for the network ID, you were interested in the part of the IP address matching the 1s in the subnet mask, for the host ID you are interested in the parts of the IP address matching the 0s in the subnet mask. For the 1s in the subnet mask, you would represent it as a 0 in the host ID. As these would be "zeroes on the left," they are not written in the host ID.

Exercises 3.4 and 3.5 will illustrate this concept.

EXERCISE 3.4 Identifying the Network ID and Host ID Given the IP Address and the Subnet Mask—1

For the IP address 192.168.100.131, with the subnet mask 255.255.255.224, what is the network ID and host ID?

1. As a first step, we need to convert both the IP address and the subnet mask into their binary representations. Table 3.19 shows the conversion of each of the octets separately.

Table 3.19 Converting all the Components of the IP Address from Decimal to Binary

Number in Decimal	Conversion Table								Number in Binary
	128	64	32	16	8	4	2	1	
192	1	1	0	0	0	0	0	0	11000000
168	1	0	1	0	1	0	0	0	10101000
100	0	1	1	0	0	1	0	0	01100100
131	1	0	0	0	0	0	1	1	10000011

2. We need to convert the subnet mask into its binary representation. Using the calculator to convert each of the octets separately gives us the results shown in Table 3.20.

3. Now we need to match the binary representation of the IP and subnet mask to obtain the network ID. For each 1 on the subnet mask, the resulting number in the network ID is the number in the IP address. For each 0 in the subnet mask, the resultant number in the network ID is a 0 too. This gives us the results shown in Table 3.21.

Table 3.20	Converting all the Components of the Subnet Mask from Decimal to Binary									
Number in Decimal	**Conversion Table**									**Number in Binary**
	128	64	32	16	8	4	2	1		
255	1	1	1	1	1	1	1	1		11111111
255	1	1	1	1	1	1	1	1		11111111
255	1	1	1	1	1	1	1	1		11111111
224	1	1	1	0	0	0	0	0		11100000

Table 3.21	Obtaining the Network ID by Matching the Binary Representation of the IP and Subnet Mask	
Address "Name"	**Dotted Binary Representation**	**Dotted Decimal Representation**
IP address	11000000.10101000.01100100.10000011	192.168.100.131
Subnet mask	11111111.11111111.11111111.11100000	255.255.255.224
Network ID	11000000.10101000.01100100.10000000	192.168.100.128

4. To obtain the host ID, the process is almost the same as the one used to obtain the network ID. The only difference is that you will copy, from the IP address, the bits that are zeroes in the subnet mask, as shown in Table 3.22.

Table 3.22	Obtaining the Host ID by Matching the Binary Representation of the IP and Subnet Mask	
Address "Name"	**Dotted Binary Representation**	**Dotted Decimal Representation**
IP address	11000000.10101000.01100100.10000011	192.168.100.131
Subnet mask	11111111.11111111.11111111.11100000	255.255.255.224
Host ID	00000000.00000000.00000000.00000011	0.0.0.3 = 3

Keep in mind that you will always see leading zeroes in host IDs. These are usually removed when writing the host ID.

Thus, given the IP address 192.168.100.131, and the subnet mask 255.255.255.224, the network ID is 192.168.100.128 and the host ID is 3.

EXERCISE 3.5   Identifying the Network ID and Host ID Given the IP Address and The Subnet Mask—2

For the IP address 187.124.100.45, with the subnet mask 255.255.240.0, what is the network ID?

1. We need to convert the IP address into its binary representation. Table 3.23 shows the results of using the calculator to convert each of the octets separately.

Table 3.23 187.124.100.45 Converted from Decimal to Binary

Number in Decimal	Conversion Table								Number in Binary
	128	64	32	16	8	4	2	1	
187	1	0	1	1	1	0	1	1	10111011
124	0	1	1	1	1	1	0	0	01111100
100	0	1	1	0	0	1	0	0	01100100
45	0	0	1	0	1	1	0	1	00101101

2. We need to convert the subnet mask into its binary representation. Using the calculator to convert each of the octets separately gives us the results shown in Table 3.24.

Table 3.24 255.255.240.0 Converted from Decimal to Binary

Number in Decimal	Conversion Table								Number in Binary
	128	64	32	16	8	4	2	1	
255	1	1	1	1	1	1	1	1	11111111
255	1	1	1	1	1	1	1	1	11111111
255	1	1	1	1	1	1	1	1	11111111
240	1	1	1	1	0	0	0	0	11110000

3. Now we need to match the binary representation of the IP and subnet mask to obtain the network ID. For each 1 on the subnet mask, the resulting number in the network ID is the number in the IP address. For each 0 in the subnet mask, the resultant number in the network ID is a 0 too. This gives us the results shown in Table 3.25.

Table 3.25	Obtaining the Network ID by Matching the Binary Representation of the IP and Subnet Mask	
Address "Name"	**Dotted Binary Representation**	**Dotted Decimal Representation**
IP address	10111011.10101000.01100100.00010100	187.124.100.45 ∧ logical conjuction
Subnet mask	11111111.11111111.11110000.00000000	255.255.240.0
Network ID	10111011.01111100.01100000.00000000	187.124.96.0

4. To obtain the host ID, the process is almost the same as the one used to obtain the network ID. The only difference is that you will copy, from the IP address, the bits that are zeroes in the subnet mask, as shown in Table 3.26.

Table 3.26	Obtaining the Host ID by Matching the Binary Representation of the IP and Subnet Mask	
Address "Name"	**Dotted Binary Representation**	**Dotted Decimal Representation**
IP address	10111011.10101000.01100100.00010100	187.124.100.45 ∨ logical Disjuncta
Subnet mask	11111111.11111111.11110000.00000000	255.255.240.0
Network ID	00000000.00000000.00000100.00101101	0.0.4.45 = 4.45

Keep in mind that you will always see leading zeroes in host IDs. These are usually removed when writing the host ID.

Thus, given the IP address 187.124.100.45 and the subnet mask 255.255.240.0, the network ID is 187.124.96.0 and the host ID is 4.45

The network ID is then used by routers to find the destination network in its routing tables. They will either have a direct link, or a neighboring router to send the packet, so it goes closer to its destination.

Going back to the analogy with the postal service here, the postal service in Los Angeles, USA does not need to know in detail about the address for a letter whose recipient is in Berlin, Germany. It only needs to know that it's for Europe, and send it to a partner who deals with letters in Europe.

In the same way, a computer in the network 192.168.0.0 does not have to know how to reach the network 201.124.96.0. It just needs to send the packet to its neighboring router, who will either have a direct connection to the destination, or send it through another router, until it eventually gets to its destination.

Exam Warning

The host ID part of an IP address can neither be all zeroes (as this is the network address) nor all ones (as this is a special address on the network, called broadcast address).

Class

In the simplest form, the split between network ID and host ID is made simply based on the octets. Aren't the addresses, written on dotted decimal, already separated in four blocks (octets)? The split can then be made based on those octets. We would have then three categories of addresses:

1. Addresses whose first octet is the network ID, and the other three are the host ID.

2. Addresses whose first two octets are the network ID, and the remaining two are the host ID.

3. Addresses having the first three octets representing the network ID, and the last octet being the host ID.

It's interesting to notice that each class allows for increasingly more networks, but reducing the number of available hosts. Let's dive into details for each class.

Each of these categories is called a "class," and they are called class A, B, and C. These classes comprise the addresses available for assignment to individual hosts. There are still two other classes: class D, used for multicasting, and class E, which is reserved for future use.

For each of the classes A, B, and C, which are the ones with addresses assignable to hosts, there is a default subnet mask. This mask is what breaks the address in one, two, or three octets for the network ID, and the remaining octets for the host ID.

If we use, for any given class, all possible combinations of addresses, the address space would be exhausted, with no addresses left for the other classes. For instance, if we used all the possible combinations for the class A (256 networks, each with 16,777,216 hosts), we would have used $256 \times 16,777,216 = 4,294,967,296$ addresses. No address would be left for the other classes. A division should be made so that each class could use a portion of the address space, while still leaving plenty of available addresses for the other classes. The division should be made in such a way that a computer could easily identify which are the network and the host ID, given an address. There's nothing that's interpreted quicker by a computer than binary digits.

Table 3.27 Identifying Classes Based on the First Octet's Value

Class	First Bits	Smaller Number (Binary)	Smaller Number (Decimal)	Greater Number (Binary)	Greater Number (Decimal)	Range for the First Octet
A	0	00000000	0	01111111	127	0 .. 127
B	10	10000000	128	10111111	191	128 .. 191
C	110	11000000	192	11011111	223	192 .. 223
D	1110	11100000	224	11101111	239	224 .. 239
E	1111	11110000	240	11111111	255	240 .. 255

HEAD OF THE CLASS...

Easily Finding the Class of an IP Address

It's important to have memorized the beginning and ending addresses for the first octet of classes A to C. At the very least, it's necessary to remember the binary formation of the address:

- first bit is a 0, class A
- first bits are 10, class B
- first bits are 110, class C

The division of the classes was then defined based on the first (leftmost) bits of the IP address, as Table 3.27 demonstrates.

Notice how fast an address could be inspected to identify its class. Just a quick look at its first four bits (at most) would define the class of the address.

Test Day Tip

Always remember the default (or standard) network masks for each class of address, which are the ones shown in Table 3.28.

Table 3.28 Classes A, B, and C, and their Default Subnet Masks

Class	Default Subnet Mask
A	255.0.0.0
B	255.255.0.0
C	255.255.255.0

Class A

The first category of addresses is class A. It has the first octet as the network ID, and the remaining three octets as the host ID. This leaves us, in theory, with 256 networks, and 16,777,216 hosts. This number is equal to 256 × 256 × 256. That's 256 different possible values for each of the remaining three octets.

The theoretical value of 256 networks is limited to 126. This is because the biggest class A value for the first octet is 127. But the network 127 is reserved for network tests (the most famous of its addresses is 127.0.0.1, known as the loopback address), and a zero is not allowed as a network address. Each network can have (256 × 256 × 256) − 2 addresses. This is 256 for each of the three octets representing the host ID, minus 2 for the network and broadcast address. Table 3.29 shows us these limits.

Class B

The second category of addresses is class B. This class has the first two octets as the network ID, and the remaining two octets as the host ID. This gives us 256 × 256 possible values for both the network and host ID. It is then possible to have (in theory) 65,536 networks, each having 65,536 hosts.

Table 3.29	Class A Limits
Class	**A**
Default network mask	255.0.0.0
Number of networks	126 (1 .. 126)
Number of hosts per network	16,777,214, which is 256 for the second to fourth octet (256 × 256 × 256); minus 2 (broadcast and network addresses)
First network address	1.0.0.0
First address assignable to a host	1.0.0.1 (one after the first network address)
First broadcast address	1.255.255.255 (last address of the first network)
Last network address	126.0.0.0
Last broadcast address	126.255.255.255
Last address assignable to a host	126.255.255.254 (one before the last broadcast address)

Table 3.30 Class B Limits

Class	B
Default network mask	255.255.0.0
Number of networks	16,384, which is 256 for the second octet, times 64 = 191 − 128 + 1 for the first octet
Number of hosts per network	65,534, which is 256 × 256 (for the third and fourth octets); minus 2 (broadcast and network address)
First network address	128.0.0.0
First address assignable to a host	128.0.0.1 (one after the first network address)
First broadcast address	128.0.255.255 (last address of the first network)
Last network address	191.255.0.0
Last broadcast address	191.255.255.255
Last address assignable to a host	191.255.255.254 (one before the last broadcast address)

The theoretical value is limited, as the first octet can range only between 128 and 191. This gives us the data shown in Table 3.30.

Class C

The third category of addresses is class C. This class has the first three octets as the network ID, and the remaining octet as the host ID. This gives us 256 × 256 × 256 = 16,777,216 possible values for the network ID, each network having only 256 possible addresses.

The theoretical value is limited, as the first octet can range only between 192 and 223. This gives us the limits shown in Table 3.31.

Class D

This class has addresses that are not assignable to a single host. They are used for a category of communication that is called multicast. The idea here is that a group of hosts will join a multicast group to receive multicast content. The address range is from 224.0.0.0 to 239.255.255.255.

Class E

This class is reserved for future use. It goes from 240.0.0.0 to 255.255.255.255.

Table 3.31 Class C Limits	
Class	**C**
Default network mask	255.255.255.0
Number of networks	2,097,152, which is 65,536 = 256 × 256 (for the second and third octet), times 32 = 223 − 192 + 1 (for the first octet)
Number of hosts per network	254, which is 256 (for the fourth octet); minus 2 (broadcast and network address)
First network address	192.0.0.0
First address assignable to a host	192.0.0.1 (one after the first network address)
First broadcast address	192.0.0.255 (last address of the first network)
Last network address	192.255.255.0
Last broadcast address	192.255.255.255
Last address assignable to a host	192.255.255.254 (one before the last broadcast address)

Broadcast

The typical form of communication between hosts is what is called unicast, when a host sends communication directly to a given host. Several situations demand communication between all hosts on a network segment. This is called *broadcast communication*. It's similar to an advertisement that is listened to by all hosts in that network segment. Each IP network has a broadcast address, which allows communication to be addressed to all hosts on that network.

CONFIGURING AND IMPLEMENTING...

Example of Broadcast Usage

There are several protocols which make heavy usage of broadcast. One is Dynamic Host Configuration Protocol (DHCP), the protocol for dynamic assignment of IP addresses, detailed elsewhere in this book. Another is the Address Resolution Protocol (ARP), which translates logical addresses (i.e., IP Addresses) into physical addresses (i.e., MAC—Media Access Control—addresses).

Whenever a router receives a package that is addressed to a network segment to which it is attached, it needs to find out the physical address of the intended recipient of that package. To do that, it sends a broadcast message (an ARP request) asking: "Who has the IP address x.y.w.z?" The host with that address answers the broadcast request with his physical address.

The sending of a broadcast message is actually the sending of a packet to the broadcast address of that network. It will be processed by all hosts on that segment. Another option for sending a broadcast message is to use the global broadcast address (255.255.255.255). This will reach all hosts on the local area network.

Multicast

Multicast is the communication where one host sends data to multiple hosts at once. The principle here is that the hosts that wish to take part on the multicast communication join a multicast group, typically using one of the addresses in class D. The principle is that the sender of data sends each packet only once to reach all the members of the multicast group.

The Transport Protocol most often used for multicast communication is User Datagram Protocol (UDP). As opposed to TCP, UDP is by definition not reliable, meaning some packets might be lost in transit. There are reliable multicast protocols, using packet loss detection mechanisms, also available, with the added cost of retransmissions, acknowledgements, and other mechanisms similar to the ones used by TCP, for guaranteed packet delivery.

Because packets can be lost on the typical multicast implementation, this form of communication is most often used when this can be tolerated, and continuity is more important. One good example of this is for audio/ video transmission over the Internet. Protocols such as Real-Time Transport Protocol (RTP) are used for this purpose.

Another protocol using multicast is Routing Information Protocol version 2 (RIPv2). This protocol is used by routers to exchange route information between them. The multicast address used is 224.0.0.9. This protocol is described in detail in Chapter 5.

Unicast

This is the most common form of communication between hosts. This is when communication is established between two hosts. A packet is sent from a sender to a destination host. Typically one host has dozens of unicast connections established at once. For instance, when you are connected to the Internet, with several Web sites opened at once, you will have several connections established. On a *command prompt window*, type:

```
netstat - a
```

to see all the open connections. You'll see an output similar to the one shown in Figure 3.3. I have used, besides the –a option, which shows all connections and listening ports, the –n option switch, to show numbers instead of names for ports and addresses.

Almost all application level protocols use unicast for communication. Some examples are as follows: File Transfer Protocol (FTP), Hyper-Text Transfer Protocol (HTTP), and Simple Mail Transfer Protocol (SMTP). For

FIGURE 3.3

Netstat Output

instance, when an e-mail server sends mail to another server, the steps performed are similar to these:

1. A Domain Name System (DNS) server is queried, to tell who is responsible for mail (MX—mail exchanger) for the domain somewhere.com is.

2. The IP address for the hostname obtained on step 1 is obtained from the DNS server.

3. An unicast connection is established with the MX host at somewhere.com.

4. The sending server identifies the domain from which the message originates.

5. The sending server identifies the e-mail of the message sender.

6. The sending server identifies the e-mail of the message recipient.

7. The e-mail data is sent.

At any point between steps 3 and 7, the destination server can abort the connection, typically to prevent spam, banning undesired hosts (step 3), undesired sending domains (step 4), undesired senders (step 5), undesired or nonexistent recipients (step 6), or undesired message content (step 7).

The connection established with the DNS server to resolve the host name, and obtain the mail server name for the destination address is also done through unicast.

Octet

IP addresses are simply a block of 32 bits (binary digits) written in sequence. To make things easier for us humans to write and remember, we break them apart in blocks of eight digits, separated by dots. This notation is

---

HEAD OF THE CLASS...

IP Address Limits

The largest possible number with 32 bits is 2^{32} = 4,294,967,296 (that's four billion, two hundred ninety-four million, nine hundred sixty-seven thousand, two hundred ninety-six). Yes, that's the number of IP addresses available, over 4 billion, which seemed, by the time the IP addressing was created, enough for the current and future needs.

Unfortunately, it's not enough nowadays. Assuming we'd like to give an exclusive IP address to every inhabitant of the earth (remember, it should be similar to an address used in letters, able to reach uniquely the intended recipient), there wouldn't be enough. As of July 2008, there are more than 6.5 billion people living in this tiny blue planet. And we should not forget that the devices that need IP addresses are neither people, nor computers, but all kinds of things you can imagine: cell phones, set-top boxes, laptop computers, servers, PDAs…

There are further constraints on the IP addressing that limits even more the number of assignable addresses. The answer to overcome these limits comes in two forms:

1. *Private addresses*, which are subsets of the IP address space, that can be used where there is no need for direct public (meaning Internet) visibility of the hosts. These addresses can then

be repeated as one wishes. For instance, a corporate network in New York can have its address in the range 192.168.0.0, and another network in the same city, just across the street, can have the same address range.

The way this is achieved is by preventing direct communication between these two networks (they can communicate to each other by means of intermediaries with public addresses).

There are several private addresses in each class of address, as follows:

- Class A: 10.0.0.0 to 10.255.255.255 (1 network)
- Class B: 172.16.0.0 to 172.31.255.255 (16 networks)
- Class C: 192.168.0.0. to 192.168.255.255 (256 networks)

2. *IPV6*, which is the next generation of the TCP/IP suite. The IP addressing part, in special, has IP addresses composed of 128 bits. This means there are 3.4×10^{38} (that's 3.4 times 10 followed by 38 zeros). Just for an idea, this gives 5×10^{28} (five times 10 followed by 28 zeros) addresses available for each of the approximately 6.5 billion people living on the earth.

called dotted decimal representation of an IP address. As 32 is four times eight, each block has 8 bits. Each 8-bit block is called an octet. Having four octets, they are simply called first octet, second octet, third octet, and fourth octet.

The largest number in the decimal system, having two digits, would be 99; the largest with three digits, 999, and so on. What this means is that the largest possible number for a given number of digits is simply a sequence of the largest number in the given number system. So, what is the largest 8-digit number in the binary system?

- 11111111 (that's 1—the largest number in the binary system—eight times).

- This number in decimal format is (convert it with the calculator) 255.

This effectively means that each octet can have values ranging from 0 to 255, which gives us 256 different numbers.

SUBNETTING

The original subdivision of IP addresses in classes, creating networks of fixed sizes, having either 254, 65,534 or 16,777,214 hosts each, imposes severe restrictions on the creation and interconnection of the networks. You either have a small (254 hosts), large (65,534 hosts), or gigantic (16,777,214 hosts) network. There's no choice in between. Assuming you have a network with only 20 hosts, or with 200,000 hosts, you're left without a choice.

If, when you want a network with 20 hosts, you need to use a 254-host network, or when you want to have 200,000 hosts, you need to use a 16,777,214-host network, the waste of addresses is unbelievable. And, considering the scarce nature of addresses already discussed, the issue is even worse.

To work around this issue, the concept of subnet was created. The main idea of subnetting (the act of creating subnetworks, or subnets) is that you can have networks with the size you want. You are not limited to the classfull (class A, B, C, D, and E) addresses to split an address into network and host ID. By using "nonstandard" subnet masks (masks which are not composed only of 255s and 0s), you can use parts of an octet for a network, giving you almost unlimited flexibility in the networks you can create.

To subnet a network, you take part of the bits that would originally (through the original subnet mask) be part of the host ID, and reserve them for the network ID (or subnet ID). This does not come without its price. By taking bits away from the host part of the address to assign to the network part, you are in effect reducing the number of possible hosts. If you want to create two subnets, you will take one bit off the host ID part of the address. For four subnets, you will take 2 bits, for eight subnets, you take 4 bits off the host ID part of the address, and the math goes on the same way.

Table 3.32 demonstrates the amount of bits taken off the host ID part of the address for each number of subnets created.

Remember that an IP address has 32 bits, and you always need to have at least two addresses in a host ID (one for the broadcast, and the other for the network ID).

Table 3.32	Mapping between Number of Subnets and Bits Taken Off of the Host ID
To Create this Number of Subnets	**You Take this Amount of Bits from the Host ID Part of the Address**
2	1
4	2
8	3
16	4
32	5
64	6
128	7
256	8
512	9

Continued

Table 3.32	Mapping between Number of Subnets and Bits Taken Off of the Host ID *continued*
To Create this Number of Subnets	**You Take this Amount of Bits from the Host ID Part of the Address**
1,024	10
2,048	11
4,096	12
8,192	13
16,384	14
32,768	15
65,536	16
131,072	17
262,144	18
524,288	19
1,048,576	20
2,097,152	21
4,194,304	22

This makes the smallest subnet possible having 30 bits for the network ID part of the subnet mask. This leaves four possible addresses for the host ID (two of which are assignable for a host, and the remaining two are reserved for the broadcast address and host ID). If it was originally a class A network, you would have taken 22 bits off the host ID part of the address.

The biggest subnet would have 9 bits for the network ID. It would be a division on a class A network, taking off a single bit of the host ID part of the address.

Test Day Tip

For each bit you add to the network part of the address, you are taking away one bit of the host part of the address. Each bit will then double the number of available subnets, cutting in half the number of available hosts for that network.

The first step in the process of subnetting is then deriving the new subnet mask. Once you have this new subnet mask, for the bits added to the network ID part of the mask, you will obtain all its possible values. This will give you all possible combinations of networks for the new subnets.

Exam Warning

Every network needs two addresses that shouldn't be assigned to hosts, namely the network and the broadcast address. This means that the number of hosts calculated for a given network will need to be subtracted by 2, rendering a useless subnet having 31 bits for the network ID (as you will not have addresses available for hosts).

An exception is made for point-to-point networks, where the broadcast and network ID address don't need to exist.

After that is done, zeroing all bits of the host ID will give you the network address of each subnet. Putting all bits of the host ID as 1 will give you the broadcast address of each network, two exercises to illustrate this concept. Exercise 3.6 gives a number of desired subnets, where Exercise 3.7 gives a number of desired hosts per subnet.

EXERCISE 3.6   Subnetting to a Given Number of Subnets

You are a network administrator who has the network 192.168.100.0 with the default class-C network mask (255.255.255.0) assigned to you; both all-ones and subnet zero are enabled. You need to create two subnets from this network. What is the new subnet mask? For each network, what is its network address, first assignable address, last assignable address, broadcast address?

1. To start with the process, let's represent the subnet mask in its binary format, which is

■ 11111111.11111111.11111111.00000000

To create eight subnets, you need 1 bit from the host part of the subnet mask, transforming your original subnet mask into (the new 1s are in bold)

■ 11111111.11111111.11111111.**1**0000000

This address in decimal format is 255.255.255.128

2. Now, obtain the binary representation of the original network address, which is

■ 11000000.10101000.01100100.00000000

3. Now you take each possible combination of values for the number that is now part of the network ID, combining it with the original network address. As it is a single bit, it's possible values are 0 and 1. This gives you two network addresses. The possible values for the new member of the network ID, 0 and 1, are in bold:

- 11000000.10101000.01100100.**0**0000000 → 192.168.100.0

- 11000000.10101000.01100100.**1**0000000 → 192.168.100.128

4. To obtain the broadcast address for each of the networks, you put 1s for all host ID bits, giving you (host IDs in bold):

- 11000000.10101000.01100100.0**1111111** → 192.168.100.127

- 11000000.10101000.01100100.1**1111111** → 192.168.100.255

5. To obtain the first assignable address of each network, you add 1 to the network ID (the binary representation is not important here)

- 192.168.100.1

- 192.168.100.129

6. The last assignable address is one less than the broadcast address for each network (the binary representation is not important here):

- 192.168.100.126

- 192.168.100.254

7. Putting it all together on Table 3.33, you have

- Original network: 192.168.100.0

- Original subnet mask: 255.255.255.0

- Number of subnets desired: 2

- New subnet mask: 192.168.100.128

Table 3.33 Subnet Details

	First Subnet	Second Subnet
Subnet address	192.168.100.0	192.168.100.128
First assignable address	192.168.100.1	192.168.100.129
Last assignable address	192.168.100.126	192.168.100.254
Broadcast address	192.168.100.127	192.168.100.255

It's worth noting that, where you had originally 254 (256 − 2, which is 256 original addresses minus 1 for the network address and one for the broadcast address) possible hosts in a single network, now you have two networks, each with 126 (128 − 2, which is 128, 256/2, minus 1 for the network address, and one for the broadcast address).

Exercise 3.6 showed how to subnet a given desired number of subnets. We will often be requested to subnet for a desired number of hosts per subnet. The general idea to solve both problems is the same. The following section details the difference:

- When subnetting to get a desired number of subnets, you need to decide how many bits you will borrow from the host ID part of the address, to be used on the network ID part of the address.

- When subnetting to get a desired number of hosts per subnet, you need to figure how many bits need to be kept on the host ID part of the address. The remaining will then be used for the network ID part of the address.

With that in mind, let's move to Exercise 3.7.

EXERCISE 3.7   Subnetting to a Given Number of Hosts Per Subnet

You, as a network administrator, were given the network 10.0.0.0, with a default class A subnet mask (255.0.0.0) to work with. You were asked to create subnets having each 1,000,000 (one million) hosts. How many subnets will you create? Which are their network IDs?

1. The first step to answer this question is to understand how many bits (of the original 24) of the host ID do you need to keep to be able to fit 100,000 hosts. Starting from 24, and going down, you will have what's shown in Table 3.34.

The last number of bits that is "too big" (meaning that it's the smallest one to fit the desired amount) is 20. This is the number of bits you need to keep for your host ID.

Because the original subnet mask was 255.0.0.0 (thus, having eight ones for the network ID), you are left with 24 bits for the host ID. As you need to keep 20, you will take 4 bits out of the host ID.

2. Now you know how many bits you will need to take off the host ID part of the address, you can build your new subnet mask, which will be

Table 3.34 Bits Left for the Host ID, and the Number of Hosts Available

Bits	2 Power the Number of Bits, or Number of Hosts with this Amount of Bits
24	16,777,216 (too big)
23	8,388,608 (too big)
22	4,194,304 (too big)
21	2,097,152 (too big)
20	1,048,576 (too big)
19	524,288 (too small)

- 11111111.0000000.0000000.0000000 (original subnet mask, 255.0.0.0)

- 11111111.**1111**0000.00000000.00000000 (new subnet mask, the 4 bits taken off of the host part are in bold. It is 255.240.0.0 in dotted decimal)

3. Now you will make every possible combination with the 4 bits. This gives you 16 combinations (2 power 4), which is your number of subnets. The address of each subnet is in the last column of Table 3.35.

Table 3.35 Subnet Addresses

The New 4 Bits	The Full Octet in Binary	The Full Octet in Decimal	The Subnet Address
0000	00000000	0	10.0.0.0
0001	00010000	16	10.16.0.0
0010	00100000	32	10.32.0.0
0011	00110000	48	10.48.0.0
0100	01000000	64	10.64.0.0
0101	01010000	80	10.80.0.0
0110	01100000	96	10.96.0.0
0111	01110000	112	10.112.0.0

Continued

Table 3.35	Subnet Addresses *continued*		
The New 4 Bits	**The Full Octet in Binary**	**The Full Octet in Decimal**	**The Subnet Address**
1000	10000000	128	10.128.0.0
1001	10010000	144	10.144.0.0
1010	10100000	160	10.160.0.0
1011	10110000	176	10.176.0.0
1100	11000000	192	10.192.0.0
1101	11010000	208	10.208.0.0
1110	11100000	224	10.224.0.0
1111	11110000	240	10.240.0.0

CIDR

CIDR is a way to categorize IP addresses for allocation to hosts and more efficient routing. CIDR represents the IP address and its subnet mask with a single number. Instead of having 2 four-octet numbers, the subnet mask is represented as its number of 1s. Because a subnet mask is always a contiguous sequence of 1s followed by a contiguous sequence of 0s, by giving the number of 1s, you are effectively describing the subnet mask. This number is represented after the IP address, which is separated by a forward slash.

Some examples are given in Table 3.36.

One of the advantages of using CIDR is the possibility of route aggregation. This means the internal routing tables of the routers will have a smaller number of entries. This is obtained through supernetting,

Table 3.36	Addresses Represented with the CIDR Notation			
IP Address	**Subnet Mask**	**Subnet Mask in Binary**	**Number of 1s**	**CIDR**
192.168.10.100	255.255.255.192	11111111.11111111.11111111.11000000	26	192.168.0.100/26
10.20.30.40	255.240.0.0	11111111.11110000.00000000.00000000	12	10.20.30.40/12
234.192.111.30	255.255.255.128	11111111.11111111.11111111.10000000	25	234.191.111.30/25
130.145.160.180	255.255.224.0	11111111.11111111.11100000.00000000	19	130.145.160.180/19

which is the opposite of subnetting we've seen so far. In subnetting, we borrow bits from the host part of the address to become part of the new network (subnet) address. Supernetting is the opposite. You will represent several contiguous networks with a single number. It's important to notice that all combinations of networks need to be present to be able to supernet.

Exercise 3.8 helps to illustrate the concept.

EXERCISE 3.8   CIDR and Supernetting

Suppose you have four contiguous class C networks, 192.168.100.0, 192.168.101.0, 192.168.102.0, and 192.168.103.0. The subnet mask for all of them is the default class C mask, 255.255.255.0, or in CIDR terminology, /24.

The addresses in binary format are shown in Table 3.37.

Observe that in the third octet, the addresses are exactly the same until the 6th bit. And they have all combinations possible (which are four) for the 7th and 8th bit. The combinations are 00, 01, 10, and 11.

Table 3.37 CIDR and Dotted Binary Addresses

Address in CIDR Format	IP Address in Dotted Binary
192.168.100.0/24	11000000.10101000.01100100.000000000
192.168.101.0/24	11000000.10101000.01100101.000000000
192.168.102.0/24	11000000.10101000.01100110.000000000
192.168.103.0/24	11000000.10101000.01100111.000000000

If you aggregate the four subnets into a single one, borrowing bits from the network part of the address to the host part you would have all networks represented by the address: 192.168.100.0/22. Thus you would be able to save space in the router's table.

To supernet networks, several conditions need to be fulfilled:

1. You need to have contiguous networks.

2. You need to have a number of networks that is power of two (2, 4, 8, 16, ...).

In this example, we had four networks. That's the reason why we have used 2 bits (2 power 2) from the network ID.

VARIABLE LENGTH SUBNET MASKING

Variable length subnet masking (VLSM) is what allows you to have even more flexibility on the way your subnets are created. Instead of having a fixed subnet mask for all the subnets you create over a given network, you can have subnet masks with differing sizes. This allows you to have, for instance, over a given class C network, one network with 100 hosts, one network with 60 hosts, and four with 10 hosts. How is this accomplished?

Let's elaborate on the example mentioned earlier. On a regular class C network (let's use as an example, the network 192.168.25.0), you can have 256 addresses, of which two are reserved (one for the broadcast address, and another for the network address itself). If you split the network in half, you will have two networks, capable of having each $128 - 2$ (that is, 126) hosts. The idea of VLSM is that you start subnetting to have a /25 network. The remaining /25 network would be divided further. Exercise 3.9 will show this in a step-by-step fashion.

EXERCISE 3.9   Variable-Length Subnet Masking

Given the network 192.168.25.0, with the default class C subnet mask, subnet it to obtain:

- One network with 100 hosts
- One network with 60 hosts
- Four networks with 10 hosts

1. We need to obtain the dotted-binary representation for the original network as shown in Table 3.38.

Table 3.38 Dotted-Binary Representation for the Original Network

Original Network	Dotted Binary
192.168.25.0/24	11000000.10101000.00011001.00000000

2. Because we need one network with 100 hosts, we will use the approach explained in Exercise 3.7 to find out how many bits need to be left in the host ID part of the address. We have already got only 8 bits in the host ID part of the address. Table 3.39 shows the amount of hosts we'd have available for each number of bits left in the host ID. Just remember that it's not just a matter of obtaining

Table 3.39	Hosts Available for Various Number of Bits Used
Bits in the Host ID	**Number of Hosts**
1	0
2	2
3	6
4	14
5	30
6	62
7	126
8	254

the power of 2! Two of the available addresses need to be used for special purposes (broadcast address, and network address itself, not being available for host addressing).

It's clear from Table 3.39 that we need to keep 7 bits in the host ID to fit 100 hosts in the network.

3. After the first split, we have the two networks (in bold, the bit that is now part of the subnet. It's the 1st bit on the 4th octet.) shown in Table 3.40.

Table 3.40	Networks after First Split (One for 126 Hosts, and the Other to be Further Divided)
First Split	**Dotted Binary**
192.168.25.0/25	11000000.10101000.00011001.**0**0000000
192.168.25.128/25	11000000.10101000.00011001.**1**0000000

OK, we have already got the first network, which is big enough for 100 hosts (actually, it can have 126 hosts, as shown in Table 3.38).

4. Let's divide the second network further. The network to be divided needs to have the first bit of the last octet set to one, because it's the second network from Table 3.39. Each resulting network would be able to have 62 hosts (refer to Table 3.38). As we need only 60, that is OK.

Observe that we still have 6 bits on the host part of each of the two resulting networks, giving us the abovementioned 62 possible hosts. The new network IDs are shown in Table 3.41.

Table 3.41	Networks after Second Split (One for 62 Hosts, the Other to be Further Divided)
Second Split	**Dotted Binary**
192.168.25.128/26	11000000.10101000.00011001.10000000
192.168.25.192/26	11000000.10101000.00011001.11000000

5. Now, we need four networks to fit 10 hosts on each. The amount of bits of the host ID part of the address needed to have 10 hosts is 4, because 3 bits would give us only 8 − 2 hosts, which is not enough, giving us 16 − 2 = 14 possible hosts. Refer to Table 3.38 for a refresher.

Leaving four bits for the host ID means that we will take two bits of the host ID to make the subnet. Look at Table 3.40, we had left only 6 bits for the host ID. We need to work on the second network of the table above, which is 192.168.25.192/26. In bold you have the bits used. This will give us the networks shown in Table 3.42.

Table 3.42	Networks after the Third and Last Split (Each Allowing 14 Hosts)
Third Split	**Dotted Binary**
192.168.25.192/28	11000000.10101000.00011001.11000000
192.168.25.208/28	11000000.10101000.00011001.11010000
192.168.25.224/28	11000000.10101000.00011001.11100000
192.168.25.240/28	11000000.10101000.00011001.11110000

6. The resultant networks we will have, starting from the original 192.168.25.0/24 network, along with the amount of hosts possible on each, is in the table below. Notice that the first 24 bits are the same for all networks. This means we have worked on a single /24 network, and created the amount of subnets we wished, varying their sizes. Table 3.43 shows all the networks we have created.

Table 3.43 Resultant Networks

Resultant Networks	Dotted Binary	Assignable Addresses
192.168.25.0/25	11000000.10101000.00011001.00000000	126
192.168.25.128/26	11000000.10101000.00011001.10000000	62
192.168.25.192/28	11000000.10101000.00011001.11000000	14
192.168.25.208/28	11000000.10101000.00011001.11010000	14
192.168.25.224/28	11000000.10101000.00011001.11100000	14
192.168.25.240/28	11000000.10101000.00011001.11110000	14

NAT/PAT

In today's world of enterprise networks, one of the major problems IT professionals Face is the rapidly depleting supply of globally unique Internet network addresses. Measures have been taken to slow the rate at which IP addresses are being allocated—including strategies such as CIDR, network address translation (NAT), and port address translation (PAT). This section will discuss NAT and PAT and how they can contribute to a security policy, the implications of NAT, and considerations when implementing NAT.

NAT is designed for IP address simplification and conservation. It enables private IP networks that use nonregistered RFC1918 IP addresses to connect to the Internet. NAT operates on a device, usually connecting two networks together, that allows them to communicate. Typically, one network uses RFC1918 IP addresses, which are translated into globally unique IP addresses. Other scenarios in which NAT can be utilized will be discussed later in this section.

NAT by itself is not a security measure and should not be implemented in such a fashion. A common misconception is that NAT will allow a company to "hide" its internal network. This can be an added security benefit, but should not be relied upon as the only security measure. Although typical private networks use addresses that are never intended to be publicly issued, a company's Internet service provider (ISP) may have knowledge of that particular network. If routing between the company and the ISP is not done properly, a route to the company may be leaked throughout the ISP, possibly exposing its network to the public.

NAT Overview

NAT is used when a company's internal addresses are not globally unique and thus cannot be routed on the Internet (for instance, using RFC1918 private addresses), or because two separate networks that need to communicate are using an overlapping IP address space.

NAT allows (in most cases) hosts in a private network (inside network) to transparently communicate with destination hosts (outside network) in a global or public network. This is achieved by modifying the *source address* portion of an IP packet as it traverses the NAT device. The NAT device will keep track of each translation (conversation) between the source host (inside network) and destination host (outside network), and vice versa. This means that NAT is a stateful technique and devices implementing NAT are stateful devices.

Throughout this section and in the Cisco documentation, networks will be described as being either an "inside" network or an "outside" network. An inside network is the set of networks subject to translation. All other networks are considered outside networks.

One of the variations of NAT is PAT. This solution only works if the application does not rely on an IP address in the data portion of the packet for functionality. In such cases, application layer gateways included inside the NAT (discussed later) may be needed to assist a NAT device.

The following is a list of terms used when referring to NAT and their descriptions. Keep in mind that different vendors may refer to these terms in varying contexts.

NAT

The basic configuration of NAT operates on a device, which connects two networks together. One of these networks (designated as inside) is addressed with either private RFC 1918 addresses or others which need to be converted into legal addresses before packets are forwarded to their destination network (designated as outside).

NAT is a method by which IP addresses are mapped from one address realm to another. This type of translation provides transparent routing from host to host. There are many variations of address translation that assist in translating different applications; however, all NAT implementations on various devices should share the following characteristics:

- Transparent address assignment
- Transparent routing through address translation (routing refers to forwarding packets and not exchanging routing information)
- ICMP error packet data translation

Transparent Address Assignment

NAT translates addresses from an inside network to addresses in an outside network, and vice versa. This provides transparent routing for the traffic traversing both networks. The translation in some cases may extend to transport level identifiers such as TCP/UDP ports. Address translation is done at the start of a session.

The following describes two types of address assignment:

- **Static address assignment** Static address assignment is a one-to-one address mapping for hosts connecting an inside network with an outside network for the duration of the NAT session. Static address assignment ensures that the translation table is static and not dynamic. Using static address assignment, your internal host is visible from the outside network because it is always assigned the same global IP address. This can be useful for some applications, but care must also be taken to secure each machine.

- **Dynamic address assignment** Dynamic address assignment is the process in which addresses are translated by the NAT device dynamically based on usage requirements. Once a NAT is no longer being used, it is terminated. NAT then frees that translation so the global address can be used in another translation.

Transparent Routing

Transparent routing refers to routing traffic between separate address realms (from an inside network to an outside one), by modifying address contents in the IP header to be valid in the address realm into which the traffic is routed to. A NAT device is placed at the border between two address realms and translates addresses in IP headers so that when the packet leaves one realm and enters another, it can be routed properly.

Typically, there are three phases to address translation.

- **Address Binding** Address binding is the phase in which an inside IP address is associated with an outside address, or vice versa. This assumes that dynamic NAT is being used and not static NAT. Address binding is fixed, with a pool of assigned static addresses. These addresses are dynamically assigned on a per-session basis. For example, whenever a host on the inside network must reach another host on the outside network, it will begin a session with that host. A translation will occur on the NAT device associating a global IP address on the outside network with the IP address of the host on the inside network. Once a session is created, all traffic originating from the same inside host will use an identical translation. The start of each new session will result in the creation of a new translation. A NAT device will support many simultaneous sessions. (Consult the vendor's documentation for specific information.)

- **Address Lookup and Translation** Once a translation is established for a session, all packets belonging to the session will be subject to address lookup and translation.

- **Address Unbinding** Address unbinding is the phase in which an inside host IP address is no longer associated with a global address. NAT will perform address unbinding when it believes the last session using an address binding has terminated.

An example of transparent routing is when a Company's inside network uses the subnet 192.168.1.0/24, and the outside network uses the subnet 207.139.221.0/24. Transparent routing would occur on the device that separates the two subnets. Instead of using a router to route packets based on destination address, NAT alters the source address of an IP packet originating from the inside network and changes it to a valid IP address in the outside network. The NAT device then builds a table to keep track of the translations that have occurred to maintain communications between a host on the inside network and a host on the outside network.

NAT Architectures

There are many variations of NAT that aid to different applications. The following is a list of some of the variations of NAT.

Traditional NAT or Outbound NAT

Traditional NAT is a dynamic translation that allows hosts within the inside network to transparently access hosts in the outside network. In traditional NAT, the initial outbound session is unidirectional (one-way)—outbound from the private network. Once a session has been established with a device on the outside network, bidirectional communication will occur for the duration of that session.

IP addresses of hosts in the outside network are unique, while IP addresses of hosts in the inside network use RFC 1918 private IP addresses. Because the IP addresses of the inside network are private and cannot be used globally, they must be translated into global addresses.

A traditional NAT router would allow Host A to initiate a session to Host Z, but not the other way around. Also, the address space from the global address pool used on the outside is routable, whereas the inside address space cannot be routed globally.

Because Host A originated a session from inside, any packets originating from Host Z in response to Host A will be permitted provided that the security rules on the NAT device permit it. If Host Z attempted to initiate a session with Host A, traditional NAT will not permit this because Host A has a private IP address. This IP address is reserved for private networks and will therefore never be routed globally. From the perspective of Host Z, Host A's IP address is 207.139.221.2 (the translated address). If Host Z attempts to initiate a session with this IP address, the NAT device will not be able to associate 207.139.221.2 with an inside IP address with traditional NAT. To allow Host Z to initiate a session with Host A, Static NAT (explained later) will need to be configured.

Port Address Translation

PAT extends the concept of translation one step further by also translating transport identifiers like TCP and UDP port numbers and ICMP query identifiers. This allows the transport identifiers of a number of private hosts to be multiplexed into the transport identifiers of a single global IP address. PAT allows numerous hosts from the inside network to share a single outside network IP address. The advantage of this type of translation is that only one global IP address is needed, whereas with NAT, each inside host must translate to a unique outside IP address.

> **Note**
>
> Both NAT and PAT can be combined. The advantage being that when NAT exhausts the pool of global IP addresses, PAT can then be used until one of the NAT translations times out. This method ensures that all inside hosts can be successfully translated into outside global IP addresses.

Host A on the inside network needs to communicate with Host Z on the outside network. Because these two hosts are on different networks and the inside network uses IP addresses from a private address space, NAT/PAT is needed to allow the two hosts to communicate. Unfortunately, the administrator only has a limited number of global IP addresses, many of which have already been assigned to various devices. Therefore, NAT cannot be used for translations. As an alternative, PAT can be used instead.

The steps taken to perform PAT are as follows:

1. Host A attempts to initiate a session with Host Z. Because Host Z is not on the same network as Host A, Host A must send the packet to the router (default gateway) for it to be routed correctly.

2. Once the packet reaches the inside interface of the router in which PAT is enabled, the router examines the translation table for an existing translation. Because this is a new session, the router creates a new translation record in the table. Since only one IP address is assigned to the pool of IP addresses to translate to, a unique port number is added to the *source address*. This will allow the router to keep track of the translation for the duration of the session:

   PAT Global 207.139.221.2(1576) Local 192.168.1.2

   The router then alters the IP header and changes the source address to the IP address of the outside interface of the router.

3. The packet is then transparently routed to Host Z.

4. Host Z replies to Host A by sending the packet to the outside interface of the router (*destination address*).

5. Once the packet reaches the outside interface, the router examines the IP header, checks the translation table for an existing translation. As a translation already exists in the table, the router changes the destination address to the IP address of Host A.

6. The process is repeated until the session between Host A and Host Z is terminated.

Static NAT

With static NAT, sessions can be initiated from hosts in the inside or outside network. Inside addresses are bound to globally unique addresses using static translations because the connections are established in either direction. A translation that occurs from the inside network to the outside network will be translated with the statically configured address on the NAT device. When a session must be established from an outside network to an inside network, the static translation must already be manually set up on the router. By creating a static translation, you are translating an inside IP address to a fixed outside global IP address. This translation will never change and will always remain in the translation table. For example, if there is a resource on the inside network that must be made accessible to the outside network, the global IP address of the resource can be advertised worldwide through the DNS. Because this resource has been statically translated into a global IP, this IP can be advertised in a DNS record. If the resource is a mail server, an MX record may be created in the company's zone associating the MX record with the global IP that was statically assigned to the resource in the inside network. By doing this, even though the mail server is not physically located in the outside network, it can still be accessed as if it were.

> **Note**
>
> Using this type of configuration to allow global access to resources has security-related advantages. If the NAT device is a Cisco PIX firewall or Cisco Router running FW IOS, access control lists can be used to limit the type of traffic permitted to reach the resource. Compare this with having a server that is physically placed in the outside network allowing global access. In this case, limiting the type of traffic would be very difficult, if not impossible, creating a security risk.

A session is initiated from Host Z on the outside network. Because the NAT device has a static translation for Host A's IP address to a global IP address, the NAT device can forward the packet from Host Z to Host A's static NAT public IP address. Recall that with traditional or outbound NAT, a session can only be initiated from the inside host, which causes a dynamic translation to occur on the NAT device. Once this translation has been created, only then can the outside host reply back to the inside host. Once the session times out, the inside host will need to start a new session with the outside host causing the NAT device to create a new translation and possibly allocating a new global IP address to the inside host for the duration of the session (if NAT is used). With a static NAT, the translation is always active; the global IP address will never be allocated dynamically to another host on the inside network for translation purposes.

Guidelines for Deploying NAT and PAT

When deploying NAT and PAT in a network, there are many things to take into consideration. Various factors will contribute to which type of NAT is used, factors such as the number of available global IP addresses for translations, or whether the inside network uses global or RFC 1918 IP addresses.

The following outlines some general guidelines for deploying NAT:

- How many public IP addresses are available for translation from inside IP addresses? If there are only a limited number of global IP addresses for many inside hosts (for example, eight global addresses for 250 inside hosts), PAT, or a combination of dynamic NAT and PAT, may be necessary.

- Router performance needs to be considered for all types of NAT. NAT increases the time it takes for a packet to arrive at a destination address. When a packet traverses a NAT device, the IP header must be modified. This is currently done using process switching, which places considerable load on the system.

- What type of addressing scheme is being used on the inside network? Are private RFC 1918 addresses being used? If so, then NAT will need to occur for the inside network(s) to be able to reach the outside networks.

- Not all applications will work with NAT. Be aware of what type of traffic will be translated and if the functionality of those applications will be affected by NAT. If this is the case, an ALG may need to be implemented to assist in the translation process. Application types that do not need an ALG, or where an ALG is built into Cisco's NAT implementation, are listed later in this section. Not all applications can be used with ALGs.

- A disadvantage of NAT is the loss of end-to-end IP connectivity. It becomes much harder to trace packets that undergo numerous IP address changes over multiple NAT hops. On the other hand, an advantage to this is that it becomes difficult if not impossible for hackers to determine a packet's source to trace or obtain the original source or destination addresses.

Some guidelines to follow for implementing static NAT are as follows:

- How many inside devices need to be statically translated? Remember that each global IP used for static translations cannot be used for dynamic translations.

- A security policy should be in place to limit the type of traffic permitted to reach that statically translated device. When an inside device is statically translated into a global IP address, any devices on the outside networks can initiate a session with the inside device.

Configuring NAT on Cisco IOS

Cisco's implementation of NAT functionality on a router is fundamentally the same as the implementation of NAT on a PIX firewall. Performance-wise, the NAT session limit on a router depends on the amount of DRAM available on the router, and the load on the router. Each NAT translation consumes approximately 160 bytes of DRAM. As a result, 10,000 translations would consume about 1.6 MB. This should not impose a burden on a typical router provided it is not overloaded by other processes. PAT, as described previously, is handled differently. The translations occur with one global IP address.

The translation table maintains each translation by assigning a unique port number to each translation. Because TCP/UDP port numbers are encoded in 16 bits, there are theoretically 65,536 possible values, resulting in 65,536 simultaneous sessions for each protocol.

The following section will outline the commands necessary to implement, and verify, NAT operation on a Cisco router.

Configuration Commands

This section will cover the commands necessary to implement NAT on a Cisco router.

Before NAT can be implemented, the inside and outside networks must be defined. To define the inside and outside networks, use the *ip nat* command.

```
ip nat inside|outside
```

- **Inside** indicates that the interface is connected to the inside network (the network is subject to NAT translation).

- **Outside** indicates that the interface is connected to the outside network.

Mark the interface as being on the inside or outside realms with the following:

```
interface ethernet0
ip nat inside
```

Enter interface configuration mode and designate *ethernet0* as the inside network interface.

```
interface serial1
ip nat outside
```

Enter interface configuration mode and designate *serial0* as the outside network interface.

Once the inside and outside network interfaces have been defined, an access list must be created to define the traffic that will be translated. This will only define the traffic to be translated and will not control any NAT functions by itself. To create an access list, use the *access-list* command:

access-list access-list-number **permit** source [source-wildcard]

- **Access-list-number** Number of an access list. This is a decimal number from 1 to 99.

- **Deny** Denies access if the conditions are matched.

- **Permit** Permits access if the conditions are matched.

- **Source** Number of the network or host from which the packet is being sent. Use the keyword *any* as an abbreviation for source 0.0.0.0 and source-wildcard 255.255.255.255.

- **Source-wildcard** (optional) Wildcard bits to be applied to the source. Use the keyword *any* as an abbreviation for source 0.0.0.0 and source-wildcard 255.255.255.255.

```
access-list 10 permit ip 192.168.1.0 0.0.0.255 any
```

This specifies that traffic originating from the 192.168.1.0 subnet destined for any other network should be translated. By itself, the access list will not translate the specified traffic.

A pool of IP addresses must be defined for dynamic NAT translations. To do this, use the *ip nat* command:

```
ip nat pool name start-ip end-ip {netmask netmask | prefix-
   length prefix-length}
[type rotary]
```

- **Name** Name of the pool

- **Start-ip** Starting IP address for range of addresses in address pool

- **End-ip** Ending IP address for range of addresses in address pool

- **Netmask** *netmask* Specify the netmask of the network to which the pool addresses belong.

- **Prefix-length** *prefix-length* Number that indicates how many bits of the netmask are ones.

- **Type-rotary** (optional) Indicates that the ranges of addresses in the address pool identify real, inside hosts where TCP load distribution will occur.

Define a pool of global addresses to be allocated as needed.

```
ip nat pool net-208 207.139.221.10 207.139.221.128 netmask
   >255.255.255.0
```

Specifies a pool of global IP addresses with the name *net-208* will contain the range of IP addresses 207.139.221.10 through 207.139.221.128.

To enable NAT for the inside destination address, the *ip nat inside destination* command will be used:

```
ip nat inside destination list {access-list-number | name}
   pool name
```

- **list** *access-list-number* Standard IP access list number. Packets with destination addresses that pass the access list are translated using global addresses from the named pool.

- **list** *name* Name of a standard IP access list.

- **pool** *name* Name of the pool from which global IP addresses are allocated during dynamic translation.

```
ip nat pool net-208 207.139.221.10 207.139.221.128 netmask
   >255.255.255.0
```

Define a pool of global IP addresses called *net-208* with the IP addresses 207.139.221.10 through 207.139.221.128.

```
access-list 10 permit any 204.71.201.0 0.0.0.255
```

Specify that traffic destined for the network address 204.71.201.0 will be translated to global addresses defined in the pool *net-207*.

```
ip nat inside destinationn list 10 pool net-207
```

Enable NAT for traffic defined in access list 10 to be translated to addresses from the *net-207* pool. This will translate the destination address, not the source.

To enable NAT for the inside source address, use the *ip nat inside source* command.

```
ip nat inside source {list {access-list-number | name} pool
   name
[overload] | static local-ip global-ip
```

- **List** *access-list number* Standard IP access list number. Packets with source addresses that pass the access list are dynamically translated using global addresses from the named pool.

- **List** *name* Name of the standard IP access list.

- **Pool** *name* Name of the pool from which global IP addresses are allocated dynamically.

- **Overload** (optional) Enables the router to use one global address for many local addresses (PAT).

- **Static** *local-ip* Sets up a single static translation.

- **Global-ip** Sets up a single static translation. This argument establishes the globally unique IP address which an inside host will be translated to.

Establish dynamic source translation using an access list to define the traffic to be translated based on source address.

```
ip nat pool net-207 207.139.221.10 207.139.221.128 netmask
    255.255.255.0
```

Define a pool of IP addresses with the name *net-207* and a range of IP addresses from 207.139.221.10 through 207.139.221.128.

```
access-list 10 permit ip 192.168.1.0 0.0.0.255 any
```

Specify that traffic originating from the 192.168.1.0 network will be translated.

```
ip nat inside source list 10 pool net-207
```

Enable dynamic NAT for traffic defined in access list 10 to be translated to addresses from the *net-207* pool. This will translate the source address and not the destination address. To enable static NAT translation for the inside host 192.168.1.10 to the global IP address 207.139.221.10 use the following command:

```
ip nat inside source static 192.168.1.10 207.139.221.10
```

To enable PAT in conjunction with, or instead of, NAT:

```
ip nat pool net-207 207.139.221.10 netmask 255.255.255.0
```

Define a single global IP address with the name *net-207* and an IP address of 207.139.221.10.

```
access-list 10 permit ip 192.168.1.0 0.0.0.255
```

Specify that traffic originating from the 192.168.1.0 network will be translated.

```
ip nat inside source list 10 pool net-207 overload
```

Enable PAT for traffic defined in access list 10 to be translated to the address defined in the *net-207* pool. This will translate the source address.

To enable NAT of the outside source address, use the *ip nat outside source* command:

```
ip nat outside source {list {access-list-number | name} pool
    name | static global-ip local-ip}
```

- **List *access-list-number*** Standard IP access list number. Packets with source addresses that pass the access list are translated using the global addresses from the named pool.

- **List *name*** Name of a standard IP access list
- **Pool *name*** Name of the pool from which global IP addresses are allocated
- **Static *global-ip*** Sets up a single static translation. This argument establishes the globally unique IP address assigned to an outside host.
- **Local-ip** Sets up a single static translation. This argument establishes the local IP address of an outside host as it appears to the inside world.

```
ip nat translation {timeout | udp-timeout | dns-timeout |
    tcp-timeout |finrst-timeout} seconds
```

- **Timeout** Specifies that the timeout value applies to dynamic translations except for overload translations. Default is 86,400 s (24 h).
- **Udp-timeout** Specifies that the timeout value applies to the UDP port. Default is 300 s (5 min).
- **Dns-timeout** Specifies that the timeout value applies to connections to the Domain Naming System. Default is 60 s.
- **Tcp-timeout** Specifies that the timeout value applies to the TCP port. Default is 86,400 s (24 h).
- **Finrst-timeout** Specifies that the timeout value applies to Finish and Reset TCP packets, which terminate a connection. Default is 60 s.
- **Seconds** Number of seconds the specified port translation times out.

```
ip nat translation timeout 300
```

This example specifies that translations will timeout after 300 s (5 min) of inactivity.

```
ip nat translation timeout 600
```

This specifies that NAT translations will timeout after 600 s (10 min) of inactivity.

Verification Commands

The following are commands used to verify the operation of NAT on a Cisco router:

- *show ip nat statistics* Displays NAT statistics.
- *show ip nat translations [verbose]* Displays NAT translations, where *Verbose* optionally displays additional information for each translation table entry, including how long ago the entry was created and used.

Table 3.44	Explanation of the Significant Fields from the **show ip nat statistics** Command Sample Output
Field	**Description**
Total translations	Number of translations active in the system. This number is incremented each time a translation is created and is decremented each time a translation is cleared or times out.
Outside interfaces	List of interfaces marked as outside with the **ip nat outside** command.
Inside interfaces	List of interfaces marked as inside with the **ip nat inside** command.
Hits	Number of times the software does a translations table lookup and finds an entry.
Misses	Number of times the software does a translation table lookup, fails to find an entry, and must try to create one.
Expired translations	Cumulative count of translations that have expired because the router was booted.

The following is a sample output from the *show ip nat statistics*. Table 3.44 outlines the significant fields in the sample output.

```
Router#show ip nat statistics
Total translations: 2 (0 static, 2 dynamic; 0 extended)
Outside interfaces: Serial0
Inside interfaces: Ethernet1
Hits: 135 Misses: 5
Expired translations: 2
Dynamic mappings:
-- Inside Source
access-list 1 pool net-208 refcount 2
pool net-208: netmask 255.255.255.240
    start 171.69.233.208 end 171.69.233.221
    type generic, total addresses 14, allocated 2 (14%), misses 0
```

Configuring NAT between a Private Network and the Internet

Company XYZ management has decided to allow employees access to the Internet. A leased line to their ISP has been purchased and installed, and a Cisco router has been purchased to route the company's internal traffic to their ISP. The ISP has assigned a range of 128 global IP addresses (207.139.221.0/25) to the company to use as they see fit. Administrators have used a private 192.168.1.0/24 subnet for their internal hosts.

Here are the steps to follow for the configuration example, with explanations for clarification as you go through the commands:

```
configure terminal
interface ethernet0
ip address 192.168.1.1 255.255.255.0
```

This assigns an IP address to *ethernet0 interface*.

```
ip nat inside
```

This designates *ethernet0 interface* as an inside network.

```
no shutdown
```

This serves to remove the interface from shutdown state.

```
interface serial0
ip address 207.139.221.1 255.255.255.128
Assign IP address to serial0 interface.ip nat outside
```

This designates *serial0 interface* as an outside network.

```
no shutdown
```

This removes the interface from shutdown status.

```
exit
access-list 10 permit ip 192.168.1.0 0.0.0.255
```

This specifies that traffic originating from the 192.168.1.0 network will be translated.

```
ip nat pool net-207 207.139.221.2 207.139.221.126 netmask
   255.255.255.128
```

This defines a pool of global IP addresses named *net-207* with an address range of 207.139.221.2 through 207.139.221.126 to be used for NAT.

```
ip nat pool net-207-PAT 207.139.221.127 netmask 255.255.255.128
```

This defines a single global IP address named *net-207-PAT* with address 207.139.221.127 to be used for PAT.

```
ip nat inside source list 10 pool net-207
```

This specifies that the source IP address of traffic defined in access list 10 will be NATed with IP addresses defined in the *net-207* pool.

```
ip nat inside source list 10 pool net-207-PAT overload
```

Lastly, this specifies that the source IP address of traffic defined in access list 10 will be PATed with IP addresses defined in *net-207-PAT* pool. PAT will occur once NAT has used all available addresses in the *net-207* pool. Once a translation has timed out due to inactivity, the global IP address will be reused for future NAT translations.

SUMMARY OF EXAM OBJECTIVES

IP addresses are used to identify hosts in a network. The addressing scheme needs to be such that a packet that leaves a host is able to get to its intended recipient, even if it's thousands of kilometers (and hundreds of networks in-between) apart.

IP addresses are represented as four numbers, ranging from 0 to 255, separated by dots. They are divided in a way that part of the address represents a network, and part represents a host inside a network. This allows intermediary devices (routers) to simply deliver the packet to a network, and leave the identification of the host inside that network to the destination router. This makes routers work easier, as they only need to know how to find networks, not individual hosts.

Initially, classes were created to identify where an address would be split to obtain the network and host ID part of the address. The important classes are A, B and C, having respectively, 1, 2, and 3 octets for the network ID and the remaining octets for the host ID.

As this fixed division had little flexibility, addresses started to be accompanied by a subnet mask. The subnet mask would then indicate where, in the IP address, the split would be done. Subnet masks are always a sequence of binary 1s, followed by 0s. They are "aligned" with the IP address, and the bits in the IP address, that match 1s in the network mask, are part of the network ID. The remaining bits are the host ID.

To make matters simpler, it's good to represent all addresses in binary format, which brings the need to know how to convert a decimal number to binary and back.

Even more flexibility can be obtained in the divisions by combining networks, to be represented as a single entry in a router table (through CIDR), and dividing a single network with different subnet masks (VLSM).

EXAM OBJECTIVES FAST TRACK

IP Addresses

- 32-bit addresses used to refer to any host in any network.

- Represented as four 8-bit groups, called octets.

- Split in two parts, one to identify the network and another to identify the host (called network ID, and host ID, respectively).

- Used together with a subnet mask, to identify where on the address the split between network ID and host ID will occur.

Binary Decimal Conversions

- Binary and decimal are only two of the possible numbering systems (other common ones are octal and hexadecimal).

- Conversion between binary and decimals and vice-versa can be aided by a table with the possible powers of 2.

Subnetting

- Further subdivision performed on top of network addresses.

- Allows one to tailor the network address to his specific needs.

- Obtained by borrowing bits of the host ID to be used by the network part of the address.

CIDR

- Can be used to aggregate entries on router tables.

- Combine contiguous subnets into a single entry.

- Represents the subnet mask and the IP address with a single number (IP address-forward slash-number of ones in the subnet mask).

Variable Length Subnet Masking

- Allows for further flexibility when subnetting.

- Instead of having a single subnet mask for your whole network, uses different-sized subnet masks for a single network.

NAT/PAT

- Allows networks to use fewer IP addresses on the public side of the router for accessing the Internet.

- Allows devices on the public side to see internal private devices using a one to one address pointer.

- Allows networks to use nonroutable IP addresses on the inside and one global address on the outside.

- Is not needed when IPv6 comes out.

ACKNOWLEDGEMENT

We fully acknowledge use of Chapter 5, "Network Address Translation/Port Address Translation," from *Managing Cisco® Network Security*, Second Edition, ISBN: 978-1-931836-56-2.

EXAM OBJECTIVES FREQUENTLY ASKED QUESTIONS

Q: Are all available IP addresses available to address a host?

A: No, only a subset of the IP addresses is available for public use. Only classes addresses in classes A, B, and C can be assigned to a host. This means the last assignable address would be 223.255.255.254 (if the last octet was 255, this would be the broadcast address for that network).

Q: Are there IP addresses that will never be used publicly for address assignment to hosts?

A: Yes, each class has a range of addresses to be used in private networks, meaning they won't ever be used publicly. These are 10.0.0.0 to 10.255.255.255 (class A), 172.16.0.0 to 172.31.255.255 (class B), and 192.168.0.0 to 192.168.255.255 (class C). Besides those reserved for private networks, there are the ones reserved addresses for testing, and future use, which are the 127 network, from 127.0.0.0 to 127.255.255.255, and the whole class D and E (224.0.0.0 to 255.255.255.255).

Q: Can I create a subnet mask using any number, valid for an octet, I can think of?

A: No, there are rules governing the definition of subnet masks. They need to be an uninterrupted chain of binary 1s, followed by all 0s. This means that only 255, 254, 252, 248, 240, 224, 192, 128, and 0 are valid numbers (in decimal) for an octet in a subnet mask. Once you get to the first non-255 (all 1s), the remaining octets need to be 0.

Q: When converting a number from decimal to binary, do I always need to fill in that eight-column table?

A: No, you can use one of several methods. This chapter showed the one with the eight-column table in Exercise 3.2. A different method (successive divisions) was used in Exercise 3.3. You will likely become used to the ones used in the subnet masks, and convert these from the top of your head.

Q: Are there other number systems in use, besides the decimal system?

A: Yes. The most commonly used in computing are the binary (base 2, having as valid numbers only 0 and 1) and hexadecimal (base 16, having as valid numbers 0 to 9 and A to F). Internally, computers don't ever use the decimal (base 10) number system. The octal (base 8, with number ranging from 0 to 7) is also used sometimes in computing and electronics.

Q: Is 255 the biggest decimal number one can represent in binary form?

A: No, you can represent whatever decimal number you'd like in binary. 255 is used as an upper limit, just because it's the highest value an octet can assume.

Q: Why do I need to consider subnetting in the first place?

A: The fixed-size networks created by the class-based address scheme, usually provided networks that were too big. Subnetting came as the solution to answer the needs of smaller enterprises, or to divide the networks inside buildings, or campuses.

Q: Can I use all addresses in a given network, to assign to hosts?

A: No, you always need to reserve two of the addresses. One is used to address the network itself, and the other is used as the network's broadcast address (one that will be listened to by all the hosts on that network).

Q: Is there a way to represent an IP address and subnet mask without writing both addresses?

A: Yes, this is achieved through the CIDR notation, which postfixes an IP address with a forward slash and the number of bits in the subnet mask that are 1s.

Q: Can I divide a network in variable sizes?

A: Yes, through variable-length subnet masking (VLSM).

Q: Using VLSM, can I make the divisions in the order I wish?

A: No, you need to start from the biggest networks (greater number of hosts) and progress to the smaller ones. This is mandatory because every time you divide you'll have less addresses to use.

Q: Is NAT/PAT important for the CCNA?

A: Yes, although we normally put NAT/PAT on the firewall that is better designed for this technology, Cisco wants you to be able to configure it in a router as well.

Q: What is the most likely way I will be tested on NAT/PAT?

A: You will most likely be given a simulation question on NAT or PAT.

SELF TEST

1. What is used by a host to determine the host ID on a given data packet?
   - **A.** The IP header
   - **B.** The subnet mask
   - **C.** The address class
   - **D.** The MAC address

2. Which of the following is the binary equivalent to the dotted decimal address 207.209.68.100?
   - **A.** 11001111.11010001.01000100.01100100
   - **B.** 10000111.11010001.01000100.01100100
   - **C.** 11001111.11010001.01000100.01101100
   - **D.** 11001111.11010001.11001101.01100100

3. You are a network administrator who needs to subnet a network to create nine subnets from a given class C network. How many bits will you need to borrow from the host ID part of the address?
   - **A.** 1
   - **B.** 9
   - **C.** 4
   - **D.** 3

4. For the subnet mask 255.255.255.192, which pair of addresses below is on the same subnet?
   - **A.** 192.168.1.116 and 192.168.1.224
   - **B.** 192.168.1.116 and 192.168.1.124
   - **C.** 192.168.1.16 and 192.168.1.124
   - **D.** 192.168.1.116 and 192.168.2.124

5. Which of the addresses below is a class C address?

   A. 10.20.30.40

   B. 140.30.50.65

   C. 230.20.35.14

   D. 200.17.45.15

6. Which class of IP addresses is used for multicast transmissions?

   A. Class A

   B. Class E

   C. Class B

   D. Class D

7. How many bits would you need to borrow from the host ID part of an address, to create 40 subnets?

   A. 10 bits

   B. 6 bits

   C. 4 bits

   D. 8 bits

8. Which option below contains the two class C networks you would combine to create the network 192.168.102.0/23 through CIDR?

   A. 192.168.102.0 and 192.168.104.0

   B. 192.168.102.0 and 192.168.101.0

   C. 192.168.102.0 and 192.168.100.0

   D. 192.168.102.0 and 192.168.103.0

9. What is the maximum number of subnets that you can create, on a non point-to-point network, from a class C address with the subnet mask 255.255.255.192?

   A. 32

   B. 128

   C. 8

   D. 16

10. Which of the subnet masks correspond to the CIDR notation/28?

   A. 255.255.192.0

   B. 255.255.240.0

   C. 255.255.255.192

   D. 255.255.255.240

11. Your ISP has given you four class B networks, 131.107.8.0, 131.107.9.0, 131.107.10.0, 131.107.11.0. Which network address should you use to combine those networks into a single address?

   A. 131.107.9.0/22

   B. 131.107.10.0/22

   C. 131.107.10.0/23

   D. 131.107.8.0/22

12. Which of the following is an invalid value for a subnet mask?

   A. 255.255.192.0

   B. 255.240.0.0

   C. 255.254.255.0

   D. 255.255.224.0

13. Which of the following addresses does not belong to an address range reserved for private use?

   A. 172.24.0.0

   B. 10.20.30.0

   C. 192.167.0.0

   D. 192.168.100.0

14. What is the maximum number of hosts addressable on a network having the subnet mask 255.255.255.192?

   A. 254   **C.** 30

   B. 128   **D.** 62

15. The class of networks which has the biggest number of hosts per network is?

   A. Class E   **C.** Class D

   B. Class C   **D.** Class A

16. You are designing a new network; you will be using a Cisco router on the perimeter of your network and the Internet. What type of NAT technology will you use to allow all of your inside hosts to connect to the Internet utilizing only 1 public address?

   A. NAT static

   B. NAT dynamic

   C. NAT overlapping

   D. NAT PAT

   E. I would not use NAT

17. You are the administrator of a Cisco network. All of a sudden people are saying they can't get to any sites on the Internet. Your connection to the Internet is provided by a Cisco 1721 router. At the router# you type *show ip nat translations* and see no output. What is the most likely cause of the problem?

A. The routing protocol has been disabled

B. The IP addresses have been removed

C. The PAT feature has been disabled

D. A and B

SELF TEST QUICK ANSWER KEY

1. B

2. A

3. C

4. B

5. D

6. D

7. B

8. D

9. D

10. D

11. D

12. C

13. C

14. D

15. A

16. D

17. C

Configuring Cisco Routers

INTRODUCTION

The ability to successfully configure a Cisco router is one of the most important skills a Cisco Certified Network Associate (CCNA) needs to possess. Being able to effectively navigate through the Cisco Internetwork Operating System (IOS) takes some practice, so one can become comfortable with the different modes of operation of the router. The Cisco IOS requires the student to know both the commands to perform certain tasks and what mode the router should be running in when that command is executed.

Students appearing for the CCNA exam need to be extremely comfortable using various commands to configure settings on routers. Unlike many certification exams that are strictly multiple choice types, the CCNA exam has several practical exercises. The exam is timed so a student must be comfortable enough to navigate through the router within a certain timeframe. Use the software that is packaged with this book to get the necessary practice you need to be successful on your CCNA exam. Employers are aware that students who pass the CCNA exam have practical skills that will allow them to be successful in the workplace.

CONNECTING TO THE ROUTER

Before you can configure your router, you must first connect to it. Router administrative connections can be made using the following methods: direct connection to the console port, a modem connection made to the auxiliary port, a Telnet connection made to a *management* interface of the router, a Hypertext Transfer Protocol (HTTP) connection to the *Web* interface, or through the Secure Shell (SSH) connection. The first time you connect to the router, however, you will have to use the console port of the router. Telnet to a *management* interface of the router is not possible unless it is first configured by the administrator. Neither is access to the auxiliary port. Therefore, the initial configuration of the router must be done using the directly connected console port.

- The console port is located on the back of the router. On most of the latest routers, the console port is an RJ-45 connector. You simply connect the console port to a serial port on your computer using the management cable that came with your Cisco router.

- The auxiliary port is also located on the back of the router. The auxiliary port allows router connections through a modem. This can come in very handy if you need to make a remote connection to the router, but Telnet access is not available.

- Telnet access is gained by using an Internet Protocol (IP) connection to a *management* interface of the router. You must first assign a management IP address to the router, and then enable Telnet access on that interface.

- Similar to Telnet access; SSH access is gained by using an IP connection to a *management* interface of the router. Before you can use SSH, you must assign a management IP address to the router, and then enable SSH access. Not all Cisco devices offer SSH access as a feature. This feature must be available in the IOS you are running on the device.

- Web access is gained by using a standard Web browser to connect to the Web-enabled *management* interface of the router. Not all devices and IOS version offer Web management as a feature. You will need to make sure it is available on your device before using it.

To connect to the router's console port or auxiliary port or make an SSH connection, you will need some type of terminal emulation software. You can also use terminal emulation software to Telnet to the *management* interface of the router, but most operating systems have a Telnet client built-in and do not require terminal emulation software be installed for Telnet connections. Terminal emulation software will give you visible interface for the router. We will discuss two popular terminal emulation software packages that can be used to connect to a Cisco router: HyperTerminal and Minicom.

HyperTerminal

HyperTerminal, as shown in Figure 4.1, is one of the most widely used terminal emulation packages used by Windows user to configure Cisco equipment. This is because, until recently (with Windows Vista), HyperTerminal was included free with any Windows operating system. You can still obtain HyperTerminal, but you must purchase it separately from the company which develops it.

HyperTerminal can be used for direct console connections to Cisco equipment or for Telnet access to Cisco equipment. HyperTerminal is very easy to configure. Exercise 4.1 will walk you through configuring HyperTerminal for console access to a Cisco router.

As mentioned, you also have the option to use Telnet to connect to your Cisco. Telnet access via HyperTerminal is just as easy to configure as console port access. Exercise 4.2 will walk you through the process.

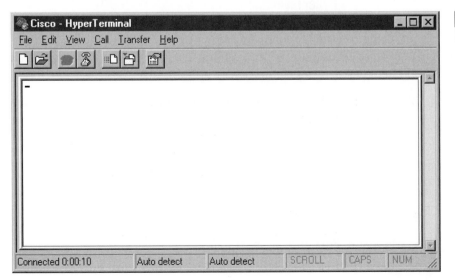

FIGURE 4.1

Windows HyperTerminal

EXERCISE 4.1   Configuring Console Port Access to a Cisco Router Using HyperTerminal

We're going to configure HyperTerminal to connect to your Cisco using the console port. Before you begin make sure you connect the console port on the router to a serial port on your computer using the appropriate cable.

1. Select **File** > **New connection**.

2. Give the connection a name and click **Enter**.

3. In the **Connect To** pane, make sure **Connect** using is set to *COM1*.

4. Click **Configure**.

5. Set **Bits per second** to 9600 bps.

6. Set **Data bits** to 8.

7. Set **Parity** to None.

8. Set **Stop bits** to 1.

9. Set **Flow Control** to None.

10. Click **OK**.

EXERCISE 4.2   Configuring Telnet Access to a Cisco Router Using HyperTerminal

We are going to walk through connecting to your Cisco router via Telnet. This does not require any special cabling, but you do need to ensure that your system has network connectivity to your router.

1. Configuring Console Port Access to a Cisco router using HyperTerminal.

2. Select **File** > **New connection**.

3. Give the connection a name and click **Enter**.

4. In the **Connect To** pane, make sure **Connect using** is set to **TCP/IP**.

5. In the **Host** address field, enter the IP of the Cisco device.

6. Make sure **Port** number is set to 23.

7. Click **OK**.

Once you have configured your HyperTerminal connection to your Cisco device, you can begin configuring it. Figure 4.1 shows you how your connected HyperTerminal session will look. Simply press the **Enter** key and you are ready to go.

Minicom

Minicom is a terminal emulation software package that runs on Linux and UNIX operating systems. Minicom is similar to Windows HyperTerminal. Minicom can be used to make console connections to your Cisco device. The settings you would use in Minicom are the same as those used in HyperTerminal.

USER EXEC MODE

When you first connect to Cisco router, you connect in *User Exec* mode. *User Exec* mode is the operating mode with the least privileges. You tell that you are in user mode by simply looking at the IOS prompt. When in user mode, the IOS prompt will end in >. By default, there is no password needed to connect to the router console using the console cable. But for security, it is recommended that you set a password.

There isn't much you can do in user mode. This is by design. You can give someone access to *User Exec* mode, but not more advanced modes. This way they can help troubleshoot issues on Cisco devices without changing the configuration. While in user mode, you will basically only have rights to view system information and perform certain troubleshooting and diagnostic commands.

Commands

To view all the commands available in *User Exec* mode, you can type ?, at the IOS prompt. Below is a sample output from this command. The actual output will vary depending on the device and IOS version.

Exec commands:

```
<1-99>           Session number to resume
access-enable    Create a temporary access list entry
clear            Reset functions
connect          Open a terminal connection
disable          Turn off privileged commands
disconnect       Disconnect an existing network connection
enable           Turn on privileged commands
exit             Exit from the EXEC
help             Description of the interactive help system
lock             Lock the terminal
```

```
login            Log in as a particular user
logout           Exit from the EXEC
name-connection  Name an existing network connection
ping             Send echo messages
power            Internal PS and RPS exec commands
rcommand         Run command on remote switch
resume           Resume an active network connection
set              Set system parameter (not config)
show             Show running system information
systat           Display information about terminal lines
telnet           Open a Telnet connection
terminal         Set terminal line parameters
traceroute       Trace route to destination
tunnel           Open a tunnel connection
where            List active connections
```

The Show *Command*

The *show* command is one of the most useful commands available in *User Exec* mode. There is a wealth of options available for the *show* command when in *User Exec* mode. If you type **sh ?** at the IOS prompt, the IOS will list all the available *show* command options.

■ *show ip route* – Use this command to view the routing table on your Cisco device.

■ *show history* – This command will show you what commands have previously been entered.

■ *show version* – This command will display information about which version of the Cisco IOS you are running.

CONFIGURING AND IMPLEMENTING...

Entering Commands in Cisco Routers
Cisco has many things in place to make entering commands easier. Most Cisco commands have abbreviations. If you type a partial command, you can use the **Tab** key to fill in the rest of the command. If you need help with the syntax of a command, you can type **?** at the end of the command. It will show you command options and syntax.

PRIVILEGED EXEC MODE

Privileged Exec mode is an escalated operating mode. It is also called *Enable* mode. This is because to enter *Privileged Exec* mode, you must enter the command *enable* at the IOS prompt. You will be able to tell that you are in privileged mode because the IOS prompt will now end with #. Once you are in privileged mode and want to return to user mode, you must enter the command *disable* at the IOS prompt. A user with *Privileged Exec* mode access can basically do almost anything on the device.

CONFIGURING AND IMPLEMENTING...

Setting Enable Passwords

It's recommended that you configure your router so that a password is required to enter privileged mode. This password is called the enable password. There are two types of enable passwords: the enable password and the enable secret. The enable password is stored in clear text, whereas the enable secret is not. The enable secret is encrypted with the MD5 algorithm. Be careful, *Privileged Exec* mode passwords are case sensitive.

Commands

To view all the commands available in *Privileged Exec* mode, you can type ?, at the IOS prompt. Below is an abbreviated sample output from this command. The actual output will vary depending on the device and IOS version.

Exec commands:

```
<1-99>            Session number to resume
access-enable     Create a temporary access list entry
access-template   Create a temporary access list entry
archive           Manage archive files
cd                Change current directory
clear             Reset functions
clock             Manage the system clock
cns               CNS agents
configure         Enter configuration mode
connect           Open a terminal connection
copy              Copy from one file to another
debug             Debugging functions (see also 'undebug')
delete            Delete a file
diagnostic        Diagnostic commands
dir               List files on a filesystem
disable           Turn off privileged commands
disconnect        Disconnect an existing network connection
dot1x             IEEE 802.1X Exec Commands
enable            Turn on privileged commands
eou               EAPoUDP
```

```
erase            Erase a filesystem
exit             Exit from the EXEC
format           Format a filesystem
fsck             Fsck a filesystem
help             Description of the interactive help system
ip               Global IP commands
lock             Lock the terminal
login            Log in as a particular user
logout           Exit from the EXEC
mkdir            Create new directory
monitor          Monitoring different system events
more             Display the contents of a file
name-connection  Name an existing network connection
no               Disable debugging functions
no               Negate a command or set its defaults
ping             Send echo messages
power            Internal PS and RPS exec commands
pwd              Display current working directory
rcommand         Run command on remote switch
reload           Halt and perform a cold restart
```

The Show Command

The *show* command is available in both *User Exec* and *Privileged Exec* modes. The options for the two modes are different however. There are two very important options that are available under *Privileged Exec* mode that are not available under *User Exec* mode.

> *Show running-config* – This command will display the configuration that is currently running on the device.

> *Show startup-config* – This command will display the configuration that is currently stored in nonvolatile random-access memory (NVRAM). When the router is restarted, the configuration is loaded from the *startup-config*.

The Copy Command

The *copy* command is used to write the current *running-config* to NVRAM or to a Trivial File Transfer Protocol (TFTP) server. The *copy* command allows you to back up and restore your configuration.

The Reload Command

The *reload* command is used to restart the device. Implementing certain configurations will require that the device be restarted. This command will allow you to remotely restart the device. You do not have to physically power cycle the system.

The *No Command*

The *no* command is one of the most powerful and useful commands available on Cisco devices. The *no* command can be used to undo almost any command that was issued or any configuration change that was performed. So, if you make a mistake when configuring your device, the *no* command will come in very handy.

GLOBAL CONFIGURATION MODE

Global Configuration mode allows you to configure global device settings. The settings you enter in *Global Configuration* mode will affect the entire router and all of its interfaces. To enter *Global Configuration* mode, you must first be in privileged mode. While in *Privileged Exec* mode, type **configure terminal** (or **config t**) at the IOS prompt to enter *Global Configuration* mode. You will be able to tell that you are in *Global Configuration* mode because the IOS prompt will now end with **(config)#**. To exit *Global Configuration* mode, simply type the *exit* command at the IOS prompt.

Global Configuration mode is where you do most of the router configuration, including the initial configuration. *Global Configuration* mode is where you give the router a name, configure a log-in banner, and set router passwords.

Commands

To view all the commands available in *Privileged Exec* mode, you can type ?, at the IOS prompt. Below is an abbreviated sample output from this command. The actual output will vary depending on the device and IOS version.

Configure commands:

```
aaa                        Authentication, authorization,
                           and accounting
access-list                Add an access list entry
alias                      Create command alias
archive                    Archive the configuration
arp                        Set a static ARP entry
banner                     Define a log-in banner
boot                       Boot commands
buffers                    Adjust system buffer pool
                           parameters
```

cp	Global CDP configuration subcommands
cef	Cisco Express Forwarding
class-map	Configure QoS Class Map
clock	Configure time-of-day clock
cluster	Cluster configuration commands
cns	CNS agents
configuration	Configuration access
control-plane	Configure control plane services
default	Set a command to its defaults
default-value	Default character-bits values
define	interface range macro definition
diagnostic	Configure diagnostic information
do	To run exec commands in config mode
dot1x	IEEE 802.1X Global Configuration Commands
downward-compatible-config	Generate a configuration compatible with older software
eap	EAP Global Configuration Commands
enable	Modify enable password parameters
end	Exit from configure mode
eou	EAPoUDP Global Configuration Commands
errdisable	Error disable
exception	Exception handling
exit	Exit from configure mode
fallback	Fallback configuration commands
file	Adjust file system parameters
help	Description of the interactive help system
hostname	Set system's network name
hw-module	Control of individual components in the system
identity	Identity Configuration Commands
interface	Select an interface to configure
ip	Global IP configuration subcommands
ixi	IXI Config command
key	Key management
kron	Kron interval facility
l2protocol-tunnel	Tunnel Layer2 protocols
lacp	LACP configuration

```
line                    Configure a terminal line
link                    Enable link state tracking
                        feature
logging                 Modify message logging
                        facilities
login                   Enable secure login checking
mac                     Global MAC configuration
                        subcommands
```

The Hostname *Command*

The *hostname* command is used to give a name to the device. This name actually shows up as part of the IOS prompt when you connect to the device. If there is no hostname specified, then a generic one will be used like *router*.

The Banner *Command*

The *banner* command is used to set a message banner. This message will be displayed when someone connects to the *administrative* interface of the device.

> **Test Day Tip**
> It's important for the exam that you understand which commands are available in each operating mode. It will make it easier for you to determine which command is expected for producing the requested result.

MANAGING INTERNETWORK OPERATING SYSTEM

The Cisco IOS is the operating system that manages Cisco routers and switches. Some commands are only available in certain versions of the Cisco IOS. Therefore, it's important that you are able to tell what version of the Cisco IOS you have. To view what version of the Cisco IOS your system is running, type the following at the IOS prompt:

```
show version (or sh ver)
```

The *show version* command will provide you with a lot of information about the device and the IOS, including the IOS version. You can see the number of interfaces on the device, the model number, the serial number, and a host of other information.

You can also find out the IOS version by looking at the IOS image filename. The IOS images are stored in flash. When the router boots, the IOS file is extracted and loaded into memory. But, you can see exactly what file IOS image file is stored in flash memory by using the following command:

```
Show flash
```

The *show flash* command will show all of the files that currently reside in flash memory, including the IOS file. The IOS image filename contains several parts. These parts are helpful in determining important information about the IOS. These parts include the following: *hardware platform, feature set, file format, IOS version number, maintenance release number,* and *train identifier*. A *train identifier* can help to further define what features are available on an IOS image.

Let's take a sample filename:

■ c2500-ipbase-l.122-1.E.bin

here,

> **c2500** is the *hardware platform*
>
> **ipbase** is the *feature set*
>
> **1** is the *file format* (compressed)
>
> **122** is the *IOS version number*
>
> **1** is the *maintenance release number*
>
> **E** is the *train identifier*

Configuration Files

The configuration changes you make while in *Global Configuration* mode will only affect the currently running configuration of the router. If the router were to be rebooted, the configuration would revert back to the preceding configuration. This is because when the router boots, it pulls its configuration from NVRAM. This configuration is called the *startup-config*. If you want to make your configuration changes permanent, you must save them to NVRAM. This can be done by typing **write memory** (or **wr mem**), or **copy running-config startup-config** (or **copy run to start**).

BACKUP AND RESTORE

As you are aware, the configuration currently running on your router is called the *running-config*. Sometime this configuration can become corrupt. This can cause your router not to function properly or not to function at all. Or more often, you may make changes to configuration and need to undo the changes. If you do not remember all the configuration changes you made, you will not be able to use the *no* command to undo them all. The key to overcoming these problems is having proper backups of your router configuration. If a situation arises where your *running-config* is no longer usable, then you can simply restore the configuration from backup.

Backing Up Configurations

There are several possible methods for backing up your Cisco device *running-config*. The most common way to back up your *running-config* is to copy it to NVRAM. NVRAM is more stable than dynamic random-access memory (DRAM), where the running-configuration is kept. What you do is copy your *running-config* to your *startup-config*. This is done using the *copy* command.

```
Copy running-configuration startup-configuration
```

Your currently running configuration will then be copied to your *startup-config* file.

Trivial File Transfer Protocol

Copying your running-configuration to NRVAM will help you if something happens to the running-configuration. It does not help you if something happens to your router itself. To protect yourself in this instance, you must copy your configuration to a separate location. One of the most common places to store your router configuration is on a TFTP server. To back up your configuration to a TFTP server enter,

```
Copy running-config tftp
```

You will be prompted for the name or address of the remote TFTP server and for a destination filename. The default name for the backup file is router_name-config.

> **Note**
> Other configuration backup options are available. To see them, type **copy running-config ?** at the IOS prompt.

Restoring Configurations

Restoring your router configuration is just as easy as backing it up. To restore the running-configuration from an NVRAM backup use the following command:

- *Copy startup-config running-config (or copy start run)*

Restoring from a TFTP server backup is just as easy. Use the following command:

- *Copy tftp running-config*

You will be prompted for the name or address of the remote TFTP server, a source filename, and a destination filename. The default destination file is running-config.

HEAD OF THE CLASS...

Restoring Configs Using File Transfer Protocol
Restoring your configuration from a TFTP server causes your router interfaces to be administratively shut down. In this mode, they are basically offline. To bring them back online, you should use the *no shutdown* command on each interface.

TROUBLESHOOTING ROUTERS

Hopefully, once you set up a router, you won't have any more problems with it. But usually, this is not the case. Sometimes, you will have problems during the initial setup or after the router has been running for a while. It's important that you understand that some of the methods can help you in troubleshooting common problems.

Troubleshooting Connection Problems

Routers are basically used to connect multiple networks. Sometimes the router itself may be online but you will experience connection problems. The router may not be able to communicate with various networks or devices. Cisco offers a few *User Exec* level commands to troubleshoot these connection issues.

- *PING* – You can use the *PING* command to send test packets to a particular device. If you get a response back, you know there is a physical connection between the two devices. If no response is returned, this could indicate a problem with the physical connection.

- *Traceroute* – The *traceroute* command is used to determine the path between two connections. Often a connection to another device will have to go through multiple routers. The *traceroute* command will return the names or IP addresses of all the routers between two devices. This also allows you to see where a packet may be misguided.

Solving Boot Problems

A less common, but more serious set of problems revolve around booting the router. If the router does not boot properly, it is basically useless. It is critical that administrators understand what can be done if their router does not boot properly. Therefore, it's also critical that you understand this for the exam.

The Configuration Register

Cisco devices contain what is called a configuration register, which is a 16-bit register that controls router behavior. You can use this to control the terminal baud rate and control broadcast addresses. But, what we are most concerned with is the fact that changing the value of the configuration can alter how the router boots. This can be a very useful tool in solving boot problems.

The first thing you need to know is how to enter read-only memory (ROM) Monitor mode, which allows you to manually manipulate files and the configuration on the router without fully booting the router. You can enter ROM Monitor mode by pressing **Ctrl-Break** as the router is booting, or setting the configuration to 2100. To do this, enter the following command:

- *Config-register 0x2100*

If you are truly in ROM Monitor mode, the IOS prompt will appear as *rommon 1>* on new routers, but *just >* on older routers. Once you are in ROM Monitor mode, you can begin manipulating the router files and router configuration.

There are several other useful configuration register settings. Table 4.1 includes a listing of some of the most commonly used ones.

Table 4.1 Cisco Configuration Register Settings

Setting	Meaning
0x2101	Load IOS from ROM
0x2100	Boot to ROM Monitor mode
0x2102	Default setting
0x2142	Ignore config in NVRAM on boot

Booting to a Different IOS Image

In some situations, your router may not boot properly because of the IOS. The IOS could have become corrupt for some reason. Or there may have been a problem trying to upgrade your IOS image. To help with this problem, Cisco devices will allow you to boot using a different OS. Two common options to boot include using a different IOS image located in flash or using an IOS image on a TFTP server.

To boot from a different IOS located in flash, type the following in ROM Monitor mode:

```
Boot system flash ios-image-name
```

To boot from an IOS image located on a TFTP server, type the following in ROM Monitor mode:

```
Boot system tftp ios-image-name tfp-server-address
```

Resetting the Router Password

Occasionally you may run into a situation where you will have to reset the password of your router. This may be because you have forgotten the password, or the password was changed by someone else and you do not know the new password. As long as you have physical access to the router, you can reset its password. It's very easy to do, although it does require a number of steps.

EXERCISE 4.3   Resetting Your Router Password

Here we will be resetting your router password. We will first bypass your startup configuration and then make the changes.

1. Connect to your router via the console cable.

2. Power off your router.

3. Power your router back on.

4. Use **Ctrl-Break** to interrupt the boot sequence. You are now in *ROM monitor* mode.

5. Type **confreg 0x2142** at the prompt. This turns on bit 6, which will cause the *NVRAM* config to be ignored.

6. Reload the router.

7. Enter privileged mode.

8. Enter *Global Configuration* mode.

9. Copy the startup config to the running config, using

```
copy start run
```

10. Change the router passwords.

11. Type **confreg 0x2102** to change the configuration register back to normal.

12. Save the current configuration to NVRAM.

13. Reload the router.

Firmware Upgrade

The firmware running on your Cisco device is the Cisco IOS. There will come a time when you will need to upgrade this firmware. This may be necessary in order to get bug fixes or to enable new router features.

The Cisco IOS is basically a file that gets loaded at device initialization. If you want to upgrade your IOS, you simply have to replace this file with a newer file. Cisco developed the Cisco IFS (Cisco IOS File System), to help you manage files on your router. You can use the Cisco IFS to copy the new IOS image to your router.

EXERCISE 4.4   Upgrade Your Router Firmware

Here we will be upgrading your router firmware. This requires us to access the flash memory in your router.

1. At the IOS prompt, type **dir**. This will list out the contents of your flash memory.

2. Type **copy tftp://<ipaddress>//ios-image-name flash:/ios-image-name**

3. Confirm the source filename. Press **Enter**.

4. Confirm the destination filename. Press **Enter**.

5. Type **sh file information flash:ios-image-name** to verify the new image was copied and is runnable.

6. Reload the router.

CONFIGURING AND IMPLEMENTING...

Deleting the current IOS image

Flash memory on your Cisco router is limited. Sometimes, to copy a new IOS to your router, you have to *delete* the current IOS from flash. This is done using the delete command. Type ***delete flash:IOS-Image-Name*** at the IOS prompt.

SUMMARY OF EXAM OBJECTIVES

Before your Cisco router can begin servicing connections, it must be configured. Before you can configure your router, you must connect to it. Cisco offers many different connection methods. Some are always available, like console connections. Some are always available, but must be configured like Telnet. Some are only available in certain versions of the IOS like SSH. No matter what connection methods your device offers, initial configuration must always be done using a console connection.

There are three main administrative modes on all Cisco devices: *User Exec* mode, *Privileged Exec* mode, and *Global Configuration* mode. Each mode offers its own set of features and functions. *User Exec* mode is the basic mode, which mostly offers the ability to view device usage and to do some basic troubleshooting. *Privileged Exec* mode offers escalated privileges, in which you can view sensitive information like device configurations. You can also perform tasks that will change the behavior of your device, like enabling debugging options. *Global Configuration* mode allows you to change the configuration of your device. You can give your device, set passwords, and perform a multitude of other configuration tasks.

Cisco devices run an operating system called the Cisco IOS. The IOS is what enables different features and functions to be performed on your device. When your Cisco device boots, the IOS image contained in flash is extracted and stored in memory. It basically runs from there.

There are two main configuration files that IOS will read; the startup-config and the running-config. The startup-config is loaded every time the IOS initializes. It is stored in NVRAM. The running-config is the configuration currently running on your Cisco device. It is basically the startup-config plus any changes you made since device initialization. The startup-config is stored in DRAM. If you want to preserve any config changes you make, you save the running-config to the startup-config. You can back up your Cisco device configuration to multiple locations. The two main back-up locations are NVRAM and an TFTP server. If your running-configuration becomes corrupt, you can restore the configuration from one of these locations.

Occasionally you may run into various issues with your Cisco router. Two of the more crucial areas where issues may occur are connectivity and bootup. Cisco provides tools for troubleshooting these issues. Connectivity issues can be troubleshot using utilities such as *PING* and *traceroute*. Boot issue can be troubleshot by changing the IOS image boot location and changing the configuration registers on your device. Firmware upgrades can be used to apply patches for known issues or bugs. Firmware upgrades can also be used to add features to your Cisco device.

EXAM OBJECTIVES FAST TRACK

Connecting to the Router

- You can connect to a Cisco router via the console port, the auxiliary port, Telnet, SSH, or HTTP.

- You will need a *Terminal Emulator* to connect to a Cisco router via the console port, via the auxiliary port, or via SSH.

User Exec Mode

- User mode is the least privileged mode of router operation.

- User mode allows you to view router statics and general information.

Privileged Exec Mode

- Privileged mode is also called *enable* mode because you use the command *enable* to enter this mode.

- Privileged mode allows you to view the router configuration.

Global Configuration Mode

- You use the command **config t** to enter *Global Configuration* mode.

- *Global Configuration* mode allows you to configure settings that will affect the entire router.

- *Global Configuration* mode is where you would give your router a name and set password.

Managing Internetwork Operating System

- The IOS is stored in flash memory on the router.
- The **show version** command is used to view information on the IOS currently running on the Cisco device.
- The running-config for Cisco devices is stored in DRAM.
- The startup-config for Cisco devices is stored in NVRAM.

Backup and Restore

- Cisco device configurations are typically backed up to NRAM and/or a TFTP server.
- The *copy* command is used to back up and restore your Cisco configuration.

Troubleshooting Routers

- You can use the *PING* and *traceroute* commands to troubleshoot connection issues.
- Setting your router configuration register to 0x2142 will allow you to bypass your NVRAM configuration settings and reset your device password.
- A Cisco device's firmware is upgraded by replacing the file that contains the IOS image.

EXAM OBJECTIVES FREQUENTLY ASKED QUESTIONS

Q: Can a simple straight-through cable be used to connect to a Cisco router console?

A: No, a special rollover cable must be used.

Q: Do all Cisco devices use the ISO?

A: No, but most Cisco routers and switches use the IOS.

Q: Can any terminal emulation software be used to connect to a Cisco?

A: You can use any American National Standards Institute (ANSI) compatible terminal emulator to connect to a Cisco device.

Q: Will the certification exam require commands to be entered freehanded?

A: Not all of the questions in the exam are multiple choices. You will be required to manually type in commands to perform specific actions.

SELF TEST

1. You have just connected to your Cisco 2500 series router. You are trying to enable debugging on your router. You are receiving the error invalid command. How can you fix the problem?
   - **A.** Use the *enable* command to enter *Privileged Exec* mode
   - **B.** Use the *config t* command to enter *Global Configuration* mode
   - **C.** Use the *disable* command to enter *Privileged Exec* mode
   - **D.** Upgrade your router firmware to a version that has debug capabilities

2. Given the following IOS image filename c2500-ipbase-l.122-1.E.bin, what feature set is running on the device?
   - **A.** The c2500 feature set
   - **B.** The IPBase feature set
   - **C.** The 122 feature set
   - **D.** The Enterprise feature set

3. Given the following IOS image filename c2600-ipbase-l.122-1.E.bin, what hardware platform is the IOS designed for?
   - **A.** The C2600 platform
   - **B.** The IPBase platform
   - **C.** The 122 platform
   - **D.** The Enterprise platform

4. One of your Cisco routers is down and you need to figure out why. Since the router is down, there is no network connectivity to the router. You also are not near the router and therefore cannot use the console port. Do you have any other options for connecting to the router to troubleshoot the issue?
   - **A.** Connect to the router using Telnet
   - **B.** Connect to the *Web administration* interface of the router
   - **C.** Establish a SSH connection to the router
   - **D.** Use a modem to connect to the auxiliary port of the router

5. You want to configure your router so that a password is required to enter *Privileged* mode. What mode must your router be in so that you can configure this requirement?
   - **A.** *User Exec* mode
   - **B.** *Global Configuration* mode
   - **C.** *Privileged Exec* mode
   - **D.** *Interface Configuration* mode

6. You made several changes to your router configuration. You tested out these changes and everything was running fine. Your route lost power and restarted itself. The changes you made seem to have disappeared. What is most likely the cause of the issue?

   A. You did not test the changes thoroughly

   B. You were in *User Exec* mode when you made the changes

   C. You were in *Privileged Exec* mode when you made the changes

   D. You did not save the configuration to NVRAM

7. You have just configured a hostname for your router. But, you are unable to save your configuration to NVRAM using the write memory command. What is most likely the issue?

   A. You must be in enable mode to save your configuration

   B. You do not have rights to save the configuration

   C. You did not configure the hostname properly

   D. You are using the wrong command to save the configuration

8. You have just configured your router with an *enable* password. But, you notice when you do a *show running-config* command, the enable password you set is visible. What can be done about this?

   A. Nothing can be done about this

   B. Configure encryption on your config file

   C. Configure an enable secret

   D. Upgrade your IOS to a more secure version

9. You have made several changes to your Cisco router configuration, but have not saved them to NVRAM, yet. You are not sure which options you configured. Is there a way for you to see what configuration changes you have made?

   A. Use the *show startup-config* command to view the configuration

   B. Use the *write memory* command to write the configuration to the screen

   C. There is no way to see the changes you made until after you save the configuration to NVRAM

   D. Use the *show running-config* command to view the configuration

10. You have just set up your Cisco router. But, you notice that the IOS prompt says *router*. Is there any way for you to change this?

A. Yes, use the router command to change the router's name

B. No, this cannot be changed

C. Yes, use the *hostname* command to give the router a name

D. Yes, install a new IOS image that is properly licensed.

11. What command can be used to view the routing table on your Cisco router?

A. *Ipconfig*

B. *Show route*

C. *Route print*

D. *Show ip route*

12. You are trying to view information about your IOS. What command will allow you to view this information?

A. *show ios*

B. *show version*

C. *show ip route*

D. *enable*

13. The configuration on your router has become corrupt. You remember that you have a backup of your configuration on a TFTP server. Which of the following commands will allow you to restore your configuration from a TFTP server?

A. *copy tftp run*

B. *copy run tftp*

C. *write mem*

D. *write tftp*

14. You want to check the contents of your router flash memory to check which IOS file you have. What command can be used to view your router's flash?

A. *dir flash*

B. *sh flash*

C. *view flash*

D. *wr mem*

15. You are having trouble with your Cisco router. You believe it is a connection issue. What command can you use to check to see your router has a network connection to another router?

A. *PING*

B. *sh route*

C. *route print*

D. *sh running-config*

16. The IOS image on your router has become corrupt. You want to boot the system from a copy of an IOS image you have on a TFTP server. Which of the following commands would allow you to do this?

    A. *copy tftp run*

    B. *boot system tftp ios-image-name tfp-server-address*

    C. *copy tftp start*

    D. *boot system flash: ios-image-name*

17. Which of the following is the default register setting for a Cisco router?

    A. *confreg 0x2100*   **C.** *confreg 0x2102*

    B. *confreg 0x2142*   **D.** *confreg 0x2002*

18. Which of the following config register settings can you use to bypass your router's NVRAM configuration file?

    A. *confreg 0x2100*   **C.** *confreg 0x2102*

    B. *confreg 0x2142*   **D.** *confreg 0x2134*

19. What command is used to exit *Privileged Exec* mode?

    A. *exit*   **C.** *enable*

    B. *no enable*   **D.** *disable*

20. You want to configure your router so that a password is required in order to connect to the console. What mode must you be in, in order to configure this requirement?

    A. *Privileged Exec* mode   **C.** *Interface Configuration* mode

    B. *Global Configuration* mode   **D.** *User Exec* mode

SELF TEST QUICK ANSWER KEY

1.	A	11.	D
2.	B	12.	B
3.	A	13.	A
4.	D	14.	B
5.	B	15.	A
6.	D	16.	B
7.	A	17.	C
8.	C	18.	B
9.	D	19.	D
10.	C	20.	B

CHAPTER 5

Routing Protocols: RIP, RIPv2, IGRP, EIGRP, OSPF

Exam objectives in this chapter

INTRODUCTION

All Cisco Certified Network Associate (CCNA) students need to understand how data is routed between two networks. There are a number of different routing protocols that Cisco routers support, including Routing Information Protocol v2 (RIPv2), Open Shortest Path First (OSPF), and Enhanced Interior Gateway Routing Protocol (EIGRP). Some routing protocols are open, such as RIPv2 and OSPF, and can be used in conjunction with other manufacture's hardware. Some routing protocols, such as EIGRP, are proprietary and can only be used when other Cisco routers are present on the network.

CCNA students should be able to distinguish between distance vector and link-state routing protocols. Understanding how these types of routing protocols communicate with neighboring routers and keep their routing tables is essential to passing the CCNA exam. CCNA students should be able to compare and contrast the different routing protocols that can be used on Cisco routers. And, equally important, given a scenario at a workplace, a

CCNA should be able to determine which routing protocol would be most effective based on the company's network configuration and needs.

ROUTING

The purpose of a network is to share information. Computers on one network can easily share information with other computers on the same network. But, it gets a little tricky when you want to share information with a system that does not reside on the same network as your system. There must be a way for the two systems to communicate. This is where routing comes in. Routing allows a system on one network to communicate with a system on another network.

One of the big advantages of routing is that the two systems do not have to know how to reach each other. There is no way one system can keep track of the whereabouts of every system it wants to communicate with. It would be virtually impossible. Therefore, routers are used to keep track of this information for you. All a system needs to know how to do is communicate with the router residing on its own network. Then the routers take care of the rest.

Network Addresses

Nowadays most networks, the Internet included, use the Transmission Control Protocol/Internet Protocol (TCP/IP) for communication. Because of this, most of the exam will focus on TCP/IP and so shall we. Each network system running TCP/IP has an IP address. This address basically specifies the location of the system. The address contains two parts. The first part of the address is the network address; the second part is the individual system address. The subnet mask is used to determine which part of the address is which. An IP address uses 32 binary digits. The subnet mask will tell you how many of these bits represent the network and how many represent the individual system.

Network addresses are what are used to specify network subnets. Locating the network is the first step in locating a particular machine. This is what routers are concerned with. Routers keep track of which network addresses are located where. A router will forward a packet to another router, until it reaches the network where the system resides.

Routing Tables

Routers and other network systems need a way of tracking destinations to different networks. This is done through the use of routing tables. A routing table will help a network system determine where it should send network traffic destined for a particular network. When a system needs to send information to a particular network, it will refer to its routing table and send the packets to the router or interface designated in the routing table.

It's key to note that routers are not the only systems that keep routing tables. Individual workstations will keep a routing table. The routing table on a workstation is generally not as detailed as the routing table on router, but it's still just as important. To view the routing table on your Windows system, type the following at the *command prompt*:

```
route print
```

Your system's routing table will look similar to the one in Figure 5.1. This workstation shows two routing tables: one for IPv4 networks and one for IPv6 networks. We will concentrate on the IPv4 table. As you can see, most of the routes of the networks have a gateway listed as Onlink. This

```
Command Prompt                                                               _ □ ×
C:\Users\derrickr>route print
===========================================================================
Interface List
 13 ...00 1f 3b 2d d7 c7 ...... Intel(R) Wireless WiFi Link 4965AGN
 10 ...00 1c 25 7c 78 69 ...... Intel(R) 82566MM Gigabit Network Connection
  1 ........................... Software Loopback Interface 1
 22 ...00 00 00 00 00 00 00 e0  Microsoft ISATAP Adapter
 19 ...02 00 54 55 4e 01 ...... Teredo Tunneling Pseudo-Interface
 29 ...00 00 00 00 00 00 00 e0  Microsoft ISATAP Adapter #4


===========================================================================

IPv4 Route Table
===========================================================================
Active Routes:
Network Destination        Netmask          Gateway       Interface  Metric
          0.0.0.0          0.0.0.0      192.168.1.254  192.168.1.102     25
        127.0.0.0        255.0.0.0           On-link        127.0.0.1    306
        127.0.0.1  255.255.255.255           On-link        127.0.0.1    306
  127.255.255.255  255.255.255.255           On-link        127.0.0.1    306
      192.168.1.0    255.255.255.0           On-link    192.168.1.102    281
    192.168.1.102  255.255.255.255           On-link    192.168.1.102    281
    192.168.1.255  255.255.255.255           On-link    192.168.1.102    281
        224.0.0.0        240.0.0.0           On-link        127.0.0.1    306
        224.0.0.0        240.0.0.0           On-link    192.168.1.102    281
  255.255.255.255  255.255.255.255           On-link        127.0.0.1    306
  255.255.255.255  255.255.255.255           On-link    192.168.1.102    281
===========================================================================
Persistent Routes:
  None

IPv6 Route Table
===========================================================================
Active Routes:
 If Metric Network Destination      Gateway
 19     18 ::/0                      On-link
  1    306 ::1/128                   On-link
 19     18 2001::/32                 On-link
 19    266 2001:0:4137:9e50:1861:1641:bb28:a647/128
                                     On-link
 19    266 fe80::/64                 On-link
 19    266 fe80::1861:1641:bb28:a647/128
                                     On-link
  1    306 ff00::/8                  On-link
 19    266 ff00::/8                  On-link
===========================================================================
Persistent Routes:
  None
```

FIGURE 5.1   *Routing Table from a Windows System*

means that the destination network is located on the same network as the system. The most significant route is the one with the destination network of 0.0.0.0. This is the *default gateway*; sometimes called the *default route* or the *gateway of last resort*. If the system is trying to reach a network that does not have a specific router, it will send the traffic to the default gateway. In general, except for the rare occasion where a workstation has been configured with a static route, traffic destined for other networks will be sent to the default gateway.

The route table on a Cisco router can be a lot more complex. You can have static routes, dynamic routes, and routes to multiple networks that are directly connected to the router. Look at the example in Figure 5.2. Not only does it show routes to multiple different networks but it also shows how the routes were learned. It will designate static routes, directly connected routes, and dynamic routes. You can see routes to three networks that are directly connected to the router. These routes are denoted by the C at the beginning of the line. This router also contains a default route. You can tell by the destination network of 0.0.0.0.

Routing Terms

Routing can be very complex, especially when you start talking about dynamically configured routes. There are lots of key terms that must be understood before you can get a full grasp on how routing truly works. So, before we move on, we need to define a few of these terms. Make sure you understand them before moving on. The exam or a live network can be quite daunting if you don't understand them.

Routing Protocols

Routing protocols are used to automatically populate routing tables. Routing protocols define how routes are calculated and how the routing tables will be populated. Routing protocols also allow routing information to be shared between routers. This is essential in ensuring that a router is aware

FIGURE 5.2

Routing Table from a Cisco Router

```
Codes: C - connected, S - static, R - RIP, M - mobile, B - BGP
       D - EIGRP, EX - EIGRP external, O - OSPF, IA - OSPF inter area
       N1 - OSPF NSSA external type 1, N2 - OSPF NSSA external type 2
       E1 - OSPF external type 1, E2 - OSPF external type 2
       i - IS-IS, su - IS-IS summary, L1 - IS-IS level-1, L2 - IS-IS level-2
       ia - IS-IS inter area, * - candidate default, U - per-user static route
       o - ODR, P - periodic downloaded static route

Gateway of last resort is 10.3.24.1 to network 0.0.0.0

     10.0.0.0/24 is subnetted, 3 subnets
C       10.3.25.0 is directly connected, Vlan1
C       10.3.24.0 is directly connected, Vlan2
C       10.3.26.0 is directly connected, Vlan3
S*   0.0.0.0/0 [1/0] via 10.3.24.1
```

of the best path for reaching a destination network. Many times there will be multiple paths to a destination network. Routers help ensure that traffic is sent along the best path.

Administrative Distance

Administrative distance defines how reliable or trustworthy a given route is. The lower the administrative distance, the more trustworthy the route is. This is important because dynamically configured routes may not always be correct. There must be a way to determine which routes to a particular destination are most likely to be correct. Statically configured routes, for example, have an administrative distance of 1. This is because routers assume that any route that is manually entered must be correct. Table 5.1 shows administrative distances for some of the more common routing protocols.

Routing Metrics

There are often many different routes to the same destination. The use of routing metrics helps a routing protocol determine which route would be the most preferred route. In a way, you can think of a metric as helping to define the cost of using a particular route. The route with the lowest cost (or best metric) is the one that the routing protocol will use to populate the routing table. Sometimes two different routes to the same destination will have the same metric. Each router and routing protocol has a different way of dealing with this. Sometimes one route will be discarded; sometimes both routes will be posted to the routing table, and the router will load balance between them.

Convergence

When a change occurs in your network topology, routing tables have to be updated. Each router will send out the contents of its routing tables to other routers. This exchange of information will happen until all routers have updated their routing tables to reflect to new network topology. This update process is known as *convergence*. Although the convergence process is taking

Table 5.1 Routing Protocol Administrative Distances

Routing Protocol	Administrative Distance
RIP	120
RIPv2	120
IGRP	100
EIGRP	90
OSPF	110

place, you will notice higher resource utilization on your routers. You may also notice that some packets may be dropped or deemed undeliverable. Because of this, the faster convergence can take place the better.

Distance Vector Routing Protocols

Distance vector routing protocols represent some of the oldest routing protocols still in use today. They, for the most part, are easy to understand. They use an algorithm called the *Bellman–Ford* to determine the preferred network path for transmission. The Bellman–Ford algorithm will help determine which network path is the shortest and most preferred route to a destination.

Routers using distance vector routing protocols will share routing information with other routers on the network. Distance vector routing protocols transmit their entire routing tables to all their directly connected neighbors. They are considered somewhat inefficient because these updates are periodically sent regardless of the network state, whether there are updates to the network topology or not.

One key point here is that distance vector routing protocols only talk to their directly connected neighbors. So each router does not have first-hand information about all the routes in its routing table. As a matter of fact, most of the routes in the routing table will be from second-hand information. Basically, in a network such as seen in Figure 5.3, Router 1 will learn about the networks connected to Routers 3 and 4 through Router 2. Similarly, Router 3 will learn about the networks connected to Router 1 through Router 2. The router does not talk to all the other routers directly. This is one reason why distance vector routing protocols generally have higher administrative distances.

Distance vector routing protocols are slow to converge. This is because all the routing information has to be processed by all routers for all the routes in the network before convergence is complete. In larger networks, this can take a lot of time. Convergence and processing routing updates can prove to be somewhat of a burden on a router's resources. So you should periodically monitor your routers to see how long this takes, to ensure it's not negatively affecting your network.

Exam Warning

To prevent router interfaces from constantly sending out updates, you can configure it to be a "passive interface." If an interface is configured as passive, it will not broadcast routing updates.

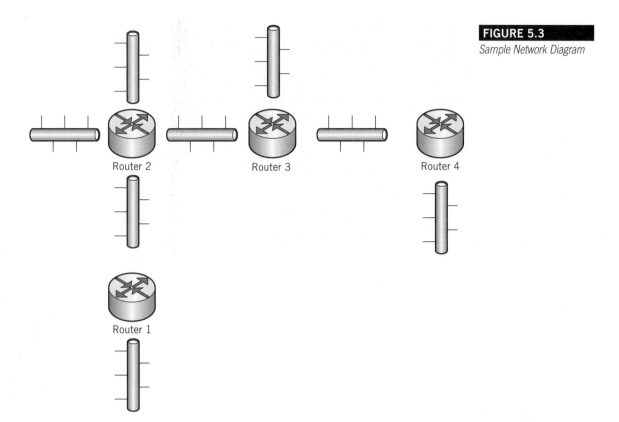

FIGURE 5.3
Sample Network Diagram

Routing Protocols

There are several routing protocols that use distance vector algorithms, especially order routing protocols. Some of the more common examples that are still used today are RIPv1, RIPv2, and Interior Gateway Routing Protocol (IGRP). We will discuss these protocols more in-depth, later in this chapter. Each protocol will be covered in its own section.

Link-State Routing Protocols

Link-state routing protocols are generally more robust than their distance vector counterparts. They are used more widely in larger networks. As the name implies, they take the actual condition of the network link into consideration when calculating the metric. They generally use a slightly more advanced algorithm for computing the best route to a destination. One commonly used algorithm is the Dijkstra Shortest Path First Algorithm.

Link-state routing protocols can transmit routing information to all other routers running the same protocol, not just directly connected neighbors.

This way, all routers are receiving first-hand information. This makes the routes more reliable. Hence, routes created by link-state routing protocols generally have lower administrative distances.

The updates sent by link-state routing protocols are called *link-state advertisements* (LSAs). These LSAs are processed by other routers on the networks. The routers then update their routing tables. Link-state routing protocols generally keep three different routing tables. The first table tracks all the router's neighbors. The second table tracks the entire network topology and all the possible routes to a destination. The third table tracks the preferred route to a destination network and is generally what is thought of when discussing routing tables.

When routers running link-state routing protocols start up, there is an initial discovery and synchronization. After the initial discovery and synchronization period, each router will send periodic hello messages. These hello messages are used to let the router's neighbors know that the router is still functioning. If a series of these hello messages are missing, then a router will be assumed to be down and unavailable.

Convergence happens much faster with link-state routing protocols than with distance vector protocols. Because routing updates only include changes to the network, there is far less processing that needs to be done when updates are sent. For this reason, link-state protocols are often preferred in larger, more complex networks.

Routing Protocols

There are also several link-state routing protocols in use today. The one we will be covering for the exam is the OSPF protocol. OSPF is one of the most widely used routing protocols today. It can be a little complex, but it is very effective in larger networks.

Hybrid Routing Protocols

Hybrid routing protocols are also sometimes referred to as advanced link-state routing protocols. This is because they improve on some of the characteristics of link-state routing protocols. Hybrid routing protocols actually combine characteristics of both distance vector and link-state routing protocols. They use characteristics of the other two types of protocols to come up with what is many times a superior protocol. Distance vector and link-state routing protocols both have their advantages and disadvantages. Hybrid routing protocols try to combine the advantages of both and leave out the disadvantages.

The problem with hybrid routing protocols is that different vendors often implement them in different manners. This can make using network equipment from multiple vendors on the same network difficult. If protocols are implemented in different ways with different vendors, the network devices may not be able to properly share information between each other. This would be a problem if you are trying to combine two networks or trying to gradually phase out older equipment.

Routing Protocols

The one hybrid routing protocol that you must be concerned with for the exam is EIGRP. EIGRP is a hybrid routing protocol implemented by Cisco. EIGRP is generally the preferred routing protocol on networks that use all Cisco equipment. EIGRP will be discussed in more detail later in the EIGRP section of this chapter.

Open Routing Protocols

Open routing protocols are protocols that use open standards that are available to everyone. Any vendor is capable of implementing the open protocols on their network devices. When these open protocols are implemented by different vendors, they have to adhere to the standard set for the protocol. There can be slight additions, but the standards must be adhered to. Because multiple vendors will implement open protocols in the same manner, devices from multiple vendors can still share routing information. This facilitates the use of devices from multiple vendors on the same network. You may give up some flexibility by implementing open routing protocols, but you gain a lot in terms of flexibility.

Routing Protocols

There are several open routing protocols available. The ones you need to know for the exam are RIPv1, RIPv2, and OSPF. These are the three most widely used. And actually RIPv1 is being phased out in favor of RIPv2. So the two most commonly used are RIPv2 and OSPF. But, we will still discuss RIPv1 for completeness.

Proprietary Routing Protocols

Proprietary routing protocols are those developed by a particular network vendor. Vendors may develop a proprietary routing protocol to address specific customer needs. Because of this, a proprietary routing protocol is often the best fit for a particular organization.

The problem with proprietary routing protocols is that they are generally vendor specific. There are a few disadvantages to this option. First, they can be difficult to implement and troubleshoot. The vendor may not provide adequate documentation around the internal workings of the protocol. Without this knowledge, you may have to consult the vendor for help implementing the protocol. Second, they are often only available on network equipment provided by the vendor who developed them. This may prevent you from being able to use multiple network vendors on your network.

Routing Protocols

Proprietary routing protocols are different for each vendor. The Cisco proprietary routing protocols that we will be concerned with are IGRP and EIGRP. Cisco designed these protocols specifically to overcome some of the limitations with other protocols. EIGRP is an enhancement of the original IGRP protocol.

RIP

RIP is one of the oldest routing protocols still in existence . RIP is a distance vector routing protocol. It adheres to most of the standards set for distance vector protocols. RIP has an administrative distance of 120. RIP works well on smaller networks but is generally considered too inefficient for larger, more complex networks.

Routing Metric

RIP only uses one metric for computing the best route to a destination. It uses *hop count* which is basically the number of routers between the source and the destination. RIP can support a maximum of 15 hops. Routes that have higher hop counts are considered invalid and are discarded.

Sometimes routes can have equal metrics. This means there may be an equal number of hops between a source and a destination, even if you take different routes. In cases where hop counts are identical for different routes, RIP will store all the routes in the routing table. Then, the router will load balance between the different routes.

Routing Updates

Routers running RIP will broadcast the contents of their routing table to their neighbors. By default, these updates will occur every 30 s. After six missed communication attempts (or 180 s), a router will consider its neighbor dead. The router will then remove all entries for that router from its routing table. It is possible to change the update timers for RIP updates, but it's not recommended. Changing the timers can cause unexpected results including increases in the time it takes for the protocol to converge or the inclusion of "dead" routes in the routing table.

RIP is a classful routing protocol. It does not send network subnet masks when sending routing updates. All networks are assumed to use the standard subnet mask for their network class. For example, an IP network starting with 10 will be assumed to use a 255.0.0.0 subnet mask. Because RIP uses classful routing, it will also do route summarization. This means that if you have your network subnetted, RIP will not report the individual subnets in its updates. This means that you cannot use only portions of a particular network or use discontiguous subnets. RIP will advertise the entire network in its updates. So, other routers will assume the entire network is available via that router not just a particular subnet.

RIPv2

RIPv2 is an enhancement to the original RIP protocol developed in 1994. RIPv2 is also a distance vector routing protocol but has a few enhancements to make it more efficient than RIPv1. Although RIPv2 is more efficient than RIPv1, it is not deemed suitable for larger, more complex networks. It simply gives you more flexibility on smaller networks.

Routing Metric

RIPv2 uses the same routing metric as RIPv1, hop count. Hop count is the number of routers between a source and destination. RIPv2 also has the same hop count limit as RIPv1. If a route has more than 15 hops, the route will be discarded as invalid.

Routing Updates

Updates with RIPv2 are sent via multicasts and not broadcasts like the original RIP protocol. The multicasts are sent using a multicast address of 224.0.0.9. This helps prevent RIP routing table advertisements from being processed by every system on the network. Only systems that listen on the multicast address of 224.0.0.9 will process the updates.

RIPv2 can also be configured to do classless routing. When configured for classless routing, RIPv2 will transmit submit masks when it sends routing updates. This allows for the use of subnetting and discontiguous networks.

RIPv2 allows for authentication to be required for updates. When authentication is enabled, each router is configured with the RIP update password.

The password sent with the RIP update must match the password configured on the destination router. If the passwords do not match, then the receiving router will not process the update.

> **Note**
> The passwords sent with RIPv2 updates are sent in clear text. You can configure your router to use a Message Digest 5 (MD5) algorithm to secure the password.

Configuring RIPv2

RIP is one of the easiest protocols to configure. This is why it's one of the most widely used. With just a few simple steps, you can have your routers configured to process RIP routing information. First, you start off by enabling RIPv2 on the router. Then, you have to specify what networks you want to enable for RIPv2. These are the networks that will be tracked via the RIPv2 protocol.

EXERCISE 5.1   Configuring RIPv2 on a Cisco Router

In this exercise, we will configure RIPv2 routing on our router and enable it for network 192.168.1.0.

1. Enter *Privileged Exec* mode with the *enable* command. Enter the enable password if you have one configured.

2. Enter *Global Configuration* mode with the *config t* command.

3. To enable RIPv2 and enter RIP configuration mode, type **router rip**.

4. Now enter *network 192.168.1.0* to enable RIP for that network. You do not need to enter a subnet mask because RIP by default is classful and the default subnet mask is assumed.

You router is now configured to run the RIPv2 protocol, and RIP routing has been set for network 192.168.1.0.

> **Exam Warning**
> By default, a router will process RIPv1 and RIPv2 updates. Forcing a router to RIPv1 will cause RIPv2 updates to be ignored.

IGRP

IGRP is a proprietary routing protocol developed by Cisco. IGRP is only available on Cisco devices. If you want to use IGRP as your only routing protocol, then all the routers on your network must be Cisco devices.

IGRP is a distance vector routing protocol, just like RIP, but is slightly more advanced and overcomes some of the limitations of using RIP. IGRP has a maximum hop count of 255. This allows IGRP to be used on much larger networks. Also IGRP has an administrative distance of 100. Therefore, its routes are considered more reliable than routes supplied by RIP.

Routing Metric

IGRP uses *composite metric*, a more advanced metric that uses a combination of multiple factors in its computation, to determine the most efficient route to a destination. By default, IRGP will use a combination of bandwidth and line delay to compute the metric for a route. You can also configure IGRP to use reliability, load, and maximum transmission unit (MTU) to compute the metric.

Routing Updates

IGRP, like many distance vector routing protocols, does not send subnet mask information but sends its entire routing table when sending routing updates. This leads to the usual limitations around the lack of support for subnets and discontiguous networks. These updates, however, are only sent every 90 s as opposed to the 30-s update time used by RIP. Additionally, IGRP routing updates are not processed by all routers running the IGRP protocol.

Autonomous Systems

When you configure IGRP on a router, you must configure an autonomous system (AS) number. An AS designates a group of routers that will share information. This AS number must match on all routers that will share routing information. Multiple ASes are used in larger networks to help segment them. In a large network, without segmentation, you might end up with very large and complex routing tables on your routers. The larger and more complex the routing tables, the longer convergence takes.

What you can do is segment your network into different groups and assign different AS numbers to different groups of routers. This will help decrease the size and complexity of the routing tables in each group. The different groups will not automatically share routing information, but you can use route redistribution to share routing information between the different ASes.

NEW AND NOTEWORTHY...

Support for IGRP

IGRP has been deprecated and is no longer supported on most Cisco routers. It has been replaced with EIGRP.

EIGRP

EIGRP is an enhancement to the original IRGP standard. EIGRP is a hybrid (or enhanced distance vector) routing protocol and one of the most widely used routing protocols used today. This is because of its robustness and efficiency.

EIGRP supports a variety of network protocols. It can provide routing support for IPv4, IPv6, Internetwork Packet Exchange (IPX), and AppleTalk. Similar to its predecessor IGRP, EIGRP has a maximum hop count of 224 and a default maximum hop count of 100. EIGRP has administrative distance of 90. This means its routes are slightly more trusted than IRGP routes and a lot more trusted than RIP routes that have an administrative distance of 120.

HEAD OF THE CLASS...

Configuring EIGRP Maximum Hop Count

The default hop count used by EIGRP is 100. To use a higher hop count, use the following command: *metric maximum-hops <1-224>*

Routing Metrics

EIGRP also uses a composite metric for determining the best route. By default, this composite metric will only use bandwidth and line delay, but it can also be configured to use load and reliability.

When EIGRP encounters routes that have the same metric, they will be added to the routing table and the routing table will load balance between them. By default, EIGRP will store up to four routes that have the same metric. But, it can be configured to store up to six.

Note

Not only can EIGRP store up to six equal paths but it can store up to six unequal paths.

Routing Updates

When a router using EIGRP comes online, the first thing it will do is try to find all its neighbors. It will then try to form an association with them. Once this association is formed, the router and its neighbors will advertise their entire routing tables to each other. But, after this initial synchronization, only updates will be transmitted between neighbors, not the entire routing table.

RTP

EIGRP uses Reliable Transport Protocol (RTP) to communicate with neighbors. When communicating with neighbors, EIGRP will first send out information to its neighbors using the multicast address of 224.0.0.10. EIGRP will keep a list of neighbors who have replied to the message. If a reply is not sent back from one of its neighbors, then EIGRP will start using unicasts to talk to the neighbor. After 16 attempts, if there is no response back, the neighbor will be considered dead and removed from the router's list of neighbors.

ASes

EIGRP uses AS numbers to determine which updates will be processed by each router. For EIGRP updates to be processed, two systems must share the same AS number. This helps cut down on the amount of updates being processed by each router. They will only process updates with the correct AS number.

CONFIGURING AND IMPLEMENTING...

Implementing EIGRP Neighbors

For two routers running EIGRP to exchange routing information, they must not only have the same AS number but they must also use the same routing metric. Unless both are the same, the routers will not establish a neighborship. A neighborship is an established relationship between two EIGRP routers. This is how EIGRP routers know whom to send updates to.

DUAL

EIGRP uses the Diffusing Update Algorithm (DUAL) for determining the best routes to a destination. The DUAL supports classless routing. Therefore, EIGRP will include subnet mask information in routing updates. This allows for variable-length subnet mask (VLSM) and the use of discontiguous networks.

Using the DUAL, EIGRP keeps track of three tables:

- **neighbor table** The neighbor table holds a list of all the routers EIGRP has established a neighborship with.

- **topology table** The topology table keeps track of the entire network topology. It stores all the information about all the routes that the router has received from its neighbors, even duplicate routes.

- **route table** The routing table is the table that stores information about the best routes to a particular destination.

The DUAL not only tracks the best route to a destination, it also maintains a table with backup routes. These backup routes are stored in the topology table. The use of backup routes helps to greatly decrease the time needed for convergence. If a topology change occurs that affects a primary route in an EIGRP routing table, EIGRP will simply place the backup route in the routing table as the new preferred route. This makes convergence almost immediate.

Exam Warning

You can route redistribution, to allow routing information to be shared among differ-ent ASes. These routes however will be considered "external" EIGRP routes and will have an administrative distance of 170.

Configuring EIGRP

Configuring EIGRP can be somewhat complex, but the base configuration is much simpler. Although it's more complicated than a base RIP configu-ration, it's still not terribly difficult. You have to enable EIGRP and set an AS number.

EXERCISE 5.2   Configuring EIGRP on a Cisco Router

In this exercise, we will enable EIGRP on the router with an AS number of 10 and enable EIGRP for network 192.168.1.0.

1. Enter *Privileged Exec* mode with the *enable* command. Enter the enable password if you have one configured.

2. Enter *Global Configuration* mode with the *config t* command.

3. To enable EIGRP and enter EIGRP configuration mode, type **router eigrp 10**.

4. Now enter *network 192.168.1.0.*

Your router is now configured for EIGRP. EIGRP will process routing information for network 192.168.1.0.

OSPF

OSPF protocol is a link-state routing protocol developed in 1988. OSPF is an open routing protocol; therefore, it can be used on just about any router. This is one distinct advantage it has over EIGRP, which is only available on Cisco routers.

OSPF is one of the most robust routing protocols being used today. It supports both IPv4 and IPv6 networks and is able to support very large networks. It has an unlimited hop count and an administrative distance of 110. This means OSPF routes are considered more reliable than RIP routes but less reliable than EIGRP routes.

Routing Metrics

OSPF uses bandwidth for calculating the metric and route cost. The route cost is calculated by dividing 10^8 by the bandwidth of the link. Table 5.2 shows bandwidth and the OSPF cost for some common network links.

OSPF uses the bandwidth in bits per second (bps) when calculating the OSPF cost. This is why Fast Ethernet and Gigabit Ethernet both come out to 1. OSPF does allow you to change factors used for calculating the cost. This will allow you to be more granular in differentiating between different network links, especially links whose bandwidth is more than 100 Mbps.

Exam Warning

For the exam, be sure you know how to calculate OSPF cost for a given link.

Routing Updates

OSPF is a classless routing protocol. Subnet masks are transmitted with the network updates. This means that OSPF supports VLSM and discontiguous

Table 5.2 OSPF Link Cost Table

Link Type	Bandwidth	OSPF Cost
56 Kbps	56K	1785
T1	1.544 Mbps	64
E1	2.048 Mbps	48
Fast Ethernet	100 Mbps	1
Gigabit Ethernet	1000 Mbps	1

networks. OSPF uses the Dijkstra algorithm for computing routes and sharing routing information.

ASes and Areas

Similar to EIGRP, OSPF uses the idea of AS number to group routers together. Routers must share the same AS number to share routing updates. This helps to isolate update traffic. OSPF takes this one step further and further divides ASes into subgroups called *areas*. Detailed routing information is shared between the routers in a given area. You can then configure OSPF so that summarized routes are sent to other routers in different areas, but within the same AS.

It starts with area 0. Area 0 is considered the backbone area and is the central distribution point for routing information. As seen in Figure 5.4, you would then have other areas that connect to this backbone area. These other areas are connected to the backbone area via a router called *area border router*.

The area border routers are responsible for transmitting routing information for the area it is responsible for. They can be configured to only send summarized routers back to the backbone routers. This helps speed convergence. In a situation where only one network within an area goes down, the area border router will not have to send out updates for the other areas. This is because the other areas do not know about individual networks; they only received the summary route. This allows convergence to happen much quicker.

FIGURE 5.4

OSPF Area Diagram

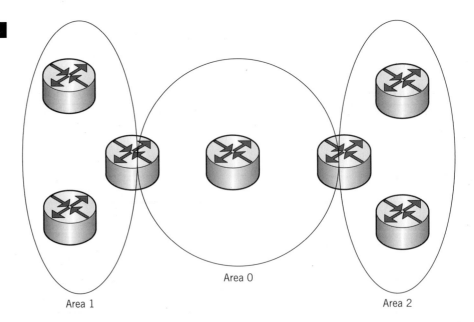

Area 0

Area 1

Area 2

OSPF tracks routers by the use of a router ID. The router ID is basically the highest IP address assigned to any interface on the router. OSPF will not send updates to all the routers it has established a neighborship with, but only to those neighbors it has established an adjacency with.

Stub Areas

Stub areas help to further decrease the amount of routing update traffic being sent over your network. A stub area has only one pathway in or out. There is one router configured as an area border router for this area. Instead of sending full route updates to the other routers within the area, the area border router will only send one route to represent a path to all networks outside the area, a default gateway route. The other routers within the area will always send traffic to this default gateway if they want to access networks outside the area. Be careful, this only works properly if there is only one pathway in or out of the area.

Route Summarization

Another way OSPF allows you to reduce update traffic is through the use of summary routes. Summary routes allow you to condense the routes for multiple contiguous networks into one route. Most costly with OSPF, this is done through area 0. The area 0 border router will summarize multiple routes into a single route and advertise them into the backbone area. This way, each individual route is not advertised into area 0.

Designated Routers

OSPF also uses the concept of designated routers (DRs). DRs are designated to coordinate topology updates. At initialization, a DR, and a backup designated router (BDR) are elected. When a topology change occurs, the update is sent to the DR. Then, the DR will update the rest of the routers in the area. Without a DR, each router would have to update its neighbor. If the routers are interconnected, this can lead to multiple redundant updates. Having DR will help eliminate this problem.

Warning

OSPF behaves differently on different network topologies. The default timers and discovery methods are different on broadcast multiaccess, nonbroadcast multiaccess, and point-to-point networks. It's important that you understand the differences when you actually go to implement OSPF.

Configuring OSPF

OSPF is one of the more robust routing protocols available. Along with the robustness comes complexity. This complexity is reflected in its configuration. When you configure OSPF, you have to configure a process ID and an area number. The process ID is just used by the router to track OSPF instances on the router.

EXERCISE 5.3   Configuring OSPF on a Cisco Router

In this exercise, we will enable OSPF on the router with a process ID of 1 and area 0. We will also enable OSPF for network 192.168.1.0.

1. Enter *Privileged Exec* mode with the *enable* command. Enter the enable password if you have one configured.

2. Enter *Global Configuration* mode with the *config t* command.

3. To enable OSPF and enter OSPF configuration mode, type **router ospf 1**.

4. Now enter *network 192.168.1.0 0.255.255.255 area 0*.

Your router is now configured for OSPF. OSPF will process routing information for network 192.168.1.0.

COMPARISON AND CONTRAST OF CISCO ROUTING PROTOCOLS

For the exam, it's important that you understand the difference between the routing protocols discussed. Table 5.3 outlines key facts about each of the protocols. Some other key points to remember are:

- RIPv1 and RIPv2 are only suitable for smaller networks. Larger networks should use IGRP, EIGRP, or OSPF, preferably EIGRP or OSPF.

- RIP routing is generally easier to configure than EIGRP or OSPF.

- IGRP and EIGRP are proprietary protocols that are only available on Cisco equipment. If your network will be using non-Cisco equipment, you should use RIPv1, RIPv2, or OSPF.

- RIPv1 and IGRP are no longer generally used. They have been replaced by their successors, RIPv2 and EIGRP, respectively.

Table 5.3	Routing Protocol Comparison				
	RIPv1	**RIPv2**	**IGRP**	**EIGRP**	**OSPF**
Administrative distance	120	120	100	90	110
Uses VLSM	No	Yes	No	Yes	Yes
Maximum hop count	15	15	255	224	None
Protocol type	Distance vector	Distance vector	Distance vector	Hybrid	Link-state
Metric	Hop count	Hop count	Bandwidth, line delay, reliability, load, and MTU	Bandwidth, line delay, load, and reliability	Bandwidth
Update interval	30 s	30 s	90 s	On change	On change
Update type	Entire table	Entire table	Entire table	Changes	Changes
Update mechanism	Broadcast	Multicast	Broadcast	Multicast	Multicast
Convergence	Slow	Slow	Medium	Fast	Fast
Automatic route summarization	Yes	No	Yes	No	No
Manual route summarization	No	Yes	No	Yes	Yes
Neighbor authentication	No	Yes	No	Yes	Yes
Routing algorithm	Bellman–Ford	Bellman–Ford	Bellman–Ford	DUAL	Dijkstra

SUMMARY OF EXAM OBJECTIVES

Routing helps move information from one network to another. Computer systems and network equipment have routing tables that designate where traffic destined for a particular network should be directed. Routers rely on routing protocols to help keep this routing information up to date. Routing protocol help prevent the need for manual updates to routing tables.

There are three main types of routing protocols: distance vector, link-state, and hybrid. Each type of routing protocol offers its own advantages and disadvantages. Distance vector protocols are generally seen as less efficient than link-state or hybrid protocols. This is why you typically see distance vector protocols in smaller networks and link-state or hybrid protocols in larger networks.

RIP is one of the oldest distance vector routing protocols that is still in use. There are two versions of RIP: RIPv1 and RIPv2. RIPv2 made some improvements over RIPv1, but there are still limitations. RIP is still very effective in smaller networks. You miss out on some of the efficiencies you might gain with other protocols, but the administrative overhead is low.

Both IGRP and EIGRP are Cisco proprietary protocol. IGRP is a distance vector protocol, and EIGRP is a hybrid protocol. EIGRP made several improvements over IGRP in terms of routing algorithms and route transmissions. EIGRP is considered one of the ideal routing protocols to use if you are using Cisco equipment.

OSPF is a robust link-state protocol and ideal for supporting large networks. It uses feature like AS numbers and areas to segment the network into a hierarchical model for routing updates. This helps to reduce network usage and router usage during update periods. The implementation of OSPF can be somewhat complex, but its benefits in large networks outweigh its complexity.

EXAM OBJECTIVES FAST TRACK

Routing

- Routing is used to send information from one network to another.

- Routers use routing tables to hold routing information.

- Routing protocols are generally classified as link-state, distance vector, or hybrid protocols. Each type has its own advantages and disadvantages.

- Administrative distance designates how trustworthy a network route in a routing table is. The lower the administrative distance, the more trustworthy the route is.

- Routing metrics are used to determine which route to a given destination is most favorable and should be considered the preferred route. The preferred route is what is entered into the routing table.

RIP

- RIPv1 is one of the oldest routing protocols still in use today.

- RIPv1 is a classful, distance vector routing protocol.

- RIPv1 has an administrative distance of 120.

- RIPv1 uses the Bellman–Ford algorithm for route computation. It uses hop count as the only metric. It has a maximum hop count of 15.

- RIPv1 uses broadcasts for sending routing updates.

RIPv2

- RIPv2 is an enhancement to the original RIP protocol.

- RIPv2 is a classless, distance vector routing protocol.

- RIPv2 has an administrative distance of 120.

- RIPv2 uses the Bellman–Ford algorithm for route computation. It uses hop count as the only metric. It has a maximum hop count of 15.

- RIPv2 uses multicasts for sending routing updates.

IGRP

- IGRP is a Cisco proprietary, classful, distance vector routing protocol.

- IGRP has an administrative distance of 100.

- IGRP has a default maximum hop count of 100, but this default can be increased to allow a maximum hop count of 255.

- IGRP uses the Bellman–Ford algorithm for route computation.

- IGRP can use the following metrics: bandwidth, line delay, reliability, load, and MTU.

EIGRP

- EIGRP is an enhancement to the original IGRP protocol.

- EIGRP is a Cisco proprietary, classless, hybrid routing protocol.

- EIGRP has an administrative distance of 90.

- EIGRP has a maximum hop count of 224.

- EIGRP can use the following metrics: bandwidth, line delay, load, and reliability.

- EIGRP uses the RTP for establishing communication with neighbors.

- EIGRP uses the DUAL for doing routing updates.

OSPF

- OSPF is an open standard, classless, link-state routing protocol.

- OSPF uses ASes and areas to divide networks into easier to manage units.

- OSPF has an administrative distance of 110.

- OSPF has an unlimited hop count.

- OSPF uses bandwidth for its metric.

- OSPF uses the Dijkstra algorithm for route selection.

- OSPF route summarization will allow you to minimize the number of routes advertised into area 0.

Comparison and Contrast of Cisco Routing Protocols

- EIGRP and OSPF are the best protocols to use for larger networks.

- IGRP and EIGRP are Cisco proprietary protocols.

- EIGRP and RIPv2 should be used in place of IGRP and RIPv1.

EXAM OBJECTIVES FREQUENTLY ASKED QUESTIONS

Q: Can a router run multiple routing protocols?

A: Yes, routers can be configured with more than one protocol.

Q: Can a single routing table contain routes supplied by different routing protocols?

A: Yes, a routing table can have routes from many different sources and routings protocols. This is where the administrative distance comes into play. The administrative distance will show how trustworthy routes from different sources are.

Q: What is required to support discontiguous networks?

A: To support discontiguous networks, a routing protocol must send subnet mask information in its routing updates.

Q: What's the difference between classful and classless routing protocols?

A: Classless routing protocols send subnet mask information in routing updates. Classful routing protocols do not.

Q: What's the difference between a regular area and a stub area?

A: Stub areas must have only one path in and path out of the area.

Q: What's the difference between an autonomous system and an area?

A: Autonomous systems are subdivided into smaller segments called areas.

Q: Can EIGRP be used on non-Cisco equipment?

A: No, EIGRP is only available on Cisco equipment.

Q: Is IGRP still in use today?

A: IGRP is not in general use today. It has been replaced with EIGRP. But, there are still some routers running older IOS versions that still use IGRP.

SELF TEST

1. Your Windows system is having trouble connecting to another system. You suspect it is a routing issue. How can you view the routing table on your system?
   A. By typing **route print** at the *command prompt*
   B. By typing **winipcfg** at the *command prompt*
   C. By typing **ipconfig** at the *command prompt*
   D. By typing **show ip route** at the *command prompt*

2. Multiple users on your network are having issues connecting to other subnets. You believe the problem to be an issue with routing. How can you check your router to ensure your router's routing table is populated correctly?
   A. Use the *ipconfig* command
   B. Use the *route print* command
   C. Use the *show ip route* command
   D. Use the *winipcfg* command

3. Routes configured by which of the following routing protocols is considered the most reliable.
   A. RIPv1
   B. RIPv2
   C. EIGRP
   D. OSPF

4. You have a very large network. You are using the RIPv1 protocol for routing updates. You notice that the route to one of your remote subnets is showing up on some, but not all your routers. Also, other routes are showing up on these routers as they should. What is most likely the problem?

   A. You need to configure VLSM

   B. You are using non-Cisco equipment on your network

   C. The link must be down

   D. You have exceeded to maximum hop count of 15

5. You are using the RIPv1 routing protocol on a small network. Your network uses a subnetted 10.x addressing scheme. You notice that users on different subnets are unable to talk to each other. What is most likely the issue?

   A. RIPv1 does not support VLSM

   B. Your network is too large

   C. One of your network switches is down

   D. RIPv1 is no longer a supported routing protocol. It has been replaced with RIPv2.

6. Which of the following is a link-state routing protocol?

   A. RIPv1   **C.** EIGRP

   B. RIPv2   **D.** OSPF

7. Which of the following are distance vector routing protocols?

   A. RIPv2   **C.** EIGRP

   B. IGRP   **D.** OSPF

8. You are in the process of designing your network. You want to minimize the amount of traffic generated by routing updates. Therefore, you want to choose a routing protocol that only sends topology updates not the entire routing table during an update. Which of the following routing protocols should you use?

   A. RIPv1   **C.** IGRP

   B. RIPv2   **D.** EIGRP

9. You are designing a new network. The network will consist of many discontiguous network segments. You want to use a routing protocol that accurately reports these networks in the routing table. Which of the following routing protocols can be used in your implementation?

   A. RIPv1   **C.** IGRP

   B. RIPv2   **D.** OSPF

10. Your network contains numerous subnets. The links of these sub-nets are all the same size. But some of the links are always more heavily loaded than others. Because of this, you want to use load as your routing metric. Which of the following routing protocols can you use on your network?

A. RIPv2

B. RIPv1

C. IGRP

D. OSPF

11. You are implementing a large network. Your network will consist of both Cisco and non-Cisco routers. Which of the following routing protocols would best fit your network?

A. IGRP

B. EIGRP

C. RIPv2

D. OSPF

12. You are designing a network. You need to use a routing protocol that will support up to 250 hops. Which of the following routing protocols will meet this requirement?

A. RIPv1

B. RIPv2

C. IGRP

D. EIGRP

13. Which of the following routing protocols has the lowest administrative distance?

A. RIPv1

B. RIPv2

C. IGRP

D. OSPF

14. You are implementing an OSPF network. One of your network links will be a 56K link. What will be the OSPF cost of this link?

A. 56

B. 1785

C. 48

D. 560

15. Where are EIGRP backup routes stored?

A. In the backup route table

B. In the primary routing table

C. In the neighborship table

D. In the topology table

16. You have configured your OSPF topology to use stub areas. What routing information will be sent from the area border router of the stub area to the rest of the routers in the area?

A. Summarized routes for the networks outside the stub area

B. Only a default route will be advertised

C. Individual routes for all the networks outside the stub area will be advertised

D. No routes will be advertised inside the stub area

17. You are implementing an OSPF network. One of your routers has interfaces with the following IP addresses: 192.168.1.1, 192.168.2.1, 172.16.32.1, and 10.3.2.1. What will be the router ID?
   A. 192.168.1.1   **C.** 172.16.32.1
   B. 192.168.2.1   **D.** 10.3.2.1

18. You are designing a very large new network. Some of your networks will use the IPX protocol. Which of the following routing protocols should you use?
   A. RIPv2   **C.** EIGRP
   B. IGRP   **D.** OSPF

19. How often are RIPv2 routing updates sent?
   A. Every 30 s   **C.** Every 90 s
   B. Every 60 s   **D.** Only on topology updates

20. You are implementing an OSPF network. One of your links will have a bandwidth of 1.544 Mbps. What will be the OSPF cost of the link?
   A. 1544   **C.** 1785
   B. 64   **D.** 640

SELF TEST QUICK ANSWER KEY

1. A
2. C
3. C
4. D
5. A
6. D
7. A and B
8. D
9. B and D
10. C

11. D
12. C
13. C
14. B
15. D
16. B
17. B
18. C
19. A
20. A

Implementing RIP, Version 2

INTRODUCTION

Routing Information Protocol (RIP), version 2, is a non-proprietary distance vector protocol that is easy to implement in a network infrastructure. All CCNA students need to know how to successfully implement RIP 2 on a Cisco router. During the CCNA exam, test takers may be presented with simulations that require them to successfully configure RIP 2 routing.

For CCNA students to successfully implement RIP 2 on a Cisco network, they should know the commands for implementing, configuring, and troubleshooting RIP 2. Individuals with their CCNA certificates should also know how to secure routers using RIP 2 with Message Digest (MD5) authentication. Use the simulation materials provided with this book to acquire sufficient practice implementing RIP 2 prior to taking the CCNA exam. Knowing how to implement RIP 2 is a required skill for passing the CCNA exam, as well as an important skill for individuals working with Cisco equipment in the industry.

RIP, VERSION 2

Routing Information Protocol is a distance vector routing protocol that is based on RFCs 1338, 1723, and 2453. A *distance vector* is a decentralized routing algorithm that requires that each router in the network inform its neighboring router about the networks and other routers within its proximity. When a router sends a routing table, the receiving routing picks the router advertisement with the lowest metric, and then adds this route to its routing table for re-advertisement. To find the route with the lowest metric or shortest path, Routing Information Protocol uses the Bellman-Ford algorithm.

Each router that uses this algorithm has to maintain its own distance table, which contains information regarding distances and shortest paths. The entries in the routing table are always updated, since neighboring routers will exchange route information which each other. The routing table contains information about directly connected neighbors and remote destination networks in the topology. Each entry in the table contains the path and distance (metric), and before a router can send packets to a destination network, the router must check these entries in the routing table.

A remote network can have multiple links, which means its router will have multiple neighbors. Compare this to driving from Texas to California. Many paths or routes are available to travel from Texas to California and back. Even Web sites such as Expedia and MapQuest can provide you with multiple routes or paths. When you're driving, multiple paths can allow you to enjoy scenery or avoid traffic. In the routing world, multiple paths also have benefits, especially if a route is down.

Characteristics of RIP

When RIP 2 sends updates, the router sends its entire routing table to all directly connected routers. The router will do this every 30 seconds on all interfaces where RIP is enabled. If a certain network or route goes down before the 30-second interval completes, the router can send a triggered update. RIP 2 sends its updates via broadcast or by using a Class D multicast address of 224.0.0.9. You can modify the time interval when a router sends its RIP updates.

Before a router decides which path it will take, it checks whether other routing protocols are configured. If two routing protocols provide route information to the same destination network, the router will select the routing protocol with the lowest administrative distance. An *administrative distance* is a measure of the trustworthiness of the source. A lower value is preferred over a higher one. Table 6.1 provides an overview of administrative distances. You can view administrative distances with the *show ip route* command.

RIP 2 is also able to *summarize routes*. Summarizing Internet Protocol (IP) addresses means you have fewer routes available in the routing table because you are using a combination of IP addresses. A smaller routing table means faster route propagation and faster updates.

For example, if a router's routing table contains the routes 192.168.20.0/24, 192.168.21.0/24, 192.168.22.0/24, and 192.168.23.0/24, you can summarize these routes to the 192.168.20.0/22 network.

To enable route summarization on an interface, use the *ip summary-address rip ip_address subnet_mask* command, where *ip_address* and *subnet_mask* identify the routes to be summarized, as shown in Figure 6.1.

For example, if you want to summarize the networks starting from 192.168.20.0, use the command *ip summary-address rip* as shown in Figure 6.2.

Table 6.1 Overview of Administrative Distances

Source	Administrative Distance
Connected interface	0
Static route	1
Enhanced Interior Gateway Routing Protocol (EIGRP)	90
Interior Gateway Routing Protocol (IGRP)	100
Open Shortest Path First (OSPF)	110
RIP	120

```
R1#config t
Enter configuration commands, one per line.  End with CNTL/Z.
R1(config)#int s0/0
R1(config-if)#ip summary-address rip ?
  A.B.C.D  IP address

R1(config-if)#ip summary-address rip ▌
```

FIGURE 6.1

Overview of the ip summary-address *Command*

```
R1#config t
Enter configuration commands, one per line.  End with CNTL/Z.
R1(config)#int s0/0
R1(config-if)#ip summary-address rip 192.168.20.0 255.255.255.0
R1(config-if)#^Z
R1#▌
```

FIGURE 6.2

Example of the ip summary-address *Command*

FIGURE 6.3

Overview of the show ip protocols *Command*

```
R1#sh ip pro
Routing Protocol is "rip"
  Sending updates every 30 seconds, next due in 17 seconds
  Invalid after 180 seconds, hold down 180, flushed after 240
  Outgoing update filter list for all interfaces is not set
  Incoming update filter list for all interfaces is not set
  Redistributing: rip
  Default version control: send version 2, receive version 2
    Interface              Send  Recv  Triggered RIP  Key-chain
    FastEthernet0/0         2     2
    Serial0/0               2     2                    rtra
  Automatic network summarization is in effect
  Address Summarization:
    192.168.20.0/24 for Serial0/0
  Maximum path: 4
  Routing for Networks:
    192.168.10.0
    192.168.20.0
  Routing Information Sources:
    Gateway          Distance      Last Update
    192.168.20.2          120       00:00:06
  Distance: (default is 120)

R1#
```

If you want to verify which routes are summarized for an interface, use the *show ip protocols* command, as shown in Figure 6.3.

RIP uses the following four update timers:

- **Route update timer** This specifies when a RIP-enabled router will broadcast its entire routing table to its neighboring router. The default value is 30 seconds.

- **Route invalid timer** This specifies the amount of time that elapses before a RIP-enabled router no longer receives any updates from a particular route, making this route invalid. The default value is 180 seconds.

- **Route holddown timer** This specifies how long a RIP-enabled router will keep an invalid route in the routing table. The default value is 180 seconds.

- **Route flush timer** As a route is marked invalid a RIP-enabled router will immediately delete this route. But it waits until the flush timer has expired. After this time, the router will remove the invalid route from the routing table. The default value is 240 seconds.

```
R1#config t
Enter configuration commands, one per line.  End with CNTL/Z.
R1(config)#router rip
R1(config-router)#timers ?
  basic  Basic routing protocol update timers

R1(config-router)#timers ▌
```

FIGURE 6.4

Overview of the timers
basic *Command*

Exam Warning

Remember all the default values of the RIP timers:

- Route update timer: 30 seconds
- Route invalid timer: 180 seconds
- Route holddown timer: 180 seconds
- Route flush timer: 240 seconds.

You can adjust the RIP timers by using the ***timers basic*** *update invalid holddown flush* command in router configuration mode, as shown in Figure 6.4.

Advantages and Disadvantages of RIP 2

RIP 2 offers several advantages:

- It supports classless routing, which means the subnet mask is included in the routing advertisements.
- It provides route summarization.
- It supports plain text and MD5 authentication for routing updates.
- It allows you to send updates using multicast instead of broadcast.

The disadvantages of RIP 2 include the following:

- RIP is not scalable in large and very large networks with 15 routers or more.
- The maximum hop count for RIP routers is 15.
- Networks with a hop count of 16 or more are considered unreachable.

Cisco networks using RIP have a slow recovery time after a topology change. In fact, it can take a couple of minutes before all of the RIP routers in the network have the same information. Furthermore, when an update occurs, the router cannot forward packets. This means the longer it takes for a RIP router to update, the longer it takes those packets to be forwarded. This can result in packet loss or retransmissions.

Exam Warning

Remember that RIP 2 works with fewer hops, rather than the available bandwidth or the number of routers the packet needs to follow to reach the destination.

In Exercise 6.1, you will configure RIP 2, configure RIP 2 timers, and verify RIP 2 configuration.

EXERCISE 6.1   Restoring a Single File from a Time Machine Volume

This simple exercise will walk you through the process of changing the default RIP update timers on an R1 router.

1. Change the route update timer to 15 seconds, the route invalid timer to 30 seconds, the route holddown timer to 45 seconds, and the route flush timer to 60 seconds, as shown in Figure 6.5.

```
R1#config t
Enter configuration commands, one per line.  End with CNTL/Z.
R1(config)#router rip
R1(config-router)#timers basic 15 30 45 60 75
R1(config-router)#^Z
R1#
```

FIGURE 6.5   *Changing the Command Timers*

The last parameter (75) in the *timers basic* command is a value that specifies the length of time for which the routing updates will be postponed.

2. To verify the configuration, use the *show ip protocols* command. Figure 6.6 shows the output.

As Figure 6.6 shows, the RIP update timers are changed.

```
R1#sh ip pro
Routing Protocol is "rip"
  Sending updates every 15 seconds, next due in 11 seconds
  Invalid after 30 seconds, hold down 45, flushed after 60
  Outgoing update filter list for all interfaces is not set
  Incoming update filter list for all interfaces is not set
  Redistributing: rip
  Default version control: send version 2, receive version 2
    Interface            Send  Recv  Triggered RIP  Key-chain
    FastEthernet0/0       2     2
    Serial0/0             2     2                    rtra
  Automatic network summarization is in effect
  Address Summarization:
    192.168.20.0/24 for Serial0/0
  Maximum path: 4
  Routing for Networks:
    192.168.10.0
    192.168.20.0
  Routing Information Sources:
    Gateway         Distance      Last Update
    192.168.20.2       120        00:00:11
  Distance: (default is 120)

R1#
```

FIGURE 6.6

Output of the show ip protocols *Command*

CONFIGURING RIP 2

Figure 6.7 shows three routers, named R1, R2, and R3. Before each router will advertise its known networks, you need to enable RIP and specify the networks you want to advertise.

To activate the RIP process, you can use the *router(config)#router rip* command. By default, RIP sends only version 1 packets, but it can receive version 1 and version 2 packets. If you want to configure your router to send only version 2 packets, use the *router(config-router)#version 2* command.

The next step is to specify the directly connected networks on your router. You can only advertise directly attached networks. You can use the ***network***

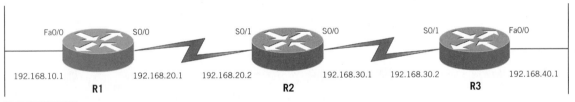

FIGURE 6.7   *Routers and Their Known Networks*

network-number command to specify the network, where *network-number* is equal to the network you want to advertise. For example: *router(config-router)#****network**** network-number*.

If you activate an interface for RIP announcements, the router will send out all networks on that interface. So, if you refer back to Figure 6.1, this means R2 adds the networks it learned from R3 to its routing table, and sends them out to R1. R2 will also learn about networks from R1 and will add those learned networks to the R2 routing table. Next, R2 sends all the networks that it learned to R3. If all the RIP routers on the network have the same information, the routers are *converged*, which means the routing tables on all the routers are the same.

> **Exam Warning**
> RIP 2 is a classless protocol, and it includes subnet masks and summarizes routes by default.

In Exercise 6.2, you will configure the R1 router with a hostname, assign an IP address to an interface, and enable an interface. Before you start, take a look at the network diagram in Figure 6.8.

In this network, there are three Cisco 2600 series routers, each with a Fast Ethernet interface. In addition, R1 and R3 have a Serial interface (WIC-1T), and R2 has two Serial interfaces (see Table 6.2).

Figure 6.9 shows the configuration required for R1.

In Figure 6.10, you can see that RIP 2 is currently disabled on R1.

Table 6.2 Configuration Information for Routers R1, R2, and R3

Router Name	Fast Ethernet Address	Interface Type	Serial 0 Address	Serial 1 Address	Subnet Mask
R1	192.168.10.1	DTE	192.168.20.1		255.255.255.0
R2		DCE	192.168.20.2		255.255.255.0
R2		DCE		192.168.30.1	255.255.255.0
R3	192.168.40.1	DTE		192.168.30.2	255.255.255.0

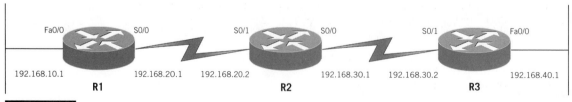

FIGURE 6.8 *Network Diagram for Configuring All Three Routers*

```
Router>en
Router#config t
Enter configuration commands, one per line.  End with CNTL/Z.
Router(config)#hostname R1
R1(config)#int fa0/0
R1(config-if)#ip address 192.168.10.1 255.255.255.0
R1(config-if)#no shut
R1(config-if)#int s
*Mar  1 00:01:49.051: %LINK-3-UPDOWN: Interface FastEthernet0/0, changed state t
o up
*Mar  1 00:01:50.051: %LINEPROTO-5-UPDOWN: Line protocol on Interface FastEthern
et0/0, changed state
R1(config-if)#int s0/0
R1(config-if)#ip address 192.168.20.1 255.255.255.0
R1(config-if)#no shut
R1(config-if)#^Z
R1#
```

FIGURE 6.9   *Configuration Required for the R1 Router*

```
R1#show ip route
Codes: C - connected, S - static, R - RIP, M - mobile, B - BGP
       D - EIGRP, EX - EIGRP external, O - OSPF, IA - OSPF inter area
       N1 - OSPF NSSA external type 1, N2 - OSPF NSSA external type 2
       E1 - OSPF external type 1, E2 - OSPF external type 2
       i - IS-IS, su - IS-IS summary, L1 - IS-IS level-1, L2 - IS-IS level-2
       ia - IS-IS inter area, * - candidate default, U - per-user static route
       o - ODR, P - periodic downloaded static route

Gateway of last resort is not set

C    192.168.10.0/24 is directly connected, FastEthernet0/0
C    192.168.20.0/24 is directly connected, Serial0/0
R1#
```

FIGURE 6.10   *Routing Table Information of the R1 Router with RIP 2 Disabled*

In Figure 6.10, the letter *C* in front of the route means the network is directly connected. These routes were created in the routing table when you configured the interface with an IP address and brought the interface up.

EXERCISE 6.2   Configuring All Three Routers

Let's start by configuring the R2 router.

1. Configure the hostname.

2. Configure the Fast Ethernet interface.

3. Configure the Serial interfaces.

4. Enable RIP 2 on the router.

Figure 6.11 shows the code required to configure an IP address and to enable the interface on the R2 router.

```
Router>en
Router#config t
Enter configuration .commands, one per line.  End with CNTL/Z.
Router(config)#hostname R2
R2(config)#int s0/0
R2(config-if)#ip address 192.168.20.2 255.255.255.0
R2(config-if)#clockrate 64000
R2(config-if)#no shut
R2(config-if)#
*Mar  1 00:05:33.635: %LINK-3-UPDOWN: Interface Serial0/0, changed state to up
*Mar  1 00:05:34.635: %LINEPROTO-5-UPDOWN: Line protocol on Interface Serial0/0,
 changed state to up
R2(config-if)#int s0/1
R2(config-if)#ip address 192.168.30.1 255.255.255.0
R2(config-if)#clockrate 64000
R2(config-if)#no shut
R2(config-if)#^Z
R2#
```

FIGURE 6.11   *Configuration Overview for the R2 Router*

Figure 6.12 shows that RIP 2 is currently disabled.

```
R2#show ip route
Codes: C - connected, S - static, R - RIP, M - mobile, B - BGP
       D - EIGRP, EX - EIGRP external, O - OSPF, IA - OSPF inter area
       N1 - OSPF NSSA external type 1, N2 - OSPF NSSA external type 2
       E1 - OSPF external type 1, E2 - OSPF external type 2
       i - IS-IS, su - IS-IS summary, L1 - IS-IS level-1, L2 - IS-IS level-2
       ia - IS-IS inter area, * - candidate default, U - per-user static route
       o - ODR, P - periodic downloaded static route

Gateway of last resort is not set

C    192.168.30.0/24 is directly connected, Serial0/1
C    192.168.20.0/24 is directly connected, Serial0/0
R2#
```

FIGURE 6.12   *Routing Table Information for the R2 Router with RIP 2 Disabled*

With the R2 router properly configured, now it's time to configure the R3 router.

5. Configure the hostname.

6. Configure the Fast Ethernet interface.

7. Configure the Serial interface.

8. Enable RIP 2 on the router.

Figure 6.13 lists the code required to configure an IP address and to enable the interface on the R3 router.

```
Router>en
Router#config t
Enter configuration commands, one per line.  End with CNTL/Z.
Router(config)#hostname R3
R3(config)#int fa0/0
R3(config-if)#ip address 192.168.40.1 255.255.255.0
R3(config-if)#no shut
R3(config-if)#5
*Mar  1 00:07:50.507: %LINK-3-UPDOWN: Interface FastEthernet0/0, changed state t
o up
*Mar  1 00:07:51.507: %LINEPROTO-5-UPDOWN: Line protocol on Interface FastEthern
et0/0, changed state to u
R3(config-if)#int s0/0
R3(config-if)#ip address 192.168.30.2 255.255.255.0
R3(config-if)#no shut
R3(config-if)#^Z
R3#
```

FIGURE 6.13   *Configuration Overview for the R3 Router*

In Figure 6.14, you can see that RIP 2 is currently disabled on the R3 router.

```
R3#show ip route
Codes: C - connected, S - static, R - RIP, M - mobile, B - BGP
       D - EIGRP, EX - EIGRP external, O - OSPF, IA - OSPF inter area
       N1 - OSPF NSSA external type 1, N2 - OSPF NSSA external type 2
       E1 - OSPF external type 1, E2 - OSPF external type 2
       i - IS-IS, su - IS-IS summary, L1 - IS-IS level-1, L2 - IS-IS level-2
       ia - IS-IS inter area, * - candidate default, U - per-user static route
       o - ODR, P - periodic downloaded static route

Gateway of last resort is not set

C    192.168.30.0/24 is directly connected, Serial0/0
C    192.168.40.0/24 is directly connected, FastEthernet0/0
R3#
```

FIGURE 6.14   *Routing Table Information for the R3 Router with RIP 2 Disabled*

Follow these steps to configure the R1 router.

  9. Select the interface.

 10. Enable RIP 2 broadcasts.

11. Enable RIP 2.

12. Advertise the networks.

Figure 6.15 shows the commands used to configure an IP address and enable the interface on the R1 router.

FIGURE 6.15

Configuration Overview for the R1 Router

```
R1#config t
Enter configuration commands, one per line.  End with CNTL/Z.
R1(config)#int s0/0
R1(config-if)#ip rip v2-broadcast
R1(config-if)#router rip
R1(config-router)#version 2
R1(config-router)#network 192.168.10.0
R1(config-router)#network 192.168.20.0
R1(config-router)#^Z
R1#
```

In the next series of steps, you'll enable RIP 2 on the R2 and R3 routers. You'll start with the R2 router.

13. Select the interfaces.

14. Enable RIP 2 broadcasts.

15. Enable RIP 2.

16. Advertise the networks.

Figure 6.16 shows the commands used to enable RIP 2 on the R2 router. Now enable RIP 2 on the R3 router.

FIGURE 6.16

Configuration Overview for Enabling RIP 2 on the R2 Router

```
R2#conf t
Enter configuration commands, one per line.  End with CNTL/Z.
R2(config)#int s0/0
R2(config-if)#ip rip v2-broadcast
R2(config-if)#int s0/1
R2(config-if)#ip rip v2-broadcast
R2(config-if)#router rip
R2(config-router)#version 2
R2(config-router)#network 192.168.20.0
R2(config-router)#network 192.168.30.0
R2(config-router)#^Z
R2#
```

17. Select the interface.

18. Enable RIP 2 broadcasts.

19. Enable RIP 2.

20. Advertise the networks.

In Figure 6.17, you can see all the commands used to enable RIP 2 on the R3 router.

```
R3#config t
Enter configuration commands, one per line.  End with CNTL/Z.
R3(config)#int s0/0
R3(config-if)#ip rip v2-broadcast
R3(config-if)#router rip
R3(config-router)#version 2
R3(config-router)#network 192.168.30.0
R3(config-router)#network 192.168.40.0
R3(config-router)#^Z
R3#
```

FIGURE 6.17

Configuration Overview for Enabling RIP 2 on the R3 Router

Neighbors

A RIP router sends out its routing table using broadcast (RIP, version 1 or version 2) or multicast (version 2) addresses. If you want to prevent RIP traffic from being received by any router on the network except for neighboring routers, you need to configure the interface as passive, as shown in Figure 6.18.

Use the following commands to configure your router to not advertise the 192.168.40.0 network on the Serial 0/1 interface. The *passive-interface* command will prevent routes from being sent out on interface S0/1, but will not prevent the router from receiving updates on that interface.

```
R3#config t
R3(config)#router rip
R3(config-router)#network 192.168.40.0
R3(config-router)#passive-interface serial 0/1
```

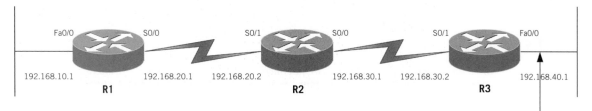

FIGURE 6.18   *Network Diagram for Configuring a Passive Interface*

How RIP Discovers Routes

In Figure 6.19, the R1 router is directly connected to networks 192.168.10.0 and 192.168.20.0, and will learn about other networks from the R2 router. Since R2 is directly connected to 192.168.20.0 and 192.168.30.0 from R1, network 192.168.30.0 is one hop away. R3 is directly connected to networks 192.168.30.0 and 192.168.40.0. R1 will also learn about these networks from R2 and R3. From R1, network 192.168.40.0 is two hops away and can be reached if R1 sends all of its packets to R2.

Table 6.3 summarizes the current state of the routing tables on the current network.

When R1 receives an update from its neighbor R2, R1 compares the received update with its own entries in the routing table. If R1 receives a better route (which means a lower metric) R1 will update its routing table with the better route.

You already know that R3 is directly connected to networks 192.168.30.0 and 192.168.40.0. In the next scenario, suppose that 192.168.40.0 goes down. R3 will detect the network failure and will no longer forward any packets on interface F0/0. R1 and R2 are currently not aware that network 192.168.40.0 is unavailable, so these routers still forward traffic destined for network 192.168.40.0 to R3, as you can see in Figure 6.20 and Table 6.4.

Normally, you would expect that R3 will inform R2 that network 192.168.40.0 is not available, but this is not always the case.

Suppose that R2 sends out its routing table before R3 can do so. This means R3 receives information from R2 stating that network 192.168.40.0

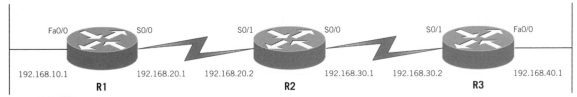

	Fa0/0	S0/0		S0/1		S0/0		S0/1		Fa0/0
	192.168.10.1	192.168.20.1	192.168.20.2			192.168.30.1	192.168.30.2			192.168.40.1
	R1			**R2**				**R3**		

FIGURE 6.19 *Network Diagram Showing the RIP Discover Routes*

Table 6.3	Overview of Routing Information								
Network	**Interface**	**Metric**	**Network**	**Interface**	**Metric**	**Network**	**Interface**	**Metric**
192.168.10.0	Fa0/0	0	192.168.20.0	S0/0		192.168.30.0	S0/0	0
192.168.20.0	S0/0	0	192.168.30.0	S1/0		192.168.40.0	Fa0/0	0
192.168.30.0	S0/0	1	192.168.10.0	S0/0		192.168.20.0	S0/0	1
192.168.40.0	S0/0	2	192.168.40.0	S1/0		192.168.10.0	S0/0	2

FIGURE 6.20 *Network Diagram Depicting How Network 192.168.40.0 Goes Down*

Table 6.4 Overview of Routing Information When Network 192.168.40.0 Is Down

Network	Interface	Metric	Network	Interface	Metric	Network	Interface	Metric
192.168.10.0	Fa0/0	0	192.168.20.0	S0/0		192.168.30.0	S0/0	0
192.168.20.0	S0/0	0	192.168.30.0	S1/0		192.168.40.0	Fa0/0	Down
192.168.30.0	S0/0	1	192.168.10.0	S0/0		192.168.20.0	S0/0	1
192.168.40.0	S0/0	2	192.168.40.0	S1/0		192.168.10.0	S0/0	2

Table 6.5 Routing Information When R2 Sends Out Its Routing Information before R3

Network	Interface	Metric	Network	Interface	Metric	Network	Interface	Metric
192.168.10.0	Fa0/0	0	192.168.20.0	S0/0	0	192.168.30.0	S0/0	0
192.168.20.0	S0/0	0	192.168.30.0	S1/0	0	192.168.40.0	Fa0/0	2
192.168.30.0	S0/0	1	192.168.10.0	S0/0	1	192.168.20.0	S0/0	1
192.168.40.0	S0/0	2	192.168.40.0	S1/0	1	192.168.10.0	S0/0	2

can be reached if R3 sends its packets to R2. R3 will change its routing information to that shown in Table 6.5 and 6.6.

Since R3 receives new information from R2, R3 will increment the hop count by 1.

R2 now receives information from R3 and hears that network 192.168.40.0 can be reached via R3. R2 will modify its routing table and will increment the hop count by 1.

R2 sends out its routing table to R1, and R1 updates its routing table and changes the route of network 192.168.40.0 with a hop count of 4.

At this point, the routing tables on all routers are incorrect. All routers "think" that network 192.168.40.0 is still reachable, but actually network 192.168.40.0 is down.

If a packet is sent from network 192.168.10.0 to network 192.168.40.0, the packet will never reach the destination network and will bounce between

Table 6.6	Overview of Routing Table							
Network	**Interface**	**Metric**	**Network**	**Interface**	**Metric**	**Network**	**Interface**	**Metric**
192.168.10.0	Fa0/0	0	192.168.20.0	S0/0	0	192.168.30.0	S0/0	0
192.168.20.0	S0/0	0	192.168.30.0	S1/0	0	192.168.40.0	Fa0/0	0
192.168.30.0	S0/0	1	192.168.10.0	S0/0	3	192.168.20.0	S0/0	1
192.168.40.0	S0/0	2	192.168.40.0	S1/0	1	192.168.10.0	S0/0	2

the routers until the packet dies. A packet will die if the hop count is greater than 15. This is what we call a *routing loop*.

Unicast Communications

Under normal circumstances, RIP 1 uses broadcast addresses and RIP 2 uses multicast addresses to send routing updates. This causes a problem on non-broadcast networks. To configure RIP 2 routing updates in a non-broadcast environment, use the ***neighbor** ip_address* command:

```
Router# config t
Router(config)# router rip
Router(config-router)# neighbor 192.168.10.2
```

Authentication

RIP 2 supports two modes of authentication: plain text authentication and MD5 authentication. The default is plain text authentication, and you should not use it in an environment where security is an issue. The password is sent in clear text in every RIP 2 packet.

Plain Text Authentication

Before you can use plain text authentication, you need to know the commands for performing this action. To enable authentication on the router, follow these steps:

1. Define a key chain and give the key chain a name.

   The key chain determines the set of keys you can use on an interface. If you don't configure a key chain, authentication cannot be performed on the selected interface.

   The following key chain identifies a group of authentication keys. Use this command in global configuration mode. The syntax is ***key chain** name-of-chain*. For example:

   ```
   Router(config)# key chain routera
   ```

To remove the key chain, use the *Router(config)#**no key chain routera*** command.

2. Define the key on the key chain.

You use a key to identify an authentication key on a key chain. Use this command in key chain configuration mode. A key can be in the range from 0 to 2147483647. The syntax is ***key** number*. For example:

Router(config-keychain)# **key 1**

To remove the key that is currently being used, use the *Router(config-keychain)# **no key 1*** command.

3. Specify the password used in the key.

This is the actual password used and it needs to be identical on the remote router. The maximum length of the string is 80 characters, and the string can contain lowercase, uppercase, and alphanumeric characters. The first character cannot be a number, however. The syntax is ***key-string** your_string*. For example:

Router(config-keychain-key)# **key-string accessdenied**

To remove the key, use the *Router(config-keychain-key)#**no key-string accessdenied*** command.

4. Specify the authentication mode.

You should use this command in interface configuration mode to specify the type of authentication used in the RIP 2 packets. The syntax is ***ip rip authentication mode** auth_mode*. For example:

Router(config-if)# **ip rip authentication mode text**

To remove authentication, use the *Router(config-if)#**no ip rip authentication text*** command.

5. Enable authentication on an interface.

You should use this command to enable authentication for RIP 2 packets and specify which keys you want to use to protect the RIP packets. Use this command in interface configuration mode. The syntax is ***ip rip authentication key-chain** chain_name*. For example:

Router(config-if)# **ip rip authentication key-chain routera**

To remove the authentication key, use the *Router(config-if)#**no ip rip authentication key-chain routera*** command.

Exam Warning

Remember how to configure your router to authenticate routing updates.

Test Day Tip

You can route update authentication only with RIP, version 2.

In Exercise 6.3, you will configure your router with RIP 2 using plain text authentication.

EXERCISE 6.3   Configuring A Router with Rip 2 Using Plain Text Authentication

Our network consists of three routers: R1, R2, and R3. All of them are running RIP 2 and periodically exchange their routing information. Your task is to configure the routers so that all RIP 2 routing information packets are authenticated using plain text authentication.

First, you'll need to configure RIP 2 plain text authentication on the R1 task list.

1. Define a key chain and give it a name.

2. Define the key on the key chain and specify the password to be used in the key.

3. Select interface s0/0 and configure the interface to use plain text authentication.

4. Enable authentication on interface s0/0.

Figure 6.21 shows the R1 configuration.

FIGURE 6.21

R1 Configuration Overview for Plain Text Authentication

```
R1#config t
Enter configuration commands, one per line.  End with CNTL/Z.
R1(config)#key chain rtra
R1(config-keychain)#key 1
R1(config-keychain-key)#key-string accessdenied
R1(config-keychain-key)#int s0/0
R1(config-if)#ip rip authentication mode text
R1(config-if)#ip rip authentication key-chain rtra
R1(config-if)#^Z
R1#
```

Now you'll configure RIP 2 plain text authentication on the R2 task list.

5. Define a key chain and give it a name.

6. Define the key on the key chain and specify the password to be used in the key.

7. Select interface s0/0 and configure the interface to use plain text authentication.

8. Enable authentication on interface s0/0.

9. Select interface s0/1 and configure the interface to use plain text authentication.

10. Enable authentication on interface s0/1.

Figure 6.22 shows the R2 configuration.

```
R2#config t
Enter configuration commands, one per line.  End with CNTL/Z.
R2(config)#key chain rtrb
R2(config-keychain)#key 1
R2(config-keychain-key)#key-string accessdenied
R2(config-keychain-key)#int s0/0
R2(config-if)#ip rip authentication mode text
R2(config-if)#ip rip authentication key-chain rtrb
R2(config-if)#int s0/1
R2(config-if)#ip rip authentication mode text
R2(config-if)#ip rip authentication key-chain rtrb
R2(config-if)#^Z
R2#
```

FIGURE 6.22

R2 Configuration Overview for Plain Text Authentication

Follow this last set of steps to configure RIP 2 plain text authentication on the R3 task list.

11. Define a key chain and give it a name.

12. Define the key on the key chain and specify the password to be used in the key.

13. Configure the interface to use plain text authentication.

14. Select interface s0/0 and enable authentication on that interface.

Figure 6.23 shows the R3 configuration.

FIGURE 6.23

R3 Configuration Overview for Plain Text Authentication

```
R3#config t
Enter configuration commands, one per line.  End with CNTL/Z.
R3(config)#key chain rtrc
R3(config-keychain)#key 1
R3(config-keychain-key)#key-string accessdenied
R3(config-keychain-key)#int s0/0
R3(config-if)#ip rip authentication mode text
R3(config-if)#ip rip authentication key-chain rtrc
R3(config-if)#^Z
R3#
```

If a router is configured to use plain text authentication for IPv2 updates, the passwords will be sent in clear text.

Test Day Tip

When you use plain text authentication, be sure that the key string and authentication mode are the same on the neighboring routers.

MD5 Authentication

Before you can use MD5 authentication, you need to familiarize yourself with the commands for performing this action. To enable authentication on the router, follow these steps:

1. Define a key chain and give the key chain a name.

   The key chain determines the set of keys that can be used on an interface. If you don't configure a key chain, authentication cannot be performed on the selected interface.

   This key chain is used to identify a group of authentication keys. Use the command in global configuration mode. The syntax is ***key chain*** *name-of-chain*. For example:

   Router(config)# **key chain routera**

   To remove the key chain, use the *Router(config)#**no key chain routera*** command.

2. Define the key on the key chain.

   You use a key to identify an authentication key on a key chain. Use this command in key chain configuration mode. The syntax is *key number*. A key can be in the range from 0 to 2147483647. For example:

Router(config-keychain)# **key 1**

To remove the key that is currently being used, use the *Router(config-keychain)#**no key 1*** command.

3. Specify the password used for the key.

   This password needs to be identical on the remote router. The maximum length of the string is 80 characters, and the string can contain lowercase, uppercase, and alphanumeric characters. The first character cannot be a number, however.

   The router will use this password to create a hash with a fixed length of 128 bits. The syntax is ***key-string** your_string*. For example:

   Router(config-keychain-key)# **key-string accessdenied**

   To remove the key, use the *Router(config-keychain-key)#**no key-string accessdenied*** command.

4. Specify the authentication mode.

   You should use this command in interface configuration mode to specify the type of authentication used in the RIP 2 packets. The syntax is **ip rip authentication mode** *auth_mode*. For example:

   Router(config-if)# **ip rip authentication mode md5**

   To remove authentication, use the *Router(config-if)#**no ip rip authentication mode md5*** command.

5. Enable authentication on an interface.

   You should use this command in interface configuration mode to enable authentication for RIP 2 packets and specify which keys you want to use to protect the RIP packets. The syntax is **ip rip authentication key-chain** *name-of-chain*. For example:

   Router(config)# **ip rip authentication key-chain routera**

   To remove the authentication key, use the *Router(config-if)@**no ip rip authentication key-chain routera*** command.

   In Exercise 6.4, you will configure RIP 2 authentication using MD5 authentication.

EXERCISE 6.4   Configuring Rip 2 Authentication with MD5

Our network consists of three routers: R1, R2, and R3. All routers are running RIP 2 and periodically exchange their routing information. Your task is to configure the routers so that all RIP 2 routing information packets are authenticated using MD5 authentication.

First you'll configure RIP 2 MD5 authentication on the R1 task list.

1. Define a key chain and give it a name.

2. Define the key on the key chain and specify the password to be used in the key.

3. Select interface s0/0 and configure the interface to use MD5 authentication.

4. Enable authentication on interface s0/0.

Figure 6.24 shows the commands used to configure RIP 2 MD5 authentication on the R1 router.

FIGURE 6.24

R1 Configuration Overview for MD5 Authentication

```
R1#config t
Enter configuration commands, one per line.  End with CNTL/Z.
R1(config)#key chain rtra
R1(config-keychain)#key 1
R1(config-keychain-key)#key-string accessdenied
R1(config-keychain-key)#int s0/0
R1(config-if)#ip rip authentication mode md5
R1(config-if)#ip rip authentication key-chain rtra
R1(config-if)#^Z
R1#
```

Now you'll configure RIP 2 MD5 authentication on the R2 task list.

5. Define a key chain and give it a name.

6. Define the key on the key chain and specify the password to be used in the key.

7. Select interface s0/0 and configure the interface to use MD5 authentication.

8. Enable authentication on interface s0/0.

9. Select interface s0/1 and configure the interface to use MD5 authentication.

10. Enable authentication on interface s0/1.

Figure 6.25 shows the commands used to configure RIP 2 MD5 authentication on the R2 router.

```
R2#config t
Enter configuration commands, one per line.  End with CNTL/Z.
R2(config)#key chain rtrb
R2(config-keychain)#key 1
R2(config-keychain-key)#key-string accessdenied
R2(config-keychain-key)#int s0/0
R2(config-if)#ip rip authentication mode md5
R2(config-if)#ip rip authentication key-chain rtrb
R2(config-if)#int s0/1
R2(config-if)#ip rip authentication mode md5
R2(config-if)#ip rip authentication key-chain rtrb
R2(config-if)#^Z
R2#
```

FIGURE 6.25

R2 Configuration Overview for MD5 Authentication

Follow this last series of steps to configure RIP 2 MD5 authentication on the R3 task list.

11. Define a key chain and give it a name.

12. Define the key on the key chain and specify the password to be used in the key.

13. Select interface s0/0 and configure the interface to use plain text authentication.

14. Enable authentication on interface s0/0.

Figure 6.26 shows the commands used to configure RIP 2 MD5 authentication on the R3 router.

```
R3#config t
Enter configuration commands, one per line.  End with CNTL/Z.
R3(config)#key chain rtrc
R3(config-keychain)#key 1
R3(config-keychain-key)#key-string accessdenied
R3(config-keychain-key)#int s0/0
R3(config-if)#ip rip authentication mode md5
R3(config-if)#ip rip authentication key-chain rtrc
R3(config-if)#^Z
R3#
```

FIGURE 6.26

R3 Configuration Overview for MD5 Authentication

MD5 authentication is more secure than plain text authentication, because the password is not sent in clear text.

> **Test Day Tip**
> When you use MD5 authentication, be sure that the key string, key number, and authentication mode are the same on the neighboring routers.

VERIFYING RIP 2 CONFIGURATIONS

RIPv2 enhances the RIP protocol by using multicast to send the routing updates as well as allowing authentication and route summarization to be utilized. This section covers the commands to enable version 2 of the RIP routing protocol.

The show Commands

Use the following commands to verify the RIP 2 configuration settings.

show ip rip database

You can use the *show ip rip database* command to summarize the address entries in the RIP 2 database. To disable the command use *no show ip rip database*.

Figure 6.27 shows the command being used to view the RIP database.

show ip route

You can use the ***show ip route*** command to display which routing entries are currently available in the routing table.

Verifying the Routes on All Routers

Now that you've configured all the routers, you can verify the configuration as follows.

FIGURE 6.27

Output of the show ip rip database *Command for R1*

```
R1#sh ip rip database
192.168.10.0/24     auto-summary
192.168.10.0/24     directly connected, FastEthernet0/0
192.168.20.0/24     auto-summary
192.168.20.0/24     directly connected, Serial0/0
192.168.30.0/24     auto-summary
192.168.30.0/24
    [1] via 192.168.20.2, 00:00:10, Serial0/0
192.168.40.0/24     auto-summary
192.168.40.0/24
    [1] via 192.168.20.2, 00:00:10, Serial0/0
R1#
```

In Figure 6.28, you can see the command used to display the content of the R1 routing table.

The routing entries starting with *R* are routes learned by RIP.

In Figure 6.29, you can see the command used to display the content of the R2 routing table.

In Figure 6.30, you can see the command used to display the content of the R3 routing table.

```
R1#sh ip route
Codes: C - connected, S - static, R - RIP, M - mobile, B - BGP
       D - EIGRP, EX - EIGRP external, O - OSPF, IA - OSPF inter area
       N1 - OSPF NSSA external type 1, N2 - OSPF NSSA external type 2
       E1 - OSPF external type 1, E2 - OSPF external type 2
       i - IS-IS, su - IS-IS summary, L1 - IS-IS level-1, L2 - IS-IS level-2
       ia - IS-IS inter area, * - candidate default, U - per-user static route
       o - ODR, P - periodic downloaded static route

Gateway of last resort is not set

R    192.168.30.0/24 [120/1] via 192.168.20.2, 00:00:18, Serial0/0
C    192.168.10.0/24 is directly connected, FastEthernet0/0
R    192.168.40.0/24 [120/1] via 192.168.20.2, 00:00:18, Serial0/0
C    192.168.20.0/24 is directly connected, Serial0/0
R1#
```

FIGURE 6.28   *Output of the* show ip route *Command on R1*

```
R2#sh ip route
Codes: C - connected, S - static, R - RIP, M - mobile, B - BGP
       D - EIGRP, EX - EIGRP external, O - OSPF, IA - OSPF inter area
       N1 - OSPF NSSA external type 1, N2 - OSPF NSSA external type 2
       E1 - OSPF external type 1, E2 - OSPF external type 2
       i - IS-IS, su - IS-IS summary, L1 - IS-IS level-1, L2 - IS-IS level-2
       ia - IS-IS inter area, * - candidate default, U - per-user static route
       o - ODR, P - periodic downloaded static route

Gateway of last resort is not set

C    192.168.30.0/24 is directly connected, Serial0/1
R    192.168.10.0/24 [120/1] via 192.168.20.1, 00:00:00, Serial0/0
R    192.168.40.0/24 [120/1] via 192.168.30.2, 00:00:14, Serial0/1
C    192.168.20.0/24 is directly connected, Serial0/0
R2#
```

FIGURE 6.29   *Output of the* show ip route *Command on R2*

```
R3#sh ip route
Codes: C - connected, S - static, R - RIP, M - mobile, B - BGP
       D - EIGRP, EX - EIGRP external, O - OSPF, IA - OSPF inter area
       N1 - OSPF NSSA external type 1, N2 - OSPF NSSA external type 2
       E1 - OSPF external type 1, E2 - OSPF external type 2
       i - IS-IS, su - IS-IS summary, L1 - IS-IS level-1, L2 - IS-IS level-2
       ia - IS-IS inter area, * - candidate default, U - per-user static route
       o - ODR, P - periodic downloaded static route

Gateway of last resort is not set

C    192.168.30.0/24 is directly connected, Serial0/0
R    192.168.10.0/24 [120/1] via 192.168.30.1, 00:00:15, Serial0/0
C    192.168.40.0/24 is directly connected, FastEthernet0/0
R    192.168.20.0/24 [120/1] via 192.168.30.1, 00:00:15, Serial0/0
R3#
```

FIGURE 6.30   *Output of the* show ip route *Command on R3*

TROUBLESHOOTING RIP 2

If for some reason the routing tables on your routers are not correctly updated, you'll need to troubleshoot the problem. This section discusses the commands required for troubleshooting the RIP 2 update process.

Debug Commands

A number of debug commands are available to enable you to troubleshoot RIP 2.

debug ip rip

You can use the *debug ip rip* command to display RIP 2 routing transactions. This command is also useful when neighboring routers are enabled for RIP 2 and authentication is not currently configured; in this case, you can use the *debug ip rip* command to view the RIP 2 authentication-related problems. To disable the command, use *no debug ip rip*.

Before the R1, R2, and R3 routers can accept updates from neighboring routers, all routing information needs to be authenticated. As you can see in the output shown in Figure 6.31, plain text authentication is not secure on R1 because the password used for authentication is sent in clear text.

In Figures 6.32 and 6.33, you can see from the output that plain text authentication is not secure on R2 or R3 for the same reasons.

As you can see, the routing updates are sent in clear text.

```
R1#debug ip rip
RIP protocol debugging is on
R1#
*Mar  1 00:30:15.051: RIP: received packet with text authentication accessdenied
*Mar  1 00:30:15.055: RIP: received v2 update from 192.168.20.2 on Serial0/0
*Mar  1 00:30:15.055:       192.168.30.0/24 via 0.0.0.0 in 1 hops
*Mar  1 00:30:15.055:       192.168.40.0/24 via 0.0.0.0 in 1 hops
*Mar  1 00:30:16.139: RIP: sending v2 update to 224.0.0.9 via FastEthernet0/0 (1
92.168.10.1)
*Mar  1 00:30:16.139: RIP: build update entries
*Mar  1 00:30:16.139:    192.168.20.0/24 via 0.0.0.0, metric 1, tag 0
*Mar  1 00:30:16.139:    192.168.30.0/24 via 0.0.0.0, metric 1, tag 0
*Mar  1 00:30:16.143:    192.168.40.0/24 via 0.0.0.0, metric 1, tag 0
*Mar  1 00:30:20.983: RIP: sending v2 update to 255.255.255.255 via Serial0/0 (1
92.168.20.1)
*Mar  1 00:30:20.983: RIP: build update entries
*Mar  1 00:30:20.983:    192.168.10.0/24 via 0.0.0.0, metric 1, tag 0
```

FIGURE 6.31   *Output of the* debug ip rip *Command on R1 Using Plain Text Authentication*

```
R2#debug ip rip
RIP protocol debugging is on
R2#
*Mar  1 00:31:38.595: RIP: received packet with text authentication accessdenied
*Mar  1 00:31:38.595: RIP: received v2 update from 192.168.20.1 on Serial0/0
*Mar  1 00:31:38.595:       192.168.10.0/24 via 0.0.0.0 in 1 hops
*Mar  1 00:31:45.939: RIP: received packet with text authentication accessdenied
*Mar  1 00:31:45.939: RIP: received v2 update from 192.168.30.2 on Serial0/1
*Mar  1 00:31:45.939:       192.168.40.0/24 via 0.0.0.0 in 1 hops
*Mar  1 00:31:49.919: RIP: sending v2 update to 255.255.255.255 via Serial0/1 (1
92.168.30.1)
*Mar  1 00:31:49.919: RIP: build update entries
*Mar  1 00:31:49.919:    192.168.10.0/24 via 0.0.0.0, metric 1, tag 0
*Mar  1 00:31:49.919:    192.168.20.0/24 via 0.0.0.0, metric 1, tag 0
*Mar  1 00:32:05.815: RIP: sending v2 update to 255.255.255.255 via Serial0/0 (1
92.168.20.2)
*Mar  1 00:32:05.815: RIP: build update entries
*Mar  1 00:32:05.815:    192.168.30.0/24 via 0.0.0.0, metric 1, tag 0
*Mar  1 00:32:05.815:    192.168.40.0/24 via 0.0.0.0, metric 1, tag 0
*Mar  1 00:32:07.955: RIP: received packet with text authentication accessdenied
*Mar  1 00:32:07.959: RIP: received v2 update from 192.168.20.1 on Serial0/0
*Mar  1 00:32:07.959:       192.168.10.0/24 via 0.0.0.0 in 1 hops
```

FIGURE 6.32   *Output of the* debug ip rip *Command on R2 Using Plain Text Authentication*

```
R3#debug ip rip
RIP protocol debugging is on
R3#
*Mar  1 00:31:53.295: RIP: sending v2 update to 224.0.0.9 via FastEthernet0/0 (1
92.168.40.1)
*Mar  1 00:31:53.295: RIP: build update entries
*Mar  1 00:31:53.295:    192.168.10.0/24 via 0.0.0.0, metric 1, tag 0
*Mar  1 00:31:53.295:    192.168.20.0/24 via 0.0.0.0, metric 1, tag 0
*Mar  1 00:31:53.299:    192.168.30.0/24 via 0.0.0.0, metric 1, tag 0
*Mar  1 00:31:55.171: RIP: sending v2 update to 255.255.255.255 via Serial0/0 (1
92.168.30.2)
*Mar  1 00:31:55.171: RIP: build update entries
*Mar  1 00:31:55.171:    192.168.40.0/24 via 0.0.0.0, metric 1, tag 0
*Mar  1 00:31:58.119: RIP: received packet with text authentication accessdenied
*Mar  1 00:31:58.119: RIP: received v2 update from 192.168.30.1 on Serial0/0
*Mar  1 00:31:58.119:       192.168.10.0/24 via 0.0.0.0 in 1 hops
*Mar  1 00:31:58.119:       192.168.20.0/24 via 0.0.0.0 in 1 hops
*Mar  1 00:32:19.619: RIP: sending v2 update to 224.0.0.9 via FastEthernet0/0 (1
92.168.40.1)
*Mar  1 00:32:19.619: RIP: build update entries
*Mar  1 00:32:19.619:    192.168.10.0/24 via 0.0.0.0, metric 1, tag 0
*Mar  1 00:32:19.619:    192.168.20.0/24 via 0.0.0.0, metric 1, tag 0
*Mar  1 00:32:19.623:    192.168.30.0/24 via 0.0.0.0, metric 1, tag 0
```

FIGURE 6.33 *Output of the* debug ip rip *Command on R3 Using Plain Text Authentication*

Verifying MD5 Authentication

Before routers R1, R2, and R3 can accept updates from neighboring routers, all routing information needs to be authenticated. MD5 authentication uses a one-way hashing algorithm. The router will not use the actual password as entered in the configuration to authenticate every update, but rather will use a 128-bit value which is based on the password, as shown in Figure 6.34 for the R1 router, Figure 6.35 for the R2 router, and Figure 6.36 for the R3 router.

Figure 6.37 shows the output of the *debug ip rip* command to verify that the authentication was not correctly configured.

debug ip routing

You can use the *debug ip routing* command to get more information on routing table updates and route cache updates. To disable the command use *no debug ip routing*.

```
R1#debug ip rip
RIP protocol debugging is on
R1#
*Mar  1 00:49:09.747: RIP: received packet with MD5 authentication
*Mar  1 00:49:09.747: RIP: received v2 update from 192.168.20.2 on Serial0/0
*Mar  1 00:49:09.747:      192.168.30.0/24 via 0.0.0.0 in 1 hops
*Mar  1 00:49:09.751:      192.168.40.0/24 via 0.0.0.0 in 1 hops
*Mar  1 00:49:14.947: RIP: sending v2 update to 224.0.0.9 via FastEthernet0/0 (1
92.168.10.1)
*Mar  1 00:49:14.947: RIP: build update entries
*Mar  1 00:49:14.947:      192.168.20.0/24 via 0.0.0.0, metric 1, tag 0
*Mar  1 00:49:14.947:      192.168.30.0/24 via 0.0.0.0, metric 1, tag 0
*Mar  1 00:49:14.951:      192.168.40.0/24 via 0.0.0.0, metric 1, tag 0
*Mar  1 00:49:25.283: RIP: sending v2 update to 255.255.255.255 via Serial0/0 (1
92.168.20.1)
*Mar  1 00:49:25.283: RIP: build update entries
*Mar  1 00:49:25.283:      192.168.10.0/24 via 0.0.0.0, metric 1, tag 0
```

FIGURE 6.34   *Output of the* debug ip rip *Command on R1 Using MD5 Authentication*

```
R2#debug ip rip
RIP protocol debugging is on
R2#
*Mar  1 00:50:18.207: RIP: received packet with MD5 authentication
*Mar  1 00:50:18.207: RIP: received v2 update from 192.168.20.1 on Serial0/0
*Mar  1 00:50:18.207:      192.168.10.0/24 via 0.0.0.0 in 1 hops
*Mar  1 00:50:32.443: RIP: sending v2 update to 255.255.255.255 via Serial0/0 (1
92.168.20.2)
*Mar  1 00:50:32.443: RIP: build update entries
*Mar  1 00:50:32.443:      192.168.30.0/24 via 0.0.0.0, metric 1, tag 0
*Mar  1 00:50:32.443:      192.168.40.0/24 via 0.0.0.0, metric 1, tag 0
*Mar  1 00:50:40.179: RIP: sending v2 update to 255.255.255.255 via Serial0/1 (1
92.168.30.1)
*Mar  1 00:50:40.179: RIP: build update entries
*Mar  1 00:50:40.179:      192.168.10.0/24 via 0.0.0.0, metric 1, tag 0
*Mar  1 00:50:40.179:      192.168.20.0/24 via 0.0.0.0, metric 1, tag 0
*Mar  1 00:50:41.567: RIP: received packet with MD5 authentication
*Mar  1 00:50:41.567: RIP: received v2 update from 192.168.30.2 on Serial0/1
*Mar  1 00:50:41.567:      192.168.40.0/24 via 0.0.0.0 in 1 hops
```

FIGURE 6.35   *Output of the* debug ip rip *Command on R2 Using MD5 Authentication*

```
R3#debug ip rip
RIP protocol debugging is on
R3#
*Mar  1 00:49:24.323: RIP: sending v2 update to 224.0.0.9 via FastEthernet0/0 (1
92.168.40.1)
*Mar  1 00:49:24.323: RIP: build update entries
*Mar  1 00:49:24.323:    192.168.10.0/24 via 0.0.0.0, metric 1, tag 0
*Mar  1 00:49:24.323:    192.168.20.0/24 via 0.0.0.0, metric 1, tag 0
*Mar  1 00:49:24.327:    192.168.30.0/24 via 0.0.0.0, metric 1, tag 0
*Mar  1 00:49:24.995: RIP: received packet with MD5 authentication
*Mar  1 00:49:24.999: RIP: received v2 update from 192.168.30.1 on Serial0/0
*Mar  1 00:49:24.999:        192.168.10.0/24 via 0.0.0.0 in 1 hops
*Mar  1 00:49:24.999:        192.168.20.0/24 via 0.0.0.0 in 1 hops
*Mar  1 00:49:28.875: RIP: sending v2 update to 255.255.255.255 via Serial0/0 (1
92.168.30.2)
*Mar  1 00:49:28.875: RIP: build update entries
*Mar  1 00:49:28.875:    192.168.40.0/24 via 0.0.0.0, metric 1, tag 0
```

FIGURE 6.36   *Output of the* debug ip rip *Command on R3 Using MD5 Authentication*

```
R2#debug ip rip
RIP protocol debugging is on
R2#
*Mar  1 00:34:36.043: RIP: sending v2 update to 255.255.255.255 via Serial0/1 (1
92.168.30.1)
*Mar  1 00:34:36.043: RIP: build update entries
*Mar  1 00:34:36.043:    192.168.10.0/24 via 0.0.0.0, metric 1, tag 0
*Mar  1 00:34:36.043:    192.168.20.0/24 via 0.0.0.0, metric 1, tag 0
*Mar  1 00:34:42.955: RIP: received packet with MD5 authentication
*Mar  1 00:34:42.955: RIP: ignored v2 packet from 192.168.30.2 (invalid authenti
cation)
*Mar  1 00:34:44.423: RIP: sending v2 update to 255.255.255.255 via Serial0/0 (1
92.168.20.2)
*Mar  1 00:34:44.423: RIP: build update entries
*Mar  1 00:34:44.423:    192.168.30.0/24 via 0.0.0.0, metric 1, tag 0
*Mar  1 00:34:44.423:    192.168.40.0/24 via 0.0.0.0, metric 1, tag 0
```

FIGURE 6.37   *Output of the* debug ip rip *Command with Incorrect Authentication Configuration*

SUMMARY OF EXAM OBJECTIVES

In this chapter, we discussed the characteristics of RIP 2. We looked at how a RIP 2-enabled router sends out its routing table, discussed how a RIP 2-enabled router can send routing updates via broadcast or multicast addresses, and compared RIP 1 and RIP 2 as well as highlighted the new route summarization, classless routing, and authentication capabilities in RIP 2.

We also discussed how to enable RIP on a router, and reviewed how to configure a router with the appropriate IP addresses. In addition, we took a close look at neighbors and how routers exchange their routing tables.

Another important topic in this chapter concerned how to configure a RIP 2-enabled router to support plain text authentication and authentication using the MD5 algorithm. In this section of the chapter, we discussed how to verify the configuration of a RIP 2-enabled router and focused on displaying the contents of the routing table.

To round out the chapter, we discussed the various iterations of the *debug* command, which you can use to get more detailed information regarding how RIP 2-enabled routers exchange their routing information. Use this tool if you expect problems when routing updates are not received or when key chains are not correctly configured.

EXAM OBJECTIVES FAST TRACK

RIP, Version 2

- The multicast address of RIP 2 is 224.0.0.9.

- The four RIP 2 update timers are the route update timer, which specifies when a RIP-enabled router will broadcast its entire routing table to its neighboring router; the route invalid timer, which specifies the amount of time that elapses before a RIP-enabled router no longer receives any updates from a particular route, making this route invalid; the route holddown timer, which specifies how long a RIP-enabled router will keep an invalid route in the routing table; and the route flush timer, which specifies when an invalid RIP-enabled router should be removed from the routing table.

- RIP 1and RIP 2 are different in a few ways. For instance, RIPv2 supports multicast and authentication.

Configuring RIP 2

- To configure RIP 2 routing, you need to enter the *router RIP* command in global configuration mode. Next, use the *network networked* command to specify all networks to which the router is directly connected.

- The *passive-interface* command prevents routes from being sent on a particular interface.

- Use the *neighbor* command to allow a RIP router to send its updates via unicast instead of broadcast. This can be useful in a non-broadcast network such as Frame Relay.

Verifying RIP 2 Configurations

- To view the contents of a routing table, use the *show ip route* command.

- To verify the RIP 2 update timers, use the *show ip protocols* command.

Troubleshooting RIP 2

- You can use the *debug* command to retrieve more detailed information in real time on RIP version packets and authentication failures.

EXAM OBJECTIVES FREQUENTLY ASKED QUESTIONS

Q: What is important for the exam?

A: You have to be familiar with the configuration commands and the debugging commands.

Q: Which commands are important?

A: Be sure to understand the following commands: *show ip protocols*, *debug ip rip*, and *router rip*.

Q: What do I need to know about RIP 2?

A: Remember how RIP 2 works and read the characteristics of RIP 2. Then you will be fine.

Q: Do I need to know the differences between RIPv1 and RIPv2?

A: Remember that RIPv1 sends a broadcast every 30 seconds, and has an administrative distance of 120. And RIPv2 is able to send routing updates via multicast and also has an administrative distance of 120.

SELF TEST

1. Which command enables Routing Information Protocol?
   A. *router RIP*
   B. *router RIP 10.0.0.0*
   C. *enable router RIP*
   D. *router RIP enable*

2. Which of the following describes RIP 2?
   A. It sends multicast updates to 224.0.0.7.
   B. It is a distance vector protocol that uses the hop count as its metric.
   C. It provides clear text and MD5 authentication.
   D. Its default holddown timer is 240 seconds.

3. You want to see the routes that only RIP 2 has discovered. Which command should you use?
   A. *show ip protocol*
   B. *show ip interface*
   C. *show ip route*
   D. *show ip route RIP*

4. Which command displays RIP 2 routing updates when a RIP-enabled router exchanges information with its neighbor?
   A. *show ip route*
   B. *show ip protocols*
   C. *debug ip RIP*
   D. *debug ip protocols*

5. Which command should you use to verify the new routes learned by your RIP 2-enabled router?
   A. *Router#show ipaddress*
   B. *Router#show ip route*
   C. *Router#show ip interface brief*
   D. *Router#debug ip protocol*

6. At which time interval does a RIP 2-enabled router send its routing updates by default?
   A. 30 seconds
   B. 45 seconds
   C. 60 seconds
   D. 90 seconds

7. Which subnet mask is represented by the /28 notation?
   A. 255.255.255.0
   B. 255.255.255.240
   C. 255.255.255.224
   D. 255.255.255.192

8. What is the CIDR notation for subnet mask 255.255.240.0?
   - **A.** /16
   - **B.** /24
   - **C.** /20
   - **D.** /32

9. What is the administrative distance for RIP 2?
   - **A.** 90
   - **B.** 100
   - **C.** 110
   - **D.** 120

10. Which statements are correct regarding RIP 2?
    - **A.** It has the same maximum hop count as RIP 1.
    - **B.** It uses broadcasts for its routing tables.
    - **C.** It's a classless routing protocol.
    - **D.** It does not send the subnet mask in updates.

11. Which of the following routes will be used to forward data if the routing table contains entries for static, RIP, IGRP, and OSPF routes?
    - **A.** IGRP route
    - **B.** Static route
    - **C.** RIP route
    - **D.** OSPF route

12. In the following output, you can see the result of *debug ip rip*. Which of the following statements is true?

```
R1#debug ip RIP
RIP protocol debugging is on
20:40:32: RIP: received v1 update from 192.168.20.5 on
    Serial0
20:40:32: 192.168.30.0 in 1 hops
20:40:32: 192.168.40.0 in 16 hops (inaccessible)
20:40:34: RIP: sending v1 update to 255.255.255.255 via
    Ethernet0 (192.168.10.1)
20:40:34: subnet 192.168.20.0, metric 1
20:40:34: RIP: sending v1 update to 255.255.255.255 via
    Serial0 (192.168.1)
20:40:34: subnet 192.168.20.0, metric 1
```

   - **A.** A ping from R1 to any host on IP subnet 192.168.40.0 would be successful.
   - **B.** A ping to IP address 192.168.20.5 would be successful.
   - **C.** At least two interfaces on R1 are participating in RIP.
   - **D.** The routing sends updates via multicast.

13. Which of the following commands will prevent routes from being out on interface S0, but will not prevent the router from receiving updates?

A. *Router(config)#int s0*

  Router(config-if)#no routing

B. *Router(config)#int s0*

  Router(config-if)#passive-interface

C. *Router(config)#router RIP*

  Router(config-router)#passive-interface s0

D. *Router(config)#router RIP*

  Router(config-router)#no routing updates

14. The networks connected to R1 have been summarized as a 192.168.176.0/21 route and have been sent to R1. Which two destination addresses will R1 forward?

A. 192.168.194.166   **D.** 192.168.183.255

B. 192.183.42   **E.** 192.168.179.10

C. 192.168.159.55   **F.** 192.168.184.86

15. You want to enable RIP 2 to send out routing updates via multicast instead of broadcast addresses. Which command should you use?

A. *Router(config)#ip RIP-v2 multicast*

B. *Router(config-if)#ip RIP-v2 multicast*

C. *Router(config)#no ip RIP v2-broadcast*

D. *Router(config-if)#no ip RIP v2-broadcast*

16. You want to specify a neighboring router on your RIP 2-enabled router. Which command should you use?

A. *Router(config-router)#neighbor 192.168.10.2*

B. *Router(config)#neighbor 192.168.10.2*

C. *Router(config-router)#ip RIP neighbor 192.168.10.2*

D. *Router(config)#ip RIP neighbor 192.168.10.2*

17. Which command should you use to verify the default RIP 2 update timers?

A. *Router(config)#show ip RIP timers*

B. *Router(config-router)#show ip RIP timers*

C. *Router#show RIP timers*

D. *Router#show ip protocols*

18. You want to turn off RIP 2 on all your routers. Which command should you use?

   A. *Router(config)#no RIP enable*

   B. *Router(config-if)#no RIP enable*

   C. *Router(config)#no router RIP*

   D. *Router(config-if)#no router IP*

19. You configured your routers with MD5 authentication and you suspect that your RIP 2-enabled routers are receiving updates. You need to verify whether all RIP 2-enabled routers are using the same key chain. Which command should you use?

   A. *Router#show ip protocols*

   B. *Router(config)#show ip protocols*

   C. *Router(config-if)#show ip protocols*

   D. *Router(config)#show ip RIP authentication*

20. You need to verify which RIP version is currently configured on your router. Which command should you use?

   A. *Router(config)#show ip protocols*

   B. *Router#show ip protocols*

   C. *Router(config)#show ip RIP version*

   D. *Router#show ip RIP version*

SELF TEST QUICK ANSWER KEY

1.	A	**11.**	B
2.	B, and C	**12.**	B, and C
3.	D	**13.**	C
4.	C	**14.**	B, and E
5.	B	**15.**	C
6.	A	**16.**	A
7.	B	**17.**	D
8.	C	**18.**	C
9.	D	**19.**	A
10.	A, and C	**20.**	B

Implementing the OSPF Protocol

INTRODUCTION

A common challenge that presents itself to administrators from many IT organizations is how to go about effectively and adequately planning for and managing the network in their enterprise. To be successful at network administration, your first priority should be to utilize the time to map out your current network infrastructure. To develop an effective plan on how to progress, typically, you should first discover the answers to the following questions:

How many routers does my environment require?

What should my logical segments look like?

What should my virtual segments look like?

What will my security model look like?

What protocol should I select for the environment?

A network infrastructure plan of action ensures that you choose the appropriate protocol and configurations for your organization. To develop your plan, you first need to know the current router configuration in your organization; where the routers are located, what roles they perform, and what protocols they are running. You must take the time to address all the impacts on your infrastructure to effectively plan. Once you have collected the appropriate information from your environment, you will be able to begin the planning that is involved in either adjusting your existing topology or deploying a new routing topology.

In this chapter, you will learn specifically about the Open Shortest Path First (OSPF) protocol. Topics will include the following: the advantages and disadvantages of utilizing OSPF, what to consider when performing your planning steps, how to configure OSPF, tools you can use to manage your OSPF environment, as well as troubleshooting strategies, which can all be used to assist you in the network management.

THE OSPF PROTOCOL

OSPF is a nonproprietary link-state protocol that enabled administrators to configure their routing environment for efficiency and link-state awareness which allows for more accurately routed data moving throughout your network infrastructure. If you are interested in becoming Cisco Certified Network Associate (CCNA) certified, you need to be comfortable implementing OSPF. You may be presented with simulations that require successful configuration of OSPF routing; hence, to be prepared, you should become proficient with the commands used in OSPF. Another important concept for you to be familiar with is securing routers using OSPF with MD5 authentication.

One of the first things you must understand is what is meant when OSPF is described as a link-state protocol. Routers utilizing link-state protocols function by creating a big picture view of the network by creating a map depicting connectivity. Each router can then perform its own calculations to determine the best next hop for every possible destination in the network. These best next hops make up the device's routing table, which it consults as it passes data through the network. By continually being updated and aware of the state of the network links between nodes, each router can keep its routing table current and efficient.

We will cover many topics in this chapter, but the first thing to keep in mind is that prior knowledge may assist you as we move through the chapter. For instance, if you have an understanding of the election process, and are comfortable configuring a device as a designated router (DR), you will be better equipped to efficiently implement OSPF on a routed network. Efficiency is a key goal when implementing OSPF and an important part of making OSPF work for you involves fine tuning the protocol. The priority and loopback addresses are examples of settings that can be adjusted when configuring OSPF to make a network more efficient. The simulation materials provided with this book will help individuals gain sufficient practice in implementing OSFP before appearing for the CCNA examination. Knowing how to implement OSPF is required for becoming CCNA certified, as well as for working with Cisco routers in the field.

OSPF Version 2 is documented in Request For Comments (RFC) 1583 and is sanctioned by the Internet Engineering Task Force (IETF). It is intended to become Internet's preferred interior routing protocol.

Advantages

OSPF uses a shortest path first (SPF) algorithm to compute routes in the routing table. The SPF algorithm computes the shortest (least cost) path between the router and all the networks of the internetwork. SPF-calculated routes are always loop-free. Due to these contributing factors OSPF is efficient; OSPF requires very little network overhead, even in very large internetworks.

Many organizations have routing devices from a variety of different vendors. If your organization has multiple routers from different manufacturers, it is heterogeneous and you cannot use Enhanced Interior Gateway Routing Protocol (EIGRP) since it is proprietary to Cisco. In this situation, your options are Routing Information Protocol (RIP), Routing Information Protocol v2 (RIPv2), or OSPF. If your organization has a large network, then typically OSPF would be utilized. Another option is a service known as *route redistribution*, which is a translation service between routing protocols.

OSPF is an industry open standard, which means that any vendor who so desires, can incorporate OSPF into their routing devices. Since no one company controls OSFP and it is not proprietary, any company is free to utilize it. By choosing OSPF, you have the ability to scale to a large and complex network while continuing to utilize different makes of routers while still having them functioning harmoniously.

Changes to routing paths in an OSPF network are propagated quickly. Instead of exchanging routing table entries like RIP routers, OSPF routers maintain a map of the internetwork that is only updated after a change to the network topology occurs. This map, called the link-state database, is synchronized between all the OSPF routers and is used to compute the routes in the routing table.

Neighboring OSPF routers form an adjacency, which is a logical relationship between routers, to synchronize the link-state database. Changes to internetwork topology are efficiently flooded across the entire internetwork to ensure that the link-state database on each router is synchronized and accurate at all times. Upon receiving changes to the link-state database, the routing table is recalculated. After initialization, OSPF only sends updates on routing table sections which have changed; it does not send the entire routing table, reducing network traffic overhead.

Routing table size can be further reduced by using *route summarization*, which is the process of taking multiple routes and lumping or consolidating them into a single advertisement. By reducing the required number of advertisements, the routing table will have fewer entries, which reduce the size of the table and helps in efficiency when determining the appropriate route.

Route summarization is also known as supernetting or route aggregation. Typically in routing tables there are many rows of individual subnets listed with their corresponding next hop addresses. Route summarization simplifies the routing table by taking sequential groups of subnets and rolling them up into a single supernetted address. By this way, when the router is evaluating what the next hop should be for a data packet, it has fewer entries to peruse and select from.

For example, let us say that the following subnets are viable routes that all have the same targeted next hop:

- 192.168.1.0/24

- 192.168.2.0/24

- 192.168.3.0/24

To improve the routing table efficiency, we can supernet these four addresses into a single address and subnet mask that will be advertised instead of each of these individually. To achieve this, the first thing we will look at is coming up with the summarized address, and then at the summarized subnet mask.

So to determine the summarized address, we have to get a little dirty with binary. Here we go:

1. Take the following four addresses and convert them into binary.

```
192.168.1.0 = 11000000 10101000 00000001 00000000
192.168.2.0 = 11000000 10101000 00000010 00000000
192.168.3.0 = 11000000 10101000 00000011 00000000
```

2. Next examine the bits from left to right. Draw a line at the point at which the binary bits diverge in value.

```
192.168.1.0 = 11000000 10101000 000000 | 01 00000000
192.168.2.0 = 11000000 10101000 000000 | 10 00000000
192.168.3.0 = 11000000 10101000 000000 | 11 00000000
```

3. Now convert the bits to the left of the line back into decimal and you have the summarized network address. In this case the summarized network address is: 192.168.0.0.

4. The final step is to determine the subnet mask. To do this, you need to turn on all the bits to the left of the line. This will give us a subnet mask of 255.255.252.0.

```
192.168.1.0 = 11111111 11111111 111111 | 01 00000000
192.168.2.0 = 11111111 11111111 111111 | 10 00000000
192.168.3.0 = 11111111 11111111 111111 | 11 00000000
```

5. So the summarized address in this case is 192.168.0.0. 255.255.252.0

OSPF networks can be logically segmented by organizing the network into areas. This results in decreased size of the routing tables. Areas are administratively defined and each area is identified by an assigned number. Routers can belong to multiple areas since areas are interface specific, but typically it is recommended that a single router belong to no more than 3 areas.

Test Day Tip

Remember the smaller the size of the routing tables, the faster the routers will be able to determine the best possible route. This is one of the many benefits OSPF has.

A router is categorized depending on how it is connected in the environment and on what types of traffic the router is capable of routing. The following are the types of OSPF routers:

- **Internal router** An internal router has all the interfaces connect to the same area. All internal routers have same link-state databases.

- **Backbone router** A backbone router has at least one interface connected to area 0. Some may function as internal routers for area 0 with all interfaces connected to the backbone, whereas others may belong to more than one area. Belonging to multiple areas classifies them additionally as area border routers (ABRs).

- **Area border router** ABRs are routers that have interfaces attached to multiple areas. These routers maintain separate link-state databases for each area that they are connected to. They are capable of routing traffic destined for or arriving from other areas.

- **Autonomous system boundary router (ASBR)** ASBRs are the routers that have at least one interface to the external network, which may or not be an OSPF system. Since this autonomous network can be non-OSPF, the ASBRs are capable of route redistribution, which means that these routers can import routing information from non-OSPF networks and distribute it in the same OSPF network for which it is responsible, as well as taking routing information from the OSPF network and distributing it into the non-OSPF system.

Test Day Tip

Often in the exams, the router types are referred to by their abbreviated acronym, and other times by their full names. For example, be sure to be able to quickly pick out that an ABR is an area border router and that an ASBR is an autonomous system boundary router.

All OSPF networks have at least 1 area. The default area is given the number 0 and functions as the backbone as additional areas are added. All other areas connect through area 0, and each defined area has its own link-state database. See Figure 7.1 for a sample OSPF topology.

As a rule of thumb, you should take into consideration your network's unique characteristics when deciding how many routers should exist per area. Consider things such as the type of equipment you are using, the expected load on a given segment, the anticipated configuration of OSPF, and the kinds of media in use for each area. Analysis of these facts will assist you in coming up with a maximum number of routers per area that works best for you.

To further reduce the amount of routing information flooded into areas, OSPF also allows the use of *stub areas*. A stub area can contain a single entry and exit point (a single ABR), or multiple ABRs when any of the ABRS can be used to reach external route destinations. Routing from stub areas to the outside world is based on a default route and stub areas are usually configured not to carry external routes.

Creating a stub area reduces the overhead needed by the routers within the stub area, and these types of areas can be useful when a topology is simple and resources are limited. Due to the simplified routing configuration within a stub area, it is possible that traffic may be routed through a

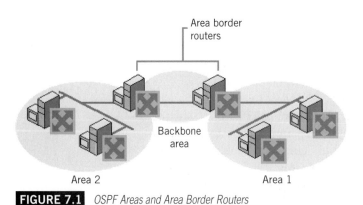

Area border routers

Backbone area

Area 2

Area 1

FIGURE 7.1 *OSPF Areas and Area Border Routers*

suboptimal path to its destination, since not all path options are considered. All OSPF routers inside a stub area have to be configured as stub routers.

OSPF has the following specific advantages:

- OSPF-calculated routes are always loop-free.

- OSPF can scale to large or very large internetworks.

- Reconfiguration for network topology changes is faster.

- Using areas, OSPF can be logically segmented.

- OSPF is a nonproprietary industry open standard protocol used by many vendors.

Disadvantages

One of the main disadvantages of OSPF is that it is complex to configure; OSPF requires proper planning and it can be difficult to configure and administer. In smaller environments, OSFP may not be worth the planning time and configuration investment for the return. Simpler protocols like RIP can be just as effective in smaller network infrastructures. Another major disadvantage of OSPF is that it is a resource heavy protocol. Depending on the infrastructure, equipment in use many need to be evaluated carefully before deploying OSFP to confirm that the routing devices can handle the extra load.

OSPF has the following specific disadvantages:

- OSPF is very processor intensive.

- OSPF maintains multiple copies of routing information, increasing the amount of memory needed.

- OSPF is not as easy to learn as some other protocols.

- Using areas, OSPF can be logically segmented.

In the case where an entire network is running OSPF and one link within it is "bouncing" every few seconds, OSPF update traffic would increase substantially on the network overhead by informing every other router *every* time the link changed state. As the size of the link-state database increases, memory requirements and route computation times increase as well. To address this scaling problem, OSPF divides the internetwork into areas that are connected to each other through a backbone area. Each router only keeps a link-state database for those areas that are connected to the router. ABRs connect the backbone area to the other areas.

CONFIGURING OSPF

To successfully configure OSFP, you have to be familiar with the way OSPF was meant to be deployed and also have a thorough understanding of how routers configured with OSPF work together to route network traffic. Many of the configurations options for OSPF have associated design decision points as we will see. In this section, we will discuss the components to keep in mind when designing your OSPF environment. As we get into the details of the "How to configure OSPF" as well as the "Why to configure it in a certain fashion," you should keep your own environment in mind. Soon you will be able to make appropriate decisions on the topology and the settings to configure within your OSPF infrastructure.

The first thing to be aware of are the reasons behind setting up OSPF environments in a hierarchical design. The main things that you must take into account when planning and designing your OSPF environment are as follows:

- Decreasing routing overhead

- Speeding up convergence

- Confining network instability to single areas of the network

The information we cover in the next sections will allow you to make design decisions that will be driven by these three main factors. Keep these factors in mind, as we discuss how OSPF Neighbors relate to each, the OSPF states, and OSPF authentication.

Neighbors

What is an OSPF Neighbor? Do they bring over casseroles for dinner on Saturday nights and complain when you walk your dog on their lawn? Not quite, but the concept of human neighbors and routing neighbors is similar in some ways.

You share the building or block where you live with other people, and thus these people are referred to as your neighbors. In the land of routers and OSPF, routers can become "OSPF Neighbors" if they simply have an interface connected on a common network.

For example, two routers connected on a point-to-point serial link could be neighbors. Routers configured for OSPF will send out hello packets on a regular interval. As soon as a router finds itself in the hello packet of another router, then the two are officially neighbors. So to relate this back to our human neighbor analogy, we all know that until you officially meet and learn the name of that person down the hall, you don't officially consider him or her as a neighbor. On routers, the following items must match on the two devices before a pair of routers are considered to be OSPF neighbors:

- Subnet mask used on the subnet
- Subnet number (as derived using the subnet mask and each router's interface Internet Protocol (IP) address)
- Hello Interval
- Dead Interval
- Area ID
- Stub area flag
- Must pass authentication checks (if in use)

If any of these parameters differ, the routers do not become OSPF neighbors.

Once the two routers consider themselves as neighbors, this allows for a pathway to the next step in router relationships: adjacency. *Adjacency* is the next step after neighboring and it is what allows two routers to share additional information. We will discuss adjacency a little later in the chapter.

Nonbroadcast Multiple Access Networks

A *nonbroadcast multiple access* (NBMA) network is a network to which multiple computers and devices are attached, but data is transmitted directly from one computer to another over a virtual circuit or across a switched fabric. NBMA does not support multicast or broadcast traffic. Some common examples of nonbroadcast network media include asynchronous transfer mode (ATM), frame relay, and X.25.[1]

NBMA is one of four network types in the OSPF communications protocol. NBMA is used to accurately model X.25 and frame relay environments in multiple-access networks, where there are no intrinsic broadcast and multicast capabilities. The other OSPF network types: broadcast, point-to-point, and point-to-multipoint will be covered later.[2]

In an NBMA configuration, OSPF sends hello packets (packets sent periodically to establish and confirm neighbor relationships between routers) to each router one at a time rather than multicasting them. The hello timer (which tells the router how often to send hello packets) is extended from 10 to 30 seconds and the dead router timer (which tells the router how long to wait before it decides that a neighboring router is not functioning) is extended from 40 to 120 seconds.[2]

Hello Protocol

The Hello protocol is used for establishing and maintaining router neighbor relationships. Hello packets are used for neighbor discovery and recovery. They also indicate that a client is still operating and network ready through keep-alives. So back to our neighbor down the hall, once you establish a relationship, you will find out information about your neighbors such as their names. Let's say you meet Eric and Jane Stevens for the first time in the elevator. You have acknowledged their existence by learning their names and they have most likely acknowledged yours by learning your name as well. By laying these basic foundations a relationship of information sharing and friendship can now begin. To bring this back to routers, OSPF's primary means of identifying its neighbors starts with its Hello protocol.

OSPF-enabled routers send multicast hellos with a destination address 224.0.0.5 on all OSPF-enabled interfaces. On multiaccess networks, which are networks supporting more than two routers, the Hello protocol selects a DR and a backup designated router (BDR). OSPF sends out hellos every 10 seconds on a broadcast link, which contains more than two nodes on the segment and 30 seconds on a nonbroadcast with only two nodes on the same segment. Exceptions exist for nonbroadcast multiaccess networks.

By exchanging a regular Hi! with your neighboring humans, you are aware that they are alive and well, and they are aware of your status as well. With OSPF, verifying the continuing operation of the network is accomplished via the Hello protocol. OSPF uses these small "hello" packets to verify link operation without transferring large tables. Every OSPF speaker sends out small hello packets in each of its interfaces every 10 seconds. It is through receipt of these packets that OSPF neighbors initially learn of each other's existence.

After the initial exchange of hellos, the routers add each other to their respective *Neighbor Tables*, which acts as a list of connected OSFP-enabled routers. Hello packets are not forwarded or recorded in the OSPF database, but if none are received from a particular neighbor for 40 seconds, that neighbor is marked down. Sort of like when you don't see your neighbor for a few days, you might mark them in your mind as being out of town, on vacation. The hello timer values can be configured, although they must be consistent across all routers on a network segment. In OSPF, link-state advertisements (LSAs) are then generated, resulting in links through a down router being marked as DOWN. This allows the router to recalculate and make an educated decision on what the best next hop should be for any given destination.

LSAs do age. The originating router advertises an LSA again after it has remained unchanged for 30 minutes. If an LSA ages to more than an hour, it is flushed from the databases. As the entry flushes out of all neighboring routers, the down path will no longer be considered. These timer values are called architectural constants by the RFC.

OSPFs various timers interact as follows:

- If a link goes down for 20 seconds, then comes back up, OSPF will not take notice.

- If a link flaps constantly, but at least one of every four hello packets make it across, OSPF does not take notice.

- If a link goes down for anytime from a minute to half an hour, OSPF floods an LSA when it goes down, and floods another LSA when it comes back up.

- If a link stays down for more than half an hour, LSAs originated by remote routers (that have become unreachable) begin to age out. When the link comes back up, all these LSAs will be flooded again.

- If a link is down for more than an hour, any LSAs originated by remote routers will have aged out and been flushed. When the link comes back up, it will be as if it were brand new.

Router Adjacencies

When routers meet the conditions to become OSPF neighbors, they next move into a state of adjacency. After the initial hello exchange between two routers, an exchange of network information begins, and after routers have synchronized their information, they are considered adjacent.

The fact that the routers consider themselves adjacent means that they will move beyond just simply hello exchange and will actually begin to transmit database content. Routers must go through various states from the initial relationship "hello" that transitions through a process before forming a "full" adjacency. Once a full adjacency is achieved, tables between routers must be kept updated to prevent loops and routing errors. LSAs are re-sent when a change occurs, or every 30 minutes to keep routing information "fresh."

There are multiple states that a neighbor relationship can pass through depending on the conditions of the network at the time. Hellos between routers continue to be sent periodically and the adjacency is maintained as long as hellos are exchanged. Missing hello messages result in a router declaring the adjacency being declared dead. As soon as OSPF identifies a problem, it modifies its LSAs accordingly and sends the updated LSAs to the remaining neighbors with full adjacencies.

Being event-driven, this LSA process intrinsically improves convergence time and reduces the amount of information that needs to be sent across the network. A key piece of information exchange in LSAs is the OSPF metric information. Many OSPF vendors assign each link a cost of 10. Cisco makes cost inversely proportional to a 100 Mbs. The following formula can be used in or to determine the OSPF link cost for a specific segment:

$$Cost = 100,000,000 \text{ bps/LinkSpeed}$$

An administrator can always override the default cost but should be considered carefully. Consistency is important, and one reason changing the default may be required, would be for compatibility with other vendor equipment; that is, configure differently for OSPF cost or possibly because the link is more than 100 Mbps. The cost value is always applied to the outgoing interface. The routing process will select the lowest cumulative cost to a remote network.

Sometimes, the metric is equivalent for multiple paths to a destination. In this case, OSPF will load balance over each of the equivalent interfaces. Cisco routers will automatically perform equal-cost load balancing for up to four paths, but this parameter can be increased by configuration to as many as 16 paths.

Designated Router

A *DR* is the router interface elected among all routers on a particular multiaccess network segment, generally assumed to be broadcast multiaccess. Special techniques, often vendor-dependent, may be needed to support the DR function on NBMA media. It is usually wise to configure the individual virtual circuits of an NBMA subnet as individual point-to-point lines. Also keep in mind that the techniques used are implementation-dependent.

Do not confuse the DR with an OSPF router type. DR is a role assumed by the elected router. A given physical router can have some interfaces that are designated (DR), others that are backup designated (BDR), and others that are nondesignated. Since there must always be a DR on any given subnet, if no router is DR or BDR for any given subnet, an election process takes place to select the DR first and then a second election is held for the BDR. The election process will be described in a later section.[3]

DRs exist for the purpose of reducing network traffic by providing a source for routing updates. The DR maintains a complete topology table of the network and sends the updates to the other routers via multicast. All routers in an area will form a slave/master relationship with the DR. They will form adjacencies with the DR and BDR only. Every time a router sends an update, it sends it to the DR and BDR on the multicast address 224.0.0.6. The DR will then send the update out to all other routers in the area, to the multicast address 224.0.0.5. This way all the routers do not have to constantly update each other, and can rather get all their updates from a single source.

The use of multicasting further reduces the network load. DRs and BDRs are always set up/elected on broadcast networks. DRs can also be elected on NBMA networks such as frame relay or ATM. DRs or BDRs are not elected on point-to-point links (such as a point-to-point WAN connection) because the two routers on either sides of the link must become fully adjacent and the bandwidth between them cannot be further optimized.

Backup Designated Router

A *BDR* is the router that becomes the DR if the current DR has a problem or fails. The BDR is the OSPF router with second highest priority at the time of the last election.[3]

Election Process

In any OSPF environment, there is a need for a DR and a BDR per subnet. The DR and BDR are roles that interfaces are elected to which defines which interfaces are responsible for certain activities on each segment. If no router is DR or BDR on a given segment, the DR is first elected, and then a second election is held to determine the BDR.

In an election, the interface with the highest priority becomes the DR for any given segment. The BDR is elected in a subsequent election, so typically the router interface with the second highest priority is elected as the BDR for the segment. Any time a DR fails, the BDR will automatically take over as the new DR and an additional election is held to determine the new BDR.

As the administrator, you do have the ability to influence the outcome of any given election. Priority values can be configured per interface and be set to any value desired. The priority values range between 0 and 254, with a higher value increasing its chances of becoming DR or BDR. The default value for all interfaces is 1; however you can also decide to configure an interface not to participate in elections, effectively setting its priority to 0. Remember that the DR is elected based on its having the highest priority hello packets.

A few things to keep in mind about elections:

- If two or more routers tie with the highest priority setting, the router sending the hello with the highest Router ID (RID) wins. An *RID* is the highest logical IP address configured on a router, and if no logical/loopback IP address is set, then the router uses the highest IP address configured on its active interfaces. For example, 192.168.0.1 would be higher than 10.1.1.2.

- If an OSPF router with a higher priority than the existing DR and BDR comes online after the election has taken place, it will not become DR or BDR until either the DR or the BDR fail.

- If the current DR becomes unavailable then the current BDR becomes the new DR and a new election takes place to find a new BDR. If the new DR then becomes unavailable and the original DR is available again, the original DR then becomes the active DR again, but no change is made to the current BDR.

Configuring the Loopback Address

For any OSPF process to initialize, it must be able to define an RID for the entire OSPF process. Once the router-wide data structures are built, it is then necessary to define the networks that the router will advertise and the area numbers into which these networks will be advertised.

There are several potential sources for the RID. The most common stable source is the IP address set on loopback 0. If more than one loopback address is defined, the internetwork operating system (IOS) will select the numerically highest IP address configured on a *loopback* interface. For example, 192.1.1.1 is numerically higher than 172.255.255.254. In other words, it is the IP address on the *loopback* interface that breaks ties, not the number of the *loopback* interfaces. In other words, loopback 1 is not automatically preferred to loopback 0.[4]

A few key points to remember about defining the RID using the loopback address:

- The highest loopback address is used in preference to a real interface address.

- A *loopback address* is a virtual interface and is automatically up, so it cannot fail with this method for choosing an RID more stable as well.

You can configure multiple loopbacks on a single router, so it becomes important to be able to determine, which will result in the generation of the RID. Table 7.1 depicts a router configured with multiple *loopback* interfaces.

In this scenario, the router would end up with a RID of 5.6.7.8, since it is the highest of the three addresses listed in the table.

If no *loopback* interfaces are defined, the OSPF process uses the numerically highest IP address value on an active physical interface. If no physical interfaces are active and configured with an IP address, the OSPF code will not initialize. In recent IOS versions, the router issues an error message if it cannot find a RID. Older versions simply do not initialize OSPF.

If there is only a single *loopback* interface, its IP address will always be the RID. In Table 7.2, the router has two serial interfaces that are active and have a higher IP value than the configured loopback address. In this case, the RID will be 1.2.3.4, since it is the only *loopback* interface, and the *loopback* interfaces are used preferentially over real interface addresses.

If there were no *loopback* interfaces configured, the numerically highest *active* interface would be used. The router depicted in Table 7.3 does not have any *loopback* interfaces configured. In evaluating the three interfaces based on IP address, first, you will see that Serial Interface 0 has the highest IP address; however, it is not an active interface indicated by the *shutdown* state. Since the value used for the RID must come from an active interface only Ethernet

Table 7.1 Router ID (RID) with Multiple Loopbacks

Loopback Interface 0	Loopback Interface 1	Loopback Interface 2
int loop 0	int loop 1	int loop 2
ip addr 1.2.3.4	ip addr 5.6.7.8	ip addr 2.3.4.6

Table 7.2 Router ID (RID) with a Single Loopback

Loopback Interface 0	Serial Interface 0	Serial Interface 1
int loop 0	int ser 0	int ser 1
ip addr 1.2.3.4	ip addr 5.6.7.8	ip addr 2.3.4.6

Table 7.3 Router ID (RID) with No Loopback and Highest IP shutdown

Ethernet Interface 0	Serial Interface 0	Serial Interface 1
int eth 0	int ser 0	int ser 1
ip addr 1.2.3.4	ip addr 5.6.7.8	ip addr 2.3.4.6
No shutdown	Shutdown	No shutdown

Interface 0 and Serial Interface 1 can be evaluated for the RID. Since Serial interface 1 has the higher IP address the RID for this device will be 2.3.4.6.

It is a good practice to configure the *loopback* interface on each of your routers to allow for an interface that will always be up and available to determine the RID and initiate the OSPF protocol without error. This task is performed by typing **interface loopback** <#> at the *Global Configuration* mode prompt, where the # represents the number of the *loopback* interface from 0 to 2,147,483,647.

Figure 7.2 is an example of how to configure the loopback across three different routers.

Changing Priority

In multiaccess networks, the router with the highest priority value is chosen as the DR, which acts as the central point of LSAs exchange. Then the router with second highest priority typically becomes the BDR. As the administrator, you may at times have a preference as to which interfaces participate in elections and become the DR and the BDR.

By using the priority command, you can set a priority value manually on any interface. The default priority for an OSPF interface is **1**. The range is from 0 to 255 and a value of **0** indicates that the interface will not participate in the DR election.

The following command configures a priority value on an interface:

■ *Router(config)#**interface** interface-number*

■ *Router(config-if)#**ip ospf priority** priority-value*

Exam Warning

Remember, if you do not want a specific interface on a router participating in the election, you must set its priority to 0.

FIGURE 7.2

How to Configure Loopback Addresses

```
London(config)#interface loopback 0
London(config-if)#ip address 192.168.31.11 255.255.255.255
London(config-router)#end

Ottawa(config)#interface loopback 0
Ottawa(config-if)#ip address 192.168.31.22 255.255.255.255
Ottawa(config-router)#end

Brasilia(config)#interface loopback 0
Brasilia(config-if)#ip address 192.168.31.33 255.255.255.255
Brasilia(config-router)#end
```

OSPF States

When *OSPF* adjacency is formed, a router goes through several state changes before it becomes fully adjacent with its neighbor. Those states are defined in the OSPF RFC 2328. We will review each of the states and their meaning. These can be helpful in troubleshooting OSPF as we will see later in this chapter.

Down

Down is the first OSPF neighbor state. It means that no information (hellos) has been received from this neighbor, but hello packets can still be sent to the neighbor in this state.

During the fully adjacent neighbor state, if a router doesn't receive hello packet from a neighbor within the RouterDeadInterval time or if the manually configured neighbor is being removed from the configuration, then the neighbor state changes from Full to Down. The default RouterDeadInterval is four times the Hello Interval.[5]

Attempt

The *attempt* state is only valid for manually configured neighbors in an NBMA environment. In the attempt state, the router sends unicast hello packets every poll interval to the neighbor, from which hellos have not been received within the dead interval.[5]

Init

The *Init* state specifies that the router has received a hello packet from its neighbor, but the ID of the receiving router was not included in the hello packet. When a router receives a hello packet from a neighbor, it should list the sender's RID in its hello packet as an acknowledgement that it received a valid hello packet.[5]

Full (Also Known as Adjacency)

In the *Full* state, routers are fully adjacent with each other. All the router and network LSAs are exchanged and the databases of the router are fully synchronized.

Full is the normal state for an OSPF router. If a router is stuck in another state, it is an indication that there are problems in forming adjacencies. The only exception to this is the two-way state, which is normal in a broadcast network. Routers achieve the Full state with their DR and BDR only. Neighbors always see each other as two-way.

At the end of the Full stage, the DR and BDR for broadcast and nonbroadcast multiaccess networks are elected.[5]

Two-Way

The *two-way* state designates that bidirectional communication has been established between two routers. Bidirectional means that each router has seen the other's hello packet. This state is attained when the router receiving the hello packet sees its own RID within the received hello packet's neighbor field.

At this state, a router decides whether to become adjacent with this neighbor. On broadcast media and nonbroadcast multiaccess networks, a router becomes full only with the DR and the BDR; it stays in the two-way state with all the other neighbors. On point-to-point and point-to-multipoint networks, a router becomes full with all connected routers.[5]

ExStart

Once the DR and BDR are elected, the actual process of exchanging link-state information can start between the routers and their DR and BDR. In this *ExStart* state, the routers and their DR and BDR establish a master/slave relationship and choose the initial sequence number for adjacency formation.

The router with the higher RID becomes the master and starts the exchange, and as such, is the only router that can increment the sequence number. Note that one would logically conclude that the DR/BDR with the highest RID will become the master during this process of master/slave relation. Remember that the master/slave election is on a per-neighbor basis.

Exam Warning

Remember that the DR/BDR election might be purely by virtue of a higher priority configured on the router instead of highest RID. Thus, it is possible that a DR plays the role of slave.

Exchange

In the *exchange* state, OSPF routers exchange database descriptor (DBD) packets. DBDs contain LSA headers only and describe the contents of the entire link-state database. Each DBD packet has a sequence number which can be incremented only by a master, which is explicitly acknowledged by the slave. Routers also send link-state request packets and link-state update packets (which contain the entire LSA) in this state. The contents of the DBD received are compared to the information contained in the routers link-state database to check if new or more current link-state information is available with the neighbor.[5]

Loading

In the *loading* state, the actual exchange of link-state information occurs. Based on the information provided by the DBDs, routers send link-state request packets. The neighbor then provides the requested link-state information in link-state update packets. During the adjacency, if a router receives an outdated or missing LSA, it requests that LSA by sending a link-state request packet. All link-state update packets are acknowledged.[5]

> **Exam Warning**
> Be aware that receiving a DBD packet from a neighbor in the init state will also a cause a transition to two-way state.

Authentication

By default, routers that utilize OSPF do not authenticate before passing routing exchanges across a network. The term *null* authentication is used to describe this authentication-less exchange. If you desire a more secure interaction between routers you have two choices for implementation: *plain text* authentication and *message digest* (MD5) authentication.

In this section, we will discuss the details of both of these authentication mechanisms and review the details of configuration for each of them. Something to keep in mind is that all areas in an OSPF autonomous system must physically connect to the backbone area, which is typically area 0. However, in cases where this physical connection is not possible, you can use a virtual link to connect to the backbone through a nonbackbone area. You can also use virtual links to connect two parts of a partitioned backbone through a nonbackbone area. It is possible and sometimes desired to enable OSPF authentication on these types of links.

> **Test Day Tip**
> Be sure to remember that any encryption adds overhead to your routers as they process traffic. If your organization doesn't have a need for the additional security, spend time to seriously evaluate these settings before implementing them.

Plain Text Authentication

The first and the simplest authentication type that we will discuss is plain text authentication, which is sometimes referred to as *simple password* authentication. Just as the name suggests plain text authentication sends the passwords through the network as clear text.

In OSPF, simple password authentication is enabled per area, and all of the routers in the area must have the key configured to participate in routing within the area. The most obvious issue with this authentication type is that since the passwords are clear text, they can be easily obtained by a packet sniffer.

Let's take a look at how this authentication type is configured. When configuring plain text authentication there are two commands that must be executed:

1. *ip ospf authentication-key <password>*

2. *area <#> authentication*

In Exercise 7.1, you will configure plain text authentication to secure a virtual link as well as configuring the *loopback* interface on your router.

EXERCISE 7.1   Configuration of the *Loopback* Interface and OSPF Authentication

In this exercise, we will perform two configuration steps. The first step will be to configure *loopback* interface 0 on your router. Follow these steps to enable and configure the *loopback* interface.

1. Log on to your router and enter the *global config* mode.

2. At the *(config)* prompt type **interface loopback 0** and press the **Enter** key on your keyboard.

3. At the *(config-if)* prompt type **ip address 192.168.1.2 255.255.255.255** and then press the **Enter** key.

4. At the *(config-router)* prompt type **end** and press the **Enter** key.

The second part of this exercise will have you enable OSPF plain text authentication. Follow these steps to enable and configure plain text authentication.

1. Log on to your router and enter *global config* mode.

2. At the *(config)* prompt type **interface Ethernet0** and press the **Enter** key on your keyboard.

3. To enable OSPF authentication on this interface type **ip ospf authentication-key Syngress**.

4. To configure area 0 for plain text password authentication type **router ospf 2** and then press the **Enter** key.

5. Next input the networks to run OSPF by typing **192.168.1.0 0.255.255.255 area 0** and then press the **Enter** key.

6. And finally type in **area 0 authentication** and then press the **Enter** key.

Figure 7.3 displays the interface configuration for Router 1.1.1.1 and Figure 7.4 displays the interface configuration for Router 3.3.3.3. The images show that Router 3.3.3.3 does not have an interface in area 0 but connects virtually to area 0. This configuration makes Router 3.3.3.3 a virtual ABR, so you would enable authentication for area 0 on Router 3.3.3.3.

MD5 Authentication

In addition to plain text passwords, there is another option available for securing your OSPF environment. In many corporations, where security is

Router 1.1.1.1

```
hostname r1.1.1.1

interface Loopback0
 ip address 1.1.1.1 255.0.0.0

interface Ethernet0
 ip address 4.0.0.1 255.0.0.0
 ip ospf authentication-key cisco

!--- This command configures the authentication key (password)
!--- on the interface as "cisco".


interface Serial0
 ip address 5.0.0.1 255.0.0.0
 clockrate 64000

!

 router ospf 2
 network 4.0.0.0 0.255.255.255 area 0
 network 5.0.0.0 0.255.255.255 area 1
 area 0 authentication

!--- This command enables plain authentication for area 0
!--- on the router.

area 1 virtual-link 3.3.3.3 authentication-key cisco

!--- This command creates the virtual link between Router
!--- 1.1.1.1 and Router 3.3.3.3 with plain text authentication
enabled.
```

FIGURE 7.3

Router 1.1.1.1

FIGURE 7.4

Router 3.3.3.3

```
                                    Router 3.3.3.3
hostname r3.3.3.3

interface Loopback0
 ip address 3.3.3.3 255.0.0.0

interface Ethernet0
 ip address 12.0.0.3 255.0.0.0

interface Serial0
 ip address 6.0.0.3 255.0.0.0

!


 router ospf 2
 network 12.0.0.0 0.255.255.255 area 2
 network 6.0.0.0 0.255.255.255 area 1
 area 0 authentication

!--- This command enables plain authentication for area 0
!--- on the router.

 area 1 virtual-link 1.1.1.1 authentication-key cisco

!--- This command creates the virtual link to area 0 via
!--- transit area 1 with plain text authentication enabled.
```

a concern, using a plain text password is out of the question, and in those cases, MD5 authentication can be used instead.

As an administrator, you must configure two variables for MD5: a key ID and a key (password). The MD5 algorithm computes a hash value from the contents of the OSPF packet and configured a key. This hash value is transmitted in the packet, along with the key ID and a nondecreasing sequence number. The nondecreasing sequence number assists in protecting against replay attacks.

The receiver, which knows the same password as the sender, gets the packet containing the hash and the key ID and using these items calculates its own hash value. By verifying that the two resulting hashes match, the receiver has successfully identified that the sender is trusted and accepts and transmits the packet.

Since additional processing must take place on both the side of the sender and the receiver, adding MD5 authentication does create additional overhead for the routers in the area. However, one additional benefit of using MD5 authentication over simple passwords is that if the administrator would like to change the password that an area is utilizing, a disruption of service does not occur with MD5. When the first router has its keys changed, the routers will transmit packets multiple times, each utilizing a different key until all of the routers are configured with the new key. With simple passwords, once you change the password value on the first router it is no longer able to communicate with the rest of the area until the key is updated on subsequent routers.

HEAD OF THE CLASS...

Security Is of the Utmost Importance!

MD5 produces a 128-bit message digest hash from the variable length input string provided. This digest hash is the value that is compared between routers to verify the identity. MD5 makes only a single pass over the input string to generate the resulting hash. One thing to keep in mind with MD5 is that, in recent years, it has been found that different strings can result in the same output hash. Also, there have been tools developed that can be used to hack MD5 hashes and discover the input string values. These tools can use methods like dictionary or brute force attacks to determine the password value that is in use.

What this means to you is that if security is of the utmost importance in your environment relying solely on router authentication to keep your environment secure is unwise. You need to be sure to take additional measures to protect your routing infrastructure. Good physical security cannot be overstated. If someone with mal intent is able to gain physical access to your routers, the next step of performing a malicious act becomes easier. Accessing the console to change configuration values or even rebooting your routers will result in disruption of network service, and performing actions such as these becomes possible once physical access has been obtained.

Another thing to remember is that when physical access is not possible, remote access may be. Configuring strong password values for remote connectivity mechanisms is critical to keep your routing environment free from unauthorized access.

Deploying a Network Intrusion Detection System (NIDS) on your network to alert you when hacking attempts are taking place may also be warranted. An NIDS can help determine when someone is performing actions that are intrusive, such as port scans or network sniffing and alerts you when these actions occur.

Let's take a look at how this authentication type is configured. When configuring MD5 authentication, there are two commands that must be executed, and a third command is required if you are enabling MD5 on a virtual link. The first command enables OSPF MD5 authentication on the interface. The second command configures a specific area for MD5 authentication under the "router ospf<process-id>" config. If you would like to configure MD5 authentication to secure a virtual link scenario you must also configure MD5 on the virtual link. The following are the three commands to execute:

1. *ip ospf message-digest-key <keyID> MD5 <key>*

2. *area <#> authentication message-digest*

3. *area <#> virtual-link <router> message-digest-key <key ID> MD5 <key>*

> **Exam Warning**
>
> The authentication key that the configuration uses defines the key (the password) that is inserted directly into the OSPF header. The key is inserted into the header when the Cisco IOS Software originates routing protocol packets. You can assign a separate password to each network on a per-interface basis. All neighboring routers on the same network must have the same password to exchange OSPF information.

Figure 7.5 and Figure 7.6 shown below depict two routers, Router 1.1.1.1 and Router 3.3.3.3. As seen in the configuration below, Router 3.3.3.3 has no interface in area 0 but connects virtually to area 0. This configuration makes Router 3.3.3.3 a virtual ABR, so you should enable authentication for area 0 on Router 3.3.3.3.

FIGURE 7.5

Router 1.1.1.1

Router 1.1.1.1

```
hostname r1.1.1.1

interface Loopback0
 ip address 1.1.1.1 255.0.0.0

interface Ethernet0
 ip address 4.0.0.1 255.0.0.0
 ip ospf message-digest-key 1 md5 cisco

!--- This command configures the MD5 authentication key
!--- on the interface as "cisco".

interface Serial0
 ip address 5.0.0.1 255.0.0.0
 clockrate 64000

!

 router ospf 2
 network 4.0.0.0 0.255.255.255 area 0
 network 5.0.0.0 0.255.255.255 area 1
 area 0 authentication message-digest

!--- This command enables MD5 authentication for area 0
!--- on the router.

 area 1 virtual-link 3.3.3.3 message-digest-key 1 md5 cisco

!--- This command creates the virtual link between Router
!--- 1.1.1.1 and Router 3.3.3.3 with MD5 authentication enabled.
```

```
                          Router 3.3.3.3
hostname r3.3.3.3

interface Loopback0
 ip address 3.3.3.3 255.0.0.0

interface Ethernet0
 ip address 12.0.0.3 255.0.0.0

interface Serial0
 ip address 6.0.0.3 255.0.0.0

!


 router ospf 2
 network 12.0.0.0 0.255.255.255 area 2
 network 6.0.0.0 0.255.255.255 area 1
area 0 authentication message-digest

!--- This command enables MD5 authentication for area 0
!--- on the router.

area 1 virtual-link 1.1.1.1 message-digest-key 1 md5 cisco

!--- This command creates the virtual link to area 0 via
!--- the transit area 1 with MD5 authentication enabled.
```

FIGURE 7.6

Router 3.3.3.3

VERIFYING OSPF CONFIGURATIONS

Before pressing the **GO** button on a new OSPF deployment, it is always a good idea to test out your planned configurations in an isolated test lab, whenever possible. This will allow you to deploy your configurations and verify that all is functioning as expected.

If you do not have a test-lab environment available, you must still do the best that you can to try and trial your proposed configurations. Many vendors have utilities available to assist you in confirming that your configuration is set up properly. One such tool, which is available from Cisco, is called the Output Interpreter Tool (OIT). It supports certain *show* commands. You can use the OIT to view an analysis of *show* command output. You must be a registered member of Cisco's Website to download the OIT. Consult with your hardware vendor to determine what is available for your brand of routing devices.

In the coming sections, we will explore commands that can be used to verify your OSPF configurations.

Utilizing the *Show* Command

The show commands can help you verify that your router environment is configured properly by allowing you to display the configuration settings a multitude of different ways. The *show* command enables you to monitor OSPF operation on your system. Using the show commands with different strings provides you with information on your router's OSPF state and configuration.

The task you are performing with this monitoring command is that you are requesting information from the router, which is then displayed on the screen. The resulting outputs of each request may vary depending on the additional string input that you provide, but you should understand that this command cannot be used for configuration. It is only for viewing information.

The show commands provide information on the actual state and configuration of your system. In the forthcoming sections, we will discuss in detail and display examples on how the *show* command can help you determine the current configuration of your routers, which can then help you identify and get ahead of issues that may arise in your environment.

Test Day Tip

The *show* command has multiple options that can be used to pull configuration data from your routers. For the exam it is a good idea to focus on getting familiar with the commands in general, as well as getting some experience with a good number of the strings.

Examples of the Show Command

In this section, we will be discussing the *show* command in greater detail. We will take a look at some of the options that are available, which allow us to view our configuration information. By specifying protocol-specific commands, we are able to focus on our OSPF configuration. The *show* command can provide information on the following OSPF items:

- Routing processes
- Border routers
- Database
- Interfaces
- Neighbors
- Virtual links
- Internal statistics
- Multiprotocol label switching (MPLS) tunnels and opaque LSAs

You can use the output filtering feature of the *show* command to include or exclude lines of output based on a text string you specify. Each of the next sections will focus on a particular string of the *show* command.

Using the *Show* Command for Plain Text Authentication

This section will utilize the *show ip ospf virtual-links* command first and then follow up with the *show ip route* command. We will walk through each output identifying points of interest, including the configuration of plain text authentication. In Figure 7.7, you can see the output of the *show ip ospf virtual-links* command with commentary included.

Notice that the output shown in Figure 7.7 shows that OSPF hellos are suppressed. This means that once the virtual link is up, no hellos are

FIGURE 7.7

Sample Output from the show ip ospf virtual-links *Command*

```
r3.3.3.3# show ip ospf virtual-links

Virtual Link OSPF_VL0 to router 1.1.1.1 is up

!--- The status of the virtual link displays.

   Run as demand circuit
   DoNotAge LSA allowed

!--- This specifies that OSPF runs as a demand circuit over
virtual links,
!--- and so link-state advertisements (LSAs) are not
refreshed (not aged out).

   Transit area 1, via interface Serial0, Cost of using 128
   Transmit Delay is 1 sec, State POINT_TO_POINT,
   Timer intervals configured, Hello 10, Dead 40, Wait 40,
Retransmit 5
     Hello due in 00:00:01
     Adjacency State FULL (Hello suppressed)

!--- The status of the neighbor adjacency displays.

     Index 1/2, retransmission queue length 0, number of
retransmission 1
     First 0x0(0)/0x0(0) Next 0x0(0)/0x0(0)
     Last retransmission scan length is 1, maximum is 1
     Last retransmission scan time is 0 msec, maximum is 0
msec
   Simple password authentication enabled

!--- The type of authentication that is enabled displays.
!--- The authentication type is simple password.
```

exchanged. OSPF suppresses the hellos because it considers virtual links to be demand circuits. Normally, OSPF sends hellos every 10 seconds and refreshes its LSAs every 30 minutes. However, even this amount of traffic is undesirable on demand circuits. The use of OSPF demand circuit options suppresses hello and LSA-refresh functions. As a result, any changes that you make to the OSPF authentication do not take effect until you clear the OSPF process with the *clear ip ospf process* command. An example is a change of the authentication type on the routers.

OK, now examine Figure 7.8 to see the results of executing the *show ip route* command with commentary.

Using the *Show* Command for MD5 Authentication

This section will display the use of the *show ip ospf virtual-links* command first and then follow up with the *show ip route* command. We will walk through each output identifying points of interest, this time the key is to keep an eye out for the MD5 Authentication configuration. Figure 7.9 displays the *show ip ospf virtual-links* output and commentary.

Now let's take a look at the **show ip route** output when MD5 authentication is enabled. Figure 7.10 displays the results of running the *show ip route* command when MD5 is enabled.

Reviewing the *show ip ospf* Command

The *show ip ospf* command can be utilized to display general information about OSPF routing processes. The following items can be viewed by running *show ip ospf*:

```
r3.3.3.3# show ip route

Codes: C - connected, S - static, I - IGRP, R - RIP, M - mobile, B - BGP
       D - EIGRP, EX - EIGRP external, O - OSPF, IA - OSPF inter area
       N1 - OSPF NSSA external type 1, N2 - OSPF NSSA external type 2
       E1 - OSPF external type 1, E2 - OSPF external type 2, E - EGP
       i - IS-IS, L1 - IS-IS level-1, L2 - IS-IS level-2, ia - IS-IS inter ar
       * - candidate default, U - per-user static route, o - ODR
       P - periodic downloaded static route
Gateway of last resort is not set
C 3.0.0.0/8 is directly connected, Loopback0
O 4.0.0.0/8 [110/138] via 6.0.0.2, 00:31:08, Serial0
O 5.0.0.0/8 [110/128] via 6.0.0.2, 22:55:44, Serial0
C 6.0.0.0/8 is directly connected, Serial0
C 12.0.0.0/8 is directly connected, Ethernet0
```

FIGURE 7.8   *Sample Output from the* show ip route *Command*

```
r3.3.3.3# show ip ospf virtual-links

Virtual Link OSPF_VL1 to router 1.1.1.1 is up

!--- The status of the virtual link displays.

  Run as demand circuit
  DoNotAge LSA allowed

!--- This specifies that OSPF runs as a demand circuit over
virtual links,
!--- and so LSAs are not refreshed (not aged out).

  Transit area 1, via interface Serial0, Cost of using 128
  Transmit Delay is 1 sec, State POINT_TO_POINT,
  Timer intervals configured, Hello 10, Dead 40, Wait 40,
Retransmit 5
    Hello due in 00:00:01
    Adjacency State FULL (Hello suppressed)

!--- The status of the neighbor adjacency displays.

    Index 1/2, retransmission queue length 0, number of
retransmission 0
    First 0x0(0)/0x0(0) Next 0x0(0)/0x0(0)
    Last retransmission scan length is 0, maximum is 0
    Last retransmission scan time is 0 msec, maximum is 0
msec
  Message digest authentication enabled

!--- The type of authentication that is enabled displays.
!--- The authentication type is MD5.
```

FIGURE 7.9

Sample Output from the show ip ospf virtual-links Command

```
r3.3.3.3# show ip route

Codes: C - connected, S - static, I - IGRP, R - RIP, M - mobile, B - BGP
       D - EIGRP, EX - EIGRP external, O - OSPF, IA - OSPF inter area
       N1 - OSPF NSSA external type 1, N2 - OSPF NSSA external type 2
       E1 - OSPF external type 1, E2 - OSPF external type 2, E - EGP
       i - IS-IS, L1 - IS-IS level-1, L2 - IS-IS level-2, ia - IS-IS inter ar
       * - candidate default, U - per-user static route, o - ODR
       P - periodic downloaded static route
Gateway of last resort is not set
C 3.0.0.0/8 is directly connected, Loopback0
O 4.0.0.0/8 [110/138] via 6.0.0.2, 00:02:41, Serial0
O 5.0.0.0/8 [110/128] via 6.0.0.2, 00:02:51, Serial0
C 6.0.0.0/8 is directly connected, Serial0
C 12.0.0.0/8 is directly connected, Ethernet0
```

FIGURE 7.10   *Sample Output from the show ip route Command*

- **Routing process** This specifies the process ID.

- **Router** This specifies the router types: internal, area border, or ASBRs.

- **OSPF Statistics** This specifies the packets sent and received.

- **TOS type** This specifies the number of types of service supported.

- **SPF timers** This specifies the timers configured on the router.

- **Maximum path splits** This specifies the maximum equal-cost paths supported.

- **Areas** This specifies the areas configured and their parameters.

- **Number of areas** This specifies the number of areas in the router.

In Exercise 7.2, we will utilize the *show* command to view OSPF configuration information.

EXERCISE 7.2   Utilizing the *Show* Command

In this exercise, we will utilize the *show* command to display router configuration information.

1. Log on to your router and type **enable**.

2. At the # prompt type ***show ip ospf*** and press the **Enter** key on your keyboard.

3. Review the results shown

4. Next type ***show ip ospf database*** and press the **Enter** key.

5. Review the results shown.

Figure 7.11 displays sample output from the *show ip ospf* command with imbedded commentary describing the sections of the output.

Reviewing the *show ip ospf border-routers* Command
You can utilize *show ip ospf border-routers* command to display a list of OSPF border routers and their information, which includes the following:

- **Destination** This specifies the destination's RID.

- **Next Hop** This specifies the next hop toward the destination.

```
r3.3.3.3# show ip ospf virtual-links

Virtual Link OSPF_VL0 to router 1.1.1.1 is up

!--- The status of the virtual link displays.

  Run as demand circuit
  DoNotAge LSA allowed

!--- This specifies that OSPF runs as a demand circuit over
virtual links,
!--- and so link-state advertisements (LSAs) are not refreshed
(not aged out).

  Transit area 1, via interface Serial0, Cost of using 128
  Transmit Delay is 1 sec, State POINT_TO_POINT,
  Timer intervals configured, Hello 10, Dead 40, Wait 40,
Retransmit 5
    Hello due in 00:00:01
    Adjacency State FULL (Hello suppressed)

!--- The status of the neighbor adjacency displays.

    Index 1/2, retransmission queue length 0, number of
retransmission 1
    First 0x0(0)/0x0(0) Next 0x0(0)/0x0(0)
    Last retransmission scan length is 1, maximum is 1
    Last retransmission scan time is 0 msec, maximum is 0 msec
  Simple password authentication enabled

!--- The type of authentication that is enabled displays.
!--- The authentication type is simple password.
```

FIGURE 7.11

Sample Output from the
show ip ospf virtual-links
Command

- **Router Type** This specifies the router type of the destination: either an ABR or ASBR or both.

- **Route Type** This specifies the type of this route: either an intraarea or interarea route.

- **Area** This specifies the area ID of the area that this route is learned from.

Figure 7.12 displays sample output from the *show ip ospf border-routers* command with imbedded commentary.

Reviewing the *show ip ospf database* Command

There are times when you might need to display the OSPF database for a particular area to ensure the proper configuration. Utilize the *show ip ospf*

FIGURE 7.12
Sample Output from the show ip ospf border-routers Command

```
host1#show ip ospf border-routers
Destination NEXT HOP    Interface      Router Type   Route Type Area
5.5.0.250    5.5.6.250   fastethernet0  ABR/ASBR      INTRA      0.0.0.0
5.5.0 250    4.4.4.250   fastethernet0  ABR/ASBR      INTRA      0.0.0.1
6.6.6.250    4.4.4.13    fastethernet0  ABR           INTRA      0.0.0.1
```

database command to display either the full OSPF database or a summary of it.

- Link ID

- for router links, this is set to the router's OSPF RID

- for network links, this is set to the IP interface address of the network's DR

- for type 3 summary LSAs, this is set to an IP network number

- for type 4 summary LSAs, this is set to an ASBR's RID

- for type 5 externals, this is set to an IP network number

- Adv Router—advertising router's ID

- Age—link-state age

- Seq#—link-state sequence number (detects old or duplicate LSAs)

- Checksum—Fletcher checksum of the complete contents of the LSA

Figure 7.13 depicts sample output from the *show ip ospf database* command with imbedded commentary.

Reviewing the *show ip ospf database opaque-area* Command

Use this command to display lists of information about the terminal equipment (TE) opaque LSAs. The TE router address LSA describes a stable IP address on the originating router that can be used for TE purposes, such as setting up TE LSPs to this address. The TE link LSA describes TE information about an interface on the originating router such as,

- **LS age** This specifies the age of LSA.

- **Options** This specifies the optional capabilities supported by the described portion of the routing domain.

- **LS Type** This specifies the type of LSA; opaque area TE router address or opaque area TE link LSA.

- **Link State ID** This specifies the link-state ID of the opaque LSA.

- **Advertising Router** This specifies the RID of the router that originated the LSA.

- **LS Seq Number** This specifies the link-state sequence number to identify duplicate or old LSIDs.

- **Checksum** This specifies the checksum of the complete contents of the LSA.

- **Length** This specifies the length of the LSA in bytes.

- **TE router ID** This specifies the TE RID of the originating router.

- **Link type** This specifies the link type as point-to-point or multiaccess.

- **Link ID** For point-to-point interfaces, this is the RID of the router at the remote end; for multiaccess interfaces, this is the address of the DR.

- **Local Address** This specifies the IP address of the local interface for the link.

- **Remote Address** This specifies the IP address of the remote (neighbor's) interface for the link.

- **TE Metric** This specifies the link metric for traffic engineering purposes; can be different from the standard OSPF link.

- **Max BW** This specifies the maximum bandwidth that can be used on this link in this direction.

- **Max Reservable BW** This specifies the maximum bandwidth that can be reserved on this link; can exceed the maximum bandwidth in the event of oversubscription.

- **Max Unreserved BW** This specifies the amount of bandwidth not yet reserved at each

```
host1#show ip ospf database
OSPF Database

  Router Link States (Area 0.0.0.0)

  Link ID       ADV Router    Age   Seq#        Checksum
5.1.101.1     5.1.101.1     932   0x80000069  0x102f
192.168.1.13 192.168.1.13 1763  0x80000099  0xaa4e
192.168.1.10 192.168.1.10 285   0x80000087  0xada6
192.168.1.11 192.168.1.11 401   0x80000087  0xaba5
192.168.24.6 192.168.24.6 622   0x800005bf  0x6087
Network Link States (Area 0.0.0.0)

  Link ID       ADV Router    Age  Seq#        Checksum
56.56.56.220 5.6.6.1        499 0x80000069  0x26a0
192.168.1.12 192.168.254.6 622 0x8000009e 0xebc2

  Summary Link States (Area 0.0.0.0)

  Link ID ADV Router    Age Seq#        Checksum
4.4.4.0  5.5.0.250     497 0x8000005a 0x2ca6
4.4.4.0   192.168.1.13 528 0x80000059 0x 45d

  AS Summary Link States (Area 0.0.0.0)

  Link ID ADV Router    Age Seq#        Checksum
5.5.0.250 192.168.1.13 491 0x80000002 0xe9d4

  AS External Link States

Link ID ADV Router Age Seq#        Checksum
8.8.8.0 5.5.0.250  502 0x8000005f 0x2d67

  Router Link States (Area 0.0.0.1)

Link ID       ADV Router    Age Seq#        Checksum
5.5.0.250     5.5.0.250     498 0x80000067 0xdec1
192.168.1.13 192.168.1.13 505 0x800000a5 0x3b32
Network Link States (Area 0.0.0.1)

Link ID       ADV Router    Age Seq#        Checksum
4.4.4.13      192.168.1.13  505 0x80000001 0x410b
5.1.0.0       192.168.1.13  940 0x80000059 0x82c4
5.2.0.0       5.5.0.250     495 0x80000001 0x51bf
5.2.0.0       192.168.1.13  932 0x80000059 0x76cf
5.3.0.0       5.5.0.250     495 0x80000001 0x45ca
5.3.0.0       192.168.1.13  932 0x80000059 0x6ada
56.56.56.0    5.5.0.250     495 0x80000062 0xc469

AS Summary Link States (Area 0.0.0.1)
Link ID   ADV Router Age Seq#        Checksum
5.5.0.250 5.5.0.250  496 0x80000001  0x51c0
```

FIGURE 7.13   *Sample Output from the show ip ospf database Command*

of the eight priority levels; each value is less than or equal to the maximum reservable bandwidth.

- **Color** This specifies the bitmask that identifies the administrative group membership for this link; a link that is a member of more than one group will have multiple bits set.

```
host1#show ip ospf database opaque-area


        Opaque-area Link States (Area 0.0.0.0)



  LS age: 914
  Options:    (TOS-capable, No Type7-LSA,
ExternalRoutingCapability, No
  Multicast Capability, No External Attributes    LSA)
  LS Type: Opaque-Area (TE Router Address)
  Link State ID: 1.0.0.0(Instance)
  Advertising Router: 100.1.1.1
  LS Seq Number: 0x80000003
  Checksum: 0xd293
  Length: 28
  TE Router-ID: 100.1.1.1



  LS age: 919
  Options:    (TOS-capable, No Type7-LSA,
ExternalRoutingCapability, No
  Multicast Capability, No External Attributes    LSA)
  LS Type: Opaque-Area (TE Links)
  Link State ID: 1.0.0.1(Instance)
  Advertising Router: 100.1.1.1
  LS Seq Number: 0x80000003
  Checksum: 0xf66e
  Length: 124
  Link Type: P2P
  Link ID: 1744896257
Local Address 14.1.1.2
Remote Address 14.1.1.1
TE Metric 0
Max BW 1000 kb/sec (125000 Bps)
Max Reservable BW 1000 kb/sec (125000 Bps)
Max Unreserved BW : pri 0 1000 kb/sec (125000 Bps)
Max Unreserved BW : pri 1 1000 kb/sec (125000 Bps)
Max Unreserved BW : pri 2 1000 kb/sec (125000 Bps)
Max Unreserved BW : pri 3 1000 kb/sec (125000 Bps)
Max Unreserved BW : pri 4 1000 kb/sec (125000 Bps)
Max Unreserved BW : pri 5 1000 kb/sec (125000 Bps)
Max Unreserved BW : pri 6 1000 kb/sec (125000 Bps)
Max Unreserved BW : pri 7 1000 kb/sec (125000 Bps)
Color 0
```

FIGURE 7.14 *Sample Output from the show* ip ospf border-routers *Command*

Figure 7.14 displays sample output from the *show ip ospf database opaque-area* command.

Reviewing the *show ip ospf interface* Command

There are times when you need to verify that the configuration on your interfaces is correct. You can use the *show ip ospf interface* command to display a list of OSPF interfaces and their properties, which includes the following:

- **Interface value (FastEthernet)** This specifies the status of the physical link and the operational status of the protocol.

- **Internet Address** This specifies the interface IP address.

- **Area** This specifies the area identifier: IP address.

- **Network type** This specifies the type of network: broadcast, NBMA, point-to-point, or point-to-multipoint.

- **Authentication type** This specifies the authentication type: none, simple, or MD5.

- **Interface cost** This specifies the metric for OSPF transmission.

- **Transmit Delay** This specifies the time between transmissions from the specified interface.

- **Interface State** This specifies the current state of the specified interface.

- **Priority** This specifies the router's priority on the specified interface.

- **Designated Router** This specifies the designated RID and respective interface IP address.

- **Backup Designated Router** This specifies the designated RID and respective interface IP address of the backup router.

- **Interface timer intervals** This specifies the configuration of timer intervals: Hello, Dead, Wait, and Retransmit.

- **Neighbors** This specifies the number of neighbors and their state; adjacent neighbors.

Figure 7.15 displays sample output from the *show ip ospf interface* command. You can see each of the above items depicted.

Reviewing the *show ip ospf internal-statistics* Command

To display internal OSPF statistics, such as allocation failures for different OSPF components you can utilize the *show ip ospf internal-statistics* command. Here are some of the items you can view with this command:

- **LSA bytes allocated** This indicates the number of bytes allocated for LSAs.

- **Router LSA bytes allocated** This indicates the number of bytes allocated for router LSAs.

- **Summary bytes allocated** This indicates the number of bytes allocated for summary LSAs.

- **Neighbor RTX bytes allocated** This indicates the number of bytes allocated for neighbor retransmissions.

```
host1#show ip ospf interface
FastEthernet0 is up, OSPF line protocol is up
OSPF interface configuration:
  Internet Address 192.168.1.250, Area 0.0.0.0
  Network type BROADCAST, No authentication
  Cost: 1
  Transmit Delay is 1 sec, Interface State DROTHER, Priority 1
  Designated Router (Interface address) 192.168.1.107
  Backup Designated Router (Interface address) 192.168.1.214
  Timer intervals configured, Hello 10, Dead 40, Wait 120, Retransmit 5
  Neighbor Count is 2, Adjacent neighbor count is 2
  Adjacent with neighbor 192.168.1.107 (Designated Router)
  Adjacent with neighbor 192.168.254.7 (Backup Designated Router)
```

FIGURE 7.15   *Sample Output from the show ip ospf interface Command*

- **Timers bytes allocated** This indicates the number of bytes allocated for OSPF timers.

- **OSPF total bytes free** This indicates the total number of bytes free.

- **OSPF heap total bytes allocated** This indicates the total number of bytes allocated from the OSPF heap.

- **Neighbor allocation failures** This indicates the number of neighbor allocation failures.

- **LSA allocation failures** This indicates the number of LSA allocation failures.

- **LSA HDR allocation failures** This indicates the number of LSA header allocation failures.

- **DB Request allocation failures** This indicates the number of database request allocation failures.

- **RTX allocation failures** This indicates the number of neighbor retransmission allocation failures.

- **LS Ack allocation failures** This indicates the number of LSA acknowledgement packet allocation failures.

- **DD Pkt allocation failures** This indicates the number of database description packet allocation failures.

- **OSPF interface allocation failures** This indicates the number of interface allocation failures.

- **OSPF general packet allocation failures** This indicates the number of general packet allocation failures.

Figure 7.16 contains sample output from the *show ip ospf internal-statistics* command.

Reviewing the *show ip ospf neighbors* Command

If you need to be able to determine which routers are seen as neighbors, you can utilize the **show ip-ospf neighbors** command. The command is run on a per-interface basis. Here are some of the items you can view:

- **Neighbor ID** This indicates the neighbor's RID.

- **Pri** This indicates the router priority of neighbor.

- **State** This indicates the OSPF neighbor's state.

- **DR** Designated router.

```
host1#show ip ospf internal-statistics
 Routing Process OSPF 1 with Router ID 5.72.3.1
 Internal OSPF Statistics, bytes allocated/free:
       LSA bytes allocated:    216
       Router LSA bytes allocated:    936
       Summary bytes allocated:    0
       Neighbor RTX bytes allocated:    0
       Timers bytes allocated:    352
       Ospf total bytes free:    824368
       Ospf heap total bytes allocated:    1048576
 Internal OSPF Statistics, allocation failures:
       Neighbor allocation failures:    0
       LSA allocation failures:    0
       LSA HDR allocation failures:    0
       DB Request allocation failures:    0
       RTX allocation failures:    0
       LS Ack allocation failures:    0
       DD pkt allocation failures:    0
       OSPF interface allocation failures:    0
       OSPF general packet allocation failures:    0
```

FIGURE 7.16 *Sample Output from the show* ip ospf internal-statistics *Command*

```
host1#show ip ospf neighbors
   Neighbor ID  Pri  State           DeadTime   Address    Interface
   10.0.8.1     1    TWO-WAY/DR Other 00:00:39  10.0.76.1  fastEthernet11/0
   10.0.71.1    1    FULL/DR          00:00:42  10.0.76.2  fastEthernet11/0
   10.0.96.1    1    FULL/BDR         00:00:28  10.0.76.4  fastEthernet11/0
```

FIGURE 7.17 *Sample Output from the show* ip ospf neighbors *Command*

- **BDR** Backup designated router.

- **DR Other** This indicates the neighbor to a designated router or a BDR.

- **Dead Time** This indicates the interval since last hello packet from neighbor.

- **Address** This indicates the IP address of the neighbor's interface.

- **Interface** This indicates the name of the specified interface and its port number; for example, *FastEthernet0*.

Figure 7.17 shows the neighbor results generated from running the **show ip ospf neighbors** command.

Reviewing the *show ip ospf remote-neighbor interface* command

Just as viewing OSPF neighbor information can be helpful, viewing which interfaces on a router are associated with remote neighbors can also be useful. To view the statistics of an interface pertaining to a remote neighbor, utilize the *show ip ospf remote-neighbor interface* command.

Figure 7.18 is a sample output from the *show ip ospf remote-neighbor interface* command.

Reviewing the *show ip ospf spf-log* Command

Remember that as the network administrator, it is your job to ensure that your OSPF deployment is deployed in an efficient manner. Some hallmarks of efficiency are shorter routing tables, fast recalculations of routing traffic, and short delays in router traffic.

To judge how efficiently your routers are performing in their day-to-day tasks, you can use the *show up ospf spf-log* command. It will show you how often and why the router has run a full SPF calculation. This command can be very useful in viewing the historical activity of your network that performs the SPF calculations. The following are some of the items you will be able to view:

- **Intra SPF log** This specifies a log for SPF calculations run to compute intraarea LSAs.

- **Inter SPF log** This specifies a log for SPF calculations run to compute interarea LSAs.

```
host1#show ip ospf remote-neighbor interface
OSPF remote-neighbor 221.221.221.221 interface
configuration:
 Update-source loopback0
 Remote-neighbor reachable: yes
 Area 0.0.0.0
 Network type POINT-TO-POINT, No authentication
 Cost: 1
 Transmit Delay is 1 sec, Interface State POINT-TO-POINT,
Priority 1
 No designated router on this network
 No backup designated router on this network
 Timer intervals configured, Hello 10, Dead 40, Wait 40,
Retransmit 5
 Neighbor Count is 1, Adjacent neighbor count is 1
  Adjacent with neighbor 221.221.221.221
```

FIGURE 7.18 *Sample Output from the show ip ospf border-routers Command*

```
host1#show ip ospf spf-log

Intra SPF log
When      Duration     LSA Router Id      Triggers
00:04:42 0.000         23.23.23.3         Protocol Off
00:04:38 0.000         23.23.23.3         LSA Add
00:04:34 0.000         12.12.12.2         LSA Add
00:04:30 0.010         23.23.23.3         LSA Update
00:03:51 0.000         23.23.23.3         Protocol Off
00:03:47 0.000         23.23.23.3         LSA Add
00:03:43 0.000         12.12.12.2         LSA Add
00:03:39 0.000         23.23.23.3         LSA Update

Inter SPF log
When      Duration     LSA Router Id      Triggers
00:04:46 0.010         23.23.23.3         Protocol Off
00:04:42 0.000         23.23.23.3         LSA Add
00:04:38 0.000         12.12.12.2         LSA Add
00:04:34 0.000         23.23.23.3         LSA Update
00:03:55 0.000         23.23.23.3         Protocol Off
00:03:51 0.000         23.23.23.3         LSA Add
00:03:47 0.000         12.12.12.2         LSA Add
00:03:43 0.000         23.23.23.3         LSA Update

External SPF log
When      Duration     LSA Router Id      Triggers
00:04:47 0.000         23.23.23.3         Protocol Off
00:04:43 0.000         23.23.23.3         LSA Add
00:04:39 0.000         12.12.12.2         LSA Add
00:04:35 0.010         23.23.23.3         LSA Update
00:03:56 0.000         23.23.23.3         Protocol Off
00:03:52 0.000         23.23.23.3         LSA Add
00:03:48 0.000         12.12.12.2         LSA Add
00:03:44 0.000         23.23.23.3         LSA Update
```

FIGURE 7.19

Sample Output from the show ip ospf spf-log Command

- **External SPF log** This specifies a log for SPF calculations run to compute routes outside the OSPF routing domain.

- **When** This specifies the amount of time since a full SPF calculation took place given in hours:minutes:seconds; the previous 20 calculations are logged.

- **Duration** This specifies the number of milliseconds to complete this SPF run; the elapsed time is in actual clock time, not CPU time.

- **LSA Router ID** This specifies that whenever a full SPF calculation is triggered by a new LSA, the RID is stored in the router.

- **Triggers** This specifies the list of reasons that triggered a full SPF calculation.

Figure 7.19 depicts a sample output from the *show ip ospf spf-log* command.

```
host1#show ip ospf virtual-links
Virtual link to router 192.168.1.13 in state POINT-TO-POINT
Transmit Delay is 1 sec
Timer intervals configured, Hello 10 sec, Dead 40 sec,
Retransmit 5 sec
```

FIGURE 7.20   *Sample Output from the show* ip ospf virtual-linksh *Command*

Reviewing the *show ip ospf virtual-linksh* Command

If you have virtual links in place in your OSPF environment, you can utilize this command to display the parameters and the current state of OSPF virtual links. This command is excellent for understanding what state your routers are in and how it sees its state of the virtual link to be. The following are the items you can view:

- **Virtual link to router** This identifies the OSPF neighbor and the current state of the virtual link.

- **Transmit Delay** This specifies the time between transmissions from the specified interface.

- **Timer intervals** This specifies the timer intervals configured for the link: Hello, Dead, and Retransmit.

Figure 7.20 displays the output of the *show ip ospf virtual-linksh* command.

TROUBLESHOOTING OSPF

Every administrator's nightmare is the routers that won't router and the resulting errors messages received by users because their data cannot move from point A to point B on the network. It always gets the phone ringing and forces you to buckle down and determine what the issue is. Once you figure out what the problem is, typically, correcting the problem is the easy part. Discovering the problem can take ages, if you are not looking in the right places.

In this section, we will cover some debugging commands that you can employ to troubleshoot OSPF. Ideally you will be able to stop running around with your hands in the air screaming, and instead settle in to utilize these commands, which can assist you in getting to the root of the issue that much quicker.

Debug Commands

Debug commands are the tools you want to turn to when things are behaving strangely in your environment. They provide information on problems with the network or the system, and with a few well-placed commands allow you to unravel a mystery configuration that may be resulting in problems on your network.

The debug commands provide information on the following OSPF items:

- Adjacencies

- Designated router

- General events

- LSAs

- Neighbors

- Packets received

- Packets sent

- Route events

- SPF events

In the next sections, we will discuss various debug commands, which will allow you to review various OSPF configuration settings.

Reviewing the debug ip ospf *Command*

The *debug ip ospf* command is used to display information on selected OSPF events. This command has many keywords that allow you to specify a variety of OSPF events. You can set the level of severity for the events that you want displayed: 0 to 7. You also have the ability to set the verbosity of the messages that you want displayed. There are three possible levels: low, medium, and high.

The following is a sample command string:

```
debug ip ospf adj
```

EXERCISE 7.3   Utilizing the *DEBUG* Command

In this exercise, we will utilize the **debug** command to display router information.

1. Log on to your router and type **enable**.

2. At the # prompt type **debug ip ospf** and press the **Enter** key on your keyboard.

3. Review the results shown.

4. Next type **undebug ip ospf** and press the **Enter** key.

Reviewing the ospf log-adjacency-changes Command

There are times when more logging is useful, particularly when you are trying to troubleshoot an issue. You can use the *ospf log-adjacency-changes* command to enable the logging of changes in the state of an OSPF neighbor.

The following is a sample command string:

```
ospf log-adjacency-changes
```

Use the no version to disable the logging of changes in the state of an OSPF neighbor.

Reviewing the undebug ip ospf Command

Debug mode is useful for troubleshooting, but once you have sorted out the issue and are ready to let things run normally again is it a good idea to toggle debugging off again. To toggle debugging off for a specific event utilize the *undebug ip ospf* command. This command will cancel the display of information on a selected event, and the same OSPF variables can be designated as in the *debug ip ospf* command.

The following is a sample command string:

```
undebug ip ospf adj
```

SUMMARY OF EXAM OBJECTIVES

OSPF is a diverse and scalable routing protocol that can bring many benefits to your environment. It is able to detect the UP/DOWN state of links in your environment and update Link-State tables as appropriate. OSPF allows state-specific routing to take place, which leads to an environment where routing delays occur on a much less frequent basis.

OSPF utilizes areas to divide the network. There is always at least one area in any OSPF topology, and additional areas can be created as required. Areas allow you to reduce the size of the routing tables that each router holds. By reducing the size of the routing tables, you promote efficiency during traffic routing.

Each router in an OSPF environment takes on a role which dictates the functions it will perform. The simplest role is an Internal Router. This router type has all of its interfaces connected to a single area and it only holds the routing table for the area it is connected to even if there are other areas in the network. If a router is configured to have its interfaces connected in multiple areas, then it is known as an ABR. ABRs hold the routing table information for each area they are connected to and can pass traffic between areas. An ASBR is connected to your OSPF network and to an external environment, which may or may not be OSPF. The ASBR can import routing information from non-OSPF networks and distribute the same in OSPF network. It can also take routing information from your OSPF networks and propagate those to the external environment.

OSPF routers use the Hello protocol to identify neighboring routers. Once neighboring routers have been identified, the routers will check for matching criteria to develop adjacency. Adjacent routers share routing table database information. Each area in an OSPF network will have an elected DR and a BDR. These roles exist to function as a center point from which routing table updates flood the network. You can impact the results of elections by manually setting priority values. A priority of 0 prevents participation in the election, otherwise the highest value wins the election.

OSPF routers can be configured to utilize authentication if desired. There are two choices available: plain text authentication and MD5 authentication. To view a router's configuration you can utilize the *show* command, which has multiple string variables that allow you to view different settings within the configuration. For troubleshooting, you can utilize the *debug* command.

EXAM OBJECTIVES FAST TRACK

The OSPF Protocol

- OSPF is a link-state routing protocol.

- OSPF is an open standard, which means that any vendor can utilize it.

- OSPF is a scalable protocol, which keeps its routing tables efficient by segmenting the network into areas.

- OSPF routers are grouped into areas. Link-state tables are specific to an area and ABRs bridge areas by being connected into multiple areas and routing information between areas.

- Routers seek neighbors to develop adjacencies that lead to routing table exchanges.

Configuring OSPF

- A router must have an RID in order for OSPF to function properly. The RID is derived from a *loopback* interface as first preference, but will use other active interfaces if the loopback has not been configured. The highest interface IP address becomes the Designated Router.

- Routers use the Hello protocol to discover their neighbors.

- Neighboring routers develop adjacencies, which lead to routing table exchanges.

- DRs and BDRs collect LSA updates from the other routers and flood the network with updates to the routing tables.
- OSPF allows the configuration of authentication between routers. There are two possible authentication choices: plain text authentication and MD5 authentication.

Verifying OSPF Configurations

- You can use the *show* command to display your current router configurations.
- The status of the routing table database can be viewed by utilizing the *show* command.
- Displaying internal statistics can assist in identifying historical behavior of your environment, which in turn can assist you in identifying problematic areas and addressing them proactively.
- *Show ip ospf interface* will allow you to display your interfaces and their configuration to verify if they are correct.

Troubleshooting OSPF

- Troubleshooting OSPF can be performed with the help of the *debug* command.
- Additional logging can be enabled through the *debug* command.
- In order for routers on the same segment to communicate when there is authentication configured, all the routers must be configured to use the same protocol and the same password and key values.
- Different manufacturers oftentimes offer tools for download to assist in troubleshooting.
- You can set the severity level of debug logging for the events you want displayed from 0 to 7.

EXAM OBJECTIVES FREQUENTLY ASKED QUESTIONS

Q: My network is running RIP now, why should I consider OSPF?

A: OSPF is a much more scalable protocol than RIP, so for larger, more complex environments, it can be a good choice. It is however more complex than RIP and needs advanced configuration to run well.

Q: What is a DR?

A: A DR is a role that is assigned through election. Once elected to DR all other routers send LSA updates to the DR, which in turn floods the network with the changes.

Q: Why would I need multiple areas?

A: Remember that there is a single area by default in any OSPF environment. Additional areas would be required in larger environments to keep the routing tables efficient. Segmenting the network allows each router to be responsible for less, therefore improving processing speed.

Q: What is an OSPF neighbor?

A: An OSPF router identifies its neighbors by comparing its own configuration values to the values of other routers through the Hello protocol. Neighbors are used to determine adjacency, which leads to the exchange of routing table information. So, essentially, an OSPF neighbor is a routing with matching configurations.

Q: If a DR fails does the BDR take over for it?

A: Yes, BDRs will take over the DR on a segment if the DR fails.

Q: I have a mixture of routers in my environment, can I still use OSPF?

A: The probability is that yes, you can still use OSPF. OSPF is an open standard and any manufacturer can choose to incorporate it into their devices. It is a good idea to verify with the manufacturer first, but the majority of router manufacturers in existence today incorporate RIP into their devices.

Q: What does it mean when a router is in the Full state with another router?

A: The two routers have full adjacency and are swapping routing table database information. Typically, routers only achieve the Full state with their DR and BDR.

Q: Why would I use the *show* command?

A: You can use the *show* command to display the current configuration of your router. It allows you to verify that the configuration is accurate.

Q: Can I utilize the *show* command to change router configuration information?

A: No, the *show* command is purely for viewing the configuration information on your router, and cannot be used to change anything.

Q: What happens when a link goes down in OSPF?

A: Since OSPF is a link-state routing protocol, the down link will be detected and all the routers in the segment will update their routing tables so as to avoid the down link.

Q: Why would I want to modify the log settings on my router to collect additional information about neighboring routers. Also, how can I accomplish this?

A: By having a historical view of the status of a router's neighbors, it assists you with identifying possible reoccurring problem areas in the network that may need to be addressed. Utilize the *debug* command to enable logging for neighboring router states.

Q: What is an RID and how is it configured?

A: The RID uniquely identifies each router and it is not configured. The router selects its RID from its interfaces. A *loopback* interface is the first choice, but if the *loopback* interface has not been configured, the router will evaluate its active interfaces to determine its RID. The highest IP value is used.

SELF TEST

1. As the network administrator of a mid-sized company you have the opportunity to redesign your network from the ground up as part of a datacenter relocation project. One of the things you are currently trying to decide is which protocol you should implement on your routers. You have a mixture of Cisco and Juniper routers in your environment, and you want to be sure that whatever you select will work well on both. Which of the following facts about your environment will lead you to select OSPF as your protocol of choice?

   A. You believe you will require a maximum of six hops in your organization.

   B. You prefer simplicity in configuration, your staff does not have a lot of time, or an advance skill set in configuring routers.

   C. Your environment has many slow and unstable connections.

   D. Requirement for VLSM support

2. In your environment, you notice that traffic from Miami that is destined for New York is routing from Miami through your routers in Kansas City. The traffic is then leaving Kansas City and heading through Illinois to finally end up in New York. You have connectivity on the network from Miami to Charlotte and then straight on to New York from Charlotte, and you are wondering why the routers are selecting the seemingly longer route. Which of the following Cisco OSPF formulas can be used to calculate an interface's cost to assist you in understanding the chosen route?

A. 100,000,000/Bandwidth in bits per second

B. 100,000,000/Bandwidth in kilobits per second

C. 100,000,000/Bandwidth in megabits per second

D. There is no formula for OSPF cost; it depends solely on the interface type.

3. Which of the following is used to calculate the OSPF path cost?

A. Number of Hops **C.** Bandwidth and Clicks

B. Bandwidth only **D.** Bandwidth, Reliability, and Load

4. Your environment is configured with four routers and multiple segments. The first router is the DR for a broadcast segment, and the second router is the BDR. The first router reboots unexpectedly. While the first router is rebooting, the second router becomes the DR. What describes the first router's role when it comes back online?

A. The first router will start an election when it comes back online to become the DR.

B. The first router will come back online and become the DR, the second router will be downgraded back to BDR status.

C. The first router will come back online as a DROTHER.

D. The first router will come back online as a BDR.

5. Which of the following *must* match between potential OSPF neighbors for an adjacency to form? Select all that apply.

A. The Area Number

B. Authentication Method

C. Interface Name

D. Stub Flag Setting

E. Process ID

F. Administrative Password

G. RID

6. You have four routers on your network. One of your routers detects that a neighbor is down. What will this router do with this link-state change information?

   A. It will send an LSA update to 224.0.0.5.

   B. It will send an LSA update to 224.0.0.12.

   C. DROTHERs do not send any kind of link change notifications.

   D. It will send an LSA update to 224.0.0.6.

7. An OSPF environment can consist of 1 or more areas. When multiple areas are present, which of the following statements is true?

   A. Internal routers are responsible for routing information redistribution.

   B. ABRs have all interfaces in the same area.

   C. ASBR is responsible for redistribution of routing information in an OSPF network.

   D. Multiple areas cannot be configured in OSPF environments.

8. You have not configured a *loopback* interface on your router. What criteria will be used to determine the RID?

   A. The highest IP address from the active interfaces only

   B. You must configure the loopback address to have an RID.

   C. The lowest IP address from the active interfaces only

   D. The highest IP address on all interfaces

9. You have noticed that support tickets from users reporting network issues in a certain area of your OSPF environment seem be increasing, and oftentimes they come in as groups of users at the same time. You are trying to determine what exactly is taking place on your routers to determine whether or not there is a network-based problem. What could you do to assist with tracking down this issue?

   A. Begin recording neighbor changes with the *ospf log-adjacency-changes* command.

   B. Utilize the *show* command to view the traffic partners and their statistics. Run the *show log-all-neighbors-state* command.

   C. Deploy a packet sniffer and analyze the traffic to determine when the network goes down.

   D. Utilize *show down* to determine which router is having difficulty.

10. How frequently do routers utilizing OSPF send out LSA updates? Select all that apply.

    A. When a route changes

    B. Every 10 seconds

    C. Once a day

    D. Every 30 minutes

11. You recently added a new router to your environment and have configured it and put it on your test network. You cannot seem to get traffic from other routers to successfully send packets through the new router. You suspect the wrong authentication type has been enabled. Which of the following commands will allow you to view the configured authentication type?

    A. *show ip ospf*

    B. *show ip ospf encryption*

    C. *show ip ospf stats*

    D. *show ospf*

12. An election is taking place in your router environment. There are four routers on the segment. How many DRs and BDRs will you end up with, when the election has completed?

    A. 4 DRs and 0 BDRs. The BDRs are only elected after a failure to the DR site.

    B. 2 DRs and 2 BDRs. Each role has a duplicate in case of failure.

    C. 1 DR and 1 BDR. One of each role is elected.

    D. DRs and BDRs are not selected during elections. They are assigned based on interface connectivity.

13. You would like to create a stub area in an attempt to reduce traffic in a problematic portion of your network. Traffic flow is often slow and router performance is poor. Which in the following are characteristics of a stub area? Choose all that apply.

    A. Have a default gateway configured

    B. Hold a copy of every area's routing table information

    C. Have a single entry and exit point

    D. Only contain external routes

14. By dividing the network into areas, the routing table that each router has to be aware of can be reduced in size resulting in greater efficiency. What additional process is performed by the routers to further reduce the size of the routing tables?

    A. Path truncation

    B. Route summarization

    C. Efficiency processing

    D. Route reduction

15. You currently have three routers and you have to add a new router onto your network to expand to a new building. You would like to set up the router to be sure that it is in working order. After configuring all of the interfaces and getting it plugged up to the network, you configure the OSPF protocol with the plain text password in use on the network. How long will it take for the new router to begin receiving its first hello packets?

    A. From 1 to 2 hours depending on the current network load

    B. A maximum of 10 seconds

    C. You must first reboot the router after configuring OSPF before any hello packets will be received.

    D. A maximum of 100 seconds

SELF TEST QUICK ANSWER KEY

1. C		**9.** A	
2. A		**10.** A, and D	
3. B		**11.** A	
4. C		**12.** C	
5. A, B, and D		**13.** A, and C	
6. D		**14.** B	
7. C		**15.** B	
8. A			

REFERENCES

1. *Wikimedia Foundation, Inc*. Nonbroadcast multiple-access network. <http://en.wikipedia.org/wiki/Nonbroadcast_Multiple_Access_Network>; Accessed 15.04.09.

2. *TechTarget*. NBMA. <http://searchnetworking.techtarget.com/sDefinition/ 0,,sid7_gci838049,00.html>; Accessed 15.04.09.

3. *Cisco any*. OSPF router types. <http://www.ciscoany.com/2008/12/16/ ospf-router-types/>; Accessed 15.04.09.

4. *Certification Zone*. Prerequisites to OSPF Startup. <http://www .certificationzone.com/cisco/newsletter/SL/nla_12-13-04_ospf.html>; Accessed 15.04.09.

5. *eTutorials.org*. Understanding OSPF Fund?ment?ls. <http://etutorials.org/Misc/ccnp +bsci+exam+certification+guide/Part+III+OSPF/Chapter+5.+Understanding+S imple+Single-Area+OSPF/Foundation+Topics/>; Accessed 15.04.09.

Implementing the EIGRP

INTRODUCTION

Enhanced Interior Gateway Routing Protocol (EIGRP) is a proprietary, advanced distance vector routing protocol that an individual with a Cisco Certified Network Associate (CCNA) certification needs to be able to implement in a network infrastructure. Unlike Routing Information Protocol v2 (RIPv2) and Open Shortest Path First (OSPF), EIGRP will only be used on networks with Cisco equipment. Although EIGRP requires Cisco equipment, it does not require the Transmission Control Protocol/Internet Protocol (TCP/IP) to be used. This is good news, as the number of revisions to IP networks in the coming years will not necessitate a corresponding revision of networks using EIGRP. EIGRP can also be used on networks running protocols other than TCP/IP, such as AppleTalk or Internetwork Packet Exchange/Sequenced Packet Exchange (IPX/SPX).

CCNAs should know the commands used in conjunction with configuring, verifying, and debugging EIGRP to successfully implement the EIGRP on a Cisco network. Individuals with their CCNA should also know how to secure routers using EIGRP with Message Digest 5 (MD5) authentication. The simulation materials provided with this book will help individuals get sufficient practice implementing EIGRP prior to taking the CCNA examination. In summary, knowing how to effectively implement EIGRP is an important skill for any CCNA working in the industry.

THE EIGRP

EIGRP is an advanced distance-vector routing protocol that addresses many of the limitations of other routing protocols, including those of its predecessor, Interior Gateway Routing Protocol (IGRP). It is an interior gateway protocol that can be scaled to support many different network sizes and topologies. It is a very diverse, sophisticated protocol that uses minimal network resources and can provide rapid, efficient convergence when changes occur in the network. It is sometimes referred to as a hybrid routing protocol because it was designed to incorporate features from both distance-vector and link-state routing protocols.

As an enhanced, later generation of IGRP, EIGRP uses the same underlying distance-vector functionality as IGRP uses. It sends traditional distance-vector information to other routers about destination networks and how to reach them. EIGRP, however, goes well beyond the capabilities of IGRP by providing improved operating efficiency, as well as supporting network technologies such as classless IP and variable-length subnet masks (VLSMs). EIGRP distinguishes itself by improving on existing distance-vector characteristics and adding link-state functionality. Although EIGRP doesn't send link-state advertisements (LSAs) like the popular link-state routing protocol OSPF, it performs link-state tasks such as synchronizing routing tables when a router starts up and exchanging only incremental updates about network changes after startup. EIGRP also provides support for multiple routed protocols, including IP version 4 and IP version 6, with something called *Protocol-Dependent Modules* (PDMs). Note: PDMs also provide support for IPX and AppleTalk, but they aren't included on the CCNA exam.

Advantages

There are many advantages to using EIGRP in our networks. Here are some of EIGRP's features and benefits:

- Uses minimal network resources very efficiently

- Sends incremental routing updates rather than the entire routing table

- Provides for rapid convergence

- Includes subnet mask information in its routing updates

- Supports loop-free classless interdomain routing (CIDR)

- Supports VLSMs

- Supports effective route summarization

- Implements more efficient route discovery and maintenance

- Provides efficient discovery of neighbors

- Suitable for all sizes of networks, including very large networks

- Allows for configuration of multiple autonomous systems (ASes) on one router

- Provides load-balancing capabilities across equal-cost and unequal-cost routes

- Allows for communication between discontiguous networks

- Communicates using Reliable Transport Protocol (RTP)

- Uses Diffusing Update Algorithm (DUAL) to choose the best path

EIGRP is very efficient in how it uses network resources. Unlike IGRP and RIP, EIGRP doesn't send periodic routing updates. EIGRP sends information only when something changes, only about the change, and only to neighboring EIGRP routers that need to know about the change. This means that on a stable network, the only traffic transmitted by EIGRP is a small hello packet that is sent periodically to check on the status of other EIGRP routers and interfaces. For this reason, EIGRP's impact on the network is minimal.

Another powerful feature of EIGRP is the capability for rapid convergence. Because EIGRP can maintain information on up to six alternate routes to a destination network at the same time, recovering from a network change is very quick and, in some cases, nearly instantaneous. EIGRP obtains information from neighboring routers and builds a topology table to hold the information. In the case of a change in the network, EIGRP can quickly obtain an alternate route from the table.

EIGRP also has the capability to be scaled for use on networks of almost any size. By default, EIGRP supports up to 100 hops, but it can be configured to support as many as 255 hops. EIGRP's capability to send information only about routing changes in its update packets, and its capability for rapid convergence, makes it a suitable and efficient protocol for use in very large networks. It can also support discontiguous subnets, expanding network design flexibility even further.

The capability that EIGRP has to include subnet mask information in its routing advertisements makes it possible to use EIGRP for classless routing, VLSMs, and route summarization. This allows organizations to conserve address space by using subnet masks that more closely fit the needs of their networks. IGRP's advertisements include classful address information, limiting its usefulness on many of our networks today. EIGRP gives us the flexibility to take advantage of some of the powerful technologies that have been developed since IGRP's inception.

EIGRP, like IGRP, is configured using the concept of ASes. *ASes* are contiguous groups of routers that exchange routing information with each other, using the same routing protocol. Only routers with the same AS will exchange routing information with each other. By separating routers in very large networks into multiple ASes, network topologies can be simplified, routing tables can be shortened, and the speed and efficiency of routing processes such as convergence can be optimized. To communicate between different ASes, the routers can be configured to redistribute the routing information.

Exam Warning

When troubleshooting EIGRP for the exam, you may get questions describing a situation where you've added a new router to the network and installed EIGRP, but no routing updates are being exchanged between the new router and the existing routers. The first thing you want to check is the AS number. Make sure that the AS is configured the same for EIGRP on all the routers. Remember, the routers won't exchange routing updates if they aren't in the same AS. To correct the problem, don't forget to remove the incorrect AS by executing the *no router eigrp <AS>* command in *Global Configuration* mode before you configure the correct AS with the *router eigrp <AS>* command.

The four key components that combine to give EIGRP its advanced capabilities are

1. Neighbor discovery/recovery

2. RTP

3. DUAL finite-state machine

4. Modular architecture for routed protocols, using PDMs

EIGRP routers dynamically learn about other routers on their directly attached networks using neighbor discovery. When a neighbor router is no longer functioning on the network, routers discover the neighbor is no longer accessible through the use of hello packets. If a router receives hello packets from a neighbor, the neighbor is reachable and the two can exchange information. If a router sends hello packets to a neighbor and doesn't receive anything back after a few times, the neighbor is considered to be dead. This is a very efficient method of periodically checking on neighbor routers while using minimal network resources.

All routes advertised by all neighbors are tracked by the DUAL finite-state machine. DUAL chooses loop-free, efficient paths based on distance information and adds routes to the routing table. The distance information used to determine the best paths are called *metrics*. DUAL can also determine the next best path if something changes. It can look at alternate routes already existing in the table, and if alternate paths are not readily available, it has the capability to look for other paths.

Most routing protocols require a separate implementation for each network layer protocol that is to be routed. For example, there are two different versions of OSPF for IP version 4 (OSPFv4) and IP version 6 (OSPFv6). PDMs make it possible for EIGRP to support multiple network layer protocols without the need for different versions or implementations. The PDMs use separate tables to hold the routing information for each protocol. If you are running both IPv4 and IPv6, for example, EIGRP will maintain a separate set of tables for each version of IP.

RTP

EIGRP uses a Cisco-proprietary protocol called *RTP* to manage the communications between routers. Cisco designed RTP to deliver different types of EIGRP packets quickly and reliably using multicasts and unicasts. Not all types of packets require reliable delivery and some don't expect replies. Packets have reliability information built into their headers. If the packet header shows that the packet requires reliable delivery, RTP is responsible for keeping track of which routers receive or don't receive the transmitted data.

Using the Class D multicast address of 224.0.0.10, traffic is sent to the other EIGRP routers on the network. For each multicast that is sent, the router keeps a list of neighbors who have replied. RTP is designed to quickly resend packets that haven't been acknowledged to keep convergence times short. If no replies are received from a neighbor, the sending router uses unicasts to resend, and keep resending, the same data to that neighbor. If there is still no reply after the unicasts have sent 16 times, the neighbor is declared dead. This process is sometimes referred to as *reliable multicast*.

Routers keep track of the information that has been sent by including sequence numbers in the packet headers. The sequence numbers make it possible for the routers to detect out-of-sequence traffic, as well as old and redundant information. Because EIGRP is a quiet protocol, only sending information about routing changes when the changes occur, it is necessary for EIGRP to have a method for detecting information that could corrupt the routing database. The sequence numbers make that possible.

Disadvantages

EIGRP clearly has a number of features that make it an efficient, a sophisticated, and a powerful routing protocol. So, why doesn't everyone use EIGRP? Well, there is one thing about EIGRP that can be a serious limitation. The disadvantage to EIGRP is that it is a Cisco-proprietary protocol. If your network is a mixed environment with Cisco routers and routers from other vendors, only the Cisco routers will be able to communicate using EIGRP. The non-Cisco routers won't be able to use, or understand, EIGRP.

CONFIGURING EIGRP

EIGRP is configured from two different modes. Router configuration mode is used for specifying the networks to run EIGRP and configuring global parameters. Other factors, such as summaries and metrics, are configured in interface configuration mode. To enable EIGRP on our router, we use the *router eigrp <AS>* command in *Global Configuration* mode. Then, in router configuration mode, we execute *network* commands for each of the networks the router is connected to that are to be a part of the EIGRP network. See Figure 8.1 for more information on ASes and networks in EIGRP networks.

Figure 8.1 shows the layout of our company. The company is housed in three separate buildings, each with its own local network and router. In addition to the three networks in the three buildings, we have two additional subnets that connect the headquarters (HQ) router to the other two locations. The router at the headquarters office is called *HQ* and has three interfaces. Ethernet 2 connects to the internal network in the HQ building. Ethernet 0 and Ethernet 1 provide connections to the other two buildings. The routers called company1

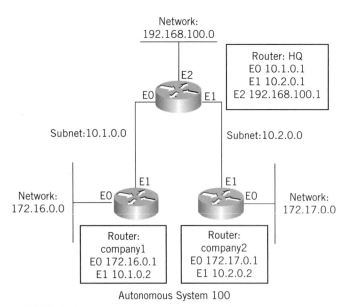

FIGURE 8.1 *Autonomous Systems and Networks in EIGRP*

and company2 each have a connection from Ethernet 1 to the HQ router and on Ethernet 0, a connection to the local network in their respective buildings.

Without any routing configured on the routers, each router knows about the two networks it is directly connected to (three networks for the HQ router). The routers determine what their directly connected networks are based on the IP addresses and subnet masks configured on the interfaces. We are going to configure EIGRP on each router to make it possible for everyone to see everyone else. Our EIGRP configuration is going to give the routers information about all of their connected networks they need to communicate to the other routers. The entire company is using AS 100 because we want all routers to communicate with all other routers. We will include the AS number in our configurations.

The steps for configuring EIGRP are

1. Enter *Global Configuration* mode.

2. Enable EIGRP and define the AS.

3. Execute *network* statements in router configuration mode; for all networks, the router is connected to that are to be included in EIGRP.

4. Repeat Steps 1 through 3 for each of the other two routers.

See Exercise 8.1 for more information on enabling EIGRP and configuring ASes and networks.

EXERCISE 8.1   Enabling EIGRP

In this exercise, we're going to configure EIGRP for the network shown in Figure 8.1.

First, we'll configure the HQ router:

1. Enter *Global Configuration* mode:

   HQ# **configure terminal**

2. Enable EIGRP and define AS 100:

   HQ(config)# **router eigrp 100**

3. Execute *network* statements for all networks the router is connected to that are to be included in the EIGRP configuration:

   HQ(config-router)# **network 10.0.0.0**
   HQ(config-router)# **network 192.168.100.0**

Now, we'll configure EIGRP on the company1 router:

1. Enter *Global Configuration* mode:

company1# **configure terminal**

2. Enable EIGRP and define AS 100:

company1(config)# **router eigrp 100**

3. Execute *network* statements for all networks the router is connected to that are to be included in the EIGRP configuration:

company1(config-router)# **network 10.0.0.0**
company1(config-router)# **network 172.16.0.0**

And, finally, we'll configure EIGRP on the company2 router:

1. Enter *Global Configuration* mode:

company2# **configure terminal**

2. Enable EIGRP and define AS 100:

company2(config)# **router eigrp 100**

3. Execute *network* statements for all networks the router is connected to that are to be included in the EIGRP configuration:

company2(config-router)# **network 10.0.0.0**
company2(config-router)# **network 172.17.0.0**

All three of our routers are now configured for EIGRP AS 100. They will exchange routing information with each other for the networks defined in the *network* commands. This will make it possible for everyone to see and access all the networks. Notice that we used classful addresses (all subnet and host bits off) for our *network* statements. EIGRP by default is a classful routing protocol but can be configured to support classless addressing.

To remove EIGRP from a router, we execute the *no router eigrp <AS>* command in *Global Configuration* mode. For example:

HQ(config)# **no router eigrp 100**

This will remove the entire EIGRP configuration from the router.

Once we've configured EIGRP on our network, how do we know if it's working? We can look at the routing tables on each router to see the EIGRP route information. The *show ip route* command displays the IP routing table. We'll look at the routing table on the HQ router:

```
HQ# show ip route
10.0.0.0/16 is subnetted, 2 subnets
C    10.1.0.0 is directly connected, Ethernet0
C    10.2.0.0 is directly connected, Ethernet1
D    172.16.0.0 [90/2795456] via 10.1.0.2, 00:05:15, Ethernet0
D    172.17.0.0 [90/2795456] via 10.2.0.2, 00:05:15, Ethernet1
C    192.168.100.0 is directly connected, Ethernet2
```

In the routing table, we see three networks directly connected to the HQ router, indicated by the C at the beginning of each line. There are also two routes with Ds at the beginning of the line. The *D* indicates that the information about those routes came from EIGRP or, more specifically, from the DUAL, which is why those routes are identified with Ds. To the right of the network numbers for each of the EIGRP routes, we see two numbers in square brackets, separated by a slash, [90/2795456]. The first number, 90, is the default administrative distance for EIGRP internal routes, and the second number is the metric that EIGRP calculated and assigned to the route. The metric is the distance information calculated and used by EIGRP to make routing decisions. An *administrative distance* is a number assigned to a type of route that helps to prioritize which type of route will be used to reach a destination network when more than one type of route exists.

The administrative distance is essentially a reliability factor. It is a number that is assigned to a type of route to identify how reliable that type of route is considered to be. The lower the distance, the more reliable the type of route is considered to be, and the more priority that route is given when there are multiple types of routes that could be used to the same destination network. For example, if your router is running both RIP and EIGRP and the same networks have been configured for both routing protocols, the routes that you will see in the routing table will be EIGRP routes because EIGRP has a lower distance (90) than RIP (120).

To look at the EIGRP configurations that we created in Exercise 8.1, we would use the *show ip protocols* command on each router. Here is the information displayed for the HQ router:

```
HQ# show ip protocols
Routing Protocol is "eigrp 100"
    Outgoing update filter list for all interfaces is not set
    Incoming update filter list for all interfaces is not set
    Default networks flagged in outgoing updates
```

```
Default networks accepted from incoming updates
EIGRP metric weight K1=1, K2=0, K3=1, K4=0, K5=0
EIGRP maximum hop count 100
EIGRP maximum metric variance 1
Redistributing: eigrp 100
Automatic network summarization is in effect
Maximum path: 4
Routing for Networks:
   10.0.0.0
   192.168.100.0
Routing information sources:
   Gateway Distance Last Update
   10.1.0.2 90 01:28:35
   10.2.0.2 90 01:28:35
Distance: internal 90 external 170
```

Next, we'll look at the *show ip protocols* information for company1:

```
company1# show ip protocols
Routing Protocol is "eigrp 100"
   Outgoing update filter list for all interfaces is not set
   Incoming update filter list for all interfaces is not set
   Default networks flagged in outgoing updates
   Default networks accepted from incoming updates
   EIGRP metric weight K1=1, K2=0, K3=1, K4=0, K5=0
   EIGRP maximum hop count 100
   EIGRP maximum metric variance 1
   Redistributing: eigrp 100
   Automatic network summarization is in effect
   Maximum path: 4
   Routing for Networks:
      10.0.0.0
      172.16.0.0
   Routing information sources:
   Gateway Distance Last Update
   10.1.0.1 90 02:02:13
Distance: internal 90 external 170
```

And, finally, let's check the EIGRP configuration on company2:

```
company2# show ip protocols
Routing Protocol is "eigrp 100"
   Outgoing update filter list for all interfaces is not set
   Incoming update filter list for all interfaces is not set
   Default networks flagged in outgoing updates
   Default networks accepted from incoming updates
```

```
EIGRP metric weight K1=1, K2=0, K3=1, K4=0, K5=0
EIGRP maximum hop count 100
EIGRP maximum metric variance 1
Redistributing: eigrp 100
Automatic network summarization is in effect
Maximum path: 4
Routing for Networks:
    10.0.0.0
    172.17.0.0
Routing information sources:
Gateway Distance Last Update
10.2.0.1 90 01:12:50
Distance: internal 90 external 170
```

For all three of our routers, the output from the *show ip protocols* command shows us the active routing protocol is EIGRP and the AS that's configured is 100. The *show ip protocols* command also displays information telling us the networks that each router has configured to participate in EIGRP and the gateways (addresses on other routers) that the router has received updates from. The last line, called *Distance*, refers to the default administrative distance that applies when EIGRP obtains its routing information from other routers in the same AS (internal 90) or from routers outside the AS (external 170).

The administrative distance of 170 for external routes refers to routing updates received by EIGRP from manual or automatic redistribution. Basically, traffic initiated within the same AS is internal and traffic initiated outside of the EIGRP AS is external. External routes can be initiated from another EIGRP AS or from another routing protocol, such as RIP. *Redistribution* is a method of translating from one protocol type to another. For example, if you configure EIGRP to redistribute RIP on a router, that router can translate between routers running only EIGRP and routers running only RIP. This makes it possible to use EIGRP even if you have some routers that won't support EIGRP.

EIGRP will do automatic redistribution for IGRP. If you have routers running IGRP and you install EIGRP, with the same AS, on those routers, EIGRP can automatically redistribute those routes and communicate with IGRP. This makes it possible to transition from IGRP to EIGRP more gradually. As we've been talking about, EIGRP is based on IGRP but has many more features and benefits than IGRP, so, if you are running IGRP on your network, it will probably be well worthwhile to upgrade to EIGRP.

In fact, with the latest versions of the Cisco Internetwork Operating System (IOS), IGRP has been eliminated. Because of the greatly advanced features of EIGRP, IGRP has been deprecated, meaning Cisco considers it obsolete. However, running IGRP and EIGRP with EIGRP's automatic redistribution is a temporary solution. Remember, information originated outside of the EIGRP AS, including information received from IGRP, is considered external. For that reason, routing information received from IGRP will have an administrative distance of 170, which isn't very good. You will still want to get all your routers transitioned to EIGRP as soon as possible.

Test Day Tip

There are times when you may not want EIGRP to advertise route information out all interfaces; for example, if you have a connection to the Internet. You control this by configuring passive interfaces. A passive interface in EIGRP doesn't send or receive information. This is done with the *passive-interface <interface>* command in router configuration mode. To stop interface Serial 0/0 from sending or receiving EIGRP information for AS 100, we would execute these commands:

Router1(config)# **router eigrp 100**
Router1(config-router)# **passive-interface serial 0/0**

Route Summarization in EIGRP

Another line we're going to look at from the *show ip protocol* information is the line that says *Automatic network summarization is in effect.* By default, EIGRP provides auto-summarization at the classful network boundaries. That means if you have multiple subnets from one network connected to your router, EIGRP will summarize all the subnets into one route for the full, classful network and send routing updates for the entire, summarized network rather than sending updates for each individual subnet. With this scenario all the traffic for any of the subnets will be sent via the same route. See Figure 8.2 for an example of auto-summarization.

In Figure 8.2, Router1 is connected to three subnets on the 172.16.0.0 Class B network. By auto-summarizing to the classful boundary, Router1 will advertise the entire 172.16.0.0 classful network instead of the three subnets individually. All traffic going to any of the subnets will travel across the one link between Router2 and Router1, and by summarizing the three subnets into the one classful

FIGURE 8.2 *Auto-Summarization in EIGRP*

network, which will be one entry in the routing table instead of three, the routing tables are kept shorter and more efficient. An EIGRP summary route has a default administrative distance of 5, which gives it a high priority among potential route types.

To make EIGRP classless, automatic route summarization has to be disabled. Earlier versions of the Cisco IOS enabled auto-summarization by default. In more recent versions, it is disabled by default. To disable auto-summarization, you use the *no auto-summary* command in router configuration mode:

Router1(config-router)# **no auto-summary**

This will prevent EIGRP from summarizing routes to the classful boundaries. Then, to get the benefits of route summarization, after you disable auto-summarization, you can configure manual route summaries based on your network needs.

> **Test Day Tip**
>
> The ability to calculate route summaries is an important skill for a CCNA. To shorten routing tables and optimize routing performance on networks, route summarization is a valuable tool and is used on many networks. Summary routes are used in most other routing protocols as well as in EIGRP, and calculating summary route addresses and masks is handled the same. The method to configure summary routes, however, varies.

Manual route summarization is done on a per interface basis and can be done on any router(s) on your network. Because you can summarize to any bit in the address, this gives you a lot of flexibility and control over the size of your routing tables. See Figure 8.3 for more information on route summarization.

Without route summarization configured, Router1 would advertise each of its individual-connected networks separately. With auto-summarization enabled, the networks would still be advertised separately because the router auto-summarizes to the classful boundaries which would be the full Class C networks. The networks are already at their classful boundaries. However, by configuring manual summarization on Router1's FastEthernet 0/0 (F0/0) interface, we can tell Router1 to advertise all four of its connected networks in one advertisement.

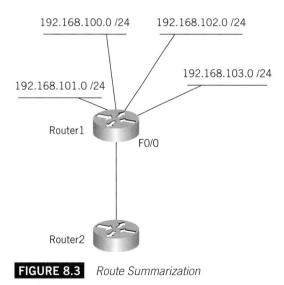

FIGURE 8.3 *Route Summarization*

HEAD OF THE CLASS....

Calculating a Summary Route Address and Mask

To calculate the address and mask for a summary route, we're going to have to do some binary math. I'm sure you remember that each number in an IP address is the decimal representation of 8 bits. A bit that is turned off has a value of 0, and a bit that is turned on has one of the values in Table 8.1, depending on its position in the 8 bits. The first (leftmost) bit in any octet, if it's turned on, has a value of 128. The second bit in any octet, if it's turned on, has a value of 64, and so on. To convert the decimal number to binary, you find the combination of bits whose total value equals the decimal number you are converting from and you turn those bits on. When converting from decimal to binary, always work from left to right, using the highest-value bits that you can.

We're going to see how it works by calculating the summary route to be advertised by Router1 (refer to the network diagrammed in Figure 8.3). Let's start by converting Router1's four network addresses to binary. We'll start by converting the first octet, 192, to binary. Working from left to right, we're going to turn on the first bit, with a value of 128, because 128 will go into 192.

192
1 _ _ _ _ _ _ _

We've now accounted for 128 of our 192, so we still need 64 more to get the total of 192 (192 – 128). Still working from left to right, the second bit has a value of 64. We'll turn on the bit with the value of 64.

192
1 1 _ _ _ _ _ _

If we add together the values of the 2 bits we've turned on, 128 + 64, we get a total of 192, so we have all the on bits we need. We'll turn the remaining bits in the octet off, and we'll have the binary equivalent of 192.

192
1 1 0 0 0 0 0 0

Then, we need to do the same thing for each of the other three octets. When the first network address is converted to binary, we get the following:

168
1 0 1 0 1 0 0 0

100
0 1 1 0 0 1 0 0

0
0 0 0 0 0 0 0 0

Here are the four network addresses in dotted decimal, followed by the binary for each address.

192.	168.	100.	0
11000000.	10101000.	01100100.	00000000

192.	168.	101.	0
11000000.	10101000.	01100101.	00000000

192.	168.	102.	0
11000000.	10101000.	01100110.	00000000

192.	168.	103.	0
11000000.	10101000.	01100111.	00000000

Now that we have our addresses in binary, we need to figure out the summary address and mask. We're going to look at all the binary addresses and compare the bits. What we're looking for is the common bits for all the addresses we're summarizing. It's easy to see that the first 16 bits are the same for all four networks because the decimal numbers are the same (192.168). Now, let's look at the third octet for all the addresses.

11000000. 10101000. **011001I00**. 00000000
11000000. 10101000. **011001I01**. 00000000
11000000. 10101000. **011001I10**. 00000000
11000000. 10101000. **011001I11**. 00000000

In the third octet, we can see that the first 6 bits are the same for all four addresses. There is a total of 22 bits that are the same for all four network addresses.

Table 8.1	Decimal Value of On Bits							
Position of Bit	1st	2nd	3rd	4th	5th	6th	7th	8th
Decimal Value	128	64	32	16	8	4	2	1

If we convert those 22 bits back to decimal, we'll have our summary address. To convert from binary to decimal, we're going to add the values of all the on bits in each octet. Here are the 22 common bits that we're working with:

11000000. 10101000. 011001

In the first octet, we'll add together the values of the first 2 bits which give us 192 (128 + 64). In the second octet, we'll add the first bit (128), the third bit (32), and the fifth bit (8) to get 168. And, in the third octet, we have the second bit (64), the third bit (32), and the sixth bit (4) which adds up to 100. The remaining 10 bits in the address, which don't match for our networks, will be turned off, so they will all have a value of zero. The entire summary address in binary is

11000000. 10101000. 011001**00. 00000000**

Notice that the last 2 bits in the third octet and all 8 bits in the fourth octet are off because they aren't part of the 22 common bits that all our networks share. When we add together the values of all the on bits, we get the following dotted decimal address for our summary address:

192.168.100.0

Now, we need a mask to go with our summary address. To figure out the mask, we're going use the same leftmost 22 bits that we used to get our summary address. For the mask, we'll turn all those 22 bits on:

11111111. 11111111. 11111100. 00000000

So, the first 22 bits are turned on in the mask. Converting this binary address to decimal gives us:

11111111. 11111111. 11111100. 00000000
255. 255. 252. 0

Our summary address and mask are

192.168.100.0
255.255.252.0

This can also be written as follows:

192.168.100.0/22

The/22 is the total number of bits turned on in the subnet mask. This slash (/) number is sometimes referred to as a CIDR number.

The steps to configure a summary route are

1. Enter *Global Configuration* mode.

2. Enter router configuration mode.

3. Disable auto-summarization if it is on.

4. Enter interface configuration mode.

5. Execute the *ip summary-address eigrp* <*summary-address*> <*mask*> command.

EXERCISE 8.2 Configuring a Summary Route

Now, we're ready to configure our summary route on Router1 in Figure 8.3.

1. Enter *Global Configuration* mode:

   Router1# **configure terminal**

2. Enter router configuration mode:

   Router1(config)# **router eigrp 100**

3. Disable auto-summarization if it is on:

Router1(config-router)# **no auto-summary**

4. Enter interface configuration mode:

Router1(config-router)# **interface fastethernet0/0**

5. Execute the *ip summary-address eigrp <AS> <summary-address> <mask>* command:

Router1(config-if)# **ip summary-address eigrp 100 192.168.100.0 255.255.252.0**

With this configuration complete, Router1 will use one entry in its routing table for all four networks.

In this example, we used four separate networks and summarized them into one larger network. This could also be done with multiple subnets within a network and even with subnets of different sizes connected to one router. Different-sized subnets on one router are configured using VLSMs.

CONFIGURING AND IMPLEMENTING...

CIDR

The calculation we just did in the "Calculating a Summary Route Address and Mask" sidebar, where we combined four Class C networks into one address to be used as a summary route, could also be used as an example of CIDR. This would allow us to combine the four separate classful networks into one larger, classless network (it no longer fits within the classful boundaries). The /22 (or 255.255.252.0 in dotted decimal format) tells the router that the first 22 bits in the source and destination addresses are all that are to be compared to determine if the devices are on the same network. If those 22 bits

match, the router will know the devices are on the same network and not to forward the packets to another network.

You may also hear this referred to as supernetting. With subnetting, we borrow host bits to be used for networking (subnetting), which involves turning on some of the host bits in the mask. With supernetting, we are going in the other direction. Instead of going to the right and turning on more bits in our subnet mask, we're going to the left into our network bits and turning some of them off. This allows you to create larger and more flexible networks than the boundaries of classful addressing permit.

Neighbor Discovery

Once EIGRP has been installed on the routers in our network, the routers will discover the neighboring routers that they will be communicating with on the network. This process is called *neighbor discovery*. When a router starts up on the EIGRP network, the new router forms adjacencies or neighborships with neighboring routers. By default, if the directly connected routers are in different ASes, they don't exchange information with each other. In large networks, this can greatly cut down on communications generated between routers and reduce the size of routing tables. Redistribution between ASes can be manually configured to allow communication between routers in different ASes.

Neighbors are discovered with the use of hello packets. When a router receives a hello packet and returns an acknowledgement (ACK) to the router that sent the original hello packet, they establish a neighborship. This is when neighboring routers exchange their entire routing tables with each other. Once EIGRP has discovered the neighboring routers and they have exchanged complete routing tables, the state of the neighboring routers and interfaces is monitored by sending periodic hello packets. Then, from this point on, the routers exchange only incremental routing information and only when something changes.

Neighbor Table

Neighbor information is stored in a router's EIGRP neighbor table. The *neighbor table* is a list of adjacent neighbors and the neighboring interface and address, along with additional details about each neighbor. The current state of each neighbor is included in the table. You'll also find the neighbors' holdtimes listed in the neighbor table. Hello packets advertise the holdtime for the neighbor, which is the length of time the neighbor is to be treated as functional and reachable. If the holdtime expires without a hello packet being received from the neighbor, DUAL is notified of the change.

Another item included for each entry in the neighbor table is the last sequence number received from the neighbor. RTP requires sequence numbers to identify out-of-sequence data packets and ACKs. RTP also uses a transmission list from the address table to determine how to queue packets for possible retransmission to each neighbor. The optimal interval for retransmission is identified with round-trip timers maintained for each neighbor.

The neighbor table is dynamically created and stored in random access memory (RAM). Every time a router starts up, the table is recreated. If you are running more than one network layer protocol on your router, there is a separate neighbor table for each PDM. The neighbor table is sometimes referred to as the *neighborship table*. To display the IP-EIGRP neighbor table, use the following command:

```
Router1# show ip eigrp neighbors
IP-EIGRP Neighbors for process 100
```

Address	Interface	Holdtime (secs)	Uptime (h:m:s)	Q Count	Seq Num	SRTT (ms)	RTO (ms)
172.16.100.1	Ethernet1	13	0:00:41	0	11	4	20
172.16.110.2	Ethernet0	14	0:02:01	0	10	12	24
172.16.110.2	Ethernet0	12	0:02:02	0	4	5	20

Topology Table

The topology table is used to store information about all known routes received from all neighbors. If a neighbor is advertising a possible route, it must be using that route to forward packets to the destination network. The PDMs are responsible for putting information into the topology table.

The topology table is a database of possible routes. It provides the information that is used to select the best possible route, which is copied into the routing table. The best metric along all possible paths to the remote network is called the *feasible distance* (FD). The FD is the metric (reported or advertised distance) reported by the neighbor plus the metric to the neighbor reporting the route. The best route, called the *successor*, is the route with the lowest metric to the destination network. This is the route that is copied into the routing table.

If the successor route goes away, DUAL will search the topology table for a backup route. The topology table is where EIGRP stores the information for up to six alternate routes to a particular network. The backup routes are called *feasible successors*. The feasible successors stored in the topology table are what makes it possible for EIGRP to converge rapidly or even instantly. If there is no feasible successor in the table, a multicast is sent out to find a new route. Changes are made to the topology table if another router provides information about an alternate route.

Topology tables are stored in RAM and are re-created whenever a router starts up. Routing tables obtain all their information from the topology table. The *show ip eigrp topology* command shows us the topology table:

```
HQ# show ip eigrp topology
IP-EIGRP Topology Table for AS(100)/ID(10.2.0.1)
Codes: P - Passive, A - Active, U - Update, Q - Query, R -
    Reply, r - reply Status, s - sia Status
```

```
P 10.1.0.0/24, 1 successors, FD is 2172416
    via Connected, Serial0/0
P 10.0.0.0/8, 1 successors, FD is 2172416
P 10.2.0.0/24, 1 successors, FD is 2172416
    via Connected, Serial0/1
P 172.17.0.0/16, 1 successors, FD is 2172416
    via 10.2.0.2 (2172416/28160), Serial0/0
P 172.16.0.0/16, 1 successors, FD is 2172416
    via 10.1.0.2 (2172416/28160), Serial0/0
P 192.168.100.0/24, 1 successors, FD is 2172416
    via Connected, FastEthernet0/0
```

The Ps at the beginning of each entry show that the routes are Passive routes, meaning DUAL isn't looking for new information for the route. Then, you see the address and mask for the destination network and how many successor routes there are to the network. FD is the metric that DUAL calculated for that route. And, just like in the routing table, the information after the word via is next-hop information for where to send packets destined for the network.

Building the Initial EIGRP Routing Tables

We've looked at some of the pieces that come into the picture when EIGRP is creating adjacencies and the tables that hold different types of information used in the process. Now, we're going to look at how the routing table comes together. Here are the steps involved in building the routing table for the first time:

1. A new router starts up.

2. The new router sends hello packets out of every interface.

3. A neighbor replies by sending update packets.

4. The new router sends ACK packets for the updates it receives.

5. Using the information received in the updates, the new router builds its topology table.

6. The new router sends updates to all its neighbors.

7. Each neighbor responds with ACKs for the updates they receive.

8. The DUAL determines the best route and backup routes based on the EIGRP metric calculations for each destination network.

9. The best route and backup routes are added to the topology table.

10. The best route for each destination is copied into the routing table as the successor route.

When making route determinations, DUAL looks at internal, external, and summary routes.

The EIGRP Metric

By default, the factors EIGRP considers when calculating its metric are as follows:

- Bandwidth

- Delay

EIGRP can also be configured to include the following in its calculations:

- Reliability

- Load

Bandwidth is the smallest bandwidth between the router and the destination network, and *delay* refers to the cumulative interface delay along the route. Another related factor that isn't included in the calculations for the metric, but that comes up when configuring things like redistribution, is the maximum transmission unit (MTU). The MTU is also included in the information exchanged between neighbor routers. The *MTU* refers to the smallest MTU value along the route to the destination network.

DUAL

One of the most powerful components of EIGRP is the DUAL. DUAL is used for selecting and maintaining the best possible path to each destination network and handling these tasks in a completely loop-free manner. This makes it possible for all routers affected by a network change to synchronize updates at the same time and routers that are not affected by the change to remain out of the recomputation process. This also contributes to EIGRP's capability for rapid convergence. In fact, convergence time using DUAL rivals that of any other existing routing protocol.

The DUAL finite state machine keeps track of all routes advertised by all neighbors to make effective decisions on which routes to place in the routing table. DUAL uses the metric information to select the successor for the routing table and the feasible successors to include in the topology table. If no feasible successors exist in the topology table when the successor is no longer available, DUAL determines if other routers are still advertising the destination. If so, a recomputation occurs to select a new successor.

An entry is copied from the topology table to the routing table when there is a feasible successor. All paths to the destination network that have the minimum costs are considered to be a set. Any neighbors from the set with an advertised metric less than the current metric in the routing table are considered to be feasible successors. If a neighbor's advertised metric changes or a change occurs to the network, it may be necessary to reevaluate the set of feasible successors. This is not considered a route recomputation.

Anytime DUAL can obtain a feasible successor that already exists in the topology table, rapid convergence can occur. If it's necessary to perform a route recomputation, the convergence will be delayed. Route entries in the topology table are either in a Passive state or in an Active state. A route is in an Active state if there are no feasible successors and is a route computation occurring.

A route recomputation begins with a router sending a query packet to all neighboring routers. The neighbors then either reply that they have feasible successors or return their own query to say that they are in the process of a route recomputation. The router cannot change the next-hop information for a route if the route is in an Active state. The route will return to Passive state once all the replies have been returned for the query, then DUAL can select the new successor.

PDMs

EIGRP can be used to support multiple network layer (routed) protocols: IP version 4, IP version 6, IPX, and AppleTalk. There are a number of options that can be configured for EIGRP that are protocol-independent and that function much the same regardless of the routed protocol(s) being used. The PDMs handle the responsibilities of supporting their respective routed protocols. The IP-EIGRP module takes care of sending and receiving EIGRP packets that are encapsulated in IP. IP-EIGRP also analyzes the EIGRP packets and informs DUAL of the information received. It asks DUAL to make routing decisions and stores the results of those decisions in the IP routing table. It also handles redistribution of routes learned by other IP routing protocols.

Packet Types

There are five types of packets that EIGRP uses to communicate with neighboring routers. Each type of packet has its own purpose and function. Some of the packet types are transmitted reliably, meaning that a response is expected, and others do not require responses. Information in the packet header defines if the packet type is to be transmitted reliably or not. For the packets that are transmitted reliably, RTP is responsible for assuring that replies are received or following up if replies are not received.

The five types of packets are:

- Hello

- Acknowledgement

- Update

- Query

- Reply

Hello

Hello packets are multicast packets that are used for neighbor discovery and recovery. Hellos do not require an ACK so are not considered to be transmitted reliably. Hello packets are sent periodically between routers to learn about neighbor routers on the directly connected network. They also allow the router to monitor the state of existing neighbor routers. This is how the router learns if a neighbor router has gone down.

By default, hello packets are sent every 5 s. The exception to this is slow (considered to be T1 speed or slower), nonbroadcast connections, where the hello packets are sent every 30 s by default. The interval for how frequently hello packets are sent is configurable as is the length of time the router should consider the sender valid if it doesn't receive any other communication. This is called the *holdtime* and, by default, is three times the hello interval. Configuration changes for hello interval and holdtime is made on a per interface basis for a particular AS. To change the interval for sending hello packets, execute the *ip hello-interval eigrp <AS> < seconds>* command in interface configuration mode. To change the holdtime, the command is *ip hold-time eigrp <AS> <seconds>*, also in interface configuration mode. On very large or congested networks, the holdtime might not be sufficient for all routers to receive their hello packets from their neighbors, so it might be necessary to increase the holdtime. Here, we change the hello interval and holdtime on the FastEthernet 0/0 interface of Router1:

```
Router1# configure terminal
Router1(config)# interface fastethernet0/0
Router1(config-if)# ip hello-interval eigrp 100 15
Router1(config-if)# ip hold-time eigrp 100 45
```

Acknowledgement

ACK packets are a type of hello packet that doesn't include data. They contain nonzero acknowledgement numbers. Where regular hello packets are sent as multicasts, ACKs are sent using unicast addresses. When routers receive update packets, they return ACKs to confirm that they received the updates. The ACK numbers are used to match updates with ACKs.

Update

Updates advertise information about destinations and how to reach the destinations. Updates can be sent as multicasts or unicasts depending on their purpose. Unicast updates are sent when new neighbors are discovered so that the neighbor can build its topology table. If a link cost change occurs, updates are sent as multicasts. Updates are always transmitted reliably.

Query

When a destination has no feasible successors, query packets are generated by the router to request route information to the destination from the neighbors. Queries are sent as multicasts unless they are sent as a response to another query. That type of query packet is sent as a unicast and is sent back to the source of the original query. Query packets are transmitted reliably.

Reply

Reply packets are sent back to the source of the query packets. Replies are sent to tell the query's originator not to recompute the route because feasible successors do exist. The purpose of the reply packet is to stop the originator of the query from going into Active state. Reply packets are also transmitted reliably.

Authentication

By default, no authentication is enabled for EIGRP, but route authentication can be configured on your routers. Once authentication is configured, routers must be validated based on predetermined passwords before they can exchange route information and participate in routing. This is a security measure used to prevent the introduction of false or unauthorized routing information. This process is also sometimes referred to as *neighbor authentication* or *neighbor router authentication*. Before you can configure authentication, EIGRP must be enabled.

MD5 Authentication

The type of authentication that EIGRP supports is MD5 authentication. MD5 authentication adds keyed information into each EIGRP packet that is sent. The receiving router uses the keyed information to confirm that the source of the packet is really who they say they are. To configure MD5 authentication, you configure an authenticating key (sometimes referred to as a password) and a key ID on the source and destination routers. Here are the steps to configure MD5 authentication for EIGRP:

1. Enter *Global Configuration* mode.

2. Enter interface configuration mode.

3. Enable MD5 authentication in EIGRP packets.

4. Enable authentication of EIGRP packets (this identifies the key to be used on this interface).

5. Exit to *Global Configuration* mode.

6. Identify a key chain, using the same name as in Step 4 (the key chain is a group of possible keys).

7. In key chain configuration mode, identify the key number (this is the identifier for the key).

8. In key chain key configuration mode, identify the key string.

9. Repeat Steps 1 through 7 on the other router.

Figure 8.4 shows the diagram of a network with two routers that will use MD5 authentication for EIGRP.

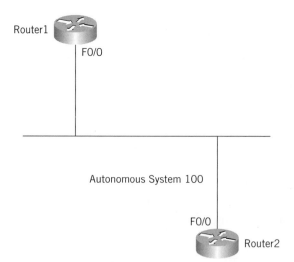

FIGURE 8.4

Configuring MD5 Authentication

Router1

F0/0

Autonomous System 100

F0/0

Router2

EXERCISE 8.3   Configuring EIGRP MD5 Authentication

In this exercise, we're going to configure MD5 authentication on the two routers in Figure 8.4.

Configuring Router1:

1. Enter *Global Configuration* mode:

   Router1# **configure terminal**

2. Enter interface configuration mode:

   Router1(config)# **interface Fastethernet 0/0**

3. Enable MD5 authentication in EIGRP packets:

   Router1(config-if)# **ip authentication mode eigrp 100 md5**
   ! The 100 is the EIGRP AS.

4. Enable authentication of EIGRP packets:

   Router1(config-if)# **ip authentication key-chain eigrp 100 ourkey1**
   ! ourkey1 is the name of the key

5. Exit to *Global Configuration* mode:

   Router1(config-if)# **exit**

6. Identify a key chain, using the same name as in Step 4:

   Router1(config)# **key chain ourkey1**

7. In key chain configuration mode, identify the key number:

   Router1(config-keychain)# **key 1**

8. In key chain key configuration mode, identify the key string:

   Router1(config-keychain-key)# **key-string 1234567890**

9. Repeat Steps 1 through 8 on the other router.

Configuring Router2:

1. Enter *Global Configuration* mode:

   Router1# **configure terminal**

2. Enter interface configuration mode:

   Router1(config)# **interface Fastethernet 0/0**

3. Enable MD5 authentication in EIGRP packets:

   Router1(config-if)# **ip authentication mode eigrp 100 md5**

4. Enable authentication of EIGRP packets:

   Router1(config-if)# **ip authentication key-chain eigrp 100 anotherkey2**

5. Exit to *Global Configuration* mode:

   Router1(config-if)# **exit**

6. Identify a key chain, using the same name as in Step 4:

   Router1(config)# **key chain anotherkey2**

7. In key chain configuration mode, identify the key number:

   Router1(config-keychain)# **key 1**

8. In key chain key configuration mode, identify the key string:

   Router1(config-keychain-key)# **key-string 1234567890**

We have now configured MD5 authentication on our routers as shown in Figure 8.4. The routers will use the key information to make sure they know who they are talking to.

VERIFYING EIGRP

Once we've configured EIGRP on our router, there are a number of commands that we can use to verify that everything is configured correctly. We'll verify that EIGRP has been enabled on the router, that we've used the correct AS number, and that we've typed in the correct information in our *network* commands. We can also verify other options that we've configured for EIGRP, such as summary routes and MD5 authentication. Let's look at some *show* commands to verify our EIGRP configurations. (Note: Some of the examples of the commands only show part of the output. Some of the information that doesn't apply to the topic has been omitted.)

Show Commands

One of the best places to start when verifying your EIGRP configuration is with the *show ip protocols* command. This command will show you quite a bit of information about EIGRP, including the AS that EIGRP is configured to use. You can also look at the networks that have been configured to be included in the EIGRP process, as well as IP addresses of source devices that have sent information to your router. In addition to EIGRP, you will see configurations for any other routing protocols that are active on the router. In Exercise 8.4, we'll look at the *show ip protocols* command to verify an EIGRP configuration.

EXERCISE 8.4   Verifying EIGRP Configuration

```
Router1# show ip protocols
Routing Protocol is "eigrp 100"
    Outgoing update filter list for all interfaces is not set
    Incoming update filter list for all interfaces is not set
    Redistributing: eigrp 100
    Automatic network summarization is in effect
    Routing for Networks:
        172.16.0.0
        192.168.0.0
    Routing Information Sources:
        Gateway Distance Last Update
        192.168.100.2  90  0:01:36
        192.168.200.2  90  0:03:24
        172.16.100.2   90  0:02:04

    Distance: internal 90 external 170
```

The information from this command tells us the only currently running routing protocol is EIGRP and that it is configured for AS 100, so we can verify that we configured the correct AS from that section. It also tells us that EIGRP will auto-summarize routes to the classful boundaries and that the auto-summary option hasn't been turned off with the *no auto-summary* command. The *Routing for Networks:* section lists the networks EIGRP will include in the information it is advertising to other routers, so we can verify we configured those correctly. Listed under *Gateway,* we can look at the other routers' addresses that we've received updates from and when the last update was sent from each of those routers. Finally, we can confirm the administrative distance being used for each of the routes to the neighboring routers and see if the router considers it an internal route or an external route.

Another *show* command that you will find very useful when verifying EIGRP configuration is the *show ip route* command. This command displays the IP routing table with all the IP routes the router is currently using to forward packets to destination networks. Here is what the *show ip route* command looks like:

```
Router1# show ip route
Codes: I - IGRP derived, R - RIP derived, O - OSPF derived,
    C - connected, S - static, E - EGP derived, B - BGP
      derived,
    * - candidate default route, IA - OSPF inter area route,
    i - IS-IS derived, ia - IS-IS, U - per-user static route,
    o - on-demand routing, M - mobile, P - periodic downloaded
      static route,
    D - EIGRP, EX - EIGRP external, E1 - OSPF external type 1
      route,
    E2 - OSPF external type 2 route, N1 - OSPF NSSA external
      type 1 route,
    N2 - OSPF NSSA external type 2 route
Gateway of last resort is not set10.0.0.0/24 is subnetted,
    10 subnets
C 10.0.100.0 is directly connected, FastEthernet0/1
C 10.0.110.0 is directly connected, FastEthernet0/0
D 10.0.120.0 [90/3184437] via 10.0.170.2, 00:01:05, Serial0/0
D 10.0.130.0 [90/3184437] via 10.0.170.2, 00:01:05, Serial0/0
D 10.0.140.0 [90/3184437] via 10.0.170.2, 00:01:05, Serial0/0
D 10.0.150.0 [90/3184437] via 10.0.170.2, 00:01:05, Serial0/0
D 10.0.160.0 [90/3184437] via 10.0.170.2, 00:01:05, Serial0/0
C 10.0.170.0 is directly connected, Serial0/0
D 10.0.180.0 [90/3184437] via 10.0.170.2, 00:01:05, Serial0/0
D 10.0.190.0 [90/3184437] via 10.0.170.2, 00:01:05, Serial0/0
```

When we execute this *show ip route* command, we can see that this router knows about 10 subnets in the 10.0.0.0/24 network. The three subnets that have Cs in front of them are subnets directly connected by way of the interfaces shown at the end of each entry. The lines with Ds at the beginning are the subnets that EIGRP discovered (the D stands for DUAL). Each of the EIGRP routes shows the default administrative distance of 90 for EIGRP internal routes. The second number in the brackets with the 90 is the metric that EIGRP has calculated and assigned to that route. For the EIGRP routes, the *via* address is the next hop address that the router will use to send packets destined for the listed network.

We can also execute the *show ip route* command to look at only EIGRP routes by adding *eigrp* to the end of the command:

```
Router1# show ip route eigrp
10.0.0.0/24 is subnetted, 10 subnets
D  10.0.120.0 [90/3184437] via 10.0.170.2, 00:01:05, Serial0/0
D  10.0.130.0 [90/3184437] via 10.0.170.2, 00:01:05, Serial0/0
D  10.0.140.0 [90/3184437] via 10.0.170.2, 00:01:05, Serial0/0
D  10.0.150.0 [90/3184437] via 10.0.170.2, 00:01:05, Serial0/0
D  10.0.160.0 [90/3184437] via 10.0.170.2, 00:01:05, Serial0/0
D  10.0.180.0 [90/3184437] via 10.0.170.2, 00:01:05, Serial0/0
D  10.0.190.0 [90/3184437] via 10.0.170.2, 00:01:05, Serial0/0
```

To look at the interfaces configured for EIGRP, we'll use the *show ip eigrp interfaces* command. This command will show us a list of the interfaces configured for EIGRP and some information about each interface:

```
Router1# show ip eigrp interfaces
IP EIGRP interfaces for process 1
                Xmit Queue Mean Pacing Time Multicast Pending
Interface Peers Un/Reliable SRTT Un/Reliable Flow Timer Routes
Di0  0     0/0   0 11/434   0       0
Et0  1     0/0   337 0/10   0       0
SE0:1.16 1     0/0   10    1/63 103   0
Tu0  1     0/0   330 0/16   0       0
```

To look at our eigrp neighbors table, we execute the *show ip eigrp neighbors* command:

```
Router1# show ip eigrp neighbors
IP-EIGRP Neighbors for process 100
Address          Interface   Holdtime   Uptime    Q Count   Seq Num   SRTT   RTO
                             (secs)     (h:m:s)                       (ms)   (ms)
172.16.100.2     Ethernet1     13       0:00:41      0         11       4     20
172.16.110.2     Ethernet0     14       0:02:01      0         10      12     24
172.16.110.1     Ethernet0     12       0:02:02      0          4       5     20
```

The *Holdtime* indicates how long the router will wait for a hello packet to come from that neighbor. The length of time that the neighbor has been a neighbor is shown in the *Uptime* field. The *queue (Q)* field will tell you how many outstanding packets are in the queue. The sequence number (Seq Num) is for the last update from the neighbor. Smooth round-trip timer (SRTT) shows how long a round-trip between this router and the neighbor should take. In other words, how long to wait for a reply from the neighbor when a multicast is sent out. The retransmission time out (RTO) shows how long the router will wait before retransmitting a packet that's in the retransmission queue.

We can use the *show ip eigrp neighbors detail* command to see a little more information about our neighbors:

```
Router1# show ip eigrp neighbors detail
IP-EIGRP neighbors for process 101
H   Address          Interface   Hold   Uptime     SRTT   RTO    Q     Seq    Type
                                        (sec)      (ms)          Cnt   Num
3   172.16.100.2     Et0/0       12     00:04:48   1832   5000   0     14
                                        Version 12.2/1.2, Retrans:0, Retries:0
Restart time 00:01:05
0   10.0.1.1         Fa0/0       11     00:04:07   768    4608   0     4  S
                                        Version 12.2/1.2, Retrans: 0, Retries: 0
2   10.0.3.2         Fa0/0       13     1w0d       1      3000   0     6  S
                                        Version 12.2/1.2, Retrans: 1, Retries: 0
1   10.0.9.2         Fa0/0       12     1w0d       1      3000   0     4  S
                                        Version 12.2/1.2, Retrans: 1, Retries: 0
```

The *H* field shows the order that the neighbors were discovered.

To look at all the routes received from all our neighbors, we can look at the topology table:

```
Router1# show ip eigrp topology
IP-EIGRP Topology Table for process 100
Codes: P - Passive, A - Active, U - Update, Q - Query,
R - Reply, r - Reply status
P 172.16.90.0 255.255.255.0, 2 successors, FD is 0
    via 172.16.80.28 (46251776/46226176), Ethernet0
    via 172.16.81.28 (46251776/46226176), Ethernet1
    via 172.16.80.31 (46277376/46251776), Serial0
P 172.16.81.0 255.255.255.0, 1 successors, FD is 307200
    via Connected, Ethernet1
    via 172.16.81.28 (307200/281600), Ethernet1
    via 172.16.80.28 (307200/281600), Ethernet0
    via 172.16.80.31 (332800/307200), Serial0
```

The Ps at the beginning of each line indicate that each of the routes is in Passive state. When a route is in an Active state, it is looking for a route to the network because it has lost the route it was using. Next are the addresses of the destination networks. Feasible successors, or backup routes, are also listed in the topology table. The FD is the calculated metric for the route. The numbers in parenthesis next to each route are the FD and the advertised distance.

To check the status of all our interfaces and make sure they're all up:

```
HQ# show ip interfaces brief
Interface       IP-Address      OK?  Method  Status  Protocol
FastEthernet0/0 192.168.100.1   YES  manual  up      up
FastEthernet0/1 192.168.110.1   YES  manual  up      up
Serial0/0       10.1.0.1        YES  manual  up      up
Serial0/1       10.2.0.1        YES  manual  up      up
```

To look at traffic statistics for eigrp packets being sent and received for this router, we use the *show ip eigrp traffic* command:

```
Router# show ip eigrp traffic
IP-EIGRP Traffic Statistics for process 77
   Hellos sent/received: 218/205
   Updates sent/received: 7/23
   Queries sent/received: 2/0
   Replies sent/received: 0/2
   Acks sent/received: 21/14
```

As you can see, there are several *show* commands that allow you to verify that your EIGRP configuration is correct and that EIGRP is working properly.

TROUBLESHOOTING EIGRP

Now, let's look at how to go about troubleshooting and dealing with EIGRP problems. There are four primary categories of issues to consider:

1. Neighbor relationships

2. Network topology

3. EIGRP routes in the routing table

4. Protocol parameters

When troubleshooting EIGRP, we can start with the *show* commands described in the previous section "Show Commands." This will allow us to verify if all our neighbors are showing up in the neighbor table. We can also check our routing table and our topology table to make sure all the route information is correct.

When troubleshooting neighbor problems, sometimes it's helpful to clear the neighbor table and let the router recreate it. To clear a neighbor table:

```
Router1# clear ip eigrp neighbors
```

If there is a specific neighbor that you want to remove from the address table, you can add the IP address of the neighbor at the end of the command.

Router1# **clear ip eigrp neighbors 172.16.100.1**

Other problems that can occur may be specific to parameters or options that you've configured for EIGRP. For example, if authentication with MD5 isn't correct, you can see a number of problems with EIGRP, including the inability for routers to communicate with other routers.

Debug Commands

There are a number of *debug* commands that we can use to monitor EIGRP packets crossing our routers. Debug allows us to watch particular types of traffic, so we can get an idea of what information is being sent and received and watch for problems. Let's start by looking at the *debug ip eigrp* command. This command lets us watch all EIGRP packets coming into and going out of the router. Note: Be careful when using this command as it can generate a lot of information and cause performance issues on your network.

```
Router1# debug ip eigrp
IP-EIGRP: Processing incoming UPDATE packet
IP-EIGRP: Ext 192.168.3.0 255.255.255.0 M 386560 - 256000
    130560 SM 360960 - 256000 104960
IP-EIGRP: Ext 192.168.0.0 255.255.255.0 M 386560 - 256000
    130560 SM 360960 - 256000 104960
IP-EIGRP: Ext 192.168.3.0 255.255.255.0 M 386560 - 256000
    130560 SM 360960 - 256000 104960
IP-EIGRP: 172.69.43.0 255.255.255.0, - do advertise out
    Ethernet0/1
IP-EIGRP: Ext 172.69.43.0 255.255.255.0 metric 371200 -
    256000 115200
IP-EIGRP: 192.135.246.0 255.255.255.0, - do advertise out
    Ethernet0/1
IP-EIGRP: Ext 192.135.246.0 255.255.255.0 metric 46310656 -
    45714176 596480
IP-EIGRP: 172.69.40.0 255.255.255.0, - do advertise out
    Ethernet0/1
IP-EIGRP: Ext 172.69.40.0 255.255.255.0 metric 2272256 -
    1657856 614400
IP-EIGRP: 192.135.245.0 255.255.255.0, - do advertise out
    Ethernet0/1
```

```
IP-EIGRP: Ext 192.135.245.0 255.255.255.0 metric 40622080 -
   40000000 622080
IP-EIGRP: 192.135.244.0 255.255.255.0, - do advertise out
   Ethernet0/1
```

To turn this command off:

Router1# **no debug ip eigrp**

A *debug* command that we can use to specifically monitor EIGRP events and notifications is *debug ip eigrp*:

```
Router1# debug ip eigrp notifications
*Oct  4  11:39:18.092:EIGRP:NSF:AS2.  Rec  RS  update  from
   135.100.10.1,
00:00:00. Wait for EOT.
*Oct 4 11:39:18.092:%DUAL-5-NBRCHANGE:IP-EIGRP(0) 2:Neighbor
   135.100.10.1 (POS3/0) is up:peer NSF restarted
```

To turn this command off:

Router1# **no debug ip eigrp notifications**

SUMMARY OF EXAM OBJECTIVES

EIGRP is a Cisco-proprietary, advanced distance-vector routing protocol that incorporates features from both distance-vector and link-state routing. EIGRP synchronizes routing tables on startup, then only sends incremental updates when network changes occur, making it possible for EIGRP to use minimal network resources. Because EIGRP can maintain up to six alternate routes to a destination in its table at the same time, it can converge very rapidly when network changes occur.

EIGRP's capability to carry subnet mask information in its update packets makes it possible for EIGRP to support classless addressing, VLSMs, and route summarization. EIGRP is highly scalable and supports very large and discontiguous networks. Large networks can be broken up into multiple ASes for more efficient routing and easier management. Routers configured with the same AS number will exchange information with each other.

There are four key components that combine to give EIGRP its advanced capabilities:

1. Neighbor discovery/recovery

2. RTP

3. DUAL

4. PDMs

Hello packets find neighbors and monitor their status. When neighbors are discovered, the routers establish an adjacency or neighborship. Routing table information is exchanged with new neighbors and maintained with incremental updates when there are changes. Information about neighbors is maintained in the neighbor table.

RTP is a Cisco-proprietary protocol that is used to manage the communications between routers. RTP uses multicasts and unicasts to quickly, efficiently, and reliably deliver different types of EIGRP packets. RTP uses the multicast address of 224.0.0.10 to send traffic to other EIGRP routers. RTP uses sequence numbers to detect out-of-sequence and old or redundant information.

EIGRP is configured from two modes: router configuration mode and interface mode. Global EIGRP parameters are configured in router configuration mode, and options such as summaries and metrics are configured per interface in interface mode. EIGRP is enabled with the *router eigrp <AS>* command in *Global Configuration* mode, and then the networks to be included in EIGRP are configured with *network <network-number>* commands in router configuration mode. An interface can be configured not to send or receive EIGRP packets with the *passive-interface <interface>* command in router configuration mode. To verify an EIGRP configuration, use the *show ip protocols* command.

EIGRP does automatic route summarization to the classful boundaries. Manual route summarization can also be configured to shorten route tables and make them more efficient. Summary route addresses and masks are calculated by finding the common bits in the networks or network segments being summarized.

The topology table holds information about all known routes received from all neighbors. The best route is copied to the routing table and is the route that's used. That route is called the successor. The topology table also has backup routes that can be used if the best route fails. The backup routes are called feasible successors. The FD, or metric, is used to determine which routes are the best and which are feasible backups. EIGRP uses bandwidth and delay as the default factors when calculating metrics. Reliability and load can also be configured to be used in the calculations.

The DUAL is used to select and maintain the best routes to the destination networks. It is DUAL's responsibility to handle routing without loops. DUAL selects successors and feasible successors and obtains information from neighbors if a route goes down and there are no feasible successors. If routes can't be found to a destination, a recalculation occurs. Routes are in Active state if the route is being recalculated or Passive state if not.

PDMs are used by EIGRP to support multiple network layer protocols, such as IP version 4 and IP version 6. PDMs maintain separate tables for each protocol and handle sending and receiving EIGRP encapsulated within the appropriate protocol.

EIGRP uses five types of packets to communicate with neighbor routers. Hello packets are used for neighbor discovery and recovery. By default they are sent every 5 s. Acknowledgements are hello packets without data that are returned in response to update packets. Updates carry routing information. Queries are used to request route information from neighbors, and replies are sent in response to queries.

MD5 authentication can be enabled for EIGRP. MD5 authentication uses keyed information to confirm the identity of the source router. MD5 authentication is configured on all the source and destination routers that will be communicating with each other.

There are several *show* and *debug* commands used to verify EIGRP configurations. The *show ip route* command displays the IP routing table, and *eigrp* can be added to the end of the command to see only EIGRP routes. *Show ip eigrp interface* shows information about the EIGRP configuration on the interfaces. The neighbor table is displayed with the *show ip eigrp neighbors* command. EIGRP traffic statistics can be shown with the *show ip eigrp traffic* command. When troubleshooting EIGRP networks, the *debug ip eigrp* command shows a great deal of information about EIGRP packets crossing the router. *Debug ip eigrp notifications* is used to monitor EIGRP events and notifications.

EXAM OBJECTIVES FAST TRACK

The EIGRP

- EIGRP is an advanced distance-vector routing protocol that uses features from both distance-vector and link-state routing protocols.

- EIGRP is very efficient in its use of network resources because it sends only incremental updates to neighboring routers when there is a change to the network.

- EIGRP can maintain multiple routes to the same network in its topology table at the same time, allowing for rapid convergence in the case of a failure.

- Technologies such as classless addressing, VLSMs, and route summarization are supported because EIGRP can carry subnet mask information in its updates.

- Four primary components combine to make EIGRP an efficient, advanced protocol: neighbor discovery/recovery, RTP, DUAL, and PDMs.

- The DUAL calculates loop-free routes to destination networks.

- Neighborships or adjacencies are formed between routers when a new router comes up.

- The neighbor table holds information about each neighbor and its connected address and interface.

- RTP handles communication between routers, ensuring reliability for the types of packets that require it.

- PDMs allow EIGRP to support different types of network layer protocols, such as IPv4 and IPv6.

Configuring EIGRP

- EIGRP is enabled with the *router eigrp <AS>* command in *Global Configuration* mode.

- Routers must be configured with the same AS number to communicate with each other.

- The *network* commands identify the networks to be included in the EIGRP configuration.

- With the *passive-interface <interface>* command executed in router configuration, an interface can be configured not to send or receive EIGRP packets.

- By default, EIGRP auto-summarizes routes to the classful boundaries.

- To make EIGRP a classless routing protocol, execute the *no auto-summary* command in router configuration mode.

- Manual summary routes shorten routing tables by incorporating multiple networks or network segments into one routing table entry.

- Neighbors are discovered using hello packets.

- Periodic hello packets are used to monitor the state of neighboring routers and their interfaces.

- The topology table is a database of all known routes received from all neighbors.

- The best possible route to a destination network (successor route) is copied from the topology table to the routing table.

- DUAL uses metrics to select successors and feasible successors.

- DUAL looks for information about backup routes (feasible successors) to destination networks in the topology table.

- If feasible successors exist in the topology table, rapid convergence is possible.

- If there are no feasible successors in the topology table, multicasts are sent to request route information.

- Routes are in a Passive state unless a route computation is occurring; then they are in an Active state.

- The next-hop information for a route can't be changed while the route is in an Active state. When all queries have been sent and all replies have been received from other routers, the state of the route returns to Passive, and DUAL can select the successor.

- EIGRP routes have a default administrative distance of 90 for internal routes and 170 for external routes.

- Internal routes are originated within the same AS.

- External routes are originated outside of the AS, whether in another EIGRP AS or from another routing protocol.

- EIGRP does automatic redistribution for IGRP if the ASes are the same number.

- MD5 authentication can be configured to validate the identity of sending and receiving devices.

Verifying EIGRP

- The *show ip protocols* command can be used to verify configuration information for EIGRP.

- To look at the routing table, execute the *show ip route* command.

- EIGRP routes are indicated by a *D* for DUAL in the routing table.

- There are *show* commands to display all the EIGRP tables (neighbor, topology, and routing).

- The *show eigrp interfaces* command is used to verify EIGRP configuration on an interface.

- Traffic statistics for EIGRP can be displayed with the *show ip eigrp traffic* command.

Troubleshooting EIGRP

- The categories for troubleshooting EIGRP are neighbor relationships, network topology, EIGRP routes, and protocol parameters.

- Clearing the neighbor table with the *clear ip eigrp neighbors* command will cause the router to rebuild the table.

- *Debug* commands provide information about EIGRP packets crossing the router.

EXAM OBJECTIVES FREQUENTLY ASKED QUESTIONS

Q: What are the benefits of EIGRP?

A: There are many powerful benefits included with EIGRP. Here are a few of the highlights: minimal use of network resources, loop-free routing, rapid convergence, support for classless addressing, and VLSMs.

Q: What does neighbor discovery do?

A: Neighbor discovery/recovery is used by routers to dynamically find neighboring routers on the network to exchange routing information. Routers communicate with their neighbors with small, periodic hello packets to make sure that the neighbors are still reachable on the network. If the router receives replies to the hello packets from a neighbor, it is assumed that the neighbor is available for communication.

Q: What is DUAL?

A: DUAL is the algorithm that's used to calculate routes and determine the best, loop-free path to a destination network. DUAL also calculates backup routes to the destination network and puts the information into the topology table.

Q: What are successors and feasible successors?

A: The successor is the best possible route to a destination network. This is the route that is copied from the topology table to the routing table. The feasible successors are the backup routes. These routes are maintained in the topology table, and in the case of a network failure, DUAL can converge rapidly by failing over to an existing feasible successor.

Q: What are the differences among a neighbor table, a topology table, and a routing table?

A: The neighbor table holds information about the directly connected neighbor routers and interfaces. The topology table contains all known routes from all neighbors. The routing table shows all routes that are currently being used to send packets to destination networks. The EIGRP routes in a routing table are the best path routes in the topology table, copied to the routing table.

Q: Can EIGRP be configured to support authentication?

A: Yes, EIGRP supports the MD5 authentication method.

SELF TEST

1. You are interested in the information that EIGRP sends from and receives to your routers, so you've turned on EIGRP debugging on one of your routers. Everything seems to be working fine on the network, but you've been watching the screen for several minutes and nothing is happening. What is the most likely cause of the lack of debug information?

   A. Debug isn't working properly.

   B. EIGRP isn't working properly.

   C. The network isn't working properly.

   D. The network is stable.

2. You are getting ready to bring up EIGRP on your routers. You want all the routers to exchange routing information with each other. What do you need to do during your EIGRP installations on the routers to make this happen?

   A. Configure all the routers with the same AS number.

   B. Configure all the routers with incremental AS numbers (that is, the first router would be AS number 1, the second router would be AS number 2, and so on).

   C. Install EIGRP but don't include any AS number.

   D. In the EIGRP configurations, list the names of all the routers to exchange information with each other.

3. You are in the process of configuring EIGRP on your routers. What would be the correct command to enable EIGRP on each of your routers?

    A. (config)#**enable eigrp**   **C.** (config)#**router eigrp 12**

    B. (config)#**router eigrp**   **D.** (config)#**eigrp no shutdown**

4. As part of the process of troubleshooting problems on your network, you are looking at debug information for EIGRP. You keep seeing the address 224.0.0.10 in the debug information. What does that address mean?

    A. It's an address that is assigned to EIGRP processes.

    B. It's the broadcast address that EIGRP uses to send updates.

    C. It's the address of the router you're running debug on.

    D. It's a multicast address EIGRP uses to send updates to neighboring routers.

5. Figure 8.5 is a diagram of your network. You are configuring EIGRP on your network, and you are starting by configuring Router2. You've executed the *router eigrp 100* command to enable EIGRP on the router for AS 100. You are now at the *(config-router)#* prompt. After you finish configuring Router2, you will configure Router1 and Router3 to complete the configuration. What *network* command(s) need to be executed on Router2 so that Router2 will do its part to make sure all network and subnet information for the entire network will be advertised throughout your entire network once all the routers have been configured?

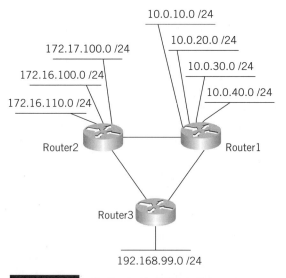

FIGURE 8.5   *Configuring the Network Statements*

A. *network 10.0.10.0*

    network 10.0.20.0

    network 10.0.30.0

    network 10.0.40.0

    network 192.168.99.0

B. *network 10.0.0.0*

    network 192.168.99.0

C. *network 172.0.0.0*

D. *network 172.16.0.0*

    network 172.17.0.0

E. *network 10.0.0.0*

    network 172.16.0.0

    network 172.17.0.0

    network 192.168.99.0

6. You just brought up a new router on your network, but it can't see the rest of the network. You configured EIGRP on the new router, but when you check the routing table, you notice that there are no EIGRP routes listed. The other routers were already running EIGRP, and everything was working fine. What is the first thing you should probably check in your EIGRP configuration?

    A. That debug is turned on.

    B. That there isn't a *shutdown* command in the EIGRP configuration.

    C. That the same AS is configured on the new router as what is already on the existing routers.

    D. That you've added the address of the new router into the EIGRP configuration on the other routers.

7. You're looking at the information that EIGRP works with in the routing processes it performs. You are executing commands on one of the routers on your network to look at the EIGRP databases. What is the command you would use to look at information about the other routers your router exchanges routing information with?

    A. *show eigrp routers*

    B. *show ip eigrp neighbors*

    C. *show eigrp neighbors*

    D. *show ip route*

8. You're looking at the topology table to see information on all possible routes to destination networks. Some of the routes that you see in the topology table are also in the routing table. What are those routes called?

    A. Successors

    B. Selected routes

    C. Feasible successors

    D. Feasible distances

9. Some of the routes in the routing table don't appear to be the best routes to you. You're trying to figure out how EIGRP came up with the routes that it put into the routing table, so you are trying to duplicate the router's calculations. What are the two factors EIGRP uses by default to calculate its metrics?

   A. Bandwidth and load
   B. Bandwidth and reliability
   C. Bandwidth and delay
   D. Delay and reliability
   E. Reliability and load

10. You are in the process of verifying your EIGRP configurations on your routers. What is the command you would execute to confirm that EIGRP is configured correctly?

    A. *show ip route eigrp*
    B. *show ip eigrp neighbors*
    C. *show ip eigrp topology*
    D. *show ip protocols*

11. Figure 8.6 is a diagram of your company network. Packets don't seem to be routing correctly across your network, so you are troubleshooting EIGRP. You've checked the configurations of EIGRP on all the routers, they are all running the same AS, and all the *network* statements are correct to exchange all routing information among all routers. Now you're looking at the configuration for Router1, and you've determined that EIGRP is auto-summarizing routes because the *no auto-summary* command is not listed in the configuration. What network address(es) should Router1 be advertising to the other two routers?

    A. 172.16.0.0, 172.17.0.0, and 10.0.0.0
    B. 172.0.0.0 and 10.0.0.0

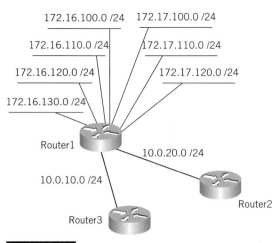

FIGURE 8.6 *Verifying Auto-Summarization*

    C. 172.16.100.0, 172.16.110.0, 172.16.120.0, 172.16.130.0, 172.17.100.0, 172.17.110.0, and 172.17.120.0

    D. 172.16.0.0

12. Now that you know the benefits of EIGRP, you have decided to implement it on your network. Up to this point, all the routing has been handled with static routes. Your only concern is that one of your routers connects directly to the Internet, and you don't want to advertise routing information about your network out to the Internet. What is the command that you would use to prevent routing information from being advertised to the Internet?

    A. shutdown in interface configuration mode

    B. *passive-interface* in interface configuration mode

    C. *passive-interface <interface>* in router configuration mode

    D. *disable* in interface configuration mode

13. Part of the network that you've inherited at your new job is shown in Figure 8.7. Your new boss wants you to clean up the router configurations as much as possible, and one of the things you've decided to do is configure summary routes on every interface on every router where it makes sense. You need to calculate the summary address and mask to apply to interface FastEthernet 0/0 on Router1 in the diagram. What is the address and mask that you should have come up with?

    A. 192.168.12.0 255.255.252.0   **C.** 192.168.12.0 255.255.255.0

    B. 192.168.0.0 255.255.255.0   **D.** 192.168.15.0 255.255.252.0

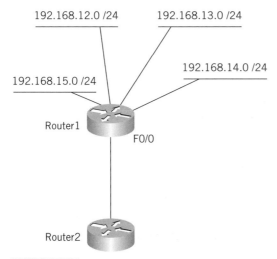

FIGURE 8.7 *Calculating a Summary Address and Mask*

14. While cleaning up the configurations on your routers, you are configuring summary routes everywhere it is appropriate. What command do you use to configure a summary route for EIGRP?

    A. *ip summary-address eigrp <summary-address> <mask>* in router configuration mode

    B. *ip summary-address eigrp <AS> <summary-address> <mask>* in *Global Configuration* mode

    C. *ip summary-address eigrp <AS> <summary-address> <mask>* in router configuration mode

    D. *ip summary-address eigrp <AS> <summary-address> <mask>* in interface configuration mode

15. What is the powerful component of EIGRP that tracks all reported routes, manages successors and feasible successors, and implements loop-free routing?

    A. PDMs

    B. DUAL

    C. Hello

    D. MD5

16. You're troubleshooting EIGRP and trying to identify why a particular route isn't showing up in the routing table. Right now you're watching debug information to make sure all the correct packets are being sent and received. To figure out where the problem is occurring, you are verifying each step of the process EIGRP goes through. You see a lot of information about hello packets. What is the hello packet's part of the process?

    A. To send route updates

    B. To ask for route updates

    C. To respond to requests for route updates

    D. Neighbor discover/recovery

17. Security is such an important consideration on these days. You are concerned about the possibility of unauthorized or false routing information being sent to your EIGRP routers. What is the technology you would implement to prevent this from happening?

    A. MD5 Authentication

    B. Summary routes

    C. Clear text authentication

    D. Passwords

18. EIGRP isn't working correctly on your network since you brought up a new router. The messages that you're seeing in debug tell you that there's an authentication mismatch. What problem are you experiencing?

   A. A neighbor went down

   B. The MD5 keys don't match on the routers that are trying to communicate.

   C. The ASes don't match on the routers that are trying to communicate.

   D. A *network* statement wasn't typed correctly.

19. You have gotten several calls from users on one of your remote networks telling you that communicating with the other company networks has gotten extremely slow. In the process of troubleshooting the problem with the network, how would you figure out the path being used to send packets from your network to the remote network?

   A. Look at the neighbors with the *show ip neighbors* command.

   B. Look at the interfaces with the *show ip interfaces* command.

   C. Look at the routing table with the *show ip route* command.

   D. Look at your physical network diagram.

20. You're looking at the information in the IP routing table and it looks like the route to one of your remote networks is not the best or most efficient route. How can you look at the information on all the EIGRP routes your router knows about to the destination network to see if the router knows about the route you believe is the best one?

   A. *show all routes*

   B. *show ip eigrp topology*

   C. *show all ip routes*

   D. *show ip route eigrp*

21. You're looking at the information in the IP routing table to determine how packets are being delivered to different destination networks. You've identified the entries beginning with Cs as directly connected and the entries beginning with Ss as static routes. There are several entries with Ds at the front. What type of routes are those?

   A. Detoured routes that the router is redirecting

   B. Direct routes from point-to-point

   C. EIGRP routes

   D. RIPv2 routes

22. There seems to be an unusual amount of traffic on your network and you're trying to track down the problem. You're looking at the topology table, and you want to make sure that the routes aren't being recalculated. What are you looking for in the first column of the topology table to see if the routes are recalculating?

A. The R for Recalculate or the N for Not Recalculating

B. The A for Active or the P for Passive

C. An X in the field

D. A blank field

23. You have configured summary routes on some of your interfaces, and you want to verify that you've configured them correctly. How could you look at the EIGRP configuration on your interfaces?

A. *show ip eigrp interfaces* **C.** *show ip eigrp topology*

B. *show ip route* **D.** *show ip eigrp summary-routes*

24. EIGRP has been running on your network for a few days and you want to see how many and what types of EIGRP packets your router has sent and received. How would you find this information?

A. Execute the *show ip eigrp* command

B. Turn on debugging

C. Execute the *show ip eigrp traffic* command

D. Execute the *show eigrp statistics* command

25. Right now your routers are all running IGRP. After hearing about the advanced features in EIGRP, you want to change your network over to EIGRP. The problem is that you have a lot of routers, and although they are all in the same AS, some of them are at remote locations and not set up for remote access. There's just no way it would be possible to get all the routers changed to IGRP all at once. What do you need to do to transition your network to EIGRP more slowly?

A. Use the same AS on your EIGRP routers as is on your IGRP routers.

B. It wouldn't work. All the routers would have to be changed to EIGRP at the same time.

C. Execute the *convert igrp* command on the EIGRP routers as you bring them up.

D. Configure static routes to route between the EIGRP and IGRP routers.

26. You're in the process of transitioning your network from EIGRP to IGRP. So far, you've configured EIGRP on some of your routers and the rest are still running IGRP. You're trying to understand why some of the routes that are in the routing table aren't the same ones that were there before you started bringing up EIGRP on some of the routers. What is the factor that is most likely causing the change?

   A. Administrative distances

   B. Autonomous systems

   C. Something is wrong with your configuration

   D. Network numbers

27. You are looking at debug information and watching the EIGRP packets cross the router. You see information about sequence numbers and retransmits. You know these are part of the function of the EIGRP component that handles reliability. What is this component called?

   A. DUAL

   B. PDMs

   C. RTP

   D. AS

28. You are documenting your network, and you need the IP address of the devices with which the router has established an adjacency. You also need to check the queue counts for those routers. What is the command that will allow you to look at this information?

   A. *show ip eigrp adjacency*

   B. *show ip eigrp interfaces*

   C. *show ip eigrp neighbors*

   D. *show ip eigrp topology*

29. While looking at the *show ip eigrp topology* table, you see something at the end of each route that says *FD is* and is followed by a big number. What is it that you are looking at?

   A. Administrative distances for the routes

   B. Network numbers for the routes

   C. Next hop information

   D. The metric for the route

30. While troubleshooting routing problems on your network, you discover that some of the routes in the topology table have an A in the first column for Active, meaning that the routes are being recalculated. As you continue to check the topology table periodically, those routes are often showing Active. You've verified that the routers are okay and there doesn't seem to be any problem other than a very busy network. What is the command that will most likely correct the problem?

A. *ip hello-interval eigrp 100 15*

B. *ip hold-time eigrp 100 45*

C. *debug ip eigrp*

D. *show ip eigrp*

SELF TEST QUICK ANSWER KEY

1. D	**11.** A	**21.** C
2. A	**12.** C	**22.** B
3. C	**13.** A	**23.** A
4. D	**14.** D	**24.** C
5. D	**15.** B	**25.** A
6. C	**16.** D	**26.** A
7. B	**17.** A	**27.** C
8. A	**18.** B	**28.** C
9. C	**19.** C	**29.** D
10. D	**20.** B	**30.** B

Access Control Lists

INTRODUCTION

Access control lists (ACLs) are one of the fundamental building blocks of a network configuration. If you fully understand how Access lists are constructed and used, you're well on your way to providing adequate security to your network. However, if you fail to grasp how wildcard masks are used or how order of operation affects Network Address Translation (NAT), then you could very well make your network the next successful target of a hacker. Understanding this topic is important, both for the test and for your career.

Unlike many technologies you will learn as a Cisco Certified Network Associate (CCNA) candidate, ACLs are really old. Standard ACLs that match traffic based on source Internet Protocol (IP) address were part of IOS 8.3. Since IOS 9 was introduced in 1992, you know ACLs have been part of securing networks for a very long time. For comparison, the first graphical point-and-click Web browser Mosaic was introduced in 1993.

In this chapter, we'll cover the most important elements of IP ACLs with an emphasis on the material required for the CCNA exam. We'll see how the most basic ACLs are used and how ACLs have matured over the years. Other topics covered will include how to select which type of ACL to use, how to build it, how to apply it, and how to troubleshoot it when things go wrong. We'll discover some of the most common ACL errors made by network engineers and how to avoid them. Finally, although not required material for the exam, we'll learn about some of the newest ACL technology.

THE ANATOMY OF AN ACL

ACLs can be used for many things in IOS. The most obvious application is to filter network traffic. In this case, the ACL is applied to an interface and is evaluated as traffic passes through the router. If the ACL permits the traffic, the packet is allowed to pass. If the ACL denies the traffic, the packet is dropped.

However, there is more than one way to use an ACL. IOS has many other uses for ACLs — from filtering routes learned from Open Shortest Path First (OSPF) neighbors to classifying traffic for quality of service (QoS) and to limiting the scope of a *debug* command. In all these cases, the basics of how an ACL is built remain the same. But, the actual meaning of "permit" and "deny" depends on how the ACL is used. If the ACL is applied to an interface, deny will drop the packet. But, if the ACL is part of a QoS config, the same deny may cause the packet to be marked with a specific DiffServ Code Point (DSCP) value.

ACL Types

Just as there are many different ways to use an ACL, there are also many different kinds of ACLs to use. An IP ACL can't be used to filter a DECnet packet, and an Internetwork Packet Exchange (IPX) Access list isn't effective for blocking an IP fragment. Each protocol must have its own ACL type. Each type has a different set of criteria that can be used to match packets of that protocol. Table 9.1 shows the list of ACL numbers and the corresponding ACL type.

Not all IOS feature sets support all ACL types. For example, a router running "IP Base" software won't have the capability to create an IPX Access list. The IOS Packaging page at Cisco.com (www.cisco.com/en/US/products/sw/iosswrel/ps5460/index.html) can help you understand what is contained in the various features sets and how to determine your feature set based on the information available from the *show version* command.

Not all versions support all ACL types. For example, IP extended Access lists in the range 2000 to 2699 and standard Access list in the range 1300

Table 9.1	ACL Numbers and Types Available in IOS
ACL Number	**ACL Type**
1 to 99	IP standard Access list
100 to 199	IP extended Access list
200 to 299	Protocol type-code Access list
300 to 399	DECnet Access list
400 to 499	XNS standard Access list
500 to 599	XNS extended Access list
600 to 699	AppleTalk Access list
700 to 799	48-bit MAC address Access list
800 to 899	IPX standard Access list
900 to 999	IPX extended Access list
1000 to 1099	IPX SAP Access list
1100 to 1199	Extended 48-bit MAC address Access list
1200 to 1299	IPX summary address Access list
1300 to 1999	IP standard Access list (expanded range)
2000 to 2699	IP extended Access list (expanded range)

to 1999 were released with IOS version 12.0.1. Review the IOS documentation for version-specific information. A quick way to find out which ACL types are available is to enter *config* mode and use the question mark. The following is output from a router running a 12.*x* feature set supporting only IP.

```
router(config)#access-list?
   <1-99>        IP standard access list
   <100-199>     IP extended access list
   <1100-1199>   Extended 48-bit MAC address access list
   <1300-1999>   IP standard access list (expanded range)
   <200-299>     Protocol type-code access list
   <2000-2699>   IP extended access list (expanded range)
   <700-799>     48-bit MAC address access list
```

The CCNA test topics published by Cisco (www.cisco.com/web/learning/le3/current_exams/640-802.html) only cover IP Access lists, so these will be covered in this chapter.

Access Control Entries Definition and Order

At its most basic, an ACL is an ordered list of Access Control Entries (ACE). Each ACE is a single statement that defines a condition which a packet is evaluated against. If the packet satisfies the condition, the packet "matches" the ACE. When there is a match, the corresponding action (either permit or deny) is taken. If there is no match, the packet is evaluated against the next ACE in the list. ACLs cannot be nested. An ACE cannot contain or call another ACL.

ACEs are in an "ordered list," which means that they are evaluated from top to bottom. The evaluation continues until the packet is either specifically permitted or specifically denied or the end of the ACL is reached. All ACLs have an implicit "deny all" at the end—so the packet is always matched. In fact, even those ACLs that end with a "permit any" statement still have the hidden "deny all" at the end. Of course, this will never be evaluated because the packet will always match the "permit any."

Because they are evaluated in order, it should be obvious that the placement of the ACEs is important. If the first ACE matches all traffic, then the remainder of the ACL will never be evaluated. This makes it especially important to understand how packets are matched—so you can be sure to avoid the very common mistake of incorrectly matching traffic.

IP ACE Criteria

There are many elements of an IP packet that can be matched in an ACE. The most obvious is the IP address itself. Standard ACLs allow only the source IP address of the packet to be matched. Extended ACLs can match packets based on the source, the destination, or both. The ACE uses an IP address/wildcard mask pair for address matching.

IP Matching Using Wildcard Masks

For many, the most challenging part of creating an ACL is to choose the correct wildcard mask to match the desired IP addresses. A wildcard mask is similar to the inverse of a subnet mask, but it is not required that the 1 bit be left-contiguous. It is used with an IP address to define which traffic is permitted or denied.

Recall from Chapter 3 that IP addresses and subnet masks can be expressed as binary bits (each with a value of 0 or 1). A *subnet mask* is a series of leftmost contiguous bits used to identify the network portion of an IP address. In contrast, a *wildcard mask* is most often a series of rightmost contiguous bits used to identify the portion of an IP address that is *ignored* during the matching process.

For example, assume you have an IP address of 213.18.37.15 with a subnet mask of 255.255.255.0. The subnet mask would identify the network portion of the IP address as 213.18.37.0 and the host portion as 18.

Exam Warning

Don't make too much out of the similarities between a subnet mask and a wildcard mask. They are similar, but they perform very different functions. Be sure you understand when each is required—it is essential for passing the test.

Now assume you want to match all hosts in the subnet 213.18.37.0. You would use the inverse mask of 0.0.0.255. Table 9.2 shows a table of subnet masks and corresponding wildcard masks. The rows highlighted in gray are masks that break on an octet boundary. Although these are most commonly used, it is important for CCNA candidates to understand how the entire table works.

Table 9.2 Subnet and Wildcard Masks

CIDR Notation	Subnet Mask	Wildcard Mask
/0	0.0.0.0	255.255.255.255
/1	128.0.0.0	127.255.255.255
/2	192.0.0.0	63.255.255.255
/3	224.0.0.0	31.255.255.255
/4	240.0.0.0	15.255.255.255
/5	248.0.0.0	7.255.255.255
/6	252.0.0.0	3.255.255.255
/7	254.0.0.0	1.255.255.255
/8	255.0.0.0	0.255.255.255
/9	255.128.0.0	0.127.255.255
/10	255.192.0.0	0.63.255.255
/11	255.224.0.0	0.31.255.255
/12	255.240.0.0	0.15.255.255
/13	255.248.0.0	0.7.255.255
/14	255.252.0.0	0.3.255.255
/15	255.254.0.0	0.1.255.255
/16	255.255.0.0	0.0.255.255
/17	255.255.128.0	0.0.127.255

Continued

Table 9.2 Subnet and Wildcard Masks *continued*

CIDR Notation	Subnet Mask	Wildcard Mask
/18	255.255.192.0	0.0.63.255
/19	255.255.224.0	0.0.31.255
/20	255.255.240.0	0.0.15.255
/21	255.255.248.0	0.0.7.255
/22	255.255.252.0	0.0.3.255
/23	255.255.254.0	0.0.1.255
/24	255.255.255.128	0.0.0.127
/25	255.255.255.192	0.0.0.63
/26	255.255.255.224	0.0.0.31
/27	255.255.255.240	0.0.0.15
/28	255.255.255.248	0.0.0.7
/29	255.255.255.252	0.0.0.3
/30	255.255.255.254	0.0.0.1
/31	255.255.255.255	0.0.0.0

This table makes it obvious that using wildcard masks is very easy if the range you wish to mask contains all hosts in a particular network. In that case, you simply apply the wildcard mask that corresponds to the subnet mask (for example, its' inverse).

Test Day Tip

Try to understand the pattern rather than memorizing the table. If you know why the table is built as it is, you can recreate the appropriate wildcard mask easily while taking the test. Why do you not need a calculator to figure out the wildcard mask? Working with subnet masks has probably made you good at determining how many host addresses are available for each mask. For example, 255.255.255.240 creates networks with 16 hosts. The wildcard mask is simply one less than this—0.0.0.15. The mask 255.255.255.252 creates a network of four addresses, and 0.0.0.3 is the wildcard mask. Remember this simple rule and you can figure the wildcard mask very easily.

The job of matching a range is also easy if the range falls on an octet boundary (/0, /8, /16, /24, /32) as you can see in Table 9.3. For example, if you specify an IP address/wildcard mask pair of 2.2.2.0/0.0.0.255, the ACE

Table 9.3 Wildcard Mask Used on the Octet Boundary

Wildcard Mask	Range to Match
255.255.255.255	Match any host
0.255.255.255	x.0-255.0-255.0-255
0.0.255.255	x.x.0-255.0-255
0.0.0.255	x.x.x.0-255
0.0.0.0	Match-specific host

would match all IP addresses in the range 2.2.2.0 to 2.2.2.255. If you specify the pair 2.2.0.0/0.0.255.255, the ACE would match addresses in the range 2.2.0.0 to 2.2.255.255.

The combination of IP address and wildcard mask can be used to match specific hosts or a range of hosts. These ranges can be the same as a subnet, but they can as easily be a range larger or smaller than the subnet. For example, assume you have the following IP address/wildcard mask pair—192.168.32.16/0.0.0.15. The ACE would match hosts 192.168.32.16 to 192.168.32.31. The actual host subnet may have a /16 mask (255.255.0.0), but the ACE in this case was used to match a small subset of 16 hosts within the large subnet.

The wildcard mask also can be used to match a range larger than the subnet. For example, if you were using a block of 16 contiguous networks all using the /28 subnet mask, you could use a 0.0.0.255 wildcard mask to match all IP addresses in all networks with a single ACE.

Here's a real world example. Assume you use the following 16 networks:

- 10.1.2.0/28

- 10.1.2.16/28

- 10.1.2.32/28

- …

- 10.1.2.240/28

All the hosts in these networks can be matched in a single ACE using the IP address and wildcard mask—10.1.2.0/0.0.0.255

To be a bit more generic, wildcard mask bits that are set to 0 are "care" bits and those set to 1 are "don't care" bits in the matching process. Table 9.4 is an example of how the bit matching actually works. Consider the example where you have the IP address/wildcard mask pair of 10.1.3.176/0.0.0.15. Which addresses match depend on whether the binary bits match the "care" bits.

Table 9.4	An Example of Wildcard Mask Bit Matching			
Example	**Fourth Octet**	**Bit Representation**		
10.1.3.176	176	1 0 1 1	0 0 0 0	
	Wildcard mask	Care	Don't care	
0.0.0.15	15	0 0 0 0	1 1 1 1	
		Examples		Result
10.1.3.177	177	1 0 1 1	0 0 0 1	Matches
10.1.3.180	180	1 0 1 1	0 1 0 0	Matches
10.1.3.187	187	1 0 1 1	1 0 1 1	Matches
10.1.3.193	193	1 1 0 0	0 0 0 1	Fails

For simplicity, in this example only the fourth octet is considered, but in reality all bits of the IP address are compared in the same way. The first 4 bits of the fourth octet of 10.1.3.180 match the first 4 bits of the fourth octet of our reference IP address 10.1.3.176. This is true of .177 and .187 too. In fact, all hosts in the range 10.1.3.176 to 10.1.3.191 will match because they all have the first 4 bits of 1101. 10.1.3.193 has the first 4 bits of 1100 (193 = 1100001 in binary and 193 in decimal). Of course, addresses such as 9.1.3.177 would fail too because the wildcard mask is 0.0.0.15. In this case, the first, second, and third octets must match all 8 bits.

Getting Fancy with Wildcard Masks

A few paragraphs ago, it was written that a wildcard mask is *most often* a series of rightmost contiguous bits. Although this is true in practice, it is definitely not required. The wildcard mask is extremely flexible in allowing you to match only the hosts you want (which is essential if the ACL is used for security), but the notation can also get complex when the range of hosts is not trivial. Consider a few more challenging examples in Table 9.5.

Exam Warning

It is a very common mistake to use a normal subnet mask in an ACE instead of a wildcard mask, especially when you're under pressure (like during a test). When creating an ACL, get in the habit of mentally creating a list of addresses that will be matched using the "1s are don't care bits" rule. This will help you double-check to make sure you haven't fallen into this trap. One thing to note, Cisco firewalls use normal subnet masks in ACLs. Go figure!

Table 9.5	Less Obvious Examples of a Wildcard Mask	
IP Address	**Wildcard Mask**	**Range Matched**
2.2.2.2	255.255.255.255	0.0.0.0 - 255.255.255.255
2.2.2.2	0.255.0.0	2.0.2.2 - 2.255.2.2
2.2.2.2	128.0.128.0	0-127.2.0-127.0
2.2.2.2	0.46.0.23	Break out the calculator!

Wildcard Shortcuts

There are a few special keywords that can be used as a shortcut in an ACE definition. These include as follows:

- x.x.x.x/255.255.255.255 can be specified with the keyword *any*. Used with any IP address, because this wildcard mask in binary is all 1s, this matches all IP addresses.

- x.x.x.x/0.0.0.0 can be specified with the keyword *host*. Used with any IP address, because this wildcard mask in binary is all 0s, this matches only the given address and no others.

Filtering on Other Elements of the Packet

In addition to IP addresses, extended ACLs allow many other parts of the IP packet to be used to match within the ACE. These include protocol, source and destination port, DSCP, IP precedence, IP options, and so forth. This section discusses the most important of these options.

Protocol

As you know from the Open Systems Interconnection (OSI) Reference Model coverage in this book, the IP is not monolithic. Transmission Control Protocol (TCP) and User Datagram Protocol (UDP) are upper layer protocols that are carried inside IP. In addition, Internet Control Message Protocol (ICMP) is a utility protocol that uses the IP packet for transport. These are the most common but are definitely not the complete list. In fact, any integer between 0 and 255 can be used to represent a protocol, but several common ones can also be referenced by a keyword. In addition to ip, tcp, udp, and ICMP, other protocol keywords that can be used in an extended IP Access list include eigrp, gre, igmp, ospf, and pim.

Ports

Both UDP and TCP use port numbers to identify which upper-layer protocol should receive the incoming packet. For example, if a packet is handed to the

Table 9.6	Commonly Used Port Names in ACE Matching	
Protocol	**Port Name**	**Port Number**
TCP	Telnet	23
	smtp	25
	www	80
UDP	dns	53
	tftp	69
	Snmp	161
	Syslog	514

TCP stack with the destination port number of 23, the protocol knows that it should forward this packet to the Telnet application running on the host.

ACEs can match packets based on the source and/or destination port numbers. Port numbers range from 0 to 65,535. To make configuration easier, IOS allows you to substitute a name for a few well-known ports. A few of the most common port names are given in Table 9.6. For a full list of which names are supported by your version of IOS, refer to the Cisco software documentation (www.cisco.com/web/psa/products/index.html?c=268438303). For a list of default port numbers used in the transport layer, refer to the Internet Assigned Numbers Authority (IANA) Web site that maintains the list (www.iana.org/assignments/port-numbers).

To make ACL matching more efficient, IOS allows you to use some common mathematical operators when specifying port numbers. They include as follows:

- **eq** (equal) exactly matches the specified port.

- **neq** (not equal) matches all but the specified port.

- **gt** (greater than) matches any port greater than the specified port.

- **lt** (less than) matches any port smaller than the specified port.

- **range** (range of ports) matches any port within an inclusive range of ports.

QoS Information

The Differentiated Services Code Point (DSCP) is a field in the header of an IP packet. This field (defined in Request for Comments (RFC) 2474 and

RFC2475—www.ietf.org/rfc/rfc2474.txt) is used to mark a packet to ensure it is handled correctly by each device in the network, without each having to individually evaluate the contents of the packet. Once marked, the packet can be treated (queued, dropped, and so forth) differently from other packets based on a QoS policy defined by administrators. The DSCP value is 6 bits and can range from 0 to 63.

The DSCP field superseded the IP Precedence value (3 bits can represent values from 0 to 7) and the type of service (TOS) field (4 bits ranging from 0 to 15). Both are defined in RFC791—www.ietf.org/rfc/rfc791.txt. These are used in a similar way as DSCP—to mark traffic to influence per hop behavior throughout the network.

An IP ACL can match packets that have been marked by any of these QoS values. This is a very common way to implement QoS policy—such as, dropping low-priority traffic over a backup circuit, for example.

State Information

The TCP is stateful—roughly meaning that the communications between hosts are negotiated and there is a connection between them. The connection is brought up, data is transferred, and then the connection is torn down.

One useful ACE element is matching based on whether a packet is part of an "established" connection. Figure 9.1 shows how this can be done. An inbound ACL is configured on port A that permits only established packets. In this example, Elizabeth can send any packet to Katherine, but Elizabeth can't send packets to Katherine without those packets being part of an established connection.

To be specific, the router will match traffic when the "established" keyword is specified only if the ACK or RST flags are set in the TCP header. This feature is very useful for securing an Internet connection because it allows inbound packets in response to outbound connection requests (for example, Web access) but blocks all others.

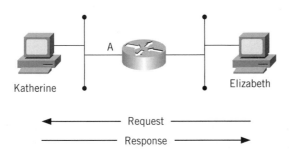

FIGURE 9.1

Using the Established Keyword

ACL DETAILS AND EXAMPLES

Now that you understand what elements can be used in an ACE, it's time to consider how to put the ACL together. IP ACLs come in two types—standard and extended. Starting in IOS version 11.2, ACLs can be configured either with numbers or with names. This section will cover syntax and provide examples and then discuss several ACL enhancements that make ACL management a bit easier.

Recall that ACLs are an ordered list of ACEs. As new ACEs are added, they are appended to the end of the list. An ACL can contain one or a great many ACEs. They are entered in the router configuration one ACE at a time.

Standard ACLs

The easiest ACL to define is the standard type, which can match packets based only on the source IP address. The syntax for a numbered standard ACE is given below. Keywords are displayed in normal text while variables are shown in italics.

```
access-list access-list-number {permit | deny} {host | source
    wildcard | any}
```

Here are a few examples and a short explanation of each:

```
access-list 3 permit 10.1.1.0 0.0.0.255
```

This ACE permits traffic sourced from IP addresses in 10.1.1.0/24, which includes 10.1.1.0 to 10.1.1.255.

```
access-list 88 deny 10.1.2.16 0.0.0.15
```

This ACE denies traffic sourced from IP addresses in 10.1.2.16/28 (0001 of fourth octet), which includes 10.1.2.16 to 10.1.2.31.

```
access-list 99 permit 10.0.0.0 0.255.255.255
```

This ACE permits traffic sourced from IP addresses in 10.0.0.0/8, which includes 10.0.0.0 to 10.255.255.255.

```
access-list 1 permit host 1.1.1.1
```

This ACE permits traffic source only from host 1.1.1.1.

```
access-list 10 deny any
```

This ACE denies all traffic.
This is not correct:

```
access-list 101 permit 10.1.1.0 0.0.0.255
```

Because the Access list number 101 is an extended ACL, the source-only matching in this ACE is not accepted by the command-line interface (CLI).

At first, the source-only nature of the matching may seem rather limiting. However, in some situations, matching based on source IP is all that is necessary. For example, assume you want to allow users only on a certain internal subnet to access the Internet. Because it's not possible to list all hosts on the Internet in an ACL, there's no benefit to specifying a destination in the ACE.

In fact, in some cases, matching on source IP is all that is possible. For example, consider creating an ACL to be used to block incoming Simple Network Management Protocol (SNMP) requests on the router. Because this traffic is destined for the router itself, only a standard ACL can be applied to the SNMP commands in the CLI.

Extended ACLs

If the simplicity of the standard ACL is not sufficient to provide the access control required, extended ACLs allow far greater matching capability. These ACLs can match on source and destination addresses in the packet, source and destination ports, protocols, and a variety of other fields.

> **Test Day Tip**
>
> It's not required that you memorize the exact syntax of every command covered on the test. The CCNA exam is not intended to measure your memory capacity. By performing the exercises in this book and studying the examples, you will be able to tell the level of detail required to pass the exam. Don't worry if you don't know all possible values of *icmp-type* in an extended ACL.

The syntax of an ACE in an extended ACL is much more complex because the fields in the packet depend on the protocol. The criteria for a TCP ACL are very different from one that matches ICMP traffic. For that reason, IP, ICMP, TCP, and UDP all have different syntax. The basic syntax for a numbered extended ACE is given below. Keywords are displayed in normal text, whereas variables are shown in italics.

IP

```
access-list access-list-number {deny | permit} protocol
    source source-wildcard destination destination-wildcard
    [precedence precedence] [tos tos] [log]
```

TCP

```
access-list access-list-number {deny | permit} tcp source
    source-wildcard [operator [port]]
destination    destination-wildcard    [operator    [port]]
    [established] [precedence precedence]
[tos tos] [log]
```

UDP

```
access-list access-list-number {deny | permit} udp source
    source-wildcard [operator [port]]
destination destination-wildcard [operator [port]] [prece-
    dence precedence] [tos tos] [log]
```

ICMP

```
access-list access-list-number {deny | permit} icmp source
    source-wildcard
destination destination-wildcard [icmp-type | [[icmp-type
    icmp-code] | [icmp-message]]
[precedence precedence] [tos tos] [log]
```

The following are a few examples and a short explanation of each:

```
access-list 101 permit ip 10.1.1.0 0.0.0.255 10.1.2.0
    0.0.0.255
```

This ACE permits all IP traffic sourced from IP addresses in 10.1.1.0/24 destined to IP addresses in 10.1.2.0/24. This ACL matches all IP traffic including TCP and UDP.

```
access-list 188 deny gre host 10.1.1.1 any
```

This ACE denies GRE-encapsulated traffic sourced from IP address 10.1.1.1 to any destination.

```
access-list 150 permit tcp 10.3.3.0 0.0.0.255 10.0.0.0
    0.255.255.255 eq 23
```

This ACE permits TCP traffic sourced from IP addresses in 10.3.3.0/24 to IP addresses in 10.0.0.0/8 with a destination port of 23 (Telnet).

```
access-list 122 permit tcp 192.168.32.0 0.0.31.255 192.0.0.0
    0.255.255.255 established log
```

This ACE permits TCP traffic sourced from IP addresses in 192.168.32.0/19 destined to IP addresses in 192.0.0.0/8, but only when the ACK or RST flags are set. In addition, this ACE will log the match at the informational level.

```
access-list 111 deny udp host 172.16.3.3 range 1 1023 any
   gt 1023
```

This ACE denies UDP traffic from 172.16.3.3 to any destination when the source port is between 1 and 1023 and the destination port is greater than 1023.

```
access-list 151 permit udp any any precedence 5
```

This ACE permits UDP traffic from any source to any destination when the IP Precedence value is set to 5.

```
access-list 177 permit icmp host 192.168.4.4 host 172.16.1.1
   echo-reply
```

This ACE permits ICMP traffic 192.168.4.4 to 172.16.1.1 when the ICMP type is "echo-reply." This keyword is one of many available. This ACE permits responses to Packet Internet Groper (PING).

```
access-list 188 deny icmp any any unreachable
```

This ACE denies all ICMP unreachable messages.

Limitations of Numbered ACLs

Because ACEs are evaluated in order, it is very important to make sure that the ACEs are ordered properly. With numbered ACLs, all new ACEs are added to the end of the existing list of ACEs.

This yields several well-known drawbacks of numbered ACLs.

- There is no way to remove a single ACE from a numbered ACL.

- There is no way to reorder ACEs.

- There is no way to insert a new ACE in the middle of an existing numbered ACL.

To deal with these limitations, router administrators are forced to delete the entire ACL and reapply the configuration with the proper ACEs in the desired order. But, this has its own problems.

Removing a standard or extended numbered Access list is done using the "no" form of the command. For example, the following command will delete the entire Access list including all ACEs. Attempting to remove a single ACE will result in the entire ACL being removed.

```
Router(config)# no access-list 5
```

This makes ACL management difficult especially if the ACL is currently applied to an interface. When an ACL that is applied to an interface is removed, the ACL stops functioning and all traffic is permitted.

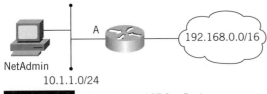

NetAdmin
10.1.1.0/24

FIGURE 9.2   *Removing an ACE Can Be dangerous*

Removing and re-adding an ACL with the unwanted ACE removed, even when done in a script, is dangerous. The reason is that ACEs start working immediately after being entered into the configuration. Imagine a network administrator in Figure 9.2 who has a Telnet session to the router to remove an ACE from the ACL applied inbound (from the router's perspective) on interface A.

The original ACL looks like this

```
Access-list 101 deny tcp 10.1.1.0 0.0.0.255 192.169.0.0
   0.0.255.255 eq 80
Access-list 101 deny tcp 10.1.1.0 0.0.0.255 192.169.0.0
   0.0.255.255 eq 25
Access-list 101 permit ip any any
```

This ACL blocks Web (tcp/80) and smtp (tcp/25) traffic from 10.1.1.0/24 to 192.168.0.0/16 but permits everything else.

The administrator performs these steps:

```
Router#conf t
Enter configuration commands, one per line. End with CNTL/Z.
Router(config)# no access-list 101
Router(config)# access-list 101 deny tcp 10.1.1.0 0.0.0.255
   192.169.0.0 0.0.255.255 eq 80
Connection to host lost.
```

Yikes! The administrator was ironically safe in removing the ACL—because the interface with the nonexistent ACL permits all traffic. But, when the first ACE was added (and became effective immediately), he or she failed to remember that there was an implicit *deny all* at the end of each ACL. He or she's been kicked off the router, and no users on 10.1.1.0/24 can access 192.168.0.0/16. This problem may not be severe in some situations, but imagine if you were working in a hospital on a router at a remote location. Many security-conscious environments (like military or financial institutions) can't allow even a short amount of time to go by without an ACL on their router interfaces.

To get around this, network engineers devise network management policies to get around the limitation. For example, all ACL management can be performed through out-of-band management interface (like through a dial-up modem or console connection). To avoid having an open ACL even for a short time, the ACL maintenance can be scheduled during a downtime window when the interface can be shut down while the ACL is changed.

There is another trick that experienced administrators use to recover from ACL configuration mistakes especially when working with remote routers. IOS permits a router reboot to be scheduled. Although not the most graceful way of returning to a known-good configuration, it can save you from extended downtime or an embarrassing call to a local site contact when you have messed up an ACL and knocked yourself off a Telnet session. Even the most seasoned router jockeys make these mistakes.

The *reload in* command is followed by a length of time (minutes or hours:minutes). In this example, admin has decided to give himself or herself 10 minutes to complete the change. If he or she doesn't cancel the reboot before that time, the router will automatically reboot and return to the known-good startup config. The reload is cancelled with the *reload cancel* command.

```
Router#reload in 10
System configuration has been modified.
Save? [yes/no]: yes
Building configuration...
[OK]
Reload  scheduled  for  02:45:51  GMT  Thu  Oct  9  2008  (in
    10 minutes) by admin on vty0 (10.2.2.2)
Reload reason: Reload Command
Proceed with reload? [confirm]
Router#conf t
Enter configuration commands, one per line. End with CNTL/Z.
<Do dangerous ACL reconfiguration here>
Router(config)#end
Router#reload cancel
Router#
***
*** --- SHUTDOWN ABORTED ---
***
```

Named Access Lists

Named Access lists do a good job at overcoming the limitations of numbered ACLs. With named lists, it's possible to add or delete an ACE in the middle of an existing ACL that is applied to an interface and working. With a little effort, the add/delete ability is capable of providing a workable (albeit cumbersome) method of reordering ACEs.

Luckily, once you've mastered numbered ACLs, named Access lists are easy to understand. This is because the syntax is not significantly different.

Unlike numbered ACLs, both types of named ACLs begin with the same command:

```
Router (config)# ip access-list {extended | standard} name
```

This command places the administrator in ACL configuration mode, with one of two prompts depending on the ACL type.

```
Router(config-ext-nacl)#
Router(config-std-nacl)#
```

At this point, the syntax is very similar to a numbered ACL except that the Access list *access-list-number* syntax is removed from the beginning of each ACE. For example, here is the syntax of a TCP ACE configured in extended named ACL mode.

```
Sequence-number permit | deny tcp source source-wildcard
    [operator [port]]
destination    destination-wildcard    [operator    [port]]
    [established]
[precedence precedence] [tos tos] [log]
```

The real benefits of named ACLs stem from the sequence number that was added at the beginning of the ACE. This number, which can be any integer from 1 to 2147483647, specifies the location within the ACL that the ACE is placed. In other words, the sequence number allows for the order of evaluation to be controlled.

If no sequence number is specified when the ACE is configured, the default is to append the ACE to the end of the ACL (similar to a numbered ACL) and assign a sequence number that is 10 greater than the largest sequence number.

Removing an ACE is accomplished by using "no" keyword in the configuration and giving a sequence number of the ACE to delete:

```
Router (config-ext-nacl)# no 20
```

It's not difficult to see how these capabilities address the main weaknesses of numbered ACLs. Consider the following example: An Access list EXAMPLE is configured that denies traffic from two hosts and permits traffic from the 10/8 network. The implicit deny-all ACE at the end of the ACL will match any other source address.

```
Router(config)#ip access-list standard EXAMPLE
Router(config-std-nacl)#deny 10.1.1.1
Router(config-std-nacl)#deny 10.2.2.2
Router(config-std-nacl)#permit 10.0.0.0 0.255.255.255
Router(config-std-nacl)#end
```

Notice in the *show* command that a sequence number has been prepended to each ACE by default.

```
Router#show ip access-list EXAMPLE
Standard IP access list EXAMPLE
    10 deny 10.1.1.1
    20 deny 10.2.2.2
    30 permit     10.0.0.0, wildcard bits 0.255.255.255
```

Now assume you want to remove the second ACE in the list—to permit traffic from 10.2.2.2. The rest of the example shows how this is accomplished.

```
Router#conf t
Enter configuration commands, one per line. End with CNTL/Z.
Router(config)#ip access-list standard EXAMPLE
Router(config-std-nacl)#no 20
Router(config-std-nacl)#end
Router#sh ip access-list EXAMPLE
Standard IP access list EXAMPLE
    10 deny 10.1.1.1
    30 permit     10.0.0.0, wildcard bits 0.255.255.255
```

It's not possible to change the sequence number of an existing ACE. So, reordering ACEs becomes an exercise in adding and removing ACEs. Here's an example of the proper way to reorder an ACE. Notice that the second ACE (sequence number 20) will never match because the host 10.1.1.1 is contained within the network that is matched by the first ACE.

```
Router(config)#ip access-list extended EXAMPLE
Router(config-ext-nacl)#deny  tcp 10.0.0.0 0.255.255.255  any
    range 20 21
Router(config-ext-nacl)#permit tcp host 10.1.1.1 any eq 20 21
Router(config-ext-nacl)#deny ip any any
Router(config-ext-nacl)#end
Router#show ip access-list EXAMPLE
Extended IP access list EXAMPLE
    10 deny tcp 10.0.0.0 0.255.255.255 any range ftp-data ftp
    20 permit tcp host 10.1.1.1 any eq ftp-data ftp
    30 deny ip any any
```

To move ACE 20 before ACE 10, it is necessary to change the sequence number to some number less than 10. In this case, sequence number 5 is used. The *show* command now shows the ACEs in the correct order so that host 10.1.1.1 can use File Transfer Protocol (FTP) without being blocked by the deny statement.

```
Router#conf t
Enter configuration commands, one per line. End with CNTL/Z.
Router(config)#ip access-list extended EXAMPLE
Router(config-ext-nacl)#no 20
Router(config-ext-nacl)#5 permit tcp host 10.1.1.1 any
   eq 20 21
Router(config-ext-nacl)#end
Router#show ip access-list EXAMPLE
Extended IP access list EXAMPLE
   5 permit tcp host 10.1.1.1 any eq ftp-data ftp
   10 deny tcp 10.0.0.0 0.255.255.255 any range ftp-data ftp
   30 deny ip any any
```

Notice that the example shows ACE 20 being removed before ACE 5 is added. This is significant because you can't add a second ACE, even with a different sequence number, which is the same as an existing ACE. IOS will not warn you of a problem—it simply ignores the error. This would be the result if the statements were reversed.

```
Router(config)#ip access-list extended EXAMPLE
Router(config-ext-nacl)#5 permit tcp host 10.1.1.1 any eq
   ftp-data ftp
Router(config-ext-nacl)#no 20
Router(config-ext-nacl)#end
Router#show ip access-list EXAMPLE
Extended IP access list EXAMPLE
   10 deny tcp 10.0.0.0 0.255.255.255 any range ftp-data ftp
   30 deny ip any any
```

Although named ACLs are very useful, they can't always be used. Some features in IOS still only support numbered ACLs. One extraordinarily helpful troubleshooting feature of IOS is limiting "debug ip packet" output using an ACL. This can only be accomplished using a numbered ACL.

Renumbering ACE Sequence Numbers

Now that ACEs can be added with a sequence number, you may find it necessary to add an ACE between two ACEs with sequential numbers. For example, assume you have an ACL with the following sequence numbers and you want to add an ACE to be evaluated in between.

```
Router#show ip access-list EXAMPLE
Extended IP access list EXAMPLE
   10 permit ip host 10.1.1.1 any
   11 permit ip host 30.1.1.1 any
```

IOS allows you to renumber sequence numbers of named ACLs by speci-fying the starting sequence number and the number interval. This example changes the previous ACL so that the starting sequence number is 5 and the interval between successive ACEs is 20. This will give you plenty of space to add the new ACE.

```
Router(config)#ip access-list resequence EXAMPLE 5 20
Router (config)#end
Router #show ip access-list EXAMPLE
Extended IP access list EXAMPLE
    5 permit ip host 10.1.1.1 any
    25 permit ip host 30.1.1.1 any
```

ACL comments

Adding inline documentation to ACLs is possible using remark ACEs. Remarks are treated like any other ACE—meaning they are appended to the end of the ACL and have an associated sequence number in a named ACL. The syntax is similar too.

For a named ACL, add a remark using the syntax:

```
ip access-list { standard | extended } name
    remark remark
```

For a numbered ACL, add a remark using the syntax:

```
access-list access-list-number remark remark
```

The trouble with adding comments to an ACL is that it is difficult in practice to tie a comment to another ACE. For example, assume you want to add a remark for each ACE in a numbered ACL. This isn't easy to do because any new ACE is appended to the end of the ACL, so you end up hav-ing all your remarks at the end rather than near the ACE which you want to document. Named ACLs are easier because you have sequence numbers, but it's still a challenge. It is not possible to append a remark off the end of an ACE (like you can in many programming languages), but this would be a nice feature.

APPLYING AN ACL

At this point, you know a lot about defining ACLs—how to select between standard or enhanced, when to use named and numbered, how to manipu-late ACEs, and so forth. But, ACLs don't do anything until they are applied. Now it's time to actually put the ACL in place. An ACL can be applied to an interface or a line (vty, console, tty, aux) or can be used in a variety of other ways from controlling dynamic routes to NAT and QoS.

Test Day Tip

It's a network design best practice to apply ACLs close to the source of the traffic. There is no sense in letting packets flow through your network if you intend to drop them once they reach their destination.

Applying an ACL to an Interface

One of the most common ways an ACL is used is to control traffic flowing in or out of an interface. First, it's important to know the big rule of applying ACLs. You can only apply one ACL per protocol per interface per direction. Think about each part of this rule:

> **One ACL**
> > **Per protocol**
> > > **Per interface**
> > > > **Per direction**

There are a lot of rules implicit in this statement:

1. You can't apply two inbound IP ACLs on the same interface (it doesn't matter if they are one named and one numbered, or one standard and one extended, or one tcp and one UDP—you still can't do it).

2. You can apply one inbound IP ACL and one outbound IP ACL to the same interface.

3. You can apply one inbound IP ACL and one inbound IPX ACL to the same interface.

An ACL is applied to an interface with the following syntax. To remove the ACL, use the **no** form of the command.

```
interface interface
   ip access-group {number | name} {in | out}
   no ip access-group {number | name} {in | out}
```

Traffic direction is an important concept when applying an ACL. When considering in which direction to filter traffic (inbound or outbound), always keep in mind that the direction is from the perspective of the router. "Out" traffic has already been through the router and is leaving the interface. "In" traffic is arriving at the interface and has not yet gone through the router.

There is no longer a default direction. Years ago, an ACL could be applied to an interface without specifying a direction (in or out), and "out" was the default direction. All new IOS versions require that a direction be explicit.

Exam Warning

You can't apply two IP ACLs to an interface that evaluate traffic flowing in the same direction. If you try, the CLI will replace your current ACL with the one you added. Always check the interface to see if an ACL is already applied. If so, combine your new ACEs into the existing ACL, but remember that ACE order is important because they are evaluated from top to bottom.

Applying an ACL to a Terminal Line

An important part of securing a network is to control access to the network device itself. This was especially true when routers were heavily used for access services but is not less important today. Access services included such things as follows:

- Terminal services: Terminals and hosts connecting over local address table (LAT) or TCP.

- Asynchronous IP routing: PCs connecting over a modem running Serial Line Internet Protocol (SLIP) or Point-to-Point Protocol (PPP).

- Remote node services: Remote wide area network (WAN) links over asynchronous interfaces running SLIP or PPP.

To support these services, Cisco routers and switches have four types of terminal lines:

- Console ports use a CON or CTY line, which is normally used for out-of-band device access for configuration and troubleshooting. The console port is normally an RJ-45 port on the device that connects to a flat blue or black console cable that connects to a PC serial interface.

- Asynchronous ports use TTY lines that function as asynchronous interfaces. These are available only on access servers (like a Cisco 5100), and they support modems to allow dial-in sessions over protocols like SLIP and PPP.

- Auxiliary ports use AUX lines and are typically used for modem access for administrators needing out-of-band device access, similar to a console port but over a phone line. These ports are available on many router models, not just access servers.

- Virtual Terminal ports use VTY lines that support incoming Telnet connections into the device. These are sometimes also used for LAT and protocol translation, but this is not common these days.

Access lists can be used to control access to and through these interfaces, but the syntax is slightly different from a normal interface. An ACL is applied to a line with the following syntax. To remove the ACL, use the **no** form of the command.

```
line {line-number | aux | console | vty }
    access-class {number | name} {in | out}
    no access-class {number | name} {in | out}
```

Each type of device has a different mix of line types, so the way you reference your line will depend on the platform. Here's an example of creating an ACL to limit Telnet access into a router.

```
access-list 5 permit 10.1.3.0 0.0.0.255
access-list 5 permit 10.200.0.0 0.0.0.255
!
line vty 0 4
    access-class 5 in
```

In this example, there are two management networks defined in the ACL—10.1.3.0/24 and 10.200.0/24. These networks contain all the devices that should be allowed to Telnet into the router. This router has five terminal lines, numbered 0 through 4. These are assigned to incoming Telnet session,—so only five simultaneous sessions are allowed. The example shows the ACL being applied to all five lines, similar to an *interface range* command. It's important to configure the same access policy on all vty lines because a user could end up connecting to any available line. Use the *show line* command to view which lines are available on your device.

It may seem odd that you can apply an ACL to a console port—because the link is serial and not IP. You would be right—it is odd. The ACL can be applied but it doesn't function.

Other Ways to Apply ACLs

In addition to controlling traffic through a router and blocking nefarious access to a network device, Access lists are used for a variety of other jobs. The following are some examples that show how an ACL is defined and applied. This is not an exhaustive list of all features that need ACLs to function. Rather these are a few of the most common features that use ACLs.

Controlling Access via SNMP

SNMP is a protocol used by network management systems to monitor and control network-attached devices. Ciscoworks, HP Openview, and other management stations all use SNMP.

SNMP access can be granted on a network device in two ways—read-only and read-write. Read-only access allows the management station to poll the device for statistics and other information, but it does not allow anything to be changed. Read-write access allows the management station to make changes to the configuration of the device.

It's obviously a good idea to make sure you trust the devices allowed to make changes to your configuration, but some versions of SNMP use only a simple shared password to permit access. To make this more secure, an ACL can be applied, which limits the source IP addresses that can use SNMP.

The following example limits read-write SNMP access to a management virtual local area network (VLAN) (10.100.20.0/24) and a single host (10.2.2.2). This uses a numbered standard ACL that limits access based on the source of the SNMP request. An extended ACL can't be used with SNMP because the destination of the request will always be the router itself.

```
access-list 99 permit 10.100.20.0 0.0.0.255
access-list 99 permit host 10.2.2.2
!
snmp-server community MySecret RW 99
```

Using ACLs with NAT

NAT is a feature of a network device that maps "internal" addresses to "external" addresses. This feature allows, for example, a network to access the Internet while using private address space. It can also be used to connect networks when they use overlapping addresses.

ACLs are used in the router configuration to define which addresses should be translated and which should not. In the following example, the extended ACL denies traffic destined for the private IP address ranges defined in RFC1918. All other traffic is permitted. It's important to understand that "denied" traffic isn't dropped. Rather, when NAT is being configured, denied traffic is not translated and "permitted" traffic is translated.

```
ip access-list extended NoNAT
   deny ip any 10.0.0.0 0.255.255.255
   deny ip any 172.16.0.0 0.15.255.255
   deny ip any 192.168.0.0 0.0.255.255
   permit ip any any
!
ip nat inside source list NoNAT interface Serial0/0/1:0
   overload
```

Controlling Route Distribution Using ACLs

Dynamic routing protocols allow routers to share information about the network with other routers to allow them to select the best path to reach a destination. In a small network with only a few links and a few destinations, all routers can easily know about all others. However, as the number of links and destinations rises, the number of possible paths can become a problem.

Because no router performs well during protocol convergence after a network change, it is wise to minimize the amount of routing information a router needs to process. This is accomplished with IP address summarization. And the key to making summarization work is the ability to limit routes sent to neighbors. This is accomplished with an Access list but applied in a different way.

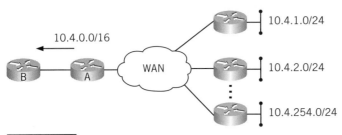

In the following example, Cisco's Enhanced Interior Gateway Routing Protocol (EIGRP) is being used. Refer to Figure 9.3 that shows a WAN with each remote site using a /24 network out of the 10.4.0.0/16 range. Router A could send all 254 networks to Router B, but there is no need for this. Instead, Router A will send only 10.4.0.0/16 and block all others.

FIGURE 9.3   *Using ACLs to Enable Routing Protocols to Summarize*

The configuration below only shows how the ACL limits the routes from being sent to Router B. The summary route would still need to be defined and redistributed into the routing protocol—but that's not essential for understanding how the ACL works.

```
router eigrp 1
   distribute-list SUMMARIZE out GigabitEthernet0/1
!
ip access-list standard SUMMARIZE
   permit 10.4.0.0
   deny    10.4.0.0 0.0.255.255
   permit any
```

A standard ACL is used because there is no concept of a "destination" (which must be defined in an extended ACL) when you are matching routes. The first ACE permits the 10.4.0.0 route, which will match the 10.4.0.0/16 summary. Note that this ACE would also permit 10.4.0.0/24, but this is not assigned to one of the remotes. It would cause no harm to allow both 10.4.0.0 routes to be sent to Router A, but it is just untidy.

The second ACE blocks all routes where the first two octets are 10.4. Of course, this would also match the summary, but this was already permitted by the first ACE. The second ACE blocks all the remote site routes from being sent to Router B.

The third ACE is only necessary if there are routes outside of 10.4.0.0/16 which need to be sent to Router B. This could include the address space being used on the WAN links or a separate range used for a different WAN.

Building a Virtual Private Network with ACLs

A Virtual Private Network (VPN) is an encrypted tunnel built between private networks typically built over an insecure or private network like the Internet. The VPN device on each end (router, firewall, and so forth) must know which networks on the near side are allowed to speak to which networks on the far side of the VPN. ACLs service this function.

Figure 9.4 shows two routers creating a VPN tunnel over the Internet. The goal is to create a VPN that will encrypt traffic between 10.4.1.0/24 and 10.4.2.0/24.

The configuration sample below is from Router A, which shows an ACL specifying a source range of 10.4.1.0/24 and a destination of 10.4.2.0/24. This ACL is applied to the crypto map using the *match address* command.

```
crypto map VPN 10 ipsec-isakmp
   set peer 2.2.2.2
   set transform-set 3DES
   match address RemoteRouter1
!
ip access-list extended RemoteRouter1
   permit ip 10.4.1.0 0.0.0.255 10.4.2.0 0.0.0.255
```

For the VPN to operate correctly, there needs to be ACL "symmetry." This means the ACL on Router B needs to be opposite of the ACL

FIGURE 9.4

Using ACLs to Configure a VPN

in the example—with 10.4.2.0/24 as the source and 10.4.1.0/24 as the destination. Both routers use the ACL to decide which traffic should flow through the VPN, so the symmetry ensures there is full connectivity in both directions.

ACCESS LIST ENHANCEMENTS

As IOS has matured and features have been added, ACLs have also been enhanced. Different types of ACLs have been introduced to solve specific problems, and the hardware and IOS have been enhanced to run ACLs more efficiently. In addition, there is some very exciting new ACL technology that has recently been released. This section will briefly cover some of the most important changes made to the ACL.

Hardware Processing

With the capability to match on various elements within the IP header, the extended ACL is much more powerful. But, the additional capabilities come at a cost—especially on busy routers. Evaluating each packet as it flows through an interface consumes CPU cycles and can place heavy demands on router resources, especially when there are many ACEs in an ACL.

Originally, an ACL was processed by the CPU one line at a time for each packet. As the number of ACEs grew, performance decreased. The first improvement was a "compiled ACL," which is available on high-performance routers (for example, 7200 and 7500). This feature (called *Turbo ACL*) used internal data structures and simultaneous pattern matching to increase performance. But, even with Turbo ACLs, processing was still performed by the CPU.

Some platforms (for example, 12000 and 6500) now perform ACL processing in special application-specific integrated circuit (ASIC) chips. The main CPU is no longer in the processing path of the ACL, so the number of ACEs on these platforms is not a drag on performance.

Time-Based ACLs

One great feature added to ACLs was the capability to turn on and off an ACE based on time. This allows you to establish different access policies based on the time—during and after working hours, for example. Time-based ACLs were added to IOS release 12.0.1.T.

In the following example, a time-based ACL is defined to allow Web traffic (tcp/80) to flow between 172.16.1.0/24 and 172.16.2.0/24 only during working hours.

```
interface FastEthernet0/0
    ip address 172.16.1.1 255.255.255.0
    ip access-group 111 in
!
access-list 111 permit tcp 172.16.1.0 0.0.0.255 172.16.2.0
    0.0.0.255 eq www time-range WORKHOURS
!
time-range WORKHOURS
    periodic weekdays 8:00 to 17:00
```

The most critical element of time-based ACLs is ensuring your router has the correct time! You may create a perfect ACL, but if your time is not right, your security policy won't work. The ACL relies on the router's system clock. Use Network Time Protocol (NTP) for synchronization, and ensure the correct time zone and daylight-savings-time values are configured.

Reflexive ACL and Context-Based Access Control

Reflexive ACLs were added to IOS release 11.3. Basically, they allow two ACLs to be linked in such a way that traffic which flows out can trigger an inbound ACL to allow the response traffic. This link is based on the session information in the packet. Interestingly, this is one of the only features that require a named ACL—numbered ACLs won't work.

Context-Based Access Control (CBAC) was introduced in IOS release 12.0.5.T and largely replaced the need for reflexive ACLs. CBAC requires the Cisco IOS Firewall feature set.

CBAC evaluates packets as they flow through the router and dynamically adds ACEs to an inbound ACL to allow the response traffic. This is based on TCP connections and UDP flow state information. Figure 9.5 shows how CBAC works.

In the following example, CBAC is configured to inspect the protocols defined in the *ip inspect* statement as traffic flows outbound on

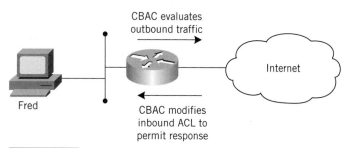

FIGURE 9.5 *CBAC Dynamically Manages the Inbound ACL in Response to Outbound Traffic*

FastEthernet4. As this happens, CBAC recognizes the session information of the outbound packets and prepends ACEs to the Firewall ACL, which permit the return traffic.

```
ip inspect name Internet udp
ip inspect name Internet icmp
ip inspect name Internet ftp
ip inspect name Internet tcp
ip inspect name Internet http
!
interface FastEthernet4
   description Internet
   ip access-group Firewall in
   ip inspect Internet out
!
ip access-list extended Firewall
   deny ip any any
```

Notice that the Firewall ACL blocks all traffic. This means that the configuration requires CBAC to function to allow any incoming packets. Without an outbound request, no packets are allowed inbound.

Dynamic ACLs

To call a Dynamic or "Lock and Key" ACL an enhancement is a bit of a stretch since the feature was first introduced in IOS Release 11.1. However, because dynamic ACLs rely on extended ACLs in addition to the Telnet application and authentication, they are definitely a way of using ACLs in a novel way to solve a particular problem.

A dynamic ACL is applied to an interface just like any other ACL. The ACL blocks traffic from flowing through the interface until a user telnets to the router and is authenticated. Once they are successfully authenticated, an ACE is dynamically added to the ACL, which permits the user through for the duration of a timeout period or until the connection is idle for a certain amount of time.

In practice, this feature was very useful for extranet connections where a company wanted to grant external users limited access to internal resources for a temporary period of time. Dynamic ACLs aren't used much any more because client VPNs (IPSec or SSL) provide the same functionality along with encryption.

Flexible Packet Matching

One of the newest and most exciting enhancements to ACL technology is called *Flexible Packet Matching* (FPM) and was introduced in IOS Release

12.4.4T. This feature allows users to match on any bit pattern at any part of the packet—including the header or payload deep inside the packet. Network managers are no longer constrained to predefined packet fields to define matching criteria. This is why FPM is considered a "next generation ACL."

Combinations of elements can be combined allowing complex matching rules—using such things as packet length, pattern matching, and traditional attributes such as ports. For example, the MS-SQL Slammer worm sends 376-byte UDP packets to port 1434. The attack packets all have a specific byte pattern at a specific offset. This is called the worm's *signature*. The following is an example of using the CLI to define the Slammer signature.

```
class-map type access-control match-all SQL-SLAMMER
   match field UDP dest-port eq 0x59A
   match field IP length eq 0x194
   match start 13-start offset 224 size 4 eq 0x4011010
```

These filters can be created in the CLI or defined in XML format and imported from an external server. Using an external server makes rapid deployment of new signatures possible, which means FPM is a tool exceptionally useful for controlling the spread of virus and worms. Unfortunately, FPM is stateless, which means that the tool can't track dynamically negotiated ports.

Excellent examples and documentation can be found in the FPM Web site (www.cisco.com/go/fpm).

ACL TROUBLESHOOTING

Troubleshooting Access lists and troubleshooting *with* Access lists are important skills for a CCNA candidate to learn. Both will be covered in this section. We'll consider what can go wrong and review how to use IOS commands to see the ACL working. Finally, the ultimate IOS troubleshooting tool—the *debug* command—will be used to see inside ACL operation, and an ACL will be used to limit the output of other *debug* commands.

What Can Go Wrong with ACLs

Each time an ACL is applied, it's intended to perform a specific purpose. If that purpose is not satisfied, then there is obviously something wrong. Each method of applying an ACL, whether it is filtering routes or classifying traffic for QoS, has a different method of troubleshooting when the ACL does not appear to work. The CCNA exam focuses on using ACLs for filtering traffic, as it flows through a router, so the discussion here will be limited to that.

An ACL applied to an interface is intended to permit and/or block packets. There are three typical problems that can occur:

- No packets are blocked when some packets should be blocked.

- All packets are blocked when only some packets should be blocked.

- The wrong packets are blocked.

Verifying the Configuration

When no packets are blocked, the problem is often that the ACL is not applied properly. It's important to make sure that the correct ACL is applied to the correct interface. To accomplish this, it's necessary for you to not only see the ACL in the configuration but also to see how IOS is actually working with the ACL. *Show* commands are the best source of information.

The *show running-config* command is the most popular way to see how the router is configured. However, it is sometimes difficult to see errors especially when the configuration spans many lines. The configuration of a 6500 switch can easily span for many hundreds of lines—so it's critical that you know where to look for the error.

IOS does provide shortcuts to certain parts of the configuration, which can help narrow your search for a mistake. The *show running-configuration interface <interface>* command is a good place to start. If you know an ACL should be applied to a specific interface, you can use this command to limit the command output to only that interface.

- Look for the *ip access-group* command in the running-config to verify that the ACL is applied to the proper interface.

Once it is determined that the ACL is applied, you need to confirm that it is the correct ACL. Recall that a nonexistent ACL can be applied to an interface, but all packets are permitted. Be careful of this when you are configuring a router because mistyping the name of an ACL can make for a confusing few hours troubleshooting why your ACL isn't working.

- Make sure the ACL number or name in the *ip access-group* command is exactly right—both spelling and case must match exactly.

Exam Warning

Named ACLs are case sensitive. If you define a named ACL correctly, then apply it to an interface using the wrong case—the ACL won't function. In this case, the ACL is treated like it does not exist and all packets will pass.

- Make sure the ACL direction defined in the *ip access-group* command is what is intended. The direction is from the perspective of the router.

Now that you know the ACL appears correctly in the running-config, you should verify that the router is acting on the ACL. Use the *show ip interface <interface>* command to confirm that the router is acting on the ACL configuration as you expect it should. As shown below, you can use the pipe character to limit the output.

```
Router# show ip interface FastEthernet 4 | include access
  list
   Outgoing access list is not set
   Inbound access list is Firewall
```

Seeing the ACL in Action Using Hit Counters

Now that you have verified that the configuration is correct, it is time to see the router work. The *show ip access-list {name | number}* command is most useful for this task.

```
Router#show ip access-list Firewall
Extended IP access list Firewall in
   10 permit udp any any eq bootpc (45531 matches)
   20 permit udp any any eq isakmp (2898 matches)
   30 permit udp any any eq non500-isakmp
   40 permit esp any any (5191543 matches)
   50 permit gre any any (253196 matches)
   60 permit icmp any any (48 matches)
```

Notice that the output of this command shows the number of packets that have been matched by this ACL. This is the most useful information when troubleshooting ACLs. However, nothing is perfect. The output can sometimes be terribly misleading. There are two common reasons for this:

- The same ACL can be applied to more than one interface. The *show ip access-list {name | number}* output displays aggregate counters that include how many ACE matches that are for all the interfaces that use that ACL.

- Packets that are processed in hardware do not increment the counters.

You can successfully work around both problems.

To resolve the first problem, use a variant of this command—*show ip access-list interface <interface>*. This command limits the output to only the ACLs that are applied to the specified interface, which is a nice shortcut.

More importantly, the counters displayed reflect only the hits on the ACL for that interface, not for all interfaces.

The problem of ACL counters not incrementing because of hardware processing is a bit more difficult to solve because you normally want the ACL to be handled in the fastest way possible. However, when troubleshooting, it may be necessary to force packets to be processed in software, so counters will increment. This is accomplished with the following interface configuration command:

```
Router(config-if)#no ip route-cache
```

Always remember to re-enable route-cache on the interface after troubleshooting is complete. Hardware processing can be a huge performance boost when available (for example, PFC on Catalyst 6500), so it should be used when available.

Exam Warning

When viewing ACL counters, there is no way to tell when the matches occurred. The counters could have incremented weeks earlier and not reflect the current traffic passing through the interface. When troubleshooting, it is often necessary to clear the counters to check for new matches. This is done in enable mode using the following command:

Router# clear access-list counters {*name* | *number*}

The benefits of ACL counters to troubleshooting can't be overemphasized. This is why it is often useful to include an explicit "deny any" ACE at the end of an ACL. Recall that each ACL ends with an implicit *deny any* ACE, so the command isn't important to the proper functioning of the ACL. However, the one benefit of adding this ACE explicitly is the counter. Without the explicit ACE, it's not possible to tell how many packets have been dropped because they reach the end of the ACL. Adding this ACE makes it easy to see this counter, which can be essential in troubleshooting.

Seeing the ACL in Action Using Log Output

Sometimes counters aren't enough to find a problem. Often, it is helpful to see exactly when an ACE is matched and see information about the specific packet. In the "ACL Details and Examples" section, ACL syntax was covered. One command line option wasn't discussed fully. At the end of each ACE, the "log" keyword can be added. Enabling this feature will write a log entry each time the ACE is matched.

Be very careful when enabling logging in a production network. This keyword can be used on a single ACE—so it won't affect the ACL as a whole. IOS rate limits logging messages by default, so the risk of overloading the router is not as great—but it is always a good policy to be careful.

The log keyword must be used with some form of router logging—buffered, terminal, syslog, and so forth. The messages are generated at the information level, so they will only appear if the log is configured to echo informational messages (severity = 6).

Here is an example of the message when an ACE is matched. In this case, the router has monitor logging enabled (which echoes messages to the Telnet session as long as "terminal monitor" is enabled as it is below). In addition, the router logs messages to its buffer and a syslog server.

```
Router(config)# ! Enable terminal line (monitor) logging
Router(config)# logging monitor informational
Router(config)# ! Enable logging to router buffer
Router(config)# logging buffered informational
Router(config)# ! Enable Syslog server
Router(config)# logging trap informational
Router(config)# logging 10.2.3.4
Router(config)# ip access-list extended TEST
Router(config-ext-nacl)# permit icmp host 1.1.1.1 any log
Router(config-ext-nacl)# end
Router# terminal monitor
```

The message seen when an ICMP packet is matched by the ACE includes the ACL name, the match information (permitted or denied), and the source and destination IP addresses. The 8 in the output shows the packet was ICMP type 8—a PING packet. If the logging is being rate limited, you would see a packet count greater than 1.

```
Oct 13 02:47:13.254: %SEC-6-IPACCESSLOGDP: list TEST permitted
    icmp 1.1.1.1 -> 2.2.2.2 (8/0), 1 packet
```

Common Pitfalls with ACLs

There are several common mistakes that administrators make when troubleshooting ACLs. The most obvious is testing with the wrong type of traffic. Most network administrators test with ICMP (specifically the *PING* and *trace* commands). In fact, these are such widely used commands that it is often forgotten that an ACL is protocol specific.

Even if a PING succeeds, the ACL could be blocking TCP traffic. In this case, using PING can be useful for verifying that basic IP connectivity is available, but it won't help in diagnosing a problem with an ACE that filters Telnet (TCP/23).

In a similar way, the ACL could be blocking ICMP (which is common on Internet-connected routers) and permitting other protocols like Hypertext Transfer Protocol (HTTP) (TCP/80). Simply because a PING is unsuccessful, it does not necessarily mean that other traffic isn't flowing properly.

Test Day Tip

During troubleshooting scenarios with ACLs, be mindful of which tools you use to diagnose the problem. *PING* and *trace* can be helpful to determine if basic IP connectivity is working but may yield misleading results if you are troubleshooting connectivity of other protocols.

One very common ACL troubleshooting mistake is to forget that the source of an ICMP packet is the egress interface of the router. Assume you are working on Router A in Figure 9.6 trying to figure out why Elizabeth can't access files on Katherine's PC. You suspect the inbound ACL on Router B is blocking the traffic. If you initiate a PING packet on Router A to Katherine, the packet that reaches the ACL would be sourced from 10.2.2.2—which is on a different subnet from Elizabeth.

The better way to troubleshoot in this scenario would be to specify the source of the PING packet to make sure it accurately reflects the problem you are trying to diagnose. In this case, the following command would provide more accurate test results.

```
Router-A# ping 10.3.3.3 source 10.1.1.1
```

Feature Order of Operation and Its Affect on ACLs

Using ACLs with features such as QoS, NAT, and encryption (crypto) is very tricky. The problem is that these features often change the IP headers of the packets. For example, when configured on an Internet router, NAT normally changes the source IP address of outbound packets. If you are configuring an ACL on the outbound interface, should you specify the original source address or the modified source address of the packet? The answer is that it depends on the order of operation of NAT.

In the case of NAT and encryption, the order of operation depends on whether the traffic flows inside-to-outside or outside-to-inside (www.cisco. com/en/US/tech/tk648/tk361/technologies_tech_note09186a0080133ddd. shtml). However, in both cases, the address translation occurs between when the inbound ACL and outbound ACL is checked. For example, when configuring an ACL with NAT, specify the real source IP address space in the

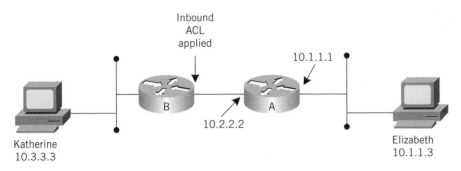

FIGURE 9.6
*Using the Wrong
Source Address When
Troubleshooting ACLs*

ACE if you are configuring an inbound ACL to match outgoing traffic, or the translated source IP address space in the ACE if you are configuring an outbound ACL to match outgoing traffic.

The QoS order of operation is described in this white paper (www.cisco. com/en/US/tech/tk543/tk757/technologies_tech_note09186a0080160fc1. shtml).

Debugging

For many, the *debug* command is the most indispensable and irreplaceable troubleshooting tool in IOS. Although it can provide an enormous amount of information, an experienced administrator can use the *debug* commands to narrow in on a problem quickly and efficiently.

The *show* commands described above and the **log** keyword in an ACE already provide a lot of information about how the ACL itself is operating. Yet, there may be times when this is not enough. You may need to see exactly what's happening to the packets as they flow through the router.

But be very careful. So many packets pass through a busy production router that using debug can generate so much data and consume so many resources that the process can literally crash the router. The ACL can be used to narrow the debug output. Even when using ACLs, the *debug* command can be dangerous, so use this command with great care.

The *debug ip packet* command is useful for displaying packets, as they flow through the router. The command displays not only forwarded packets (those that pass through the router) but also received and generated packets (those that are destined for, or generated by, the router itself).

IP packet debugging is enabled with the following syntax in *Privileged Exec* mode. Note that named Access lists are not supported. To stop the debugging, use the **no** form of the command.

```
debug ip packet [access-list-number] [detail]
no debug ip packet [access-list-number] [detail]
```

Or, you can use one of the two forms that disable all debugging.

```
no debug all
undebug all
```

Just as hit counters are not incremented with hardware switched packets, the *debug ip packet* command will not display packets that are fast switched—only process switched packets are captured. So, it is sometimes necessary to disable fast-caching on an interface before enabling this *debug* command. If you forget, you may see only the first packet, which is sometimes all that IOS requires to build a fast switching path. Also, the *terminal monitor* command is necessary if you want to see the packets echoed to a Telnet session.

The following is an example of how to use an ACL to filter the output of a *debug ip packet* command. First, a standard or extended numbered ACL is created, and then the *debug* command is invoked with the ACL number which limits the output. If the ACL was not used, the router would echo all packets—a potentially disastrous result. A single PING from 10.6.4.4 to 10.11.1.1 produced the example output.

```
Router(config)# access-list 160 permit ip host 10.6.4.4 host
    10.11.1.1
Router(config)# interface FastEthernet0/0
Router(config-if)# no ip route-cache
Router(config-if)# end
Router# undebug all
All possible debugging has been turned off
Router# debug ip packet 160 detail
IP packet debugging is on (detailed) for access list 160
Router# terminal monitor
Router#
Oct 14 02:42:04.423: IP: tableid=0, s=10.6.4.4 (FastEthernet0/0),
    d=10.11.1.1 (Multilink1), routed via FIB
Oct 14  02:42:04.423:  IP:  s=10.6.4.4  (FastEthernet0/0),
    d=10.11.1.1 (Multilink1), g=10.17.11.2, len 60, forward
Oct 14 02:42:04.423: ICMP type=8, code=0
Router# no debug all
All possible debugging has been turned off
```

The output includes a lot of information about the packet, including

- which interface the packet comes from (FastEthernet0/0) and where it is going (Multilink1), and to which IP it is being sent next (10.17.11.2).

- what happens to the packet (forward, access denied, and so forth).

- details about the packet—60 bytes long and ICMP type = 8 (PING).

Note that the ACL is not applied to any interface. This is unnecessary because the *debug* command isn't echoing packets on a single interface. Rather, it is capturing packets that match the ACL on the CPU, so it is essentially able to see all interfaces at once.

Don't forget to re-enable route-cache on the interface once debugging is complete. You don't want to leave your packets being process switched.

Exam Warning

It may appear odd in the example that the *no debug all* command was entered before and after the debug was done. The first command is unnecessary, but getting into this habit can save you! Imagine if you made a mistake in the ACL which resulted in permitting all traffic, then you enabled the debug. Immediately your screen is filled with debug output, and you are unable to type the command necessary to stop it. By entering the *no debug all* command before doing the debug, you can use the CLI history to easily stop the debug. Simply press the up-arrow twice (which recalls the command before the debug was started) and then press **Enter** to accept the command.

SUMMARY OF EXAM OBJECTIVES

This chapter covered the history and development of Access lists—from standard ACLs to the newest technology of FPM. Not all the material will be required to pass the CCNA exam, but a full understanding of ACLs is essential to running a successful network. ACLs can be difficult, especially if you are unfamiliar or uncomfortable with IP addressing. Practice in both ACLs and addressing is the only way to build the confidence to do well on the exam.

You will need to know how ACLs are built and applied. You'll need to master how to apply the rules of ACLs—not simply the syntax. You'll need to know how ACEs are added and deleted, the differences between standard and extended ACLs, and how order of operation affects the addressing in an ACE. All these skills will become second-nature as you work with ACLs. But for those just starting out, practice is the essential ingredient.

ACLs are considered one of the trickiest topics on the CCNA exam. It's easy to make mistakes when you have to compare a long collection of commands. Learn what's in this chapter, practice, relax, and have fun.

EXAM OBJECTIVES FAST TRACK

The Anatomy of an ACL

- Each type of numbered ACL has a range of numbers associated with it. Numbers 1 to 99 (and 1300 to 1999) are assigned to standard IP address lists and 100 to 199 (and 2000 to 2699) are assigned to extended IP Access lists.

- An ACL is made up of an ordered list of ACEs. Each packet is evaluated against the ACEs from top to bottom until there is a match, where the packet will either be permitted or be denied.

- An implicit "deny all" is appended to the end of each ACL. This guarantees that all packets will match at least one ACE.

- IP ACEs use wildcard masks in matching source and destination addresses. These function in a similar way as a subnet mask but can't be considered equivalent because they are not tied to an interface address.

- When an ACE evaluates addresses using wildcard masks, bits set to 1 must match ("care") and bits set to 0 are ignored ("don't care"). ACEs can use many fields in a packet for evaluation criteria. The most common include source and destination addresses, protocol, ports, QoS, and state information.

ACL Details and Examples

- Standard Access lists match only based on the source IP address of the packet. Extended Access lists can match on source and destination address, in addition to port, protocol, and many other fields.

- With extended ACLs, each protocol (ip/tcp/udp/icmp) has a different set of criteria that can be used for matching packets. This means the ACE syntax is unique to each protocol.

- Numbered ACLs have several limitations including the inability to reorder ACEs or add/remove a single ACE.

- Sequence numbers on named ACLs are used to add and remove individual ACEs, which resolves the limitations of numbered ACLs.

- Comments can be added to both named and numbered ACLs, but they managed as other ACEs and aren't tied to a specific ACE.

Applying an ACL

- There is an important rule to remember for applying an ACL—one ACL per protocol per interface per direction.

- The direction of the ACL is from the perspective of the router. With an ACL applied inbound ("in"), packets are evaluated as they enter the router.

- Use access-group to apply an ACL to an interface and access-class to apply an ACL to a line.

- Access lists are also used to control many other elements of the router operation, including filtering routing updates, controlling SNMP access, determining interesting traffic for NAT, and so forth.

Access List Enhancements

- On many platforms, ACLs can now be evaluated in hardware, which reduces the time and resources necessary to process large numbers of ACEs.

- Time-based ACLs are useful for making security policy changes based on recurring time and date ranges. To use this feature, it's important to make sure the router has the correct time and date. Use NTP with the correct time zone settings to make sure the ACLs work properly.

- CBAC is part of the IOS Firewall feature set and is used to dynamically modify incoming Access lists to permit response traffic from an outbound request. This tool protects your internal network by blocking all but requested traffic from the untrusted network.

- FPM is the next generation of ACL technology, which allows matching on complex combinations of criteria. An important advancement available in FPM is the ability to match on byte patterns anywhere in the header or body of a packet. This makes FPM useful for virus and worm control.

ACL Troubleshooting

- Commands such as *show run* and *show ip interface* provide the best first place to look for configuration errors such as an ACL that is applied in the wrong direction (in versus out) or a misspelled ACL name (remember they are case sensitive).

- ACL hit counters displayed with *show ip access-list* are great for troubleshooting, but counters may not increment when packets are switched in hardware. Keep this in mind when using this command to verify the ACE is matching packets.

- Use the log keyword on an ACE to enable ACL logging to buffer (seen in *show log*), to a syslog server, to the console, or to a Telnet session (if you remember the *terminal monitor* command).

- When using features, such as NAT, encryption, and QoS, be aware that the order of operation is especially important to ACL processing. If NAT changes the source or destination address, make sure you take this into account when defining the ACE.

- The *debug ip packet* command should be used with an ACL to avoid overwhelming the router. Even with an ACL, be very careful when using this command in a production network.

EXAM OBJECTIVES FREQUENTLY ASKED QUESTIONS

Q: Can an ACL call another ACL?

A: No—ACLs can't be nested. And because you can only use one ACL per interface per protocol per direction, you may need to integrate ACEs from several security policy requirements to satisfy your needs.

Q: Why doesn't the CLI complain when I incorrectly specify the wild-card mask using rightmost contiguous digits like a subnet mask?

A: Because what you have entered is a *valid* (albeit incorrect) wildcard mask. A wildcard mask tells IOS which bits in the ACE-provided IP address should be matched (bit = 0) and which should be ignored (bit = 1). These can be any bits—they do not have to be left-contiguous (which would essentially be the inverse of a subnet mask).

Q: Why aren't higher-layer protocols like FTP or WWW allowed in the protocol field of an extended ACL?

A: Because these are treated as ports not protocols. IOS has many predefined ports (like 80 for WWW) that can be matched, but this is configured in a TCP or UDP ACL.

Q: Can Access lists filter on ttl or fragments?

A: Yes, this capability is in 12.4(2)T and is described here—www.cisco.com/en/US/docs/ios/12_4t/12_4t2/htaclttl.html.

Q: Because an extended ACL can match on source IP address (like a standard ACL) in addition to a number of other fields, why would I ever want to use a standard ACL?

A: In most cases, you can use an extended ACL if you prefer because you can duplicate the logic of a standard ACL. However, in some instances (like an SNMP community filter), a standard ACL is required.

Q: If an IP ACL matches ICMP traffic, why would I need a specific ICMP ACL?

A: Because the extended ICMP ACL enables you to match based on protocol-specific fields including the ICMP type and message.

Q: When I try to delete a single ACE in a numbered ACL, it ends up deleting the entire ACL. What's wrong?

A: That's the way it works and it's a common problem. To get around this, use a named ACL so you can add and remove ACEs using sequence numbers.

Q: What is the safest way to manage an ACL in a production network?

A: Use an out-of-band approach by connecting through the console port. You can remove the ACL from the interface before changing it but that leaves your interface unprotected. Some security-conscious companies prefer to shut down the interface to ensure nonfiltered traffic doesn't slip through during maintenance.

Q: How large can an ACL get?

A: Very large; the named ACL sequence numbers range from 1 to 2147483647, but I doubt you will ever need that many! It's a good idea to minimize the number of ACEs (for manageability at least), but hundreds of ACEs on an ACL is possible in a large network.

Q: Which is the best direction in which to filter traffic?

A: That depends. Filtering on inbound will permit or drop packets before they reach the router, so they don't consume resources and so forth. However, you may need the packets to be filtered after they enter the router—for example, dropping packets in response to a QoS policy that shapes outbound traffic. The direction of the ACL is always relative to the router.

Q: Why would I ever want an outbound ACL on a terminal line?

A: The router CLI allows users to Telnet to other devices. If this functionality is not desired for security reasons, you can block outbound Telnets by applying an outbound ACL to VTY lines. If you try when an ACL is blocking this, you receive the message "% Connections to that host not permitted from this terminal."

Q: What's a good way to find out if an ACL is being used in the config?

A: This is more difficult than it first appears because an ACL can be used in number of different ways. One way is to search the config for the ACL name (doesn't work well with numbered ACLs) by using output modifiers

```
Router# show running-config | include ACLNAME
```

If the only output is the ACL definition, the ACL name does not appear in the config and can be safely removed.

Q: Does the number of ACEs affect how long it takes to forward packets through the router?

A: Yes, on some platforms more than others. Larger devices, such as the Catalyst 6500, support ACL processing in special ASIC hardware, so the number of ACEs doesn't have a large effect on packet processing delay. Lower-end hardware still process ACEs in software, which consumes CPU. This does have at least some impact on processing delay.

Q: Do time-based ACLs work during daylight savings time?

A: Yes, as long as this is configured properly on the router. Make sure you use a solid NTP server to sync the routers clock and configure the correct time zone and DST parameters in the CLI. Only if these are correct will time-based ACLs work properly.

Q: How can you see the "dynamic" Access list that is being manipulated by CBAC? The *show ip access-list* command only shows me the ACEs that are statically configured—not the dynamic ACEs being added by CBAC.

A: The best way to see this is with the *show ip inspect sessions* command. It shows both established sessions and those that are closing because they are "old."

Q: Is FPM supported on low-end routers?

A: On some—yes with IOS release 12.4(4)T running Advanced Security, Advanced IP Services, and Advanced Enterprise feature sets. The Cisco 871, 1700, 1800, 2600, and 2800 are all supported, but they need the memory and flash to run the correct version and feature set.

Q: My ACL configuration looks right in the running-config, but the ACL isn't working. What could be wrong?

A: A number of things can go wrong. Make sure to verify your configuration using other *show* commands like *show ip interface*—to confirm the ACL is applied and in the correct direction. Also, make sure your ACLs are spelled correctly and the letter case is the same. To ensure the ACL definition matches the application command, get in the habit of using copy/paste.

Q: My hit counters aren't incrementing even though I've disabled hardware processing on the interface.

A: Your traffic may be reaching the end of the ACL and being dropped by the implicit "deny any" ACE. There is normally no counter for this ACE—so the drops are silent. Add an explicit "deny any" to your ACL and retest.

Q: My ACL isn't matching Telnet traffic even though I know the port number is correct.

A: Don't overlook that the ACE may not be matching traffic because it's not written correctly. Common problems include swapping source and destination ports. For example, Telnet is matched by specifying a TCP ACE and using destination port 23, but this only matches traffic that is flowing from the originator of the Telnet session. Return traffic is matched with a TCP ACE using source port 23.

Q: I don't want debugging output to be sent to the router's log. How can I stop this?

A: Change your logging config to buffer severity level 6 or lower (for example, "logging buffered informational"). Logging at debug level (severity = 7) is useful sometimes, but it can quickly fill up the router log.

SELF TEST

1. Which is the correct syntax for a numbered ACL?

   A. `access-list 14 permit ip 10.1.1.0 0.0.0.255`

   B. `access-list 14 permit tcp 10.1.1.0 0.0.0.255 10.2.2.0 0.0.0.255`

   C. `access-list 101 permit tcp 10.1.1.0 0.0.0.255 10.2.2.0 0.0.0.255`

   D. `access-list 101 permit ip 10.1.1.0 0.0.0.255`

2. Which set of ACEs is mostly likely in the correct order?

   A. `access-list 10 permit host 10.1.1.1`
   `access-list 10 permit 10.0.0.0 0.255.255.255`
   `access-list 10 deny 10.1.1.0 0.0.0.255`

   B. `access-list 10 permit 10.0.0.0 0.255.255.255`
   `access-list 10 deny 10.1.1.0 0.0.0.255`
   `access-list 10 permit host 10.1.1.1`

   C. `access-list 10 permit host 10.1.1.1`
   `access-list 10 deny 10.1.1.0 0.0.0.255`
   `access-list 10 permit 10.0.0.0 0.255.255.255`

   D. `access-list 10 deny 10.1.1.0 0.0.0.255`
   `access-list 10 permit host 10.1.1.1`
   `access-list 10 permit 10.0.0.0 0.255.255.255`

3. Which ACE will correctly match traffic sourced from all the following hosts, and no others – 172.16.1.4, 172.16.1.5, 172.16.1.6, and 172.16.1.7

   A. `access-list 2 permit 172.16.1.4 255.255.255.252`

   B. `access-list 2 permit 172.16.1.0 0.0.0.252`

   C. `access-list 2 permit 172.16.1.0 0.0.0.3`

   D. `access-list 2 permit 172.16.1.4 0.0.0.3`

4. What is the primary difference between an extended IP ACL and an extended TCP ACL?

    A. An IP ACL can match all IPs, including ICMP, TCP, and UDP. But, it can't match on source or destination port.

    B. An IP ACL allows you to match based on whether the session is established, but TCP ACLs do not.

    C. A TCP ACL does not support source and destination port checking, but the IP ACL does.

    D. An IP ACL can match on DSCP information (TOS or precedence) but TCP ACLs can not.

5. What is the best way to define ACEs to match on an inclusive range of destination TCP ports between 1025 and 1028?

    A. `access-list 101 permit tcp any gt 1025 any`
       `access-list 101 permit tcp any lt 1028 any`

    B. `access-list 101 permit tcp any any gt 1025`
       `access-list 101 permit tcp any any lt 1028`

    C. `access-list 101 permit tcp any any range 1025 1028`

    D. `access-list 101 permit tcp any range 1025 1028 any`

6. What are the limitations of numbered ACLs?

    A. There is no way to remove a single ACE and no way to reorder ACEs.

    B. There is no way to remove a single ACE, no way to add an ACE in a specific spot in the ACL, and no way to reorder ACEs.

    C. There is no way to add an ACE, but it is possible to remove a specific ACE.

    D. ACEs in numbered ACLs can be manipulated just as they can in named ACLs.

7. Which of the following TCP ACEs use the correct syntax?

    A. `access-list 101 permit tcp 10.5.4.0 255.255.255.0`
       `172.16.3.0 eq 23`

    B. `access-list 101 tcp permit 10.5.4.0 0.0.0.255`
       `172.16.3.0 eq 23`

    C. `access-list 101 permit tcp 10.5.4.0 255.255.255.0`
       `172.16.3.0 0.0.0.3 eq 23`

    D. `access-list 101 tcp permit 10.5.4.0 0.0.0.255`
       `172.16.3.0 0.0.0.3 eq 23`

8. What is the best way to add an ACE to the middle of the list of ACEs in the following named ACL?

```
Router # show ip access-list TEST
Standard IP access list TEST
    10 permit 10.1.1.1
    20 permit 10.1.1.2
    30 permit 10.1.1.3
    40 permit 10.1.1.5
```

   A. Delete the ACL and recreate it with the new ACEs in the proper sequence.

   B. `permit 10.1.1.4 no 40`
   `permit 10.1.1.5`

   C. `35 permit 10.1.1.4`

   D. `40 permit 10.1.1.4`

9. If you have IPX, IP, and DECnet addresses on an interface, how many ACLs can be applied to that interface?

   A. 6   **C.** 2

   B. 3   **D.** 0

10. You want to apply an ACL named TEST inbound on a FastEthernet interface. Which of the following is the correct way to do this?

   A. `ip access-group test in`   **C.** `ip access-class TEST in`

   B. `ip access-group in TEST`   **D.** `ip access-group TEST in`

11. Refer to Figure 9.7. You want to block all read/write SNMP access to the router, except from a single management VLAN. What is the best way to accomplish this?

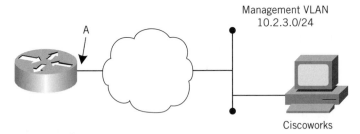

FIGURE 9.7 *Using an ACL to Block SNMP Access to the Router*

A. Create an extended ACL with the source being the management VLAN and the destination being the router's IP on interface A. The ACL should block destination ports udp/161 and udp/162 and be applied inbound on interface A.

B. Create an extended ACL with the destination being the management VLAN and the source being the router's IP on interface A. The ACL should block destination ports udp/161 and udp/162 and be applied outbound on interface A.

C. Create a standard ACL that only permits traffic from the management VLAN. The ACL should be applied to the router's VTY lines.

D. Create a standard ACL that permits only traffic from the management VLAN. The ACL should be appended to the end of the *snmp-server community* command in the configuration.

12. You are building an ACL to control incoming EIGRP routes. You want to permit the summary route 10.2.32.0/20, block any more specific routes, and permit all others. How would you define and apply this ACL?

A. `ip access-list standard ACCEPT_SUMMARY`
      `permit 10.2.32.0`
      `deny 10.2.32.0 0.0.15.255`
      `permit any`
   `router eigrp 1`
      `distribute-list ACCEPT_SUMMARY in`

B. `ip access-list standard ACCEPT_SUMMARY`
      `permit 10.2.32.0 255.255.240.0`
      `deny 10.2.32.0 0.0.15.255`
   `router eigrp 1`
      `distribute-list ACCEPT_SUMMARY in`

C. `ip access-list standard ACCEPT_SUMMARY`
      `deny 10.2.32.0 0.0.15.255`
      `permit 10.2.32.0`
      `permit any`
   `router eigrp 1`
      `distribute-list ACCEPT_SUMMARY in`

D. ```ip access-list standard ACCEPT_SUMMARY
      deny 10.2.32.0 0.0.15.255
      permit 10.2.32.0 255.255.240.0
      permit any
   router eigrp 1
      distribute-list ACCEPT_SUMMARY out```

13. Time-based ACLs are a good way to implement security policy that changes based on time and date. Where does the router get the time it uses to match incoming traffic, and what is the best way to ensure the policy works properly?

    A. Time-based ACLs get the time from a NTP server. To ensure this is accurate, NTP should synchronize with a stratum 1 or 2 time-source. Time zone and daylight-savings-time offsets are provided by the NTP server.

    B. Time-based ACLs get the time from the router's system clock. To ensure this is accurate, NTP should be used for synchronization. Time zone and daylight-savings-time offsets are provided by NTP, so there is no need to adjust for local time.

    C. Time-based ACLs get the time from the router's system clock. To ensure this is accurate, NTP should be used for synchronization and correct time zone and daylight-savings-time values must be configured.

    D. Time-based ACLs get the time from an NTP server. To ensure this is accurate, NTP should synchronize with a stratum 1 or 2 timesource, but time zone and daylight-savings-time values must be configured on the router to adjust to local time.

14. How does CBAC protect internal hosts?

    A. CBAC allows response traffic by evaluating TCP sequence numbers to verify a session is in progress. Only internal hosts can initiate sessions.

    B. CBAC evaluates outbound traffic and dynamically prepends ACEs to an inbound ACL to permit response traffic.

    C. CBAC evaluates outbound traffic and creates a session host map to allow internal hosts to freely request sessions to external hosts and permit only response traffic flowing in the other direction.

    D. CBAC inspects outbound traffic and builds a TCP session table that permits inbound traffic without the need for an ACL.

15. How are Dynamic or "Lock and Key" ACLs used?

   A. Dynamic ACLs begin by evaluating packets in software, but as flows are built packets can then be matched by an ASIC in hardware without requiring as many router resources.

   B. Dynamic ACLs provide a way to change an ACL in response to application traffic—like FTP dynamically negotiating ports.

   C. Dynamic ACLs can match not only header fields, but also on packet payload by using bit pattern matching, packet length, and so forth.

   D. Dynamic ACLs require a user to connect and authenticate to the router using an application (for example, Telnet) before the ACL permits traffic.

16. You are troubleshooting an ACL using the *show ip access-list* command, but you see the hit counters are not incrementing. What could be wrong and how do you fix it?

   A. On some platforms, hit counters don't increment when the packets are processed in hardware. This can't be "fixed," but you can temporarily disable hardware processing during troubleshooting by using "no ip route-cache" on the interface.

   B. Many older routers don't support ACL hit counters. The command still works but does not provide accurate output.

   C. ACL hit counters depend on a service running on the router. This is enabled by default but can be enabled if it is disabled by using the command *service acl-hitcount*.

   D. The availability of ACL hit counters depend on the IOS feature pack running on the router. The firewall feature packet is required to fully support ACL hit counters.

17. Without doing a *show running-config*, what is the best way to determine which ACLs are applied to an interface and in what direction?

   A. Create a testing scenario where you can initiate traffic from both sides of the suspected ACL which will tell you if a certain protocol is allowed. For example, if TCP/23 is allowed, you should be able to create a Telnet session from a PC off one side of the router to the router's far-end IP address.

   B. Use the *show ip access-list detail* command. The output will provide detail about each interface, whether an Access list is applied and in which direction.

C. Use the *show ip access-list interface <interface>* command or the *show ip interface <interface>* command. Both will show which ACLs are applied and the direction.

D. Use the *show protocols <interface>* command, which will provide detail about each interface, whether an Access list is applied, and in which direction.

18. Refer to Figure 9.8. Katherine is unable to access the Web server. You have a Telnet session with the router and are trying to troubleshoot the problem. You ping the server using the following command and get a successful response. What is the best next step in the troubleshooting process?

```
Router#ping 2.2.2.2
Type escape sequence to abort.
Sending 5, 100-byte ICMP Echos to 2.2.2.2, timeout is 2
    seconds:
!!!!!
Success rate is 100 percent (5/5), round-trip min/avg/
    max = 68/72/84 ms
```

FIGURE 9.8

Troubleshooting an Internet Connectivity Problem

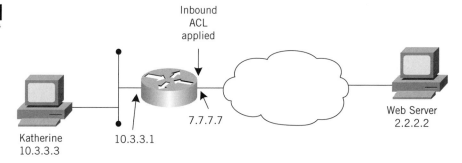

A. Use the IOS extended *PING* command to initiate a ping sourced from the 10.3.3.1 address.

B. Use the IOS *trace* command to determine the path taken through the network to the Web server.

C. Call the Web server administrator and determine if any server-side ACLs are in place.

D. Visit Katherine's PC to determine if a personal firewall may be blocking the traffic.

E. Remove the inbound ACL and retest.

19. Refer to Figure 9.9. You want to create an outbound ACL to limit Elizabeth's access to the Internet. Your policy for this user forbids her to use Telnet (tcp/23) but permits Web surfing (tcp/80) or any other application. Her NATted IP is 7.7.7.8. Which of the following is the correct ACL?

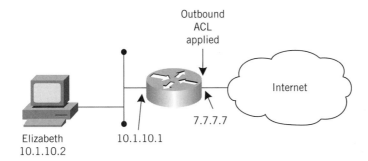

Outbound
ACL
applied

Internet

7.7.7.7

Elizabeth
10.1.10.2

10.1.10.1

FIGURE 9.9

Configuring ACLs with NAT

   A. `access-list 101 deny tcp host 10.1.10.2 any eq 23`
      `access-list 101 permit tcp host 10.1.10.2 any`
   B. `access-list 101 permit ip host 7.7.7.8 any eq 80`
      `access-list 101 deny ip host 7.7.7.8 any eq 23`
   C. `access-list 101 deny tcp host 7.7.7.8 any eq 23`
      `access-list 101 permit ip host 7.7.7.8 any`
   D. `access-list 101 permit ip host 10.1.10.2 any eq 80`
      `access-list 101 deny ip host 10.1.10.2 any eq 23`
      `access-list 101 permit ip host 10.1.10.2 any`

20. You have a Telnet session to a router and you've enabled *debug ip packet <access-list-number>* to troubleshoot a problem you're having with an application not working. A *show debug* confirms that the debug is active. Yet, no output is seen even though you are convinced by looking at the ACL hit counters that traffic is passing that matches the ACL in the debug. What could be wrong?

   A. You've forgotten that debug output is unavailable over a Telnet session. You need to connect to the router using a console cable.

   B. You've forgotten to enable the *terminal monitor* command to echo the debug output to the Telnet session.

   C. There is an ACL applied to the VTY interface that is blocking the output of the debug command.

   D. You've forgotten to enable "logging buffered" which is necessary for the output to be echoed to the Telnet session.

SELF TEST QUICK ANSWER KEY

1.	C	11.	D
2.	C	12.	A
3.	D	13.	C
4.	A	14.	B
5.	C	15.	D
6.	B	16.	A
7.	C	17.	C
8.	C	18.	A
9.	A	19.	C
10.	D	20.	B

IPv6

INTRODUCTION

More networks will be migrating from Internet Protocol version 4 (IPv4) to Internet Protocol version 6 (IPv6) over the next several years. Cisco has always been a leader in using the latest technologies, and they have taken a real lead as a company by developing equipment that supports the IPv6 protocol stack. The latest versions of the Cisco Internetwork Operating System have support for many IPv6 features, including IPv6 Routing Information Protocol (RIP) and IPv6 access control lists.

There are many reasons for the migration to IPv6 including the limitations of an IPv4 address space. The limit of the IPv4 address space is further complicated by the number of devices, such as cell phones and personal digital assistants (PDAs), which now require an IP address. As the number of Internet users continues to proliferate, the IP address space needs to be increased somehow. IPv6 is a solution that helps to address the problems caused by the lack of IPv4 address space. The United States Department of Defense is planning to start to migrate their systems to an IPv6 environment starting in 2008. In summary, the limitations of the IPv4 address space have caused a need for the move to IPv6. Cisco is aware of the need for companies to move to IPv6 infrastructure and is one of the companies that is leading the way in the transition to the IPv6 world.

NEED FOR IPv6

IPv6, also known as IP next generation (IPng), was developed because of the inevitable, and rapidly approaching, exhaustion of IPv4 addresses. There are a total of about 4.3 billion IPv4 addresses, with large blocks of those addresses set aside for special purposes, and unavailable for assigning to network devices. The vast majority of the remaining, assignable addresses are already in use. The need for IP addresses is increasing very rapidly—much faster than was anticipated when IPv4 was originally created. IP addressing has expanded far beyond the boundaries of earlier, more traditional networks, where each networked device required one IP address to communicate with other devices on the network.

These days, network devices often have more than one IP address. Computers may have multiple network adapters, each with a unique IP address. Routers usually use at least one unique IP address for each interface, so a router with several interfaces can easily use a large block of addresses. In addition to the multitudes of devices connected to an organization's network, many people have multiple computers at home, each requiring one or more IP addresses to connect to a household network. Then there are virtual hosts using even more of the limited supply.

Beyond the obvious network devices, there are a number of other IP-addressed devices that have become extremely popular in these busy times. Over the last few years, the use of mobile phones, PDAs, notebooks, tablets, and gaming consoles has absolutely exploded, with no likelihood of the growth slowing anytime soon. IP-addressed industrial appliances and IP-capable home appliances are becoming more and more common. Add in the IP addressing needs for transportation—automobiles and Internet access on some airplanes and trains, for example—and it becomes pretty easy to see why we are running out of IPv4 addresses so quickly. There simply aren't enough IPv4 addresses to go around for our current needs, not to mention future needs.

The Internet is growing very rapidly, with more and more people connecting every day. Rapid, continuing growth of the Internet is inevitable. Near the end of 2008, the world's population was approximately 6.7 billion, with less than 25% of those people online. Currently, some countries have only a small presence on the Internet, with many more of their companies and individuals wanting to get connected. Classless interdomain routing (CIDR), variable length subnet masks (VLSMs), private addressing, and network address translation (NAT) have extended the life of IPv4, but we will run out of addresses at some point in the next few years, some estimates say as early as 2010 or 2011. The main reason we need IPv6 is that it solves the problem of our dwindling supply of IP addresses. In fact, IPv6 provides a huge number of addresses (3.4×10^{38}) that, at least in theory, should last indefinitely. In addition, IPv6 has other features and benefits that make it a superior protocol to IPv4.

Differences from IPv4

The basic framework of IPv6 is similar to IPv4, but there are many differences between the two protocols, starting with the address itself. IPv6 has a much larger address space, 128 bits to IPv4s 32 bits. The addresses also look very different. See Table 10.1 for an example of an IPv4 address, displayed in dotted decimal and binary formats.

IPv6 addresses contain elements that aren't used in IPv4 addresses. First, IPv6 addresses include letters as well as numbers. This is because an IPv6 address is represented by eight 16-bit hexadecimal fields. Hexadecimal is a

Table 10.1 Example of IPv4 Address

Dotted Decimal Format	Binary Format
192.168.12.200	11000000.10101000.00001100.11001000

base 16 numbering system that uses the numbers 0 through 9 and the letters a through f (or A through F, the letters aren't case-sensitive). You are probably familiar with hexadecimal from working with Media Access Control (MAC) addresses, which are hardware addresses used on *Ethernet* interfaces. IPv6 addresses are considerably larger than MAC addresses (IPv6's 128 bits compared to 48 bits for a MAC address), but it's all hexadecimal. The relationship between MAC addresses and IPv6 addresses goes beyond the hexadecimal format, because the MAC address is often included as part of the IPv6 address for the device. Another noticeable difference between IPv6 and IPv4 addresses is that, in IPv6, the fields are separated with colons instead of periods.

With IPv4 we got used to working with dotted decimal addresses and you may be wondering why IPv6 addresses aren't also displayed in decimal format. The problem with using decimal for IPv6 addresses is that the addresses would be quite long and difficult to work with. IPv4 addresses are made up of four 8-bit fields. Using 8-bit fields in IPv6 would result in 16 numbers. Hexadecimal allows us to display more bits in a shorter address. Table 10.2 compares decimal, hexadecimal, and binary values and shows how to convert between them.

Table 10.2 Decimal, Hexadecimal, and Binary Conversions

Decimal	Hexadecimal	Binary
0	0	0000
1	1	0001
2	2	0010
3	3	0011
4	4	0100
5	5	0101
6	6	0110
7	7	0111
8	8	1000
9	9	1001
10	A	1010
11	B	1011
12	C	1100
13	D	1101
14	E	1110
15	F	1111

Table 10.3	Example of IPv6 Address	
Hexadecimal Format	**Binary Format**	
2001:0db8:1a2b:0011:0000: 0000:345c:de67	0010000000000001:0000110110111000. 0001101000101011:0000000000010001: 0000000000000000:0000000000000000: 0011010001011100:1101111001100111	

Displaying the address from Table 10.3, below, in 8-bit, dotted decimal format would look like this:

32.1.13.184.26.43.0.17.0.0.0.0.52.92.222.103

As you can see, dotted decimal would just be too difficult to work with. If you look at the address in Table 10.3 you can see that hexadecimal makes the address look a little easier and, in the "IPv6 addresses" section, we're going to look at some ways to make the hexadecimal addresses more user friendly still. Table 10.3 shows the IPv6 address in hexadecimal and binary formats.

As you can see, especially when compared to an IPv4 address, an IPv6 address can be rather intimidating. After all, it's pretty easy to keep track of an organization's IPv4 addresses because it isn't too difficult to memorize the few groups of IPv4 addresses your organization may use. On the other hand, IPv6 addresses don't look very easy to memorize or to work with. A little later in this chapter, in the section entitled "IPv6 Addresses," we will take a closer look at the IPv6 addresses and make them a lot less daunting. We will look at shortened expressions of the address. We'll also break down an IPv6 address so that those numbers and letters make some sense.

IPv6's much larger address space provides us with a number of advanced features that aren't included in IPv4. Here is a list of some of the high points of IPv6's features:

- Built-in mobility and security standards
- Better aggregation
- Capability for multihoming to multiple ISPs
- Plug and play for network devices
- Easier renumbering of devices
- A simpler packet header
- More efficient routing
- Better performance
- Transition methodologies for migrating from IPv4 to IPv6

Suffice it to say that IPv6 is a considerable advancement from IPv4.

The enhanced IPv6 mobility and security features address some of the limitations of IPv4. It's very common in our time for people to access the corporate network from a variety of remote locations. Wireless access is very widely available and workers have a need to be able to connect with their office networks from anywhere they are traveling. IPv6's mobility features allow devices to roam between networks without losing connectivity. In fact, entire networks can very easily be moved from one fixed infrastructure to another.

Another feature that is built into IPv6 is IP security (IPsec). Cisco networking devices running IPv6 security features provide protection against network degradation or failure, as well as protecting against data loss or compromise. With IPsec, we also get the benefit of data authentication services in addition to data confidentiality. IPsec offers secure end-to-end data transmission over IP networks by encrypting the data at the IP packet level. Although some security for IPv4 is accomplished with add-ons, this standards-based security solution is native for IPv6.

The autoconfiguration capabilities of IPv6 will simplify network administration. IPv6 addresses can be autoconfigured in a couple of ways and can include the device's MAC address as part of the IP address. Devices can become part of the network in a plug-and-play fashion, not requiring manual intervention. Modifying addresses and renumbering devices has been simplified. This ability will streamline network migrations; for example, when changing Internet service providers (ISPs). With IPv4, network migrations are often very tedious projects, sometimes requiring network administrators to work many hours on weekends or late at night to avoid disrupting network operations and users.

An IPv6 packet has a much simpler header, consisting of only half the number of fields as in an IPv4 packet's header. The simpler header provides a number of advantages. The header provides for better routing efficiency for increased performance and scalability. The simplified header also allows for easier aggregation of addresses which will go a long way in shortening routing tables and improving performance. There is no need for checksum processing because checksums are not included in the new header. Another welcome change to the header is the elimination of broadcasts.

The three address types used by IPv4 are as follows:

- Unicast addresses

- Multicast addresses

- Broadcast addresses

IPv6 also uses three main types of address, although one type is different from IPv4. The three address types used by IPv6 are as follows:

- Unicast addresses

- Multicast addresses

- Anycast addresses

Devices communicate with other individual devices by sending packets to the unicast address of the device, which works the same as in IPv4. A unicast address is assigned to a *singe* interface, such as an individual network interface card (NIC) on a computer. The Cisco IOS supports the following types of IPv6 unicast addresses:

- Aggregatable global address

- Link-local address

- IPv4-compatible IPv6 address

- Unique local address

We'll talk a lot more about unicast addresses in the section entitled "Address Space."

Multicasting is a very important method of communication in IPv6. IPv6 uses multicasting to accomplish many tasks. Multicast addresses are used to send packets to a group of interfaces, such as a group of computers. Multicasting is used for functions like streaming media and video conferencing, and many IPv6 routing protocols use multicasts to send updates to groups of routers. Multicasting in IPv6 is much like multicasting in IPv4, although IPv6 has a much larger range of addresses for multicasting and uses multicasting more extensively than IPv4.

The last type of IPv4 address is a broadcast that can cause a number of problems on networks. Because broadcast packets are sent to all devices on the network or subnetwork, they can use a lot of bandwidth. When broadcast storms (uncontrolled floods of broadcast packets forwarded across the network) occur, they can use virtually all of the bandwidth on the network, causing the entire network to slow to a crawl or stop functioning altogether. In addition, broadcasts interrupt devices while they are trying to do other things. Every device on the network has to stop what it's doing to respond when broadcasts are sent out. The problems created by broadcasts are eliminated with IPv6 because it uses multicasts instead of broadcasts. As a result, communication is more specific with IPv6. This provides for improved performance and efficiency on IPv6 networks.

The third type of address in IPv6 is an anycast. With anycast addressing, you can assign the same IPv6 address to multiple devices. When traffic is sent to the anycast address, it is routed to the closest device with that address. The routers determine the closest device based on information in their routing tables. This provides improved options for load balancing or content delivery services over those available with IPv4.

As you can see, IPv6 is a much improved upgrade from IPv4. It has a much larger address space to provide for many more addresses and it provides solutions for other limitations of IPv4. IPv6 supports functionality that was not included in IPv4. Some improvements included in IPv6, for example the simplified header and the elimination of broadcasts, improve network performance.

Interoperability with IPv4

The benefits of IPv6 certainly give us a lot of incentive for changing our networks from IPv4 to IPv6. This migration, however, can involve a great deal of time and effort and, in some cases, cost to bring our existing network devices and applications to a point where they are IPv6-compliant. Transitioning from IPv4 to IPv6 within an organization may be a slow, gradual process. As you transition your networks to IPv6, there are a number of mechanisms available to maintain interoperability with IPv4 until you are ready to completely transition to IPv6. This allows you to utilize the benefits of IPv6 while maintaining the functionality of your IPv4 networks and applications.

Worldwide, the transition to IPv6 will be an even slower process. The organizations that do transition their networks to IPv6 may need to access IPv4 networks and the IPv4 Internet. The gradual transitioning-to-IPv6 process will require some type of interoperability between IPv6 and IPv4. Luckily, there are several migration strategies available to allow for a gradual transition to IPv6, giving us the ability to begin utilizing the advanced features of version 6, while maintaining the functionality of version 4.

Included in these migration options is dual stacking, where a device is running IPv4 and IPv6 at the same time, allowing the device to communicate with both IPv4 and IPv6 networks. We also have some tunneling mechanisms that allow us to communicate between networks running different versions of IP. For example, we can encapsulate IPv6 packets within IPv4 packets, essentially making the IPv6 packets look like IPv4 packets. This makes it possible to communicate between IPv6 networks when there is an IPv4 network in between.

Dual-Stacks

Dual stacking is the most common method used for interoperability between IPv4 and IPv6. With dual stacks, both the IPv4 and the IPv6 protocol stacks are enabled on the device at the same time. Devices that are dual stacked can communicate with other IPv4 devices and other IPv6 devices just as easily. A dual-stack network with all routers and hosts running both IPv4 and IPv6 is the Cisco and Internet Engineering Task Force (IETF) recommended transitioning method. A single network running both protocols is easier to set up and work with than a separate physical topology for IPv4 and logical topology for IPv6, using tunnels.

With the dual-stack method, IPv4 and IPv6 run alongside one another, and each is independent of the other. The two protocols share network resources but function as completely separate protocols. Dual stacking allows the device to continue functioning in the IPv4 network, and to add the newer IPv6 capabilities as they are implemented on the network. When IPv4 is no longer needed, you can remove the IPv4 protocol stacks from the devices and be fully configured for IPv6.

CONFIGURING AND IMPLEMENTING...

Confirming the IPv6 Capabilities in Your Version of the Operating System

Before you can start implementing IPv6/IPv4 interoperability, IPv6 addresses, and others, you have to be sure that your version of the Cisco IOS supports IPv6 and the IPv6 functionality you want to implement. There are many different versions of the operating system being used in the world today and not all of them have IP version six capabilities. The routers that do have IPv6 included in the operating system might not have all of the capabilities you are interested in configuring either. To check your operating system for IPv6 capabilities, type the *show ipv6 ?* command at the privileged prompt:

> company# **show ipv6 ?**

If the operating system supports IPv6, you will see a list of options that can be used with the *show ipv6* command. If you get an error message, the operating system doesn't include IPv6.

Even if IPv6 is included in your copy of the IOS, there have been many changes to IPv6 and to the IPv6 functionality of Cisco's IOS. Different versions of the operating system support different functions of IPv6. The commands and output look different on different versions of operating system. Although using the latest version of the IOS gives you all of the up-to-date changes to the Cisco IPv6 functionality, it isn't always practical to bring all of the organization's routers up to the latest version.

This is why it's a good idea to research the capabilities of your version(s) of the IOS before beginning to implement IPv6. That way you'll know how IPv6 can be configured and if all of your routers will be compatible. To check the version of the IOS on your router, use the *show version* command at the privileged exec prompt. Cisco's Web site contains information about specific IPv6 capabilities available in different versions of the operating system at www.cisco.com/en/US/docs/ios/ipv6/configuration/guide/ip6-roadmap.html

It's easy to configure dual stacking on Cisco routers. The steps are as follows:

1. Enter global configuration mode.

2. Turn on IPv6 forwarding.

3. Configure IPv4 and IPv6 addresses on the interface(s) you want to be dual stacked.

See Exercise 10.1 for more on configuring dual stacks on a Cisco router.

EXERCISE 10.1   Configuring Dual Stacking on Cisco Routers

In this exercise, we will configure dual stacking on the *Fastethernet0/0* interface of a router called company.

1. Enter global configuration mode:

   company# **configure terminal**

2. Enable IPv6 on the router:

   company(config)# **ipv6 unicast-routing**

3. Move to interface configuration mode for the *Fastethernet0/0* interface:

   company(config)# **interface Fastethernet0/0**

4. Configure the IPv6 address:

   company(config-if)# **ipv6 address 2001:db8:1a2b:11::345c:de67/64**

5. Configure the IPv4 address:

   company(config-if)# **ip address 192.168.12.200 255.255.255.0**

When we're ready to go all IPv6 and the dual stacking is no longer required, we simply remove the IPv4 address from the interface:

company(config-if)# **no ip address 192.168.12.200 255.255.255.0**

To disable IPv6 routing on the router, we execute the *no ipv6 unicast-routing* command at the global configuration prompt:

company(config)# **no ipv6 unicast-routing**

To disable IPv6 only on the interface, we execute the *no ipv6 address* <address>/<prefix-length> command in interface configuration mode.

company(config-if)# **no ipv6 address 2001:db8:1a2b:11::345c:de67/64**

Tunneling

Another mechanism that can be used while transitioning from IPv4 to IPv6 is a technique known as *overlay tunneling*. Where dual-stacks involve enabling both IPv4 and IPv6 to communicate with both IPv4 and IPv6 devices and networks, tunneling encapsulates IPv6 packets within IPv4 packets. When this encapsulation takes place, it is identified by a protocol type of 41 in the IP header. The packet includes an IPv4 header with no options, followed by an IPv6 header, then the data. This method makes it possible to communicate between isolated IPv6 networks, across an IPv4 network. Essentially, this process disguises the IPv6 packets as IPv4 packets to make them compatible with the IPv4 network.

You may have subnets or portions of your networks that have been upgraded to IPv6, while other segments are still IPv4. You need a method for communicating across the IPv4 segments. Even more challenging is communicating between your IPv6 networks when it's necessary to cross IPv4 networks under someone else's control. If you have no input as to when those networks will be upgraded, you can use tunneling and it won't matter that those networks are IPv4 networks. Overlay tunnels can be configured between border routers or a border router and a host. Regardless of what devices are used as endpoints for your tunnels, they must be configured with dual-stacks.

Tunnels can be manual or dynamic. Manual IPv6 tunnels must be configured on both ends, with the source and destination addresses defined. Dynamic tunnels look at the packet destination and routing information to automatically create the tunnel. A manual tunnel basically creates a permanent link between two IPv6 networks or domains, allowing them to communicate securely across an IPv4 backbone.

6to4 tunnels are simple, point-to-point tunnels designed to carry only IPv6 packets. See Figure 10.1 for an example of a manual 6to4 tunnel.

The steps for configuring a 6to4 tunnel are as follows:

1. Create a *tunnel* interface.

2. Assign an IPv6 address to the *tunnel* interface you just created.

3. Define the source address for the beginning point of the tunnel.

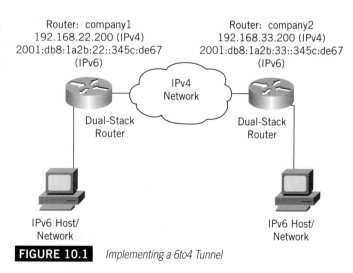

Router: company1
192.168.22.200 (IPv4)
2001:db8:1a2b:22::345c:de67
(IPv6)

Router: company2
192.168.33.200 (IPv4)
2001:db8:1a2b:33::345c:de67
(IPv6)

IPv4 Network

Dual-Stack Router

Dual-Stack Router

IPv6 Host/ Network

IPv6 Host/ Network

FIGURE 10.1   *Implementing a 6to4 Tunnel*

4. Define the destination address, or ending point, of the tunnel.

5. Define the type of traffic to be carried across the tunnel.

6. Repeat steps 1 through 5 on the router at the other end of the tunnel.

EXERCISE 10.2   Configuring 6to4 Tunneling

Now we're going to take a look at how to configure the tunnel shown in Figure 10.1. The routers company1 and company2 are the two ends of our point-to-point tunnel. To configure a tunnel between the two devices, they must be dual stacked. Here's how we configure the tunnel on our routers:

Configuring the tunnel on company1:

Create a *tunnel* interface:

company1(config)# **interface tunnel 0**

Set an IPv6 address on the *tunnel* interface:

company1(config-if)# **ipv6 address 2001:db8:1a2b:22::345c:de67/64**

Define the source of the packets being sent through the tunnel (this end of the tunnel):

company1(config-if)# **tunnel source 192.168.22.200**

Define the destination of the packets being sent through the tunnel (the other end of the tunnel):

company1(config-if)# **tunnel destination 192.168.33.200**

Define the type of traffic to be sent through the tunnel:

company1(config-if)# **tunnel mode ipv6ip**

Repeat all of the aforementioned steps on the router on the other end of the tunnel.

Configuring the tunnel on company2:

company2(config)# **interface tunnel 0**
company2(config-if)# **ipv6 address 2001:db8:1a2b:33::345c:de67/64**
company2(config-if)# **tunnel source 192.168.33.200**
company2(config-if)# **tunnel destination 192.168.22.200**
company2(config-if)# **tunnel mode ipv6ip**

After completing this tunnel configuration, the devices on the IPv6 networks can send data back and forth across the IPv4 network.

There are a couple of things to keep in mind when using these tunnels. Although the tunnels are a great way to provide interoperability with IPv4 while you are in the process of transitioning to IPv6, it should be viewed as a temporary solution. Also, if the IPv4 network has an NAT translation point, you can run into problems with your tunnel as most implementations of NAT don't support this transitioning strategy.

To verify the configuration of your tunnel, use the command:

```
company1# show interface tunnel 0
Tunnel0 is up, line protocol is up
  Hardware is Tunnel
  MTU 1514 bytes, BW 9 Kbit, DLY 500000 usec,
    reliability 255/255, txload 1/255, rxload 1/255
  Encapsulation TUNNEL, loopback not set
  Keepalive not set
  Tunnel source 192.168.22.200 (Ethernet0/0), destination
    192.168.33.200
    fastswitch TTL 255
  Tunnel protocol/transport GRE/IP, key disabled, sequencing
    disabled
  Tunnel TTL 255
  Checksumming of packets disabled, fast tunneling enabled
  Last input 00:00:14, output 00:00:04, output hang never
  Last clearing of "show interface" counters never
  Input queue: 0/75/0/0 (size/max/drops/flushes); Total
    output drops: 0
  Queueing strategy: fifo
  Output queue :0/0 (size/max)
  5 minute input rate 0 bits/sec, 0 packets/sec
  5 minute output rate 0 bits/sec, 0 packets/sec
    4 packets input, 352 bytes, 0 no buffer
    Received 0 broadcasts, 0 runts, 0 giants, 0 throttles
    0 input errors, 0 CRC, 0 frame, 0 overrun, 0 ignored,
      0 abort
    8 packets output, 704 bytes, 0 underruns
    0 output errors, 0 collisions, 0 interface resets
    0 output buffer failures, 0 output buffers swapped out
```

To remove the tunnel, execute the *no interface tunnel <tunnel-number>* command on each router:

```
company1(config)# no interface tunnel 0
```

As the transition from IPv4 to IPv6 slowly continues, many companies will have the need to communicate between their new IPv6 networks and existing IPv4 networks, whether within their organization or with outside IPv4 networks and the IPv4 Internet. This gradual migration to IPv6 has been addressed with dual-stack and tunneling solutions.

IPv6 ADDRESSES

When we compared IPv6 to IPv4, we took a brief look at an IPv6 address. We saw that an IPv6 address is much larger than an IPv4 address (128 bits for version 6 and 32 bits for version 4). We also looked at the visual difference, where IPv4 addresses are represented in dotted decimal and IPv6 addresses are represented in hexadecimal. As was mentioned earlier, an IPv6 address is represented by eight 16-bit hexadecimal fields. Hexadecimal uses the numbers 0 through 9 and the letters a through f. The letters are not case sensitive, so you may see capital or lowercase letters in an IPv6 address.

HEAD OF THE CLASS...

Making IPv6 Addresses More "User-Friendly"

At first look, an IPv6 address is pretty intimidating. They're much larger than IPv4 addresses and have more fields to deal with. Let's look at some ways to make expressing an IPv6 address more user-friendly. Let's see what we can do with the IPv6 address we looked at in Table 10.3:

2001:0db8:1a2b:0011:0000:0000:345c:de67

This address definitely looks complicated. As long as we follow a few rules, though, there are some things we can do to make it easier to work with, starting with shortened ways of expressing the address. The first thing we can do is to get rid of some of the zeros in the address. The leading zeros in any field are optional. By eliminating the leading zeros, we can shorten the address to:

2001:db8:1a2b:11:0:0:345c:de67

It's already starting to look better. We've shortened it by a several digits by removing those extra zeros.

Another rule that we can apply to shorten it further applies any time we have contiguous fields of all zeros. We can replace any number of contiguous fields of all zeros with "::" so long as we only do that once in an address. We want to use it where we have the most con-

tiguous fields of all zeros. For our example, the address now looks like this:

2001:db8:1a2b:11::345c:de67

Let's look at another example of the correct way to use the "::" when replacing multiple fields of all zeros:

2001:db8:0000:0000:0000:0000:345c:de67

With the contiguous fields of all zeros replaced with "::" our address now looks like this:

2001:db8::345c:de67

Here is an example of an incorrect way to use the "::"

2001:db8:0000:0000:0034:0000:0000:0000

would be incorrectly represented as:

2001:db8::34::

This example shows you why you can only use "::" once in an address. In this case, the network devices wouldn't know where to fill in all of the missing zeros in this address. We have five of our eight fields represented by two sets of "::". We can't tell from looking at the address where the three contiguous fields of zeros belong and where the two contiguous fields of zeros belong. To represent the address correctly, one of the double colons in this address would need to be replaced with the correct number of fields, with single

zeros in each. Generally, you want to replace the section with the most contiguous zeros with the "::"
   2001:db8:0:0:0034::
   Here are some more examples of valid IPv6 addresses written in a shortened format:
   FF01:0:0:0:0:0:0:1 => FF01::1

0:0:0:0:0:0:0:1 => ::1
0:0:0:0:0:0:0:0 => ::
   So, how's that for making IPv6 addresses more user-friendly? We've shortened the last two addresses to a "::1" and just a "::". That's even better than IPv4 addresses.

Now we're going to take a much more in-depth look at IPv6 addresses. Let's break an address down and look at the different parts of the address. Different sections of an IPv6 address have different functions. Figure 10.2 shows what the primary sections in an IPv6 address represent.

2001	09b8	1a2b	0011	0000	0000	345c	de67
Global Prefix			Subnet		Interface ID		

FIGURE 10.2   *IPv6 Address Example with Sections Defined*

Although IPv6 addresses look a lot different than IPv4 addresses, some of the characteristics of the IPv6 addressing scheme are essentially the same as in IPv4. The primary functions of an IP address, whether version 4 or version 6, is to identify an interface on the network, and to provide information for routing. Because IP addresses are assigned to interfaces, some devices will have more than one address. Routers, for example, will usually have an IP address assigned to each interface.

Exam Warning

Even with IPv6 having 128 bits of address space you may still be given subnetting questions.

Just as IPv4 has addresses reserved for special functions, IPv6 also has special addresses. See Table 10.4 for a description of the special, reserved addresses in IPv6.

The last three special addresses in Table 10.4 include a slash and a number, a CIDR-type notation, at the end of the addresses. The /32 and the /16 are prefix numbers, identifying the first 32 bits as the prefix of the first two addresses, and the first 16 bits as the prefix of the last address, similar to the network portion of the address in IPv4. In the two addresses with the /32, the /32 indicates that the first 32 bits must match for the address (2001:db8 are the first 32 bits for the first address and 3FFF:FFFF are the first 32 bits for the second address) to be part of the defined range. And, for the last address, /16 means the first 16 bits (2002) must match for the address to be part of the defined range of 6to4 transitioning system addresses.

Table 10.4	IP Version 6 Special Addresses
Special IPv6 Addresses	**Description**
0:0:0:0:0:0:0:0	Shortened expression = :: Unspecified address (/128 prefix). With a /0 prefix, this is the same thing as 0.0.0.0 0.0.0.0 in IPv4. This address is the IPv6 equivalent of "any" and is used when setting up a default route to tell the router where to send packets destined for any network not already listed in the routing table.
0:0:0:0:0:0:0:1	Shortened expression = ::1 Loopback address, localhost. When packets are sent to this device, IPv6 loops them back to the same interface (the *loopback* interface, a software only interface). The equivalent of 127.0.0.1 in IPv4.
2001:db8::/32	This prefix is reserved for examples and documentation. These are nonroutable addresses.
3FFF:FFFF::/32	This prefix is also reserved for examples and documentation.
2002::/16	6to4 transition system. Allows IPv6 packets to be sent across an IPv4 network, without configuring explicit point-to-point tunnels. Used for point-to-multipoint tunnels.

There is another special type of address that you may come across in dual-stack IPv6/IPv4 networks called an *ipv4-mapped addresses*. This address type includes the IPv4 address in the last 32 bits. These addresses have all zeros in the first five fields (the first 80 bits), all ones in the next field (16 bits), and the last 32 bits represent an IPv4 address. For example, to create the IPv4-mapped address for 192.168.100.200, we get ::ffff:c0a8:64c8 for our IPv6 address. Another way of writing an IPv4-mapped address is for the last 32 bits to be written in standard dotted decimal format. The IPv6 address using this method of IPv4 mapping is ::ffff:192.168.100.200.

Every interface configured with IPv6 must have at least one loopback address (::1/128) and one link-local address (used only for communicating on the local link). A single interface may have multiple addresses of any type (unicast, multicast, and/or anycast). You can see there are a number of rules for how to use IPv6 addresses. There are many Requests for Comment (RFCs) to define the rules for different aspects of IPv6 addressing. The RFC that describes the architecture of IPv6 is RFC 4291.

Address Space

The extremely large address space available with IPv6 provides a lot of flexibility for address space allocation. The Internet Assigned Numbers Authority

(IANA) is the organization responsible for managing IPv6 address space and allocating addresses. The IANA has divided the overall address space into blocks for different purposes, with the IPv6 unicast space using the vast majority of all of the IPv6 addresses. In fact, the entire IPv6 address range, with the exception of the FF00::/8 prefix, makes up the unicast space. FF00::/8 is the prefix for IPv6 multicasting addresses.

Unicasts are a one-to-one type of communication, generally delivered to an individual interface on the network. IPv6 does allow one address to be assigned to multiple interfaces for load-balancing functions, though, so unicasts are sometimes delivered to more than one interface. The IANA assigns blocks of unicast addresses to ISPs and Regional Internet Registries (RIRs) who break the blocks of addresses down further and assign the smaller blocks to their clients. Currently, the unicast addresses that have been assigned by the IANA are only in the 2000::/3 range. There are several types of unicast communications, each with its own reserved range of addresses.

- **Global unicast addresses** The type of unicast addresses that are assigned by the IANA (2000::/3) are global unicast addresses.

- **Reserved unicast addresses** There are multiple groups of unicast addresses reserved by the IETF.

- **Link-local unicast addresses** Link-local unicast addresses are private addresses with a prefix of FE80::/10.

- **Unique local addresses** Unique local addresses are also private addresses, developed to replace a unicast address type called *site-local addresses*. Site-local addresses were denounced September 2004.

Global Unicast Addresses

The global unicast address space is a full 1/8 of the total IPv6 address space and is the largest block of assigned addresses. The global unicast addresses are designed for organizations, ISPs, and RIRs to structure the addresses hierarchically. Global unicast addresses start with 2001. Figure 10.3 shows the format of a global unicast address.

The first three bits in a global unicast address are a fixed value of 001 (2000::/3). The global routing prefix is the unique routing prefix in a specific organization's site. The first 48 bits (three fixed bits of 001 and the 45 its in the global routing prefix) are used to identify a site prefix, assigned to a specific site of an organization. A site is a group of subnets and links. Routers on the IPv6 Internet use these

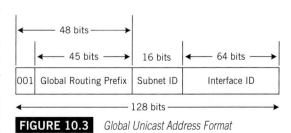

FIGURE 10.3 *Global Unicast Address Format*

addresses to forward packets with matching 48-bit prefixes to routers for the organization's site. The organization's site can be further broken down into subnets using the subnet identifier. Each site can create up to 65,536 subnets or levels of hierarchical addressing for more efficient routing. Finally, the interface identifier is a 64-bit field assigned to a specific interface.

Global unicast addresses function much like IPv4 public, routable addresses. They are globally-unique addresses, with an unlimited scope on the worldwide Internet. Internet routers route packets with global source and destination addresses to the routers of the site using the 48-bit destination prefix.

Exam Warning

On the exam in IPv6 troubleshooting, you may get questions that state this device cannot see the network. Why? Always start your troubleshooting by looking at the IPv6 address, if it does not start with 2001: it is not a globally routed IPv6 address and that may be the problem. The next two things you want to look at are the prefix and the subnet bits. For the device to see the network it must have the same number of prefix bits and the subnet bits must match the other devices on the network.

Link-Local Unicast Addresses

Link-local addresses are private addresses with a scope that's limited to the link (specific physical network). The link-local address is unique only on the link and the addresses are not routable outside of the link. Because all link-local addresses have the same prefix, routers would not have any information they could use to determine where to route the packets. For this reason, routers will not route link-local addresses at all, even within internal networks. Link-local addresses can be used to set up test networks, or any internal network when global addresses are not needed. They are used for automatic address configuration, neighbor discovery, and router discovery.

Link-local addresses are not a new concept. Beginning with Windows 98, Microsoft enabled autoconfiguration of clients with Automatic Private IP Addressing (APIPA). The range of link-local addresses in IPv4 is 169.254.0.0/16. Figure 10.4 displays the address format for the IPv6 link-local address.

The specific address space used for link-local addresses is FE80::/10. The lowest (last) 64 bits in the link-local address identify the specific interface. When communicating with

FIGURE 10.4   *Link-Local Address Format*

link-local addresses, you must specify the outgoing interface because all of the interfaces use FE80::/10.

Unique Local Unicast Addresses

Another type of IPv6 unicast address that is not intended to be routed globally is the unique local address, although these addresses are likely to be unique. Unique local addresses can be routed within sites and, in a limited fashion, between some sites. Unique local addresses are almost exactly like IPv4 private addresses.

Unique local addresses contain a randomly-generated, globally-unique prefix, unlikely to be duplicated anywhere. They also contain a well-known prefix, to facilitate filtering the packets at the site's boundaries. These addresses make it possible to combine or interconnect sites privately without creating address conflicts and without the necessity of renumbering interfaces. The format of the IPv6 unique local address is shown in Figure 10.5.

The address space used for IPv6 unique local addresses is FC00::/7. The field marked L in the diagram indicates if the address is locally assigned. If the value in the field is 1, the address has been locally assigned. At some time in the future, the 0 value may have significance but, at the current time, it isn't in use. The global identifier is generated using a pseudorandom algorithm and is used to create a globally-unique prefix. The pseudorandom allocation of global IDs ensures that there is no relationship between the various numbers that are generated. The numbers are not designed to be aggregated. This helps to clarify that these routers are not intended to be routed.

Multicast Addresses

Multicasts are a one-to-many communication. When packets are sent to multicast addresses those packets are delivered to all interfaces identified by the multicast address. Multicasts are used frequently in IPv6 and multicast communications are very important to the functioning of many aspects of IPv6. They work much the same in IPv6 as they do in IPv4, but IPv6 uses a much larger range of addresses for multicasting. In addition to the way IPv4 uses multicasts, IPv6 also uses multicasts instead of broadcasts, eliminating the problems caused by broadcast traffic in IPv4. Multicasts allow much more efficient use of the network. Figure 10.6 displays the format of a multicast address.

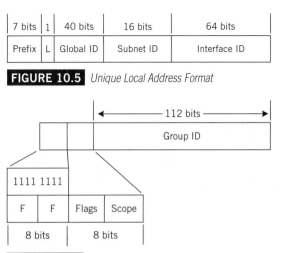

FIGURE 10.5 *Unique Local Address Format*

FIGURE 10.6 *Multicast Address Format*

Multicast addresses begin with 8 bits, all turned on, which is written as FF in hexadecimal. The next two fields are the flags and scope fields, each of which is 4 bits long. The third bit in the flags field indicates prefix. This flag allows for part of the group address to include the source network's unicast prefix. This creates a globally unique group address. The last bit in the flags field indicates if the address is permanent (value of the bit is 0) or temporary (value of the bit is 1). There are a number of addresses permanently assigned to particular types of multicast traffic, valid over a specified scope value. There are many ranges of addresses permanently assigned for multicasting functions. Table 10.5 lists a sampling of some of the commonly used, permanent multicast addresses.

The scope field in the multicast address relates to the subset of the network the address belongs to. There are a total of 15 scopes defined in IPv6. Some of the more common scopes are as follows:

1 = node

2 = link

5 = site

8 = organization

E = global

Anycast Addresses

The last type of IPv6 addresses we're going to talk about is new with IPv6. These addresses are called anycast addresses. Anycasts are one-to-nearest or one-to-one-of-many communications. Multiple interfaces are assigned the same IPv6 address. The source device sends packets to the anycast address and

Table 10.5 Permanent Multicast Addresses

Scope	Address Space	Description
Node-Local	FF01::1	All nodes address
Node-Local	FF01::2	All routers address
Link-Local	FF02::1	All nodes address
Link-Local	FF02::2	All routers address
Link-Local	FF02::9	All RIP routers address
Link-Local	FF02::1:2	All-DHCP-agents
Site-Local	FF05::2	All routers address
Site-Local	FF05::1:3	All-DHCP-servers

the routers decide which device with that address is the closest. The range of addresses used for anycasting comes from the unicast address space.

All nodes with the address should provide uniform services to get the benefit of anycast addressing. Anycast addresses can be used beneficially for load balancing, automatic failover, and content delivery services. Anycast addresses can also be used when a network is multihomed to several ISPs that have multiple connections to each other. The global routing prefix allows aggregation upwards, eventually to the ISP. Figure 10.7 shows the format of the anycast address.

n bits	128-n bits
Subnet Prefix	Interface ID

FIGURE 10.7 *Anycast Address Format*

The number of bits used in the subnet prefix field is variable and will determine how many bits are used in the interface identifier portion of the address (128 total bits minus the bits in the subnet prefix). When a unicast address is deliberately assigned to more than one interface, it automatically becomes an anycast address. The interfaces with the anycast address assigned will share some type of a network prefix. This is what determines the network area where the anycast routes are advertised. An anycast address can also be created by using the *ip address <address>/<prefix> anycast* command in interface configuration mode:

```
company# configure terminal
company(config)# interface Fastethernet0/0
company(config-if)# ipv6 address 2001:db8:1:1:ffff:ffff:ffff:ffff/64 anycast
```

Aggregating Addresses

The much bigger address space available in IPv6 allows for a larger allocation of addresses for organizations and for ISPs. This provides ISPs with enough addresses so that they can aggregate the prefixes of all of their customers to announce a single prefix to the IPv6 Internet. The larger address space also allows organizations to define a single prefix to identify their entire site and aggregate the addresses to the single prefix. Address aggregation provides a number of benefits:

- By aggregating prefixes in the global routing table, routing tables can be kept much smaller.

- Aggregation allows much more efficient, scalable routing.

- Smaller routing tables from address allocation provides for improved bandwidth functionality for network and Internet traffic.

To expand network functionality and take advantage of the benefits IPv6 provides, routing efficiency and scalability will become more and

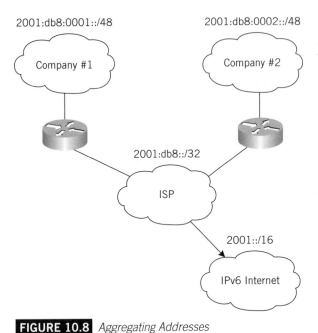

2001:db8:0001::/48

2001:db8:0002::/48

Company #1

Company #2

2001:db8::/32

ISP

2001::/16

IPv6 Internet

FIGURE 10.8 *Aggregating Addresses*

more critical. As the Internet continues to grow at such a rapid rate, address aggregation will keep routing tables shorter and improve Internet operations. Figure 10.8 shows an example of how address aggregation works.

Company1 and Company2 both connect to the ISP in the center of the diagram. The ISP can aggregate the traffic coming from the 2001:db8:0001 and 2001:db8:0002 prefixes and advertise only the /32 prefix (2001:db8), which includes both customers' traffic, to the IPv6 Internet.

CONFIGURING AN IPv6 ADDRESS

Now that we've looked at the different types of addresses used in IPv6 and talked about how those addresses can be aggregated to shorten routing tables and improve performance, it's time to look at how we assign IPv6 addresses to our network devices. IPv6 addresses can be assigned statically or dynamically. We can use static addresses that contain a manually-assigned interface identifier or IPv6 can create an address using something called a 64-bit Extended Universal Identifier (EUI-64) in the lower 64 bits of the address. The EUI-64 is a method of taking the device's MAC address and creating an Internet identifier from it. We'll see how that works a little later in the EUI-64 section. Devices can address themselves automatically using stateless autoconfiguration, which also incorporates EUI-64 as part of the address. Devices can also be autoconfigured statefully, meaning information about the addresses is stored on the server, using Dynamic Host Configuration Protocol (DHCP) for IPv6.

Autoconfiguration of Addresses

One of the features in IPv6 that is going to save network administrators a lot of work is the ability to have IPv6 addresses assigned to our network devices for us. First, we're going to take a look at the process IPv6 uses to autoconfigure devices statelessly, which requires little or no work on our part. Then, we'll look at DHCP for IPv6.

Stateless Autoconfiguration

Stateless autoconfiguration of addresses enables plug-and-play networking of devices and reduces administrative overhead. The device creates a preliminary address which is verified for uniqueness, and the device is then able to communicate on the network without the need for manual intervention. Cisco uses the EUI-64 format for stateless autoconfiguration of interfaces.

There are four steps in the process of stateless autoconfiguration to create a link-local address:

1. An interface identifier is generated.

2. A tentative address is created.

3. The address is verified as unique on the link.

4. If the address is confirmed to be unique, it is assigned to the interface.

In Step 1, an interface identifier is generated. The MAC address of the interface is modified using the EUI-64 method of padding a MAC address and creating a 64-bit interface ID from a 48-bit MAC address. It is initially assumed that this address is unique. However, there have been instances of manufacturers shipping batches of NICs with the same MAC address, so there is a slight possibility that the address won't be unique on the link.

In Step 2, the device needs to obtain prefix information for its address. The host sends a router solicitation (RS) message requesting prefix information. The RS message is an Internet Control Message Protocol (ICMP) message type 133 and is sent to the multicast address of the routers. In response, the router sends a multicast message called a router advertisement (RA) to the multicast address of the hosts. The RA is an ICMP message type 134. The RA includes the prefix information and other network information. The interface identifier generated in Step 1 is appended to the prefix information to create the 128-bit link-local address for the interface. The address is tagged as tentative until it can be verified as unique.

A process called *duplicate address detection* (DAD) is used in Step 3 to determine if the address is unique. The system sends ICMP packets containing neighbor solicitation messages across the link. The tentative address is the destination address and the source address is the unassigned address "::". If another interface is already using the tentative address, the device responds with a neighbor advertisement message. If this happens, the tentative address can't be used because it's already assigned to another device.

Finally, in Step 4, if the address is unique, it is assigned to the interface. If it isn't unique, manual intervention is required to create a unique address.

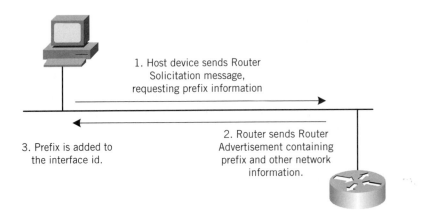

FIGURE 10.9

Generating an Autoconfigured Address

Figure 10.9 displays the communication process between the host and the router, described in Step 2.

Routers send periodic RAs to tell other devices about prefixes and other network information. Rather than wait for the next periodic RA, however, host devices send RS messages causing the routers to generate RAs when needed.

To check the configuration of IPv6 addresses on an interface, execute the *show ipv6 interface <interface-number>* command. Here is an example of the *show ipv6 interface* command to see the configuration and status of the *Fastethernet0/0* interface:

```
company# show ipv6 interface ethernet 0/0
Ethernet0 is up, line protocol is up
IPv6 is enabled, link-local address is 2001:0DB8::/32
Global unicast address(es):
2000:0DB8::2, subnet is 2001:0DB8::/64
Joined group address(es):
FF02::1
FF02::2
FF02::1:FF11:6770
MTU is 1500 bytes
ICMP error messages limited to one every 500 milliseconds
ICMP redirects are enabled
ND DAD is enabled, number of DAD attempts: 1
ND reachable time is 30000 milliseconds
ND advertised reachable time is 0 milliseconds
ND advertised retransmit interval is 0 milliseconds
ND router advertisements are sent every 200 seconds
ND router advertisements live for 1800 seconds
ND advertised default router preference is Medium
Hosts use stateless autoconfig for addresses.
```

DHCP for IP Version 6

DHCP for IPv6 is a stateful method of autoconfiguration, meaning information about the addresses is stored on the server. In addition to IP addresses, DHCP servers can pass other parameters to the host devices. For this reason, DHCP servers add additional flexibility to the automatic configuration process. DHCP provides more control over network configurations than stateless or serverless addressing. Although stateless autoconfiguration is very convenient, there are a number of benefits provided by DHCP that are not provided by stateless autoconfiguration alone. DHCP can pass additional configuration options to the hosts, including Domain name server (DNS) information, and domain names. DHCPv6 can make renumbering devices a much easier process and, using dynamic DNS, can be used for automatic domain name registration of network devices. Because of the additional configuration capabilities offered by DHCP, it's likely that DHCP will continue to be used as extensively in IPv6 as it is in IPv4.

DHCPv6 is an updated version of DHCP for IPv4, with added support for IPv6 addressing and the benefits of the new IPv6 features. DHCPv6 can be used on its own or in conjunction with stateless autoconfiguration to send additional IPv6 configuration information to the hosts. How DHCPv6 works is very similar to DHCP for version 4, with a few exceptions. Here are the steps involved in the DHCPv6 process:

1. The host device detects the presence of routers on the link.

2. If a router is found, the RA is checked to see if DHCP can be used.

3. If the RA indicates that DHCP can be used or if there is no router,

4. A DHCP solicit message is sent to the multicast address for all-DHCP-agents.

In DHCP for version 4, DHCP requests are sent as broadcasts. DHCPv6 has been updated to use multicasting instead because IPv6 doesn't use broadcasts.

The nature of how IPv6 operates compared to IPv4 is different in some respects because of the much larger address space available with IPv6. Addresses, and even entire prefixes, can be allocated to devices for a much longer time period than in IPv4. The need for static allocation of addresses has increased to access home servers and traveling devices via DNS servers. Sites with multiple links sometimes require flexibility in the prefixes they obtain, such as in prefix length. Improvements to DHCPv6 have addressed these needs.

Some of these needs for addressing and prefix assignment have required a stateful form of DHCP to store the information on the DHCP servers.

The Cisco IOS implementation of DHCPv6 is a stateless form of DHCPv6 ("DHCPv6-lite"). To meet these requirements, Cisco's DHCPv6 function includes the prefix delegation (PD) and DNS options, allowing the routers to distribute prefixes and DNS server and domain name information. Although Cisco's DHCPv6 software doesn't provide all of the capabilities of a stateful DHCPv6 server, such as maintaining address information, it has the ability to pass configuration parameters to DHCPv6 clients.

Enabling IPv6

Refer to Exercise 10.3 for the steps to go through to enable IPv6 and configure an IPv6 address on an interface.

EXERCISE 10.3 **Enabling IPv6 and Configuring IPv6 Addresses**

1. Access global configuration mode:

   company# **configure terminal**

2. Enable IPv6 forwarding on the router:

   company(config)# **ipv6 unicast-routing**

3. Move to interface configuration mode:

   company(config)# **interface Fastethernet0/0**

4. Enable IPv6 on the interface and cause a link-local address to be automatically generated.

   company(config-if)# **ipv6 enable**

Remember, link-local addresses aren't routable so this command enables the device to communicate only with the other devices on the local link, or physical network. Here are the steps to configure a global unicast address on the interface.

   company(config-if)# **ipv6 address 2001:db8:1a2b:11::345c:de67/64**

This command specifies the entire 128-bit IPv6 address.

Alternatively, you can specify the prefix information for the address and allow the router to create the interface identifier automatically by modifying the interface's MAC address.

   company(config-if)# **ipv6 address 2001:db8: 1a2b:11::/64 eui-64**

To disable IPv6 on the router, execute the *no ipv6 unicast-routing* command at the global configuration prompt:

company(config)# **no ipv6 unicast-routing**

To disable IPv6 on an individual interface, the command *no ipv6 enable* is executed in interface configuration mode:

company(config-if)# **no ipv6 enable**

To remove the global IPv6 address from the interface without disabling IPv6, leaving the automatically-generated link-local address intact, use the *no ipv6 address* command in interface configuration mode. For example, to remove the IPv6 address we assigned to *Fastethernet0/0*, we would execute the command:

company(config-if)# **no ipv6 address 2001:db8:1a2b:11::345c:de67/64**

EUI-64

The EUI-64 option has been mentioned a few times now, so let's take a look at exactly what it is. The EUI-64 format uses the interface's MAC address, pads the MAC address, and creates an interface identifier from the padded MAC address. An interface identifier is 64 bits long and a MAC address is 48 bits long so padding the MAC address gives us the 64 bits we need for the interface identifier. The MAC address is padded by inserting FFFE into the middle, between the Organization Unique ID (OUI) and the serial number. Here is an example of a MAC address before it is modified:

00-10-AB-23-45-67

After the address has been modified using the EUI-64 standard it looks like this:

02-10-AB-FF-FE-23-45-67

MAC addresses used in the Cisco IOS are displayed as three 16-bit hexadecimal fields. For example, a MAC address used on a router interface would look something like this:

0010:AB23:4567

After the address is modified, it looks like this:

0210:ABFF:FE23:4567

In addition to the FF FE that is added into the middle of the MAC address, the second digit is now a 2. The 2 indicates that the address is a global unicast address. The seventh highest-order bit in the interface identifier is

FIGURE 10.10 *Modified EUI-64 Address*

called the Universally Unique/Locally Unique (U/L) bit. The purpose of this bit is to specify if the address is intended to remain local or if it is to be a global address. An on ("1") bit indicates that the address is a global unicast address. If the bit is off (a "0" bit), the address is intended to remain local. The seventh bit has a value of 2 when the bit is turned on. That's why the value of the second hexadecimal digit is now 2. More information on modified EUI-64 addresses is detailed in Figure 10.10.

Configuring the EUI-64 portion of the address is automatic in the case of the link-local address that is generated when an interface is enabled for IPv6. Here are the commands you would execute in the Cisco IOS:

> company(config)# **interface Fastethernet0/0**
> company(config-if)# **ipv6 enable**

These commands enable IPv6 on the *Fastethernet0/0* interface and cause a link-local address, with the modified EUI-64 interface ID to be automatically created.

Link-Local

Link-local addresses are internal, private addresses that are only accessible on the particular link. The address space used by link-local addresses is FE80::/10. The lowest (last) 64 bits in the link-local address identify the specific interface. When communicating with link-local addresses, you must specify the outgoing interface because all of the interfaces use FE80::/10.

Devices on the network automatically build a link-local address during the initialization process for an IPv6 NIC. Link-local addresses are also assigned automatically when a unique local or aggregatable global address is assigned to an interface. This is possible because the link-local prefix is fixed in length and well known (FE80::/10). The interface identifier portion of the address uses the EUI-64 numbering convention.

Link-local addresses can also be configured manually when you want to assign a link-local address other than the automatically-generated address to an interface. For example, when a device goes through the autoconfiguration process, it uses DAD to determine if the address is unique. It sends neighbor solicitation messages across the link to the address it is trying to autoconfigure. If another device replies, the address is not unique and can't be assigned. In that case, a static address has to be used. To create a manual link-local address on an interface, you would execute the *ipv6 address <address>/<prefix-length> link-local* command in interface configuration mode:

```
company(config)# interface Fastethernet0/0
company(config-if)# ipv6 address fe80::11:2ab:cd3:e10/64 link-local
```

Unnumbered

IPv6 can be enabled on an interface without assigning an explicit IPv6 address to the interface. An unnumbered interface uses the global IPv6 address of another interface as the source of the packets it sends. IPv6 is enabled on an unnumbered interface by using the *ipv6 unnumbered <interface-type><interface-number>* command in interface configuration mode. The interface with the global address to be used as the source address is the interface identified in the command. The *ipv6 unnumbered* command works a lot like the *ip unnumbered* command in IPv4, just updated to support IPv6. The configuration to create an unnumbered interface is

```
company(config)# interface serial0/0
company(config-if)# ipv6 unnumbered Fastethernet0/0
```

This configuration enables IPv6 on the *serial0/0* interface and identifies the *Fastethernet0/0* interface's address as the one to be used as the source address for packets originating from the *serial0/0* interface.

To disable IPv6 on the *serial0/0* interface, execute the *no ipv6 unnumbered* command in interface configuration mode:

```
company(config-if)# no ipv6 unnumbered
```

IPv6 DNS Mappings

To make working with IPv6 addresses easier, we're going to want to implement IPv6 name resolution. Name resolution is an extremely important component of IPv4 networks and, with the more complicated addresses for IPv6, it's even more critical for IPv6 networks. IPv6 allows us to configure host tables on our routers, as does IPv4. The format of the command is the same, just using IPv6 addresses. The syntax of the command we'll use to create static host-name-to-IPv6-address mappings is

```
IPv6 host <name> [<port>] <IPv6address> [<IPv6address> <IPv6
    address> ...]
```

The *<name>* field refers to the name of the device you want to map to the IPv6 address(es). The *<port>* field is an optional part of the command that allows you to include the port number you wish to connect to when you telnet to the device. The last part of the command is one or more IPv6 addresses associated with the device. When you connect to the device using the name from the host table entry, the router attempts to connect using the addresses in the order listed. Here is an example configuration for creating a host table:

company(config)# **ipv6 host company1 2001:db8:1a2b::345c:de67**
company(config)# **Ipv6 host company2 2001:db8:3a4b::c543:de10**

We can look at our host table by doing the *show hosts* command, which will display default domain name, style of name lookup service, list of name server hosts, and cached list of host names and addresses.

```
company# show hosts
Default domain is not set
Name/address lookup uses static mappings
Host          Port    Flags        Age    Type    Address(es)
company1      None    (perm,OK)    0      IP      2001:db8:1a2b::345c:de67
company1      None    (perm, OK)   0      IP      2001:db8:3a4b::c543:de10
```

To remove an entry from the host table, we use the *no ipv6 host <name> <address>* command:

company(config)# **no ipv6 host company1 2001:db8:1a2b::345c:de67**

DNS is the most commonly-used method for mapping names to IPv6 addresses. DNS is a critical component of all IP networks because it is necessary for Transmission Control Protocol/Internet Protocol (TCP/IP) applications to be able to obtain the IP addresses for all of the devices needing to be accessed. Knowing all of the IPv6 addresses out there is not possible for anyone (it isn't possible for IPv4 addresses either, but IPv6 addresses are even worse), so we need some method of accessing devices without having to keep track of the IP addresses. DNS servers provide the mapping between the much-easier names for devices and their IP addresses. Applications also use DNS servers to provide them with information on resources.

Unlike most of the other protocols we've talked about in this chapter, there is no IPv6 version of DNS. IPv6-usable DNS servers maintain mapping information for resolving names to IPv6 addresses and for reverse mappings from IPv6 addresses to DNS names. They may also provide mappings for IPv4 addresses. To provide name resolution for IPv6, DNS servers must support a different record type than is used in IPv4. To work with IPv6 DNS servers must be able to work with IPv6 "AAAA" (referred to as quad A) resource record types and, if the DNS server will also resolve for IPv4, it must support IPv4 "A" record types as well.

The command for defining the DNS servers for the router to query for name resolution is the same as in IPv4, except the address of the server in our example is an IPv6 address. To configure the DNS server, use the *ip name-server* command. The syntax of the command is

```
ip name-server <server1address> [<server2address>
      <server3address> ...]
```

and the example of how to configure it looks like this:

```
company(config)# ip name-server 2001:db8:a12::10
company(config)# ip domain-lookup
```

The *ip domain-lookup* command enables the DNS service. By default, DNS is enabled so you only need to execute this command if the DNS service has been disabled.

IPv6 ACLs

Access control lists (ACLs) filter packets, allowing or denying access to services or resources. In the Cisco IOS, ACLs are referred to as access lists and are used to filter traffic and control access on the router and on the network. IPv6 ACLs work a lot like IPv4 ACLs except, of course, that they filter based on IPv6 addresses and ports. As with IPv4 ACLs, inbound and/or outbound packets can be filtered.

Cisco's earlier implementations of IPv6 provided the ability to configure ACLs much like standard IP access lists in IPv4. Lists provided basic traffic filtering, such as source and destination addresses, inbound and outbound on an interface. These earlier IPv6 ACLs ended with an implicit *deny any* statement, as do IPv4 ACLs. As Cisco's IPv6 IOS component has evolved, so have the IPv6 ACLs. Later versions of the IOS allow filtering on source and destination addresses, plus filtering based on IPv6 option headers and optional, upper-layer protocol type information, similar to extended IP access lists for IPv4.

IPv6 ACLs are configured using access list configuration mode, accessed with the *ipv6 access-list <list-name>* command. ACLs are created with permit and deny statements, then the list is applied to the interface or other location where it is to be used to filter the traffic. IPv6 ACLs are named lists. In IPv4, we can create access lists with names or numbers to identify the list. IPv6 ACLs don't support numbered lists. The name can't start with a number and can't contain spaces or quotes and IPv4 and IPv6 ACLs can't have the same name. IPv6 ACLs end with the following implicit statements:

```
permit icmp any any nd-na
permit icmp any any nd-ns
deny ipv6 any any
```

The two ICMP permit statements are necessary for the IPv6 neighbor discovery process. The last statement denies all other IPv6 packets not explicitly permitted elsewhere in the list. IPv6 ACLs can filter packets based on the following protocol types:

- TCP

- UDP

- Stream Control Transmission Protocol (SCTP)

- ICMPv6

Ports and ranges of ports can be filtered just like in IPv4 access lists. The equal to (*eq*), less than (*lt*), greater than (*gt*), not equal to (*neq*), and range options are still available in IPv6 ACLs. Logging information to the console about the packets being matched is still available as is the ability to redirect the logging information. At the global configuration prompt, use the command, *ipv6 access-list <list-name>* to enter access list mode. Here is an example of how to configure an IPv6 ACL:

```
company(config)# ipv6 access-list in-list-1
company(config-ipv6-acl)# permit 1abc:11::/32 any
company(config-ipv6-acl)# permit 1abc:12::/32 any
company(config-ipv6-acl)# sequence 35 permit tcp any any eq smtp
company(config-ipv6-acl)# permit udp any any eq domain
```

This list is identified by the name *in-list-1*. The first two statements in the list permit packets coming from the source addresses 1abc:11::/32 and 1abc:12::/32, going to any destination. The last two statements permit smtp (e-mail) and domain (DNS) packets coming from any source and going to any destination.

One thing that does look a little different than in IPv4 ACLs is the *sequence 35* at the beginning of the *permit udp* command. When the list is created the statements will be automatically sequenced by 10s (10, 20, 30, etc.). To add a statement with a sequence other than the default sequence, use *sequence* and the number to tell the router where to put the statement. The phrase "*sequence 35*" can be at the beginning of the command or at the end of the command. The *sequence* option gives us the ability to add statements into the list where we need them and to resequence the list if necessary. Named extended access lists in IPv4 also have this ability although you include only the sequence number and not the word "sequence" in your IPv4 ACL commands.

If we had multiple access lists on our router and wanted to look at all of them, we could execute the *show access-lists* command. To display our access list called in-list-1, we use the *show ipv6 access-lists <list-name>* command:

```
company# show ipv6 access-list in-list-1
IPv6 access list in-list-1
permit IPv6 1abc:11::/32 any sequence 10 (10 matches)
permit IPv6 1abc:12::/32 any sequence 20 (2 matches)
permit tcp any any eq smtp sequence 35 (600 matches)
permit tcp any any eq domain sequence 40 (998 matches)
```

The number of matches in parentheses at the end of each statement is the count of packets that matched the statement since the last time the counters were reset. To reset the counters, use this command:

company# **clear ipv6 access-list in-list-1**

Once the ACL is created, it is applied to define the traffic it is to filter. To apply our list to inbound traffic on our *Fastethernet0/0* interface, we configure the following:

company(config)# **interface Fastethernet0/0**
company(config-if)# **ipv6 traffic-filter in-list-1 in**

Another place we might want to apply our access list is to filter packets coming into our virtual terminal (vty) lines. This limits who has access to the router itself, for functions like telnet for router management. To apply the ACL to inbound traffic on our vty lines, numbered 0 through 4:

company(config)# **line vty 0 4**
company(config-line)# **ipv6 access-class in-list-1 in**

To remove a statement from our access-list, we execute the *no <sequence-number>* command within ACL configuration mode:

company(config-ipv6-acl)# **no 35**

To remove the entire list, we execute the *no ipv6 access-list <list-name>* command, at the global configuration prompt:

company(config)# **no ipv6 access-list in-list-1**

To remove the access list from our virtual terminal lines, we enter:

company(config-line)# **no ipv6 access-class in-list-1 in**

IPv6 Routing

Routing in IPv6 is much like routing in IPv4. The router maintains an IPv6 routing table that it uses to determine how to forward packets. We can configure static routes and dynamic routes, like in IPv4. Configuring static routes in IPv6 uses the same command format that we use in IPv4. To set up a static route, execute the following command:

```
IPv6 route <destination-network>/<prefix-length>
<next-hop-address|interface> [<distance>]
```

The last part of the command before the optional distance is either a next hop address on a remote router, or an interface on this router. Here are some examples of how to configure static routes on the router called company. The first static route tells the router to send packets intended for the 2001:db8:a12:3::/64 network to the next hop address, 2001:db8:a12:4::2/64.

```
company(config)# ipv6 route 2001:db8:a12:3::/64 2001:db8:a12:4::2/64
```

The following example of a static route tells the router to send packets intended for the 2001:db8:a12:3::/64 network out the *Fastethernet0/0* interface:

```
company(config)# ipv6 route 2001:db8:a12:3::/64 Fastethernet0/0
```

To look at the static routing information in a routing table, we use the *show IPv6 static* command:

```
company# show ipv6 static
IPv6 Static routes
Code: * - installed in RIB
* 3AB0::/16, interface Ethernet1/0, distance 1
* 4AB0::/16, via nexthop 2001:1::1, distance 1
    5AB0::/16, interface Ethernet3/0, distance 1
* 5AB5::/16, via nexthop 4AB0::1, distance 1
    5AB5::/16, via nexthop 98::1, distance 1
* 5AB5::/16, interface Ethernet2/0, distance 1
* 6AB0::/16, via nexthop 2007::1, interface Ethernet1/0, distance 1
```

The RIB indicated by the asterisk in front of some of the routes, refers to the IPv6 Routing Information Base, a master database of routes.

To display the entire IPv6 routing table, including all types of routes currently designated as the closest routes for that router, use the *show route* command, specifically for IPv6.

```
company# show ipv6 route
IPv6 Routing Table - 9 entries
Codes: C - Connected, L - Local, S - Static, R - RIP, B - BGP
I1 - ISIS L1, I2 - ISIS L2, IA - IIS interarea
L     4AB0::2/128 [0/0]
          via ::, Ethernet1/0
C     4AB0::/64 [0/0]
          via ::, Ethernet1/0
LC    4AB1::1/128 [0/0]
          via ::, Loopback0
L     5AB0::2/128 [0/0]
          via ::, Serial6/0
C     5AB0::/64 [0/0]
          via ::, Serial6/0
S     5AB2::/48 [1/0]
          via 4000::1, Null
L     FE80::/10 [0/0]
          via ::, Null0
```

To remove a static route, use the *no ipv6 route* command for the route you want to remove in global configuration mode:

```
company(config)# ipv6 route 2001:db8:a12:3::/64 2001:db8:a12:4::2/64
```

In addition to static routes, routes can be created dynamically in IPv6, as they can in IPv4. Dynamic routing is accomplished by installing a Dynamic Routing Protocol and configuring it. The steps for configuring routing protocols are as follows:

1. Create the routing process.

2. Enable the routing process on the interfaces.

3. Customize the routing protocol for your specific network.

Most of the routing protocols that we use in IPv4 have been updated for use in IPv6. Many functions and configurations included in IPv4 routing protocols are nearly the same in the IPv6 versions. Routing protocols that depend on broadcasts to function will not work in IPv6 because IPv6 doesn't use broadcasts but there are many routing protocols available for use in IPv6 that use multicasting. Some examples of IPv4 routing protocols updated for use in IPv6 are as follows:

- RIP

- Enhanced Interior Gateway Routing Protocol (EIGRP)

- Open Shortest Path First (OSPF)

- Integrated Intermediate System-to-Intermediate System (IS-IS)

IPv6 RIP

One of the routing protocols widely used in IPv4 that is available in an updated version for IPv6 is RIP. RIP is an Interior Gateway Protocol (IGP), meaning that it is used within a particular autonomous system. The updated version of IPv6 RIP is also referred to as RIPng (RIP next generation). IPv6 RIP is based on RIPv2 and still includes the primary features of RIPv2. As in RIPv2, IPv6 RIP is a Distance-Vector Routing Protocol, with a maximum hop count of 15. It still uses split horizon, poison reverse, and other techniques to avoid routing loops. In addition to the characteristics it inherited from IPv2, IPv6 RIP supports IPv6 addresses and prefixes, IPv6 addresses for next hop, and IPv6 for transport.

IPv6 RIP still uses multicasting to send updates and is still User Datagram Protocol (UDP)-based, although it has a new UDP port assignment (port 521). The multicasting address of FF02::9 that IPv6 RIP uses to send updates is the all RIP routers group. Routers keep the next-hop address of neighboring routers for every destination network in their routing tables. IPv6 RIP also keeps track of next-hop address information but uses link-local addresses rather than global addresses.

Configuring IPv6 RIP is accomplished a little differently from configuring RIPv2. With RIPv2, *network* statements are used to enable the advertising of networks. In IPv6 RIP, network statements have been eliminated. Instead, advertising is enabled directly on the interface within interface configuration mode. IPv6 RIP itself can be enabled directly from the interfaces, without the need to access router configuration mode, although there are still other commands that are executed at the router configuration prompt. When IPv6 RIP is enabled on an interface, a routing process is automatically created. The command syntax for enabling RIP on an interface is: *ipv6 rip tag enable*. The *tag* is a group name that identifies the RIP process that's running. Here is an example of how to configure RIP on an interface:

```
company(config)# interface Fastethernet0/0
company(config-if)# ipv6 rip process1 enable
```

This is how you would enable RIP using router configuration mode. You would also access router configuration mode if you needed to set or change a global parameter, such as a redistribute.

```
company(config)# ipv6 router rip process1
company(config-router)#
```

> **Test Day Tip**
>
> Remember that in IPv4 you set up RIP with only the *router rip* command and then the *network* command at the router(config-router)# prompt. In IPv6 you turn on the RIP protocol with the *ipv6 router rip groupname* command then go to the interfaces that you want to participate in the rip protocol and issue the *ipv6 rip groupname enable* command to start the broadcasting of rip routes.

In the Cisco IOS, each RIPv6 process maintains its own local routing table, called a *Routing Information Database* (RIB). The RIPv6 RIB contains lowest-cost routes collected by RIPv6 from neighboring network devices. Expired routes being advertised to RIPv6 neighbors by the RIPv6 process are also included in the RIB. All routes that haven't expired are entered into the master RIP RIB, unless the same route was discovered by another routing protocol and already exists in the master RIB with a lower administrative distance. To display configuration information about all current RIP processes, use the *show ipv6* rip command:

```
company# show ipv6 rip
RIP process "process1", port 521, multicast-group FF02::9,
   pid 55
   Administrative distance is 25. Maximum paths is 4
   Updates every 30 seconds, expire after 180
   Holddown lasts 0 seconds, garbage collect after 120
   Split horizon is on; poison reverse is off
   Default routes are not generated
   Periodic updates 8883, trigger updates 2
Interfaces:
   Ethernet2
   Redistribution:
RIP process "process2", port 521, multicast-group FF02::9,
   pid 61
   Administrative distance is 120. Maximum paths is 4
   Updates every 30 seconds, expire after 180
   Holddown lasts 0 seconds, garbage collect after 120
   Split horizon is on; poison reverse is off
   Default routes are not generated
   Periodic updates 8883, trigger updates 0
Interfaces:
   None
Redistribution:
```

To display the RIP routes in the IPv6 routing table, use the *show ipv6 route* command with the *RIP* keyword:

```
company# show ipv6 route RIP
IPv6 Routing Table - 5 entries
Codes: C - Connected, L - Local, S - Static, R - RIP, B - BGP
I1 - ISIS L1, I2 - ISIS L2, IA - IIS interarea
R     4AB0::/64 [0/0]
           via ::, Ethernet1/0
R     4AB1::1/128 [0/0]
           via ::, Loopback0
R     5AB0::2/128 [0/0]
           via ::, Serial6/0
R     5AB0::/64 [0/0]
           via ::, Serial6/0
R     5AB2::/48 [1/0]
           via 4000::1, Null
```

To remove a particular RIP process from an interface, execute the *no ipv6 rip* command for the process you want to remove in interface configuration mode:

company(config-if)# **no ipv6 rip process1 enable**

To remove a RIP process from the router altogether, use the following command:

company(config)# **no ipv6 router rip process1**

IPv6 OSPF

OSPF is a link-state routing protocol that is popular in IPv4 and that has been updated for IPv6. OSPF for IPv6 is actually OSPFv3, as OSPFv2 is the routing protocol used in IPv4 networks. The basics of OSPF haven't changed and there are many similarities between OSPF2 and OSPF3. OSPF was developed for large networks or Autonomous Systems divided into hierarchical areas. As a link-state routing protocol, OSPF uses the shortest path first (SPF), or Dijkstra, algorithm for calculations. OSPF gets an overall picture of the topology of the network by advertising link-state information throughout the network.

With OSPFv2, the router ID (RID) was obtained from the highest IP address configured on the router. OSPFv3 handles the RID differently. When you are configuring OSPFv3, you assign the RID, area ID, link-state ID as part of the configuration process. These values are going to look similar to OSPFv2 because they are 32-bit values like IPv4 addresses, but they aren't obtained from the IP addresses. Other changes to OSPF with version 3 are in the packet headers. Values are assigned, added, and removed in a fashion that makes it possible for OSPFv3 to be routed over almost any network layer protocol.

OSPFv3 makes use of IPv6 by using link-local addresses for next-hop attributes and adjacencies. Updates and acknowledgements are still sent as multicasts, now using FF02::/5 for the OSPF routers multicast group, and FF02::/6 for the OSPF-designated routers multicast group. Where OSPFv2 networks and interfaces are configured in the router configuration mode, OSPFv3 has been updated like most of the other IPv6 protocols to configure interfaces and networks attached to the interfaces in interface configuration mode. And, like other IPv6 routing protocols, other OSPFv3 options are still configured at the (config-router) prompt.

To start IPv6 OSPF routing process #10, and create a router ID, the commands are as follows:

(config)# **ipv6 router ospf 10**
(config-router)# **router id 1.1.1.1**

Or, to configure the OSPF process in interface configuration mode,

(config-if)# **ipv6 ospf 10 area 0.0.0.0**

This one statement starts OSPF process #10 and assigns the interface to area 0.0.0.0.

To disable OSPF on the router,

(config)# **no ipv6 router ospf 10**

Now we want to look at the routing table to see our OSPF routes:

```
company# show ipv6 route
IPv6 Routing Table - 7 entries
O 2001:DB8:1A2B:11::/64 [110/65]
via FE80::21A:7FFF:FE35:ACE9, Serial0/0/1
O 2001:DB8:1A2B:12::/64 [110/128]
via FE80::21A:7FFF:FE35:ACE9, Serial0/0/1
O 2001:DB8:1A2B:13::/64 [110/128]
via FE80::21A:2FFF:FE35:ACE9, Serial0/0/1
C 2001:DB8:1A2B:14::/64 [0/0]
via ::, Serial0/0/1
L 2001:1A2B:3C4D:121:CF2:ABC9:DEDE:A3B4/128 [0/0]
via ::, Serial0/0/1
L FE80::/10 [0/0]
via ::, Null0
L FF00::/8 [0/0]
via ::, Null0
```

To display general information about IPv6 OSPF, use this command:

```
company# show ipv6 ospf
Routing Process "ospfv3 1" with ID 10.1.1.1
SPF schedule delay 5 secs, Hold time between two SPFs 10
  secs
  Minimum LSA interval 5 secs. Minimum LSA arrival 1 secs
  LSA group pacing timer 240 secs
  Interface flood pacing timer 33 msecs
  Retransmission pacing timer 66 msecs
  Number of external LSA 0. Checksum Sum 0x000000
  Number of areas in this router is 1. 1 normal 0 stub 0 nssa
```

```
Area BACKBONE(0)
  Number of interfaces in this area is 1
  MD5 Authentication, SPI 1000
  SPF algorithm executed 2 times
  Number of LSA 5. Checksum Sum 0x02A005
  Number of DCbitless LSA 0
  Number of indication LSA 0
  Number of DoNotAge LSA 0
  Flood list length 0
```

Use the *show ipv6 ospf database* command to view the OSPFv3 database:

company# **show ipv6 ospf database**

```
    OSPFv3 Router with ID (172.16.4.4) (Process ID 1)
              Router Link States (Area 0)
ADV Router   Age   Seq#          Fragment  ID  Link  countBits
172.16.4.4   239   0x80000003                   1      B
172.16.6.6   239   0x80000003      0       1           B

        Inter Area Prefix Link States (Area 0)
ADV Router      Age      Seq#           Prefix
172.16.4.4      249      0x80000001     FEC0:3344::/32
172.16.4.4      219      0x80000001     FEC0:3366::/32
172.16.6.6      247      0x80000001     FEC0:3366::/32
172.16.6.6      193      0x80000001     FEC0:3344::/32
172.16.6.6      82       0x80000001     FEC0::/32

        Inter Area Router Link States (Area 0)
ADV Router    Age    Seq#          Link ID      Dest RtrID
172.16.4.4    219    0x80000001    50529027     172.16.3.3
172.16.6.6    193    0x80000001    50529027     172.16.3.3

        Link (Type-8) Link States (Area 0)
ADV Router    Age    Seq#          Link ID    Interface
172.16.4.4    242    0x80000002    14         PO4/0
172.16.6.6    252    0x80000002    14         PO4/0

        Intra Area Prefix Link States (Area 0)
ADV Router  Age  Seq#         Link ID  Ref-lstype  Ref-LSID
172.16.4.4  242  0x80000002   0        0x2001      0
172.16.6.6  252  0x80000002   0        0x2001      0
```

VERIFYING IPV6

There are a number of commands that we can use to verify that IPv6 is configured correctly on our routers. We want to verify that IPv6 has been enabled on the router and that the interfaces have been configured correctly for IPv6. We also want to check the IPv6 addresses on the interfaces. We will be using several *show* commands to verify our configurations. (Note: Some of the examples of the commands only show part of the output. Some of the information that doesn't apply to the topic has been omitted.)

Show Commands

One of the best places to start verifying our configurations is with the *show running-config* command. Because the running-config is a script file that contains all of the commands the router is currently using, all of the IPv6 configuration commands we've entered will be displayed by looking at our running-config. We're looking for the *ipv6 unicast-routing* command to make sure we enabled IPv6 routing. This is also one place that we can check our IPv6 addresses on our interfaces.

```
company# show running-config
Building configuration...
Current configuration:
Current configuration : 3441 bytes
!
version 12.2
service timestamps debug datetime localtime
service timestamps log datetime localtime
no service password-encryption
!
hostname company
!
IPv6 unicast-routing  ! here's where we turned on ipv6 on the router
!
!
interface FastEthernet0/0
IPv6 address 2001:db8:1a2b:11::345c:de67/64  ! this is the ipv6
    address for this interface
```

To check the configurations on our interfaces, we can use the *show ipv6 interface* command that will display status and configuration information for all of our IPv6 interfaces. We can see whether IPv6 is enabled on the interfaces and verify the link-local and global addresses for the interfaces. To look at the configuration for a specific interface, we would include the specific interface we want to look at in the command. Refer to Exercise 10.4 for further information on how to verify your IPv6 address configurations.

EXERCISE 10.4   Verifying IPv6 Address Configurations

To verify your IPv6 address configurations you will use the *show ipv6 interface* command.

1. Execute the command.

2. Verify that the IPv6 addresses are correct.

```
company# show ipv6 interface Fastethernet0/0
Fastethernet0/0 is up, line protocol is up
IPv6 is enabled, link-local address is 2001:0DB8::/29 ! Here's the
    link-local ip address
Global unicast address(es):
2000:0DB8::2, subnet is 2001:0DB8::/64 !Here's the global unicast address
Joined group address(es):
FF02::1
FF02::2
FF02::1:FF11:6770
MTU is 1500 bytes
ICMP error messages limited to one every 500 milliseconds
ICMP redirects are enabled
ND DAD is enabled, number of DAD attempts: 1
ND reachable time is 30000 milliseconds
ND advertised reachable time is 0 milliseconds
ND advertised retransmit interval is 0 milliseconds
ND router advertisements are sent every 200 seconds
ND router advertisements live for 1800 seconds
ND advertised default router preference is Medium
Hosts use stateless autoconfig for addresses.
```

The *brief* format of the *show ipv6 interfaces* command can be used to verify global addresses and status of the interfaces:

```
company# show ipv6 interface brief
Ethernet0 is up, line protocol is up
Ethernet0 [up/up]
unassigned
Ethernet1 [up/up]
2001:0DB8:200:/29
Ethernet2 [up/up]
2001:0DB8:300:/29
Ethernet3 [up/up]
2001:0DB8:500:/29
```

You can display the information about all of your neighboring devices from the neighbor discovery (ND) cache, by executing the *show ipv6 neighbor* command. You can also specify an IPv6 address or an interface to get specific information. Here is the information for the *Ethernet 0* interface:

```
company# show ipv6 neighbors ethernet 0
IPv6 Address              Age   Link-layer Add  State  Interface
2000:0:0:cc2::55          0     0011.12ab.cd3   REACH  Ethernet0
FE80::20:31FF:FE6a:772    0     0003.a0d6.dcd   REACH  Ethernet0
2001:11::31               -     0022.db11.121   REACH  Ethernet2
```

Verifying IPv6 routing protocols running on the router can be accomplished with the *show ipv6 protocols* command:

```
company# show ipv6 protocols
IPv6 Routing Protocol is "connected"
IPv6 Routing Protocol is "static"
IPv6 Routing Protocol is "isis"
Interfaces:
Ethernet0/0
Ethernet0/1
Serial/0/
Loopback1 (Passive)
Loopback2 (Passive)
Redistribution:
```

Finally, to display the IPv6 routes that the router knows about, use the *show ipv6 route* command to see the IPv6 routing table:

```
company# show ipv6 route
IPv6 Routing Table - 9 entries
Codes: C - Connected, L - Local, S - Static, R - RIP, B - BGP
I1 - ISIS L1, I2 - ISIS L2, IA - IIS interarea
B       3AB0::/64 [20/0]
            via FE80::A1B2:33FF:FE02:48C0, Serial2/0
L       4AB0::2/128 [0/0]
            via ::, Ethernet1/0
C       4AB0::/64 [0/0]
            via ::, Ethernet1/0
LC      4AB1::1/128 [0/0]
            via ::, Loopback0
L       5AB0::2/128 [0/0]
            via ::, Serial6/0
C       5AB0::/64 [0/0]
            via ::, Serial6/0
S       5AB2::/48 [1/0]
            via 4000::1, Null
```

```
L        FE80::/10 [0/0]
            via ::, Null0
L        FF00::/8 [0/0]
            via ::, Null0
```

TROUBLESHOOTING IPV6

Now that we have our IPv6 configured on the router and we've verified our configuration using the show commands, we're going to take a look at how we can troubleshoot IPv6 problems. The show commands we just executed to verify the configuration are a good place to start when we're troubleshooting because we want to verify that we've configured everything correctly before we start looking any further. Once we've confirmed that everything is configured correctly, we'll check connectivity with the other devices on our network, just like we do in IPv4. We'll use the *ping* and *traceroute* commands for IPv6. First the *ping* command will test basic connectivity to the destination IPv6 address.

company# **ping ipv6 2001:db8::11/64**

Refer to Table 10.6 for an explanation of the characters that you might see when pinging in IPv6.

Table 10.6 Meanings of Characters in Ping Results

Character	Description
!	Each exclamation point indicates receipt of a reply.
.	Each period indicates that the network server timed out while waiting for a reply.
?	Unknown error.
@	Unreachable for unknown reason.
A	Administratively unreachable. Usually means that an ACL is blocking traffic.
B	Packet too big.
H	Host unreachable.
N	Network unreachable (beyond scope).
P	Port unreachable.
R	Parameter problem.
T	Time exceeded.
U	No route to host.

Now *traceroute* will show us the path the packets are taking to get to the destination device.

company# **traceroute ipv6 2001:db8::11/64**

There are several troubleshooting commands that give us the ability to clear counters and caches and look at particular types of traffic and information. These are the *clear* and *debug* commands.

Clear Commands

The *clear* commands allow you to monitor counts of particular types of traffic crossing your router and to look at cached information collected by your router. By using the *clear* commands, you can start the counters at zero, and you can empty existing caches so that the router recreates the information. When you're troubleshooting problems, looking at some of this information can be invaluable. Here are some of the most commonly used *clear* commands and descriptions of what each of the commands clears.

company# **clear ipv6 traffic**

Resets IPv6 traffic counters.

company# **clear ipv6 route ***

Deletes all routes from the IPv6 routing table (Note: Clearing all routes will cause the router to rebuild the entire routing table which uses a lot of CPU.)

company# **clear ipv6 route 2001:db8:123a:b4::/64**

Clears this specific route from the IPv6 routing table.

company# **clear ipv6 rip**

Deletes routes from the IPv6 RIP routing table and RIP routes in the IPv6 routing table.

company# **clear ipv6 neighbor**

Deletes all entries in the IPv6 neighbor discovery cache, except static entries.

company# **clear ipv6?**

Displays a list of all types of IPv6 information that can be cleared.

Debug Commands

Debug lets us watch particular types of traffic crossing the router. The traffic is crossing your router whether you have debug turned on or not, but debug lets you watch it and see what's included. Note: Be careful when using *debug* commands because they get a high priority in the CPU and can cause serious performance degradation or even cause the router to reboot. To disable any type of debug, repeat the command with the word *no* before it. For example, to turn on debugging for IPv6 icmp, the command is *debug ipv6 icmp*. To turn debugging for IPv6 icmp, the command is *no debug ipv6 icmp*. Here are some *debug* commands you will find useful for troubleshooting IPv6.

company# **debug ipv6 icmp**

Displays debugging information about IPv6 ICMP (except neighbor discovery).

company# **debug ipv6 nd**

Displays debug information about IPv6 ICMP neighbor discovery.

company# **debug ipv6 packet**

Displays debug information about IPv6 packets.

company# **debug ipv6 routing**

Displays debug information about IPv6 routing table updates and route cache updates.

company# **debug ipv6 rip**

Displays debug information about IPv6 RIP.

company# **debug ipv6?**

Displays a list of the types of IPv6 traffic you can debug.

company# **no debug all**

A quick alternative to turning off each individual type of traffic you are debugging, *no debug all* turns off all possible debugging.

SUMMARY OF EXAM OBJECTIVES

IPv6 was originally developed to solve the problem of the inevitable exhaustion of IPv4 addresses. In addition to the much larger address space provided by IPv6, it also includes a number of other benefits that are not provided by IPv4, such as autoconfiguration of addresses, built-in security and mobility technologies, and better aggregation capabilities. The transition from IPv4 to IPv6 has been, and will continue to be, a very slow process. IPv6 includes some transitioning mechanisms to make it possible for organizations to communicate between IPv4 and IPv6 devices and networks while the gradual migration to IPv6 occurs. Dual-stacks allow both the IPv4 and IPv6 protocol stacks to be configured on a device at the same time so the device can communicate with IPv4 devices and networks and IPv6 devices and networks. Tunneling strategies make it possible to send data between isolated IPv6 networks when an IPv4 network exists in the middle.

The much larger address space provided by IPv6 comes from 128 bits per address compared to IP4v's 32-bit addresses. IPv6 addresses are represented by eight 16-bit hexadecimal, colon-separated fields. The addresses can often be expressed in a shortened format by eliminating the leading zeros in each field and using "::" to replace the longest string of contiguous, all-zero fields. An IPv6 address has three sections, each with its own purpose. The first 48 bits represent the global prefix, which is similar to the network portion of an IPv4 address. The next 16 bits are the subnet portion of the address and the last 64 bits are the interface identifier.

There are three primary types of addresses that make up the IPv6 address space. Unicast addresses are assigned to network interfaces, and are used for one-to-one communications. Multicasts are used extensively in IPv6 and IPv6 uses a much larger address space for multicasts than IPv4. The final type of address used in IPv6 is the anycast. An anycast address is assigned to multiple devices. Packets sent to the anycast address will be delivered to the closest device with the address. Broadcasts have been eliminated in IPv6, which has also eliminated the problems caused by broadcast traffic.

Almost the entire IPv6 address space is used for unicast addresses. The only exception is the multicast address space of FF00::/8. There are different types of unicast addresses. Aggregatable global unicast addresses are public, routable addresses, unique on the worldwide Internet. They make up 1/8 of the entire IPv6 address space and are managed by the IANA, who assigns blocks of these addresses to RIRs and ISPs who break them down further to lease to their clients. The addresses assigned by the IANA so far are only in the 2000::/3 range.

Reserved unicast addresses are used by the IETF and make up multiple blocks of addresses. Link-local unicast addresses are private addresses only usable on the link, used for autoconfiguration, neighbor discovery, and router discovery. Their part of the address space is FE80::/10. The last type of unicast address is a unique local address, which is almost exactly like an IPv4 private address. Unique local addresses can be routed within a site and, in a limited fashion, between sites.

Configuring IPv6 addresses can be accomplished manually with static addresses or automatically, using either stateless autoconfiguration or stateful autoconfiguration with a DHCPv6 server. Stateless autoconfiguration is accomplished by network hosts requesting prefix information from a router and using EUI-64—inserting FFFE in the middle of a 48-bit MAC address—to create an interface identifier. This stateless method of autoconfiguration can be used on its own or in conjunction with a DHCPv6 server to pass additional options to the devices.

Autoconfiguration assigns a link-local address on the device, which is only usable on the link. To communicate outside of the link, a global unicast address has to be assigned to the device. IPv6 is enabled on a router using the *ipv6 unicast-routing* command. Enabling IPv6 on an interface is accomplished with the *ipv6 enable* command or by configuring an IPv6 address on the interface. An IP address is configured on an interface with this command: *ipv6 address <address>/<prefix-length>* or this command: *ipv6 address <prefix>/<prefix-length> eui-64*.

Name resolution is important to make devices reachable by name. Host tables can be configured on the routers with static entries and the *name-server* command identifies DNS servers that the router can query for name-to-IPv6-address mapping information. IPv6 also provides support for named ACLs to filter packets and control access to services and devices on the network.

IPv6 handles routing similarly to IPv4, with static routes and dynamic routing. Most of the IPv4 routing protocols have been updated to provide support for IPv6. To configure a routing protocol in IPv6, you create the routing process, enable the protocol on the interfaces, and configure the protocol for your specific network. IPv6 RIP is a Distance-Vector Routing Protocol, based on RIPv2 and still functions much like it does in IPv4. IPv6 OSPF is a Link-State Routing Protocol that has been updated for IPv6.

There are a number of *show* commands available for verifying configuration of IPv6. The *show running-config* command can be used to verify that IPv6 has been enabled, and you can verify IPv6 addresses using the *show ipv6 interface* command. There are also *show* commands that you can use to check your routing table (*show ipv6 route*) and to verify the configuration of your routing protocol.

When troubleshooting IPv6, you can use the *ping ipv6* and *traceroute ipv6* commands to check connectivity to other IPv6 devices. The *debug* commands allow you to watch specific types of traffic crossing your router and the *clear* commands let you reset counters and clear out caches of information.

EXAM OBJECTIVES FAST TRACK

Need for IPv6

- IPv6 is a 128-bit addressing system, providing an address space many times larger than the 32 bits in an IPv4 address, effectively solving the problem of the not-too-distant exhaustion of IPv4 addresses.

- IPv6 provides a number of advantages over IPv4, including easier aggregation of addresses, built in mobility and security technologies, and autoconfiguration of addresses.

- IPv6 provides for interoperability of IPv4 and IPv6 and mechanisms for transitioning gradually from IPv4 to IPv6 with dual stacking and tunneling options.

IPv6 Addresses

- IPv6 addresses are represented by eight 16-bit hexadecimal fields.

- IPv6 addresses can be expressed in a shortened format by eliminating leading zeros in each field and replacing the largest group of contiguous fields of all zeros with "::".

- IPv6 uses multicast addresses, anycast addresses, and three types of unicast addresses (global, link-local, and unique local), and has eliminated the need for broadcasts.

- Link-local addresses are private addresses used only on the link for autoconfiguration, neighbor discovery, and router discovery.

- Each type of address has its own range of numbers within the overall address space.

Configuring an IPv6 Address

- Before IPv6 addresses can be configured on the router, IPv6 routing must be turned on with the *ipv6 unicast-routing* command.

- IPv6 nodes autoconfigure their addresses statelessly by obtaining prefix information from the router and creating an *EUI-64* interface identifier by padding the MAC address with FFFE between the OUI and the serial number.

- Static IPv6 addresses are assigned to a router interface using the *ipv6 address* command.

- IPv6 can be enabled on an interface without a specific IPv6 address using the *ipv6 unnumbered* command, and identifying another interface to be used for the source address of packets originated from the unnumbered interface.

- Global Unicast addresses are public routable addresses assigned to individual interfaces.

- An interface can have multiple addresses of any type.

- Traffic sent to an anycast address is sent to the closest device of multiple devices with the same address.

Verifying IPv6

- Use the *show running-config* command to verify you enabled IPv6 routing by looking for the *ipv6 unicast*-routing command.

- Most *show* commands used to verify IPv6 configuration options include *ipv6* in the command; for example, *show ipv6 interface* to display IPv6 addresses and information about the interfaces.

- IPv6 uses the neighbor discovery process for finding neighboring IPv6 devices and, using the *show ipv6 neighbor* command which displays the neighbor discovery cache, can help you verify IPv6 connections.

- The *show ipv6 route* command displays the IPv6 routing table and can be modified to display particular types of routes.

Troubleshooting IPv6

- The *ping ipv6* and *traceroute ipv6* commands allow you to test connectivity between devices and follow the path the packets take to get to the destination just like *ping* and *traceroute* do in IPv4.

- There are a number of *clear* commands that allow you to reset counters and clear cached information to obtain fresh troubleshooting information.

- The *debug* commands allow you to watch particular types of traffic crossing your router to troubleshoot what information is being sent or received correctly.

EXAM OBJECTIVES FREQUENTLY ASKED QUESTIONS

Q: Is anybody really using IPv6 yet?

A: Yes, although it's still a very small percentage, there are people using IPv6. Some organizations, military and government agencies, and mobile phone service providers, are using IPv6 widely. As far as the Internet is concerned, toward the end of 2008, Google determined that there is a little more than 0.2% of Internet users on IPv6. And, remember, the 2008 Summer Olympic Games in Beijing was a very public implementation of IPv6.

Q: Is IPv6 harder to work with than IPv4?

A: Once you have an understanding of the IPv6 addresses, you'll find there are a number of things that make IPv6 easier to work with. Autoconfiguration of addresses can reduce administrative overhead and the much larger address space eliminates the need for configuring and managing extras and add-ons.

Q: Hasn't the use of private addresses eliminated the need for IPv6?

A: The use of private addresses has helped to lengthen the lifespan of IPv4, but the public addresses are still being used at such a rapid rate that running out is inevitable. Plus, the additional benefits of IPv6 also provide incentive for transitioning to IPv6.

Q: What if I install IPv6 on my network and everything doesn't work properly?

A: That's one of the benefits of using dual stacking and transitioning more slowly to IPv6. If your devices are dual stacked they can still communicate using IPv4 just like they do now. You don't have to eliminate the IPv4 stacks until you've had an opportunity to test IPv6 and make sure everything is working.

Q: What is a link-local address?

A: Link-local addresses are essentially private addresses of a sort that are used within a particular link, or physical network. These addresses cannot be routed so they are truly specific only to a particular link. Link-local addresses are the automatically generated addresses that are created when IPv6 is configured on a device. IPv6 link-local addresses are very much like the IPv4 APIPA used in most implementations of Microsoft Windows starting with Windows 98 (the 169.254.0.0/16 address space).

Q: How do I get global IPv6 addresses?

A: From your ISP. The IANA allocates blocks of addresses to RIRs and ISPs, who further break down the address blocks and lease the smaller blocks to their customers.

Q: What is an anycast?

A: Anycast addresses are a new type of address for IPv6. An anycast address is assigned to multiple devices with the same services. When traffic is sent to an anycast address the routers determine which device with that address is the closest and route the packets to that device. Anycast addresses can be used to create redundancy, provide load balancing, and improve content delivery services.

Q: What is an EUI-64?

A: The EUI-64 is a standard that uses an Ethernet device's MAC address and modifies it to be used as the 64-bit interface identifier portion of an IPv6 address. The hexadecimal digits FFFE are added into the middle of the 48-bit MAC address, between the OUI and the serial number.

Q: How do I know an IPv6 address is a link-local address?

A: The address space for link-local addresses is with FE80::/10.

Q: Does DNS work the same in IPv6 as it does in IPv4?

A: Essentially, DNS works the same. DNS maps names to IPv6 addresses and vice-versa, just like it does in IPv6. IPv4 and IPv6 use different record types (A for IPv4 and AAAA for IPv6) so a DNS server that is providing mappings must support the record type of each protocol it is mapping for.

Q: What is an administrative distance?

A: An administrative distance is a reliability factor that is assigned to a type of route. Administrative distances are from 0 through 255. The lower the administrative distance for a route, the more reliable that type of route is considered to be and the more priority it is given. With static routes administrative distances can also be used to force priority of particular routes.

Q: Can I still use ping and traceroute to test connectivity and troubleshoot in IPv6?

A: Yes. The only difference is that you have to add IPv6 to the command like you do with a number of other IPv6 commands. So the commands would be *ping ipv6 <device-name-or-address>* and *traceroute ipv6 <device-name-or-address>*.

SELF TEST

1. You're ready to start the process of transitioning your network to IPv6. You have multiple locations with several hundred computers, printers, and other devices that currently are all configured

for IPv4. You aren't sure if all of the applications or devices on your network are IPv6 compatible. What will be the easiest and least disruptive method for you to use to start the transitioning process?

A. 6to4 tunneling

B. Dual stacking

C. Dynamic overlay tunneling

D. IPv4/IPv6 translation

2. Your company has transitioned all of its networks to IPv6 addressing. The home office is connected to two satellite offices across the Internet, as shown in Figure 10.11. What tunneling type is your company using?

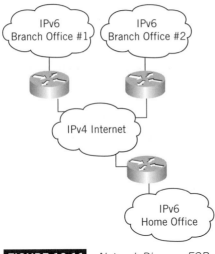

FIGURE 10.11   *Network Diagram FOR SELF-TEST QUESTION #2*

A. IPv6 VPN

B. Dual stacking

C. 6to4 tunneling

D. 4to6 tunneling

3. You have started the process of setting up IPv6 on your networks. You are ready to start implementing IPv6 on your routers. What is the command that you would execute on each router to turn on IPv6?

A. *ipv6 enable*

B. *enable ipv6*

C. *mode ipv6*

D. *ipv6 unicast-routing*

4. You need to set an IPv6 address on an interface on your router. It needs to be an address that can be routed across the Internet. What type of address do you need to assign to the interface?

   A. Link-local address

   B. Unique local address

   C. Multicast address

   D. Global unicast address

   E. Reserved address

5. You need to assign the address 2001:0db8:0000:0000:0000:eb00:0000:0002 to an interface on your router. You don't want to type the entire address out. What is the correct shortened expression for the address?

   A. 2001:db8::eb:0:2   **C.** 2001:db8::eb00:0:2

   B. 2001:db8:::eb00::2   **D.** 2001:db8:0::eb00:2

6. You have a very busy ftp server on your network that serves users in three different buildings. It's no longer able to keep up with the demands on it so you are adding two additional ftp servers to take some of the load off of the existing ftp server. All of the ftp servers will serve up the same files but you want your users to be able to access the ftp server that's closest to them so there is some load balancing taking place. What type of an address do you need to assign to your ftp servers to accomplish this?

   A. Anycast   **C.** Link-local

   B. Multicast   **D.** Loopback

7. When you execute the command *debug ipv6 routing* you see information that includes the IPv6 address FE80::0011:22FF:FE37:1234 in the information on your screen. What type of IPv6 address are you looking at?

   A. Global unicast   **C.** Link-local

   B. Loopback   **D.** Multicast

8. You have been given the address 2001:db8::eb00:0:2 to apply to your router. What is the command to assign this address to an interface on your router?

   A. ip address 2001:db8::eb00:0:2 /64

   B. ipv6 address 2001:db8::eb00:0:2 /64

   C. configure interface 2001:db8::eb00:0:2 /64

   D. configure address 2001:db8::eb00:0:2

9. You are verifying the autoconfigured IPv6 address on a host computer on the network. You obtain the MAC address for the device which is 0010:AB23:4567. What is the correct global-unicast interface identifier that was automatically created using the EUI-64 modification?

   A. 0010:ABFF:FE23:4567

   B. 0210:ABFF:FE23:4567

   C. 0010:AB23:4567

   D. 210.23.256.0

   E. 0000:0010:AB23:4567

10. One of the computers on your network is unable to access the rest of the network. One of the steps in your troubleshooting process is to ping the local host or loopback address. What is the command you use?

    A. ping ipv6 127.0.0.1   **C.** ping ipv6 ::1

    B. ping 0.0.0.0   **D.** ping ipv6 0::0

11. You are going to set up a test network to get an idea how IPv6 works before deploying it on your network. You want to enable IPv6 on your serial interfaces and they need private addresses like the other devices on your test network. Which command would you use to enable IPv6 and have a private address automatically created on the serial interfaces?

    A. *ipv6 enable*   **C.** *ipv6 local address*

    B. *ipv6 enable address*   **D.** *enable unicast-routing*

12. The company networks have been set up for IPv6. You've installed IPv6 addresses on all of the devices and now you need to be able to route packets between your different networks so everyone can access all of the resources on all of the network devices. What's the next thing you need to do to make this happen?

    A. Give everyone a list of all of the IPv6 addresses.

    B. Set up host tables to map names to the IPv6 addresses.

    C. Create access control lists to give people access.

    D. Enable and configure a Dynamic Routing Protocol.

13. You've decided to use RIP to dynamically build your routing tables on your routers. What is the command to enable RIP on the routers?

    A. company(config)# ipv6 router rip process1

    B. company(config-router)# enable RIP

    C. company# enable rip

    D. company(config)# router rip

14. You want to use another, quicker method of bringing up RIP on the router than the *ipv6 router rip <tag>* command executed in global configuration mode. The command is:

    A. company(config)# *router rip process1*

    B. company(config-router)# *enable*

    C. company(config-if)# *ipv6 rip process1 enable*

    D. company(config)# *router ipv6 rip*

15. RIP doesn't seem to be working correctly on your network so you are looking at RIP debug information to try to identify the problem. You keep seeing the address FF02::/9 in the debug information. What does that address mean?

    A. It's RIPs loopback address.

    B. It's all of the local-link addresses on your network.

    C. It's a multicast address for all RIP routers.

    D. It's a broadcast address that RIP uses to send updates.

16. You have one IPv6 address that you're using on your router. It's assigned to your *Ethernet 0* interface. Now you need to configure IPv6 on your serial interface, but you don't want to use another address. Instead, you'd like the packets sent from the serial interface to use the *Ethernet 0* interface address as their source address. What's the command to configure this on the router?

    A. company(config-if)# *ipv6 enable*

    B. company(config-if)# *ipv6 unicast-routing*

    C. company(config-if)# *ipv6 address copy Ethernet 0*

    D. company(config-if)# *ipv6 unnumbered Ethernet 0*

17. The global unicast prefix your company uses is 2001:db8::/64. You need to put an IPv6 address on your *Ethernet 0* interface on your router. You want the router to create an interface identifier from the interface's MAC address. What is the command to configure this on your router?

    A. ip address 2001:db8:: /64

    B. ipv6 address 2001:db8::/64 MAC

    C. ipv6 address 2001:db8::/64 EUI-64

    D. ipv6 address 2001:db8::/64

    E. ip address 2001:db8::/64 MAC

18. All of the devices on your network have been assigned IPv6 addresses and you are testing connectivity across your network. When you type the command *ping ipv6 pc24* from the router you get a reply back from the computer called pc2 instead of the computer called pc24. What is the most likely cause of the problem?

    A. An entry in your host table is incorrect.

    B. RIP obtained incorrect information about where to send the packets.

    C. pc24 is forwarding packets to pc2.

    D. pc24 has an ACL on it.

19. Now that you have IPv6 set up on your network, you need to set up some ACLs to control access to your devices and particular services on the network. What command could you use to begin configuring an ACL for IPv6?

    A. *ipv6 access-list 4000*

    B. *ipv6 acl*

    C. *ipv6 access-list inbound-list*

    D. *permit any any*

20. There are three implicit statements at the end of IPv6 ACLs. The last line is an implicit *deny any any* to deny any IPv6 that hasn't been explicitly permitted previously in the list. What do the other two statements permit?

    A. Inbound and outbound e-mail

    B. IPv6 pings and telnet

    C. Multicasts and anycasts

    D. Two icmp message types for neighbor discovery

21. You want to limit access to your router via telnet. You've created an ACL called *stay-out*, permitting only administrators. How do you apply the ACL to control access to the router itself?

    A. The *ipv6 traffic-filter stay-out in* command at the (config-line) prompt.

    B. The *ipv6 access-class stay-out in* command at the (config-ipv6-acl) prompt.

    C. The *ipv6 access-class stay-out in* command at the (config-line) prompt.

    D. The *ipv6 access-group stay-out in* command at the (config-line) prompt.

22. You are configuring some new routing options on your routers to route IPv6. You want to make sure all of your networks appear in the routing table and you want to see what types of routes are being used to access the networks. What is the command you would use to get this information?

    A. *show ip route*

    B. *show ipv6 route*

    C. *show ipv6 static*

    D. *ipv6 route*

23. You have been comparing Dynamic Routing Protocols and you are trying to decide if a Distance-Vector or Link-State Routing Protocol is best. You know that Distance-Vector Protocols use distance calculations to obtain routing information. How does a link-state protocol such as OSPF obtain routing information?

    A. The same way a Distance-Vector Protocol does only faster

    B. With link-state advertisements

    C. By using fast convergence

    D. By querying a DHCP server

24. You're verifying the IPv6 configuration on your router. The first thing you want to check is to make sure IPv6 has been enabled on the router. How would you accomplish this?

    A. The *show running-config* command

    B. The *show ipv6 ?* command

    C. The *show ip protocols* command

    D. The *show ipv6 enable* command

25. You aren't able to communicate between your router and the other IPv6 devices on your network. You've checked the configurations on the host devices, so now you need to check your IPv6 address configurations on your router. When verifying your IPv6 address configurations, what command will you use?

    A. *show ipv6 address*

    B. *show ip address*

    C. *show ipv6 interface*

    D. *show ipv6 route*

26. While troubleshooting your network and verifying connectivity, you execute the *ipv6 ping* command. When you try to ping some devices you get the exclamation marks (!!!!) that indicate you're getting replies to your pings. But, with other devices, you're getting U's (UUUU). What do the U's mean when you are trying to do an ipv6 ping?

   A. The server timed out waiting for a reply

   B. Unknown error

   C. Network unreachable

   D. No route to host

27. While you're troubleshooting the IPv6 traffic crossing your network you want to look at traffic information for IPv6. You know there are commands that can show you statistics and other information as well as commands you can use to clear existing information and start fresh. How does the *clear ipv6 traffic* command help you?

   A. Resets the IPv6 counters

   B. Disables IPv6

   C. Drops all IPv6 packets

   D. Resets the IPv6 routing table

28. You're interested in the process the routers go through to gather information about other routers and how they are able to communicate with each other. You know neighbor discovery is an important part of how routers discover each other and you want to watch what types of information is exchanged. How can you do this?

   A. show discovery info

   B. show IPv6 nd

   C. debug IPv6 nd

   D. debug IPv6 neighbors

29. How would you get rid of the IPv6 routing table so the router can recreate its routing table and start fresh? You want to do this without restarting the router.

   A. clear IPv6 route*

   B. clear IPv6 router

   C. erase IPv6 route

   D. no IPv6 route

30. How would you quickly make sure that all debugging has been turned off?

   A. no debug

   B. no debug all

   C. debug off

   D. no debug IPv6

SELF TEST QUICK ANSWER KEY

1. B		**11.** A		**21.** C	
2. C		**12.** D		**22.** B	
3. D		**13.** A		**23.** B	
4. D		**14.** C		**24.** A	
5. C		**15.** C		**25.** C	
6. A		**16.** D		**26.** D	
7. C		**17.** C		**27.** A	
8. B		**18.** A		**28.** C	
9. B		**19.** C		**29.** A	
10. C		**20.** D		**30.** B	

Configuring Cisco Switches

INTRODUCTION

Years ago, companies started to replace their hubs with switches because of the superior performance that switches offer. Cisco switches in particular boast many advanced features, including virtual LANs (VLANs), which are designed to help companies improve their network performance, and port security, which is intended to help administrators better secure their networks.

To obtain CCNA certification you need to be able to configure, manage, and maintain switches. You are also expected to be able to use switches to help make a company network more efficient and secure. Although the process of configuring a Cisco switch is similar to that of configuring a router, many of the commands involved are different and are unique to switches.

This chapter will cover the process of configuring Cisco Catalyst switches. First I will provide an overview of switching technology, and then you'll get your hands dirty configuring, maintaining, and troubleshooting a switch. In addition, the simulation software that accompanies this book addresses Cisco Internetwork Operating System (IOS) switch commands.

| Application |
| Presentation |
| Session |
| Transport |
| Network |
| Datalink |
| Physical |

FIGURE 11.1

The Physical Layer, Where You Can Find Repeaters and Hubs

SWITCHING CONCEPTS

In the past, company networks typically contained numerous Ethernet devices. Among these devices were *repeaters*, which worked at Layer 1 (the physical layer) of the network and were designed to boost the electrical signal on the wire to expand the network. Along with repeaters, Layer 1 also usually contained *hubs*, which basically were multiport repeaters and could be used to create star networks (see Figure 11.1).

Although hubs were increasingly being used to handle network traffic, they suffered from numerous limitations. For instance, a hub is a simple device; it connects all computers on a network to each other. Because it works at Layer 1 and connects hosts on the network to one single Ethernet segment, if a host on a hub wants to communicate with the network the host sends traffic to the hub and the hub forwards the traffic to all of the ports on the hub. To get a better idea of how this works, take a look at Figure 11.2. When host A sends traffic to host C, the hub will forward the traffic to every host that is connected to the hub.

Because a hub is not intelligent, it cannot make decisions regarding where to forward network traffic based solely on Media Access Control (MAC) addresses. Furthermore, when you use hubs on your network, all of the computers on the network will be placed into one large collision domain. The more hosts on your network, the more collisions you will have. Therefore, if a host wants to send traffic the host needs to ensure that no other hosts are currently sending traffic on the network. This is because Ethernet uses Carrier Sense Multiple Access with Collision Detection (CSMA/CD) to communicate across the network. (We will discuss collision domains in more detail later in this chapter.)

If you have a large network with a lot of hosts connected to it, chances are good that the network will experience a lot of collisions and a lot of retransmissions. This results in slow performance. A better solution is to replace your hub with switches to reduce the number of collision domains. A switch

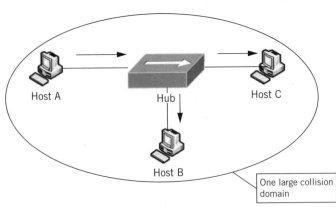

FIGURE 11.2 *Schematic Design of a Hub*

operates at Layer 2 (the datalink layer) and divides the network into smaller networks, or segments (see Figure 11.3). A switch also creates a virtual circuit between two hosts, allowing the devices to operate at the maximum speed allowed by using all of the available bandwidth. Furthermore, unlike a hub, a switch will use MAC addresses to make decisions regarding where to forward network traffic.

| Application |
| Presentation |
| Session |
| Transport |
| Network |
| Datalink |
| Physical |

FIGURE 11.3

The Datalink Layer, Where You Can Find Switches

Switching Modes

When a switch receives a frame, the switch will decide what to do with it. To increase the performance of the network, it is important to keep latency as low as possible. *Latency* is the time between sending and receiving a frame. For the CCNA exam, it is important that you know the following three switching modes:

- **Cut-through** Cut-through switching does not copy the entire frame into the switch's buffer, but rather will forward the frame when the switch receives the first six bytes of the frame. Because the MAC address is part of the first six bytes, the switch can forward the frame based on information in the MAC address table. Cut-through switching will not calculate cyclic redundancy check (CRC) values, so if a switch receives a frame that is corrupted, it will still forward the frame.

- **Fragment-free** Fragment-free switching is a modification of cut-through switching. When a switch receives a frame, the switch will wait until the first 64 bytes are received and then will forward the frame to the destination port based on the information in the MAC address table.

- **Store-n-forward** Store-n-forward switching is basically the same as frame forwarding. When a switch receives a frame, the switch will copy the entire frame into its memory buffers and will calculate the CRC. If the CRC calculation is correct, the switch will forward the frame to the destination port based on the information found in the MAC address table. If the frame is corrupt, the frame will be dropped. An Ethernet frame can be of any size, so the latency in store-n-forward switching depends on the size of the frame. Also, although store-n-forward switching is the slowest switching method, it is also usually the most accurate.

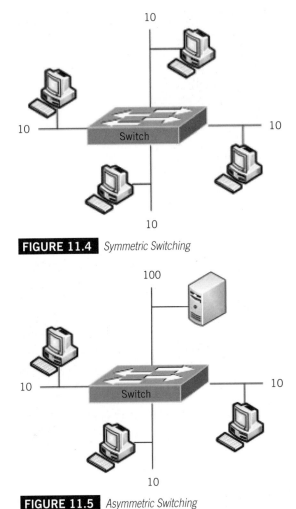

FIGURE 11.4 *Symmetric Switching*

FIGURE 11.5 *Asymmetric Switching*

Symmetric Versus Asymmetric Switching

In addition to switching modes, it is also important for test takers to understand the differences between symmetric and asymmetric switching. *Symmetric switching* provides connections with the same bandwidth and is optimized for a peer-to-peer or workgroup environment (see Figure 11.4).

Asymmetric switching, also called 10/100 switching, is optimized for client/server communications so that multiple clients can simultaneously connect to the server.

As you can see in Figure 11.4, with symmetric switching all hosts on the network are connected to a switch and have the same amount of bandwidth available. Symmetric switching requires more bandwidth on the server switchport, since more hosts can communicate with the server. As you can see in Figure 11.5, with asymmetric switching all hosts on the network are connected to the switch using a 10 Mbit switchport, except for the server, which is connected to the switch using a 100 Mbit switchport.

Content-Addressable Memory

All Cisco Catalyst switches use content-addressable memory (CAM) to store the MAC addresses used for switching. When a switch receives a frame, the switch reads the frame and places the source MAC address into the CAM table together with a timestamp. The switch will later use the MAC address table to forward the frame to the correct switchport. If a host is moved from one switchport to another, the switch will update only the timestamp, since the MAC address is already listed in the MAC address table.

The following gives you an example of the command used to view the MAC address.

For instance, you can use the *show mac-address-table ?* command to display all of the available parameters (see Figure 11.6).

You can use the *show mac-address-table* command (without the question mark) to display the entries in the MAC address table, as shown in Figure 11.7.

Use the *show mac-address-table count* command to display the number of addresses in the MAC address table, as shown in Figure 11.8.

```
Switch#show mac-address-table ?
  address        address keyword
  aging-time     aging-time keyword
  count          count keyword
  dynamic        dynamic entry type
  interface      interface keyword
  multicast      multicast info for selected wildcard
  notification   MAC notification parameters and history table
  static         static entry type
  vlan           VLAN keyword
  |              Output modifiers
  <cr>

Switch#show mac-address-table
```

FIGURE 11.6

Commands Supported with the show mac-address-table ? *Command*

Issuing the command *clear mac-address-table* will clear the MAC addresses from the cache, as shown in Figure 11.9.

As mentioned earlier, a switch will make its decisions regarding where to forward network traffic based on the MAC addresses stored in the MAC address table. A switch can have dynamic or static MAC addresses. When a switch receives information from a new host and the MAC address is not in the MAC address table, the switch will *dynamically* add the MAC address into the MAC address table. This entry will stay in the MAC address table until the switch does not hear from the host for a certain period of time (300 seconds by default), or until the MAC address table is manually cleared. A *static* MAC address is a MAC address that is manually added to the switch's MAC address table. Static MAC addresses enhance security, since you can decide which hosts are allowed to access your network.

```
Switch#show mac-address-table
          Mac Address Table
-------------------------------------------

Vlan    Mac Address       Type        Ports
----    -----------       --------    -----
 All    0012.d913.3700    STATIC      CPU
 All    0100.0ccc.cccc    STATIC      CPU
 All    0100.0ccc.cccd    STATIC      CPU
 All    0100.0cdd.dddd    STATIC      CPU
   1    0004.23d4.7742    STATIC      Fa0/1
Total Mac Addresses for this criterion: 5
Switch#
```

FIGURE 11.7   *Viewing the Contents of a MAC Address Table*

```
Switch#show mac-address-table count

Mac Entries for Vlan 1:
-------------------------
Dynamic Address Count  : 0
Static  Address Count  : 1
Total Mac Addresses    : 1

Total Mac Address Space Available: 8189

Switch#
```

FIGURE 11.8   *Determining the Number of MAC Addresses in the MAC Address Table*

```
Switch#clear mac-address-table ?
  dynamic         dynamic entry type
  notification    Clear MAC notification Global Counters

Switch#clear mac-address-table dynamic
Switch#
```

FIGURE 11.9 *Clearing the MAC Address Table*

Exam Warning

The default timeout value for a dynamically learned MAC address is 300 seconds.

MAC Flooding

MAC flooding, which often can be compared to Address Resolution Protocol (ARP) cache poisoning, occurs when a switch is overloaded with MAC addresses. In such a scenario, the switch often drops into "hub" mode. When the switch receives a frame while in hub mode, the destination MAC address cannot be found in the MAC address table and the switch can no longer learn about the MAC addresses in the table. As a result, the switch will broadcast the frame to every switchport, and the frame will be received by every host that is connected to that switch.

Exam Warning

When a switch drops into hub mode, a malicious user can sniff network traffic to view all of the traffic forwarded by the switch.

Test Day Tip

To prevent MAC flooding attacks on your network, you have to implement port-based security.

Layer 2 Switches

As mentioned earlier, a Layer 2 switch operates at the datalink layer, which means the switch forwards traffic based on MAC addresses. When a Layer 2 switch forwards traffic, the switch will not modify the original frame. The only exception is when you implement Quality of Service (QoS) on your switch. In that case, the switch will modify the Differentiated Services Code Point (DSCP) bits in the Internet Protocol (IP) header.

Test Day Tip

If your network contains hubs, you can easily replace them with switches without changing cables and network interface cards.

As shown in Figure 11.10, if host A wants to communicate with host B, the switch creates a *virtual connection* to allow traffic between the two ports where hosts A and B are connected. If hosts C and D want to communicate at the same time, the switch will also create a virtual connection between the switchports where hosts C and D are connected.

If hosts A and B are on the same subnet and hosts C and D are on another subnet, host A cannot set up a connection with either host C or host D. This is because a Layer 2 switch cannot forward frames if the frame is destined for another network.

A Layer 2 switch creates a dedicated connection between the sender and receiver and can operate at full-duplex speed with simultaneous connections. This means that when hosts A and B in Figure 11.10 have a full-duplex connection, hosts C and D can communicate at the same time with each other over a full-duplex connection.

Typically, a Layer 2 device is not adequate for modifying the IP header, so communication between two different subnets cannot occur. If communication needs to occur between subnets or virtual networks, you need a router. A router operates at Layer 3 and can change IP headers.

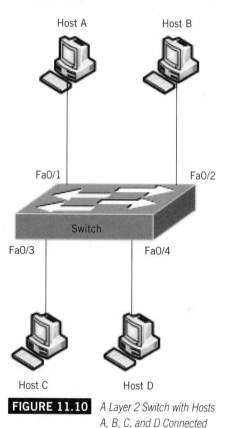

FIGURE 11.10   *A Layer 2 Switch with Hosts A, B, C, and D Connected*

Exam Warning
A Layer 2 switch operates only at the datalink layer.

Layer 3 Switches

Layer 3 switches are relatively new devices. A Layer 3 switch also has routing capabilities and can use routing protocols. Based on the information in the routing table, a Layer 3 switch can send a packet from one network to another

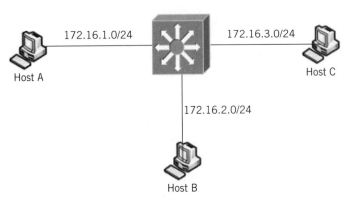

network. As depicted in Figure 11.11, you can connect hosts using a different IP address to a Layer 3 switch.

Before a host on one network can forward traffic on another network, the switch needs to check the IP header of the packet. To do this, the switch will have to look in the routing table, decrement the Time to Live (TTL) value, and forward the packet to the correct switchport.

FIGURE 11.11   *A Layer 3 Switch with Hosts A, B, and C Connected*

> **Test Day Tip**
> A Layer 3 switch operates at both the datalink and network layers.

Collision Domains

Before we discuss collision domains in detail, let's define *collision*. When two hosts send traffic at the same time, a collision occurs. When a collision occurs on a network, both hosts start a timer. This timer generates a random number, which signifies the amount of time the host must wait before it can transmit traffic again on the network.

When a lot of collisions occur on a network, a lot of traffic will be destroyed. Then, when the host needs to transmit its traffic again, network performance will suffer. Such a situation typically occurs in Ethernet environment where hubs are installed, because such environments have one large collision domain.

Collisions are a normal characteristic of networks. You cannot stop all collisions from occurring, as that would be unrealistic. A better goal is to try to minimize that number of collisions that take place. To do so, you need to divide your Ethernet segment into smaller collision domains, which will result in fewer hosts per collision domain. To accomplish this, you have to use a switch. Every switchport has its own collision domain. This means that if you connect, for example, four hosts to four different switchports, you will have four collision domains (see Figure 11.12).

As shown in Figure 11.12, every host is connected to a separate switchport and has its own collision domain.

There is a method for reducing the size of collision domains. That method is called microsegmentation, and we'll discuss it next.

Microsegmentation

Microsegmentation is a method for dividing your network using multiple switches. Therefore, if two hosts communicate with each other, only two nodes are coexisting with each collision domain: One node is the host and the other one is the switch. An advantage of using microsegmentation is that every node will have the full amount of bandwidth available so that communications can occur with the maximum available port speed. Also, with microsegmentation every host on the network is dedicated to an individual switchport and lives in its own collision domain.

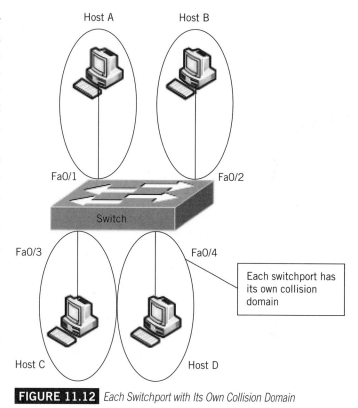

Broadcast Domains

When all hosts on the same network can reach each other via broadcasts, this is called a *broadcast domain*. Broadcasts are not new when it comes to networks. If, for example, a certain host needs to know the MAC address of another host, the sending host sends out an ARP broadcast. This broadcast is processed by all hosts on the same broadcast domain.

FIGURE 11.12 *Each Switchport with Its Own Collision Domain*

When you connect all hosts on the same switch, those hosts are members of the same broadcast domain. If you connect multiple switches together, those hosts again belong to the same broadcast domain. Too many broadcasts on a network will result in slow performance, since every broadcast on your network must be processed by every host on your network.

If you want to limit your broadcast domain, you can divide it by using routers. A router will not typically forward a broadcast from one broadcast domain to another.

> **Test Day Tip**
> The more collision domains you have on your network, the more you'll reduce the number of collisions on your network.
>   The more broadcast domains you have on your network, the slower your network performance will be.

CONFIGURING SWITCHES

Now that you understand the concepts related to switches, it's time to learn how to configure switches. In the following sections, you will learn how to interpret the light-emitting diodes (LEDs) on a switch, as well as how to configure a switch.

Understanding the LED Indicators

On the front of every switch are several LEDs which can help you to monitor the activity and performance of the switch. Figure 11.13 shows the front view of the Cisco Catalyst 2950 switch, and identifies all of the buttons you can use to troubleshoot the switch.

The following LEDs are available:

- **System LED** This LED turns green when the switch is powered on and is functioning correctly.

- **Redundant Power Supply (RPS) LED** This LED lets you know whether the RPS is being used.

- **Port Mode LEDs** These LEDs indicate the current state of the MODE button (outlined in Table 11.1).

- **Port Status LEDs** Depending on the status of the Port Mode LEDs, these LEDs can have different meanings, as discussed next.

When you connect a power cable to your switch, the switch initiates a series of tests. These tests are called Power-On Self-Tests (POSTs) and they indicate the preboot sequence of a switch. During a POST all switchports (the Port Status LEDs in Figure 11.13) are green. During the initialization phase the Port Status LEDs turn amber for about 30 seconds while the switch tries to discover the network topology. After the POST completes, each Port Status LED is turned OFF. If the test fails for some reason, the LED of the

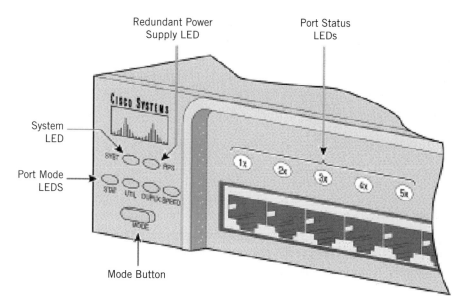

Redundant Power
Supply LED

Port Status
LEDs

System
LED

Port Mode
LEDS

Mode Button

FIGURE 11.13

*Overview of the LEDs
Available on the Cisco
Catalyst 2950 Switch*

Table 11.1 Overview of Port Mode LEDs

Port Mode LEDs	Color	Description
STAT	OFF	No link
	Solid green	Link is operational.
	Flashing green	Port is sending or receiving data.
	Alternating green/amber	Link failure
	Solid amber	Port is not forwarding frames or is shut down.
UTL	OFF	If each LED is OFF the port is working at 50 percent of the total bandwidth.
		If the rightmost LED is OFF, the switch is using less than 50 percent of the total bandwidth.
		If the two rightmost LEDs are OFF, the switch is using less than 25 percent of the total bandwidth.
	Green	The switch is using 50 percent or more of the total bandwidth.
FDUP	OFF	The switchport function is on half-duplex.
	Green	The switchport function is on full-duplex.
100	OFF	The switchport function is at 10 Mbps.
	Green	The switchport function is at 100 Mbps.

switchport will turn amber. If the System LED is green, it means the POST was successful. If the System LED is amber, it means the POST has failed for some reason. If the Port Status LEDs turn green, the switch establishes a link between a host and the switchport. This just means that there is a physical connection (cable) between the switchport and a host. If no host is connected to a switchport, the Port Status LEDs are turned off.

Connecting to the Switch

You can configure a switch in several ways. The following subsections provide an overview of the connection types which are used most frequently.

HyperTerminal

One way in which you can configure a switch is through Windows HyperTerminal. Beforehand, however, you must connect the switch to your computer by plugging a rollover cable into your computer's Serial DB-9 port.

If you want to connect to your switch using a console cable, you can connect the cable's serial adapter to your computer's serial port (the COM port) and plug the RJ-45 connector into the console port of your switch (see Figure 11.14).

Once you've connected your switch to your computer, follow these steps to configure your switch through HyperTerminal:

1. Select **Program | Accessories | Communications | HyperTerminal**. HyperTerminal will launch and a Connection Description dialog box will be displayed.

2. Enter a name for the connection (as shown in Figure 11.15) and click **OK**. The **Connect To** dialog box will be displayed.

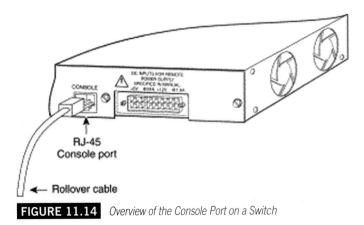

FIGURE 11.14 *Overview of the Console Port on a Switch*

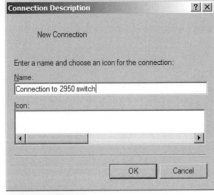

FIGURE 11.15 *Entering a Connection Name in the Name Text Box*

3. In the **Connect To** dialog box, select **COM1** in the **Connect using** drop down and click **OK**, as shown in Figure 11.16.

4. The **COM1 Properties** dialog box will display (see Figure 11.17). In the **COM1 Properties** dialog box, select **9600** in the **Bits per second** drop down, **8** in the **Data bits** drop down, **None** in the **Parity** drop down, **1** in the **Stop bits** drop down, and **Xon / Xoff** in the **Flow control** drop down, and then click **OK**.

5. Press the **Enter** key to modify the configuration of your switch. At this point, your switch should be configured appropriately.

FIGURE 11.16 *Selecting the COM Port*

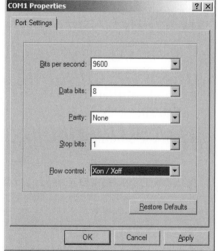

FIGURE 11.17 *Configuring Port Settings for COM1*

Minicom

As an alternative to HyperTerminal, you can configure your switch through Minicom, a Linux-based serial communications program. To install Minicom under Red Hat Linux, use the command *yum install minicom*. Then, follow these steps:

1. Connect your console cable to your switch and to your Linux machine.

2. Type **minicom –s** to launch Minicom in Setup mode.

3. From the menu that appears, select **Serial port setup**.

4. Change the hardware flow control from yes to no by pressing the **F** key.

5. Select the **E** key to select **9600 baud**.

6. Press **Enter** twice in succession.

7. Save the setup as **df1**.

8. Select **Exit** to leave the setup.

Cisco Network Assistant

You also can configure and manage your Cisco switch by using Cisco Network Assistant. (With this Windows-based application, you can manage devices such as routers and access points as well.) Cisco Network Assistant is free of charge and you can download it from the Cisco Web site, at www. isco.com/ en/US/products/ps5931/. Once you've downloaded Cisco Network Assistant, follow these steps:

1. Double-click **cna-windows-k9-installer-5.3.exe** to start the installation process.

2. On the **Initial** page, specify a **Directory Name** (see Figure 11.18) and click **Next**.

3. On the **Summary** page (see Figure 11.19), click **Finish** to complete the installation.

4. Select **Cisco Network Assistant** from the **Programs** menu.

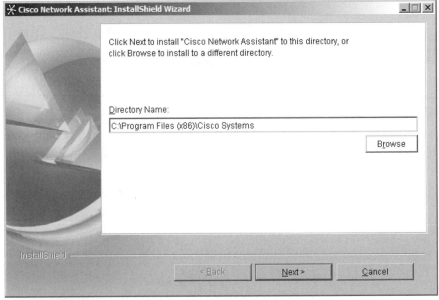

FIGURE 11.18   *Specifying the Installation Location for Cisco Network Assistant*

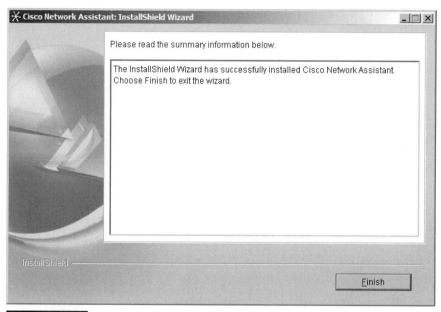

FIGURE 11.19 *Summary Information After Installation*

5. On the **Connect** dialog box, in the **Connect To** text box, type the IP address of the switch you want to manage and click **Connect** (see Figure 11.20).

6. In the **Authentication** dialog box (see Figure 11.21), specify your credentials and click **OK**.

   The application will start. On the right-hand side of your screen you will see a toolbar with buttons labeled Configure, Monitor, Troubleshoot, and Maintenance (see Figure 11.22).

7. To configure your switch, click the **Configure** button.

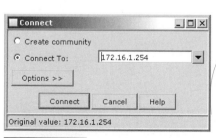

FIGURE 11.20 *Specifying the IP Address of the Switch to Which to Connect*

FIGURE 11.21 *Specifying Credentials to Authenticate*

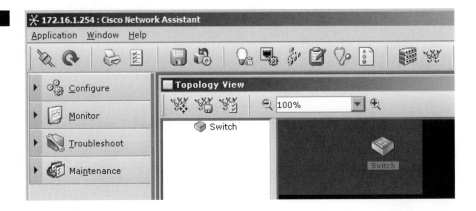

8. In the **Port Settings** dialog box, click the **Configuration Settings** tab to configure each switchport (see Figure 11.23).

9. To change the settings for a switchport, select the port and then click the **Modify** button.

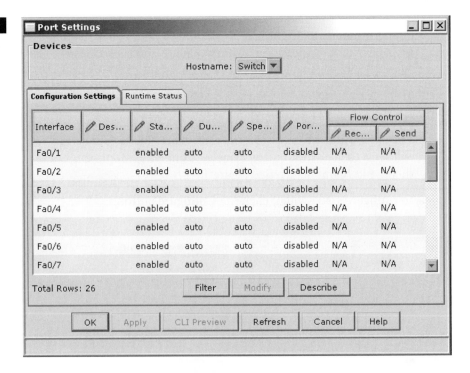

10. In the **Modify Port Settings** dialog box that appears, modify the port settings using the pull-down menus and click **OK** to implement your changes (see Figure 11.24).

Another nice feature of the Cisco Network Assistant program is the Front Panel, which you can access by selecting **Monitor | Views | Front Panel** from the toolbar. This tool gives you a graphical view of the front side of the switch (see Figure 11.25). This can be handy if you suspect a problem with a particular switchport.

In Figure 11.25, the first LED is colored green (although you cannot see this, as this is a black-and-white book). The green color signifies that a host is connected to that switchport.

FIGURE 11.24   *Modifying a Switchport*

FIGURE 11.25   *The Front of a Cisco Catalyst 2950*

Commands

Like routers the switches have different modes for command line access. They are User Exec, Privileged Exec, and Configuration modes. In this section we will expand on what each mode does.

User Exec Mode

When you connect to a switch, you enter User Exec mode. User Exec mode provides some limited access to monitoring commands, but it does not allow you to configure a switch via configuration commands. The prompt for User Exec mode access is *Switch>*. Follow the prompt with a question mark (?) to retrieve a list of the commands available for use (see Figure 11.26).

```
Switch>?
Exec commands:
  access-enable    Create a temporary Access-List entry
  clear            Reset functions
  connect          Open a terminal connection
  disable          Turn off privileged commands
  disconnect       Disconnect an existing network connection
  enable           Turn on privileged commands
  exit             Exit from the EXEC
  help             Description of the interactive help system
  lock             Lock the terminal
  login            Log in as a particular user
  logout           Exit from the EXEC
  name-connection  Name an existing network connection
  ping             Send echo messages
  rcommand         Run command on remote switch
  resume           Resume an active network connection
  set              Set system parameter (not config)
  show             Show running system information
  ssh              Open a secure shell client connection
  systat           Display information about terminal lines
  telnet           Open a telnet connection
  terminal         Set terminal line parameters
--More--
```

One of the commands available for use is the *show* command, which will retrieve information on an interface, for example, or the version of the Cisco IOS software running on the switch. To leave User Exec mode use the *logout* or *quit* command.

Before users can connect to your switch via the console port, it is advisable that you configure a User Exec mode password (see Figure 11.27).

```
Switch#config t
Enter configuration commands, one per line.  End with CNTL/Z.
Switch(config)#line con 0
Switch(config-line)#password accessdenied
Switch(config-line)#end
Switch#
00:01:07: %SYS-5-CONFIG_I: Configured from console by console
Switch#
```

```
Switch>en
Password:
Switch#
```

When a user connects to your switch, a user-level password is required (see Figure 11.28).

Privileged Mode

Privileged mode provides you with full access to all commands, including those for configuring, monitoring, and managing your switch. The prompt for Privileged mode is *Switch#*. Figure 11.29 shows a list of the commands available for use in Privileged mode.

```
Switch#?
Exec commands:
  access-enable     Create a temporary Access-List entry
  access-template   Create a temporary Access-List entry
  archive           manage archive files
  cd                Change current directory
  clear             Reset functions
  clock             Manage the system clock
  cns               CNS agents
  configure         Enter configuration mode
  connect           Open a terminal connection
  copy              Copy from one file to another
  debug             Debugging functions (see also 'undebug')
  delete            Delete a file
  dir               List files on a filesystem
  disable           Turn off privileged commands
  disconnect        Disconnect an existing network connection
  dot1x             Dot1x Exec Commands
  enable            Turn on privileged commands
  erase             Erase a filesystem
  exit              Exit from the EXEC
  format            Format a filesystem
  fsck              Fsck a filesystem
--More--
```

FIGURE 11.29

Retrieving a List of All Commands Available for Use in Privileged Mode

From Privileged mode, you can make any changes to the running configuration. When you save these changes to the startup configuration, all settings will be stored even if you reboot your switch. To leave Privileged mode, you can use the *disable* or *exit* command.

Test Day Tip

To go from User Exec mode to Privileged mode, use the command *enable* or *en*.

With all of this knowledge under your belt, it's time now to work through an exercise. In Exercise 11.1, you will configure your switch with a few basic settings.

EXERCISE 11.1   Configuring your Switch with Some Basic Settings

1. Set the hostname of the switch to **SW1**.

2. Configure the console password of the switch as **accessdenied**.

3. Configure a Message of the Day (**MOTD**) banner for the switch.

4. Configure your switch with an IP address and a default gateway, and enable the VLAN 1 interface.

5. Copy your current configuration changes to NVRAM.

Figure 11.30 shows the commands for configuring the switch with the aforementioned settings.

```
Switch#config t
Enter configuration commands, one per line.  End with CNTL/Z.
Switch(config)#hostname SW1
SW1(config)#line con 0
SW1(config-line)#password accessdenied
SW1(config-line)#banner motd #
Enter TEXT message.  End with the character '#'.
Only authorized access is allowed
#
SW1(config)#int vlan1
SW1(config-if)#ip address 172.16.1.254 255.255.255.0
SW1(config-if)#no shut
SW1(config-if)#exit
SW1(config)#
00:08:43: %LINK-3-UPDOWN: Interface Vlan1, changed state to up
00:08:44: %LINEPROTO-5-UPDOWN: Line protocol on Interface Vlan1, changed state t
o up
SW1(config)#ip default-gateway 172.16.1.1
SW1(config)#end
SW1#copy ru
00:09:10: %SYS-5-CONFIG_I: Configured from console by
SW1#copy run sta
Destination filename [startup-config]?
Building configuration...
[OK]
SW1#
```

FIGURE 11.30   *Commands Required for Exercise 11.1*

Understanding Port-Based Security

If a malicious user connects to your network, the user's computer will probably receive an IP address and this computer can send a denial of service (DoS) attack, which can result in network outages. To prevent an unauthorized user from connecting to your network you need to configure your switch with port-based security.

Port-based security is a Layer 2 security feature which protects your switch in the following ways:

- It allows only traffic from a known MAC address.

- It restricts the number of MAC addresses that can connect through a switchport.

Exam Warning

A hacker can use a tool such as Macshift or the UNIX command *ifconfig* to "spoof" his MAC address, so although port-based security is a good way to improve security, it is not foolproof.

You enable port-based security in Port Security Interface mode. Figure 11.31 lists the commands you can use to configure port-based security.

When you connect additional hosts to your switch, a lot of MAC addresses will be available in the MAC address table. Each MAC address will be associated with a switchport. MAC addresses can be dynamic, secured, or static:

- A *dynamic* MAC address is a MAC address that the switch learned and is basically the first host that connects to the switchport. The switch will remove the MAC address from the MAC address table when no response is received within a certain time.

```
Switch#config t
Enter configuration commands, one per line.  End with CNTL/Z.
Switch(config)#int fa0/1
Switch(config-if)#switchport port-security ?
  aging          Port-security aging commands
  mac-address    Secure mac address
  maximum        Max secure addresses
  violation      Security violation mode
  <cr>

Switch(config-if)#switchport port-security
```

FIGURE 11.31

Port-Based Security Options

- A *secured* MAC address is a MAC address that was manually entered into the MAC address table and is associated with a secured port.

- A *static* MAC address is a MAC address that was manually entered into the MAC address table but is not removed when you reset your switch.

Test Day Tip

You can configure a switchport in access mode or trunk mode. But you can enable port-based security only on a switchport that is configured in access mode, not a trunk port.

When your switch dynamically learns MAC addresses the switch will keep the addresses for a certain amount of time (known as the *aging time*). Unused MAC addresses are automatically removed from the MAC address table after the aging time expires. Table 11.2 shows the contents of a MAC address table.

You can specify the aging time per VLAN or for all VLANs as a group. Use the *show mac-address-table aging-time* command to verify the aging time currently in use (see Figure 11.32).

As you can see in Figure 11.33, you can change the default aging time by using the command *mac-address-table aging-time {seconds}*.

Table 11.2 Contents of a MAC Address Table

MAC Address	VLAN ID	Switchport
00:04:23:D4:77:42	1	Fa0/1
00:04:23:D4:77:43	1	Fa0/2
00:04:23:D4:77:44	1	Fa0/3

When you configure port-based security on your switch and a malicious user tries to connect to the switch, the switch can do one of the following:

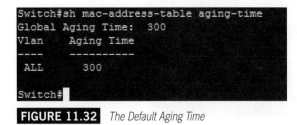

```
Switch#sh mac-address-table aging-time
Global Aging Time:   300
Vlan    Aging Time
----    ----------
 ALL       300

Switch#
```

FIGURE 11.32 *The Default Aging Time*

- It can disable the port permanently or for a specific amount of time. The port will be placed in the Shutdown state.

- It can drop traffic from unauthorized hosts, and the port will be placed in the Restrict state.

```
Switch#config t
Enter configuration commands, one per line.  End with CNTL/Z.
Switch(config)#mac-address-table aging-time ?
  <0-0>           Enter 0 to disable aging
  <10-1000000>  Aging time in seconds

Switch(config)#mac-address-table aging-time 600
Switch(config)#
```

FIGURE 11.33

Defining an Aging Time

■ When the limit of the maximum number of learned MAC addresses
  is reached, the switch will still forward traffic from known MAC
  addresses but will drop traffic from unknown MAC addresses. The
  port will be placed in the Protect state.

Figure 11.34 shows all three of these violation modes.

```
Switch#config t
Enter configuration commands, one per line.  End with CNTL/Z.
Switch(config)#int fa0/1
Switch(config-if)#switchport port-security violation ?
  protect    Security violation protect mode
  restrict   Security violation restrict mode
  shutdown   Security violation shutdown mode

Switch(config-if)#switchport port-security violation
```

FIGURE 11.34

Port-Based Security Violation Options

Exam Warning

If you need to configure a switchport in access mode, use the command *switchport
mode access*.

Allowing Traffic from a Known MAC Address

If you configure your switch to only allow traffic from a known MAC Address,
this allows traffic to the switch only from a well-known MAC address. You
can configure each switchport to allow one or more MAC addresses. In this
case, you can specify the maximum number of hosts that can connect using
that specific port. Configuring multiple MAC addresses per port is also useful when you connect a wireless access point to your switch. This allows
access to your wireless network only from known MAC addresses, and can
be combined with 802.1x authentication for additional security.

In the next section, you will learn which commands can be used to configure the switchports using port-security.

For instance, you can use the command *switchport port-security mac-address {mac-address}* to allow a specific MAC address to access your switch (see Figure 11.35). If you do not specify this command, the switch will dynamically learn the MAC address from the first host that connects to your switch.

```
Switch#config t
Enter configuration commands, one per line.  End with CNTL/Z.
Switch(config)#int fa0/1
Switch(config-if)#switchport port-security mac-address ?
  H.H.H   48 bit mac address
  sticky  Configure dynamic secure addresses as sticky

Switch(config-if)#switchport port-security mac-address 00:04:23:d4:77:42
Switch(config-if)#
```

FIGURE 11.35 *Configuring the Switchport with a Fixed MAC Address*

Use the command *switchport port-security maximum {max-value}* to specify the maximum number of allowed MAC addresses per switch port (see Figure 11.36). This means that when another client computer with a different MAC address connects to your switch, the switch will continue to operate until the maximum number of allowed MAC addresses is reached.

As you can see in Figure 11.37, you can use the command *switchport port-security violation* to configure your switch with a violation mode when the maximum number of MAC addresses is reached.

FIGURE 11.36

Configuring the Maximum Number of Allowed MAC Addresses per Switchport

```
Switch#config t
Enter configuration commands, one per line.  End with CNTL/Z.
Switch(config)#int fa0/1
Switch(config-if)#switchport port-security maximum ?
  <1-132>  Maximum addresses

Switch(config-if)#switchport port-security maximum 1
Switch(config-if)#
```

FIGURE 11.37

Display Port-Based Security Violation Mode

```
Switch#config t
Enter configuration commands, one per line.  End with CNTL/Z.
Switch(config)#int fa0/1
Switch(config-if)#switchport port-security violation ?
  protect   Security violation protect mode
  restrict  Security violation restrict mode
  shutdown  Security violation shutdown mode

Switch(config-if)#switchport port-security violation shutdown
Switch(config-if)#
```

When you don't change the port-based security violation mode, the default behavior is to shut down the switchport.

Exam Warning

By typing **switchport port-security**, you accept the default values, which means you're allowing only one MAC address and only from the first host computer that connects to your switch. If there is a violation, the switch shuts down the port.

In Exercise 11.2, you will configure your switch with port-based security to allow only traffic from a specific host.

EXERCISE 11.2   Conguring your Switch for Port-Based Security

1. Configure switchports 1 through 12 to allow only one MAC address per switchport, and configure each switchport so that if a violation occurs, the switchport will be shut down. You currently do not have a list of MAC addresses, so the switch must take the first MAC address that connects to a port.

Figure 11.38 shows the commands used to configure port-based security violation mode.

```
Switch#config t
Enter configuration commands, one per line.  End with CNTL/Z.
Switch(config)#int range fastethernet 0/1 - 12
Switch(config-if-range)#switchport port-security maximum 1
Switch(config-if-range)#switchport port-security violation shutdown
Switch(config-if-range)#
```

FIGURE 11.38

Configuring Port-Based Security Violation Mode

2. When you connect a host to a secured port, the switch will record the MAC address. To get an overview of the secured MAC addresses from the MAC address table, enter the command **show port-security address** (see Figure 11.39).

3. Enter the command **show port-security interface fa0/1** to determine the status per port (see Figure 11.40).

Figure 11.41 shows you some information about a switchport where no host is currently connected.

```
Switch#sh port-security address
            Secure Mac Address Table
-----------------------------------------------------------------
Vlan    Mac Address         Type                    Ports     Remaining Age
                                                              (mins)

----    ----------          ----                    -----     ------------
  1     0004.23d4.7742      SecureDynamic           Fa0/1         -
-----------------------------------------------------------------
Total Addresses in System (excluding one mac per port)    : 0
Max Addresses limit in System (excluding one mac per port) : 1024

Switch#
```

FIGURE 11.39   *Displaying the Secured MAC Addresses from the MAC Address Table*

```
Switch#show port-security int fa0/1
Port Security                 : Enabled
Port Status                   : Secure-up
Violation Mode                : Shutdown
Aging Time                    : 0 mins
Aging Type                    : Absolute
SecureStatic Address Aging    : Disabled
Maximum MAC Addresses         : 1
Total MAC Addresses           : 1
Configured MAC Addresses      : 0
Sticky MAC Addresses          : 0
Last Source Address           : 0004.23d4.7742
Security Violation Count      : 0

Switch#
```

FIGURE 11.40   *Displaying the Configuration Settings of a Secured Switchport*

```
Switch#show port-security int fa0/2
Port Security                 : Enabled
Port Status                   : Secure-down
Violation Mode                : Shutdown
Aging Time                    : 0 mins
Aging Type                    : Absolute
SecureStatic Address Aging    : Disabled
Maximum MAC Addresses         : 1
Total MAC Addresses           : 0
Configured MAC Addresses      : 0
Sticky MAC Addresses          : 0
Last Source Address           : 0000.0000.0000
Security Violation Count      : 0

Switch#
```

FIGURE 11.41   *A Switchport with No Host Connected*

Managing a Switch via a Web-Based Interface

You can also manage your switch through your Web browser. To do so, follow these steps:

1. Make sure JavaScript is installed and enabled on your client computer and that all the files to configure your switch via html are available on your switch. You can verify this with the *show flash* command at the # prompt of your router. If you see html in the list you have the files.

2. Download the image of your choice from the Cisco Web site (www. cisco.com/public/sw-center/sw-ios.shtml). This file must be a

CMS image (a .tar file). The Cluster Management Suite (CMS) is a feature to manage the switch via a web browser. The CMS uses the html directory to extract all .html files. Before you can download IOS images for your switch, you must have a support contract.

3. Make sure enough memory is available on the switch (see Figure 11.42) by erasing previous IOS images or adding more memory into the switch.

4. Make sure all previous .html files on your switch are removed. Use the command *delete flash:html/** to perform this operation (see Figure 11.43).

```
Switch#dir html
Directory of flash:/html/

No files in directory

7741440 bytes total (294400 bytes free)
Switch#
```

FIGURE 11.42 *Contents of the HTML Directory in Flash*

```
Switch#delete flash:html/*
Delete filename [html/*]?
No such file
Switch#
```

FIGURE 11.43 *Deleting All HTML Files from Flash*

5. Execute the *archive tar* command to copy the .tar file. After the copy process, the archive command will automatically extract all files to the appropriate directory (see Figure 11.44). Be sure that there is enough free memory available on your switch!

```
Switch#$ /xtract tftp://172.16.1.10/c2950-i6k2l2q4-tar.121-22.EA12.tar flash:
Loading c2950-i6k2l2q4-tar.121-22.EA12.tar from 172.16.1.10 (via Vlan1): !
extracting info (112 bytes)
extracting c2950-i6k2l2q4-mz.121-22.EA12.bin (3722038 bytes)
```

FIGURE 11.44 *Extracting the .tar File to Flash*

6. Write all changes to memory by using the command *write memory* (see Figure 11.45).

7. Reload your switch with the *reload* command. After the switch reload, enable the HTTP server with the command *ip http server* (see Figure 11.46).

```
Switch#write memory
Building configuration...
[OK]
Switch#
```

FIGURE 11.45 *Saving all Configuration Changes*

```
Switch#config t
Enter configuration commands, one per line.  End with CNTL/Z.
Switch(config)#ip http server
Switch(config)#
```

FIGURE 11.46 *Enabling the HTTP Server*

8. Open your favorite Web browser. In the address bar, type the IP address of your switch and press **Enter**. This loads the default home page and opens the Cisco Device Manager (see Figure 11.47).

From this window, you can manage your switch by using the toolbar on the left-hand side, under Contents.

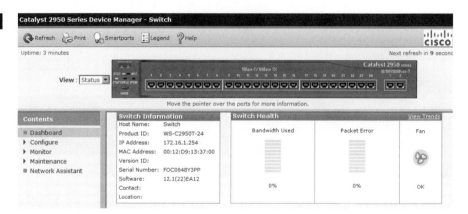

MAINTAINING SWITCHES

When you power on a switch for the first time, you can configure the switch by using the System Configuration Dialog Wizard. This wizard will guide you through the necessary configuration steps.

It is also possible to configure a switch manually. You can configure a switch with a hostname by using the command *hostname name_of_host*. Alternatively, you can configure a switch with an IP address. This can be useful for managing the switch remotely. To verify the currently assigned IP address, use the command *show interfaces vlan vlan_id*.

Finally, to save your configuration information, use the command *copy running-config startup-config*. This command will save your configuration to NVRAM.

To view the current configuration of your switch use the command *show running-config*, and to erase the switch configuration use the command *erase startup-config*.

Displaying the List of Available Commands

You can display a list of all available commands by typing a question mark (?) in the command-line interface (CLI). The available commands depend on the version of the Cisco IOS software installed on your switch.

The Cisco Web site lists all available commands for maintaining switches. For example, a list of all the available commands for a Cisco Catalyst 2950 can be found here: http://www.cisco.com/en/US/docs/switches/lan/catalyst2950/software/release/12.1_22ea/CR/cli1.html

Upgrading the Firmware

Before you upgrade your switch, be sure that you have a copy of your current IOS software. To verify the current IOS software running on your switch, use the command *show version*.

Figure 11.48 shows what you'll see during the boot process. On the third line of Figure 11.48, you can see that the switch is running Version 12.1(22) of the EA10a Release Software (fc2). Refer to the Cisco Web site (www.cisco.com/public/sw-center/sw-ios.shtml) to get more information on IOS software releases (see Figure 11.49).

Before you upgrade your switch, it's a good idea to copy the current IOS to a host running a Trivial File Transfer Protocol (TFTP) server by using the command *copy flash tftp*.

```
Switch#sh version
Cisco Internetwork Operating System Software
IOS (tm) C2950 Software (C2950-I6K2L2Q4-M), Version 12.1(22)EA10a, RELEASE SOFTW
ARE (fc2)
Copyright (c) 1986-2007 by cisco Systems, Inc.
Compiled Tue 24-Jul-07 17:37 by antonino
Image text-base: 0x80010000, data-base: 0x8067E000

ROM: Bootstrap program is C2950 boot loader

Switch uptime is 3 hours, 23 minutes
System returned to ROM by power-on
System image file is "flash:/c2950-i6k2l2q4-mz.121-22.ea10a.bin"


This product contains cryptographic features and is subject to United
States and local country laws governing import, export, transfer and
use. Delivery of Cisco cryptographic products does not imply
third-party authority to import, export, distribute or use encryption.
Importers, exporters, distributors and users are responsible for
compliance with U.S. and local country laws. By using this product you
agree to comply with applicable laws and regulations. If you are unable
to comply with U.S. and local laws, return this product immediately.

--More--
```

FIGURE 11.48   *Overview of the Boot Process*

Tools & Resources

Downloads

1 Select Product > 2 Select Software Type > 3 Select Software > 4 Download

Switches > Cisco Catalyst 2950C 24 Switch > IOS Software > 12.1.22-EA12 > C2950 EI AND SI IOS CRYPTO AND WEB BASED DEVICE MANAGER

Download Image

DOWNLOAD

Details	
Release	12.1.22-EA12
Filename	c2950-i6k2l2q4-tar.121-22.EA12.tar
Release Date	15/Jul/2008
Security Advisories	Security Advisories
Minimum Memory	DRAM:16MB Flash:8MB
Size	5580 KB
Router Checksum	0xc3b9
MD5	40687d9f9f1ca3405a8955992593e3ed

FIGURE 11.49   *The Cisco Web Page Where You Can Download IOS Images*

Now we'll walk through the steps required to upgrade the firmware of your switch. For this short exercise, all configurations are being done from a Cisco Catalyst 2950 switch and the host is configured with an IP address in the same subnet as the switch.

1. Retrieve the name of the current image file by typing the command *show boot* (see Figure 11.50).

FIGURE 11.50

Displaying the Boot Configuration Files

```
Switch#show boot
BOOT path-list:
Config file:           flash:/config.text
Private Config file:   flash:/private-config.text
Enable Break:          no
Manual Boot:           no
HELPER path-list:
NVRAM/Config file
      buffer size:     32768
Timeout for Config
         Download:     0 seconds
Config Download
      via DHCP:        disabled (next boot: disabled)
Switch#
```

2. In Figure 11.50, no software image is defined in the boot path. To display the image file type use the command *show flash*. Figure 11.51 shows the IOS images available in Flash.

```
Switch#show flash

Directory of flash:/

    2  -rwx     3719152  Mar 01 1993 00:45:13 +00:00  c2950-i6k212q4-mz.121-22.e
a10a.bin
    3  -rwx        1681  Mar 01 1993 00:03:13 +00:00  config.text
    4  -rwx          24  Mar 01 1993 00:03:13 +00:00  private-config.text
    5  -rwx         556  Mar 01 1993 01:28:09 +00:00  vlan.dat

7741440 bytes total (4017664 bytes free)
Switch#
```

FIGURE 11.51 *Overview of the IOS Images Available in Flash*

3. Verify that enough free memory is available on the switch. If insufficient memory is available, you can make a copy of the current IOS to a TFTP server. Otherwise, you can rename the current IOS (see Figure 11.52).

```
Switch#rename flash:c2950-i6k212q4-mz.121-22.ea10a.bin flash:c2950-i6k212q4-mz$
Destination filename [c2950-i6k212q4-mz.121-22.ea10a.old]?
Switch#
```

FIGURE 11.52 *Renaming the IOS Image in Flash*

4. Verify that the file renaming process was successful (see Figure 11.53).

5. Disable access to the switch by using a Web browser (see Figure 11.54).

```
Switch#dir flash:
Directory of flash:/

    2  -rwx     3719152  Mar 01 1993 00:45:13 +00:00  c2950-i6k212q4-mz.121-22.e
a10a.old
    3  -rwx        1681  Mar 01 1993 00:03:13 +00:00  config.text
    4  -rwx          24  Mar 01 1993 00:03:13 +00:00  private-config.text
    5  -rwx         556  Mar 01 1993 01:28:09 +00:00  vlan.dat

7741440 bytes total (4017664 bytes free)
Switch#
```

FIGURE 11.53 *Showing the Flash Content*

FIGURE 11.54

Disabling the HTTP Services

```
Switch#config t
Enter configuration commands, one per line.  End with CNTL/Z.
Switch(config)#no ip http server
Switch(config)#
```

6. Use the command *archive tar* to extract the new IOS image into Flash memory (see Figure 11.55).

   Figure 11.56 shows the output.

FIGURE 11.55

Extracting the IOS Image to Flash

```
Switch#$ /x tftp://172.16.1.10/c2950-i6k2l2q4-tar.121-22.EA12.tar flash:
```

```
Switch#$ /x tftp://172.16.1.10/c2950-i6k2l2q4-tar.121-22.EA12.tar flash:
Loading c2950-i6k2l2q4-tar.121-22.EA12.tar from 172.16.1.10 (via Vlan1): !
extracting info (112 bytes)
extracting c2950-i6k2l2q4-mz.121-22.EA12.bin (3722038 bytes)!!!!!!!!!!!!!!!!!!!!
!!!!!!!!!!!!!!!!!!!!!!!!!!!!!!!!!!!!!!!!!!!!!!!!!!!!!!!!!!!!!!!!!!!!!!!!!!!!!!!!!!!
!!!!!!!!!!!!!!!!!!!!!!!!!!!!!!!!!!!!!!!!!!!!!!!!!!!!!!!!!!!!!!!!!!!!!!!!!!!!!!!!!!!!
!!!!!!!!!!!!!!!!!!!!!!!!!!!!!!!!!!!!!!!!!!!!!!!!!!!!!!!!!!!!!!!!!!!!!!!!!!!!!!!!!!!!
!!!!!!!!!!!!!!!!!!!!!!!!!!!!!!!!!!!!!!!!!!!!!!!!!!!!!!!!!!!!!!!!!!!!!!!!!!!!!!!!!!!!
!!!!!!!!!!!!!!!!!!!!!!!!!!!!!!!!!!!!!!!!!!!!!!!!!!!!!!!!!!!!!!!!!!!!!!!!!!!!!!!!!!!!
!!!!!!!!!!!!!!!!!!!!!!!!!!!!!!!!!!!!!!!!!!!!!!!!!!!!!
```

FIGURE 11.56 *Output from the Extraction Process*

7. After downloading the new IOS image, the switch will automatically extract the IOS image file. Enable the HTTP services again for Web-based management (see Figure 11.57).

FIGURE 11.57

Enabling the HTTP Services Again

```
Switch#config t
Enter configuration commands, one per line.  End with CNTL/Z.
Switch(config)#ip http server
Switch(config)#
```

8. Specify the new IOS image to be used by using the *boot* command. After the switch has finished reloading, use the command *show flash* (see Figure 11.58) to retrieve a list of the available image files.

9. Restart your switch by using the *reload* command (see Figure 11.59). After the switch has restarted, verify the IOS version with the command *show version*.

```
Switch#sh fla
04:54:56: %SYS-5-CONFIG_I: Configured from console by c
Switch#sh fla

Directory of flash:/

    2  -rwx     3719152  Mar 01 1993 00:45:13 +00:00  c2950-i6k2l2q4-mz.121-22.e
a10a.old
    3  -rwx        1681  Mar 01 1993 00:03:13 +00:00  config.text
    4  -rwx          24  Mar 01 1993 00:03:13 +00:00  private-config.text
    5  -rwx         556  Mar 01 1993 01:28:09 +00:00  vlan.dat
    6  -rwx         112  Mar 01 1993 04:47:06 +00:00  info
    7  -rwx     3722038  Mar 01 1993 04:49:42 +00:00  c2950-i6k2l2q4-mz.121-22.E
A12.bin
    8  drwx        1280  Mar 01 1993 04:52:44 +00:00  html

7741440 bytes total (7168 bytes free)
Switch#config t
Enter configuration commands, one per line.  End with CNTL/Z.
Switch(config)#boot system flash:c2950-i6k2l2q4-mz.121-22.EA12.bin
Switch(config)#
```

FIGURE 11.58 *Contents of Flash, and Specifying the Boot File*

```
Cisco Internetwork Operating System Software
IOS (tm) C2950 Software (C2950-I6K2L2Q4-M), Version 12.1(22)EA12, RELEASE SOFTWA
RE (fc1)
Copyright (c) 1986-2008 by cisco Systems, Inc.
Compiled Tue 08-Jul-08 00:03 by amvarma
Image text-base: 0x80010000, data-base: 0x80680000

ROM: Bootstrap program is C2950 boot loader

Switch uptime is 0 minutes
System returned to ROM by power-on
System image file is "flash:c2950-i6k2l2q4-mz.121-22.EA12.bin"


This product contains cryptographic features and is subject to United
States and local country laws governing import, export, transfer and
use. Delivery of Cisco cryptographic products does not imply
third-party authority to import, export, distribute or use encryption.
Importers, exporters, distributors and users are responsible for
compliance with U.S. and local country laws. By using this product you
agree to comply with applicable laws and regulations. If you are unable
to comply with U.S. and local laws, return this product immediately.

 --More--
```

FIGURE 11.59 *Overview of the Boot Process with the New IOS Image*

Backing Up and Restoring Configurations

It is important to back up your switch configurations and know how to restore a switch to a saved configuration. In this section we will cover the commands and concepts that will allow you to back up and restore configurations on Cisco switches.

Backing Up Configurations

Before you modify your switch, it's a good idea to copy the current configuration to a host running a TFTP server. You can do this using the *copy running-config tftp* command.

Assuming that you're using a Cisco Catalyst 2950 switch and that the host is configured with an IP address in the same subnet as the switch, start by typing the *enable* command at the prompt, and then copy the running configuration file to the TFTP server. Enter the IP address of the TFTP server, as well as a destination filename; by default, this is the hostname of the switch with *–confg* at the end (see Figure 11.60).

FIGURE 11.60

Copying the Running Configuration to a TFTP Server

```
Switch>enable
Switch#copy running-config tftp:
Address or name of remote host []? 172.16.1.10
Destination filename [switch-confg]?
!!
2734 bytes copied in 4.316 secs (633 bytes/sec)
Switch#
```

Depending on the size of the configuration, it can take several seconds or, perhaps, minutes, before the configuration is copied to the TFTP server.

Test Day Tip

An exclamation point (!) indicates a successful transfer of User Datagram Protocol (UDP) packets from a switch to a TFTP server.

Restoring Configurations

If you need to restore your switch configuration because the configuration file was corrupted or you made some configuration changes you cannot reverse, you need to retrieve your original configuration file back from the TFTP server. The easiest way to do this is by using the command *copy tftp startup-config* (see Figure 11.61) then reloading the router. The Startup-config is the only configuration that is overwritten when you copy to it. If you were to copy to the running-config you would only be adding the copy from the server to the ram. It would not fix the problem.

The backup configuration file will now be copied to Dynamic Random Access Memory (DRAM) (running-config). If you want to keep this configuration the next time you start your switch, you still need to copy the data from DRAM to NVRAM (startup config) with the command *copy running-config startup-config* (see Figure 11.62).

The startup-config stores configuration information used when you boot your switch. The running-config is configuration information used when you make configuration changes to your switch.

```
User Access Verification

Password:
CM_Router3>en
Password:
CM_Router3#copy tftp start
Address or name of remote host []? 10.10.1.199
Source filename []? ccnabook.txt
Destination filename [startup-config]?
Accessing tftp://10.10.1.199/ccnabook.txt...
Loading ccnabook.txt from 10.10.1.199 (via Ethernet0): !
[OK - 8514 bytes]
[OK]
8514 bytes copied in 9.668 secs (881 bytes/sec)
CM_Router3#reload
Proceed with reload? [confirm]
```

FIGURE 11.61 *Copying the Configuration File from the TFTP Server to the Switch*

```
Switch#copy running-config startup-config
Destination filename [startup-config]?
Building configuration...
[OK]
Switch#
```

FIGURE 11.62 *Copying the Running Configuration to the Startup Configuration*

TROUBLESHOOTING SWITCHES

When you need to troubleshoot a switch, the first thing you need to do is verify the physical connection and that you used the right cable when you connected the host to the switch. Next, verify that the switchport is correctly configured. When you connect a host to a switch, the switchport must be configured in access mode. To verify the physical connection of a switch, use the command *show interfaces fastethernet0/1*. If the line protocol is down, the physical connection is probably at issue.

Using the *show* Commands

You can use the *show* command to display the current configuration of your switch. When you make some changes to your switch, all the changes will be visible in the running configuration.

When you use *show*, you can add a question mark (?) to the end to retrieve a list of all the commands supported (see Figure 11.63).

You can use the *show interfaces* command to get detailed information regarding all the interfaces. To get detailed information on a particular interface—for instance, the fa0/1 interface—use the command *show interface fa0/1* (see Figure 11.64).

```
Switch#show ?
  access-lists        List access lists
  accounting          Accounting data for active sessions
  aliases             Display alias commands
  arp                 ARP table
  auto                Show Automation Template
  boot                show boot attributes
  buffers             Buffer pool statistics
  cdp                 CDP information
  class-map           Show QoS Class Map
  clock               Display the system clock
  cluster             Cluster information
  cns                 CNS agents
  configuration       Contents of Non-Volatile memory
  controllers         Interface controller status
  crypto              Encryption module
  data-corruption     Show data errors
  debugging           State of each debugging option
  dhcp                Dynamic Host Configuration Protocol status
  dot1x               Dot1x information
  dtp                 DTP information
  env                 Environmental facilities
  errdisable          Error disable
 --More--
```

```
Switch#show interface fa0/1
FastEthernet0/1 is up, line protocol is up (connected)
  Hardware is Fast Ethernet, address is 0012.d913.3701 (bia 0012.d913.3701)
  MTU 1500 bytes, BW 100000 Kbit, DLY 100 usec,
     reliability 255/255, txload 1/255, rxload 1/255
  Encapsulation ARPA, loopback not set
  Keepalive set (10 sec)
  Full-duplex, 100Mb/s, media type is 100BaseTX
  input flow-control is unsupported output flow-control is unsupported
  ARP type: ARPA, ARP Timeout 04:00:00
  Last input 03:07:47, output 00:00:01, output hang never
  Last clearing of "show interface" counters never
  Input queue: 0/75/0/0 (size/max/drops/flushes); Total output drops: 0
  Queueing strategy: fifo
  Output queue: 0/40 (size/max)
  5 minute input rate 0 bits/sec, 0 packets/sec
  5 minute output rate 0 bits/sec, 0 packets/sec
     819 packets input, 83081 bytes, 0 no buffer
     Received 126 broadcasts (12 multicast)
     0 runts, 0 giants, 0 throttles
     0 input errors, 0 CRC, 0 frame, 0 overrun, 0 ignored
     0 watchdog, 12 multicast, 0 pause input
     0 input packets with dribble condition detected
     7668 packets output, 697123 bytes, 0 underruns
```

You can use the *show running-config* command to get a detailed list of the current configuration of your switch, or you can use the *show running-config int fa0/1* command to retrieve limited information regarding a specific interface port (see Figure 11.65).

Use the *show port-security* command to get a list of all secured switch-ports (see Figure 11.66).

```
Switch#show running-config int fa0/1
Building configuration...

Current configuration : 107 bytes
!
interface FastEthernet0/1
 switchport mode access
 switchport nonegotiate
 switchport port-security
end

Switch#
```

FIGURE 11.65 *Retrieving Configuration Information for the fa0/1 Interface*

```
Switch#sh mac-address-table
          Mac Address Table
-------------------------------------------

Vlan    Mac Address      Type        Ports
----    -----------      --------    -----
All     0012.d913.3700   STATIC      CPU
All     0100.0ccc.cccc   STATIC      CPU
All     0100.0ccc.cccd   STATIC      CPU
All     0100.0cdd.dddd   STATIC      CPU
  1     0004.23d4.7742   STATIC      Fa0/1
Total Mac Addresses for this criterion: 5
Switch#
```

FIGURE 11.66 *Contents of the MAC Address Table*

Using the *clear* Commands

You can use the *clear* command to erase information. When you use the *clear* command, you can add a question mark (?) to the end to retrieve a list of all the commands supported (see Figure 11.67).

```
Switch#clear ?
  access-list        Clear access list statistical information
  access-template    Access-template
  arp-cache          Clear the entire ARP cache
  cdp                Reset cdp information
  cns                CNS agents
  controllers        Clear interface controller info
  counters           Clear counters on one or all interfaces
  crypto             Encryption subsystem
  host               Delete host table entries
  interface          Clear the hardware logic on an interface
  ip                 IP
  kerberos           Clear Kerberos Values
  lacp               Port channel information
  line               Reset a terminal line
  logging            Clear logging buffer
  mac                MAC forwarding table
  mac-address-table  MAC forwarding table
  pagp               Port channel information
  port-security      Clear secure information
  radius             Clears radius server information
  spanning-tree      Clear spanning tree parameters
  storm-control      Clear storm control counters
--More--
```

FIGURE 11.67

Overview of the Options for the clear *Command*

Use the command *clear port-security all* to clear all MAC addresses from the MAC address table (see Figure 11.68). Afterward, you can use the command *show mac-address-table* to verify that all of the items were removed from the MAC address table.

Solving Boot Problems

If you experience problems using commands on your switch, you could be using an incorrect boot image file. To retrieve a list of the currently loaded boot files, use the command *show boot* (see Figure 11.69).

FIGURE 11.68

Clearing the MAC Address Table

```
Switch#clear port-security ?
  all        All secure MAC addresses
  configured Configured secure MAC address
  dynamic    Secure MAC address auto-learned by hardware
  sticky     Secure MAC address either auto-learned or configured

Switch#clear port-security all
Switch#sh mac-address-table
          Mac Address Table
-------------------------------------------

Vlan    Mac Address      Type        Ports
----    -----------      --------    -----
 All    0012.d913.3700   STATIC      CPU
 All    0100.0ccc.cccc   STATIC      CPU
 All    0100.0ccc.cccd   STATIC      CPU
 All    0100.0cdd.dddd   STATIC      CPU
Total Mac Addresses for this criterion: 4
Switch#
```

FIGURE 11.69

Overview of Boot Configuration Information

```
Switch#sh boot
BOOT path-list:            flash:c2950-i6k2l2q4-mz.121-22.EA12.bin
Config file:              flash:/config.text
Private Config file:      flash:/private-config.text
Enable Break:             no
Manual Boot:              no
HELPER path-list:
NVRAM/Config file
       buffer size:       32768
Timeout for Config
          Download:       0 seconds
Config Download
       via DHCP:          disabled (next boot: disabled)
Switch#
```

To retrieve a list of all the IOS images available on your switch, use the command *show flash* (see Figure 11.70).

As you can see in Figure 11.70, two IOS images are available. If you would like another image, use the command *boot system* to boot the switch with an IOS image of your choice (see Figure 11.71).

```
Switch#sh flash

Directory of flash:/

    2  -rwx    3719152  Mar 01 1993 00:45:13 +00:00  c2950-i6k2l2q4-mz.121-22.ea10a.bin
    4  -rwx       2907  Mar 01 1993 00:53:50 +00:00  config.text
    5  -rwx        556  Mar 01 1993 01:28:09 +00:00  vlan.dat
    6  -rwx        112  Mar 01 1993 04:47:06 +00:00  info
    7  -rwx    3722038  Mar 01 1993 04:49:42 +00:00  c2950-i6k2l2q4-mz.121-22.EA12.bin
    8  drwx       1280  Mar 01 1993 04:52:44 +00:00  html
   29  -rwx         46  Mar 01 1993 04:55:49 +00:00  env_vars
   30  -rwx         24  Mar 01 1993 00:53:52 +00:00  private-config.text

7741440 bytes total (5632 bytes free)
Switch#
```

FIGURE 11.70   *Overview of Available Files in Flash*

```
Switch#config t
Enter configuration commands, one per line.  End with CNTL/Z.
Switch(config)#boot system flash:c2950-i6k2l2q4-mz.121-22.ea10a.bin
Switch(config)#end
Switch#
```

FIGURE 11.71   *Instructing the Switch to Boot from a Specific IOS Image*

Another problem that can occur is that your switch reboots in ROMmon mode, and afterward it shows only the *switch:* prompt (see Figure 11.72).

To determine what is causing this problem, use the *set* command, as shown in Figure 11.73.

As you can see in Figure 11.73, the *MANUAL_BOOT* variable is set to *Yes*. This causes the switch to boot in manual mode. Use the command *set MANUAL_BOOT no* to change this variable (see Figure 11.74).

The next step is to issue the *boot* command to continue to load your switch (see Figure 11.75).

At this point, the switch should be loading with the correct IOS image.

In addition to these configurations, you also can reset your switch from the factory default settings. *However, this procedure will erase everything from your switch.*

```
C2950 Boot Loader (C2950-HBOOT-M) Version 12.1(11r)EA1, RELEASE SOFTWARE (fc1)
Compiled Mon 22-Jul-02 17:18 by antonino
WS-C2950T-24 starting...
Base ethernet MAC Address: 00:12:d9:13:37:00
Xmodem file system is available.
Initializing Flash...
flashfs[0]: 27 files, 2 directories
flashfs[0]: 0 orphaned files, 0 orphaned directories
flashfs[0]: Total bytes: 7741440
flashfs[0]: Bytes used: 7735808
flashfs[0]: Bytes available: 5632
flashfs[0]: flashfs fsck took 15 seconds.
...done initializing flash.
Boot Sector Filesystem (bs:) installed, fsid: 3
Parameter Block Filesystem (pb:) installed, fsid: 4

The system is not configured to boot automatically.  The
following command will finish loading the operating system
software:

    boot

switch:
```

FIGURE 11.72 *Overview of Boot Process in ROMmon mode*

```
switch: set
BOOT=flash:c2950-i6k212q4-mz.121-22.ea12.bin
MANUAL_BOOT=yes
switch:
```

FIGURE 11.73 *Determining the Boot Configuration Problem with the set Command*

```
switch: set MANUAL_BOOT no
switch:
```

FIGURE 11.74 *Configuring the Boot Process to Auto-Boot*

FIGURE 11.75

Showing the Boot Process

```
switch: set
BOOT=flash:c2950-i6k212q4-mz.121-22.ea12.bin
MANUAL_BOOT=no
switch: boot flash:c2950-i6k212q4-mz.121-22.EA12.bin
Loading "flash:c2950-i6k212q4-mz.121-22.EA12.bin"...####
################################################
```

If you still want to reset your switch, press and hold the **MODE** button while the switch is connected via the power cord. After two seconds, the LED indicators on the switch will start to blink. While these LEDs are blinking, continue to hold down the MODE button. After eight seconds, the LEDs will stop blinking and the switch will reboot. After reboot, the switch will start the initial setup.

Resetting a Switch Password

At some point, you will need to make some configuration changes on your switch but you may have forgotten your password. In this section, I will guide you through the process of resetting a password. (You must have physical access to the switch in order to complete these steps.)

> **Exam Warning**
>
> Although the CCNA exam will not test you on resetting a switch password, this information is still good to know. Of course, you should not share this information with hackers.

1. Connect your PC to the console port of your switch, and unplug the switch's power cord.

2. Plug in the switch's power cord and press the MODE button in the front of the switch for at least two seconds.

3. Release the MODE button after the LED above port 1 has been on for at least two seconds. The flash initialization process will be interrupted.

4. Type the following commands:

   - flash_init

   - load_helper

   - dir flash:

5. Rename the original configuration file by typing the command **rename flash:config.text flash:config.org**.

6. Reboot the switch by typing the command *boot*. This will start up your switch without reading the configuration file.

7. You will be prompted to start the setup. Type **n** to abort the initial configuration dialog.

8. Press **Enter** and type the command **enable**.

9. The switch will now be in Privileged mode. To rename the configuration file, type the command **rename flash:config.org flash:config.text**.

10. Copy the configuration file into memory by using the command **copy flash:config.text system:running-config**. At this point, the switch will be loaded with an empty configuration file and the current configuration file will be copied into memory.

11. Go to configuration mode and reset the password.

12. Store the current configuration file in memory.

Recovering a Switch Password

In some cases, you may not want to reset your password, but rather recover the password you lost or can no longer remember. Exercise 11.3 will walk you through the steps of recovering a lost or forgotten password on a Cisco Catalyst 2950 switch.

EXERCISE 11.3   Recovering a Lost or Forgotten Password

1. Press and release the MODE button. You will be prompted with the information shown in Figure 11.76.

```
C2950 Boot Loader (C2950-HBOOT-M) Version 12.1(11r)EA1, RELEASE SOFTWARE (fc1)
Compiled Mon 22-Jul-02 17:18 by antonino
WS-C2950T-24 starting...
Base ethernet MAC Address: 00:12:d9:13:37:00
Xmodem file system is available.

The system has been interrupted prior to initializing the
flash filesystem.  The following commands will initialize
the flash filesystem, and finish loading the operating
system software:

    flash_init
    load_helper
    boot

switch:
```

FIGURE 11.76 *Overview of the Manual Boot Process*

2. At the *switch*: prompt, type **flash_init**. You will see the screen shown in Figure 11.77.

3. At the *switch*: prompt, type **load_helper** and then **dir flash**: to get a list of the files available in Flash (see Figure 11.78).

```
switch: flash_init
Initializing Flash...
flashfs[0]: 27 files, 2 directories
flashfs[0]: 0 orphaned files, 0 orphaned directories
flashfs[0]: Total bytes: 7741440
flashfs[0]: Bytes used: 7735808
flashfs[0]: Bytes available: 5632
flashfs[0]: flashfs fsck took 15 seconds.
...done initializing flash.
Boot Sector Filesystem (bs:) installed, fsid: 3
Parameter Block Filesystem (pb:) installed, fsid: 4
switch:
```

FIGURE 11.77

Executing flash_init

```
switch: load_helper
switch: dir flash:
Directory of flash:/

2     -rwx   3719152    <date>        c2950-i6k2l2q4-mz.121-22.ea10a.old
4     -rwx   2734       <date>        config.text
5     -rwx   556        <date>        vlan.dat
6     -rwx   112        <date>        info
7     -rwx   3722038    <date>        c2950-i6k2l2q4-mz.121-22.EA12.bin
8     drwx   1280       <date>        html
29    -rwx   46         <date>        env_vars
30    -rwx   24         <date>        private-config.text

5632 bytes available (7735808 bytes used)
switch:
```

FIGURE 11.78   *Files Available in Flash*

```
switch: rename flash:config.text flash:config.old
switch:
```

FIGURE 11.79

Renaming the Configuration File

4. Rename the original config.text file to config.old (see Figure 11.79).

5. Continue with the boot process. After the boot process completes, type **n**.

6. Complete the exercise by specifying another password. Figure 11.80 provides an overview of the commands required to specify the new password.

FIGURE 11.80

Overview of All the Commands Used to Specify Another Password

```
Switch>enable
Switch#rename flash:config.old flash:config.text
Destination filename [config.text]?
Switch#copy flash:config.text system:running-config
Destination filename [running-config]?
2734 bytes copied in 2.272 secs (1203 bytes/sec)
Switch#config t
Enter configuration commands, one per line.  End with CNTL/Z.
Switch(config)#enable secret accessdenied
Switch(config)#line con 0
Switch(config-line)#password accessdenied
Switch(config-line)#end
Switch#
00:03:50: %SYS-5-CONFIG_I: Configured from console by console
Switch#copy run sta
Destination filename [startup-config]?
Building configuration...
[OK]
Switch#
```

SUMMARY OF EXAM OBJECTIVES

This chapter began with an overview of the differences between hubs and switches. As we discussed, a hub works at Layer 1 and a switch works at Layer 2. A switch will make its decisions based on the MAC addresses available in the MAC address table. Three switch modes are available: cut-through, fragment-free, and store-n-forward.

We also discussed the MAC address table and how to clear it, and we differentiated between a Layer 2 switch and a Layer 3 switch. In addition, we discussed the LED indicators on the Cisco Catalyst 2950 switch, and you learned that if the System LED is green, the switch is functioning normally, but if the System LED is amber, there is a possible failure.

This chapter also covered the steps for configuring a switch. We discussed the options of configuring a switch with the Windows-based HyperTerminal, with the Minicom Linux-based terminal emulation program, and with Cisco Network Assistant, a freeware tool that you can use to configure your switch via a GUI.

In addition to learning the differences between User Exec mode and Privileged mode, you also learned about port-based security, which is a Layer 2 feature designed to protect your switch against malicious users by assigning one MAC address per switchport. If the switch detects a violation, the switch can shut down, protect, or restrict the switchport.

A bit later in the chapter you learned that by running the HTTP services on your switch, you can configure and manage your switch via your favorite

Web browser. We also discussed how to upgrade the firmware of your switch. You now know that you can use the command *copy tftp flash* to copy the new IOS from your TFTP server to your switch's Flash memory.

We rounded out the chapter with a discussion of how to back up and restore the configuration of your switch, when to use the *show* and *clear* commands, how to solve boot problems, and how to configure your switch for a manual or automatic boot.

EXAM OBJECTIVES FAST TRACK

Switching Concepts

- The three LAN switch methods are called cut-through, fragment-free, and store-n-forward.

- Cut-through switching does not copy the entire frame into the switch's buffer, but rather will forward the frame when the switch receives the first six bytes of the frame. Because the MAC address is part of the first six bytes, the switch can forward the frame based on the information from the MAC address table.

- Fragment-free switching is a modification of cut-through switching. When a switch receives a frame, the switch will wait until the first 64 bytes are received and then will forward the frame to the destination port based on the information in the MAC address table.

- Store-n-forward switching is basically the same as frame forwarding. When a switch receives a frame, the switch will copy the entire frame into its memory buffers and will calculate the CRC. If the CRC calculation is correct, the switch will forward the frame to the destination port based on the information found in the MAC address table. If the frame is corrupt, the frame will be dropped.

Configuring Switches

- Switches feature light-emitting diodes (LEDs). The color of the LED can help you determine the status of your switch.

- When the LED is green the switchport is functioning normally. When the LED is amber, the switchport is disabled or shut down.

- Switches offer two modes. In User Exec mode, all you can do is view the configuration. In Privileged mode, you can modify the configuration of the switch.

- You can configure your switchport for port-based security. Use the command *switchport port-security* to accept the default settings.

Maintaining Switches

- Use the command *show boot* to show the boot configuration of your switch.

- Use the command *show version* to display the current IOS version running on your switch.

- Use the command *copy running-config tftp* to copy the current configuration of your switch to a TFTP server.

- Use the command *copy tftp startup-config* to copy the configuration from a TFTP server to your switch.

- Use the command *show flash* to get a list of all the files available in flash memory.

Troubleshooting Switches

- Use the *show ?* command to retrieve a list of all the options used.

- To retrieve the configuration of your switch, use the *show running-config* command.

- To retrieve the startup configuration of your switch, use the *show startup-config* command.

EXAM OBJECTIVES FREQUENTLY ASKED QUESTIONS

Q: Should I know all the commands used to configure port-based security?

A: Yes, you need to practice all of these commands to understand how port-based security works.

Q: Can I get help while taking the exam by typing a question mark (?) after each command?

A: No, you cannot receive help on the commands used in the labs.

Q: Will I need to know the difference between User Exec and Privileged modes?

A: Absolutely. This is one of the most important things you need to understand before you work with a switch or router.

Q: Will the exam contain any simulation questions?

A: Yes. A few questions will ask you to configure a switch via the command line. Keep in mind that simulation questions require extra time to complete, so plan your time accordingly.

Q: Can I go back to a previous question while taking the exam?

A: No, you cannot go back to a previous question. You also cannot review your answers.

Q: How much time do I have to take the exam?

A: In total, you have 90 minutes to take the exam. Come to the exam well prepared; don't wait until a day or two before your exam to start studying. Take your time and read the questions slowly.

SELF TEST

1. Which of the following statements regarding hubs are true?
   A. They operate at the datalink layer.
   B. They increase the number of collisions.
   C. Layer 2 addresses are used to make forwarding decisions.
   D. Signals are distributed through all ports except the source port.

2. Which switching mode creates the most latency and offers the best error detection?
   A. Cut-through
   B. Store-n-forward
   C. Fragment-free
   D. Adaptive cut-through

3. Which of the following is used to build a dynamic MAC address table?
   A. Source IP address
   B. Destination IP address
   C. Source MAC address
   D. Destination MAC address

4. What does it means when the System LED is amber?
   A. The POST is running.
   B. The POST has failed.
   C. The POST was successful.
   D. The switch has experienced a fatal error.

5. How can a switch be configured to prevent unauthorized hosts to access your network?

   A. Assign a MAC address to a switchport.

   B. Add unused switchports to VLAN 1.

   C. Use port-based security to allow only the first host to access the network.

   D. Shut down all unused ports.

6. Which command do you use to back up the IOS of your switch to a PC?

   A. *Switch#copy tftp flash*

   B. *Switch#copy flash tftp*

   C. *Switch(config)#copy tftp flash*

   D. *Switch(config)#copy flash tftp*

7. If a host is powered down, how long will the MAC address in the MAC address table stay on your switch?

   A. 30 seconds   **C.** 600 seconds

   B. 300 seconds   **D.** 120 seconds

8. Which commands can you use to change from Global Configuration mode to Privileged Exec mode?

   A. Logout   **D.** Quit

   B. Disable   **E.** End

   C. Exit

9. You lost the password of your Cisco Catalyst 2950 switch and you need to initiate the password recovery procedure. What do you do?

   A. Rename the Flash file.

   B. Hold down the MODE button during switch startup.

   C. Connect a PC via a console cable, and after startup press Ctrl+Break.

   D. Enter the setup program by deleting the switch configuration file.

10. Which protocol do you use to upgrade an IOS image from a Cisco Catalyst 2950?

    A. HTTP   **C.** Telnet

    B. SNMP   **D.** TFTP

11. You need to connect your PC to the console port of your switch. Which cable do you use?

   A. Crossover cable

   B. Straight cable

   C. Rollover cable

   D. Serial cable

12. What does port-based security use to allow or deny access to a switchport?

   A. Source IP address

   B. Destination IP address

   C. Source MAC address

   D. Destination MAC address

13. What are the three modes of port-based security?

   A. Restrict   **E.** Protect

   B. Stop   **F.** Close

   C. Start   **G.** Disable

   D. Shutdown

14. Which of the following is a reason why a switch does not add the broadcast address to its MAC address table?

   A. A broadcast address will never be the source address of a frame.

   B. A broadcast is never forwarded by a switch.

   C. Broadcast addresses are not compatible with the switching table.

   D. A switch will drop broadcasts to avoid broadcast storms.

15. You need to execute the command *show mac-address-table*. In which mode(s) can you execute this command?

   A. User mode

   B. Enable mode

   C. Global Configuration mode

   D. Setup mode

   E. Interface Configuration mode

16. You need to reboot your switch. Which command do you use?

   A. *Switch>reboot*

   B. *Switch#reboot*

   C. *Switch(config)#reboot*

   D. *Switch#reload*

17. What type of memory is used to store the configuration of your switch?
    - **A.** ROM
    - **B.** RAM
    - **C.** NVRAM
    - **D.** Flash

18. What command copies the configuration information from RAM to NVRAM?
    - **A.** *copy running-config tftp*
    - **B.** *copy tftp running-config*
    - **C.** *copy running-config startup-config*
    - **D.** *copy startup-config running config*

19. Which of the following is true about switches and hubs for network connectivity?
    - **A.** Switches increase the number of collision domains.
    - **B.** Hubs increase the number of collision domains.
    - **C.** Switches do not forward broadcasts.
    - **D.** Hubs dedicate more bandwidth per host than switches.

20. What will an Ethernet switch do when it receives a frame and the MAC address of the destination host is in the MAC address table?
    - **A.** The switch will forward the frame to all switchports except the source switchport.
    - **B.** The switch will forward the frame to the specific switchport.
    - **C.** The switch will drop the frame.
    - **D.** The switch will delete the MAC address from the MAC address table.

SELF TEST QUICK ANSWER KEY

1. B, and D	**8.** C, and E	**15.** A, and B
2. B	**9.** B	**16.** D
3. C	**10.** D	**17.** C
4. B	**11.** C	**18.** C
5. A, and D	**12.** C	**19.** A
6. B	**13.** A, D, and E	**20.** B
7. B	**14.** A	

Spanning-Tree Protocol

INTRODUCTION

This chapter will cover the Spanning-Tree Protocol (STP), how the protocol works, and consider its strengths and weaknesses. We'll see how the protocol has evolved in the past three decades to answer those weaknesses. The frames and timers that affect the operation of the STP will be described with an emphasis on the material Cisco requires that Cisco Certified Network Associate (CCNA) candidates understand. Finally, we'll discover what can go wrong in a network at Layer 2 (where STP operates) and see how to troubleshoot STP.

STP is an important topic for network engineers to understand because of the ubiquity of Ethernet itself. To put the subject of the chapter in a greater context, it is worthwhile to understand a bit about the history of Ethernet, especially the challenges faced by its designers.

By the early 1990s, Ethernet had emerged from the pack of competing standards to become the most widely deployed local-area network (LAN) technology. Even after IBM increased the speed of Token Ring to 16 Mbps, the performance benefits of switched Ethernet convinced many network managers to adopt it. As time passed, Ethernet's increasing speeds and cheaper hardware proved too compelling and Token Ring networks were largely replaced.

This competition between protocols came at a time when networks were getting larger and more important to the business. These trends drove two new challenges for networks: (1) additional bridges were added to support the growing number of hosts and (2) additional links between bridges were added to provide redundancy.

To deal with these issues, IBM proposed Source Route Bridging as the 802.5 standard. This protocol allowed parallel paths between bridges in the same LAN because the end host was responsible for selecting the path through the network. Ethernet faced the same problems and the 802.1d subcommittee was created to solve them. The outcome of that effort was transparent bridging and the original STP.

STP was invented by Dr. Radia Perlman, a network engineer at Digital Equipment Corporation in the late 1980s. Her contributions were so important that admirers honor Dr. Perlman, who now works for Sun Microsystems, by calling her "Mother of the Internet."

ETHERNET FRAME FORWARDING

Before we consider STP, it is essential to understand how frames are forwarded by transparent bridges (or switches which are simply multiport bridges). In this chapter, I'll use the terms bridge and switch interchangeably. Switches are not hubs. They do not simply flood an incoming frame mindlessly out every port. Rather, an Ethernet bridge is often called a "learning" bridge because it discovers on which segment a host resides by listening to incoming frames.

As a frame enters the switch, it records the source media access control (**MAC**) address and the receive port in the content-addressable memory (CAM) table. Cisco documentation also refers to the CAM as the "MAC forwarding table" and in Internet operating system (IOS) as "mac-address-table."

Figure 12.1 shows how the CAM table affects frame forwarding. If the switch knows that Fred is located off port 1, it can intelligently forward frames destined for Fred out port 1 without sending the frame out ports 2 and 3. If Katherine was sending frame to Fred, the switch would know that Fred is located off port 1, and it would know enough not to forward the frames to port 3, so Elizabeth would not need to receive them. This traffic segmentation is a big benefit to switched Ethernet.

During normal operation, a switch needs to continue learning about its environment. Hosts can not only join and leave the network but they can also move between segments on the network. For example, consider two wireless access points connected to two ports of the same switch. If a wireless host roams between the Access Points (APs), traffic coming from the host will be seen as moving between the switchports. The Ethernet network sees this traffic on the new port and overwrites the old CAM information (address/port) with the new information to reflect the new port where the host is located.

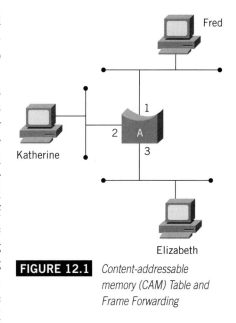

FIGURE 12.1 *Content-addressable memory (CAM) Table and Frame Forwarding*

If the switch does not know where host A is located, it floods the frame out all ports, except for the port where it received the frame. This behavior ensures that traffic destined to hosts that haven't yet transmitted on the network still reaches their destination. Broadcasts and multicasts are flooded too.

Exam Warning

It is important to understand the basic operation of frame flooding on an Ethernet switch. If the destination **MAC** address of the frame does not have an entry in the CAM table, the switch will flood the frame out each port except for the port where the frame was received. When virtual LANs (VLANs) are implemented, the frame is flooded out each port in the VLAN except for the port where the frame was received.

The switch also records a timestamp when the address/port entry was placed in the CAM. This is called the CAM aging time. Each time a frame is received that matches an existing CAM entry, the aging time is updated. If no new frame is received before the timestamp gets too old (the default is 5 minutes), the entry is removed from the CAM table. This process ensures the switch doesn't maintain old and possibly incorrect information in the forwarding table. For more practice with CAM tables and Ethernet forwarding, refer to Exercise 12.1.

EXERCISE 12.1   Understand How CAM Tables Affect Ethernet Frame Forwarding

Refer to Figure 12.1. For the following series of frames, I'll keep track of the CAM table of switch A. Then, I'll decide how the switch handles each frame—whether it is flooded or sent to a specific port. Assume all frames are unicast.

1. Fred sends a frame to Katherine.
   Source **MAC** of Fred is learned off port 1.
   No current CAM entry for Katherine, so frame flooded out port 2 and 3.

2. Katherine responds by sending a frame to Fred.
   Source **MAC** of Katherine is learned off port 2.
   CAM entry shows Fred off port 1, so frame is sent only to port 1.

3. Fred sends another frame to Katherine.
   CAM entry for Fred already exists, so the timestamp of the entry is updated.
   CAM entry shows Katherine off port 2, so frame is sent only to port 2.

Now create your own scenario. Draw a diagram of a switched network with multiple segments off each switch and multiple hosts off each segment. Come up with your own frame sequence and record how the switched network handles the frames.

Consider this—if Host1 and Host2 are both on the same segment (off the same port on the switch), how is a frame handled by the switch when it receives the frame? Answer—The switch creates a CAM entry with the source **MAC** of the sender (if necessary) and floods the frame out each of its ports (except for the port where it received the frame) if it doesn't have a CAM entry for the destination host. If it knows the destination is off the same port where it received the frame, the switch drops the frame.

The Problems with Loops in Ethernet Networks

If a switch does not have a CAM entry for the destination **MAC** address of an incoming frame, it is flooded out every port on the switch except for the port where the frame was received. While this flooding behavior ensures that frames reach their destination, it causes some very unpleasant results when parallel links are simultaneously forwarding frames.

Consider the Ethernet frame that consists of a preamble, destination, and source **MAC** addresses, protocol type field, data, and a frame check sequence (FCS). There is no "hop count" value to modify as the frame flows through the network. Bridging in Ethernet is "transparent," which means that the network makes no changes to the forwarded frame. Thus, a frame looks the same to a receiving bridge regardless of the number of times it has looped.

Exam Warning

It is a common misconception that frames are modified as they flow through a switch. This is true only if the packet is *routed*. A frame flowing through a switch or bridge at Layer 2 (from one port to another in the same VLAN) is not modified. The source and destination **MAC** addresses in the frame header are the same before and after the frame is forwarded.

In contrast, routing protocols implement some type of "hop count" check to ensure the network recognizes and properly handles looping frames. At each hop of the network, the packet is modified by the router. At some point, the routing protocol's concept of infinity (16 hops in Routing Information Protocol [RIP]) is breached and the packet is dropped.

Are bridge loops worse than routing loops? Absolutely! With a routing loop, a packet may loop forever, but there will only be one copy, whereas with a bridge loop, it is possible for frames to proliferate. Consider the looped topology in Figure 12.2 and keep in mind that the bridges don't know that the others exist. There is no "L2 routing protocol."

In this scenario, Fred is a network user who sends a frame to a previously unknown destination that is received by all three bridges. Each of the bridges receives the frame and updates their individual CAM tables to note that Fred can be found on the receiving port on segment 1. Then they queue the frame for transmission on segment 2. Let's say that Bridge A is the first to transmit the frame with no changes to segment 2. Bridges B and C hear the new frame and dutifully update their CAM table to say that Fred can now be found on segment 2, and queue the frame for transmission to segment 1.

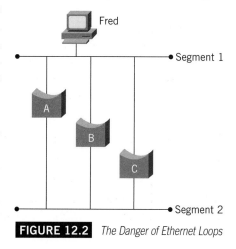

FIGURE 12.2   *The Danger of Ethernet Loops*

You can probably see where this is going. There was only a single frame sent by Fred, but the frame very quickly has multiplied as it loops between segments. The smallest Cisco Catalyst 2960 branch office edge switch has a forwarding rate of 2.7 million packets per second (mpps). In other words, this process is extremely fast. Loops crash networks! So that's why the STP goes to great lengths to build a loop-free topology.

WHAT IS A SPANNING TREE AND HOW DOES IT ELIMINATE LOOPS?

Remember that redundancy is good. It is essential to a well-designed network because it ensures that the network can stay up even as links and devices inevitably fail. So, STP has one goal of creating a fully-connected but loop-free topology. But what does this mean?

A network is similar to the mathematical concept of a connected graph. The "spanning tree" of a graph (network) is the collection of edges (links) that connect all the vertices (Ethernet bridges) without a cycle (loop). Consider the network with redundant links in Figure 12.3 and a spanning tree of that network in Figure 12.4.

Notice that the spanning tree of the graph is "fully-connected." There is no part of the graph that can't be reached from any other part of the graph. If you were a computer connected to one of the edges, you would be able to

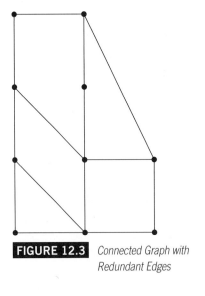

FIGURE 12.3   *Connected Graph with Redundant Edges*

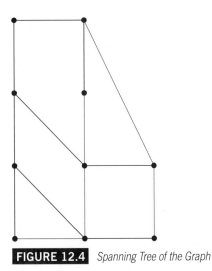

FIGURE 12.4   *Spanning Tree of the Graph*

successfully communicate to any other computer connected to any other edge. Also notice that the spanning tree is "loop-free." Between any two points on the network, there is only a single path through which the traffic flows.

The STP creates the "fully-connected and loop-free" topology (which is a fancy way of saying a subset of the network with these two properties) by finding loops and blocking interfaces. The original STP is very mature, widely implemented, robust, and vendor neutral. Now, we will dig into the protocol details. Before you move on, refer to Exercise 12.2 and try your hand at creating spanning trees and minimum spanning trees.

EXERCISE 12.2   Understand Spanning Trees

It is important for the CCNA candidate to understand what a spanning tree is and what function it performs. Draw your own connected graphs with redundant edges like Figure 12.3. Try to be creative in how the vertices are connected together. Now, draw the graph again as a spanning tree.

Once you're comfortable with that, make your graph more complex by adding more redundancy and more vertices (try 12). Note how much longer it takes you to find a spanning tree and consider how adding bridges and links add to the complexity of the STP algorithm in the network. This is the main reason why building in excessive redundancy to a network is not a good idea.

See if you can find more than one spanning tree in your graphs. A well-connected graph will have a number of spanning trees to choose from.

Finally, add a "weight" to each edge—just a number from 1 to 10. A minimum spanning tree is one with a weight equal or less than all the other possible spanning trees. Try to find the minimum spanning tree in several of your graphs.

STP: The Details

It is necessary for a bridge to understand enough about the rest of the network topology so that it can recognize when one of its ports is part of a loop. To do this, the STP chooses a single reference point in the network and then finds all redundant paths to that point. Once found, certain ports on redundant paths are blocked by the bridge so that a spanning tree is created; a fully-connected and loop-free topology. The reference point in the network is the root bridge.

Recall from "The Problems with Loops in Ethernet Networks" section that transparent bridges can't determine from a data frame whether it has passed through another bridge. Thus, there must be some "out of band" way for the bridges to communicate with each other (so they can gather the information necessary to find and prevent the loops).

This is accomplished with Bridge Protocol Data Units (Bpdus). These frames are sent by bridges to a well-known multicast address out each port every 2 seconds. All bridges that are running STP listen for this address and know to process the Bpdu. Unlike some multicast addresses, Bpdus are addressed to a link-local address. This means that the bridge does not forward the Bpdu to other ports. Thus, a bridge only communicates through Bpdus with its directly connected neighbor bridges.

> **Test Day Tip**
> Don't get bogged down in the details. A CCNA candidate is not expected to memorize the exact makeup of the Bpdu frame. Rather, focus on the fields that are meaningful to the STP algorithm, which are emphasized in this section.

Bpdus come in the following two types:

1. Configuration Bpdus

- Used by the bridge to build a spanning tree

2. Topology Change Notification (TCN) Bpdus

- Used by the bridge to advertise network changes

A Bpdu frame has a normal data link layer header. What makes the frame important is the data carried inside the Bpdu field. Figure 12.5 shows the elements that make up the Bpdu field that is carried inside the Bpdu frame.

There are a few of these elements that are important to understand before we move on. They are as follows:

- **Root ID** This field indicates the root bridge priority (a 2-byte value that can be administratively configured) and its' address, a 6-byte

Protocol Identifier (2 bytes)	Version (1 byte)	Message Type (1 byte)	Flags (1 byte)	Root ID (8 bytes)	Root Path Cost (4 bytes)	Bridge ID (8 bytes)	Port ID (2 bytes)	Message (2 bytes)	Max Age (2 bytes)	Hello Time (2 bytes)	Forwarding Delay (2 bytes)

FIGURE 12.5 Bpdu *Field*

value (48-bits) and is often a **MAC** address from one of the bridge's ports.

- **Root Path Cost** This field indicates the cost from the sending bridge to the root bridge.

- **Bridge ID** This field includes the sending bridge's priority and address.

Root Bridge Election

Surprisingly, these three pieces of information are all that are required for the STP to choose a root bridge and find all redundant paths in the network. It is called a "root" bridge because all paths on the spanning tree are rooted at that point. The root bridge is elected based on a comparison of the Bridge IDs of all the bridges in the network.

Whichever bridge has the *lowest* Bridge ID becomes the root bridge. Recall that the Bridge ID is the concatenation of the Bridge Priority (2 bytes) and a **MAC** address (6 bytes). It is important to remember that the Bridge Priority is the high-order bits of the ID, which means that it is more significant in the comparison.

In other words, the bridge with the lowest Bridge Priority becomes the root bridge. If the Bridge Priorities are equal, the switch with the lowest **MAC** address becomes the root bridge. Once you understand this concept, the actual election process is pretty simple.

> ### Exam Warning
> A common mistake is to think that the higher Bridge ID wins the root election. It is actually the *lowest* Bridge ID. And, the "most significant" part of the Bridge ID is the priority—so the *lowest* Bridge Priority yields the *lowest* Bridge ID. Only when the Bridge IDs are equal does the *lowest* **MAC** address make a difference in the root election. Don't forget that.

When it is powered on, each bridge assumes it is the root bridge. Before the switch starts receiving or sending any user traffic, it sends Bpdus to all its connected neighbors with its own priority and address in the Bridge ID and Root ID fields. At the same time, it's also listening to Bpdus sent by its neighbor bridges. If it receives a Bpdu with a lower Root ID, it substitutes the better Root ID for its own in the Bpdus it is sending out. Eventually, all the bridges have the same Root ID.

Once elected, the root bridge is the only one to originate configuration Bpdus. The rest of the bridges in the network simply replace the Bridge ID field with their own information and forward the Bpdu out all their ports. This has one very important effect on the STP—that the timers set on the root are used by all bridges throughout the network. You may have noticed that the Bpdu frame also includes timer values. Since the root bridge is the only one which originates configuration Bpdus, these timers are set on the root. How these values are set on the other bridges in the network is completely irrelevant.

What happens if a new bridge joins the network once the election is complete? The process runs all over again. It's probably obvious that, as a design goal, it is a good idea to minimize the number of times this process occurs in a production network.

Path Cost and Root Port Selection

Now that a root bridge has been elected, the STP needs to calculate the best path it has to the root. This requires a metric so that redundant paths (loops) can be compared and the least attractive path eliminated. That metric is the STP root Path Cost.

To build a meaningful root Path Cost, each port in the network is assigned a port cost. By default, this value is inversely proportional to the port bandwidth as shown in Table 12.1. The root Path Cost is actually the sum of all the port costs along the path toward the root. This calculation selects the best (lowest cost) path to the root.

There is a process by which the root Path Cost is built.

1. The root bridge advertises a root Path Cost of 0 in configuration Bpdus.

2. When the root's neighbor receives the Bpdu, it adds the receiving port's port cost to the root Path Cost.

3. Then the bridge forwards the Bpdu with the new root Path Cost to all its neighbors.

4. As the Bpdu flows downstream through the network, the root Path Cost grows at each subsequent bridge.

Table 12.1 Default STP Port Costs for Common Bandwidths

Port Speed	Default Port Cost
10 Mbps	100
100 Mbps	19
1 Gbps	4

A bridge in a well-connected network may receive many Bpdus. However, it knows that its best path to the root is through the port that receives the Bpdu with the lowest root Path Cost. This port is called the root port.

> **Exam Warning**
>
> The port cost of the *receiving* port is added to the root Path Cost before the Bpdu is sent along to the next switch. The port cost of the sending port is not involved in the calculation.

Designated Ports

What happens if a bridge receives a Bpdu with a higher root Path Cost on a nonroot port? In that case, the bridge knows there is a suboptimal path to the root bridge through that port. It also knows that two bridges serve this particular segment and both have a viable path to the root bridge. And finally, it knows there is a loop.

Only one port needs to forward traffic to and from this segment, so it is necessary to determine which of the bridges should perform this task. This is the job of the designated port.

The designated port is determined by comparing the root Path Cost. Whichever bridge advertises the port on the shared segment with a lower root Path Cost has the designated port for that segment. If the root Path Cost is equal, whichever bridge has the lower Bridge ID will have the designated port.

Because the root bridge will always (of course) have the lowest Path Cost to the root bridge, all the root bridge ports are designated ports.

Loop Elimination

Now that a root bridge has been elected, root ports on each switch have been selected, and designated ports chosen on each shared segment, it is time to get down to the business of blocking ports. The decision is relatively easy: All ports that are not a root port or a designated port are placed in the blocking state, which will be covered in the Port States and STP Timers section below. In this state, a port is not allowed to send or receive traffic. Thus, this ensures the loop is eliminated and a spanning-tree is the result.

This entire process is called "convergence." The time the network takes to converge depends on the number of bridges and links in the network. During convergence, the network does not forward user traffic because, as we have seen, it doesn't take long for a loop to bring down the network. So it should make sense that it is a good idea to limit the number of bridges and links in a network. This is one good reason to not over-engineer your network. Too much redundancy is not necessarily a good thing from a convergence standpoint.

The network pays a heavy price to ensure a loop-free topology. The original STP takes 50 seconds to recover from some link failures. That's obviously a very long time, but the time is justified because of how bad loops are to an Ethernet network. STP enhancements have made a lot of progress to speed convergence and keep our networks both loop-free and forwarding traffic.

Port States and STP Timers

Before we go through an example of STP in action, you need to understand how a bridge port progresses through a variety of states as the STP operates. A port is said to "transition" between states and the length of time that a port stays in a particular state is determined by the STP timers. There are five possible port states and three important timers.

The possible port states include the following:

- **Disabled** These are ports that are administratively shut down by a network administrator or are forced to the disabled state by the switch itself (perhaps as a result of a software feature, such as port security). In some environments, administrators prefer to keep all unused ports disabled as a security measure. This state is not really considered a part of the normal STP progression.

- **Blocking** Ports enter blocking state when they first come up or when STP needs to remove a link from the topology. While blocking, a port does not send or receive normal user frames and it does not learn **MAC** addresses to populate the CAM table. But in this state, the port can still receive Bpdus, but it does not send them.

- **Listening** In *listening* state, the port still cannot send or receive user frames. However, it can now both receive and send Bpdus (so it can fully participate in STP). It is in this state that a port can become a root or designated port, or the bridge may determines that the port needs to transition back to the blocking state.

- **Learning** Even in *learning* state, a port is unable to send and receive frames. However, the port is finally allowed to listen to the source addresses of incoming frames and populate its CAM table.

- **Forwarding** A port in *forwarding* state is both sending and receiving data. And, it is also sending and receiving Bpdus.

Test Day Tip

All the details of STP may at first seem overwhelming. However, if you have prepared yourself for the test by running through some scenarios as suggested by this chapter's exercises, you'll begin to see how the timers and port states work together. It is better to understand *why* a specific port needs to be blocking than to attempt to memorize everything.

It's very important to network stability that the network converges and guarantees a loop-free topology before ports transition to the *forwarding* state. So, the timers that control the protocol are important to the proper operation of the STP. The default timer values were selected by the 802.1d group to ensure that the protocol operates correctly. For full coverage of how the standards group arrived at these timers, read Radia Perlman's excellent book, *Interconnections: Bridges, Routers, Switches, and Internetworking Protocols* (2nd Edition) (ISBN: 978-0201634488). Dr. Perlman makes it clear that while it is possible to change these values, it is extremely unwise.

Recall from the introduction to STP: The Details section that the Configuration Bpdu sent by the root bridge control the timer values used by all the bridges on the network. The STP timers are as follows:

- **Hello Time** This value determines how often Bpdus are sent out. The default Hello Time is 2 seconds, but this can be tuned from 1 to 10 seconds.

- **Forward Delay** This value is the time a port spends in both the *listening* and *learning* states. The default Forward Delay is 15 seconds, but this can be tuned from 4 to 30 seconds.

- **Max Age** This value is the time that a bridge stores a copy of a Bpdu before throwing it away. If a bridge stops receiving Bpdu on a port, the Max Age is essentially the time that it takes the bridge to recognize that a topology change has occurred. The default Max Age is 20 seconds, but this can be tuned from 6 and 40 seconds.

THE OPERATION OF STP: PUTTING IT ALL TOGETHER

We will discuss STP operation by considering the network in Figure 12.6. This network is built from several bridges interconnected with redundant Ethernet links. You will notice that there are loops, which are useful in keeping the network operational in case a link or switch fails. Figure 12.7 is the spanning tree

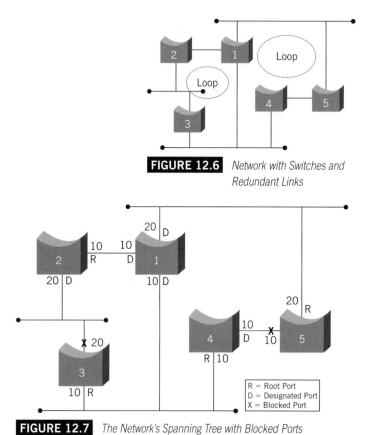

FIGURE 12.6 *Network with Switches and Redundant Links*

FIGURE 12.7 *The Network's Spanning Tree with Blocked Ports*

of the same network with the loops removed.

STP Operation at Initial Power Up

Assume that the devices in Figure 12.7 are coming up after a power failure. All bridges are now initializing. None of the bridges are administratively configured with a low priority, so the determination of a root bridge will be made on the basis of the lowest **MAC** address. All bridges begin by sending out configuration Bpdus, where they each advertise their own Priority and address in the Root ID field.

Bridge 2 receives a Bpdu from Bridge 1 on one port, and another from Bridge 3 on a different port. The Bpdu from Bridge 1 is "better" because 1 < 2 (assume here that the bridge number is equivalent to the MAC). Bridge 2 responds to this by sending out its next Bpdu to bridge 3 with Bridge 1's information in the Root ID field. Bridge 3 to 5 operate the same way, and very quickly all bridges accept the Bpdu from Bridge 1 as superior and it becomes the root bridge.

> **Test Day Tip**
> During the test, don't panic when faced with a network topology that you didn't consider during your preparation. STP operation isn't all that complicated once you know the basic rules. Simply relax and start running through the process from the beginning. Remember it's the same algorithm whether it operates on three switches or a hundred.

Once all bridges agree on a root, each must decide its best path to the root. As Bpdus are received, the Path Cost is calculated. Bridge 2 receives a Bpdu from Bridge 1 and the Path Cost is 10. Bridge 2 also receives a Bpdu from Bridge 3 and the Path Cost is 30 (the sum of the two costs of the "receive" ports—10 + 20). Bridge 2 then decides that the port which received the Bpdu with cost 10 is the root port.

Now, Bridges 2 and 3 need to decide which port on their shared segment should become the designated port. Bridge 2 sends its Bpdu to Bridge 3 with a root Path Cost of 10, since that's the sum of all the costs of the receive ports on the path to the root (which in this case is only one port). Bridge 3 sends its Bpdu to Bridge 2 with the same root Path Cost. Because these costs are equal, the bridge with the lowest Bridge ID has the designated port. Since the Priority of both bridges is equal (we stipulated that this was not manually configured earlier), the decision is based on their **MAC** address. The port on Bridge 2 becomes the designated port and the port on Bridge 3 transitions to the blocking state.

Bridges 4 and 5 need to make a similar decision on their shared segment. In this case, Bridge 5 advertises a root Path Cost of 20 to Bridge 4, and Bridge 4 advertises a root Path Cost of 10 to Bridge 5. This means that the port on Bridge 4 becomes the designated port and the port on Bridge 5 transitions to the blocking state.

Once this process takes place, the root and designated ports undergo transition through the *listening* and *learning* states, and finally transition to *forwarding*.

STP Operation after Link Failure

Let's cover what happens in the event of a link failure, considering the operational network that was just described in Figure 12.7. Assume the shared link connecting Bridge 5 to Bridge 1 has failed. As a result of this, Bridge 5 is isolated.

Even though the root bridge sends a Configuration Bpdu out every 2 seconds, Bridge 5 "remembers" the Bpdu it receives for the Max Age time: 20 seconds. So, it can take up to 20 seconds for Bridge 5 to even recognize anything is wrong. At this point, Bridge 5 transitions its blocked port toward Bridge 4 to *listening* state, where it remains for 15 seconds, then to *learning* state for another 15 seconds. Finally, Bridge 5 transitions the port to *forwarding* state and starts sending and receiving user traffic.

In this example, it has taken 50 seconds (20 + 15 + 15) for Bridge 5 to fully recover and for the STP to converge the network into a fully connected and loop-free topology.

Understanding how STP operates is really important and there is nothing better than practice to make the lesson stick. Refer to Exercise 12.3 for some ideas on how to test yourself.

EXERCISE 12.3   Practice, Practice, Practice

Build your own network similar to Figure 12.7. Start with a small number of switches and segments. Interconnect the switches so that you have some redundancy. After all, finding the spanning tree is no fun with no redundant links to disable! Add weights to each switch port and assign a number to each switch that you can use for its **MAC** address.

Once you have your topology, run through a few scenarios. For each scenario, run through the root election process, find the correct spanning tree, label all root and designated ports, and identify ports that will be blocked.

1. Assume no STP priority is configured and elect a root based on **MAC** address.

2. Pick a different switch (one-way off by itself) and assume it has the lowest **MAC** address.

3. Pick a switch and assume this has been administratively configured to be your root.

Now, take one of your completed scenarios and break a link. Run through the process as your network responds to the link failure. Try this multiple times with different links.

PROBLEMS WITH ORIGINAL STP AND SOLUTIONS

By now, the major problem with the original STP should be pretty obvious. Modern applications can't accommodate a 50-second outage as the network converges around a failure. Any voice over Internet Protocol (IP) call would certainly be dropped, web browsers would time out, storage area networking (SAN) traffic would cause errors, the support center would be flooded with calls, and the CIO would be calling you to figure out what the heck just happened.

STP Enhancements to Speed Convergence

Many multimedia applications (like voice and video over IP) require very strict service from the network in terms of availability and mean time to recovery (MTTR). These applications need very fast recovery (sometimes subsecond) and in the most extreme cases, nonstop forwarding.

But in the two decades following the STP adoption in 1990 as a standard, it wasn't always that way. The recovery time, although slow, was acceptable. Few business-critical applications were deployed that required fast recovery.

Email, one of the most popular applications, was not sensitive to short network outages.

As more and more applications came along that did need fast recovery, networking companies like Cisco responded with proprietary STP features that cut down on the convergence time. The most important STP features are *Backbonefast, Uplinkfast, Loopguard,* and *Unidirectional Link Detection* (UDLD).

Uplinkfast

The *Uplinkfast* feature was developed to speed convergence in a very common topology (an access switch with uplinks to two distribution-layer switches). As you know, one of these uplinks would be a root port and in *forwarding* state and one would be blocking. If the primary path to the root were to fail for any reason, the failure would need to be detected and the blocking port would need to undergo transition through *listening* and *learning* states (a potential 50-second outage).

Uplinkfast keeps track of all paths to the root bridge and all but the root port is kept in blocking state. If the primary path fails, the next-best path transitions immediately to the *forwarding* state. This was a major improvement over the original STP, which is why a very similar procedure was built into the next generation protocol.

> **Exam Warning**
>
> *Uplinkfast* keeps track of *all* paths to the root, not just a single backup path. The only blocked ports that are not included in the "uplink group" are ones that are self-looped, which means that the port does not provide an alternate path to the root. The lower right switch in Figure 12.8 is self-looped.

Uplinkfast should not be used on a root bridge or on switches that serve as a transit path to the root for other switches. To ensure this, when configured, *Uplinkfast* makes a few changes in the background. To influence root bridge selection, the *Uplinkfast* switch's Bridge Priority is changed to 49,152. The default Bridge Priority for Cisco switches is 32,768, so *Uplinkfast* makes it very unlikely that the switch will become the root. To stop transit traffic, the port cost of all ports is increased by 3000, which makes the path through the *Uplinkfast* switch undesirable.

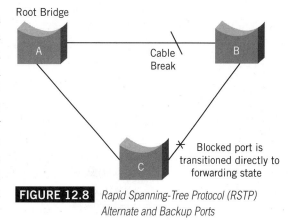

FIGURE 12.8 *Rapid Spanning-Tree Protocol (RSTP) Alternate and Backup Ports*

This feature is enabled globally, not on an individual port. This means that when *Uplinkfast* is configured, it is operational for all VLANs defined on the switch. To enable *Uplinkfast*, the syntax is as follows:

```
Switch(config)# spanning-tree uplinkfast
```

Cisco recommends that *Uplinkfast* not be used on switches that have more than 20 VLANs, because the convergence times can become unacceptable. Refer to this URL for more information—www.cisco.com/en/US/tech/tk389/tk621/technologies_tech_note09186a0080094641.shtml.

Backbonefast

Backbonefast feature speeds convergence in the event of an "indirect" link failure, as shown in Figure 12.9. A failure is indirect when it occurs on a link that is not directly connected to the switch. In Figure 12.9, from Bridge C's perspective, the failure of the AB link is indirect.

Assume that the AB link fails. B would recognize the link failure immediately. Since it has no alternate path (because C's port is blocking), Bridge B considers itself the new root and sends out Bpdus that are received by Bridge C. These Bpdus are not superior to the root's Bpdus, so Bridge C drops them. Bridge C remembers the Bpdus it receives on a port for Max Age (20 seconds). When link AB was up, Bridge B was relaying root Bpdus to Bridge C, which kept that port blocked. When the link fails, Bridge B no longer relays these Bpdus, but Bridge C won't recognize this for Max Age seconds. Once that happens, Bridge C begins sending out Bpdus from the root to Bridge B. After that, Bridge C transitions the previously blocked port through *listening* and *learning* states (another 30 seconds).

The *Backbonefast* feature doesn't eliminate all the delay, but it is capable of eliminating the Max Age wait, which drops the maximum convergence time from 50 to 30 seconds. That's not as dramatic a decrease as provided by *Uplinkfast*, but every little bit helps minimize those support calls.

With this feature enabled, a switch recognizes an indirect link failure through the reception of an inferior Bpdu and it can respond immediately. *Backbonefast* uses a Root Link Query (RLQ) protocol to check the other possible paths to the root bridge. This protocol uses a

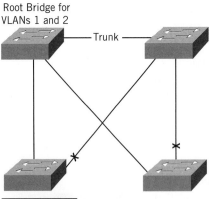

Root Bridge for VLANs 1 and 2

Trunk

FIGURE 12.9 Backbonefast

request/response frame exchange to probe upstream switches to determine if their path to the root bridge is viable. For this reason, for *Backbonefast* to function properly, it must be enabled on every switch in the network.

Backbonefast is configured globally. To enable the feature, this syntax is as follows:

```
Switch(config)# spanning-tree backbonefast
```

Portfast

Cisco released the *Portfast* feature to deal with startup problems related to STP's long delay in transitioning a port to the *forwarding* state. Using the default timers, it takes 30 seconds for a port to move through *listening* and *learning* states. This delay proved too long for some operating systems, causing Dynamic Host Configuration Protocol (DHCP) problems, Microsoft networking failures, and various IBM, AppleTalk, and Internetwork Packet Exchange (**IPX**) errors.

The basic idea behind *Portfast* is that it is unnecessary to wait for STP to determine that a new port doesn't create a loop if you know for sure that the port is connected to an end device. *Portfast* moves a newly connected port to the *forwarding* state, bypassing the *listening* and *learning* states. Because of this, it's important that administrators know where to configure this feature.

Portfast should only be configured on ports that connect to "leaf nodes," which are workstations or servers with a single NIC, IP phones, routers, and so forth. Never configure *Portfast* on a port connected to another switch or hub.

There is another often-overlooked benefit of *Portfast*. When a port first comes up, the switch sends a TCN Bpdu to the root. When it reaches the root, this frame causes the root to temporarily drop the CAM timeout from 5 minutes to 15 seconds. The intention is for the network to quickly age out CAM entries in order to properly route traffic after a topology changes. However, if it is an end-station joining the network there is no need for this. *Portfast* eliminates the TCN Bpdu.

Portfast is disabled by default on switch ports. It is enabled in *port configuration* mode with the following syntax:

```
Switch(config-if)# spanning-tree portfast
```

Portfast can also be enabled globally on all ports:

```
Switch(config)# spanning-tree portfast default
```

Exam Warning

When *Portfast* is enabled globally, it is very important to disable *Portfast* on any ports connected to switches and hubs. There are two things to keep in mind:

1. Disable *Portfast* on uplink ports *before* the feature is enabled globally to ensure that no loops form.

2. It is a common mistake to simply remove the *portfast* command on a port with "no spanning-tree portfast" and think it is disabled. This isn't the case. To disable *Portfast* on the port, use the following command:

```
Switch(config-if)# spanning-tree portfast disable
```

These STP features are so widely used that it's important for any network engineer to understand when and where they are deployed. Refer to Exercise 12.4 for additional practice.

EXERCISE 12.4   Implementing STP Features

Refer back to your networks built in Exercise 12.3. One suggestion was to break a link, running through the STP convergence process. Take this to the next level by trying the following:

1. Figure out how long it would take for your network to converge using the default STP timers.

2. Identify where you would implement the STP features *Backbonefast*, *Uplinkfast*, and *Portfast*.

3. Run through the link recovery process again and determine how long it would take the network to converge using these features.

STP Enhancements for Stability

Slow STP convergence was not the only problem with the original STP. Since Bpdu frames aren't authenticated, security can be compromised if a nefarious host began sending Bpdus with values "superior" to the current root. Some way was needed to ensure the root of the STP could not be hijacked in this way. *Bpdu Guard* and *Rootguard* perform this function. Other features were aimed at ensuring that unidirectional links (something that became especially important as Ethernet over fiber became popular) would not cause loops. *Loopguard* and UDLD addressed this concern. The following is an overview of each of these features.

Bpdu Guard

When *Portfast* is configured on an end host port, the switch should never receive a Bpdu on that port. If someone inadvertently connects a switch or hub to this port, *Portfast* is intelligent enough to understand that a mistake has been made. After receiving a Bpdu, *Portfast* immediately puts the port in *blocking* mode and transitions the port to *listening* mode, essentially disabling *Portfast* automatically.

Some administrators would prefer that the port stay disabled, so that the configuration error can be corrected by either recabling the new switch to a non-*Portfast* port or reconfiguring the port as an uplink. When configured, *Bpdu Guard* listens for Bpdus on a *Portfast*-enabled port. If one is received, the feature immediately puts the port in *errDisabled* state. It is necessary for an administrator to reenable the port once this occurs. This is done by performing a "shutdown" and "no shutdown" on the port in *interface configuration* mode.

Like *Portfast*, *Bpdu Guard* can be enabled on an individual port or globally. To enable the feature on a specific port, this syntax is as follows:

```
Switch(config-if)# spanning-tree bpduguard enable
```

To enable *Bpdu Guard* globally, the syntax is as follows:

```
Switch(config)# spanning-tree portfast bpduguard default
```

Rootguard

The placement of the root bridge in a network is an important design decision. A poorly placed root bridge can result in extra hops as traffic traverses the network, which uses resources unnecessarily and increases latency. In the worst cases, a misplaced root can cause network instability if links that connect the root to the rest of the LAN tend to flap.

These potential problems cause many network managers to select a root that is well connected and near the "middle" of the LAN. This is accomplished normally by administratively setting the preferred root bridge's priority to a value lower than the other bridges in the network. However, what happens if a new bridge is introduced into the network that has a Bridge Priority that is even lower than what is configured on the root? The normal operation of STP will be to elect the new bridge as root.

To stop this, *Rootguard* is used to define on which ports a bridge should see the root bridge. Once configured on a port, if a bridge receives a Bpdu on that port where the Bridge ID is better than the root bridge, the port is placed in root-inconsistent state. In this state, traffic is not sent or received but the port continues to listen for Bpdus. The port will recover (by the normal transitioning through the STP states to *forwarding* mode) as soon as the Bpdus seen on the port change so that they are not superior to the root bridge.

This feature is best used on ports where you know there is not a path back to the root bridge. *Rootguard* is disabled by default. It is enabled on the port using the following syntax:

```
Switch(config-if)# spanning-tree guard root
```

Loopguard and UDLD

Loopguard and UDLD features are similar in that they both detect loops caused by unidirectional links. STP's standard loop prevention measures require two-way communications between bridges on each end of the link. However, if the link or port is faulty and only carries traffic in one direction, STP is unable to detect and eliminate the loop.

Loopguard should be configured on root or blocking ports (in other words, nondesignated ports). These ports are normally expected to receive Bpdus. This feature monitors the Bpdus, and if they suddenly stop, *Loopguard* transitions the port to "loop inconsistent" state and no traffic is passed. *Loopguard* should not be used on the same port as *Rootguard* or on *Portfast* or channeling ports.

Loopguard can be enabled globally and when this is done, the feature is intelligent enough to activate only on the correct ports. To enable the feature on a specific port, this syntax is as follows:

```
Switch(config-if)# spanning-tree guard loop
```

To enable *Loopguard* globally, the syntax is as follows:

```
Switch(config)# spanning-tree loopguard default
```

UDLD performs the same function as *Loopguard*, but in a very different way. UDLD builds a neighbor relationship with another directly connected bridge using UDLD frames that are supposed to be echoed back to the originating bridge. If the frame returns, the link is bidirectional. If the link was bidirectional and suddenly the frames are no longer returned, the link has become unidirectional.

What happens next is based on how UDLD is configured. In *Normal* mode, a syslog is generated and the port is allowed to continue passing user traffic. In *Aggressive* mode, the port is forced to *errDisabled* state and administrative access is required to bring the port back online.

Because UDLD requires a neighboring bridge to echo the UDLD frames, both devices need to have the UDLD enabled. Like the *Loopguard*, UDLD can be configured globally or on a specific port. To enable the feature on a specific port, this syntax is as follows:

```
Switch(config-if)# udld port {aggressive}
```

To enable UDLD globally, the syntax is as follows:

```
Switch(config)# udld port {aggressive | enable}
```

It is also possible to configure the message time, which controls how often UDLD messages are exchanged between bridges. The idea is to ensure UDLD handles the error condition before STP can transition the port to *forwarding* state. Like most other STP timers, it is unwise to change the default (which is 15 seconds) unless you fully understand the effect of the change.

STP PROTOCOL EVOLUTION

Nearly two decades has passed since 802.1d was completed and networks have changed a lot. Network hardware back then didn't support logical networks (VLANs), so STP ran on a single flat network. When VLANs were first introduced, STP could be still used to ensure a loop-free topology but was originally implemented as a "common spanning tree" (CST). In other words, a single instance of the spanning tree was used for the entire network. The main problem with a CST is that only a single Layer 2 topology is used.

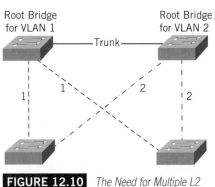

FIGURE 12.10 *The Need for Multiple L2 Topologies*

Consider the common network layout shown in Figure 12.10. VLANs 1 and 2 are defined on each switch and there are trunks carrying both VLANs throughout the network. Imagine if a single CST were used in this redundant configuration. A single root bridge would be selected and two links would be blocked to eliminate the loops. The traffic from both VLANs would flow through the same physical links while half the network sits idle.

Compare the CST with Figure 12.11, where a separate instance of the STP is run for each VLAN. All ports are still trunks but a single VLAN can be blocked on the trunk, allowing all network devices to be fully utilized. Here, there are two topologies: one for VLAN 1 and a completely different one for VLAN 2.

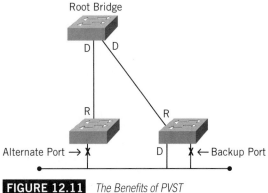

FIGURE 12.11 *The Benefits of PVST*

There are two types of Per-VLAN Spanning Tree (PVST) and both are Cisco proprietary. PVST uses Inter-Switch Link (ISL) trunking to carry VLANs between switches. PVST+ is the same as PVST but uses 802.1q as the trunking protocol. PVST+ is the default implementation on Cisco switches.

Rapid Spanning-Tree Protocol (802.1w)

STP's next generation came about when the Rapid Spanning-Tree Protocol (RSTP) was adopted by the Institute of Electrical and Electronics Engineers (IEEE) in 1998. The protocol is now part of 802.1d-2004 available from http://standards.ieee.org/getieee802/. The primary motivation behind RSTP development was the need for faster convergence. Where it can take up to 50 seconds for STP to respond to a topology change in the network, RSTP can often converge in approximately 1 second. Cisco's implementation of RSTP implements one spanning tree instance per VLAN, just like the original STP.

> **Test Day Tip**
> The CCNA objectives focus on RSTP rather than the original STP. However, it's not possible to understand RSTP without the background. So, keep this in mind during the test when faced with a question. Make sure you read the question carefully to ensure you are thinking about the right protocol.

Because of the need for RSTP to be backwards compatible with STP, much of the STP terminology and parameters are unchanged. This makes it relatively easy for anyone familiar with STP to configure and troubleshoot an RSTP network, without the need to tweak timers or configure any of the proprietary STP features.

New RSTP port states

Although STP has four port states, RSTP has only three and they are easier to learn because the state is based on what the port actually does. Compare this to standard STP where there is little difference between *listening* and *blocking* states in terms of what the port is actually doing. The RSTP states are as follows:

- **Discarding** This state corresponds to STP's disabled, *blocking* and *listening* states. In *discarding* state, the port is not learning **MAC** addresses.

- **Learning** This state is the same as STP's *learning* state.

- **Forwarding** This state is the same as STP's *forwarding* state.

New RSTP port roles

The root and designated port roles are the same in STP and RSTP. The difference between the protocols is the ports that would end up in STP's *blocking* state. In RSTP, these ports become either a backup port or an alternate port. Recall that a blocked port in STP is on a shared segment, where two or more bridges share a link. One of these ports is the designated port and the other is in the *blocking* state.

An alternate port has a viable albeit suboptimal path (based on root Path Cost) to the root bridge and can therefore take over for the root port if that path fails. Alternate ports operate very much like *Uplinkfast*. When a root port fails on a bridge, the alternate port can be transitioned immediately to the *forwarding* state without worrying that this creates a loop.

An RSTP backup port can't guarantee a unique path to the root bridge. It knows this because it is receiving "better" Bpdus from itself (recall that this can be based on a lower port priority or **MAC** address). This is also called a "self-looped" port. Figure 12.8 shows both an alternate and backup port.

RSTP uses the same process to create a spanning tree as 802.1d. How port priorities and Path Costs are used to build the topology is exactly the same. This enables RSTP to interoperate with standard 802.1d devices; however, the convergence benefits of RSTP are lost, but only for that portion of the network.

Bpdu Processing in RSTP

There are a few significant changes to the way Bpdus are used in RSTP. The frame format is the same, except that the flag byte in the original frame is now used to provide additional information to bridges receiving the Bpdu. This includes data used to tell the neighboring bridge the role and state of the port that originated the Bpdu. That may seem odd for those who know 802.1d. In the original STP, only the root bridge normally generated Bpdus (the other bridges simply forwarded the one received from the root). In RSTP, each bridge sends Bpdus every hello-time, which is still 2 seconds by default.

Even though there is no formal neighbor relationship between bridges, the Bpdus now serve as a keepalive. When a bridge fails to receive a Bpdu on a *discarding* port for three hello intervals (6 seconds), it can immediately respond to the link failure. This can happen even faster if there is a hardware indication of the outage, such as the interface going down. Part of the response to the failure is the fast aging of information in the CAM table. Remember that a discarding port requires the constant reception of Bpdus from its neighbor to stay in *discarding* state.

RSTP also changes how inferior Bpdus are handled. Recall from the previous section on Port States and STP Timers that in the original STP, a port remembers for Max Age seconds the Bpdu it receives on a port. *Backbonefast* was used to eliminate this wait when an indirect link fails. This capability is now built into the protocol itself.

Refer back to Figure 12.9. With RSTP, a bridge no longer discards an inferior Bpdu it receives on a blocking port as was the case for Bridge C. Instead, this Bpdu is immediately accepted and replaces the previous Bpdu. Since Bridge C still has a viable path to the root, this can be immediately advertised to the downstream Bridge B, which can immediately accept it.

Fast Network Convergence with RSTP

Bpdu handling alone can't provide the performance gain achieved by RSTP. What's needed is an aggressive protocol that knows more about the network and can transition to a loop-free topology after a topology change without requiring multiple timers to expire.

This added awareness comes from multiple sources. The first is a familiar source: the *Portfast* port configuration. The Cisco feature *Portfast* causes end host ports to transition immediately to *forwarding* state. In addition, port transitions on *Portfast* ports don't generate TCNs. RSTP uses the feature in a similar way and calls these "Edge ports."

RSTP also makes some assumptions about the link type based on the operational duplex of the port. Ports running in *full-duplex* mode are assumed to be point-to-point links, and half-duplex ports are assumed to be shared links. This seems reasonable, but the default behavior can be overridden if necessary on a port-by-port basis. If, for example, you require a half-duplex uplink to a switch, the port can be configured as a *point-to-point* interface. Or, if you know for sure that a shared segment does not contain a bridge, the port can be configured as a *point-to-point* interface.

These new bits of information combine with an operation called "sync" to enable quick convergence. The sync operation is only possible on point-to-point links and involves a negotiation between bridges. When a bridge receives a better Bpdu on a new port (meaning that a new path to the Root has become available), the sync process allows the bridge to negotiate with its upstream neighbor to allow that bridge to immediately place its port in *forwarding* state.

It can do this safely because the bridge has placed its downstream ports in *discarding* state, except those that are Edge ports.

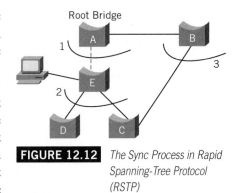

This cascading process continues downstream away from the root until there are no more non-Edge ports. What results is a topology that is exactly the same that is achieved

FIGURE 12.12 *The Sync Process in Rapid Spanning-Tree Protocol (RSTP)*

by the original STP, but without waiting on timers. It is a worthwhile exercise to create a few convergence scenarios to convince yourself that the resulting topology of STP and RSTP is the same.

Figure 12.12 shows how the RSTP convergence process works when a new link is added. Assume that the AE link is added to the topology. When connected, the new ports on both A and E are placed in *blocking* state. When E receives its first Bpdu (called a proposal) from the root, it knows that this new link has a better root Path Cost than its previous root port, so it places its non-Edge ports in *blocking* state. Then, E sends an agreement Bpdu to the root and asks it to unblock its port. Now, both ports on AE can be immediately transitioned to *forwarding* state.

This proposal/agreement process repeats with each link downstream. The decision on which port to block above would depend on the root Path Cost advertised by E toward C, compared to the root Path Cost advertised by B toward C. If EC is superior, then C's uplink to E would become its root port with the other port becoming an alternate port.

EXERCISE 12.5   Moving To RSTP

Refer back yet again to the networks you built in Exercise 12.3. Your work so far has been with 802.1d STP. Take the same networks and implement RSTP. Consider the following questions.

1. How would your topology change between 802.1d and 802.1w?

2. Which of your blocking ports would become alternate and which would become backup ports?

3. Assume one of your links fails. How would RSTP speed convergence by not discarding inferior Bpdus? Does this speed convergence in all cases? If not, when does it help?

4. Determine which ports in your network would be Edge ports and which ones would be point-to-point. Why?

5. Assume a link failure and run through the RSTP sync process. Think about which devices would be affected by the convergence and which wouldn't be affected. How is this different from 802.1d? Does the convergence yield the same topology as 802.1d?

Multiple Spanning-Tree Protocol (802.1s)

Rapid STP works well in many networks. But, as the number of VLANs increase, the resources needed for the switch to maintain an STP instance per VLAN can become a problem. Multiple Spanning-Tree Protocol (MSTP) solves this problem by bringing back the concept of a CST, but with a twist. This protocol was originally defined by IEEE as 802.1s and later incorporated in 802.1Q-2003. Most networks that require lots of VLANs don't have a unique topology per VLAN. Rather, they have a small number of topologies (often two) and many VLANs that map onto these.

Exam Warning

The number of different STP "instances" with 802.1s depends on the number of different topologies that are desired. In practice, there are usually two or three spanning trees when using MST, and all VLANs are mapped onto these. The big benefit is very low STP overhead for a large number of VLANs.

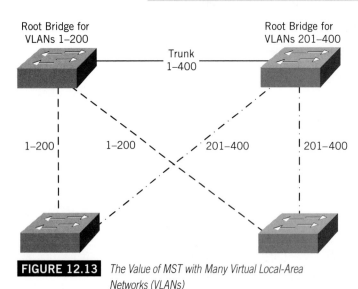

Root Bridge for
VLANs 1–200

Root Bridge for
VLANs 201–400

Trunk
1–400

1–200   1–200   201–400   201–400

For example, consider the network shown in Figure 12.13. All links trunk VLANs 1–400. One bridge is the root for VLANs 1–200, and the other is root for VLANs 201–400. In this case, there are two topologies.

With a Per-VLAN STP, there would be 400 instances of STP running on each switch. With MST, there would be two (one for each topology). As you can see, MST scales much better than PVST does.

FIGURE 12.13   *The Value of MST with Many Virtual Local-Area Networks (VLANs)*

RSTP CONFIGURATION

The configurations of STP and Rapid STP are very similar and deceptively simple. PVST+ is enabled by default on VLAN 1 on Cisco switches, which ensures a loop-free network out-of-the-box. The configuration only gets challenging when the protocol is tweaked by implementing features and modifying timers. We've already seen how features are enabled both globally and on individual ports. This section will discuss how the protocol is configured and how timers can be changed.

Selecting the *protocol* Mode and Other Global Settings

The first step in configuring STP is to decide which version of spanning tree will be run on the switch. This decision affects all VLANs on the switch. In other words, PVST+ can't be used for some VLANs, while MST or Rapid STP is used for others. If RSTP is the configured mode, then this protocol is used for all VLANs on the switch. The default is PVST+. To change the *STP* mode to Rapid STP, the syntax is as follows:

```
Switch(config)# spanning-tree mode rapid-pvst
```

The Root ID and Bridge ID are 8 bytes (64-bits), made up of a 2-byte priority and a 6-byte (48-bits) address, which is often a **MAC** address from one of the bridge's ports. In older versions of software (prior to Release 12.1(8a) E), the priority could assume any value in the range 0 to 65,535. This was because all the bits of the priority were used for the priority value.

Later versions of IOS took some bits from the priority field and used them to allow support for "extended" Ethernet VLANs (those between 1006 and 4094). Prior to this, only "normal" VLANs were allowed (those between 2 and 1001). To configure extended VLANs, the STP needs to be configured to support a 12-bit extended system ID. This is accomplished with the following syntax:

```
Switch(config)# spanning-tree extend system-id
```

Some devices (like the 7600) always run with an extended system-id, so there is no need to enable it on these devices.

Changing STP Timers

Making changes to STP timers is normally a terrible idea. The protocol is tuned to produce predictable results. Although changing timers may provide a slight improvement in convergence, the risk of catastrophic network failure normally outweighs the benefits. The convergence benefits of RSTP have made tweaking the timers much less necessary. Having said that, here's how to change the timers!

Although the STP timers can be changed on any switch, only the timers defined on the root bridge are used. Because each VLAN has its own instance of STP (regardless if it is the original STP or Rapid STP), the timers are specified along with the VLAN to which they apply. There are three configurable timers:

- **Forward Time** This is the duration of the *listening* and *learning* states. The default is 15 seconds.

```
Switch(config)# spanning-tree vlan <vlan> forward-time
```

- **Hello Time** This is interval between Bpdus. The default is 2 seconds.

```
Switch(config)# spanning-tree vlan <vlan> hello-time
```

- **Max Age** This is the length of time a bridge remembers a Bpdu. The default is 30 seconds.

```
Switch(config)# spanning-tree vlan <vlan> max-age
```

Affecting the STP Topology

There are good reasons to change the default values that affect the root bridge election process. It is almost always a good idea to administratively configure a primary and backup root bridge in the network. This ensures that the selected bridge is centrally located, well-connected, and properly protected (power, physical security, and so forth). Using the default values, it is always possible that a poorly selected bridge can be elected. If the bridge that advertises the best Bridge ID just because it has the lowest **MAC** address happens to be connected to a failing **uninterruptible power supply (UPS)**, the network would be unstable when the switch bounced.

Test Day Tip

When faced with a scenario to build or troubleshoot STP, it's best to read the question completely before jumping into the configuration. Know in advance exactly what you are trying to accomplish. You may even want to take a few notes while reading the scenario to make sure you satisfy all the question's requirements. Finally, go over the question again after you're done to make sure you've not missed anything.

The comparison of Bridge IDs is what influences the root bridge election. Whichever bridge has the *lowest* Bridge ID becomes the root bridge. Also recall that the Bridge ID is built from the Bridge Priority and a **MAC** address, with the Bridge Priority being the most significant. In other words, even though it is possible to change the **MAC** address used by STP, the better way to force a root bridge election is by lowering the Bridge Priority.

This is easily accomplished in two ways. The most direct way is to manually configure the Bridge Priority using the following command:

```
Switch(config)# spanning-tree vlan <vlan> priority <0-61440>
```

The priority value should be in multiples of 4096, so you can start at 4096 for the preferred root, 8192 for the preferred backup, and so forth. Setting the priority to 0 ensures that the bridge will never be the root.

This sets the priority directly, but you must know what other priorities are used on the network to ensure that you use the lowest value on the preferred root bridge, and the next lowest value on the backup root bridge. In practice, this isn't normally a problem. If you leave all other switches at their default value (32768 in most cases), selecting the correct values is easy.

If you don't know what priorities are used on the various bridging devices on your network, Cisco has included a macro command that configures the root based on what the bridge knows about the Bridge Priority of the current root bridge. The macro is run using the following syntax:

```
Switch(config)# spanning-tree vlan <vlan> root [primary |
    secondary]
```

Although the macro will guarantee that the bridge takes on the proper priority to assume the correct role in the network, it does not guarantee that no other switch will ever be introduced that will select a priority even lower. The macro run is a one-time event, it doesn't recheck periodically to ensure no other bridge joins with a lower value. To keep the root in place, use the *Rootguard* feature.

RSTP Interoperability with 802.1d STP

While it would be desirable to run a single STP network wide, it is often impossible to do so. Some older Cisco switches support only PVST+ (for example, Cisco 2900XL), whereas most new models support all modes (for example, Catalyst 4500 or 6500). The IEEE 802.1w committee considered the widespread use of legacy devices in networks and interoperability was built in to the new protocol.

Rapid STP is able to work with 802.1d STP, but some of the benefits are lost. This is a good thing because 802.1d bridges drop the Bpdus they receive from RSTP bridges. Each port on an RSTP bridge can determine the *spanning tree* mode running on its own segment. It does this by using a 3-second migration delay timer that starts each time a port comes up.

When the migration timer expires, the switch listens for the next Bpdu on that segment and will adjust its *STP* mode to correspond to the received Bpdu. If the bridge does change modes as a result of hearing a Bpdu, it reruns the timer. This makes sure the bridge is not flapping between modes if it hears a variety of Bpdus on the segment.

The important thing to remember about this is that when 802.1d and RSTP bridges share a segment, the RSTP bridge adjusts the spanning tree mode it runs on that port only. So, while there is a loss of fast convergence when interworking with a legacy device, it is limited to only devices downstream off that port.

RSTP Sample Configurations

The next section will show configurations of a simple network shown in Figure 12.14. In this environment, there are two distribution layer switches and two access layer switches, one running RSTP and another running 802.1d STP. Two VLANs are defined and trunked throughout the network, with RSTP used to balance the traffic load between the switches.

The following are the STP configurations of the two distribution layer switches Dist_1 and Dist_2. The example comes from WS-C4507R switches running 12.2(31)SGA. They are nearly identical except for the administratively configured spanning tree priorities, which set the root of each VLAN. Dist_1 will be the root of VLAN 10 and Dist_2 will be the backup root. Dist_2 will be the root of VLAN 20 and Dist_1 will be the backup root. Note that *Portfast* is not enabled by default on these switches so the feature doesn't need to be administratively disabled on the uplinks. Note also that since *Portfast* is not configured, *Bpdu guard* is unnecessary. Normal-mode UDLD is enabled globally.

On Switch Dist_1, we find the following configuration.

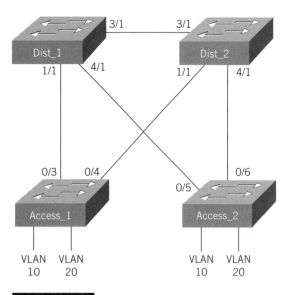

FIGURE 12.14   *Sample Configurations*

```
Dist_1#show running-config
   Building configuration…
   !
   spanning-tree mode rapid-pvst
   spanning-tree extend system-id
   udld enable
   spanning-tree vlan 10 priority 4096
   spanning-tree vlan 20 priority 8192
   !
   vlan 10,20
!
interface GigabitEthernet1/1
   description Uplink to Access_1
   switchport trunk encapsulation dot1q
   switchport trunk allowed vlan 10,20
   switchport mode trunk
!
interface GigabitEthernet3/1
   description Uplink to Dist_2
   switchport trunk encapsulation dot1q
   switchport trunk allowed vlan 10,20
   switchport mode trunk
!
interface FastEthernet4/1
   description Uplink to Access_2
   switchport trunk encapsulation dot1q
   switchport trunk allowed vlan 10,20
   switchport mode trunk
!
end
```

On switch Dist_2, we find the following configuration.

```
Dist_2#show running-config
Building configuration…
!
spanning-tree mode rapid-pvst
spanning-tree extend system-id
udld enable
!
spanning-tree vlan 10 priority 8192
spanning-tree vlan 20 priority 4096
!
vlan 10,20
!
```

```
interface GigabitEthernet1/1
   description Uplink to Access_1
   switchport trunk encapsulation dot1q
   switchport trunk allowed vlan 10,20
   switchport mode trunk
!
interface GigabitEthernet3/1
   description Uplink to Dist_1
   switchport trunk encapsulation dot1q
   switchport trunk allowed vlan 10,20
   switchport mode trunk
!
interface FastEthernet4/1
   description Uplink to Access_2
   switchport trunk encapsulation dot1q
   switchport trunk allowed vlan 10,20
   switchport mode trunk
!
end
```

Access_1 is a WS-C3560-48PS running 12.2(44)SE1 with a default Bridge Priority of 32868. Gig0/3 will be the root port of VLAN 10 and Gig0/4 will be the root port of VLAN 20. The other VLANs in the trunks will be in the *blocking* state and will be RSTP alternate ports, which can be enabled immediately if the root port fails for any reason. The *Rootguard* feature is enabled on non-uplink ports. *Loopguard*, *Portfast*, and *Bpdu Guard* are all enabled globally. Because *Portfast* is enabled globally, it must be specifically disabled on the uplinks.

On switch Access_1, we find the following configuration.

```
Access_1#show running-config
   Building configuration…
!
spanning-tree mode rapid-pvst
spanning-tree extend system-id
spanning-tree portfast bpduguard default
spanning-tree portfast default
spanning-tree loopguard default
udld enable
!
vlan 10,20
!
interface GigabitEthernet0/3
   description Uplink to Dist_1
   switchport trunk encapsulation dot1q
   switchport trunk allowed vlan 10,20
```

```
   switchport mode trunk
   spanning-tree portfast disable
!
interface GigabitEthernet0/4
   description Uplink to Dist_2
   switchport trunk encapsulation dot1q
   switchport trunk allowed vlan 10,20
   switchport mode trunk
   spanning-tree portfast disable
!
interface GigabitEthernet0/24
   description End Host
   spanning-tree guard root
!
end
```

Access_2 is a legacy WS-C2924-XL running 12.0(5)WC11. The 802.1d STP enabled by default and there is no command to change the mode like on the other switches. There is an *STP* command that allows you to select between the IBM and IEEE versions of 802.1d. IEEE is the default. The Default Bridge Priority is 49152, so there is no hope that this switch would become the root. The older switches use the "vlan database" interactive command to create VLANs, so they do not appear in the config. *Uplinkfast* is enabled because that feature will enable faster convergence if the root port fails, even in a mixed configuration. This switch doesn't support an extended system-id, so no Ethernet VLAN over 1001 is possible.

On switch Access_2, we find the following configuration.

```
Access_2#show running-config
   Building configuration…
!
spanning-tree uplinkfast
udld enable
!
interface FastEthernet0/5
   description Uplink to Dist_1
   switchport trunk encapsulation dot1q
   switchport trunk allowed vlan 10,20
   switchport mode trunk
!
interface FastEthernet0/6
   description Uplink to Dist_2
   switchport trunk encapsulation dot1q
   switchport trunk allowed vlan 10,20
   switchport mode trunk
!
```

```
interface FastEthernet0/6
  description End Host
  spanning-tree rootguard
!
end
```

STP TROUBLESHOOTING

Once spanning tree is operational in your network, it's a good idea to understand how the operation of the protocol can be viewed with IOS commands. There are a few very critical *show* commands that are needed to identify key elements of your spanning tree configuration.

Check the Operational Settings of STP

These can be viewed in the active config (in the output of a *show running-config* command), but it's also important to be able to see how the protocol is actually operating. Remember that some STP values are set globally, some are configured on the VLAN, and some are port config settings. As a result, there's not a one-stop place to find everything.

The most basic information about the global configuration can be found with the command below. It is a simple list of the active global configuration with some useful summary statistics on the number of ports in the various STP states.

```
Access_1#show spanning-tree summary
Switch is in rapid-pvst mode
Root bridge for: none
Extended system ID            is enabled
Portfast Default              is enabled
PortFast BPDU Guard Default   is enabled
Portfast BPDU Filter Default  is disabled
Loopguard Default             is enabled
EtherChannel misconfig guard  is enabled
UplinkFast                    is disabled
BackboneFast                  is disabled
Configured Pathcost method used is short
```

Name	Blocking	Listening	Learning	Forwarding	STP Active
VLAN0010	1	0	0	72	73
VLAN0020	1	0	0	71	72
2 vlans	2	0	0	143	145

Many commands show STP information for multiple VLANs. The following command provides a list of all ports on the switch that are in the *blocking* state listed by VLAN.

```
Access_1#show spanning-tree blockedports
Name           Blocked Interfaces List
VLAN0010       Gi2/1
VLAN0020       Gi2/1
Number of blocked ports (segments) in the system: 2
```

The most useful command in many situations is *show spanning-tree vlan <vlan>*. The output shows much of the important information needed when troubleshooting STP. From the example below, you can see that VLAN 10 is running Rapid STP. The root's priority, the STP timers in affect, and the root port are all shown here. In addition, the command displays the STP values that this bridge has configured, including its priority, address and STP timers. Finally, the command displays a list of interfaces, their associated STP role, their status (*forwarding* or *blocking*), the port cost, and the port type.

```
Access_1# show spanning-tree vlan 10

VLAN0010
  Spanning tree enabled protocol rstp
  Root ID    Priority    4196
             Address     00d0.0006.4400
             Cost        4
             Port        1 (GigabitEthernet1/1)
             Hello Time  2 sec Max Age 20 sec Forward Delay
                         15 sec

  Bridge ID  Priority    32868 (priority 32768 sys-id-ext
                         100)
             Address     0016.4615.0c00
             Hello Time  2 sec Max Age 20 sec Forward Delay
                         15 sec
             Aging Time  300

Interface     Role Sts Cost     Prio.Nbr Type
Gi1/1         Root FWD 4        128.1       P2p
Gi2/1         Altn BLK 4        128.65      P2p
Fa3/1         Desg FWD 19       128.129     P2p Edge
Fa3/2         Desg FWD 19       128.130     P2p Edge

// SNIP //
```

If that doesn't provide enough information, the "detail" keyword unlocks a huge amount of useful information. There are several pieces of critical information here including when the last topology change occurred, and which port triggered the change. Knowing this is really important during troubleshooting. The following is an example of using the "detail" keyword with the *show spanning-tree* command.

```
Access_1#show spanning-tree vlan 10 detail

VLAN0010 is executing the rstp compatible Spanning Tree
    protocol
Bridge Identifier has priority 32768, sysid 100, address
    0016.4615.0c00
Configured hello time 2, max age 20, forward delay 15,
    transmit hold-count 6
    Current root has priority 4196, address 00d0.0006.4400
    Root port is 1 (GigabitEthernet1/1), cost of root path is 4
    Topology change flag not set, detected flag not set
    Number of topology changes 4087 last change occurred
        1d13h ago from GigabitEthernet4/24
    Times:  hold 1, topology change 35, notification 2
            hello 2, max age 20, forward delay 15
    Timers: hello 0, topology change 0, notification 0,
            aging 300

Port 1 (GigabitEthernet1/1) of VLAN0010 is root forwarding
    Port Path Cost 4, Port priority 128, Port Identifier 128.1.
    Designated root has priority 4196, address 00d0.0006.4400
    Designated bridge has priority 4196, address 00d0.0006.4400
    Designated port id is 128.898, designated Path Cost 0
    Timers: message age 16, forward delay 0, hold 0
    Number of transitions to forwarding state: 1
    Link type is point-to-point by default
    Loop guard is enabled by default on the port
    BPDU: sent 47, received 914407

Port 65 (GigabitEthernet2/1) of VLAN0010 is alternate
    blocking
    Port Path Cost 4, Port priority 128, Port Identifier
        128.65.
    Designated root has priority 4196, address
        00d0.0006.4400
    Designated bridge has priority 8292, address
        00d0.0402.6800
    Designated port id is 128.262, designated Path Cost 3
    Timers: message age 16, forward delay 0, hold 0
    Number of transitions to forwarding state: 28
```

```
Link type is point-to-point by default
Loop guard is enabled by default on the port
BPDU: sent 89, received 13326275

Port 129 (FastEthernet3/1) of VLAN0010 is designated
  forwarding
  Port Path Cost 19, Port priority 128, Port Identifier
    128.129.
  Designated root has priority 4196, address 00d0.0006.4400
  Designated bridge has priority 32868, address
    0016.4615.0c00
  Designated port id is 128.129, designated Path Cost 4
  Timers: message age 0, forward delay 0, hold 0
  Number of transitions to forwarding state: 1
  The port is in the portfast mode by default
  Link type is point-to-point by default
  Bpdu guard is enabled by default
  Loop guard is enabled by default on the port
  BPDU: sent 519303, received 0

// SNIP //
```

Test Day Tip

Don't get overwhelmed by the amount of information displayed in the STP *show* and *debug* commands. If you have understood this chapter, all the information should be familiar to you. The output may appear excessive, but it is simply the same information displayed PER PORT.

EXERCISE 12.6   Build and Test STP

If you've got the gear, there is no better way to learn than to build the networks yourself. Gather the switching hardware, cable it up, and configure the networks you designed in Exercise 12.3.

Important—Don't experiment with spanning tree configurations on a production network. Networks don't forward frames properly during convergence, so changes to the STP configuration do impact users. Experiment with STP changes *only* in a test lab.

If you do have the gear, try these suggestions (be careful—only in test):

1. Configure RSTP throughout the network. Determine an appropriate root and backup root and administratively configure these using priorities.

2. Learn your topology. Use *show* commands to find out which ports are forwarding and which are blocked. Determine each port's STP role and figure out *why* they are in that role.

3. Affect your topology by changing port priorities to modify the root Path Cost. Check the effect of each change to the topology using your *show* commands.

4. Introduce a "better" root. Use the *show* and *debug* commands to observe as the network runs the root election process and converges.

5. Test the STP stability features by introducing a new root off a *Rootguard*-enabled port.

6. Test *Uplinkfast* and *Backbonefast* by simulating a link failure and watching the network converge.

7. Connect a switch to a *Bpdu Guard* port and check the log for messages from this feature, or configure the feature to shut down the port.

8. Introduce a loop off a *Portfast* port and see how this feature responds.

What Can Go Wrong?

STP is intended to stop one of the most disastrous events a network can encounter: A loop. If STP isn't working properly, loops can form and cause the network to crash. There are some ways to identify problems with the STP before that happens.

Most importantly, it is critical to know your STP topology. You should know which switches in your environment are roots for each VLAN. You should know which ports on each switch are blocked and why. You should follow configuration best practices (www.cisco.com/en/US/products/hw/switches/ps700/products_white_paper09186a00801b49a4.shtml) on every device in your network. If you follow good network management practices, design your network properly, and don't try to be a hero by shaving a half-second from the convergence time by fiddling with the STP timers. STP will work for you.

When troubleshooting STP, follow a layered troubleshooting approach. For example, you should know which ports in your network are uplinks. Check the interface counters on these ports to identify problems (for example, alignment, FCS, and so forth). These errors can cause lost Bpdus, which affects the stability of STP. A management application that can poll these values and notify you when they pass some administratively-defined threshold is a good idea.

IOS also has a number of tools to troubleshoot STP. The *debug* command can provide a wealth of information, but it must be used with care in a production environment. STP can generate an enormous number of events, especially when things are going wrong. When in doubt about how a *debug* command will affect your production network, it is wise to contact Cisco's Technical Assistance Center (TAC) at www.cisco.com/en/US/support/index.html.

Having said that, here is the command necessary to debug STP:

```
Access_1#debug spanning-tree ?
  all                    All Spanning Tree debugging messages
  backbonefast           BackboneFast events
  bpdu                   Spanning tree BPDU
  bpdu-opt               Optimized BPDU handling
  config                 Spanning tree config changes
  etherchannel           EtherChannel support
  events                 Spanning tree topology events
  exceptions             Spanning tree exceptions
  general                Spanning tree general
  ha                     STP HA debug commands
  mstp                   MSTP debug commands
  pvst+                  PVST+ events
  root                   Spanning tree root events
  snmp                   Spanning Tree SNMP handling
  switch                 Switch Shim debug commands
  synchronization        STP state sync events
  uplinkfast             UplinkFast events
```

You can see that debug gives you the ability to narrow the output, but that can also hide the problem. When using debug, don't forget to use the "terminal monitor" command to echo the debug output to a terminal session. If you don't use this command, the debug output may not be visible.

Also, one obvious but commonly overlooked source for information is the router log. Remember to do a "show log" to see what recent events have occurred. This assumes, however, that buffer logging is enabled. Here is the *global configuration* command to enable this:

```
Switch(config)# logging buffered 10000 debugging
```

SUMMARY OF EXAM OBJECTIVES

This chapter has covered not only the material required to pass the CCNA exam, but also what's necessary to run spanning tree successfully in your environment. STP is a challenging topic and there are a number of details that are easy to forget and overlook.

We have covered the basics of the original STP and how the protocol has evolved over time. The CCNA candidate needs to understand how to configure and troubleshoot the protocol, but this material can't be mastered until you have a good grasp of the basics.

STP is often considered one of the most difficult topics on the CCNA exam. It's a good idea to test your knowledge by creating bridging scenarios and running through various ways to affect the topology. STP is so important to the proper operation of a network that an in-depth understanding of the gory details is really useful.

EXAM OBJECTIVES FAST TRACK

Ethernet Frame Forwarding

- Ethernet bridges maintain a CAM table containing a mapping between learned source **MAC** addresses and ports.

- The CAM table allows the switch to intelligently forward frames without needing to flood traffic to all ports.

- The default CAM timeout is 5 minutes, but the CAM entry is updated each time a frame is seen from a host.

- Loops are really bad in Ethernet networks. STP provides a way to create a loop-free topology.

What Is a Spanning Tree and How Does It Eliminate Loops?

- A spanning tree is a fully-connected loop-free graph.

- A bridge is elected to "root" the spanning tree based on the lowest Bridge ID.

- Bpdus are sent between bridges, which allow them to learn about the network.

- Port costs are inversely proportional to the port bandwidth. The higher the bandwidth, the lower the port cost.

- Designated ports have the lowest root Path Cost. This is the best path to the root.

- Ports are placed in *blocking* state to eliminate loops.

The Operation of STP: Putting it all Together

- Loops are essential in network design to ensure adequate redundancy and protect against link or device failure.

- It can take up to 50 seconds for 802.1d STP to recognize a link failure and fully converge on a new topology.

- Max Age is the STP timer that controls how long the protocol "remembers" a Bpdu it receives.

Problems with Original STP and Solutions

- *Backbonefast*, *Uplinkfast*, and *Portfast* are three features developed by Cisco to provide faster STP convergence.

- *Uplinkfast* keeps track of all backup paths to the root and is able to quickly switch to a backup path if the root port fails.

- *Backbonefast* protects against "indirect" link failure by allowing the switch to quickly recognize the failure.

- UDLD and *Loopguard* offer similar protection against unidirectional links.

- *Rootguard* ensures that a port will never become the root port, which protects against a new switch advertizing itself as the root.

STP Protocol Evolution

- RSTP is defined in IEEE 802.1w and provides faster convergence than 802.1d.

- RSTP port states including *discarding*, *learning*, and *forwarding*. *Discarding* ports are either alternate or backup ports depending on if the port is self-looped.

- The benefits of Cisco's *Backbonefast* and *Uplinkfast* features are built in to RSTP.

- *Portfast* ports in RSTP are "Edge ports" and operate similar to 802.1d.

- Full-duplex links are considered "point-to-point" links and speed convergence through the RSTP sync process.

RSTP configuration

- RSTP is not available on older switches. Although the protocol is able to interoperate with 802.1d switches, the convergence benefits are lost.

- The extended system-id is necessary to support extended VLANs, numbered 1006-4096.

- Modifying the STP timers is not necessary in RSTP to get the benefits of the protocol's quick convergence.

- Modify the swtich priority or use a macro to force a well-placed switch to become the root or backup root.

STP Troubleshooting

- Use *show* commands to determine the topology of your network, find the root, learn the active port states, and so forth.

- Use STP *debug* commands very carefully. It is wise to use STP *debug* commands in a test lab only.

- Don't forget to review the routers log for STP output. SNMP and syslog messages can provide good information when troubleshooting problems.

EXAM OBJECTIVES FREQUENTLY ASKED QUESTIONS

Q: If a host never transmits a frame on the network, how does the switch ever learn about its **MAC**?

A: It doesn't. If a host never transmits, the switch must always flood frames destined to that host.

Q: How often is the CAM table updated with new information?

A: Every time a frame arrives on a port. If the **MAC**/port is already in the CAM, the timestamp is updated.

Q: How large is the CAM table?

A: This varies by platform. The 6500 can have 65536 entries in the CAM. The 2960 can support only 8173.

Q: Is there only one spanning tree for each network?

A: No—there can be many. The number of possible spanning trees depends on the number of vertices and edges. If you have a mathematical mind, you can calculate the number of trees using Kirchhoff's theorem (http://en.wikipedia.org/wiki/Kirchhoff%27s_theorem).

Q: Should I manually configure a switch to use a specific **MAC** address for the Bridge ID?

A: No. It is better to force the root and backup root using the Bridge Priority. The **MAC** is used only when the Bridge Priorities are equal.

Q: Is the root Path Cost cumulative?

A: Yes. It is the sum of all port costs calculated by the switches in a path to the root. For each hop along the way, the root Path Cost is added to the receive port cost when the Bpdu is received.

Q: How long does the root election process take place?

A: This depends on the number of switches. The more switches, the longer the election process takes.

Q: If a switch comes online with a "better" Bridge Priority, does it take over as the root?

A: Yes. Since the network doesn't forward traffic during convergence (to avoid loops), it is normally not a good idea to do this except during a maintenance window. To avoid this potentially happening by mistake or as a Denial of Service (DOS) attack, the *Rootguard* and *Bpdu Guard* features protect the root from being hijacked.

Q: How long does convergence take when the failure occurs on a directly connected link?

A: For direct failures that can be immediately recognized, convergence takes 30 seconds (15 seconds for *listening* and 15 seconds for *learning*) before the blocked port can take over.

Q: Why is it not a good idea to change the STP timers?

A: The STP protocol was designed to work properly with the default timers. Although you may be able to squeeze a tiny improvement in convergence by tweaking the timers, the risk of causing catastrophic failure by introducing a loop is possible. Better to migrate to a newer protocol like 802.1w or 802.1s.

Q: Does *Bpdu Guard* shut down a port that receives a Bpdu?

A: This depends on the mode. In *aggressive* mode, *Bpdu Guard* puts a port in *errDisabled* state and this requires administrator intervention to bring the port back up. In *normal* mode, the feature simply logs a message.

Q: Can a network use both PVST and RSTP?

A: There is a misunderstanding. PVST only means that there is an STP instance per VLAN—but it doesn't specify which flavor of STP—802.1d or 802.1w.

Q: If RSTP is configured on all switches but one legacy switch that runs 802.1d, are the convergence benefits of RSTP lost for all devices?

A: No, but a lot depends on the topology. If the legacy device is hung off an RSTP switch and doesn't have downstream RSTP devices, then the benefits are only lost to the hosts connected to the legacy switch.

Q: How can RSTP safely eliminate the *listening* state?

A: In 802.1d, the *listening* state also blocked traffic from being forwarded. The RSTP states are based on how the ports are operating, so they are actually easier to remember.

Q: Which is better—802.1w or 802.1s?

A: It depends on your environment. 802.1s is a bit more difficult to configure but scales much more than RSTP. RSTP is supported on many switching platforms and is easy to configure, but will not scale well when there are hundreds of VLANs.

Q: Which *show* commands are the most useful?

A: The *show spanning-tree summary* and *show spanning-tree vlan <vlan> detail* commands show nearly all the information that is meaningful for configuration, validation, and troubleshooting.

SELF TEST

1. You're using a network protocol analyzer to troubleshoot an application problem for a user. This tool enables you to capture all frames and you are connected to a different port but the same switch as the server. Yet, you are unable to see the application traffic frames between the application server and user don't appear. What is a potential problem that can cause this?

   A. The CAM table is not updating properly so the switch isn't forwarding traffic to your tool.

   B. The switch has CAM entries for the destination of the traffic so it isn't flooded to the port connected to your analyzer.

   C. Your analyzer isn't transmitting on the network so the switch doesn't know to send traffic to your port.

   D. The server and host aren't sending traffic to the analyzer so this configuration won't work.

2. You have a large switched network with some pretty old switches. The network seems to be operating correctly, but when evaluating network traffic, you notice that a lot of unicast traffic is being flooded to ports that don't contain the destination host. What can cause this?

   A. The STP isn't converging which is causing a loop.

   B. The frames are being sent too quickly and the old switches can't filter the frames that fast.

   C. There are too many hosts and the CAM table of the old switch is being overrun, which causes traffic to flood.

   D. Memory problems on the switch are causing a lack of frame buffers to process the traffic, which causes traffic to flood.

3. A frame is forwarded through an Ethernet switch between two ports in the same VLAN. What information changes in the frame as this happens?

   A. The source **MAC** address of the frame is changed to the switch **MAC** address

   B. The destination **MAC** address of the frame is changed to the router **MAC** address

   C. The source and destination **MAC** addresses remain the same, but destination IP address is changed to the router IP.

   D. There is no change made to the frame.

4. When a bridge loop forms, what stops frames from flowing around the loop indefinitely or proliferating?
   A. There is a hop count field in the Ethernet header that is decremented each time a frame is forwarded through a switch.
   B. When the frame is received by the router, it is sent toward its destination IP address and stops looping as a result.
   C. Breaking the loop (by removing links or turning off hardware) will stop a frame from looping.
   D. The routing protocol concept of infinity is breached and the frame is dropped.

5. Are bridge loops worse than routing loops, and why?
   A. Yes, because with a routing loop a frame may loop forever but there is only a single copy of the frame. Frames can proliferate with bridge loops, which can crash the network.
   B. No, routing loops are worse because more router resources are expended by routing a looping frame than switching a looping frame.
   C. Yes, bridge loops are worse because switching is often performed in hardware and so a frame loops much faster being switched than routed.
   D. No, routing loops are worse because they are more difficult to stop. Routing loops require a reboot of network equipment to clear.

6. You are given the opportunity to build a network for a large new building and have a lot of fiber that can be used to create a very well connected topology. Is it a good idea to build the switched network so that each switch has four possible paths to the root bridge?
   A. Yes, because more redundancy is always better for important networks.
   B. No, because the STP protocol can only support two redundant paths between switches.
   C. Yes, because STP operates more efficiently as the number of switches and links increases.
   D. No, because STP convergence takes longer as the number of switches and links increases.

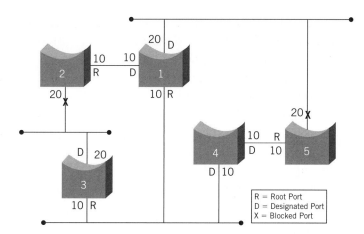

FIGURE 12.15

*Example Topology for
Questions 7 and 8*

7. Refer to Figure 12.15. Which switch is the spanning-tree root and how can you tell given the information shown in the figure?

   A. Switch 1 is the root because it has the highest cumulative port costs.

   B. Switch 4 is the root because all its ports are in the *designated* state.

   C. Switch 1 is the root because it has the smallest address.

   D. Switch 5 is the root because it has the highest address.

8. Refer again to Figure 12.15. Assume that the root port on switch 3 fails and that no proprietary feature is used to speed convergence. How long could it take for 802.1d to converge after this failure, and why?

   A. 35 seconds, because switch 2 would take 20 seconds to recognize the failure (Max Age) and 15 seconds to transition to *forwarding* state.

   B. 30 seconds, because it would take switch 3 up to 15 seconds to recognize the failure and 15 seconds to transition to *forwarding* state.

   C. 50 seconds, because it would take up to 20 seconds for switch 2 to recognize the failure and 30 seconds to transition to *forwarding* state.

   D. 30 seconds, because it would take switch 2 exactly 30 seconds to transition to *forwarding* state.

9. The root Path Cost is important to the STP algorithm because it determines the best path from any switch to the root bridge. How is the root Path Cost calculated?

    A. It is the sum of the port costs for all ports in the path from the root to the receiving switch.

    B. It is the sum of the port costs for all sending ports in the path from the root to the receiving switch.

    C. It is the sum of the port costs for all receiving ports in the path from the root to the receiving switch.

    D. The root Path Cost is equal to the port cost of the sending port on the root.

10. The *Rootguard* feature is intended to protect the placement of the root by ensuring that no other switch can take over the root by advertising itself with a better Bridge ID. Where is the *Rootguard* feature configured?

    A. *Rootguard* is configured on individual ports that you know don't have a path back to the root.

    B. *Rootguard* is configured globally only on the root and backup root bridges.

    C. *Rootguard* is configured globally on all switches in the network.

    D. *Rootguard* is configured on individual ports that you know have a path back to the root.

11. How does the *Portfast* feature eliminate startup problems for some hosts?

    A. The *Portfast* feature eliminates startup problems by stopping the switch from sending a TCN Bpdu to the root when a host connects.

    B. The *Portfast* feature eliminates startup problems by allowing the switch to transition the port directly to *forwarding* state, which eliminates the 30 second wait for *listening* and *learning* states.

    C. The *Portfast* feature eliminates startup problems by dropping the CAM timeout from 5 minutes to 15 seconds when a host connects.

    D. The *Portfast* feature eliminates startup problems by disabling the spanning tree on the port.

12. *Loopguard* and UDLD perform a similar function, but by a different method. How are these functions different and how are they similar?

    A. *Loopguard* and UDLD both block loops from forming only over 802.1q trunked ports. *Loopguard* does this by detecting invalid Bpdus and UDLD does this by detecting duplicate frames.

    B. *Loopguard* and UDLD both block loops from forming due to uni-directional links. *Loopguard* does this by detecting missing Bpdus and UDLD does this by watching for **MAC** addresses that flap between ports in the CAM table.

    C. *Loopguard* and UDLD both avoid loops from forming only over Etherchannel link bundles. *Loopguard* does this by detecting bundle instability and UDLD does this by watching for Bpdus with invalid source **MAC**s.

    D. *Loopguard* and UDLD both avoid loops from forming due to uni-directional links. *Loopguard* does this by watching for Bpdus that suddenly stop and UDLD does this by sending special frames to a neighboring switch and expecting a response.

13. What is the main limitation of a CST?

    A. A CST does not support more than a single VLAN.

    B. CST supports multiple VLANs but doesn't operate properly over 802.1q trunk ports.

    C. A CST only supports a single physical topology which doesn't fully utilize network resources.

    D. CST is not supported only older legacy switches.

14. Ports in 802.1d that would be placed in *blocking* state have been changed in RSTP. The 802.1w protocol makes these either alternate or backup ports. What is the difference between these ports?

    A. An alternate port has a backup path to the root bridge, but a backup port does not.

    B. Both alternate and backup ports have a path to the root bridge, but the path through the backup port may not be loop-free.

    C. An alternate port has a backup path to the root bridge and can be transitioned immediately to *forwarding* state. A backup port can't guarantee a unique path to the root bridge because the port is self-looped.

    D. Both alternate and backup ports have a path to the root bridge. The difference involves how the two ports send and receive Bpdus.

15. What is the primary reason that a network designer may prefer MST (802.1s) over RSTP (802.1w)?

A. In networks with many VLANs, RSTP consumes too many resources because each VLAN runs a unique instance of the STP.

B. Convergence in RSTP is slower than MST, so the 802.1s is preferred in mission critical environments.

C. The configuration complexity of RSTP makes the environment difficult to manage compared to 802.1s.

D. RSTP doesn't work well in networks that contain a lot of redundancy.

16. You want to force a specific switch to be the root of your spanning tree. What is the best way to accomplish this?

A. Implement the *Rootguard* feature to ensure only your preferred switch can become the root.

B. Lower the spanning-tree priority of your preferred root to a value lower than any other Bridge Priority.

C. Use the *Bpdu Guard* feature to block any other switch from advertising itself as a more preferred root.

D. Select a lower value **MAC** address in the Bridge ID of your preferred root to a value lower than any other bridge address.

17. You have been asked to configure STP throughout a network made up of both new and older hardware. Your design goal is to provide for the fastest convergence possible. What is the best approach to this problem?

A. Run MST (802.1s) throughout the network because it provides the widest possible support for legacy devices while maintaining fast convergence.

B. Run 802.1d throughout the network to support interoperability with the older hardware and implement *Backbonefast* to speed convergence.

C. Run RSTP (802.1w) throughout the network because it provides the widest possible support for legacy devices while maintaining fast convergence.

D. Run RSTP (802.1w) on newer devices and 802.1d on legacy devices. The two protocols are interoperable, but the convergence benefits of RSTP are lost on links to 802.1d switches.

18. You have configured RSTP throughout a small test lab and you have found that your network does not converge very quickly. What is the most likely cause?

    A. The STP timers are not the same on all switches in the network.

    B. The links between switches are not configured to be full-duplex.

    C. The root bridge is not placed properly.

    D. The port costs are not configured correctly.

19. You are troubleshooting a potential bridge loop that caused your network to crash. After rebooting all your switches to get your network back online, you begin your investigation. What is your best source of information about the problem?

    A. The *show spanning-tree vlan <vlan> detail* command will provide spanning tree statistics to help isolate a loop.

    B. The *show interface* command will show evidence of a loop by showing huge traffic that's been sent on the ports.

    C. The *debug spanning-tree all* command will provide useful information for troubleshooting the loop formation.

    D. Your *syslog* or *snmp* server logs will contain information that can help.

20. Consider Figure 12.16. You want to influence the spanning tree topology to enable servers connected to switches B and C to communicate directly without traffic flowing through the root bridge. Assume all links are the same speed. How would you modify the port costs to accomplish this?

    A. Raise the port cost on port 3.

    B. Raise the port cost on ports 4 and 5.

    C. Lower the port cost on ports 4 and 5.

    D. Lower the port cost on port 1.

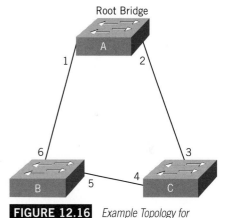

FIGURE 12.16 *Example Topology for Question 20*

SELF TEST QUICK ANSWER KEY

1.	B	**11.**	B
2.	C	**12.**	D
3.	D	**13.**	C
4.	C	**14.**	C
5.	A	**15.**	A
6.	D	**16.**	B
7.	B	**17.**	D
8.	C	**18.**	B
9.	C	**19.**	D
10.	A	**20.**	A

VLANs

INTRODUCTION

It is not enough for a Cisco Certified Network Associate (CCNA) to just be able to configure and maintain the switches in a network environment; they also need to be able to make the network efficient and secure as possible. This can be accomplished by using virtual local area networks (VLANs). VLANs allow network administrators to divide the network by designating certain ports as part of a logical network. Although several computers or devices can be connected to the same physical network, they can be all separated logically through the use of a VLAN.

CCNAs are not the only ones who need to be aware of VLANs and their impact on the network, whereas other individuals in the computer industry, such as computer forensic investigators, intrusions investigators, and penetration testers also need to have knowledge of VLANs because they need to be aware of how a network is segmented. VLAN databases can provide important details to any individual who is trying to discern the logical breakup of the network. An individual taking the CCNA exam should know how to configure and maintain VLANs. It is a good idea to use the simulation software that accompanies this book to get sufficient practice with VLANs. In summary, a CCNA needs to understand how VLANs logically divide the network and affect the traffic and security of a switched network.

VLANs EXPLAINED

The first thing that might come to mind when we mention VLANs is that somehow they don't exist physically. They do exist and they are very commonly used in the enterprise or corporate computing networks to segment networks. In the past, to separate or segment networks, we simply used separate pieces of hardware such as hubs or switches. It became very clear that when hubs and switches only come in predefined capacities such as 5, 8, 12, 24, or even 36 ports, potentially we could be wasting resources by not fully utilizing all the ports on these devices. In addition, as companies expanded and spread into different locations, it became difficult to have people in the same departments on the same LAN segments. Someone envisioned being able to change and reconfigure one device into multiple segments and VLANs were born.

Broadcast Domains

One of the problems that we must control in a network environment is the spread of broadcasts. A broadcast is a data transmission or packet that is sent to every machine. Each machine must process this packet and see whether it relates to them. An analogy might be: to hear an announcement on the PA, we all must pay attention until the point when we realize it has no importance to us. In a network, broadcasts take up valuable bandwidth that could be used to carry other data and also take up valuable processing power to determine whether the packet is important or not. A broadcast uses a very special Media Access Control (MAC) address of FF:FF:FF:FF:FF:FF. As we saw in Chapter 11, a networking device listens for its own MAC address and for the broadcast MAC address and processes these packets only. Because switches only store source MAC address in their switching tables, a broadcast MAC address is never stored in the switching table. When a switch receives a packet that is not contained in its switching table, it floods that packet to every port to find the recipient. This means that the switches do not impede any broadcasts. If we were going "old school" and using hubs, hubs merely repeat the packet to every single port. Only routers impede and do not forward broadcasts. The area of the network that is defined when a broadcast propagates from one switch or hub to another and one PC to another is known as a "broadcast domain." The more the broadcasts on the network, the less efficient and productive the network is.

There are certain networking services that rely on broadcasts that are very common such as Dynamic Host Configuration Protocol (DHCP) or Address Resolution Protocol (ARP) and therefore all broadcasts can't be eliminated. To control broadcasts, we segment networks into different pieces to control how many broadcasts are on each segment. VLANs are a natural extension to segment a network physically by segmenting the network virtually. This allows us maximum flexibility in configuration of segmenting the network to control broadcast domains.

Security

Companies often use VLANs in security situations as well. For a long time, Cisco did not officially endorse using VLANs for security but in recent documentation does talk about this. How can we use VLANs to help security? Because we are virtually segmenting the network into separate segments, we can group different networking devices on segments based on their role in our organization. For example, we might have a VLAN that specifically was set up for resources in the Human Resources (HR) department. We could control access to this particular segment so that only those PCs that require access to the HR servers can get access to them. Most organizations do use VLANs to some extent to segment sensitive resources from other VLANs on the network.

Test Day Tip

Make sure you know why VLANs are used; the test may give you scenarios where VLANs will be an important solution to the problems mentioned earlier.

Static VLANs

Static VLANs in Cisco represent a situation where ports are assigned the VLAN membership manually. This is the most common form of VLAN set up in today's enterprise. This requires an administrator of the Cisco switch to manually assign different ports into their associated VLAN membership.

Port-Based VLANs

The most common way of assigning static VLANs is through port-based assignment. What this means is that an administrator accesses the switches configuration and for individual ports, assigns the membership of these ports to VLANs. By default, all ports in a switch are assigned to what we call the administrative VLAN, VLAN 1. Unless we are going to put them into another VLAN, we can leave these ports in their default configuration.

CONFIGURING AND IMPLEMENTING...

The Industry Standard in Port-Based VLANs

When you read about dynamic VLANs next, you will see that they do have some advantages over the static VLANs discussed earlier. Keep in mind that the great majority of all implementations of VLANs is port-based. Why is this so? There is greater upfront work with dynamic VLANs, for example, you must set up and implement a server to manage VLAN membership. But probably the most common reason for not implement-ing dynamic VLANs is the continued maintenance of the VLAN membership database. Think of a corporate situation, when someone has a defective machine, that machine is swapped out with a replacement so the worker can get back to work. Maintaining the member-ship database for a large company would place a huge burden on the IT department. As such, IT departments tend to go towards port-based VLANs that have little need for maintenance after the initial setup.

Dynamic VLANs

Unlike static VLANs, dynamic VLANs are not based on port numbers. Their membership is either based on their MAC address or on the protocol they are using. This method of assigning VLANs is not as common but does have the advantage that as machines move from one port to another such as a laptop moving from one location to another, their VLAN membership will remain the same.

MAC-Based VLANs

One of the ways we can set up dynamic VLANs is by basing it on a network-ing device's MAC address. The MAC address, which should never change for a device since it is permanently set by the manufacturer and because it should be unique worldwide, is a perfect address to use to identify a specific computer system. VLANs can be assigned using the MAC address. A cen-tralized server called a VLAN Membership Policy Server is set up to contain all the MAC addresses and their associated VLAN membership. When a machine connects to the network, the switch queries the VMPS server to ascertain what VLAN the machine is a part of and then dynamically assigns the port the correct VLAN.

Protocol-Based VLANs

VLANs may also be assigned based on the protocol they are using. The concept here is to segment traffic based on the protocol that is being transmitted by the networking device. A good example of this is the current situation where often a PC and a Voice Over IP (VOIP) phone are connected together on the same port of the switch. The traffic for the phone is time sensitive and needs to have priority. Often the VOIP portion is carried on a separate VLAN than the IP traffic from the PC. Cisco allows you to segment the IP and VOIP traffic in separate VLANs and assign priority to the phone traffic using Quality of Service (QoS). Protocol-based VLANs can also be used to segment Transmission Control Protocol/Internet Protocol (TCP/IP) traffic from protocols such as IPX/ SPX and Appletalk.

NEW AND NOTEWORTHY...

Voice Over IP and VLANs

We have seen a rise in the number of companies switching to using VOIP for their telephone communications. Oftentimes, there is a single networking cable that provides service to both the phone and the PC that a person is using. This is done through daisy chaining the PC through the phone. Cisco has a built in command set for establishing VLANs for voice and data on the same cable. In addition to setting up the standard VLAN, you enter the command SWITCHPORT VOICE VLAN and then the number of the VLAN to be assigned. This combined with the command MLS QOS TRUST COS that provides priority for the VOIP traffic allows this set up.

CONFIGURING A VLAN

Configuring a VLAN in a Cisco switch is not an overly difficult process. We'll walk through the basic steps of the process, which include setting up the different numbered or named VLANs and setting the IP address for each VLAN.

Naming and Numbering the VLAN

Cisco VLANs are numbered from 1 to 4,094. The normal VLANs are numbered from 1 to 1,005. These VLANs are stored in the switches flash memory in a file called vlan.dat. In addition, there are VLANs numbered from 1,006 to 4,094 that are called the *extended VLANs*. The extended VLANs do not have as many options and are stored in the running configuration file of the switch. There are a number of VLANs that are set up in Cisco switches by default. These are set at the factory and cannot be changed by the end user. These include what we call the administrative VLAN, which is VLAN 1, and VLANs 1,002–1,005, which are for Token Ring and FDDI networks, respectively. To enable easier identification, we may also name VLANs so that they have a better description of their use.

To access the VLAN configuration menu, there are a series of steps you need to perform. As indicated in the following, you must initially enter into the *Global Configuration* mode by typing **configure terminal**, then access the VLAN menu by typing **VLAN** and then the number associated with the VLAN. To add a name to the VLAN, simply type **NAME** and then the name you wish to call it. Typing **END** will back you out of the VLAN configuration prompt. You will know you are in the *VLAN configuration* mode when your prompt changes to SWITCH (config-vlan)#. As shown in Figure 13.1, it's simple to create a VLAN such as VLAN 2.

Setting the VLAN IP Address

Setting the VLAN IP address is pretty simple as well in a Cisco switch. If you have mastered the application of assigning IP addresses to routers we use a similar process. As illustrated later, you enter *Global Configuration* mode by typing **configure terminal**, then access the specific VLAN by typing **interface VLAN** and then the VLANs number. To assign the address, the syntax is **ip address 10.1.1.1 255.0.0.0** if you wanted to set the address to 10.1.1.1/8. As shown in Figure 13.2, you could set the IP address for VLAN 2.

```
Switch>enable
Switch#configure t
Enter configuration commands, one per line.  End with CNTL/Z.
Switch(config)#vlan 2

%LINK-5-CHANGED: Interface Vlan2, changed state to upSwitch(config-vlan)#
Switch(config-vlan)#name production
Switch(config-vlan)#end
%SYS-5-CONFIG_I: Configured from console by console
Switch#show vlan

VLAN Name                             Status    Ports
---- -------------------------------- --------- ------------------------------
1    default                          active    Fa0/1, Fa0/2, Fa0/3, Fa0/4
                                                Fa0/5, Fa0/6, Fa0/7, Fa0/8
                                                Fa0/9, Fa0/10, Fa0/11, Fa0/12
                                                Fa0/13, Fa0/14, Fa0/15, Fa0/16
                                                Fa0/17, Fa0/18, Fa0/19, Fa0/20
                                                Fa0/21, Fa0/22, Fa0/23, Fa0/24
                                                Gig1/1, Gig1/2
2    production                       active
```

FIGURE 13.1   *Creating VLAN2 with the Name Production*

```
Switch>enable
Switch#configure terminal
Enter configuration commands, one per line.  End with CNTL/Z.
Switch(config)#interface vlan 2
Switch(config-if)#ip address 10.1.1.1 255.0.0.0
Switch(config-if)#no shutdown
Switch(config-if)#exit
Switch(config)#exit
%SYS-5-CONFIG_I: Configured from console by console
Switch#
```

FIGURE 13.2   *Setting the IP Address for VLAN2 to 10.1.1.1*

Test Day Tip
Make sure you understand how to access the VLAN configuration information and
set the IP address for each VLAN.

EXERCISE 13.1   Creating and Verifying VLANs

In this exercise, you will create three VLANs on your Cisco switch.

1. Type **ENABLE** to access privileged exec mode.

2. Type **CONFIGURE TERMINAL** to access global configuration
   mode.

3. Type **VLAN 2** to create VLAN 2 and access VLAN configuration
   mode.

4. Type **NAME HR** to name this VLAN HR.

5. Type **VLAN 3** to create VLAN 3.

6. Type **NAME PRODUCTION** to name this VLAN Production.

7. Type **VLAN 4** to create VLAN 4.

8. Type **NAME SALES** to name it Sales.

9. Type **Ctrl-Z** to return to privileged exec mode.

10. Type **SHOW VLAN BRIEF** to verify VLAN creation.

VLAN Frames

You are probably wondering how VLANs actually work. End networking devices normally do not know they are using VLANs. Traffic is transmitted from the end networking device to the switch, the switch then tags the data frame with a specific VLAN ID so that the switch can carry this information through its switching process. When the frame is delivered to the correct port for transmission to another end device, the tag is then removed and sent on. The VLAN IDs are used to correctly deliver the packet to its intended destination. Cisco switches may support all or some of the following implementations of VLAN tagging.

802.1Q

The most commonly used protocol for VLANs, produced by the Institute of Electrical and Electronics Engineers (IEEE), is universal standard. What this means is that two devices from different manufacturers can interoperate using 802.1Q. Because of it being an international standard, most networking devices support 802.1Q.

Test Day Tip

802.1Q is a IEEE standard and therefore is supported by most switches and even network interface cards (NICs) that can accommodate VLANs.

Interswitch Link Protocol

Cisco, before it standardized on 802.1Q, had its own protocol for VLANs called Interswitch Link (ISL). This allowed Cisco switches to only communicate VLAN information with other Cisco switches. ISL has been phased out of Cisco's IOS but may exist on older switches or older versions of the IOS.

Exam Warning

Even though Cisco has discontinued ISL on some of their new switches, they may still refer to it so be prepared.

FDDI 802.10

As mentioned earlier, Cisco switches support FDDI VLANs as well. They do this through an implementation of the IEEE standard called 802.10 for FDDI VLANs.

LANE

Certain Cisco switches also support VLANs for ATM transmission through LAN emulation called *LANE*. LANE allows ATM to function like a regular Ethernet network minus all the complexities of ATM.

VLAN DATABASES

As we mentioned earlier, the VLAN database is stored in different locations depending on whether we are using standard or extended VLANs. For VLANs 1 through 1,005, the information is stored in the flash memory of the system. The flash contains a file called vlan.dat that stores the information for the standard VLANs. It's always a good idea when reusing an old switch to delete this VLAN database file so you start out with a blank slate. For VLANs 1,006 through 4,094, the VLAN information is stored in the running-configuration of the switch.

VLAN Types

VLANs can be used on several different types of networks and Cisco by default supports many of them. They have reserved some of the standard VLAN numbers for specific types of networks. Listed below are the default numbers and networks they support.

Default

The default VLAN for Cisco switches is VLAN 1 for Ethernet. This is also what is called the administrative VLAN where the switches administrative functions can be accessed from this VLAN.

> **Exam Warning**
>
> To access the configuration of the Cisco switch via telnet or SSH, you will need to have access to VLAN 1 that is the default administrative VLAN.

FDDI Default

The FDDI default VLAN uses number 1,002 on a Cisco switch. This is used for FDDI networks and utilizes the 802.10 standard for VLANs.

Token Ring Default

The Token-Ring Default VLAN uses number 1,003 on a Cisco switch. This is used for implementing VLANs on Token Ring networks.

FDDInet Default

The FDDInet Default VLAN uses number 1,004 on a Cisco switch. This is a different implementation of VLANs for FDDI networks.

Trnet Default

The Trnet Default VLAN uses number 1,005 on a Cisco switch. This is a different implantation of VLANs for Token Ring networks.

Exam Warning

Be familiar with the fact that VLANs support FDDI and Token Ring as well as Ethernet.

Creating VLANs

Creating VLANs is a fairly easy process. From *global configuration* mode, type **VLAN** and then the number of the VLAN you wish to create. In addition, you can add a name to the VLAN by entering the command **NAME** and then the name you wish to create. As shown in Figure 13.3, you can create multiple VLANs with multiple names.

Exam Warning

VLANs do need to have numbers but don't necessarily need to have names. The names allow you easy access to be able to understand what they are used for.

```
Switch>enable
Switch#configure terminal
Enter configuration commands, one per line.  End with CNTL/Z.
Switch(config)#VLAN 2
Switch(config-vlan)#name production
Switch(config-vlan)#VLAN 3
Switch(config-vlan)#name HR
Switch(config-vlan)#VLAN 4
Switch(config-vlan)#name sales
Switch(config-vlan)#VLAN 5
Switch(config-vlan)#name IT
Switch(config-vlan)#exit
Switch(config)#
```

FIGURE 13.3 *Adding 4 VLANs to a Switch*

Adding VLANs

Once we have created the VLANs we are going to use on our switch, we still need to assign them to each individual port they will be using. Because ports can be used for both trunking (that we will explore in the next chapter) and for access, we must first set the necessary mode, and then set them for a specific VLAN. The command to enable the correct mode is *SWITCHPORT MODE ACCESS*, which sets the port in the mode for nontrunking. This is then followed by the command that actually sets the VLAN and the port will be a part of. This command is *SWITCHPORT ACCESS VLAN* and then the number of the VLAN. As shown in Figure 13.4, you set interfaces to the specific VLAN they are going to be a part of.

Test Day Tip
Make sure you know how to add VLAN information to specific ports. It is a two step process, first setting to access and then assigning the appropriate VLAN.

```
Switch>enable
Switch#configure terminal
Enter configuration commands, one per line.  End with CNTL/Z.
Switch(config)#interface fa0/1
Switch(config-if)#switchport mode access
Switch(config-if)#switchport access vlan 2
Switch(config-if)#int fa 0/2
Switch(config-if)#switchport mode access
Switch(config-if)#switchport access vlan 3
Switch(config-if)#^Z
%SYS-5-CONFIG_I: Configured from console by console
Switch#show vlan

VLAN Name                             Status    Ports
---- -------------------------------- --------- -------------------------------
1    default                          active    Fa0/3, Fa0/4, Fa0/5, Fa0/6
                                                Fa0/7, Fa0/8, Fa0/9, Fa0/10
                                                Fa0/11, Fa0/12, Fa0/13, Fa0/14
                                                Fa0/15, Fa0/16, Fa0/17, Fa0/18
                                                Fa0/19, Fa0/20, Fa0/21, Fa0/22
                                                Fa0/23, Fa0/24, Gig1/1, Gig1/2
2    production                       active    Fa0/1
3    HR                               active    Fa0/2
```

FIGURE 13.4 *Setting Multiple Interfaces with VLANs*

EXERCISE 13.2   Adding Ports to VLANs

In this exercise, you will create three VLANs on your Cisco switch.

1. Type **ENABLE** to access privileged exec mode.

2. Type **CONFIGURE TERMINAL** to access global configuration mode.

3. Type **INTERFACE FA0/1** to access FastEthernet port 0/1.

4. Type **SWITCHPORT MODE ACCESS** to set this port into a nontrunking access mode.

5. Type **SWITCHPORT ACCESS VLAN 2** to set this port to use VLAN 2.

6. Type **INTERFACE FA0/2** to access FastEthernet port 0/2.

7. Type **SWITCHPORT MODE ACCESS** to set this port into a nontrunking access mode.

8. Type **SWITCHPORT ACCESS VLAN 3** to set this port to use VLAN 2.

9. Type **INTERFACE FA0/3** to access FastEthernet port 0/3.

10. Type **SWITCHPORT MODE ACCESS** to set this port into a nontrunking access mode.

11. Type **SWITCHPORT ACCESS VLAN 4** to set this port to use VLAN 2.

12. Type **Ctrl-Z** to return to privileged exec mode.

13. Type **SHOW VLAN BRIEF** to verify VLAN assignment.

Deleting VLANs

To remove a VLAN, we must again be in *global configuration* mode and type the following command *NO VLAN* and the number of the VLAN that we want to remove. As shown in Figure 13.5, we remove VLAN 2.

Test Day Tip

Mostly, every Cisco command can be cancelled out using the word "NO" before it.

```
Switch>enable
Switch#configure terminal
Enter configuration commands, one per line.  End with CNTL/Z.
Switch(config)#NO VLAN 2
Switch(config)#^Z
%SYS-5-CONFIG_I: Configured from console by console
Switch#show vlan

VLAN Name                             Status     Ports
---- -------------------------------- ---------- -------------------------------
1    default                          active     Fa0/3, Fa0/4, Fa0/5, Fa0/6
                                                 Fa0/7, Fa0/8, Fa0/9, Fa0/10
                                                 Fa0/11, Fa0/12, Fa0/13, Fa0/14
                                                 Fa0/15, Fa0/16, Fa0/17, Fa0/18
                                                 Fa0/19, Fa0/20, Fa0/21, Fa0/22
                                                 Fa0/23, Fa0/24, Gig1/1, Gig1/2
3    HR                               active     Fa0/2
4    sales                            active
5    IT                               active
1002 fddi-default                     active
1003 token-ring-default               active
1004 fddinet-default                  active
```

FIGURE 13.5   *Removing VLAN 2 from a Switch*

VERIFYING VLANs

It is helpful to be able to list all of the VLANs that are on a switch. There are several different *show* commands that can help us look at VLANs on the switch. Using the command *SHOW VLAN BRIEF* gives you an abbreviated list of the VLANs on the System.

Verifying VLAN Assignment

In addition to looking at the VLANs, it is also important to be able to verify which ports are parts of which VLAN. We can look at individual VLAN assignments using the command *SHOW VLAN* and then either the VLAN number or name. As shown in Figure 13.6, the *SHOW VLAN BRIEF* command gives us lots of information.

```
Switch>enable
Switch#show vlan brief

VLAN Name                              Status     Ports
---- ------------------------------    ---------  --------------------------------
1    default                           active     Fa0/3, Fa0/4, Fa0/5, Fa0/6
                                                  Fa0/7, Fa0/8, Fa0/9, Fa0/10
                                                  Fa0/11, Fa0/12, Fa0/13, Fa0/14
                                                  Fa0/15, Fa0/16, Fa0/17, Fa0/18
                                                  Fa0/19, Fa0/20, Fa0/21, Fa0/22
                                                  Fa0/23, Fa0/24, Gig1/1, Gig1/2
3    HR                                active     Fa0/2
4    sales                             active
5    IT                                active
1002 fddi-default                      active
1003 token-ring-default                active
1004 fddinet-default                   active
1005 trnet-default                     active
Switch#show vlan ?
  brief  VTP all VLAN status in brief
  id     VTP VLAN status by VLAN id
  name   VTP VLAN status by VLAN name
  <cr>
```

FIGURE 13.6   *Show Commands for VLANs*

HEAD OF THE CLASS...

Are VLANs Important?

I often get asked why VLANs are so important. Are they used in the enterprise? VLANs are used to create virtual segments in our network. A network that has excessive amounts of broadcasts put an undue burden on the network. The use of VLANs is very commonplace, and you will see as a CCNA that often this is the majority of the work you perform when you are working on the LAN.

TROUBLESHOOTING VLANs

Troubleshooting VLANs centers around making sure that the ports are assigned correctly to their VLANs. There are very few configuration issues other than port assignment that might go wrong. One of the other problems that could cause issues is incorrect IP address assignment for the VLANs.

Show Commands

We've already looked at several show commands but for the most multipurpose show command, use the command *SHOW VLAN*, which gives you the name of the VLANs, port address assignment, VLAN IDS, MTU, type of connection, as well as statistics. As shown in Figure 13.7, the *SHOW VLAN* command gives us additional statistics for the VLANs.

```
Switch>enable
Switch#show vlan

VLAN Name                         Status    Ports
---- -------------------------    --------- -------------------------------
1    default                      active    Fa0/3, Fa0/4, Fa0/5, Fa0/6
                                            Fa0/7, Fa0/8, Fa0/9, Fa0/10
                                            Fa0/11, Fa0/12, Fa0/13, Fa0/14
                                            Fa0/15, Fa0/16, Fa0/17, Fa0/18
                                            Fa0/19, Fa0/20, Fa0/21, Fa0/22
                                            Fa0/23, Fa0/24, Gig1/1, Gig1/2
3    HR                           active    Fa0/2
4    sales                        active
5    IT                           active
1002 fddi-default                 active
1003 token-ring-default           active
1004 fddinet-default              active
1005 trnet-default                active

VLAN Type  SAID     MTU   Parent RingNo BridgeNo Stp  BrdgMode Transl Trans2
---- ----- -------- ----- ------ ------ -------- ---- -------- ------ ------
1    enet  100001   1500  -      -      -        -    -        0      0
3    enet  100003   1500  -      -      -        -    -        0      0
4    enet  100004   1500  -      -      -        -    -        0      0
```

FIGURE 13.7   *SHOW VLAN Command*

Test Day Tip

The *SHOW VLAN* command gives you VLAN information, assignment, and statistics.

To check the IP addressing for the VLANs, use the *SHOW RUNNING-CONFIG* command. As shown in Figure 13.8, here's a sample Running-Config file.

```
!
interface GigabitEthernet1/1
!
interface GigabitEthernet1/2
!
interface Vlan1
 ip address 10.1.1.2 255.0.0.0
!
interface Vlan3
 ip address 11.0.0.1 255.0.0.0
!
line con 0
!
line vty 0 4
 login
line vty 5 15
 login
!
!
end

Switch#
```

FIGURE 13.8   *VLAN IP Addresses from the SHOW RUNNING-CONFIG*

Test Day Tip
The running-config shows us the IP addressing information for each VLAN.

To verify the existence of the VLAN.DAT file that contains the standard VLANs, you can use the *SHOW FLASH* command. As shown in Figure 13.9, a sample vlan.dat file is located in flash memory.

Clear Commands

To clear the VLAN statistics, from priviledged exec mode, enter the command *CLEAR VTP COUNTERS*. It should also be noted to clear all the VLAN information; you should enter both of the following commands. *ERASE STARTUP-CONFIG* clears all the configuration information from the switch and will effectively erase all extended VLAN information as well as the IP address information for the VLANs. It should be noted that this will erase ALL configuration information from the switch so it should only be used when you are going to redeploy the switch to another location. To erase

```
[OK]
Switch#show flash
Directory of flash:/

    1  -rw-      4414921           <no date>  c2960-lanbase-mz.122-25.FX.bin
    2  -rw-          736           <no date>  vlan.dat


64016384 bytes total (59600727 bytes free)
Switch#
```

FIGURE 13.9   *Show Flash Command Verifying the VLAN.DAT File*

```
Switch>enable
Switch#clear vtp counters
Switch#erase startup-config
Erasing the nvram filesystem will remove all configuration files! Continue? [con
firm]
[OK]
Erase of nvram: complete
%SYS-7-NV_BLOCK_INIT: Initialized the geometry of nvram
Switch#delete flash:vlan.dat
Delete filename [vlan.dat]?
Delete flash:/vlan.dat? [confirm]

Switch#
```

FIGURE 13.10   *Clearing a Switch of VLAN Information*

the standard VLAN information, you need to issue the command *DELETE FLASH:VLAN.DAT*, which will erase the vlan.dat file from the switches flash. As shown in Figure 13.10, we clear the counters, startup-config, and the vlan.dat file from flash.

Exam Warning

Remember to clear all VLAN information, you need to erase the configuration and delete the VLAN.DAT file. Just erasing the configuration will not get rid of all the VLAN information.

SUMMARY OF EXAM OBJECTIVES

VLANs are very important to enterprise computing these days as they allow us to segment the network for different protocols, broadcast domains, and security. The proprietary Cisco VLAN Protocol InterSwitch Link has been replaced by the industry standard 802.1Q. Cisco also supports VLANs for Token Ring and FDDI networks. To create VLANs, you choose from the 4,094 choices for numbering and potentially also add a name to the VLAN. The VLAN assignment can be the more common port based assignment or can use dynamic VLANs using a VLAN Membership Policy Server. Each VLAN will represent a separate network and therefore should have a separate IP address network. The configuration information for standard VLANs 1 to 1,005 is stored in flash in a file called VLAN.DAT and those for VLANs 1,006 to 4,094 or the extended VLANs is stored in the configuration file.

EXAM OBJECTIVES FAST TRACK

VLANs Explained

- Used to control the size of broadcast domains

- Used to segment different departments with different security requirements from one another

- Used to connect the same departments over several locations into the same broadcast domain

- Used to control different network protocols so they don't interfere with one another

Configuring a VLAN

- A VLAN is created using the *VLAN #* command.

- The administrative VLAN or the VLAN that is used to access the switch configuration is VLAN 1.

- You may name the VLAN using the *NAME* command.

- To delete a VLAN, use the *NO VLAN #* command.

- To assign a port to a specific VLAN use the *SWITCHPORT MODE ACCESS* and *SWITCHPORT ACCESS VLAN #* commands.

- To assign a VLAN and IP address, use the IP ADDRESS IP.IP.IP.IP SM.SM.SM.SM substituting the appropriate IP and subnet mask.

VLAN Databases

- The normal or standard VLANs are stored in flash in a file called *VLAN.DAT*.

- The extended VLAN information is stored in the *RUNNING-CONFIG* file.

- To clear all VLAN information, you must erase the *STARTUP-CONFIG* file and delete the *VLAN.DAT* file and restart the switch.

Verifying VLANs

- To verify the VLANs on the system, use the *SHOW VLAN BRIEF* command.

- To verify the existence of the VLAN.DAT file, use the *SHOW FLASH* command.

Troubleshooting VLANs

- Troubleshooting VLANs often comes in the form of verifying the ports associated with each VLAN.

- To see what ports are assigned to each VLAN and their statistics, use the *SHOW VLAN* command.

EXAM OBJECTIVES FREQUENTLY ASKED QUESTIONS

Q: Why did Cisco move from its own protocol InterSwitch Link to the IEEE 802.1Q?

A: The switch occurred because Cisco needed the ability to interoperate with other networking devices from other manufacturers.

Q: Why is it important to segment broadcast domains?

A: Broadcasts are very common in networking in things like DHCP and ARP. This traffic causes overhead on the network.

Q: What is the administrative VLAN?

A: The administrative VLAN is the VLAN in which you can communicate with the configuration on the switch.

Q: Are there any VLANs set up by default?

A: VLAN 1 and VLANs 1,002 to 1,005 are set up by default.

Q: What VLAN is the ports setup in by default on the switch?

A: All ports are set up by default to VLAN 1.

SELF TEST

1. Your company has an Ethernet network that has been exhibiting signs of being overloaded. Of the four uses for VLANs discussed in this chapter, which one is the most appropriate?

   A. Security

   B. Broadcast domains

   C. Departmental grouping

   D. Segmenting protocols

2. Your company has an Ethernet network that has confidential information that must be protected for the HR department. Of the four uses for VLANs discussed in this chapter, which one is the most appropriate?

   A. Security

   B. Broadcast domains

   C. Departmental grouping

   D. Segmenting protocols

3. Your company has a departmental application that relies on broadcasts as its main transmission mode. Of the four uses for VLANs discussed in this chapter, which one is the most appropriate?

   A. Security

   B. Broadcast domains

   C. Departmental grouping

   D. Segmenting protocols

4. Your company has an Ethernet network which you will implement VOIP on. Of the four uses for VLANs discussed in this chapter, which one is the most appropriate?

   A. Security

   B. Broadcast domains

   C. Departmental grouping

   D. Segmenting protocols

5. There are a series of different networking devices in your corporate network. VLANs can be created on with of the following devices?

   A. HUB

   B. Network interface card

   C. Wireless access point

   D. Switch

6. Your network has several departments that are spread over several different floors in a building. HR resides on both the 1st and 3rd floor. Why would we use VLANs in this situation? There are a series of different networking devices in your corporate network.

   A. Departmental grouping

   B. Security

   C. Broadcast domains

   D. Segmenting protocols

7. You have been tasked with creating VLANs to solve broadcast issues. You access the switch and go to global configuration mode, what is the correct command for creating VLAN 3?

A. *Switch#VLAN 3*   **C.** *Switch>VLAN 3*

B. *Switch(config-if)#VLAN 3*   **D.** *Switch(config)#VLAN 3*

8. You have been tasked with setting the IP address on VLAN. You access the switch, what is the correct command for creating VLAN 3?

A. *Switch#ip address 10.1.1.1 255.0.0.0*

B. *Switch(config-if)# ip address 10.1.1.1 255.0.0.0*

C. *Switch> ip address 10.1.1.1 255.0.0.0*

D. *Switch(config)# ip address 10.1.1.1 255.0.0.0*

9. You have been tasked with setting the IP address on VLAN. You access the switch, if the VLAN is inactive, what command do you issue to activate the interface?

A. *Switch(config-if)# activate*

B. *Switch(config-if)# reactivate*

C. *Switch(config-if)# turnon*

D. *Switch(config-if)# no shutdown*

10. You have been tasked with setting up a new VLAN. You are to name this new VLAN HR. What is the correct command for creating setting the name to HR?

A. *Switch#name HR*

B. *Switch(config-if)# name HR*

C. *Switch(config-vlan)# name HR*

D. *Switch(config)# name HR*

11. You have been tasked with setting up a new VLAN, VLAN 6. You are to name this new VLAN Production. What is the correct command for creating this VLAN?

A. *Switch#vlan 4*
    Switch(config-vlan)# name production

B. *Switch(config-if)# vlan 4*
    Switch(config-vlan)# name production

C. *Switch(config-vlan)# vlan 4*
    Switch(config-vlan)# name production

D. *Switch(config)# vlan 4*
    Switch(config-vlan)# name production

12. You have been tasked with renaming an existing VLAN. You are to name this new VLAN HR. What is the correct command for creating setting the name to HR?

    A. *Switch(config-vlan)# name HR*

    B. *Switch(config-vlan)# rename HR*

    C. *Switch(config-vlan)# newname HR*

    D. *Switch(config-vlan)# vlan name HR*

13. You have been tasked with assigning port fa0/1 to VLAN 3. What is the correct command for putting this port into an access mode?

    A. *Switch(config-if)# switchport mode trunk*

    B. *Switch(config-if)# switchport mode access*

    C. *Switch(config-if)# switchport mode VLAN*

    D. *Switch(config-if)# switchport access*

14. You have been tasked with assigning port fa0/3 to VLAN 100. What is the correct command for creating setting the name to HR?

    A. *Switch(config-if)# switchport access VLAN 100*

    B. *Switch(config-if)# access VLAN 100*

    C. *Switch(config-if)# switchport 100*

    D. *Switch(config-if)# VLAN 100 add*

15. You are setting up a network where you will be having different kinds of traffic based on protocol. You should set up what type of VLAN?

    A. static   **C.** dynamic

    B. traffic   **D.** switching

16. You are setting up a network where PCs need to be assigned based on department. These PCs will not be moved, what type of VLAN should you set up?

    A. Dynamic   **C.** Port-based

    B. Traffic-based   **D.** Protocol-based

17. The standard VLANs are stored in a file on our switch. What is that file called?

    A. VLAN.SDR

    B. VLAN

    C. VLAN.SWITCH

    D. VLAN.DAT

18. The standard VLANs use only a portion of the total VLANs that are available. From what range do the standard VLANs come from?

A. 1 to 1,024

B. 1 to 1,005

C. 1 to 100

D. 1 to 4,094

19. VLANs are supported on several different network types on a Cisco Switch. Which one of the following is not supported in standard VLANs?

A. Ethernet

B. Arcnet

C. FDDI

D. Token Ring

20. Extended VLANs are configurable on Cisco switches but do not have the functionality of standard VLANs. What VLAN numbers represent extended VLANs?

A. 1,000 to 4,094

B. 1,006 to 4,094

C. 100 to 4,094

D. 1 to 4,094

21. The extended VLANs are stored in a different location than our standard VLANs. Where are extended VLANs stored?

A. Running-config

B. Flash

C. Memory

D. VLAN.DAT

22. The standard VLANs are stored in the VLAN.DAT file. Where does this file reside?

A. Running-config

B. Flash

C. Memory

D. Hard drive

23. To completely clear a switch of all VLAN information, you must erase the startup-config and do which of the following?

A. Clear the whole flash

B. Erase the Running-Config

C. Reset the memory

D. Delete the Flash:VLAN.DAT

24. There are several ways to verify VLAN assignment for the ports on the system. Choose the correct *show* command.

A. *SHOW VLAN*

B. *SHOW VLANS*

C. *VLAN SHOW*

D. *SHOW ALL VLANS*

25. You would like to view all available VLANs in an abbreviated form. Which *show* command will allow you to view the VLANs in this form?

    A. *SHOW VLAN*   **C.** *SHOW VLAN 1*

    B. *SHOW VLAN BRIEF*   **D.** *SHOW VLANS*

26. Your company has a homogenous infrastructure made up of only Cisco switches. You wish to use a proprietary Cisco only VLAN protocol, which one would you choose?

    A. 802.1Q   **C.** Inter switch link (ISL)

    B. 802.10   **D.** LANE (LAN emulation)

27. Your company has an infrastructure made up of FDDI connections. You wish to use a VLAN protocol to segment the FDDI ring networks, which one would you choose?

    A. 802.1Q   **C.** Inter switch link

    B. 802.10   **D.** LANE

28. Your company has an infrastructure made up of ATM connections which you want to control via a less complicated VLAN solution. You wish to use a VLAN protocol to segment the ATM networks, which one would you choose?

    A. 802.1Q   **C.** Inter switch link

    B. 802.10   **D.** LANE

29. Your company has an infrastructure made up of many different kinds of switching equipment for Ethernet. You wish to use a VLAN protocol to interconnect this equipment, which one would you choose?

    A. 802.1Q   **C.** Inter switch link

    B. 802.10   **D.** LANE

30. You have implemented VLANs on your network. You wish to make sure that all the ports in your switch are set to access mode. How would you verify that fact?

    A. *SHOW FLASH*   **C.** *SHOW RUNNING-CONFIG*

    B. *SHOW VLAN B1*   **D.** *SHOW VTP STATUS*

31. You have recently made changes to the VLANs in your network. You would like to clear all the statistics of VLAN information to get a fresh start. What command would allow you to reset VLAN statistics?

    A. *CLEAR VTP COUNTERS*   **C.** *ERASE FLASH*

    B. *ERASE STARTUP-CONFIG* **D.** *ERASE VLAN.DAT*

SELF TEST QUICK ANSWER KEY

1.	B	**16.**	C
2.	A	**17.**	D
3.	B	**18.**	B
4.	D	**19.**	B
5.	D	**20.**	A
6.	A and B	**21.**	B
7.	D	**22.**	D
8.	B	**23.**	A
9.	D	**24.**	B
10.	C	**25.**	C
11.	D	**26.**	B
12.	A	**27.**	D
13.	B	**28.**	A
14.	A	**29.**	C
15.	C	**30.**	A

VLAN Trunking Protocol

INTRODUCTION

Virtual local area networks (VLANs) allow network administrators to secure and more efficiently manage switched networks. Devices such as computers that are physically connected to the same switch can be logically separated through the use of VLANs. When a Cisco switch is configured, there can be several VLAN databases created on that switch. Most network infrastructures have more than one switch. What VLAN Trunking Protocol (VTP) does is allow devices on different physical switches to be connected to the same logical network or VLAN. Without the VTP, each switch would operate independently of each other with their own unique databases. VTP allows switches on a network to share their VLAN database so that devices on different physical switches can exist on the same logical network.

VLANs play an extremely important role in an efficient switched network. A Cisco Certified Network Associate (CCNA) needs to know how to configure VTP so the switches can share a common VLAN database. After switches are configured properly to use a common database via VTP, the network administrator will be easily able to separate devices logically on the network. In summary, a CCNA needs to understand how VTP is used to configure VLANs over multiple switches and understand how to use these VLAN databases to logically divide the network.

EXPLAINING VTP

We have seen in the previous chapter "VLANs" how to implement VLANs and assign specific machines to those VLANs. This chapter focuses on how to make management of VLANs simpler for Cisco network associates, so we can streamline the process. VTP is an attempt by Cisco to exchange information about VLANs between different networking devices such as switches. In addition, it provides a way for multiple VLANs to be carried from one switch to another providing a conduit or "trunk" for this to occur. In a small network, recreating several VLANs is not an issue, but when there are many VLANs, the overall maintenance of this task becomes burdensome.

Trunks

Let's first work through the concept of what a trunk is. A trunk is a link between two switches that carries more than one VLANs data. We saw in Chapter 13 that each individual port is typically assigned to a specific VLAN, and this VLAN defines who else can hear the traffic that is confined to this VLAN. A problem arises when data needs to be passed from one switch to another; for example, we have a switch on one floor that contains three VLANs and a switch on another floor that contains the same three VLANs. One method we could use to tie these two switches together would be to run a separate wire on one switch for each of the VLANs to a separate port for each of the VLANs on the other switch. Can you imagine having a dozen VLANs and having to run a dozen wires between the two switches? It is a lot of extra work. Instead, we run a single wire between the two as a conduit for information to flow from one switch to another. For the VLANs to remain in place and for the two switches to be able to keep track of what data belongs to each VLAN, a system had to be developed to add VLAN information to each packet, so the two switches could forward the data to the correct VLAN on a different switch. We'll discuss the two most common ways of doing that in a moment, but the conduit between the two switches that carries this information is called a *trunk*. To set a particular port to trunking, you need to issue the command *switchport mode trunk*. As shown in Figure 14.1, this switchport for Gigabit 1/1 has been set to trunking mode.

```
Switch>enable
Switch#configure terminal
Enter configuration commands, one per line.   End with CNTL/Z.
Switch(config)#int gig1/1
Switch(config-if)#switchport mode trunk
Switch(config-if)#
```

FIGURE 14.1

Setting a Port to Trunking Mode

Exam Warning

Make sure you know how to enable a trunk for both InterSwitch Link (ISL) and 802.1Q for your exam. The command is *switchport mode trunk* and then *switchport encapsulation dot1q* or *ISL*.

Broadcast Domains

VLANs were envisioned to separate different kinds of traffic and that separation includes separating different broadcast domains. As we discussed in Chapter 13, a broadcast domain is the area that a broadcast will propagate out to. These broadcasts also need to flow from one switch to another through a VLAN that is connected by a trunk. A packet such as a Dynamic Host Configuration Protocol (DHCP) packet that is based on broadcasts needs the capability to flow through the VLAN to every machine even though they may be connected on different switches. This is not to say that DHCP packets flow between VLANs because the only way for traffic to flow between VLANs is via a router, and a router by default blocks broadcast packets.

Relation to VLANs

VLANs have to pass data including broadcasts to the ports that are associated with the VLAN. Every port on every switch that is part of the same VLAN should be able to communicate with one another without the assistance of a router. In essence, every port is on the same LAN when they are in the same VLAN even though they may be on separate switches and even in different locations. The connection between these different switches is the trunking that we talked about above and is the reason VTP is so important.

Security through VLANs

VLANs can be used to implement security by segmenting different departments into separate segments, so one department cannot eavesdrop on the traffic from another. Trunking could alter this security if someone to get access the trunked connection. The process of jumping from one VLAN to another is called *VLAN hopping* and could be a security risk if someone has access to the trunked connection. It is very important to make sure that your trunked connections are secure so that malicious activity cannot occur.

> **Test Day Tip**
>
> Even though the concept behind VLANs seems complex, the above areas are the focus for what VLANs accomplish.

Encapsulation Methods

Cisco has several ways to incorporate VLAN traffic into trunking on switches. In Chapter 13 we discussed that for Ethernet networks, Cisco supports two different standards for VLANs, and they are the Institute of Electrical and Electronics Engineers, Inc.'s (IEEE) implementation of 802.1Q and Cisco's ISL. On Fiber Distributed Data Interface (FDDI) networks, VLANs are supported using 802.10, and for Asynchronous Transfer Mode (ATM) networks, Cisco uses LAN Emulation (LANE) Protocol. We will discuss the main two Ethernet VLAN protocols because the majority of all LANs are Ethernet.

> **Test Day Tip**
>
> Though Cisco supports four different ways to set up VLAN tagging, two—802.1Q and ISL—typically show up on the certification exam.

802.1Q

Cisco supports the industry standard for VLANs standardized by the IEEE called *802.1Q*. This format inserts a tag into each frame that lists the VLAN ID for that frame. This protocol is defined for Ethernet networks and allows the transport of VLAN frames from one switch to another through links that are set for trunking. Cisco has been transitioning its switches to this format for VLANs because it allows interoperation with equipment from other manufacturers.

ISL

Some older Cisco switches support Cisco's proprietary format for VLANs called *ISL*. Cisco's format that has been phased out of new versions of the IOS and out of newer switches used a slightly different format for identification of VLANs. ISL encapsulates the data frame with a format that indicates the VLAN. This format instead of inserting a tag has a slightly greater overhead and could only be used with other Cisco switches that supported it.

HEAD OF THE CLASS...

Why did Cisco Switch from ISL to 802.1Q?
You are probably asking why Cisco switched from its own protocol ISL to 802.1Q. There are certainly technical reasons why the switch took place, but in simple terms, they needed to interoperate with other equipment manufacturers. The IEEE 802.1Q is a standard that is supported by all major manufacturers, and therefore, Cisco could take advantage of being able to operate with existing equipment. Certainly, this switch was not in Cisco's best interest as with ISL they could have a homogenous switch infrastructure, but they were forced to do this because of consumer feedback.

VTP MODES

To exchange VLAN information with other Cisco switches, Cisco offers its own VTP. VTP exchanges information about numbering and names of VLANs among Cisco switches. VTP uses a client server model to exchange this information from one switch to another, meaning that we have a main server that is where information is changed and the client who transfers this information to itself. Cisco uses the word *domain* to describe the relationship among these servers and clients, while using it for other uses such as Web domains, Microsoft active directory domains, and many more which may be somewhat confusing. We will explore what each one of these components of Cisco's VTP infrastructure does.

> **Exam Warning**
> Make sure you understand the four standard modes for VTP: *server, client, transparent,* and *off.*

Server

Cisco uses domains to separate different areas of VTP. Each domain represents an area of influence and is headed by a VTP server. The *VTP server* is the master copy of VLAN information for its domain. Changes to VLAN information on the server will be propagated out to all clients and will replace their VLAN databases. As such, you must be very careful when changing the VTP server VLAN database as any mistakes will be compounded when this information is sent to the clients. As shown in Figure 14.2, the switch is put into VTP server mode.

```
Switch>enable
Switch#configure terminal
Enter configuration commands, one per line.  End with CNTL/Z.
Switch(config)#vtp mode server
Device mode already VTP SERVER.
Switch(config)#
```

Client

Cisco VTP clients receive their VLAN information from the VTP server. The clients merely replicate changes from the server to the VLAN database. Any changes, deletions, and additions are copied from the VTP server to the client. As shown in Figure 14.3, the switch is put into VTP client mode.

```
Switch>enable
Switch#configure terminal
Enter configuration commands, one per line.  End with CNTL/Z.
Switch(config)#vtp mode client
Setting device to VTP CLIENT mode.
Switch(config)#
```

Transparent

Cisco has a third option for VTP which is termed *transparent*. Transparent VTP switches participate in exchanging VLAN information, yet they do not actually implement the information they are exchanging. Transparent switches may have specialty needs and therefore do not need to implement VLAN changes, but they also may be a link between two other switches that do need to implement changes and therefore need to pass along the VLAN information. As shown in Figure 14.4, the switch is put into VTP transparent mode.

```
Switch>enable
Switch#configure terminal
Enter configuration commands, one per line.  End with CNTL/Z.
Switch(config)#vtp mode transparent
Setting device to VTP TRANSPARENT mode.
Switch(config)#
```

Test Day Tip

Using transparent mode does tend to show up on the exam. Make sure you understand that transparent mode forwards VTP information to other switches but does not implement the VTP database into the switch.

Off

The final option for VTP is to not participate at all in VTP. When a switch is set for off, the switch neither implements VLAN information from the VTP server nor does it transfer VTP information to other switches. Perhaps, the best term for this might be a standalone VLAN switch.

CONFIGURING VTP

Configuring Cisco VTP is a multistep process. You must first define the version of VTP that you will be using whether that be versions 1, 2, or even 3 as newer Cisco Catalyst switches could use. You must assign the switch to the VTP domain it will be a part of, so it can exchange information with other Cisco switches in the autonomous domain. We must set the mode among server, client, transparent, or off. In addition, we need to set a password for security reasons. What follows is a discussion of these areas.

Versions

There are three different versions of the proprietary Cisco VTP. Version 3 is only available on newer Cisco Enterprise switches that run the Catalyst OS or operating system. We will discuss the two versions which could be mentioned on your certification exam.

NEW AND NOTEWORTHY...

VTP Version 3 Is Here!

New versions of the Catalyst Switch Operating System support VTP version 3. Because these are the only switches that implement that, you must be using a homogenous environment of new Catalyst switches only.

Version 1

Version 1 of the Cisco VTP is the most supported version. This is the recommended protocol unless you need the additional functionality that is built into version 2. To enable version 1, use the command *vtp version 1*. As shown in Figure 14.5, the switch is configured for version 1 VTP.

```
Switch>enable
Switch#configure terminal
Enter configuration commands, one per line.  End with CNTL/Z.
Switch(config)#vtp version 1
VTP mode already in V1.
Switch(config)#
```

FIGURE 14.5

Configuring VTP Version 1

Version 2

Version 2 of the Cisco VTP is incompatible with the other two versions. VTP version 2 does add one significant difference to version 1. VTP version 2 adds support for Token Ring VLANs. To enable version 2, use the command *vtp version 2*. As shown in Figure 14.6, the switch is configured for version 2 VTP.

FIGURE 14.6

Configuring VTP Version 2

```
Switch>enable
Switch#configure terminal
Enter configuration commands, one per line.  End with CNTL/Z.
Switch(config)#vtp version 2
Switch(config)#^Z
%SYS-5-CONFIG_I: Configured from console by console
```

Exam Warning

Remember that version 1 and version 2 of VTP are not compatible and will not work with one another.

Creating a Management Domain

To set up a VTP hierarchy in your infrastructure, you must first create a management domain. The domain hierarchy that will be set up to support our server and clients will allow you to use VTP to replicate the VLAN information. To set up the VTP domain, use the following command *vtp domain*. As shown in Figure 14.7, the switch is configured for the VTP domain corporate.

FIGURE 14.7

Configuring the VTP Domain Corporate

```
Switch>enable
Switch#configure terminal
Enter configuration commands, one per line.  End with CNTL/Z.
Switch(config)#vtp domain corporate
Changing VTP domain name from NULL to corporate
Switch(config)#
```

EXERCISE 14.1

Setting VTP Domain, Mode, and Version

1. From *User Exec* mode, type the command **enable**.

2. From *Privileged Exec* mode, type the command **configure terminal**.

3. From *Global Configuration* mode, type the command **vtp domain corporate**, which will create the corporate domain.

4. From *Global Configuration* mode, type the command ***vtp mode server***, which will set the mode to server.

5. From *Global Configuration* mode, type the command ***vtp version 1***, which will set the version to version 1.

Adding a Switch to a Management Domain

To add a switch to a management domain, you must first set the switch to client mode, so it can receive VTP information using the *vtp mode* command. Then, you should specify the management domain name using the *vtp domain* command. As shown in Figure 14.8, the switch is put into VTP client mode and configured for the domain called *corporate*.

```
Switch>enable
Switch#configure terminal
Enter configuration commands, one per line.  End with CNTL/Z.
Switch(config)#vtp mode client
Setting device to VTP CLIENT mode.
Switch(config)#vtp domain corporate
Changing VTP domain name from NULL to corporate
Switch(config)#
```

FIGURE 14.8

Configuring a Switch as a VTP Client

Test Day Tip

Remember that a switch that is brought on as a client will overwrite its own VLAN information with the VLAN database from the server.

Verifying VTP Configuration

To verify the VTP configuration, use the *show vtp status* command as shown in Figure 14.9.

```
Switch>enable
Switch#show vtp status
VTP Version                     : 2
Configuration Revision          : 0
Maximum VLANs supported locally : 255
Number of existing VLANs        : 5
VTP Operating Mode              : Client
VTP Domain Name                 : corporate
VTP Pruning Mode                : Disabled
VTP V2 Mode                     : Disabled
VTP Traps Generation            : Disabled
MD5 digest                      : 0x2B 0x62 0xB6 0x19 0x6C 0xC8 0x0B 0xB3
Configuration last modified by 0.0.0.0 at 0-0-00 00:00:00
```

FIGURE 14.9

Show vtp status *Command*

VTP Password

To protect the VTP information in your infrastructure from erroneous information, it is suggested that you use a password to protect your clients from receiving false information. To set the VTP password, use the following command *vtp password*. As shown in Figure 14.10, the switch is configured with a VTP password called *password*.

```
Switch>enable
Switch#configure terminal
Enter configuration commands, one per line.  End with CNTL/Z.
Switch(config)#vtp password password
Setting device VLAN database password to password
Switch(config)#
```

Message Digest 5

To keep the password secret in a VTP domain, the switches use the Message Digest 5 (MD5) hash to protect the transmission. Cisco switches must be configured with the same domain name and same password to communicate with one another.

Exam Warning

Make sure you understand how to implement a VTP password in your management domain. The password is the only form of security for transferred VTP information.

VTP Pruning

To keep broadcasts from propagating to switches that do not contain ports in certain VLANs, Cisco has implemented a process called *pruning*. When broadcast traffic is sent switch to switch, by default it is also passed to switches that may not have any ports in that particular VLAN. We can enable pruning that automatically shapes the traffic and does not send broadcasts to switches that do not contain those VLANs. To enable pruning, all the switches in your management domain must support VTP version 2 and use the command *vtp pruning* from *Global Configuration* mode.

Pruneeligible

To have a VLAN be pruned, you have to enable the specific VLAN to be pruned using the command from *Global Configuration* mode *vtp prune-eligible 2*, which would enable pruning for VLAN 2.

Test Day Tip
Make sure you understand pruning and that it is not enabled by default. With pruning in place, then specific VLANs must be marked as pruneeligible.

INTER-VLAN ROUTING

For two VLANs to communicate with one another and still maintain their separate segments, we must use a router to accomplish this. A *router* is a device that connects two separate networks together and acts as a gateway between the two of them. A router exchanges information between the two networks based on a routing table that describes the best path to get from one network to another. When we send information from one VLAN to another, we call this *inter-VLAN routing*. This can be accomplished in several different configurations using either a separate router or a module that can be inserted in some Cisco switches called a *Route-Switch module*. A Route-Switch module is essentially just a router in a card format that was designed exclusively to exchange traffic between VLANs. In most corporate situations, we would probably use a combination of both separate routers and Route-Switch modules.

Configuring Inter-VLAN Routing

For two VLANs to communicate with one another, it is necessary to use a router to route or move the two networks together. Because the two VLANs are on different network segments and have the different address ranges, a router is necessary to connect them together and to have communication. That router can use or not use VLANs themselves, so there may be several different configurations such as the following.

Router on a Stick

A *router on a stick* is a configuration where we have a single separate router that is connected to the switch through a single port. The router uses VTP to separate different VLANs even though they are being carried on the single connection. Essentially, the information is carried out from the switch to the router tagged with one VLAN ID, is transferred to a different VLAN at the router, and then is sent back on the same link. Hence, the router looks like it is connected to the switch on a stick and got the term *router on a stick*. There are some requirements for a router on a stick configuration. The router must be connected to the switch using a high-speed ink, at least 100 MBps. Second, the router and the switch must both support the same

VLAN protocol and be configured. Third, the router must be configured with subinterfaces for each of the VLANs supported to route between them. To configure the router on a stick configuration, you access the router and start creating subinterfaces from *Global Configuration* mode, type **interface** and then the **subinterface number**, and then specify the VLAN protocol using the *encapsulation* command. Follow that with setting a specific Internet Protocol (IP) address on the subinterface using the *IP address* command. Figure 14.11 sets up FastEthernet port 0/0 with two subinterfaces and assigns them IP address of 10.0.0.1 on vlan 2 and 11.0.0.1 on vlan 3.

FIGURE 14.11

Setting up Router on a Stick Configuration

```
Router>enable
Router#configure terminal
Enter configuration commands, one per line.  End with CNTL/Z.
Router(config)#interface fa0/0.1
Router(config-subif)#encapsulation dotlq 2
Router(config-subif)#ip address 10.0.0.1 255.0.0.0
Router(config-subif)#interface fa0/0.2
Router(config-subif)#encapsulation dotlq 3
Router(config-subif)#ip address 11.0.0.1 255.0.0.0
Router(config-subif)#
```

Exam Warning

The router on a stick configuration is very common for Cisco exams on VLANs. You use one link on the router and one link on the switch that both support VLANs to route between different VLANs.

IP Route Command

Routing between VLANs can be either accomplished using a routing protocol such as Routing Information Protocol (RIP) or Open Shortest Path First (OSPF) or done using a static route on the router. To set up a routing protocol rip, you would use the *router rip* command and then assign the networks to RIP using the *network* command. Figure 14.12 shows setting RIP for inter-VLAN routing between the 10.0.0.0 and 11.0.0.0 networks.

In addition, perhaps a simpler way for routing between VLANs is using a static route. A static route is set by the administrator and has very little overhead for the router. The command to set a static route is *IP route* and then the network address and subnet mask of the destination network followed by the interface used to reach it. In Figure 14.13, we set up a static route to the network 10.0.0.0 using interface FA0/0 and a static route to network 11.0.0.0 using interface FA1/0.

```
Router>enable
Router#config t
Enter configuration commands, one per line.   End with CNTL/Z.
Router(config)#router rip
Router(config-router)#network 10.0.0.0
Router(config-router)#network 11.0.0.0
Router(config-router)#^Z
%SYS-5-CONFIG_I: Configured from console by console
Router#show ip route
Codes: C - connected, S - static, I - IGRP, R - RIP, M - mobile, B - BGP
       D - EIGRP, EX - EIGRP external, O - OSPF, IA - OSPF inter area
       N1 - OSPF NSSA external type 1, N2 - OSPF NSSA external type 2
       E1 - OSPF external type 1, E2 - OSPF external type 2, E - EGP
       i - IS-IS, L1 - IS-IS level-1, L2 - IS-IS level-2, ia - IS-IS inter area
       * - candidate default, U - per-user static route, o - ODR
       P - periodic downloaded static route

Gateway of last resort is not set

C    10.0.0.0/8 is directly connected, FastEthernet0/0
C    11.0.0.0/8 is directly connected, FastEthernet1/0
Router#
```

FIGURE 14.12   *Setting up RIP Protocol*

```
Router>enable
Router#config t
Enter configuration commands, one per line.   End with CNTL/Z.
Router(config)#ip route 10.0.0.0 255.0.0.0 fa0/0
Router(config)#ip route 11.0.0.0 255.0.0.0 fa1/0
Router(config)#^Z
%SYS-5-CONFIG_I: Configured from console by console
Router#show ip route
Codes: C - connected, S - static, I - IGRP, R - RIP, M - mobile, B - BGP
       D - EIGRP, EX - EIGRP external, O - OSPF, IA - OSPF inter area
       N1 - OSPF NSSA external type 1, N2 - OSPF NSSA external type 2
       E1 - OSPF external type 1, E2 - OSPF external type 2, E - EGP
       i - IS-IS, L1 - IS-IS level-1, L2 - IS-IS level-2, ia - IS-IS inter area
       * - candidate default, U - per-user static route, o - ODR
       P - periodic downloaded static route

Gateway of last resort is not set

C    10.0.0.0/8 is directly connected, FastEthernet0/0
C    11.0.0.0/8 is directly connected, FastEthernet1/0
Router#
```

FIGURE 14.13   *Setting up Static Routes*

> **Test Day Tip**
>
> The *IP route* command is very common for routing in Cisco. Being able to assign the static route using this command will help on many questions in the exam.

Isolating Broadcast Traffic

Routers in general do not pass broadcasts from one network to another, so in the case of VLANs, broadcasts are not passed from one VLAN to another. This isolates the broadcast traffic from one VLAN to another. This is why we can create separate broadcast domains for each VLAN yet have them continue to be connected together using a router. VLANs with inter-VLAN routing are a great solution to solve the problem of creating smaller broadcast domains.

VERIFYING AND TROUBLESHOOTING VTP

Once the configuration of VTP is complete, you need to be able to verify that your configuration is correct. There are two *show* commands that allow us to verify this information.

Show Commands

The *show* command *show vtp status* allows us to view the VTP configuration for the switch. Figure 14.14 shows the switch output of the *show vtp status* command.

FIGURE 14.14

Show vtp status *Command*

```
Switch>enable
Switch#show vtp status
VTP Version                      : 2
Configuration Revision           : 0
Maximum VLANs supported locally  : 255
Number of existing VLANs         : 5
VTP Operating Mode               : Client
VTP Domain Name                  : corporate
VTP Pruning Mode                 : Disabled
VTP V2 Mode                      : Disabled
VTP Traps Generation             : Disabled
MD5 digest                       : 0x2B 0x62 0xB6 0x19 0x6C 0xC8 0x0B 0xB3
Configuration last modified by 0.0.0.0 at 0-0-00 00:00:00
```

In addition, statistics for the VTP are available by using the *show vtp counters* command, and Figure 14.15 shows the output from the *show vtp counters* command.

```
Switch>enable
Switch#show vtp counters
VTP statistics:
Summary advertisements received      : 5
Subset advertisements received       : 2
Request advertisements received      : 0
Summary advertisements transmitted : 4
Subset advertisements transmitted  : 1
Request advertisements transmitted : 1
Number of config revision errors     : 5
Number of config digest errors       : 0
Number of V1 summary errors          : 0


VTP pruning statistics:

Trunk                Join Transmitted Join Received      Summary advts received from
                                                         non-pruning-capable device
---------------      ---------------- ----------------   --------------------------
Switch#
```

FIGURE 14.15 Show vtp counters *Command*

SUMMARY OF EXAM OBJECTIVES

This chapter focused on replicating the VLAN information across your enterprise using the Cisco proprietary VTP. VTP information is exchanged from servers to clients, and their VLAN database is updated. A *trunk* is the conduit for carrying VLAN information from one switch to another using 802.1Q, ISL, 802.10, or LANE. The VLAN names and numbers are carried using VTP. VTP management is configured in domains which consist of servers and clients. Switches may also be configured in transparent mode where they do add VLAN information to their own database or off where they do not even participate in forward VTP messages. To not send unnecessary traffic, you may also configure VTP pruning on Cisco switches.

EXAM OBJECTIVES FAST TRACK

Explaining VTP

- VTP is a Cisco proprietary protocol for exchanging VLAN information between switches.

- VTP has three different versions, which are incompatible with one another.

- VLAN information must match in both number and name across the enterprise.

- Information for VLANs is carried across multiple switches using trunk ports.

VTP Modes

- VTP server mode serves as the focal point for making VLAN changes in the network.

- VTP client mode replicates changes from the server to its own VLAN database.

- VTP transparent mode forwards VTP messages to connected switches but does not implement the VLAN database in its own database.

- VTP off mode neither forwards VTP messages nor implements the VTP information in its own database.

- VTP mode is set using the *vtp mode* command.

- A switch may be only set to one VTP mode at a time.

Configuring VTP

- Switches must be put into a management domain using the *vtp domain* command.

- Switches must be configured into a version using the *vtp version* command. Version 2 switches support Token Ring.

- A password is configured to prevent erroneous VLAN information using the *vtp password* command.

Inter-VLAN Routing

- Inter-VLAN routing can be accomplished using separate interfaces for each VLAN or a single interface in a *router on a stick* configuration.

- Inter-VLAN routing can use either a separate router or a Route-Switch module built into a switch.

Verifying and Troubleshooting VTP

- *Show vtp status* command shows the current configuration of VTP on a switch.

- *Show vtp counters* command shows the current VTP statistics for the switch.

EXAM OBJECTIVES FREQUENTLY ASKED QUESTIONS

Q: What is the difference between VTP and VLAN tagging protocols?

A: For VLAN tagging, the switches use 802.1Q, ISL, 802.10, and LANE. For exchanging VLAN information, the switches use VTP.

Q: What modes can VTP be set up for?

A: VTP operates in server, client, transparent, or off modes.

Q: When a switch is added to a management domain as a client, what happens?

A: The VLAN database on the client is updated with the VLAN information from the server.

Q: Does VTP affect the ports assignment of VLANs on the switch?

A: VTP does not affect the ports that are configured on the switch, just the VLAN database.

Q: How is VTP information secured on the switch?

A: VTP information is exchanged using MD5 protocol, and a password that prevents inauthentic VLAN information from being exchanged.

Q: Why would you prune using VTP?

A: Pruning allows broadcast packets to be prevented from being sent to switches that are not using that particular VLAN.

SELF TEST

1. Your network has a large number of VLANs which must be configured on multiple switches. Which of the following protocols allow you to replicate your VLAN information to the different switches?

   A. 802.1Q   **C.** LANE

   B. ISL   **D.** Cisco VTP

2. Your network has a large number of VLANs which must be configured on multiple switches. You wish to replicate this information on your Token Ring network that comprised older Cisco equipment. Which version of VTP would you use?

   A. Version 1   **C.** Version 3

   B. Version 2   **D.** Version 4

3. Your network has a large number of VLANs which must be configured on multiple switches. What mode must the port be put into to accomplish sending multiple VLANs data between switches?

   A. Connected   **C.** Trunk

   B. Access   **D.** STP

4. Your network has a large number of VLANs which must be configured on multiple switches. You wish to replicate this information on your Ethernet network. Which version of VTP would you use?

   A. Version 1   **C.** Version 3

   B. Version 2   **D.** Version 4

5. Your network has a large number of VLANs which must be configured on multiple switches. You wish to replicate this information on your Ethernet network. You need a focal point to make all changes to the VLAN which is Switch1. What VTP mode would you set Switch1 to?

   A. Server   **C.** Transparent

   B. Client   **D.** Off

6. Your network has a large number of VLANs which must be configured on multiple switches. You wish to replicate this information on your Ethernet network. Switch2 needs to gain its VLAN information from Switch1. What VTP mode would you set Switch2 to?

   A. Server   **C.** Transparent

   B. Client   **D.** Off

7. Your network has a large number of VLANs which must be configured on multiple switches. You wish to replicate this information on your Ethernet network. You have Switch3 that has specialized VLAN information that must not be changed. Switch3 is between Switch1 and Switch2 that need to replicate VLAN information. What VTP mode would you set Switch3 to?

   A. Server   **C.** Transparent

   B. Client   **D.** Off

8. Your network has a large number of VLANs which must be configured on multiple switches. You wish to replicate this information
   on your network. You have Switch4 that does not need to exchange
   VLAN information with others. What VTP mode would you set
   Switch4 to?

   A. Server   **C.** Transparent

   B. Client   **D.** Off

9. Your network has a large number of VLANs which must be configured
   on multiple switches. You wish to replicate this information on your
   network. You have Switch1 that will be the focal point for VLAN information. What command would you use to set this switch to this mode?

   A. *Vtp mode client*

   B. *Vtp mode server*

   C. *Vtp mode transparent*

   D. *Vtp mode off*

10. Your network has a large number of VLANs which must be config-
    ured on multiple switches. You wish to replicate this information on
    your network. To group together your VLAN information, you need
    to create what?

    A. Group   **C.** Switchblock

    B. Vtp group   **D.** Domain

11. Your network has a large number of VLANs which must be config-
    ured on multiple switches. You wish to replicate this information
    on your network. You want to create a VTP management domain
    CORP. What command would you use to create that?

    A. *VTP CORP*

    B. *VLAN VTP CORP*

    C. *VTP DOMAIN CORP*

    D. *VLAN DOMAIN CORP*

12. Your network has a large number of VLANs which must be config-
    ured on multiple switches. You wish to replicate this information on
    your network. You want to set a switch to support VTP for Token
    Ring networks. What command would you use to enable that?

    A. *Version 1*

    B. *Version 2*

    C. *Vtp version 1*

    D. *Vtp version 2*

13. Your network has a large number of VLANs which must be configured on multiple switches. You wish to replicate this information on your network. You want to set a switch to support VTP for Token Ring networks. You are concerned about security. What command would you use to protect your VLAN information using the password password?

    A. *Password password*
    C. *VLAN password password*
    B. *Vtp password password*
    D. *No vtp password password*

14. Your network has a large number of VLANs which must be configured on multiple switches. You wish to replicate this information on your network. You need to change the management domain from CORP1 to CORP2. What command would you use to accomplish this task?

    A. *VTP DOMAIN CORP1 CORP2*

    B. *VTP DOMAIN CORP2 CORP1*

    C. *VTP DOMAIN CHANGE CORP2*

    D. *VTP DOMAIN CORP2*

15. Your network has a large number of VLANs which must be configured on multiple switches. You wish to replicate this information on your network. You are having problems with a switch and want to remove its VTP password. What command would you use to remove a VTP password?

    A. *No vtp password*
    C. *No vlan password*
    B. *No password*
    D. *Vtp password null*

16. Your network has a large number of VLANs which must be configured on multiple switches. You wish to see the current state of VTP on the system. What command would you use to show the current VTP configuration?

    A. *Show vtp counters*
    C. *Show vlan*
    B. *Show vtp status*
    D. *Show running-config*

17. Your network has a large number of VLANs which must be configured on multiple switches. You wish to see what errors have occurred with VTP transmissions on the switch. What command would you use to show this statistics current VTP configuration?

    A. *Show vtp counters*
    C. *Clear vtp counters*
    B. *Show vtp status*
    D. *Show running-config*

18. Your network has a large number of VLANs which must be configured on multiple switches. You wish to see how many errors are occurring, and you want to look at current information. What command would you use to set these statistics to a clean state?

    A. *Show vtp counters*   **C.** *Clear vtp counters*

    B. *Show vtp status*   **D.** *Show running-config*

19. Your network has a large number of VLANs which must be configured on multiple switches. You wish to see how many advertisements are occurring. What command would you use to see this information?

    A. *Show vtp counters*   **C.** *Clear vtp counters*

    B. *Show vtp status*   **D.** *Show running-config*

20. Your network has a large number of VLANs which must be configured on multiple switches. You are unable to connect to switches that are using a VTP password. What command would you use to see the MD5 digest for a switch?

    A. *Show vtp counters*   **C.** *Clear vtp counters*

    B. *Show vtp status*   **D.** *Show running-config*

21. Your network has a large number of VLANs which must be configured on multiple switches. Some switches do not have ports that are in all the VLANs in the enterprise. What would you enable to keep these switches from having unnecessary broadcast traffic?

    A. VTP server   **C.** VTP pruning

    B. 802.1Q   **D.** VTP transparent

22. Your network has a large number of VLANs which must be configured on multiple switches. Some switches do not have ports that are in all the VLANs in the enterprise. You have enabled VTP pruning on these switches, yet they are still receiving traffic. What must you also do to keep these switches from receiving unnecessary broadcast traffic?

    A. Reload the switch.

    B. Make the unused VLANs pruneeligible.

    C. Enable trunking.

    D. Set the mode to server.

SELF TEST QUICK ANSWER KEY

1.	D		12.	D
2.	B		13.	B
3.	C		14.	D
4.	A		15.	A
5.	A		16.	B
6.	B		17.	A
7.	C		18.	C
8.	A		19.	A
9.	B		20.	B
10.	D		21.	C
11.	C		22.	B

Cisco WAN Configuration

INTRODUCTION

Although a majority of network administration is done within the local area network (LAN), Cisco also provides equipment that will allow companies to connect to wide area network (WAN) links. An individual looking to pass the Cisco Certified Network Associate (CCNA) examination should be aware of WAN technologies such as Integrated Services Digital Network (ISDN), Asynchronous Transfer Mode (ATM), Frame Relay, and T1. An individual pursuing a career in the field of networking also needs to know which of these technologies fall into the category of circuit-switched, packet-switched, or dedicated line.

It is also useful to have a basic understanding of the bandwidth associated with these WAN technologies. Having a general idea of facts like ATM or T3, that these WAN connections are significantly faster than ISDN or Public Switched Telephone Network (PSTN) connections is also a good idea. Knowing the various speeds associated with these WAN technologies will also help to increase your chance of success on any multiple choice questions on the CCNA exam that deal with bandwidth.

We fully acknowledge use of Chapter 3, "Cisco Hardware and IOS Basics," from Building a Cisco Network for Windows 2000, ISBN: 978-1-928994-00-8 and Chapter 3, "Using PPP to Provide Remote Network Access" from Building Cisco Remote Access Networks: 978-1-928994-13-8

To be successful on the CCNA exam, you need to be able to understand diagrams with various WAN configurations. It is important to know the mesh and hierarchical WAN network models and the three core layers associated with the hierarchical model. Finally, to be successful on the exam, you should be aware of WAN design and topology. In summary, a CCNA needs to be aware of WAN technologies and understand how they fit into the overall picture of a company's infrastructure.

WHAT IS A WAN?

A WAN is defined as two or more remote networks connected by public communication methods. Most companies are still using a carrier method called *T1*, but other methods such as *cable* and *digital subscriber line* (DSL) (via Virtual Private Networks (VPNs)) are becoming increasingly popular. As we progress through this chapter, we look at the most common methods of establishing WAN links and how they differ, as well as how they are presented on the test.

WAN Terms

Below are some of the common terms used when discussing WANs and WAN technologies. As we describe each one, we will focus not only on the test, but also on real world applications.

CPE—Customer Premise Equipment

CPE is also known as *Customer Provided Equipment*; this is the terminal, modem, adapter, or any other device that connects to the telecommunications company's connection point to the outside. Some of the devices that you may see are customer service unit/data service unit (CSU/DSU), ISDN adapters, or cable and DSL modems. On the exam, remember that any time your router connects to the outside, there will be some sort of CPE device.

CO—Central Office

This is the building owned by the telecommunications company where your point-to-point connection joins the wide area cloud. This building contains the exchange-switching equipment that connects data networks or voice networks.

Last Mile

The Last Mile refers to the distribution to individual homes and businesses of high speed, low latency data, and voice access. Technologies such as fiber optic, high-speed copper, and wireless have been used to meet the growing demand for connectivity.

Demarcation Point

Demarcation point is also known as the *demarc point*; this is the jack in the wall where the telecommunications provider meets the CPE. If you are using a T1 circuit, you will also hear this called the *Smart Jack*. For an analog modem, it is called the *Network Box* on the outside of the building and it connects you to the PSTN and would also allow you to connect your regular telephone.

Toll Network

The term *Toll network* equates to the "Trunk" lines that run from your building to the CO. It is possible that your company has multiple phone lines and phone numbers; they are carried to your building on the Trunk line. These are the primary number and all subsequent numbers, and are called the *Toll network* as this is the link that you are paying for.

Categories

When working with WAN technologies, it is important to know what category of connectivity you are dealing with. The three major types of connectivity are detailed in this section.

Circuit-Switched

These are dedicated physical circuits. The two best examples of circuit-switched are dial-up modems using Plain Old Telephone Service (POTS) or ISDN. These technologies dial a number and establish a point-to-point connection with the device on the other side. It is analogous to placing a "voice" or person-to-person phone call between two electronic devices. Although these can be considered "point to point," the endpoint can change as you connect to different endpoint devices.

Packet-Switched

In a packet-switched network, the path your data takes may change during the transmission. The path the first packet takes may not be the same path that subsequent packets take, or every packet may travel a different path. Some common methods of packet-switched networking are X.25 and ATM.

X.25 is a protocol established by the Comité Consultatif International Téléphonique et Télégraphique (CCITT), an international telecommunications organization that became the International Telecommunication Union

Telecommunication Standardization Sector (ITU-T) based in Switzerland, in the 1980s. During the 1980s and 1990s, the X.25 Protocol was widely used to connect data communications devices worldwide using a device called a *packet assembler/disassembler* (PAD). A common usage for this technology was to connect a dumb terminal to a main frame computer over a WAN link.

Exam Warning

Even though this technology may be out of date, it is important to know what a PAD is. It may show up in a number of questions. For example, what layer of the Open System Interconnection (OSI) model would you find a PAD? The answer is Layer 2; the Data Link layer. Even though packets are normally associated with the network layer of the OSI, the PAD does not use higher level addressing.

ATM was developed in the mid-1980s to deliver real-time video and voice data across WAN connections. ATM uses a cell-switching methodology to transmit high bandwidth data. This protocol was standardized by both the ITU and the ATF Forum. This protocol is also at the Data Link layer of the OSI model, and uses virtual circuits and a 5-byte header and a consistent payload size of 48 bytes, unlike Internet Protocol (IP) that uses a variable length payload. This dedicated payload size reduces overhead on the receiving side by not having to negotiate the payload size.

Test Day Tip

Remembering that the ATM Protocol uses a fixed payload size increases efficiency of the data transfer rate.

Dedicated

A dedicated circuit is also known as a *point-to-point connection*. If you have a circuit that is always available to a remote location, such as a T1 or T3 circuit, you can see devices on the other side at without having to establish the WAN connection first. A T1 line is a 24-channel link that supports 1.544 Mbps of data transfer; a T3 is equal to 28 T1 (giving you almost 45 Mbps). In this circuit type, there is only one available destination as apposed to the other two types.

WAN Types

As you prepare for your CCNA, you will need to know the individual communications technologies used in WAN connectivity. In this session, you will learn the different technologies used in WAN configuration and connectivity.

PSTN

PSTN, also known as *POTS*, is the telephone on your desk. With a device known as a *modulator/demodulator* (MODEM), you can connect your computer to a dial-up network such as EarthLink or CompuServe. Before the Internet was transformed from a private government network to a network of private computers connected by common carriers and allowed the general public to purchase connectivity with carriers such as GTE, Sprint, AT&T, and cable companies such as Comcast and Sprint, you would use the PSTN to connect to private information services. Today these services have been absorbed by the Internet and you don't see many uses for PSTN; however, you can connect a MODEM to the AUX port on the back of your router and dial in to your router to make configuration changes.

ISDN

ISDN, a digital communications service, comes in two common configurations; Basic Rate Interchange (BRI) meant for home use and Primary Rate Interchange (PRI) meant for business use. The basic difference between the two services is the number of channels available to carry traffic. With ISDN, there are two types of channels, bearer channels (B channels) that carry the data elements (either voice or computer data) and the delta channel (D channel) that handles the signaling of the circuit. ISDN uses out-of-band signaling (the D channel), where the T1 or T3 uses in-band signaling, With in-band signaling, you lose 8 Kbps of each channel for control of the circuit, and with out-of-band, you lose one channel.

> **Test Day Tip**
> When answering questions about ISDN, remember the B channels carry data. The trick I use to remember this is that they bear (like bear the load) data.

BRI is a version of ISDN that was designed to bring digital dial-up service to homes. It has two B channels of 64 Kbps each and one control channel (D channel) of 16 Kbps. It was to allow homes to connect with information services providers (pre-Internet) and voice calls with a faster connection than a MODEM could achieve. AT&T and Sprint marketed ISDN stating that "by 1998 every home in America would have ISDN"; today most homes use cable or DSL for voice and data connectivity and the number of businesses that still use ISDN BRI for a back-up connection to their WAN connections are very few.

PRI is an ISDN standard that defines 24 channels with a throughput of 1.544 Mbps (such as the T1 carrier); the major difference between PRI and T1 is that in a T1, you get 24 data channels of 64 Kbps and you lose 8 Kbps from each channel for signaling and control of the entire circuit, and in PRI ISDN, you get 23 64 K channels and lose one channel of 64 K for control. As described in the previous section, this is the difference between in-band and out-of-band control or signaling. PRIs are mostly used with telephone Primary Branch Exchange (PBX) systems.

Time-division multiplexing (TDM) is a digital transmission method that multiple bit streams are transmitted in a way that it appears that they are sent simultaneously. It is comprised of frames where a timeslot for each channel (or bit stream) and after the last timeslot completes, it starts over with the first timeslot again. TDM has been used in T1, ISDN, and other protocols over time. It is most commonly used in a synchronous data stream.

DSL

DSL is a digital connection in a point-to-point topology. The DSL line connects from your home or office to the telephone companies' CO.

HEAD OF THE CLASS...

DSL Speed Variations
The key to DSL speed is the closeness to the CO. The further away from the CO and the digital subscriber line access multiplexer (DSLAM), the slower your DSL connection will be. The maximum distance from a CO for a DSL customer is 18,000 ft.

There are two common variations of DSL: ADSL and SDSL. ADSL stands for asymmetric digital subscriber line. In ADSL you have two different speeds, a higher speed for downloads and a lower speed for upload; for example, if you had a 1 Mbps connection, you would have 768 Kbps for downloads and 256 K for uploads. This is for people who download more than they upload and prefer to have greater speeds on the download side. SDSL is symmetric digital subscriber line; this splits the bandwidth equally between upload and download. Taking the same 1 Mbps connection, you would have 512 Kbps for uploading and 512 Kbps for downloading. The DSL specifications state that DSL can operate from 1 Mbps up to 8 Mbps, depending on the equipment and distance from the CO.

Exam Warning
Note that DSL signals are not capable of being transmitted over fiber optic cables.

There are two signaling standards used in ADSL: Discrete MultiTone (DMT) and Carrierless Amplitude/Phase (CAP). The most commonly used today is DMT. In DMT, it breaks the ADSL signal into 247 4kHz channel. Imagine connecting 247 modems directly to your computer. In DMT, it uses the 247 channels to send data up and down the ADSL service and is constantly monitoring these channels. If the signal of one of these channels starts to become too degraded, it will move it to a new channel. In CAP, it creates two channels: one for upstream traffic and one for downstream traffic.

If you are using DSL, you were most likely given some filters to attach to your phone lines on jacks that are not being used for DSL; these are called *low-pass* (LP) filters. They are used to block everything above 4 kHz so that phone conversations aren't affected by DSL signals, as all voice conversations take place below the 4kHz frequency.

The ADSL Modem, called an *ADSL Transmission Unit-Remote* (ATU-R) by the phone company, connects your building to the telephone company over a copper connection. Remember maximum distance is 18,000 ft to the digital subscriber line access multiplexer (DSLAM), which then connects to the Internet service provider (ISP) switch that connects to the Internet.

Cable Modem

Cable Internet carries a digital signal between your home or office and the Internet over the same coax cable you get your television channels on. The cable companies use a shared media access method; each neighborhood has a multiplexer (MUX) that each customer connects to and that feeds back to the cable companies' CO. Each person on the MUX shares the total bandwidth with everyone else on the MUX. The speeds range from 1 Mbps to 400 Mbps on the downstream side and 384 Kbps to 20 Mbps on the upstream side.

The cable MODEM takes a digital signal and modulates it over a radio frequency and then demodulates it back to a digital signal on the other side.

NEW AND NOTEWORTHY...

Cable Modem Bandwidth Capping

When you sign up for cable Internet, you contract for a specific maximum bandwidth. Your modem is then programmed with that information. It is called *capping*; if you hack into your modem and change the programming (called "uncapping"), you may be in violation of your terms of service and in violation of laws.

As cable companies develop better neighborhood MUX technology, the shared bandwidth will continue to increase for the individual users. Today as more people are added to the MUX, speeds decrease to each user. When comparing DSL to cable, remember that you are connected point-to-point on DSL and shared access on cable.

T1/T3

T1 and T3 technology are T-carrier technologies developed by the Bell Laboratories. T1 is also known as *DS1* and the terms can be used interchangeably though they use the same technology.

T1 is comprised of 24 64Kbps channels for a gross bandwidth of 1.544 Mbps, similar to ISDN PRI. The difference, however, is you get to use all 24 channels but lose 8 Kbps for the overhead signaling. With T1, this is called *in-band signaling*. The primary protocol used over the T1 and T3 lines is Frame Relay and is a Layer 2 technology. T3 is comprised of 28 T1 circuits for a gross bandwidth of 44.736 Mbps.

E1/E3

In Europe, the European Conference of Postal and Telecommunications Administrations (CEPT) developed the standards for wide area networking, which improved upon the American standard T-carrier system. These standards are then adopted by the ITU-T, which supports speeds of 2.048 Mbps on an E1 line and 34.368 on an E3 line. Note that the E1 is faster than the American T1, but the E3 is approximately 10 Mbps slower than the T3. In America, the T1 is still the most commonly used carrier, but cable and DSL are encroaching on this.

Optical Carrier

Optical carrier (OC) uses fiber optic cable and a protocol called *Synchronous Optical Network* (SONET), and the speeds are based on the OC level. The cost of the link is based on the speed of the link. Using the SONET Protocol means there is a clocking signal required to make this protocol work effectively, when troubleshooting this signal the most common problem is the lack of the clocking signal from the service provider.

OC speeds range from 51.84 Mbps for an OC1 connection to 155 Mbps on an OC3, all the way up to 160 Gbps for an OC3072. The topology for a SONET is a dual-ring network, traffic goes one direction on one ring and the opposite direction on the other ring, so data is transmitted redundantly around the rings.

ATM

ATM was developed in the mid-1980s and is the primary carrier protocol used with the SONET technology discussed in the OC section above. ATM breaks the Layer 3 packets that can have a variable length size into fixed sized cells then transmits them over the fiber optic network. By using a fixed size, there is no need to negotiate the size of the buffer for sending and receiving the data, so it can move at higher speeds. ATM was designed to improve Voice over Internet Protocol (VOIP) and video traffic qualities, which require higher bandwidth than most traffic.

Exam Warning

Remember both ATM and OC use SONET and a dual-ring architecture. It will come up on the test in various different questions.

An ATM cell consists of a 5-byte header and a 48-byte payload; when the standard was being designed, groups from the United States wanted a 64-byte payload but were overruled by the international community. The thought was that 64 bytes was a good compromise between the large IP packets that carried lower bandwidth traffic and the 48-byte proposal for high-bandwidth voice and streaming video traffic.

Frame Relay

Frame Relay is most commonly associated with the T carrier (T1/T3) and is a Layer 2 Protocol, hence the word *Frame* in the name. It moves data from source to destination over a frame-associated cloud. The terms you will need to be familiar with are *channel service unit/data service unit* (CSU/DSU), *Frame Switch*, and *Smart Jack*.

The CSU/DSU has two different and distinct sides, one for the *channel side* and one for the *data side*. The service provider is the one concerned with the channels; remember a T1 is 24 64-Kbps channels, these channels can be combined for voice or data traffic. The data side is the primary concern of the customer and can be split with bandwidth for data uploading and downloading. There are two ways to split the bandwidth asymmetrically and symmetrically; in asymmetrical setup, you can split the bandwidth into two unequal segments—for example in a standard T1, you get 1.544 Mbps, you may want 1 Mbps for downloads and only .544 Mbps for uploading data. This will speed up downloads to your network and give some bandwidth for the upload. In symmetrical setup, you would split the bandwidth into two equal pieces.

Frame Switches are located at the providers' COs and across the Internet and pass the frames from source to destination. You do not need to focus much on these for the CCNA test.

The Smart Jack is the point where your router meets the provider's network. It uses a modified version of the RJ45 Jack called an *RJ48* and the major difference in the connector is a guiding plastic piece on one side. Another name for the Smart Jack is the demarcation point.

> **Exam Warning**
>
> Be very careful on the CCNA exam, they use Smart Jack and demarc (short for demarcation point) interchangeably.

Table 15.1 lists the fields in the Frame-Relay header. Of all the fields in the header, you need to know the most about the data-link connection identifier (DLCI); it is a 10-bit field that identifies the address of the Frame-Relay device. Most network devices autodetect the DLCI from the upstream partner. You can see the results of this auto detection with the *show frame-relay map* command (Figure 15.1), you can see the actual DLCI set to the serial line.

Notice, the DLCI is displayed both in decimal (base 10) and hexadecimal (base 16).

Table 15.1 Frame-Relay Header Information

Field Header	Description
Data link control identifier (DLCI) source	The identifying address of the source network
C/R	Command or response frame
Extended address (EA) (source)	2 bytes of additional address information
Forward explicit congestion notification (FECN)	Used to tell downstream partners about congestion on the link. 0 = no congestion, 1 = congestion
Backward explicit congestion notification (BECN)	Used to tell upstream partners of congestion on the link. Same as above; 0 = no congestion, 1 = congestion.
Discard eligibility (DE)	If there is congestion on the line and DE is set, this tells the Frame Switch it can discard if congestion is heavy.
Extended address destination	2 bytes of additional address information
Information	Additional protocols over Frame-Relay information

FIGURE 15.1

Output of Show Frame-Relay Map Command

```
R1#show frame-relay map
Serial4/2 (up): ip 172.16.1.2 dlci 102(0x64,0x1840), dynamic,
        broadcast,, status defined, active
```

When troubleshooting the Frame-Relay connection, you may have to give the support personnel at your service provider both of these numbers. Also note the status of dynamic as opposed to static (automatic set from provider as opposed to manually set by you).

If you must set the DLCI manually, you will use the following command in interface configuration mode (router(config-if)# prompt), *frame-relay map protocol protocol-address DLCI [broadcast] [ietf | cisco]*, where the protocol is IP, AppleTalk, DecNET, or IPX, and the DLCI is the device address for that interface.

WAN ENCAPSULATION FORMATS

There are two primary formats used to encapsulate WAN packets, the most common industry protocol is the Point-to-Point Protocol (PPP). It works over many WAN technologies, including analog dial-up Modems. The other is the High Level Data Link Control (HDLC) Protocol, and this is a Cisco proprietary Protocol and can only operate over Cisco routers.

PPP

Providing remote access as part of an organization's network infrastructure is becoming a common requirement today. Traveling salesmen, telecommuters, and remote offices all need to gain access to corporate network services, so they must be able to connect to a network.

PPP is one of the most popular and cost-effective methods of giving users remote access to corporate intranets and/or the Internet. Businesses and ISPs prefer giving their users dial-in or dedicated line access using PPP because of several key factors that will be covered in this chapter, including scalability, operability, and reliability. PPP is an OSI Layer 2 Protocol standard that allows two computing devices to communicate with each other using point-to-point connections such as an analog phone line, an ISDN line, or a serial link. These point-to-point connections can be client-to-network or router-to-router. The physical media that can be used to transport PPP includes unshielded twisted-pair (UTP), fiber optic, and wave transmissions, such as satellite systems. PPP is a full-duplex protocol unconcerned with transmission rates, which can be used with either synchronous or asynchronous communication lines. PPP can be used to encapsulate popular network protocols such as IP (the Internet standard) and Internetwork Packet Exchange, (IPX, Novell's native standard). This encapsulation is done by placing the OSI Layer 3 IP packet inside the PPP OSI Layer 2 frame and sending it down the transmission media to the other side where the PPP encapsulation frame is stripped away. The Layer 3 IP packet is then passed up to the next layer of the protocol stack. There are four ways PPP can be used as a Data Link layer Protocol on a Cisco router to provide access to computing resources:

- To provide dial-in access to remote users;

- To provide backup services over an asynchronous or synchronous connection in case a circuit fails between two routers;

- To provide encapsulation between two routers over a leased line;

- To provide dial-on-demand routing (DDR) services between two routers.

Exam Warning

The command to set up PPP encapsulation on a Cisco router is router(config-if)# *encapsulation ppp*

EXERCISE 15.1   Setting up PPP on a Serial Line

First go into global configuration mode.

- router#*configuration terminal*

- Then go into interface configuration for the serial line you wish to change to the PPP Protocol.

- router(config)# *interface serial 0/0*

- Then issue the command to setup PPP and exit and save the changes.

- router(config-if)# *encapsulation ppp*

- router(config-if)#^z

- router# *copy running-config startup-config*

- In this exercise, you changed the serial line on card 0 port 0 from the default PPP encapsulation to PPP.

For more on PPP, read these Request for Comments (RFCs):

- RFC 1661–Point-to-Point Protocol (PPP)

- RFC 1332–PPP Internet Protocol Control Protocol (IPCP)

- RFC 1333–PPP Link Quality Monitoring

- RFC 1334–PPP Authentication Protocols (PAP)

- RFC 1378–PPP AppleTalk Control Protocol (ATCP)

- RFC 1552–PPP Internet Protocol Exchange (IPXCP)

- RFC 1553–PPP Compressed IPX (CIPX)

- RFC 1570–PPP LCP Extensions

- RFC 1990–PPP Multilink Protocol (MP)

- RFC 1994–PPP Challenge Handshake Protocol (CHAP)

HDLC

HDLC was derived from Synchronous Data Link Control (SDLC). Although commonly referred to as a protocol, HDLC isn't a protocol at all. It's actually a Data Link layer bit-stuffing algorithm that specifies a data encapsulation method for synchronous serial links. It is also important to remember that HDLC is a Data Link layer (Layer 2) Protocol.

HDLC is used primarily in a peer-to-peer environment; one node is designated to be the primary and the others become secondary. A session can use one of the following connection modes, which determines how the primary and secondary nodes interact:

- Normal unbalanced

- Asynchronous

- Asynchronous balanced

Normal unbalanced occurs when the secondary node responds only to the primary node. Asynchronous occurs when the secondary node initiates the message, and asynchronous balanced occurs when both nodes send and/or receive over part of a duplex line.

> **Exam Warning**
> HDLC is the default for all Cisco Serial line connections—in a configuration, you will not see the *encapsulation hdlc* command as it is assumed.

HDLC is the standard method of serial communications and is the default setting for all Cisco serial ports. It has no overlay technology and simply gives a pure serial connection between two ports. There are no special abilities as in the case of Frame Relay and Point-to-Point. You will simply get two serial ports to transport to each other over HDLC—nothing more and nothing less.

WAN CONNECTION DEVICES

One of the keys to a CCNA certification is to know how the WAN is connected at each layer. In this section, we talk about the technologies and standards used in the WAN.

DTE/DCE

DTE stands for data terminal equipment and DCE stands for data circuit terminating equipment. They are two ends of the same connection. One is on the service provider side and the other is on the customer premise side. It is a serial connection that requires a synchronizing signal (Cisco calls this the *clock rate*) that controls the speed of the link. The clock rate is provided by the DCE device. In a T1 circuit the, CSU/DSU is the DTE device and the Frame-Relay switch is the DCE device.

> **Exam Warning**
> Remember which side of the link set the clock; DCE—remember C for clock!

EXERCISE 15.2 Setting Clock Rate on a DCE Router

The first step in setting the clock rate is to determine the appropriate setting. In this exercise, we set the clock rate for a full T1 link. To determine the appropriate clock rate, take the number of channels and multiply by 64,000, so a T1 is $24 \times 64,000 = 1,536,000$.

- The steps to do this are as follows:
- router#*configuration terminal*
- router(config)#*interface serial 0/0*
- router(config-if)# *clock rate 1536000*
- router(config-if)# $^\wedge z$
- router#*copy running-config startup-config*
- In this exercise, you set the clock rate for a DCE router.

Router

A router is a Layer 3 device that is responsible for the movement of data (routing) from one logical network to another. It is really a computer optimized to do this function. It has random access memory (RAM), read-only memory (ROM), a central processing unit (CPU), and a hard drive (flash memory).

There are two configurations stored in a Cisco router; the startup configuration is stored in nonvolatile RAM (NVRAM) and is only read when the router "starts" up; the other is the running configuration and it is stored in RAM while the router is operating. If you make changes to the router and do not save the running configuration into the startup configuration, the changes will be lost if the router loses power.

Modem

Modem is an acronym for modulator/demodulator. Cable and dial-up devices are modems. In the cable Internet device, there is a true modem device modulating information from the cable modem onto the wire and demodulating information coming in from the wire. There are not a lot of questions on the CCNA exam about modems; however, there are still some. One of the keys to modems is that there has to be some analog circuit in use to modulate the digital signal over. The most common analog circuits are POTS or PSTN.

CSU/DSU

CSU/DSU stands for channel service unit/data service unit. It is most commonly associated with the T1 carrier and is composed of two sides; the channel side and the data side. Remember T1 is defined as 24 65-K channels, the CSU side handles the combing or separating of the channels into voice and data segments, while the DSU side is the customers to control the amount of upstream and downstream bandwidth is allowed.

Standards

Each of the standards discussed in this section play a part in the knowledge needed for a CCNA student. Although there will not be a lot of test questions directly pointed to these standards, your understanding of them will help in answering the questions on protocols that run over these standards.

EAI/TAI 232

This standard is also known as the *RS-232* standard and is a serial (one data stream) communications method most commonly associated with modems.

It uses voltage to signify the 1s and 0s on the line, valid voltage levels for this technology are plus or minus 3 to plus or minus 15 volts. The most common connectors are DB9 and DB25. The console port on a Cisco router connects to the RS-232 port on your PC and the console port uses a rare RJ45 connector for this serial connection.

X.25

X.25 is a packet-switching network Protocol that maps to the three lower levels of the OSI model (Physical, Data Link, and Network). At the Data Link layer, it uses Link Access Procedure, Balanced (LAPB) Protocol to handle the DTE/DTC circuit negotiation. This protocol was very popular before the Frame Relay Protocol hit the scene in the early 1990s. Frame Relay was a better transmission protocol as it only dealt with the Physical and Data Link layers, so it cut down on the protective overhead needed.

Test Day Tip

The device used to connect to a X.25 network is called a *PAD*.

Remember back in Chapter 2 (OSI Model), we discussed about the session layer supporting switched virtual circuits (SVCs) and permanent virtual circuits (PVCs). X.25 can support both types of circuits.

WAN NETWORK MODELS

There are three major models used in designing WANs: the mesh, partial mesh, and the hub and spoke. In this section, we define these standards, how to implement them and their advantages and disadvantages of each topology.

Mesh

As described in Chapter 1, in the section on a mesh network in a LAN environment, all devices are connected to all the other devices. So each router would need a connection to each router in the WAN. The same formula that was used in Chapter 1 for a mesh LAN is used here also. That formula is the number of network devices (N) multiplied by the number of devices − 1 (N − 1) then divided by 2 or N (N − 1)/2.

This design allows for full interconnectivity and is vary rarely used due to the expense of the all of links required.

Advantages

If any one link goes down, communications can still occur between all devices. If one device goes down only communications to that device are lost and all other devices can still communicate with each other.

Disadvantages

The three biggest disadvantages are cost, cost, cost! The cost of the equipment, the cost of the connections, and the cost of maintaining it make it one of the most prohibitive network modes out there.

Partial Mesh

In the partial mesh network, you have a few redundant connections to allow for communications in the event of a connection failure. As opposed to the full mesh network, you don't connect to all the other devices just enough to ensure that all devices can still communicate during an outage. There is no formula for this topology and a good network designer will minimize the redundant links as much as possible to lower cost.

Advantages

The loss of a single link will, most likely, not bring the entire network down. It provides for options to allow routing protocols like Enhanced Interior Gateway Routing Protocol (EIGRP) to pick different paths when links slow-down due to heavy load, latency, or poor reliability.

Disadvantages

The biggest disadvantage again is cost; each redundant link will increase the installation and monthly maintenance cost of the WAN. Also the troubleshooting will be a little more difficult as the redundant link may mask or hide the problem. This is an area where having a logging server operating is important to report when a link goes down.

Hub and Spoke

In the hub and spoke topology, you have a core router that is the central connectivity point to all the remote offices (Figure 15.2).

In this topology, the loss of either the perimeter router (not shown) or the core router will keep all the other networks from seeing the Internet or all the other offices. As we cover the layers of the hub and spoke, we dissect the configurations and introduce you to the *ip unnumbered* command and the *ip route* command.

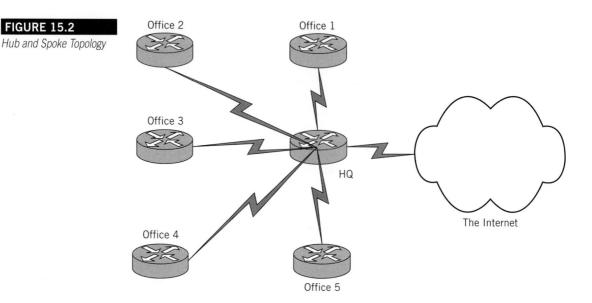

FIGURE 15.2

Hub and Spoke Topology

Components

The components of a hub and spoke topology are perimeter router, core router, and spoke router. In this section, we define each of these different routers and the unique configurations that make them function with minimal overhead and maintenance.

Perimeter Router

This router is usually provided by the ISP and is your connection to the outside world. You would normally not be responsible for this router and possibly the firewall between the outside and inside; however, you may be responsible for this firewall (and that is covered in *Firewall Policies and VPN Configurations*, ISBN: 978-1-59749-088-7, Syngress).

Core Router

The core layer router is the key to the hub and spoke topology; it connects the main office LAN to all the remote offices as well as interconnectivity of the remote offices and finally, connection of all offices and the main office LAN to the Internet. I use no routing protocols as all the routing can be programmed using static routes, with the *ip route* command.

The configuration below is a configuration from a core router in the hub and spoke. The highlighted commands illustrate the key commands in setting up a hub and spoke core router.

```
!
version 12.2
no service pad
service timestamps debug uptime
service timestamps log uptime
no service password-encryption
!
hostname Core_Rtr
!
enable secret 5 $1$dMN7$QOT/aSbp5Ecn4614wACLC1
enable password secret
!
username administrator privilege 15 password 0 &&*$(#78979738(
username backupadmin privilege 15 password 0 ##*$*#*@883872
ip subnet-zero
ip cef
!
!
ip domain-name training-911.com
ip host tftp 10.10.1.199
ip host office3 192.168.3.1
ip host office2 192.168.2.1
ip host office1 192.168.1.1
!
ip ssh time-out 90
ip ssh authentication-retries 2
!
call rsvp-sync
!
!
!
!
!
!
!
!
interface FastEthernet0/0
    ip address 10.10.1.225 255.255.0.0
    no ip route-cache
    no ip mroute-cache
    duplex half
!
```

```
interface ATM2/0
   no ip address
   shutdown
   no atm scrambling sts-stream
   no atm ilmi-keepalive
!
interface CBR2/0
   no ip address
!
interface CBR2/1
   no ip address
   shutdown
!
interface CBR2/2
   no ip address
   shutdown
!
interface CBR2/3
   no ip address
   shutdown
!
interface Serial3/0
   ip unnumbered FastEthernet0/0
   serial restart-delay 0
   clockrate 64000
!
interface Serial3/1
   ip unnumbered FastEthernet0/0
   serial restart-delay 0
   clockrate 64000
!
interface Serial3/2
   ip unnumbered FastEthernet0/0
   serial restart-delay 0
   clockrate 64000
!
interface Serial3/3
   ip unnumbered FastEthernet0/0
   serial restart-delay 0
   clockrate 64000
!
interface Ethernet4/0
   ip address 24.153.149.2 255.255.255.248
   ip access-group 101 in
   duplex full
!
```

```
interface Ethernet4/1
  no ip address
  shutdown
  duplex half
!
interface Ethernet4/2
  no ip address
  shutdown
  duplex half
!
interface Ethernet4/3
  no ip address
  shutdown
  duplex half
!
router igrp 1
  redistribute connected
  network 10.0.0.0
!
ip classless
ip route 0.0.0.0 0.0.0.0 Ethernet4/0
ip route 192.168.1.0 255.255.255.0 Serial3/1
ip route 192.168.2.0 255.255.255.0 Serial3/2
ip route 192.168.3.0 255.255.255.0 Serial3/3
no ip http server
!
logging 10.10.1.199
access-list 22  permit any log
access-list 101 denyicmp any any log
access-list 101 permit   tcp any any eq 22 log
access-list 101 denytcp any any eq telnet log
access-list 101 permit      ip any any
dialer-list 1   protocol   ip permit
dialer-list 1   protocol   ipx permit
!
dial-peer cor custom
!
!
!
!
gatekeeper
  shutdown
!
```

```
banner motd #
Cisco 7200 - Instructor Router
Warning - this router is private property
All usage of this device is monitored, logged and can be
investigated.
Any Unauthorized use may be prosocuted to the fullest extent
allowed under federal and state laws.
#
!
line con 0
   exec-timeout 0 0
   logging synchronous
   login local
line aux 0
line vty 0 4
   access-class 22 in
   exec-timeout 1 0
   login local
   transport input ssh
!
End
```

The command *ip unnumbered FastEthernet0/0* is used to tell the serial line to not assign an IP address to the interface but use the same address as the *FastEthernet* interface, thus not requiring subnetted addresses for each interface. The *show ip interface brief* command would show the same address for all interfaces on this router. This is very useful in point-to-point connections. The *show ip route* command would only show the two directly connected routes on the two *FastEthernet* interfaces, one for the main office LAN and one for the connection to the Internet.

The *ip route* commands point to each of the remote office networks allowing the router to see each network. The last command of importance is the *ip route 0.0.0.0 0.0.0.0 FastEthernet 4/0*; this command tells the router if the destination route is not in the routing table, send it out interface FastEthernet card 4 port 0 (that is what the 4/0 means). This is a special route called in Cisco speak the *Gateway of Last Restort* or default gateway in windows speak. This static route also has an * after it to show it is not a normal static route. In the routing table, the * is listed as the candidate default.

Test Day Tip

It is important for the CCNA student to know the command to set the default gateway, what the * means in the routing table and how to set manual routes.

Once this router has been completed, we can then move onto a router at a remote office, called the *spoke router*.

Spoke Router

The router at this layer is the other end of the point-to-point connection with the core router. It is very easy to set up and uses the unnumbered command and the setting up of the gateway of last resort of the core router, but it does not need a route to each of the remote offices, as the core has that information. In the configuration below, you will see only two commands in bold. These are the two commands that each spoke router would use to establish connectivity.

```
!
version 12.2
service timestamps debug uptime
service timestamps log uptime
no service password-encryption
!
hostname Office1
!
enable secret 5 $1$X1sq$.p53Nr6BoLeADjj7UXhjk1
enable password secret
!
memory-size iomem 20
ip subnet-zero
!
!
!
ip audit notify log
ip audit po max-events 100
ip ssh time-out 120
ip ssh authentication-retries 3
!
!
!
!
!
!
!
!
!
!
!
```

```
interface Ethernet0
  no ip address
  shutdown
  half-duplex
!
interface FastEthernet0
  ip address 192.168.1.1 255.255.255.0
  speed auto
  half-duplex
  no cdp enable
!
interface Serial0
  ip unnumbered FastEthernet0
!
ip classless
  ip route 0.0.0.0 0.0.0.0 Serial0
no ip http server
ip pim bidir-enable
!
!
dialer-list 1 protocol ip permit
dialer-list 1 protocol ipx permit
!
call rsvp-sync
!
dial-peer cor custom
!
!
!
!
line con 0
  exec-timeout 0 0
    login local
    password cisco
line aux 0
line vty 0 4
  password cisco
  login
!
end
```

On this router, the routing table would only have two entries; one for the local connected LAN and one for the gateway of last resort, which means if the data is not destined for the LAN, send it upstream to the core router that will know how to handle the data. If the traffic is for a remote office, the router will forward it. Also, if the data is for the main office, it will forward it. Finally, if the data is for the Internet, it will not have an entry in the routing table and will then send it out the gateway of last resort (to the ISP).

Advantages

No routing protocols need to be configured, thus reducing the overhead on each of the routers and reducing the bandwidth used to update the routing tables. This also gives your organization a single point of control for Internet traffic, so you can filter, monitor, and track Internet usage for the entire organization in one place instead of at the individual office level. The network administrator only has to update the manual routing table if an office is added or removed from the network.

Disadvantages

The only real disadvantage is you need point-to-point connectivity, which today means using a T1 or ATM; therefore, there is a bigger cost associated with this topology over using DSL lines and VPNs for connectivity.

SUMMARY OF EXAM OBJECTIVES

In this chapter, we looked at the WAN technologies and topologies a CCNA candidate needs to understand before taking the exam.

We looked at the features of T1s versus cable and DSL Internet connections, with bandwidth, connectivity standards, and related technologies. Commands for configuring clock rate and the PPP Protocol were exercised as these commands show up frequently on the CCNA exam. Some of the other WAN technologies we defined were the Last Mile, demarcation point, Smart Jack, CO, and the importance of each one to the CCNA student. We also learned the three types of circuits used, packet-switched, circuit-switched, and dedicated, and the types of signaling used across them.

In WAN types, we talked about legacy dial-up (PSTN), the three types of ISDN (PRI, BRI, and TDM), DSL, and Cable. Then we went onto the more business-related technologies like T1/T3, E1/E3 (the European standards), OC, ATM, and finally Frame Relay. With regard to the exam, know the importance of each standard as it applies to routers.

Under WAN encapsulation formats, we looked at the industry standard PPP and the Cisco proprietary HDLC; remember if all your equipment is Cisco, you can use the HDLC Protocol, but if you are connecting to non-Cisco devices, you must use the PPP Protocol, and in exercise 15.1 we changed a router from HDLC to PPP.

With WAN connection devices, we looked at the key items used to connect our offices to each other and the Internet, the importance of the DTE/DCE relationship and how to set the clock rate on a DCE device, and the importance of knowing how to set the clock rate. We determined the importance of knowing where it is set, on the DCE side; remember C for DCE and C for clock! We closed out that section with an important tip remembering what device works on a X.25 network, the PAD.

Finally in WAN network models, we compared the three major models in use today: the full mesh, the partial mesh, and the hub and spoke. In each we gave the advantages, disadvantages, and their unique attributes. In this section, we also introduced the concept of IP unnumbered and the default route, or gateway of last resort.

EXAM OBJECTIVES FAST TRACK

What is a WAN?

- CPE is the customer side of the WAN Link.

- The Smart Jack is where the customer meets the network.

- The Smart Jack can also be called the *demarcation (or demarc) point*.

- Circuit-switched network operate over ISDN or PSTN services.

- Packet-switched networks operate over ATM services.

- Dedicated networks are used for point-to-point connectivity.

- BRI—ISDN is a legacy digital service that delivered 128 Kbps to residential and business customers.

- PRI—ISDI is similar in speed to a T1 but the signaling is different; it uses out-of-band signaling as opposed to T1s in band signaling.

- DSL comes in two common formats: *Asymmetric*, where more bandwidth is set aside for down loads; *Symmetric* (where download and upload are allocated the same amount of bandwidth).

WAN Encapsulation Formats

- PPP is an industry standard protocol that can be programmed on Cisco devices.

- HDLC is Cisco's proprietary protocol and is the default protocol programmed on Serial Lines.

- Both PPP and HDLC are Layer 2 (Data Link layer) of the OSI model.

WAN Connection Devices

- DTE is the consumer/customer side of the WAN link and means data terminal equipment.

- DCE is the service provider side of the WAN link and means data circuit-terminating equipment.

- There is a signal required to synchronize the link, and it is called *clock rate*.

- Routers serial interface connect to the DTE/DCE link through a CSU/DSU.

- CSU/DSUs are Layer 2 devices and the most common protocol is Frame Relay.

- Routers operate at Layer 3 of the OSI model.

- X.25 Protocol uses a PAD device to connect to the network.

WAN Network Models

- Mesh networks have no single point of failure.

- Mesh networks have the highest equipment and link cost due to the full redundant nature.

- Partial mesh networks have less cost but more risk if certain links fail than full mesh.

- Hub and spoke networks allow for ease of routing table building.

- Hub and spoke allows for single point of control for all traffic to the Internet.

- Hub and spoke requires no overhead and bandwidth for routing updates.

EXAM OBJECTIVES FREQUENTLY ASKED QUESTIONS

Q: If X.25 and the PAD are legacy technology, why do I need to know it for the exam?

A: Even though you are not likely to find X.25 in the field, the technologies in use today are based on this technology.

Q: Can the same router be used in a hub and spoke as well as a partial or full mesh environment?

A: Depending on the programming, yes! The same router can be used in any of the topologies. However, for a core router, you are going to need more connectivity than some routers offer.

Q: Why are there multiple terms for some of the technologies, like demarcation point and Smart Jack?

A: In each case of duplicate terms for one technology, it comes from the fact that different people look at different standards (United States versus International) and get the name from that standard.

Q: Are there any ISDN questions on the current CCNA exam?

A: Yes, there are a few questions on PRI circuits and how they compare to T1. BRI is not covered much anymore.

Q: How deep do I really need to know DSL?

A: Know the two types of DSL, ADSL and SDSL, and know which of the two signaling standards is the most common DMT as apposed to CAP.

Q: Is a cable modem truly a modem, does it actually modulate and demodulate signals?

A: Yes, there is a true modulator/demodulator in the cable modem technology.

SELF TEST

1. In a typical WAN environment, your router loses connection to the service provider on Frame-Relay link. Which of the following would most likely be the cause of the loss of connection?

   A. DCE lost clock rate

   B. DTE lost clock rate

   C. ISDN lost clock rate

   D. PPP lost clock rate

2. You are studying the legacy X.25 Protocol for the CCNA exam. What is the name of the X.25 device that connects the router to the X.25 cloud?

   A. Modem

   B. Router

   C. Switch

   D. PAD

   E. Hub

3. You are setting up a point-to-point connection between your core router to a spoke router at a remote location. What is the appropriate command to set the clock rate on a Cisco router to support a full T1?

   A. *router>clockrate 1536000*

   B. *router#clockrate 1536000*

   C. *router(confiig-line)#clockrate 1536000*

   D. *router(config-if)#clockrate 1536000*

   E. *router(config)#clockrate 1536000*

4. You are diagnosing a Frame-Relay circuit that has been working for a long time. The circuit is a full T1 from your service provider operating at full speed. You think that the service provider has dropped a piece of the header information. What field in the header would most likely cause this problem?

   A. BECN

   B. FECN

   C. DE

   D. DLCI

5. You are a network administrator and you are building a new facility. You have to chose between DSL and cable for your connectivity. Which of the following is the most important factor in determining between DSL and cable?

   A. Number of repeaters between source and destination

   B. Line of sight between source and destination

   C. Distance from the CO

   D. Cost of installation

6. You are preparing for your CCNA exam and are studying the WAN terms for the test and the question that is asked is; which of the following terms means the same as Smart Jack?

   A. Central office (CO)

   B. Customer premise equipment (CPE)

   C. Demarcation point (demarc)

   D. Last Mile

   E. Toll network

7. You are designing a new network connection from your office to a new office. You only need a fractional T1 circuit for this new office. You have decided to purchase three channels of a T1. What would the clock rate be on this link?

   A. 1536000

   B. 192000

   C. 320000

   D. 64000

8. You are in charge of designing the new office and all the networking and communications equipment and circuits for the new office. You have decided to purchase a PBX for the voice communications services. Which of the following services would you order to connect to your PBX?

   A. T1

   B. ISDN—PRI

   C. DSL

   D. Frame Relay

9. You are troubleshooting a T1 connection and the provider has asked you to provide some information about the Frame-Relay connection. What command would you use to find the DLCI for the provider?

   A. *router# show frame-relay map*

   B. *router>show frame-relay map*

   C. *router(config)# show frame-relay map*

   D. *router(config-if)# show frame-relay map*

   E. *router(config-line)# show frame-relay map*

10. You are designing a new network for your company. They require 100 percent uptime even in the event of a single link failure. You are told that cost is no object. Which network model would you use to provide this functionality to your company?

    A. Full mesh

    B. Partial mesh

    C. Hub and spoke

11. You are setting a hub and spoke network and are working on the core router. You want to tell the 3rd serial port on card 0 of the router to use the same IP address as the 1st port of the FastEthernet on card 3. What command would you use?

    A. *router(config)# interface serial 3/3*

       router(config-if)# ip unnumbered fastethernet 3/0

    B. *router(config)# interface serial 3/0*

       router(config-if)# ip unnumbered fastethernet 0/3

    C. *router(config)# interface serial 0/3*

       router(config-if)#ip unnumbered fastethernet 3/0

    D. *router(config)#interface serial 3/0*

       router(config-if) ip unnumbered fastethernet 3/0

12. You are studying for your CCNA exam; you are reading the section that talks about default gateways or gateways of last resort. The question is: What character signifies that a static route is the candidate default/gateway of last resort?

    A. S&

    B. S#

    C. S*

    D. S@

13. You are setting up a network and your company has chosen to go with the Hub and Spoke topology. You are trying to determine how many routes you have to create on each spoke in a 25-spoke network. What is the number of routes you have to configure on each spoke?

    A. 25

    B. 12

    C. 0

    D. 10

    E. 1

14. You are working for a large company and are setting up a new router for a branch location. This router is to connect the company to the internet. What command would you type to set the gateway of last resort to send all traffic that does not have an entry in the routing table to pass traffic to the ISP on serial 0?

15. You are studying for the CCNA exam and are studying the WAN Configuration section. Match the following technologies with the appropriate layer of the OSI Model.

   A. Router1 Physical

   B. CSU/DSU2 Network

   C. Modem3 Data Link

SELF TEST QUICK ANSWER KEY

1.	A	**9.**	A
2.	D	**10.**	A
3.	D	**11.**	C
4.	D	**12.**	C
5.	C	**13.**	E
6.	C	**14.**	ip route 0.0.0.0 0.0.0.0 s0 or ip route 0 0 s0
7.	B	**15.**	A – 2, B – 3, C – 1
8.	B		

Configuring PPP and CHAP

INTRODUCTION

The CCNA certification exam will test a candidate's ability to install, configure, operate, and troubleshoot medium-size routed and switched networks, as well as implement and verify connections to remote sites in a wide area network (WAN). Because so many connections around the world rely on modems, cable networks, DSL, T1s and so on, it's no wonder that the first level of Cisco certification testing would cover two of today's most widely used protocols and technologies: Point-to-Point Protocol (PPP) and Challenge Handshake Authentication Protocol (CHAP).

Most Cisco gear supports such WAN protocols as Integrated Services Digital Network (ISDN), Asynchronous Transfer Mode (ATM), Frame Relay, High Level Data Link Control (HDLC), Serial Line Internet Protocol (SLIP), and X.25, among others. As you will see in this chapter, your use of these technologies will rely heavily on your ability to encapsulate and secure data transmissions. That is where PPP and CHAP come into play.

In this chapter, we will cover the fundamentals you need to know for passing the CCNA exam and for configuring routers and WAN connections with PPP and CHAP for remote access solutions. We will also look at how authentication protocols, such as CHAP and Password Authentication Protocol (PAP), work and how they are configured on Cisco devices.

UNDERSTANDING PPP AND CHAP

For the CCNA exam, you will need to know not only what functions both CHAP and PPP perform, but also how to configure these protocols and ultimately troubleshoot the myriad issues that may occur with their use.

PPP is a Layer 2 WAN protocol used for basic data encapsulation and transmission across a network. For data transmission between any two nodes (devices or routers), a data path must be established and flow control procedures must be in place to ensure that correct and accurate delivery of data is accomplished. PPP is a data link layer protocol and its basic purpose is to transport network layer packets across a data link layer point-to-point network. It is the most widely used and most popular WAN protocol today because it offers complete control of data link setup, dynamic assignment of Internet Protocol (IP) addresses, network protocol multiplexing, link testing, link configuration, error detection, and negotiation options for network layer address and data compression.

PPP uses two authentication protocols: PAP and CHAP. CHAP is preferred over PAP because, to establish identity, CHAP uses a three-way handshake comprising the local host requesting authentication, the remote host sending an encrypted response, and the local host comparing the received information and then accepting or rejecting the connection: PAP uses only a two-way handshake. Also, PAP is less secure than CHAP. With PAP, passwords are sent in clear text, whereas with CHAP they are sent encrypted and secure. Since the requesting of authentication credentials is performed only upon initial link setup and credentials are sent insecurely, PAP is not recommended for use on networks where security is a concern.

OSI Model Fundamentals

The Open Systems Interconnection (OSI) model describes how data moves throughout a network from one system to another. To understand the fundamentals of the OSI model, you should know what PPP and CHAP do as well as the role the OSI model plays in these protocols.

PPP is configured to work at the data link OSI layer and helps data transmission by utilizing a multiprotocol setup via the physical, data link, and network layers of the OSI model. As shown in Figure 16.1, the OSI model is provided as a backdrop to PPP and how it is mapped into those bottom three layers of the model.

PPP plays specific roles at the network, data link, and physical layers of the model. Like most other protocols, PPP operates first, at the physical layer: Bits are sent across the

OSI Model and PPP

Network	IPCP, IPXCP NCP
Data Link	LCP
Physical	Connection and Media

FIGURE 16.1 *Mapping PPP to the OSI Model*

medium, wire, or link, and devices such as modems function at this layer. One step above the physical layer is the data link layer. As do most protocols that operate at Layer 2, PPP uses Link Control Protocol (LCP) to handle Layer 2 functionality (LCP is the workhorse of PPP and we will cover it in detail in the next section). Meanwhile, Network Control Protocol (NCP) operates solely at Layer 3 and is responsible for the breakdown between network protocol types such as Internet Protocol Control Protocol (IPCP), also covered in detail in the next section.

Another reason PPP is one of the most commonly used WAN protocols today is because it supports both synchronous and asynchronous communications. Most computer systems today will use PPP when an option is presented. For example, when configuring a modem (which modulates and demodulates a signal between analog and digital) you will almost always use PPP. Modems operate at Layer 1, but specific transmissions require that upper-layer controls be used. Since PPP supports both synchronous and asynchronous communications, it's easy to facilitate this need. Synchronous communications are typical for point-to-point lines, whereas asynchronous communications are commonly used on dialed circuits using modems.

Test Day Tip
PPP includes the ability to dynamically assign IP addresses to a device on the other end of the PPP link. When you dial into an Internet service provider (ISP) with your modem, the ISP can dynamically assign an IP to a device.

Although PPP is a widely used and highly flexible protocol, aside from controlling and managing an encapsulated session, PPP does not provide security. This is where PAP and CHAP add to the equation. Both PAP and CHAP bring added security to the network, but CHAP offers enhanced capabilities over PAP in that CHAP enforces the use of a username and password for gaining access to the network, thereby making it more difficult for malicious parties to conduct an attack.

We will discuss both PAP and CHAP in more detail later in the chapter. For now, let's take a closer look at PPP so that when you begin to configure and/or troubleshoot your connections and Cisco devices, you know which components within PPP to examine and analyze for problems.

> **Exam Warning**
>
> Make sure for the exam that you understand which protocol maps to which layer. This may not appear as a direct question, but understanding which protocol to troubleshoot to solve a specific problem is important.

Point-to-Point Protocol (PPP)

To establish a point-to-point connection, you need a WAN link such as a T1 line which connects two remote sites, you need a termination device that connects the line to a modem or a modem to a router, and you need to configure a protocol. WAN connections are typically not the same from end to end, so it's important to know how to configure PPP on multiple same or dissimilar connection types. Luckily, the basic configuration for both is simple and common enough for almost all WAN media in use today. To use end-to-end encapsulation (and security) you would configure PPP and CHAP. You can easily connect a site that uses a T1 line to a site that uses a DSL link and use PPP and CHAP without issue.

PPP is commonly used to encapsulate a connection on a Transmission Control Protocol/Internet Protocol (TCP/IP) based network through a modem and a telephone line, a router connected to another router, and via other connection methods and media. Although the Internetwork Packet Exchange (IPX) and Sequenced Packet Exchange (SPX) protocols can be used, this is not common simply because IPX/SPX is generally used only for extreme cases of backward compatibility. Since almost all Novell-based systems have moved to the TCP/IP protocol suite, you would use this protocol only in cases where you need to accommodate a very old system or network segment that had to support it.

PPP is a simple protocol to understand and troubleshoot. Once you break it down into sections and subsections (as we will do next), it is easy to see why it has become the de facto standard in the industry.

Understanding LCP and NCP

PPP, defined in RFC 1661, replaced SLIP because of SLIP's many deficiencies, among them the fact that SLIP supports only IP and does not allow authentication and dynamic assignment of routed protocols. Unlike SLIP, PPP provides a standard method for transporting multiprotocol datagrams over point-to-point links.

PPP is composed of three main components or subsections:

- PPP operates on the physical, data link, and network layers of the OSI model. The physical layer is where the link is made and the bits are transported across the connected medium. PPP can encapsulate multiprotocol datagrams over the wire. Here, a frame format for local area network (LAN) protocol multiplexing is chosen and LCP begins to connect.

- PPP uses LCP at the data link layer of the OSI model to establish, configure, and test the data link connection for use.

- PPP uses NCP at the network layer of the OSI model. NCP is broken down further into multiple protocols. A family of NCPs is used to establish and configure different network layer protocols such as IPX, AppleTalk, and IP. IP in NCP form would be called IPCP as an example.

Test Day Tip

Commonly used NCPs are IPCP, Internetwork Packet Exchange Control Protocol (IPXCP), NetBIOS Frames Control Protocol (NBFCP), and AppleTalk Control Protocol (ATCP). The NCP defined for IP, Version 6 (or IPng—Next Generation) is IP Version 6 Control Protocol (IPv6CP).

PPP Frame Format

PPP's frame format is easy to understand if you know how to interpret a frame breakdown, as shown in Figure 16.2. In the figure, you can see the five fields of the frame, along with a start and end flag.

PPP Frame

1 Byte	1 Byte	1 Byte	1–2 Bytes	Variable	2–4 Bytes	1 Byte
Flag	Address	Control	Protocol	Data (and padding)	FCS	Flag

FIGURE 16.2

Fields of a PPP Frame

Here is a breakdown of each field:

- **Flag** The start flag in PPP uses the same format as the start flag in HDLC. It denotes the beginning of the frame, and its value is set at a binary number of 01111110.

- **Address** Because PPP is used for a point-to-point connection, the Address field uses the broadcast address of HDLC, which is 11111111, to avoid the data link address in the protocol.

- **Control** The Control field in PPP uses the same format as the U-frame in HDLC. The value is 11000000 and it is used to show that the frame does not contain sequence numbers, flow control, or error control.

- **Protocol** The Protocol field defines what is being carried in the data field (see Table 16.1 for more information).

- **Data (and Padding)** The Data field carries the user data or NCP packets. This field is sometimes called the Payload field.

- **FCS** The Frame Check Sequence field uses the same format as it does in HDLC. It contains a 2- to 4-byte cyclic redundancy check (CRC).

Table 16.1 PPP Protocol Field Values

Protocol Field	Value
0x0021	IP
0x0029	AT
0x002B	IPX
0x003D	Multilink
0x0201	802.1d Hello
0x8021	IPCP
0x8029	ATCP
0x802B	IPXCP
0xC021	LCP
0xC023	PAP
0xC025	LQR
0xC223	CHAP

- **Flag** Like the start flag, the end flag in PPP uses the same format as the end flag in HDLC. It indicates the end of the PPP frame, and its value is 01111110.

Table 16.1 provides a more detailed list of the values of the Protocol field. Codes found in this table become visible when you debug PPP and CHAP, or if you use a protocol capture and analysis tool to view the data within a PPP or CHAP packet. In the low level debug output, you can see information within the protocol field.

PPP provides a standard method for transporting multiprotocol packets over point-to-point links. PPP's Protocol field can help you troubleshoot issues, especially with upper-layer protocols. Understanding PPP's phases from link establishment to disconnection is also helpful when trying to understand and troubleshoot your WAN connectivity.

Understanding PPP Phases

While establishing the protocol, the PPP link goes through several distinct phases. These phases are specified as *Link Dead*, *Link Establishment*, *Authentication*, *Network Layer Protocol configuration*, and *Link Termination*, which then results in the Link Dead phase being repeated. Here is a breakdown of each phase so that you can better understand how the frame is read and how PPP will react based on each phase:

- **Link Dead (physical layer not ready) phase** The link necessarily begins and ends with this phase. When a carrier is detected, PPP moves into the Link Establishment phase.

- **Link Establishment phase** LCP establishes a connection through an exchange of configure packets. As soon as the Protocol field contains *c021h*, PPP moves to the Link Establishment phase. After a Configure-ACK packet is sent and received, the exchange is complete and the LCP Opened state begins. The LCP codes are one byte long. LCP options include Maximum Receive Unit (MRU), which specifies the maximum size of the information transported in bytes within the PPP packet received by the local equipment; and Magic-Number, which can show you a detected loop on a link during negotiation.

- **Authentication phase** By default, authentication is not mandatory. Authentication negotiation occurs during the Link Establishment phase, where only LCP, authentication protocol, and link quality monitoring packets are allowed. The Link Quality Report (LQR) is important to the usability of this phase. Packets are sometimes dropped or corrupted because of noise and equipment problems. LQR helps in monitoring the quality of the PPP link. All other packets received during this phase are discarded. In PAP, one side supplies both a username and a password in clear text to the peer that is authenticating it. In CHAP, one peer challenges the other peer and the peer being challenged must be able to respond with the correct answer to the challenge before passing authentication. The password in CHAP creates the answer to the challenge and is never transmitted across the wire, which makes it inherently more secure than PAP.

- **Network Layer Protocol configuration phase** After the link is established and LCP negotiates optional facilities as needed, PPP must send NCP packets to choose and configure one or more network layer protocols; after configuration, datagrams from each network layer protocol can be sent over the link. The link remains configured for communications until explicit LCP or NCP packets close the link. Each NCP can be opened and closed at any time. After an NCP reaches the opened state, PPP carries the corresponding network layer protocol packets (e.g., IPCP for NCP). Each NCP negotiates its own phase.

- **Link Termination phase** PPP can terminate a link at any time. Possible reasons for termination include loss of carrier, authentication failure, link quality failure, expiration of an idle period timer, and the administrative closing of an interface or link. LCP closes a link through an exchange or through terminate packets. While the link is closing, PPP informs the network layer protocols so that they can take appropriate action. Once the link is terminated, the Link Dead phase is reinitialized.

One of the most resource-intensive procedures in PPP negotiation occurs during LCP negotiation. Previously, Cisco IOS created a statically configured number of processes to authenticate calls. Each process handled a single call, but in some situations the limited number of processes could not keep up with the incoming call rate, resulting in some calls timing out. PPP, when used over different technologies such as ISDN, dial-up, and Frame Relay, poses different requirements to ensure interoperability.

Since so many types of connections can be used, it's important to know which connection types PPP can use and how they work together when PPP is configured.

The most common connection type that PPP uses is the Internet. PPP addresses problems of Internet connectivity by employing three main components:

- HDLC as a basis for encapsulating datagrams over point-to-point links

- LCP for setting up, configuring, and testing the data link connection

- NCP for establishing and configuring different network layer protocols (PPP is designed to allow the simultaneous use of multiple network layer protocols, among them IPv4 and v6, IPX, and AppleTalk)

Exam Warning

Make sure you know the difference between IPCP and IPv6CP. Since IPv6 is becoming more prevalent in today's networks, it's important to know when PPP's NCP IPv6CP would be used.

To get a better understanding of how PPP works, you can view the output from a debug command. Later in this chapter we will look at the commands used for PPP and CHAP debugging in more depth, but for now let's go through the steps of performing a debug and view how the PPP phases work (see Exercise 16.1). For the exam, it's important to understand not only the packet's header structure, but also know how to read data within the packet.

Test Day Tip

For the CCNA exam, you will need to know how to turn on debugging and use the resultant output to solve problems. You will also need to know that turning on debugging will take up router or switch resources; therefore, it's recommended that you use commands carefully as some impact the router more intensely than others. You should always schedule the use of most if not all debug commands, and make sure you understand how each command impacts the device, especially if it is running on a production network.

EXERCISE 16.1   Debugging and Viewing PPP Negotiations

1. Log on to Router A and turn on debugging by using the *debug ppp negotiation* command:

   ```
   RouterA#debug ppp negotiation
   PPP protocol negotiation debugging is on
   RouterA#
   ```

2. View the sample output on the router's console. As you can see, the debug process has been turned on and you will be able to view output based on PPP protocol negotiation.

   ```
   RouterA#
   *Feb 1 00:08:16.541: BR0:1 PPP: Treating connection as a
     callin
   *Feb  1 00:08:16.552: BR0:1 PPP: Phase is ESTABLISHING,
     Passive Open
   [0 sess, 0 load]
   ```

3. Next, once the ISDN connection becomes active, the BRI link in the debug shows PPP establishing a link. Since Link Establishment is processing, it's important to know that LCP will begin its process within PPP. This is common throughout most if not all PPP-based connections.

   ```
   RouterA#
   *Feb  1 00:08:16.669: BR0:1 LCP: State is Listen
   *Feb  1 00:08:17.034: BR0:1 LCP: I CONFREQ [Listen] id 7
     len 17
   ```

4. Next, once LCP begins its process, you can view the authentication starting up using PAP.

```
RouterA#
*Feb 1 00:06:17.038: BR0:1 LCP: AuthProto PAP (0x0304C023)
<-Output Omitted->
```

The process continues throughout the remaining phases. In the end, the NCPs will be configured for use. Viewing the debug sequence, you can get an idea about how PPP operates and how LCP and NCP Authentication is used in the process.

As you can see, PPP is easy to understand and troubleshoot. This is also why understanding how to troubleshoot while using the OSI model is important. Knowing which protocol maps to which layers is equally as important while running debug commands and troubleshooting output on multiple routers configured to connect branch offices to a company's main data center. It helps to understand which layers are affected and which protocols are in operation so that you can determine where a problem is occurring.

Test Day Tip

PPP operates on Layer 1 of the OSI model. PPP can operate on a variety of Data Terminal Equipment/Data Circuit-Terminating Equipment (DTE/DCE) physical interfaces, including asynchronous serial, synchronous serial, High Speed Serial Interface (HSSI), and ISDN.

Challenge Handshake Authentication Protocol (CHAP)

It's easy to authenticate for connectivity between two PPP-based devices. With PPP, you can authenticate using either PAP or CHAP. As mentioned earlier, CHAP is the preferred protocol, because CHAP uses a three-way handshake, whereas PAP uses only a two-way handshake (see Figure 16.3).

As you can see in Figure 16.3, when CHAP is used over a WAN connection the router receiving the connection sends a challenge which includes a random number. This random number is input into a Message Digest (MD5) authentication algorithm to provide an encryption key. This key is then used to send authentication information between Routers 1 and 2. Since CHAP uses encryption and has a verification mechanism in place, it is inherently secure.

FIGURE 16.3

Using CHAP

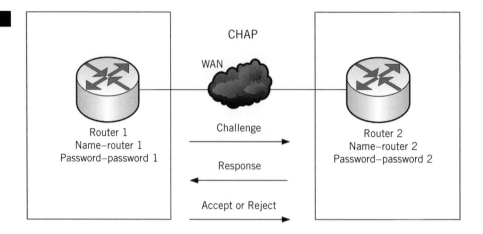

Test Day Tip

Microsoft Challenge Handshake Authentication Protocol (MS-CHAP) is nearly identical to CHAP in terms of how it operates. The main difference between the two is that Microsoft's proprietary version of CHAP is not an open standard. You will not be tested on MS-CHAP on the CCNA exam. However, you should know about its use and its proprietary nature. CHAP and PAP are open standards-based protocols. RFC 2759 covers Microsoft PPP CHAP Extensions, Version 2, in detail.

Password Authentication Protocol (PAP)

PAP is a protocol used for the basic authentication purposes of a WAN connection. When PAP is used over a WAN connection, the dialing router transmits username and password information in clear text (i.e., without encryption). In Figure 16.4, PAP is using its two-way handshake to send credentials in clear text from Router 1 to Router 2; Router 2 then either accepts or rejects the attempt.

Exam Warning

PAP is not as secure as CHAP. Always use CHAP when available to increase you security posture. For the exam, make sure you know how to configure CHAP with PPP. Also, know how to spot misconfiguration, as this is likely why you will have an authentication problem.

Unlike with PAP, when CHAP is used over a WAN connection the router receiving the connection sends a challenge which includes a random number that is later input into the MD5 hash algorithm, as noted in the preceding section. For this reason, CHAP is preferred over PAP for network connectivity.

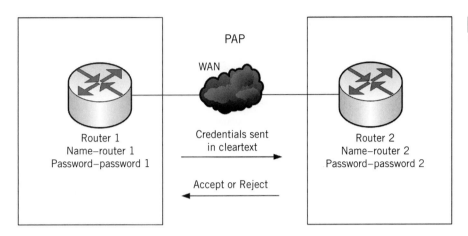

FIGURE 16.4

Viewing PAP

Test Day Tip

The MD5 algorithm can add a secure layer of encryption to your data transmissions. MD5 uses a hash function. The hash value is 128 bits and is commonly seen as a 32-digit hexadecimal number. You can learn more about MD5 in RFC 1321.

CONFIGURING AND IMPLEMENTING PPP AND CHAP ON CISCO ROUTERS

To configure PPP, first you must understand what type of connection you are making. A network diagram can help.

Note

For the CCNA exam, you will need to know how to configure PPP and CHAP/PAP on a Cisco router. For example, you may be presented with a question that shows two routers trying to connect over a WAN. You may need to either verify a particular configuration statement to rule out whether PPP or CHAP is suffering from a mis-configuration, or simply configure it from scratch on an interface at the command line. Not knowing the most basic commands and how to troubleshoot the resultant output will be a serious problem during the test. You will also have to determine the correct answers of misleading questions in which PPP is not the issue, but rather CHAP is, and vice versa.

Figure 16.5 shows a common connection with PPP and CHAP in use. Regardless of the WAN connection type (it could be a simple point-to-point T1 connection) it's imperative that you know the steps to configure PPP and CHAP.

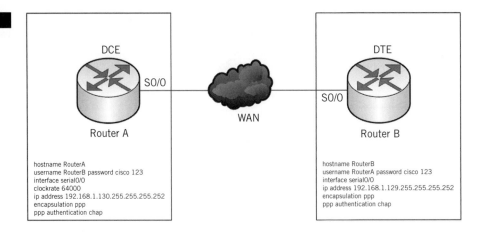

FIGURE 16.5

PPP and CHAP Sample Configuration

In Figure 16.5, it's clear that to configure PPP correctly you must configure an encapsulation statement on the interface and a username and password as a global command statement. This means you will need to configure PPP and CHAP within Interface Configuration mode and the username and password in Configure Terminal mode.

In Exercise 16.2, you will configure PPP and CHAP on two Cisco routers.

EXERCISE 16.2 Configuring PPP and CHAP on CISCO Routers

For this exercise, let's assume you have two routers, Router C and Router D, and that both need PPP and authentication such as PAP or CHAP. To specify the password to be used in CHAP or PAP caller identification, perform the following task in Global Configuration mode (this is where you will add your credential set):

1. Log on to Router C and configure the Serial 0/0 interface with an IP address of 10.1.1.1 and a mask of 255.255.255.252, PPP encapsulation, and CHAP authentication:

```
RouterC# conf t
RouterC(config)# interface s0/0
RouterC(config-if)#ip address 10.1.1.1 255.255.255.252
RouterC(config-if)#encapsulation ppp
RouterC(config-if)#ppp authentication chap
RouterC(config-if)#exit
```

2. Configure a credential set. Configure a username (which is the router you want to connect to, Router D in this example) and a password of pswd123.

```
RouterC(config)#username RouterD password pswd123
RouterC(config)#exit
```

3. Configure PPP and CHAP on Router D via the following commands:

```
RouterD# conf t
RouterD(config)# interface s0/0
RouterD(config-if)#ip address 10.1.1.2 255.255.255.252
RouterD(config-if)#encapsulation ppp
RouterD(config-if)#ppp authentication chap
RouterD(config-if)#exit
RouterD(config)#username RouterC password pswd123
RouterD(config)#exit
```

4. To configure an alternative interface on Router C for PPP and PAP, type the following at the prompt:

```
RouterC# conf t
RouterC(config)# interface s0/1
RouterC(config-if)#ip address 10.1.1.3 255.255.255.252
RouterC(config-if)#encapsulation ppp
RouterC(config-if)#ppp authentication pap
RouterC(config-if)#exit
RouterC(config)#ppp  pap  sent-username  RouterE  password
    pswd123
RouterC(config)#exit
RouterC# wr mem
```

5. Save the configuration and test all the interfaces to make sure your network can pass traffic without any issues.

PAP requires one extra configuration step. When you're doing two-way authentication you must not forget to add the *ppp pap sent-username username password password* command. If this command is not present on the receiving router and the PPP client attempts to force the server to authenticate remotely, the request for PAP credentials will fail. You can find the failure results in the *debug ppp negotiations* output.

Here is what the Serial 0/0 or 0/1 interface would look like if you chose to configure CHAP or PAP:

```
RouterC# show interface serial0/0
interface serial0/0
ip address 10.1.1.1 255.255.255.252
encapsulation ppp
ppp authentication chap
RouterC# show interface serial0/1
```

```
interface serial0/1
ip address 10.1.1.2 255.255.255.252
encapsulation ppp
ppp authentication pap
<-Output Omitted->
```

Remember when configuring CHAP that you must add a username entry for each remote system from which the local router requires authentication. If you forget this step, you will not have a functioning PPP and CHAP connection.

Exam Warning

You will be tested on PPP and CHAP thoroughly in the CCNA exam, albeit perhaps not directly. It's imperative that you know when to use PPP and CHAP, especially when presented with different types of WAN connection methods. For simulation-based questions, you will need to know the basic IOS commands from memory and how, when, and where to apply them.

Troubleshooting PPP and CHAP

Troubleshooting any network problem can be tricky. Luckily, with PPP you do not have too much data to weed through to find a problem, and if you know how to use the correct debugging commands, you will likely be able to solve just about any PPP (or CHAP) based problem quickly.

As mentioned earlier, PPP goes through the five phases of Link Dead, Link Establishment, Authentication, Network Layer Protocol configuration, and Link Termination when transporting multiprotocol packets over point-to-point links. For practical purposes, most network technicians often consider PPP as a four-phase protocol because in the Link Dead phase, PPP remains stagnant until activity occurs; as such, in this phase, there really is nothing to troubleshoot.

Once you have an active link, however, the following four phases occur in LCP, which PPP uses to handle Layer 2 functionality. Knowing how to troubleshoot each phase separately will help you understand how to isolate PPP-related issues.

- **Link Establishment phase** This phase establishes the link.

- **Link Quality Determination phase** The phase makes sure you have good link quality to transmit data.

- **Network Layer Protocol Configuration Negotiation phase** This phase correctly utilizes a network layer protocol for upper-layer transmission.

- **Link Termination phase** This phase cuts off the connection and returns the link to the Link Dead phase.

Having a solid understanding of these phases will truly help when you begin the debugging process. In your debug output you will find very low-level information that will seem cryptic unless you know how PPP operates through these phases.

When troubleshooting PPP you will find that you can isolate many problems to the first three layers of the OSI model (the physical, data link, and network layer connections). For example, it is common to have a problem with the link itself. Many times the link becomes inactive, and this is why you do not have end-to-end connectivity. If you do have a reliable link, the next issue could be either at the data link or the network layer. Since LCP works at the data link layer and NCP at the network layer, it's easy to isolate from debug output which of these is the culprit. An LCP or NCP connection can be terminated due to the following situations:

- On administrative closing of the interface (this concerns LCP only)

- When a subfunction fails, such as a physical failure causing LCP and NCP to fail, or LCP causing NCP to fail

- When negotiations fall through or do not become established

- On line loop detection, which is also a common Telco-related issue

When a link is terminated, it will lock up your device while the protocols try to renegotiate the connection.

Exam Warning

If you want to check PPP negotiation between two peers, you must first ensure that the lower-level functions are working correctly. If your WAN link is configured as an ISDN circuit, you must know how to test all layers of the ISDN before you begin to test PPP, as ISDN functions at the physical layer. You cannot start your tests on PPP until you have checked all of the ISDN services, such as the physical interface, the dial-up connection, and any termination devices.

Your first step in troubleshooting should be to use the basic *show* commands. To view PPP on an interface, you simply need to show the interface via the *show interface* command:

```
RouterA#show interface serial0/0
    Serial0 is up, line protocol is up
    Hardware is HD64570
    Internet address is 192.168.1.10/24
        MTU 1500 bytes, BW 1544 Kbit, DLY 20000 usec, rely
            255/255, load 1/255
        Encapsulation PPP, loopback not set, keepalive set (10 sec)
    LCP Open
Listen: IPCP
Open: IPCP, CDPCP
Last input 00:00:09, output 00:00:12, output hang never
Last clearing of "show interface" counters never
Input queue: 0/75/0 (size/max/drops); Total output drops: 0
Queueing strategy: weighted fair
Output queue: 0/1000/64/0 (size/max total/threshold/drops)
    Conversations  0/1/256 (active/max active/max total)
    Reserved Conversations 0/0 (allocated/max allocated)
5 minute input rate 0 bits/sec, 0 packets/sec
5 minute output rate 0 bits/sec, 0 packets/sec
    1921 packets input, 136287 bytes, 0 no buffer
    Received 1301 broadcasts, 0 runts, 0 giants, 0 throttles
    0 input errors, 0 CRC, 0 frame, 0 overrun, 0 ignored,
        0 abort
    2165 packets output, 100238 bytes, 0 underruns
    0 output errors, 0 collisions, 220 interface resets
    0 output buffer failures, 0 output buffers swapped out
    279 carrier transitions
    DCD=up  DSR=up  DTR=up  RTS=up  CTS=up
```

Note in the preceding code how the encapsulation type is set to PPP when viewing the Serial 0/0 interface; also note that LCP is open to IPCP and CDPCP (and that it is listening for IPXCP). By viewing this configuration, you can see whether you have misconfigured anything.

Exam Warning

For the CCNA exam, you will need to know how to look at configurations, interfaces, and debug output primarily to find problems relating to PPP and CHAP.

Debugging PPP

Using the debugging command-line tool in IOS can be very helpful when trying to find the cause of a problem. You should always be careful when debugging a device. You also need to know how to configure the router to be able to receive and/or manipulate the output from a debug session.

When configuring debugging on a Cisco device, you should remember that by default, all debug messages will go to the console and will not be sent to any log. Also, if your console buffer is too small or your log is set to Small, you may not capture all the information you need to see. To log debug output to the system log you need to use the *logging buffered* command in Global Configuration mode. The *show logging* command will show you the status. You can then use the *terminal monitor* command if you need to see your debug output in a Telnet session.

When debugging, you will want to set the command to enable milli-second-based timestamps on the router within which you are working, for increased accuracy. To do this, simply run the *service timestamp debug date-time* command with the *msec* option:

```
RouterA(config)# service timestamp debug datetime msec
```

Once the router is configured to check for milliseconds you can turn on debugging to check for output. To debug PPP and CHAP authentication (or another authentication protocol), issue the following command:

```
RouterA# debug ppp authentication
```

Once you issue *debug ppp authentication* you will see the following output if ISDN is configured on BRI0/0:

```
RouterA#debug ppp authentication
01:10:30: %LINK-3-UPDOWN: interface BRI0/0:1, changed state
   to up
01:10:30: BRI0/0:1 PPP: using dialer call direction
01:10:30: BRI0/0:1 PPP: treating connection as callin
01:10:30: BRI0/0:1 CHAP: O CHALLENGE id 10 len 24 from
   'RouterB'
01:10:30: BRI0/0:1 CHAP: 1 CHALLENGE id 10 len 23 from
   'RouterA'
01:10:30: BRI0/0:1 CHAP: waiting for peer to authenticate first
01:10:30: BRI0/0:1 CHAP: 1 RESPONSE id 10 len 24 from
   'RouterA'
01:10:30: BRI0/0:1 CHAP: unable to validate response,
   username RouterB not found
```

```
01:10:30: BRIO/0:1 CHAP: O FAILURE id 10 len 27 msg is
   'authentication failure'
01:10:30: BRIO/0:1 %ISDN-6-CONNECT: interface BRIO/0:1, is
   now connected to unknown
01:10:30: %LINK-3-UPDOWN: interface BRIO/0:1, changed state
   to down
<-Output Omitted->
```

This is the output of the preceding network configuration where Router A and Router B are two network segments connected via an ISDN link. When troubleshooting connectivity issues between two routers on a network using ISDN, as mentioned earlier, you should ensure that all lower-layer ISDN functionality is up and running. Remember that you can use the *debug isdn events* command to test all ISDN-related functionality. To be more specific, you can always use the Layer 2-related *debug isdn q921* or the Layer 3-related *debug isdn q931* command. The *debug dialer events* command will give you information regarding initiated and/or disconnected calls. It's important to know the status of the WAN protocol before moving to PPP or PPP-based authentication protocols such as CHAP and PAP.

ISDN was created for the purpose of enabling voice, video, and data over links, as the Plain Old Telephone System (POTS) had no capacity for video and very little for data. The B channel has a capacity for 64 kilobits per second (Kbps) and with two B channels a combined bandwidth value of 128 Kbps. The B channel is for sending data and it uses either the PPP or HDLC encapsulation method.

The CCNA exam will center on the use of PPP for B channel encapsulation. It is important to note, however, that HDLC is also a valid choice. The D channel has a standard capacity of 16 Kbps, but different vendors implement a capacity as high as 64 Kbps. The D channel utilizes Link Access Procedure D (LAPD) for its protocol, and not the PPP or HDLC encapsulation method used over B channels.

Test Day Tip

The LAPD protocol operates at Layer 2 of the OSI model. This protocol is defined in CCITT Q.920/921. In this way, LAPD works in Asynchronous Balanced Mode (ABM). ABM is used for error recovery. LAPD is an important part of ISDN to help it remain stable.

Now, let's configure a debug for authentication, since you know that ISDN is okay and the lower levels of PPP are functioning properly. Once you enter

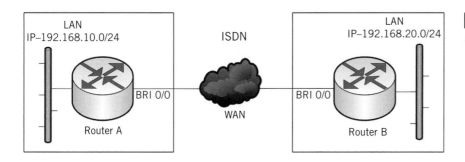

FIGURE 16.6

Debugging an ISDN Link

the *debug ppp authentication* command on Router B, as shown in Figure 16.6, you will find the source of your issue.

If you carefully examine the debug generated by the *global debug PPP authentication* command, you will see that Routers A and B can communicate over the WAN link, and that when authentication begins there is an issue with Router B's username and password. This was found from Router B's output.

Exam Warning

For the exam, you must know how to use debug commands to solve issues. Obviously, the lab scenario on the exam will be limited to some degree, but you will be able to use many troubleshooting commands to help solve problems. You will also be given problems which require in-depth knowledge of specific debug commands and their associated output.

To debug PPP and CHAP, you need to be familiar with commonly used debug commands. For instance, you would use the *debug ppp negotiations* command to troubleshoot and resolve issues with LCP communications between peers. This command will display PPP packets transmitted during PPP startup where PPP options are first negotiated.

```
RouterA# debug ppp negotations
```

You can also use the *debug ppp packet* command, which will display the PPP packets that were sent and received, and when this occurred. (This is why you should know how to set your router in milliseconds, so you can decipher fine details during troubleshooting.) The *debug ppp packet* command also displays low-level packet dumps. To debug PPP packets you can use the EXEC based command:

```
RouterA# debug ppp packet
```

You would use the *debug ppp errors* command to display output relating to protocol errors that occur while in the connection negotiation and operation phases. Protocol errors will be shown in detail. To debug PPP errors you can use the EXEC based command:

```
RouterA# debug ppp errors
```

The *debug ppp chap* command will display CHAP and PAP packet exchanges between peers. This is helpful in determining whether your peers have a misconfiguration.

```
RouterA# debug ppp chap
```

Test Day Tip

All debug commands are run in Global Configuration mode, not Interface Configuration mode.

Remember that when using debug commands you need to be careful about your environment and any adverse affects the debug may have on the environment. Use debugs with care in a production environment.

Exam Warning

Always make sure that when you use a debug command you do not cause a device to lock up or crash. Debugging usually taxes a system's resources heavily, so, for example, if you wanted to run a debug on a virtual private network (VPN) router doing software-based encryption via the command *debug ip packet*, you could freeze the system and lose access to it, thereby requiring a reboot or restart to unlock it. Use a debug command only when you know that doing so you will not cause problems; or if possible, conduct your debug session during off hours or during hours of inactivity. Use *no debug all* to turn off debugging.

SUMMARY OF EXAM OBJECTIVES

The Cisco CCNA exam will check a candidate's ability to install, configure, operate, and troubleshoot medium-size routed and switched networks, as well as implement and verify connections to remote sites in a WAN. Because so many connections are made across the world based on modems, cable networks, DSL, T1's and so on, it's no wonder that the first level of Cisco certification testing would cover the most widely used protocols and technologies in use today such as PPP and CHAP. WAN protocols supported by most Cisco gear include Integrated Services Digital Network (ISDN), Asynchronous Transfer Mode (ATM), Frame Relay, High-Level Data Link Control

(HDLC), Serial Line Internet Protocol (SLIP), X.25, and others. As you will soon see, using these technologies (such as ISDN) will rely heavily on your ability to encapsulate and secure data transmissions. That is where PPP and CHAP come into play. In this chapter, we covered the fundamentals you need to know to pass the CCNA exam and to configure routers and WAN connections with PPP and CHAP for remote access solutions.

Specifically, you learned about the differences between PPP and SLIP, its predecessor, in terms of their benefits as well as how they operate. Point-to-Point Protocol (PPP) is just one method of connecting a computer to a remote network. PPP is a point-to-point WAN protocol that works at the Data Link layer of the OSI Model. PPP is more stable than SLIP and has error checking features included. It also operates using different Network layer protocols (such as IPX from the IPX/SPX protocol suite and AppleTalk as examples) whereas SLIP only uses TCP/IP based IP. PPP (as well as SLIP) will encapsulate a datagram and other Network layer protocol information over point-to-point links. PPP will also function better than the older SLIP due to its subdivision into phases. When PPP is used on a link, it will negotiate with the other side of the link. PPP negotiation consists of three phases, which are Link Control Protocol (LCP), Authentication, and Network Control Protocol (NCP). PPP can operate on a variety of DTE/DCE physical interfaces, including asynchronous serial, synchronous serial, HSSI, and ISDN. You also learned about encapsulation and authentication, and we discussed the differences between CHAP and PAP in this regard. Because connecting up networks (especially over the Internet) can be very unsecure, authentication is needed for security purposes and this is where CHAP (Challenge Handshake Authentication Protocol) comes into play. When CHAP (or PAP) is used, credentials are transmitted with or without encryption from the sending side. When CHAP is used, a challenge which includes a random number is sent for added security. This random number is input into an MD5 algorithm to provide the encryption key with which to send authentication information between routers thus providing end to end encryption. CHAP uses encryption whereas PAP does not and offers no form of security that can be trusted. CHAP uses a 3-way handshake. This handshake is made up of the local host requesting authentication, the remote host sending an encrypted response, and the local host comparing the received information and then accepting or rejecting the connection. PAP only uses a 2-way handshake and is much less secure We rounded out the chapter with exercises that took you through the steps of debugging and viewing PPP negotiations, as well as configuring and implementing PPP and CHAP on Cisco routers.

EXAM OBJECTIVES FAST TRACK

Understanding PPP and CHAP

- PPP is a point-to-point WAN protocol that works at the data link layer of the OSI model. PPP is more stable than SLIP and includes error-checking features.

- PPP can operate on a variety of DTE/DCE physical interfaces, including asynchronous serial, synchronous serial, HSSI, and ISDN.

- When PPP is used on a link, it will negotiate with the other side of the link. PPP negotiation consists of three phases: LCP, Authentication, and NCP.

- PPP uses LCP to set up, configure, and test a data link connection.

- PPP uses NCP to establish and configure different network layer protocols. PPP is designed to allow the simultaneous use of multiple network layer protocols, including IPv4 and v6, IPX, and AppleTalk.

- PPP operates using different network layer protocols (e.g., IPX and AppleTalk), whereas SLIP uses only TCP/IP-based IP. PPP and SLIP will encapsulate a datagram and other network layer protocol information over point-to-point links. These are called NCPs.

- The phases of PPP are Link Dead, Link Establishment, Authentication, Network Layer Protocol, and Link Termination, at which point the Link Dead phase is initiated again.

- PPP uses HDLC as a basis for encapsulating datagrams over point-to-point links.

- PAP is the older of the two PPP authentication protocols. It has major security flaws, including the sending of passwords in clear text and allowing a client to choose when it sends a password.

- When CHAP is used over a WAN connection, the router receiving the connection sends a challenge which includes a random number that can be input into an MD5 hash algorithm. MD5 hashing and server control is a function of CHAP.

- CHAP uses a three-way handshake comprising the local host requesting authentication, the remote host sending an encrypted response, and the local host comparing the received information and then accepting or rejecting the connection. PAP only uses a two-way handshake and is much less secure.

- MS-CHAP is nearly identical to CHAP in terms of how it operates. The main difference between the two is that MS-CHAP is Microsoft's proprietary version of CHAP and is not an open standard. You will not be tested on MS-CHAP on the CCNA exam directly, but you should know about its use and its proprietary nature.

- CHAP and PAP are open standards-based protocols.

Configuring and Implementing PPP and CHAP on Cisco Routers

- You use the *show interface* command to verify the current state of PPP LCP negotiations.

- You use the *debug ppp negotiations* command to troubleshoot and resolve issues with LCP communications between peers. This command will display PPP packets transmitted during PPP startup where PPP options are first negotiated.

- You use the *debug ppp packet* command to display the PPP packets that are being sent and received, and when this occurs. This command also displays low-level packet dumps.

- You use the *debug ppp errors* command to display output relating to protocol errors that occur while in the connection negotiation and operation phases. Protocol errors are shown in detail.

- You use the *debug ppp chap* command to display CHAP and PAP packet exchanges between peers. This is helpful in determining whether your peers have a misconfiguration.

- You use the *debug ppp authentication* command to troubleshoot and resolve issues with authentication attempts using protocols such as CHAP and PAP.

EXAM OBJECTIVES FREQUENTLY ASKED QUESTIONS

Q: For the exam, should I know what multilink PPP is and how it works?

A: Yes, you should be familiar with multilink PPP for the exam. Specifically, you must understand how PPP operates; if you know how

PPP works, all you have to remember is that with multilink, you are basically using PPP across a type of WAN-based network with multiple links such as Frame Relay and/or ISDN. Multilink PPP (also known as MLP) is defined in RFC 1990 and is used to combine multiple WAN links into a single logical channel that is sometimes referred to as a *bundle* when describing ISDN channels. Using MLP will allow for load-balancing of traffic from multiple links as well as providing link redundancy.

Q: For the exam, will I need to know about Dial-on-Demand Routing (DDR)?

A: Yes. For the exam, you will need to know that multilink PPP is configured along with ISDN to establish DDR. DDR will provide a significant savings in cost over point-to-point links that are always available. ISDN BRI or PRI rate interfaces can be bundled with MLP to provide connectivity when needed.

Q: Can I configure PPP to use both CHAP and PAP?

A: Yes, you can configure PPP to use both CHAP and PAP authentication methods. However, the other device must not return a CHAP response. If CHAP returns a reject response, PAP will not be used.

Q: Does PPP debugging eat up so many router and/or switch resources that I will not be able to test it in a production scenario?

A: No, you can test PPP while running production routers or switches. However, if the network device on which you wish to run tests is relied on or performs a critical function, using it for this purpose may impact its performance. Therefore, before running a debug command, you should know the model of the device so that you can see whether offloaded hardware is processing specific functions. You should also know how much memory or CPU power the device has, what functions it performs, and what protocols are running and in use. Also, consider the use of the device. Is it a crucial router that is already overtaxed with work? Use caution in every scenario and you will avoid problems while testing.

Q: How secure are the authentication protocols, and can I rely on them for my network?

A: As a network engineer, you will always have to wear the secondary hat of "security analyst." *Network engineer* also implies security engineering, so it's recommended that while studying to become a

CCNA, you consider security every step of the way. It's also implied that anything released by Cisco, or any other vendor, is fair game for malicious hackers. Every IOS release for the past few years has grown exponentially in terms of security options. When working with any authentication protocol (or any protocol in general) you should always consider that it can easily be hacked. As such, you should stay on top of the Cisco updates that are released, code release caveat statements, code-based security updates, and security news.

SELF TEST

1. You are a Cisco engineer assigned to configure a WAN connection for a company. You are configuring the WAN connection utilizing PPP. When using PPP, it's important to understand the underlying protocols used to facilitate processes such as link setup and, eventually, teardown of the circuit, link, or line. In PPP, which underlying protocol is responsible for establishing and configuring as well as testing, maintaining, and terminating PPP WAN-based connections? (Choose all that apply.)

   A. NCP   **C.** CDP
   B. LCP   **D.** X.25

2. As a network consultant, you are asked to set up a secure way to connect a WAN link utilizing PPP. Which of the following statements regarding PPP authentication protocols is true? (Choose all that apply.)

   A. When CHAP is used over a WAN connection, the username and password are sent by the dialing router without encryption.

   B. When PAP is used over a WAN connection, the username and password are sent by the dialing router with encryption.

   C. When CHAP is used over a WAN connection, the username and password are sent by the dialing router with encryption.

   D. When PAP is used over a WAN connection, the username and password are sent by the dialing router without encryption.

3. Which of the following PPP sublayers is responsible for all of PPP's network layer protocol negotiations?

   A. IPCP   **C.** X.25
   B. LCP   **D.** NCP

4. What verification command can show the current state of the PPP LCP?

    A. The *debug NCPLCP* command is used to verify the current state of PPP LCP negotiations.

    B. The *test-network* command is used to verify the current state of PPP LCP negotiations.

    C. The *show interface* command is used to verify the current state of PPP LCP negotiations.

    D. The *show network-status* command is used to verify the current state of PPP LCP negotiations.

5. As a new Cisco engineer, you are configuring a set of routers using PPP. You need to configure CHAP authentication. What Cisco IOS configuration mode is used when enabling PPP authentication?

    A. Interface Configuration mode

    B. Global Configuration mode

    C. PPP Configuration mode

    D. Authentication Configuration mode

    E. CHAP Configuration mode

6. Which of the following best describes the inherent problems of PPP using PAP during the LCP phase?

    A. PAP enables the client to control the authentication attempt.

    B. PAP will send the transmission across the wire unauthenticated.

    C. PAP during the LCP phase will send out Hello packets to find the adjacent router.

    D. PAP will use CHAP for its authentication and the handoff is unsafe.

7. You are a network engineer looking to implement security on your network. Your WAN router is connected to two other routers on the other side of the world. You need to secure these three routers correctly. You would like to use a secure function of PPP to authenticate each device. A three-way handshake is preferred over a two-way handshake in terms of authentication methods available. Which PPP authentication protocol uses a three-way handshake and thus is the one you should configure on all of your network routers?

    A. NCP   **C.** PAP

    B. CHAP   **D.** LCP

8. You are a network engineer trying to resolve a particularly difficult authentication problem. You are investigating the routers involved and are using debug commands. While troubleshooting, you try to find where authentication failures are taking place within PPP. Which protocol should you analyze to find the source of the issue?

   A. PPPoE

   B. LCP

   C. IPCP

   D. CDPCD

   E. CDP

9. You are a Cisco engineer troubleshooting a PPP-based connectivity issue on an IPv6-based network. The routers were taken from an older IPv4 network and were installed on the one you are testing. You check that IPv4 is currently in use on the router and that PPP is configured. You find that you cannot communicate across your network. From the answers given, what is the reason you are not getting your routers to connect?

   A. You need to configure the correct NCP, which is IPv6CP. If you do not configure IPv6 on your routers, they will not be able to communicate over the network.

   B. You need to configure the correct LCP, which is IPv6CP. If you do not configure IPv6 on your routers, they will not be able to communicate over the network.

   C. You need to configure the correct NCP, which is IPv4CP. If you do not configure IPv6 on your routers, they will not be able to communicate over the network.

   D. You need to configure the correct LCP, which is IPNGCP. If you do not configure IPv6 on your routers, they will not be able to communicate over the network.

10. While configuring a network router, you need to find an interface in which to configure PPP for WAN communications among three separate routers. From the answers given, which interface type can you use to configure PPP? (Select all that apply.)

    A. Synchronous serial

    B. Asynchronous serial

    C. LMI

    D. HSSI

    E. ISDN

11. As a network analyst, you are working on a solution for configuring PPP, and you are connecting one TCP/IP-based network to another TCP/IP-based network. You will need to communicate between both networks using IP. Which of the following statements regarding the PPP NCP-based IPCP protocol is true? (Choose all that apply.)

    A. IPCP will pass WINS and DNS information.

    B. IPCP will pass NDS information.

    C. IPCP will handle compression.

    D. You will need to use IPCP for address assignment.

12. You are troubleshooting a WAN-based problem for your company. You want to configure an interface protocol that will allow error correction. From the answers given, which protocol listed will *not* provide error-correction features?

    A. SDLC   C. PPP

    B. HDLC   D. LAPD

13. While solving an issue on a PPP-based connection, you notice that you do not have the correct encapsulation type on a particular interface on a troubled router. If Router A has a serial interface you would like to configure with DDR, what protocol choice given should be configured? (Choose only one answer.)

    A. HDLC   C. X.25

    B. SDLC   D. PPP

14. While working as a Cisco engineer, you are assigned to help resolve an ISDN network design issue. You are not sure whether you should use PPP on the B channels. From the list of answers given, which answer provides the correct design for the solution needed?

    A. You should use PPP for the B channels and LAPD for the D channel.

    B. You should use HDLC for the B channels and PPP for the D channel.

    C. You should use CDP for the B channels and LAPD for the D channel.

    D. You should use PPP for the B channels and HDLC for the D channel.

    E. You should use LAPD for the B channels and HDLC for the D channel.

15. You are a consultant working on a new network rollout. You have three Cisco routers that will be connected together over a WAN. You need to use a protocol on the connected interfaces on each router. From the list of options, which answer clearly defines which protocol is used on Cisco-based hardware by default?

A. PPP

B. HDLC

C. LAPB

D. CDP

E. SLIP

16. You are a Cisco engineer troubleshooting a connectivity issue between two routers in a new network design. You enter the *debug ppp authentication* command on the Router B router. Based on the graphic in Figure 16.7 and, beneath that, the output received from the router, what's the most likely cause of this connectivity issue?

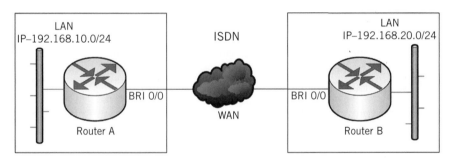

FIGURE 16.7

Debugging an ISDN Link

```
RouterA#debug ppp authentication
01:10:30: %LINK-3-UPDOWN: interface BRIO/0:1, changed state
   to up
01:10:30: BRIO/0:1 PPP: using dialer call direction
01:10:30: BRIO/0:1 PPP: treating connection as callin
01:10:30: BRIO/0:1 CHAP: 0 CHALLENGE id 10 len 24 from
   'RouterB'
01:10:30: BRIO/0:1 CHAP: 1 CHALLENGE id 10 len 23 from
   'RouterA'
01:10:30: BRIO/0:1 CHAP: waiting for peer to authenticate
   first
01:10:30: BRIO/0:1 CHAP: 1 RESPONSE id 10 len 24 from
   'RouterA'
01:10:30: BRIO/0:1 CHAP: unable to validate response, username
   RouterB not found
```

```
01:10:30: BRI0/0:1 CHAP: O FAILURE id 10 len 27 msg is
   'authentication failure'
01:10:30: BRI0/0:1 %ISDN-6-CONNECT: interface BRI0/0:1, is
   now connected to unknown
01:10:30: %LINK-3-UPDOWN: interface BRI0/0:1, changed state
   to down
<-output omitted->
```

A. Router A has only PAP configured.

B. The username and password are not properly configured on the Router B router.

C. You cannot connect two BRI interfaces together in this manner without using ISDN B channels.

D. Currently, your ISDN circuit is no longer available and is causing peers to drop authentication.

17. You are working on your company's network and you are asked to deploy an authentication scheme that can help provide the most security offered with PPP. Based on the diagram in Figure 16.8, which statement best describes CHAP functionality and why is it more secure than PAP?

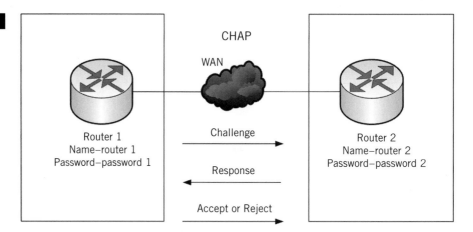

FIGURE 16.8

Viewing CHAP Used on a PPP Link

A. Using CHAP, the challenge and response used are based on the Two-Fish algorithm, thereby adding a layer of security to your authentication scheme.

B. Using CHAP, you will find that no challenge and response are used; rather, a system of key numbers connected in sequence when the receiving router receives them provides a layer of security.

   C. You should use PAP for added security; CHAP is secure only if AES encryption and a digital certificate are added.

   D. Using CHAP, the challenge and response used are based on the MD5 algorithm, thereby adding a layer of security to your authentication scheme.

18. You are working on your company's network. When asked to deploy an authentication scheme that can help secure a PPP-based link, you decide to use PAP. Based on the diagram in Figure 16.9, what should you be concerned with when deploying PAP over an unsecured PPP link?

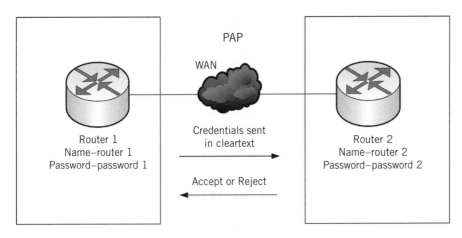

PAP

WAN

Credentials sent in cleartext →

Accept or Reject ←

Router 1
Name–router 1
Password–password 1

Router 2
Name–router 2
Password–password 2

FIGURE 16.9

Viewing PAP Used on a PPP Link

   A. The passwords for both Router 1 and Router 2 are easily guessed.

   B. Credentials are broadcast to all routers configured on the WAN, instead of to a single peer.

   C. Passwords are sent in clear text and can easily be captured by malicious users.

   D. Routers 1 and 2 cannot communicate over the WAN link without the use of Frame Relay.

19. You are a consulting engineer working on a WAN issue for a client. The client's systems are antiquated and use SLIP. You have a requirement to upgrade to PPP to support multiprotocol transmissions. What other reasons would you use PPP over SLIP? (Choose all that apply.)

   A. You want to use PPP instead of SLIP as PPP can operate at the transport layer.

   B. You want to use PPP instead of SLIP as SLIP does not function with TCP/IP.

C. You want to use PPP instead of SLIP as PPP is more stable.

D. You want to use PPP instead of SLIP as PPP has error-checking features included.

20. You are a Cisco engineer and you need to configure PPP on a set of routers. PPP can be configured to work at which OSI model layer for Internet access?

A. Data link

B. Network

C. Physical

D. Application

SELF TEST QUICK ANSWER KEY

1. A, and B
2. C, and D
3. D
4. C
5. A
6. A
7. B
8. B
9. A
10. A, B, D, and E

11. A, C, and D
12. B
13. D
14. A
15. B
16. B
17. D
18. C
19. C and D
20. A

Appendix: Self Test

Chapter 1: Introduction to Networking

1. A Cisco router at your location is no longer connecting your company to the Internet; you have noticed that users can no longer access resources on the VPN and the public Internet. You have a T1 connection to the Internet and you are the data terminal interface (DTE) side of the serial (Frame Relay) link. You have issued the show IP interface brief command and see that your CSU/DSU interface has the status of up and the protocol down. What command will tell you if the clock from the DCE is set?

   A. *Router1# show controllers s0*

   B. *Router1(config#) show controllers s0*

   C. *Router1# show clock setting*

   D. *Router1# show clockrate*

   E. *Router(config-if)# show clockrate*

   Correct Answer & Explanation: **A**. The show controllers command will show you not only you are the DTE side of the DTE/DCE but it will also show you if the clock is detected.

   Incorrect Answers & Explanations: **B**, **C**, **D**, and **E**. Answer **B** is incorrect as you cannot do show commands in global configuration mode. Answer **C** is incorrect as it only shows system clock configuration not the T1 link. Answer **D** is incorrect as there is no such command. Answer **E** is incorrect as this command does not exist and you cannot do show commands in any configuration mode.

2. A workstation in building A of an office campus network needs to obtain IP configuration information from a DHCP server in building B of the same campus. Do you need a DHCP relay server in building A to accomplish this?

   A. Yes

   B. No

Correct Answer & Explanation: **B**. In a campus area network (CAN) you are connected by switches and local connectivity instead of routers. Switches pass broadcast traffic so you do not need a relay server to obtain DHCP traffic.

Incorrect Answer & Explanation: **A** is incorrect; until you add routers between the buildings broadcast traffic will pass through the network. Once routers are added between the buildings you would then need a DHCP relay.

3. You have computers deployed into every cubicle in the office. One computer cannot access network resources on an Ethernet twisted pair network. No other users are having problems connecting to the network resources. You have tested the physical cable and there are no shorted wires or other physical problems. You have tested the NIC and also found no problems. What other factor could prohibit you from accessing the network? Pick two answers.
   A. Patch panel not wired correctly
   B. Server not online
   C. Length of wire from end-point to end-point
   D. Electromagnetic interference

   Correct Answers & Explanations: **A** and **C**. If no other users are having problems accessing network resources you have, and you have tested the cable from the computer to the socket your problems are either distance (on a twisted pair network you are limited to 100 m (about 300 feet) from end-point to end-point without something to amplify the signal) or a problem on the backbone itself. Once you have limited the problem to one device you can look at each component from the computer to the network.

   Incorrect Answers & Explanations: **B** and **D**. Answer **B** is incorrect as all other users can access the resource. Answer **D** is incorrect as EMI would affect other users.

4. You are given the number 229 in decimal notation and are asked to convert it to binary, what would the correct binary notation be?
   A. 11011110   D. 10101010
   B. 11100101   E. 11001111
   C. 00100111

   Correct Answer & Explanation: **B** (128 + 64 + 32 + 4 + 1 = 229). Remember the values of each bit and ask the 8 questions.

Incorrect Answers & Explanations: **A, C, D,** and **E.** Answer **A** is incorrect as it is equal to 222. Answer **C** is incorrect as it is equal to 39. Answer **D** is incorrect as it is equal to 170. Answer **E** is incorrect as it is equal to 207.

5. What is the maximum number of combinations that you can combine in an 8-bit number?

   A. 1,024

   B. 2,048

   C. 254

   D. 256

   E. 100

   Correct Answer & Explanation: **D.** 256 in an 8-bit number; you can have from 0 to 255, thus 256 combinations.

   Incorrect Answers & Explanations: **A, B, C,** and **E. A, B, C,** and **E** are incorrect as they are either larger or smaller than 256. 1,024 is actually 1 MB of RAM and 2,048 is 2 MB, 254 is the number of hosts you can support on a Class C network and 100 would be the first octet of one Class A network.

6. You are the administrator of a small business network. You notice that as you add workstations to the network over time the speed of the network decreases. What devices would you replace in your network with what other device to resolve this problem?

   A. Replace repeaters with hubs.

   B. Replace routers with hubs.

   C. Replace routers with switches.

   D. Replace hubs with switches.

   E. Replace switches with hubs.

   Correct Answer & Explanation: **D.** The correct answer would be **D** because hubs create collision domains and send the data signal out all the connected ports while switches only send data signals out the port that has the destination computer (determined by the MAC address).

   Incorrect Answers & Explanations: **A, B, C,** and **E.** Answer **A** is incorrect because hubs are multiport repeaters and would make no difference. Answers **B** and **C** are incorrect as routers do not connect devices on the network they connect networks together. Answer **E** is incorrect as switches are the solution to this problem and the hubs are the problem.

7. What are the five items required to have a network?
   A. Data, segment packet frame, and bits
   B. Supercomputer, mainframe computer, desktop, laptop, and handheld
   C. Sender, receiver, message, media, and protocol
   D. Video, audio, broadcast, multicast, and unicast

   Correct Answer & Explanation: **C**. The correct answer would be **C** as these are the five items you need to have for a communications network.

   Incorrect Answers & Explanations: **A**, **B**, and **D**. Answer **A** is incorrect as it is the five protocol data units in the TCP/IP communications model. Answer **B** is incorrect as it is the progression of computers from largest to smallest. Answer **D** is incorrect as it is two types of data and the three ways data can be sent.

8. As the administrator of a network you have one user that cannot see the network. Everyone else can see all of the network resources. In what order of the OSI model layers would you try and troubleshoot this problem?
   A. Application, physical, data link, session
   B. Physical, data link, session, network
   C. Physical, network, application
   D. Physical, data link, application, network
   E. None of the above as the OSI model does not pertain to troubleshooting

   Correct Answer & Explanation: **C**. The first thing to check is the physical cabling and the card working. If you have a green light on both sides the physical layer is operating correctly. Next you check the Network Protocol using commands like PING and Traceroute and finally you check the actual Application Layer Protocol you are trying to use, like the Telnet or the Ftp Protocol.

   Incorrect Answers & Explanations: **A**, **B**, **D**, and **E**. Answer **A** is incorrect because you already know the application layer has failed as the user cannot access the resources. Answer **B** is incorrect as the data link and session layers do not contribute to the troubleshooting process for this type of problem. Answer **D** is incorrect again as the data link is not useful to troubleshooting this problem and if it is not a physical problem, the application layer is already identified as being a problem. Answer **E** is incorrect as the OSI model, even though it is a theoretical model, is useful in identifying different kinds of problems.

Chapter 2: Open Systems Interconnect Model

1. What is the unique physical address (Burned In Address—BIA) that is found on all NICs called?

   A. DNS Address

   B. NAT Address

   C. IP Address

   D. MAC Address

   Correct Answer & Explanation: **D**. Every network adapter has a unique Media Access Control (MAC) address assigned to it. The MAC address is the unique ID serial number of the Ethernet card in one's computer. MAC addresses are needed in a LAN for computers to communicate; therefore, answer **D** is correct. Note that MAC addresses have nothing to do with Apple Macintosh computers.

   Incorrect Answers & Explanations: **A**, **B**, and **C**. Answer **A** is incorrect, as DNS (The Domain Name Service) translates IP addresses to hostnames across the network and the Internet. Answer **B** is incorrect, as NAT (Network Address Translation) translates one IP address on a public network to an IP address on a private (Internal) network. Answer **C** is incorrect, as an IP (Internet Protocol) address is the network layer address.

2. Which of the following is a valid MAC address?

   A. 00:05:J6:0D:91:K1

   B. 10.0.0.1 - 255.255.255.0

   C. 00:05:J6:0D:91:B1

   D. 00:D0:A0:5C:C1:B5

   Correct Answer & Explanation: **D**. A MAC address consists of six hexadecimal numbers. The highest possible hexadecimal number is FF:FF:FF:FF:FF:FF, which denotes a broadcast. The first 3 bytes contain a manufacturer code, and the last 3 bytes contain a unique station ID. Therefore, answer **D** is correct. You have to understand hexadecimal to be able to solve this, as decimal is base10, binary is a base2 system, and hex is base16. The numbers are counted from 0 to 9 and then lettered A to F before adding another digit. The letters A through F represent decimal numbers 10 through 15, respectively. Because F is the highest, then obviously an answer like C is easy to eliminate, as a quick scan of the hex shows a letter 'J' used, which is not in the base16 numbering system.

Incorrect Answers & Explanations: Answer **A** is incorrect; even though the format looks correct it is not using the HEX numbering system (Base 16) that uses 0 to 9 and A to F to represent the numbers used. Answer **B** is incorrect, as it is an IP address and subnet mask, which are network layer addresses. Answer **C** is incorrect for the same reason answer A was incorrect.

3. When working with MAC addresses, which layer of the OSI model do MAC addresses, frames, and switches associate to?

    A. Data Link   **C.** Presentation

    B. Host-to-Host   **D.** Application

Correct Answer & Explanation: **A**. The Data link layer contains two sublayers: the MAC and LLC sublayers. The LLC or Logical Link Control sublayer is responsible for providing the logic for the data link, and thus it controls the synchronization, flow control, and error checking functions of the data link layer. The MAC sublayer is responsible for providing control for accessing the transmission medium. It is responsible for moving data packets from one NIC to another, across a shared transmission medium such as an Ethernet or fiber-optic transmission medium. Physical addressing is addressed at the MAC sublayer. Every NIC has a unique MAC address, also called the physical address, which identifies that specific NIC on the network. The MAC address of a NIC usually is burned into a read-only memory (ROM) chip on the NIC card. Therefore, answer **A** is correct.

Incorrect Answers & Explanations: **B**, **C**, and **D**. Answer **B** is incorrect because Host-to-Host is not a layer in the OSI model; it is the Transport layer of the DoD model. Answer **C** is incorrect, as the presentation layer is responsible for the formatting data as well as compression and encryption. Answer **D** is incorrect, as the application layer handles top level protocols, such as SMTP and FTP.

4. From the list of choices, which of the following media access methods is used for an IEEE 802.5 network?

    A. Direct sequence   **C.** CSMA/CD

    B. Token passing   **D.** CSMA/CA

Correct Answer & Explanation: **B**. The 802.5 standard defines a Token Ring network. Token Ring uses token passing as its method of communicating on the network; therefore, answer **B** is correct.

Incorrect Answers & Explanations: Answer **A** is incorrect; direct sequence is not correct as it is not a method used by any IEEE 802 standard, this method is used to take over a network and send an entire stream as one continuous transmission. Answer **C** is incorrect, as CSMA/CD is the IEEE 802.3 standard Ethernet. Answer **D** CSMA/CA is used by AppleTalk.

5. Which OSI model layer is responsible for frame sequencing?
   - **A.** The physical layer
   - **B.** The transport layer
   - **C.** The data link layer
   - **D.** The application layer

   Correct Answer & Explanation: C. The data link layer combines bits into bytes and bytes into frames, provides access to media using MAC addresses, and detects error. Furthermore, it provides sequencing of frames. Therefore, answer **C** is correct.

   Incorrect Answers & Explanations: Answer **A** is incorrect because the physical layer handles bits, the 1s and 0s that go across the wire. Answer **B** is incorrect because the transport layer is responsible for segmenting the data. And answer **D** is incorrect, as it does not sequence data to a smaller unit; it starts the process of breaking data at the transport layer.

6. POP3 is identified by which TCP/IP port number?
   - **A.** UDP Port 21
   - **B.** TCP Port 23
   - **C.** UDP Port 25
   - **D.** TCP Port 110

   Correct Answer & Explanation: D. POP uses TCP port 110; therefore, answer **D** is correct.

   Incorrect Answers & Explanations: Answer **A** UDP port 21 is part of the FTP (File Transfer Protocol). Answer **B** is incorrect because port TCP 23 is Secure Shell SSH. Answer **C** is incorrect as TCP and UDP port 25 are part of the SMTP (Simple Mail Transfer Protocol).

7. Standards for CSMA/CD are specified by which IEEE 802 sublayer?
   - **A.** 802.1
   - **B.** 802.2
   - **C.** 802.3
   - **D.** 802.5

   Correct Answer & Explanation: C. CSMA/CD is used on multiple access networks as defined in the IEEE 802.3 specification. Using this method, devices that have data to transmit listen for an opening on the line before transmitting (Carrier Sense). That is, they wait for a time when there are no signals traveling on the cable.

When a device detects an opening, it transmits its data. Therefore, answer **C** is correct.

Incorrect Answers & Explanations: Answer **A** is incorrect, as the 802.1 standard is the IEEE LAN/MAN standard. Answer **B** is incorrect, as the 802.2 is a subset of the 802.3; it is the standard for the LLC layer of the data link layer. And **D** is incorrect, as the 802.5 is the Token Ring standards and guidelines.

8. From the choices listed, which of the following protocols represents e-mail protocols? Please choose two from the list below.
   A. POP3   **C.** IMAP4
   B. SNMP   **D.** Telnet

   Correct Answers & Explanations: **A** and **C**. POP3, IMAP4, and SMTP are common e-mail-based protocols. Therefore, answers **A** and **C** are correct.

   Incorrect Answers & Explanations: Answer **B** is incorrect, as SNMP is the Simple Network Management Protocol. Answer **D** is incorrect, as Telnet is a remote access connectivity protocol that works over TCP port 22, and all data is in clear text.

9. From the following protocols listed, select the protocol that network management applications use to monitor network devices remotely.
   A. SNMP   **C.** SMTP
   B. DNS   **D.** DHCP

   Correct Answer & Explanation: **A**. SNMP is used for communications between a network management console and the network's devices, such as bridges, routers, and hubs. This protocol facilitates the sharing of network control information with the management console. SNMP uses a management system/agent framework to share relevant network management information. This information is stored in an MIB and contains a set of objects, each of which represents a particular type of network information such as an event, an error, or an active session. SNMP uses UDP datagrams to send messages between the management console and the agents. Therefore, answer **A** is correct.

   Incorrect Answers & Explanations: Answer **B**; DNS is used for translating IP addresses to host names over the Internet. Answer **C**; SMTP is the Simple Mail Transfer Protocol. And answer **D** is the Dynamic Host Configuration Protocol.

10. When discussing the OSI model and the DoD model, which layers of the OSI model handle what you would find in the application layer of the DoD model? Choose all that apply.

A. Application

B. Presentation

C. Transport

D. Session

Correct Answers & Explanations: **A**, **B**, and **D**. The OSI model has seven layers, and the DoD model has four. The top layer of the DoD model is the application layer, but it also maps cleanly to the OSI model's top three layers, application, presentation, and session.

Incorrect Answer & Explanation: Answer **C**; the transport layer is equal to the Host–to-Host layer in the DoD model.

11. You are a network technician assigned to install a new network hub. Which layer of the OSI model does a standard hub operate at? Select only one answer.

A. Physical layer

B. Data Link layer

C. Network layer

D. Transport layer

Correct Answer & Explanation: **A**. Hubs operate at the physical layer of the OSI model. Therefore, answer **A** is correct.

Incorrect Answers & Explanations: Answer **B** is incorrect, as switches and bridges operate at the data link layer. Answer **C** is incorrect as the network layer is where routers operate. And answer **D** is incorrect, as the operating system (OS) is handled at the transport layer.

12. You are a network technician assigned to install a new network switch. Which layer of the OSI model does a standard switch (or bridge) operate at? Select only one answer.

A. Physical layer

B. Data link layer

C. Network layer

D. Transport layer

Correct Answer & Explanation: **B**. Switches and bridges operate at the data link layer of the OSI model. Therefore, answer **B** is correct.

Incorrect Answers & Explanations: Answer **A** is incorrect, as hubs and repeaters work at the physical layer. Answer **C** is incorrect, as routers work at the network layer. And answer **D** is incorrect, as the operating system (OS) operates at the transport layer.

13. You are a network technician assigned to install a new network router. Which layer of the OSI model does a standard router operate at? Choose all that apply.

   A. Physical layer   **C.** Network layer

   B. Data Link layer   **D.** Transport layer

Correct Answer & Explanation: **C**. Routers operate at the network layer of the OSI model. Therefore, answer **C** is correct. Don't get caught up with "choose all that apply," as it's only a distracter. Pay close attention to wording such as this on the CCNA exam; navigating tricky wording is also another skill that you are learning while reading this publication. Pay attention to all the layers, where they lay in the model, what happens at each layer, and which devices operate where.

Incorrect Answers & Explanations: Answer **A** is incorrect, as hubs and repeaters work at the physical layer. Answer **B** is incorrect, as switches and bridges work at the data link layer. And answer **C** is incorrect, as the operating system (OS) works at the transport layer.

14. You are a network technician assigned to install a new NIC in a PC. Which layer of the OSI model does an NIC operate at? Select only two answers.

   A. Physical layer   **C.** Network layer

   B. Data link layer   **D.** Transport layer

Correct Answers & Explanations: Answers **A** and **B**. NICs operate at the physical layer to provide media connectivity to the network and MAC/LLC connectivity at the data link layer of the OSI model. Therefore, answer **B** is correct.

Incorrect Answers & Explanations: Answer **C** is incorrect, as routers work at the network layer. And answer **D** is incorrect, as the transport layer handles the operating system (OS) to create the segments that get passed down to the network layer.

15. What is a multiport repeater called?

   A. Hub   **D.** Brouter

   B. Switch   **E.** Modem

   C. Router

Correct Answer & Explanation: Answer **A** is correct, as a hub is nothing more than a multiport repeater; it takes electrical signal in, amplifies it, and sends it out all ports.

Incorrect Answers & Explanations: Answer **B** is incorrect, as a switch is a multiport bridge. Answer **C** is incorrect, as a router is the same as a Multiport Router. Answer **D** is incorrect, as a Brouter is a router that also has the capability to be a data link (Layer 2) bridge. And answer **E** is incorrect, as a Modem is an analog device that modulates digital data over an analog line and demodulates the data back into a digital format.

Chapter 3: Subnetting, CIDR, and Variable Length Subnet Masking

1. What is used by a host to determine the host ID on a given data packet?
   A. The IP header
   B. The subnet mask
   C. The address class
   D. The MAC address

   Correct Answer & Explanation: **B**. The subnet mask is what allows a host or router to determine where to split the address in its network and host constituent parts.

   Incorrect Answers & Explanations: A, C, and D. Answer **A** is incorrect because the IP header is a part of the IP packet that contains version, source, and destination address information, among the other things. Answer **C** is incorrect because the address class would be used in a classfull environment to determine where the split occurs between host and network ID. But a typical classless environment requires a subnet mask. Finally, answer **D** is incorrect because the MAC address is used to have the physical address of a host, because an IP address is a logical address.

2. Which of the following is the binary equivalent to the dotted decimal address 207.209.68.100?
   A. 11001111.11010001.01000100.01100100
   B. 10000111.11010001.01000100.01100100
   C. 11001111.11010001.01000100.01101100
   D. 11001111.11010001.11001101.01100100

   Correct Answer & Explanation: **A**. Answer **A** converts to the correct IP address.

   Incorrect Answers & Explanations: **B**, **C**, and **D**. B, C and D are incorrect answers as they convert to different IP addresses, which are **B** is 135.209.68.100, **C** is 207.209.68.108, and **D** is 207.209.205.100.

3. You are a network administrator who needs to subnet a network to create nine subnets from a given class C network. How many bits will you need to borrow from the host ID part of the address?

A. 1

B. 9

C. 4

D. 3

Correct Answer & Explanation: **C**. Because you need to create nine subnets, you need the minimum number of bits that would allow this number of combinations. With 4 bits, you could have 16 subnets created, if the *ip subnet zero* command is issued on the router. If it isn't, then only 14 (as the all-ones and the subnet zero are not available) subnets would be available.

Incorrect Answers & Explanations: **A**, **B**, and **D**. Answer **A** is incorrect because with 1 bit you would be able to create only two (2^1) subnets. Answer **B** is incorrect because you don't even have 9 bits, as there are only 8 bits left for the host ID on a class C address. But, if you could use 9 bits, you would be able to create 512 (2^9) networks, which is far more than what you need. Finally, answer **D** is incorrect because with 3 bits, you could create only 8 (2^3) networks, which is less than what you need.

4. For the subnet mask 255.255.255.192, which pair of addresses below is on the same subnet?

A. 192.168.1.116 and 192.168.1.224

B. 192.168.1.116 and 192.168.1.124

C. 192.168.1.16 and 192.168.1.124

D. 192.168.1.116 and 192.168.2.124

Correct Answer & Explanation: **B**. The correct answer is **B** because both addresses are on the network 192.168.1.68. To obtain the network they are in, we need to convert both the subnet mask and the addresses to binary, and make sure that the bits on the IP address are equal, for the bits on the subnet mask that are 1s. This gives the following values for the options mentioned earlier.

The mask is the same for all options, which is (in binary): 11111 111.11111111.11111111.11000000. To be on the same subnet, the addresses need to be equal until the 26th bit (2nd bit of the

Answer	Address 1	Address 2	Difference
A	11000000.10101000.00000001.01110100	11000000.10101000.00000001.11100000	25th bit
B	11000000.10101000.00000001.01110100	11000000.10101000.00000001.01111100	None, right answer
C	11000000.10101000.00000001.00010000	11000000.10101000.00000001.01111100	26th bit
D	11000000.10101000.00000001.01110100	11000000.10101000.00000010.01111100	23rd and 24th bit

Table 3.44 Identifying if Two Addresses are on the Same Network

last octet). Table 3.44 shows all options, and where the network parts of the addresses differ.

To obtain the network address of each of the addresses, you just need to zero, on the IP address, the bits which are zero in the subnet mask. This is left as an exercise for you.

Incorrect Answers & Explanations: **A**, **C**, and **D**. Answer **A** is incorrect because the 25th bit is different. Answer **C** is incorrect because the address differs on the 26th bit. Finally, answer **D** is incorrect because the 23rd and 24th bits are different.

5. Which of the addresses below is a class C address?
   A. 10.20.30.40   **C.** 230.20.35.14
   B. 140.30.50.65   **D.** 200.17.45.15

Correct Answer & Explanation: **D**. A class C address has its first octet ranging from192 to 223. You just need to remember that the range, in binary, is from 11000000 to 11011111; first 3 bits are always 110.

Incorrect Answers & Explanations: **A**, **B**, and **C** are not class C addresses. **A** is a class A address (first bit is 0). **B** is a class B address (first 2 bits are always 10), and **C** is a class D address (first bits are 1110).

6. Which class of IP addresses is used for multicast transmissions?
   A. Class A   **C.** Class B
   B. Class E   **D.** Class D

Correct Answer & Explanation: **D**. A class D address is used for multicast transmissions.

Incorrect Answers & Explanations: **A**, **B**, and **C**. Options **A** and **C** are incorrect because class A and B addresses are used for regular address assignment, relying on unicast or broadcast transmissions. Option **B** is incorrect, because a class E address is reserved for future use.

7. How many bits would you need to borrow from the host ID part of an address, to create 40 subnets?

   A. 10 bits   **C.** 4 bits

   B. 6 bits   **D.** 8 bits

   Correct Answer & Explanation: **B**. With 6 bits, you can create 62 subnets (2^6).

   Incorrect Answers & Explanations: **A**, **C**, and **D**. Option **A** would allow 1,022 subnets (2^{10}), which is far more than what is needed. Option **C** would allow only 14 (2^4) subnets. Option **D** would allow 254 (2^8) subnets.

Exam Warning

The number of available subnets mentioned assumes the all-ones and subnet zero as being available (usually set through the *ip subnet-zero* router command). If they are not available, then the number is reduced by 2.

---

8. Which option below contains the two class C networks you would combine to create the network 192.168.102.0/23, through CIDR?

   A. 192.168.102.0 and 192.168.104.0

   B. 192.168.102.0 and 192.168.101.0

   C. 192.168.102.0 and 192.168.100.0

   D. 192.168.102.0 and 192.168.103.0

   Correct Answer & Explanation: **D**. We need to focus here only on the third octet. The original 24-bit subnet mask becomes a 23-bit one, and the right answer needs to keep the same 23 first bits, varying only the 24th. This is seen only with answer **D**.

   Incorrect Answers & Explanations: **A**, **B**, and **C**. Table 3.45 shows all the addresses converted to binary. You can see there that answer **A** has a difference in the 21st bit. Answers **B** and **C** have the 23rd bit different.

Table 3.45	Identifying Two Addresses That can be Combined through CIDR		
Answer	**Address 1**	**Address 2**	**Difference**
A	11000000.10101000.01100110.00000000	11000000.10101000.01101000.00000000	21st bit
B	11000000.10101000.01100110.00000000	11000000.10101000.01100101.00000000	23rd bit
C	11000000.10101000.01100110.00000000	11000000.10101000.01100100.00000000	23rd bit
D	11000000.10101000.01100110.00000000	11000000.10101000.01100111.00000000	Correct answer, they are equal up to the 23rd bit.

9. What is the maximum number of subnets that you can create, on a non point-to-point network, from a class C address with the subnet mask 255.255.255.192?

   A. 32

   B. 128

   C. 8

   D. 16

   Correct Answer & Explanation: **D**. The given network mask leaves us with 6 bits from the host ID to use for subnets. Answer **D** uses 4 ($2^4 = 16$) of the host ID bits for subnetting, still leaving two bits for host address assignment on each subnet. With these two bits, you could have two hosts on each subnet. Remember that a subnet needs to have at least two bits for host IDs, otherwise you will end up with a subnet without addresses available for assignment to hosts.

   Incorrect Answers & Explanations: **A**, **B**, and **C**. Answer **A** uses 5 ($2^5 = 32$) of the host ID bits for subnetting. This leaves a single bit for hosts. Answer **B** would require 7 ($2^7 = 128$) bits of the host ID to be borrowed for subnetting, but we only have 6 available! Answer **C** takes only 3 ($2^3 = 8$) of the host ID bits for subnetting, which is not the maximum number possible.

10. Which of the subnet masks correspond to the CIDR notation /28?

    A. 255.255.192.0

    B. 255.255240.0

    C. 255.255.255.192

    D. 255.255.255.240

    Correct Answer & Explanation: **D**. Answer **D** is correct because che/28 means that the subnet mask needs to have 28 consecutive 1s. The three first octets give you twenty-four 1s. Therefore, we need four extra 1s. As you can see going back to Table 3.1, 240 is 11110000 in binary, which makes **D** the correct answer.

Incorrect Answers & Explanations: **A**, **B**, and **C**. Answer **A** is incorrect because that number has 18 consecutive 1s only. Answer **B** is incorrect because that number has only 20 consecutive 1s. Finally, option **C** is incorrect because that number has 26 consecutive 1s.

11. Your ISP has given you four class B networks, 131.107.8.0, 131.107.9.0, 131.107.10.0, and 131.107.11.0. Which network address should you use to combine those networks into a single address?

   A. 131.107.9.0/22   **C.** 131.107.10.0/23

   B. 131.107.10.0/22   **D.** 131.107.8.0/22

Correct Answer & Explanation: **D**. The addresses are the same on the first two octets. We will combine them on the basis of the 3rd octet. Table 3.46 shows the third octet for all the addresses in binary.

Table 3.46	Third Octet from Question 11
3rd Octet in Decimal	**3rd Octet in Binary**
8	00001000
9	00001001
10	00001010
11	00001011

All possible combinations for the last two bits in the 3rd octet are present. Therefore, we can make those two bits equal to zero, obtaining the binary number 00001000, which is 8 in decimal. By doing this, we will also push the subnet mask back two bits. As we had a class C (subnet mask with twenty-four 1s) address, we will be left with 22 1s. This makes answer **D**, with the address 131.107.8.0/22 the correct answer.

Incorrect Answers & Explanations: **A**, **B**, and **C**. Answers **A** and **B** are incorrect because they don't have the last two bits equal to zero. Answer **C** is incorrect because it uses /23, and we need to have twenty-two 1s in the new subnet mask.

12. Which of the following is an invalid value for a subnet mask?

   A. 255.255.192.0   **C.** 255.254.255.0

   B. 255.240.0.0   **D.** 255.255.224.0

Correct Answer & Explanation: **C**. Answer **C** is an invalid subnet mask, as it doesn't have a contiguous set of 1s (there is 254, which is 11111110 in binary, followed by 255, which is a nonzero value).

Incorrect Answers & Explanations: **A**, **B**, and **D**. Answers **A**, **B**, and **D** are incorrect because those are all valid subnet masks. Answer **A** has eighteen 1s, and all zeros following them. Answer **B** has twelve 1s, and 20 zeroes following them. Answer **D** has twenty-one 1s, with 11 zeroes after them.

13. Which of the following addresses does not belong to an address range reserved for private use?

    A. 172.24.0.0
    B. 10.20.30.0
    C. 192.167.0.0
    D. 192.168.100.0

Correct Answer & Explanation: **C**. The private address ranges are as follows:

- 10.0.0.0 to 10.255.255.255, for class A
- 172.16.0.0 to 172.31.255.255, for class B
- 192.168.0.0 to 192.168.255.255, for class C

The only answer outside of those ranges is answer **C**, which is a public address.

Incorrect Answers & Explanations: **A**, **B**, and **D**. Those are all private addresses. Answer **A** is a class B private address. Answer **B** is a class A private address. Answer **D** is a class C private address.

14. What is the maximum number of hosts addressable on a network having the subnet mask 255.255.255.192?

    A. 254
    B. 128
    C. 30
    D. 62

Correct Answer & Explanation: **D**. The given network mask leaves us with six bits for the host ID. This means we can have 64 ($2^6 = 64$) addresses on that network, two of which are reserved for the network and broadcast addresses.

Incorrect Answers & Explanations: **A**, **B**, and **C**. Answer **A** is incorrect because, to have 254 addresses available, we would need 8 ($2^8 - 2 = 254$) bits on the host ID. Answer **B** is incorrect for two reasons. First, we would need 7 bits for the host ID to have 128 ($2^7 = 128$) available addresses, but two of those wouldn't be assignable to hosts, leaving only 126 ($2^7 - 2 = 126$) hosts addressable. Answer **C** is incorrect because we would need only 5 ($2^5 - 2 = 30$) host ID bits to have that number of hosts, but we have six available. Therefore, this is not the maximum number of addressable hosts.

15. The class of networks which has the biggest number of hosts per network is?

A. Class E

B. Class C

C. Class D

D. Class A

Correct Answer & Explanation: **A**. A class A network has three octets available for host addresses, allowing more than 16 million hosts per network. See Table 3.29 for details.

Incorrect Answers & Explanations: **B**, **C**, and **D**. Answer **B** is incorrect, because a class C network can have only 254 hosts, as Table 3.30 shows. Answers **C** and **D** are incorrect because classes D and E are not used for direct addressing of hosts.

16. You are designing a new network, and will be using a Cisco router on the perimeter of your network and the Internet. What type of NAT technology will you use to allow your entire inside hosts to connect to the Internet utilizing only one public address?

A. NAT static

B. NAT dynamic

C. NAT overlapping

D. NAT PAT

E. I would not use NAT

Correct Answer & Explanation: **D**. Answer **D** would be the correct answer; to use only one address on the public side of the router to control traffic to the Internet it would be PAT.

Incorrect Answers & Explanations: **A**, **B**, **C**, and **E**. Answer **A** is incorrect as static NAT is used to point an outside address to a single inside address to allow for traffic like e-mail to come into your network. Answer **B** is incorrect as dynamic NAT was used to allow a pool of outside addresses to be used by inside computers to get to the Internet. Answer **C** is incorrect as overlapping is used when you have publicly routable addresses on the inside, instead of the private reserved address, and you are translating that to your assigned public address on the outside. Answer **E** is incorrect, as with all IPv4 networks you use NAT.

17. You are the administrator of a Cisco network. All of a sudden people are saying they can't get to any sites on the Internet. Your connection to the Internet is provided by a Cisco 1721 router. At the router# you type *show ip nat translations* and see no output. What is the most likely cause of the problem?

A. The routing protocol has been disabled.

B. The IP addresses have been removed.

C. The PAT feature has been disabled.

D. A and B

Correct Answer & Explanation: **C**. The correct answer is **C**; the *show ip nat* command, if NAT was working, should show the table of inside private addresses and their associated port ID.

Incorrect Answers & Explanations: **A**, **B**, and **D**. Answer **A** is incorrect as most perimeter routers do not have a routing protocol on it as they are normally point-to-point connections to their ISP and use a Gateway of Last Resort for all external traffic. Answer **B** is incorrect; if you had no IP addresses on the router the *show ip nat-translations* command would still display the internal attempts to translate addresses.

Chapter 4: Configuring Cisco Routers

1. You have just connected to your Cisco 2500 series router. You are trying to enable debugging on your router. You are receiving the *error invalid* command. How can you fix the problem?

A. Use the *enable* command to enter *Privileged Exec* mode.

B. Use the *config t* command to enter *Global Configuration* mode.

C. Use the *disable* command to enter *Privileged Exec* mode.

D. Upgrade your router firmware to a version that has debug capabilities.

Correct Answer & Explanation: **A**. You must be in *Privileged Exec* mode to enable debugging. You use the *enable* command to enter *Privileged Exec* mode.

Incorrect Answers & Explanations: **B**, **C**, and **D**. Answer **B** is incorrect, because you don't need to be in *Global Configuration* mode to use debugging. Also you need to first be in *Privileged Exec* mode before you can enter *Global Configuration* mode. Answer **C** is incorrect, because the *disable* command is used to exit *Privileged Exec* mode. Answer **D** is incorrect, because *debug* commands should be available in your IOS version.

2. Given the following IOS image filename c2500-ipbase-l.122-1.E.bin, what feature set is running on the device?

   A. The c2500 feature set

   B. The IPBase feature set

   C. The 122 feature set

   D. The Enterprise feature set

   Correct Answer & Explanation: **B.** The second parameter in the IOS image file name will designate what feature set it is capable of running.

   Incorrect Answers & Explanations: **A**, **C**, and **D**. Answer **A** is incorrect, because c2500 is the hardware platform. Answer **C** is incorrect, because 122 is the IOS version. Answer **D** is incorrect, because E is the train identifier.

3. Given the following IOS image filename c2600-ipbase-l.122-1.E.bin, what hardware platform is the IOS designed for?

   A. The C2600 platform   **C.** The 122 platform

   B. The IPBase platform   **D.** The Enterprise platform

   Correct Answer & Explanation: **A.** The first parameter in the IOS file name identifies the hardware platform it was designed for.

   Incorrect Answers & Explanations: **B**, **C**, and **D**. Answer **B** is incorrect, because IPBase is the feature set. Answer **C** is incorrect, because 122 is the IOS Version. Answer **D** is incorrect, because E is the train identifier.

4. One of your Cisco routers is down and you need to figure out why. Since the router is down, there is no network connectivity to the router. You also are not near the router and therefore cannot use the console port for connecting to the router. Do you have any other options for connecting to the router to troubleshoot the issue?

   A. Connect to the router using Telnet

   B. Connect to the *Web administration* interface of the router

   C. Establish a SSH connection to the router

   D. Use a modem to connect to the auxiliary port of the router

Correct Answer & Explanation: **D**. You can connect a modem to the auxiliary port on your router. Then you can connect remotely using a telephone line.

Incorrect Answers & Explanations: **A**, **B**, and **C**. Answer **A** is incorrect, because Telnet connections require a network connection to your router. Answer **B** is incorrect, because Web connections require a network connection to your router. Answer **C** is incorrect, because SSH connections require a network connection to your router.

5. You want to configure your router so that a password is required to enter *Privileged* mode. What mode must your router be in so that you can configure this requirement?
   A. *User Exec* mode
   B. *Global Configuration* mode
   C. *Privileged Exec* mode
   D. *Interface Configuration* mode

Correct Answer & Explanation: **B**. Your router must be in *Global Configuration* mode to configure an enable password.

Incorrect Answers & Explanations: **A**, **C**, and **D**. Answer **A** is incorrect, because *User Exec* mode will not allow you to configure the enable password. Answer **C** is incorrect, because *Privileged Exec* mode will not allow you to configure an enable password. Answer **D** is incorrect, because *Interface Configuration* mode will not allow you to configure an enable password.

6. You made several changes to your router configuration. You tested out these changes and everything was running fine. Your router lost power and restarted itself. The changes you made seem to have disappeared. What is most likely the cause of the issue?
   A. You did not test the changes thoroughly.
   B. You were in *User Exec* mode when you made the changes.
   C. You were in *Privileged Exec* mode when you made the changes.
   D. You did not save the configuration to NVRAM.

Correct Answer & Explanation: **D**. When you make configuration changes, they only apply to the currently running configuration. Unless you save these changes to NVRAM, they will be lost when the router restarts.

Incorrect Answers & Explanations: **A**, **B**, and **C**. Answer **A** is incorrect, because the changes were not saved when you rebooted. Answer **B** is incorrect, because if the changes were not possible in *User Exec* mode, you would have received an error when you were configuring them. Answer **C** is incorrect, because if the changes were not possible in *Privileged Exec* mode, you would have received an error when you were configuring them.

7. You have just configured a host name for your router. But, you are unable to save your configuration to NVRAM using the *write memory* command. What is most likely the issue?

   A. You must be in enable mode to save your configuration.

   B. You do not have rights to save the configuration.

   C. You did not configure the host name properly.

   D. You are using the wrong command to save the configuration.

   Correct Answer & Explanation: **A**. You cannot save your configuration to NVRAM in *Global Configuration* mode, unless you use the *do* command. You must be in enable (or *Privileged Exec*) mode to save configuration changes, without using the *do* command.

   Incorrect Answers & Explanations: **B**, **C**, and **D**. Answer **B** is incorrect, because if you have rights to run the commands, you have rights to save the changes. Answer **C** is incorrect, because if you had entered the command incorrectly, you would have received an error message when you did it. Answer **D** is incorrect, because *write memory* is the correct command to use to save your configuration changes to NVRAM.

8. You have just configured your router with an enable password. But, you notice when you do a *show running-config* command, the enable password you set is visible. What can be done about this?

   A. Nothing can be done about this

   B. Configure encryption on your config file

   C. Configure an enable secret

   D. Upgrade your IOS to a more secure version

   Correct Answer & Explanation: **C**. Enable secret passwords are not visible when you view your configuration. You could also use the *service password-encryption* command to encrypt all passwords on the router.

Incorrect Answers & Explanations: **A**, **B**, and **D**. Answer **A** is incorrect, because you can configure an enable secret. Answer **B** is incorrect, because the option to encrypt your config file is not available. Answer **D** is incorrect, because this would happen in all IOS versions.

9. You have made several changes to your Cisco router configuration, but have not saved them to NVRAM, yet. You are not sure which options you configured. Is there a way for you to see what configuration changes you have made?

A. Use the show *startup-config* command to view the configuration.

B. Use the *write memory* command to write the configuration to the screen.

C. There is no way to see the changes you made until after you save the configuration to NVRAM.

D. Use the *show running-config* command to view the configuration.

Correct Answer & Explanation: **D**. The *show running-config* command can be used to view the configuration currently running on your Cisco device.

Incorrect Answers & Explanations: **A**, **B**, and **C**. Answer **A** is incorrect, because the *show startup-config* command will show the configuration in NVRAM. Answer **B** is incorrect, because the *write memory* command is used to save your configuration to NVRAM. Answer **C** is incorrect, because you can use the *show running-config* command to view an unsaved configuration.

10. You have just set up your Cisco router. But, you notice that the IOS prompt says *router*. Is there any way for you to change this?

A. Yes, use the *router* command to change the router's name.

B. No, this cannot be changed.

C. Yes, use the *hostname* command to give the router a name.

D. Yes, install a new IOS image that is properly licensed.

Correct Answer & Explanation: **C**. The *hostname* command is used to give your router a name. Once configured, this name will appear at the IOS prompt.

Incorrect Answers & Explanations: **A**, **B**, and **D**. Answer **A** is incorrect, because the *router* command is not used to change the name of the router. Answer **B** is incorrect, because the router's name can be changed using the *hostname* command. Answer **D** is incorrect, because the router name is not embedded in the IOS.

11. What command can be used to view the routing table on your Cisco router?

A. *Ipconfig*   C. *Route print*

B. *Show route*   D. *Show ip route*

Correct Answer & Explanation: **D**. The *show ip route* command will display the routing information on your Cisco router.

Incorrect Answers & Explanations: **A**, **B**, and **C**. Answer **A** is incorrect, because *Ipconfig* is used to view IP configuration information on Windows systems. Answer **B** is incorrect, because show route is not a complete command. Answer **C** is incorrect, because route print is used to view routing information on Windows systems.

12. You are trying to view information about your IOS. What command will allow you to view this information?

A. *show ios*   C. *show ip route*

B. *show version*   D. *enable*

Correct Answer & Explanation: **B**. The *show version* command will display information about your IOS, configuration resister, hardware platform, and much more.

Incorrect Answers & Explanations: **A**, **C**, and **D**. Answer **A** is incorrect, because *show ios* not a valid command. Answer **C** is incorrect, because *show ip route* is used to view routing information on your Cisco router. Answer **D** is incorrect, because the *enable* command is used to enter *Privileged Exec* mode.

13. The configuration on your router has become corrupt. You remember that you have a backup of your configuration on a TFTP server. Which of the following commands will allow you to restore your configuration from a TFTP server?

A. *copy tftp run*   C. *write mem*

B. *copy run tftp*   D. *write tftp*

Correct Answer & Explanation: **A**. The *copy tftp run* command will copy your configuration from a TFTP server to DRAM.

Incorrect Answers & Explanations: **B**, **C**, and **D**. Answer **B** is incorrect, because *copy run tftp* will backup your current configuration to a TFTP server. Answer **C** is incorrect, because *write mem* will copy your current configuration to NVRAM. Answer **D** is incorrect, because *write tftp* will not restore your configuration from the TFTP server.

14. You want to check the contents of your router flash memory to check which IOS file you have. What command can be used to view your router's flash?

   A. *dir flash*   **C.** *view flash*

   B. *sh flash*   **D.** *wr mem*

   Correct Answer & Explanation: **B**. The *show flash* command will show you the contents of your router's flash memory.

   Incorrect Answers & Explanations: **A**, **C**, and **D**. Answer **A** is incorrect, because *dir flash* will not show the contents of flash memory. Answer **C** is incorrect, because *view flash* will not show the contents of flash memory. Answer **D** is incorrect, because *wr mem* will save your configuration to NVRAM.

15. You are having trouble with your Cisco router. You believe it is a connection issue. What command can you use to check to see your router has a network connection to another router?

   A. *PING*   **C.** *route print*

   B. *sh route*   **D.** *sh running-config*

   Correct Answer & Explanation: **A**. The *PING* command can be used to check for basic network connections.

   Incorrect Answers & Explanations: **B**, **C**, and **D**. Answer **B** is incorrect, because *show route* is used to view routing table information on the router. Answer **C** is incorrect, because *route print* is used to view routing information on Windows systems. Answer **D** is incorrect, because *show running-config* will display the current configuration on your Cisco router.

16. The IOS image on your router has become corrupt. You want to boot the system from a copy of an IOS image you have on a TFTP server. Which of the following commands would allow you to do this?

   A. *copy tftp run*

   B. *boot system tftp ios-image-name tfp-server-address*

   C. *copy tftp start*

   D. *boot system flash: ios-image-name*

Correct Answer & Explanation: **B**. The *boot system* command is used to boot your router from an alternate location.

Incorrect Answers & Explanations: **A**, **C**, and **D**. Answer **A** is incorrect, *copy tftp run* will copy your configuration from a TFTP server to the running-config file, it will not change the boot image. Answer **C** is incorrect, because *copy tftp start* will copy your configuration from a TFTP server, it will not change the boot image. Answer **D** is incorrect, because *boot system flash: ios-image-name* attempt to boot your system using an IOS image stored in flash memory, not one stored on a TFTP server.

17. Which of the following is the default register setting for a Cisco router?
    A. *confreg 0x2100*   **C.** *confreg 0x2102*
    B. *confreg 0x2142*   **D.** *confreg 0x2002*

Correct Answer & Explanation: **C**. The default configuration register setting for Cisco routers is 0x2102. Changing this setting can affect how your router boots.

Incorrect Answers & Explanations: **A**, **B**, and **D**. Answer **A** is incorrect, because setting the configuration register to 0x2100 will force your router into *ROM Monitor* mode. Answer **B** is incorrect, because setting your configuration register to 0x2142 will cause the system to bypass the configuration in NVRAM on boot. Answer **D** is incorrect, because setting your configuration register to 0x2002 may cause the router not to boot properly.

18. Which of the following config register settings can you use to bypass your router's NVRAM configuration file?
    A. *confreg 0x2100*   **C.** *confreg 0x2102*
    B. *confreg 0x2142*   **D.** *confreg 0x2134*

Correct Answer & Explanation: **B**. Setting your configuration register to 0x2142 will cause your router to bypass your router's config file on boot.

Incorrect Answers & Explanations: **A**, **C**, and **D**. Answer **A** is incorrect, because setting the configuration register to 0x2100 will force your router into *ROM Monitor* mode. Answer **C** is incorrect, because 0x2102 is the default Cisco router configuration register setting.

Answer **D** is incorrect, because setting your configuration register to 0x2134 may cause your router not to boot properly.

19. What command is used to exit *Privileged Exec* mode?

    A. *exit*   **C.** *enable*

    B. *no enable*   **D.** *disable*

    Correct Answer & Explanation: **D**. The disable command is used to exit *Privileged Exec* (or enable) mode.

    Incorrect Answers & Explanations: **A**, **B**, and **C**. Answer **A** is incorrect, because the *exit* command is used to exit *Global Configuration* mode or disconnect from the router. Answer **B** is incorrect, because *no enable* is not a valid command. Answer **C** is incorrect, because the *enable* command is used to enter *Privileged Exec* mode.

20. You want to configure your router so that a password is required in order to connect to the console. What mode must you be in, in order to configure this requirement?

    A. *Privileged Exec* mode   **C.** *Interface Configuration* mode

    B. *Global Configuration* mode   **D.** *User Exec* mode

    Correct Answer & Explanation: **B**. You must be in *Global Configuration* mode in order to configure a console password; more specifically, you must be in line configuration mode.

    Incorrect Answers & Explanations: **A**, **C**, and **D**. Answer **A** is incorrect, because *Privileged Exec* mode will not allow you to configure router passwords Answer **C** is incorrect, because *Interface Configuration* mode will not allow you to configure router passwords. Answer **D** is incorrect, because *User Exec* mode will not allow you to configure router passwords.

Chapter 5: Routing Protocols: RIP, RIPv2, IGRP, EIGRP, OSPF

1. Your Windows system is having trouble connecting to another system. You suspect it is a routing issue. How can you view the routing table on your system?

    A. By typing **route print** at the *command prompt*

    B. By typing **winipcfg** at the *command prompt*

    C. By typing **ipconfig** at the *command prompt*

    D. By typing **show ip route** at the *command prompt*

Correct Answer & Explanation: **A**. The *route* command is used to modify the routing table on Windows system. The *route print* command will display the current routing table on your system.

Incorrect Answers & Explanations: **B**, **C**, and **D**. Answer **B** is incorrect because *winipcfg* is used to view IP configuration on older Windows systems. Answer **C** is incorrect because *ipconfig* is used to view IP configuration information on Windows systems. Answer **D** is incorrect because *show ip route* is used to view routing information on Cisco routers.

2. Multiple users on your network are having issues connecting to other subnets. You believe the problem to be an issue with routing. How can you check your router to ensure your router's routing table is populated correctly?
    A. Use the *ipconfig* command
    B. Use the *route print* command
    C. Use the *show ip route* command
    D. Use the *winipcfg* command

Correct Answer & Explanation: **C**. The *show ip route* command can be used to view the routing table on your Cisco router.

Incorrect Answers & Explanations: **A**, **B**, and **D**. Answer **A** is incorrect because *ipconfig* is used on Windows systems to view IP configuration information. Answer **B** is incorrect because *route print* is used on Windows systems to show the routing table. Answer **D** is incorrect because *winipcfg* is used on older Windows systems to show IP configuration information.

3. Routes configured by which of the following routing protocols is considered the most reliable.
    A. RIPv1   C. EIGRP
    B. RIPv2   D. OSPF

Correct Answer & Explanation: **C**. EIGRP routes are considered the most reliable. EIGRP routes have an administrative distance of 90.

Incorrect Answers & Explanations: **A**, **B**, and **D**. Answer **A** is incorrect because RIPv1 routes have an administrative distance of 120. Answer **B** is incorrect because RIPv2 routes have an administrative distance of 120. Answer **D** is incorrect because OSPF routers have an administrative distance of 110.

4. You have a very large network. You are using the RIPv1 protocol for routing updates. You notice that the route to one of your remote subnets is not showing up on some, but not all your routers. Also, other routes are showing up on these routers as they should. What is most likely the problem?

A. You need to configure VLSM.

B. You are using non-Cisco equipment on your network.

C. The link must be down.

D. You have exceeded to maximum hop count of 15.

Correct Answer & Explanation: **D**. If RIPv2 encounters a route that has a hop count greater than 15, the route will be discarded.

Incorrect Answers & Explanations: **A**, **B**, and **C**. Answer **A** is incorrect; RIPv1 does not support VLSM. Also, if VLSM was the issue, the route would not show up anywhere. Answer **B** is incorrect because RIPv1 is an open protocol and can be used on non-Cisco equipment. Answer **C** is incorrect because if the link were down, the route would not show up anywhere.

5. You are using the RIPv1 routing protocol on a small network. Your network uses a subnetted 10.*x* addressing scheme. You notice that users on different subnets are unable to talk to each other. What is most likely the issue?

A. RIPv1 does not support VLSM.

B. Your network is too large.

C. One of your network switches is down.

D. RIPv1 is no longer a supported routing protocol. It has been replaced with RIPv2.

Correct Answer & Explanation: **A**. RIPv1 does not send subnet masks with its updates and therefore does not support VLSM. Because of this, your subnets are not being properly added to the routing tables.

Incorrect Answers & Explanations: **B**, **C**, and **D**. Answer **B** is incorrect because the question states that it is a small network. RIPv1 works best on small networks. Answer **C** is incorrect because if one of your switches were down, you would be experiencing other problems as well. Answer **D** is incorrect because it is still in use today, and it can be configured on your routers.

6. Which of the following is a link-state routing protocol?

A. RIPv1   **C.** EIGRP

B. RIPv2   **D.** OSPF

Correct Answer & Explanation: **D**. OSPF is a link-state routing protocol.

Incorrect Answers & Explanations: **A**, **B**, and **C**. Answer **A** is incorrect because RIPv1 is a distance vector routing protocol. Answer **B** is incorrect because RIPv2 is a distance vector routing protocol. Answer **C** is incorrect because EIGRP is a hybrid routing protocol. It uses features of both distance vector and link-state routing protocols.

7. Which of the following are distance vector routing protocols?

A. RIPv2   **C.** EIGRP

B. IGRP   **D.** OSPF

Correct Answer & Explanation: **A** and **B**. RIPv2 and IGRP are both distance vector routing protocols.

Incorrect Answers & Explanations: **C** and **D**. Answer **C** is incorrect because EIGRP is a hybrid routing protocol. It uses features of both link-state and distance vector routing protocols. Answer **D** is incorrect because OSPF is a link-state routing protocol.

8. You are in the process of designing your network. You want to minimize the amount of traffic generated by routing updates. Therefore, you want to choose a routing protocol that only sends topology updates not the entire routing table during an update. Which of the following routing protocols should you use?

A. RIPv1   **C.** IGRP

B. RIPv2   **D.** EIGRP

Correct Answer & Explanation: **D**. EIGRP will only send topology updates in its update announcements. It does not send the contents of the entire routing table.

Incorrect Answers & Explanations: **A**, **B**, and **C**. Answer **A** is incorrect because RIPv1 sends the entire routing table in its updates. Answer **B** is incorrect because RIPv2 sends the entire routing table in its updates. Answer **C** is incorrect because IGRP sends the entire routing table in its updates.

9. You are designing a new network. The network will consist of many discontiguous network segments. You want to use a routing protocol that accurately reports these networks in the routing table. Which of the following routing protocols can be used in your implementation?

A. RIPv1   **C.** IGRP

B. RIPv2   **D.** OSPF

Correct Answer & Explanation: **B** and **D**. Both RIPv2 and OSPF support VLSM and the use of discontiguous subnets.

Incorrect Answers & Explanations: **A** and **C**. Answer **A** is incorrect because RIPv1 does not support VLSM. Answer **C** is incorrect because IGRP does not support VLSM.

10. Your network contains numerous subnets. The links of these subnets are all the same size. But some of the links are always more heavily loaded than others. Because of this, you want to use load as your routing metric. Which of the following routing protocols can you use on your network?

A. RIPv2   **C.** IGRP

B. RIPv1   **D.** OSPF

Correct Answer & Explanation: **C**. IGRP allows you to use load as part your routing metric.

Incorrect Answers & Explanations: **A**, **B**, and **D**. Answer **A** is incorrect because RIPv2 uses hop count as its only metric. Answer **B** is incorrect because RIPv1 uses hop count as its only metric. Answer **D** is incorrect because OSPF uses bandwidth as its metric.

11. You are implementing a large network. Your network will consist of both Cisco and non-Cisco routers. Which of the following routing protocols would best fit your network?

A. IGRP   **C.** RIPv2

B. EIGRP   **D.** OSPF

Correct Answer & Explanation: **D**. OSPF supports large networks and can be used on non-Cisco equipment.

Incorrect Answers & Explanations: **A**, **B**, and **C**. Answer **A** is incorrect because IGRP is proprietary and can only be used on Cisco equipment. Answer **B** is incorrect because EIGRP is proprietary and can only be used on Cisco equipment. Answer **C** is incorrect because RIPv2 should not be used on large networks.

12. You are designing a network. You need to use a routing protocol that will support up to 250 hops. Which of the following routing protocols will meet this requirement?

    A. RIPv1

    B. RIPv2

    C. IGRP

    D. EIGRP

    Correct Answer & Explanation: **C**. IGRP can support up to 255 network hops.

    Incorrect Answers & Explanations: **A**, **B**, and **D**. Answer **A** is incorrect becauseRIPv1 only supports 15 hops. Answer **B** is incorrect because RIPv2 only supports 15 hops. Answer **D** is incorrect because EIGRP only supports 224 hops.

13. Which of the following routing protocols has the lowest administrative distance?

    A. RIPv1

    B. RIPv2

    C. IGRP

    D. OSPF

    Correct Answer & Explanation: **C**. IGRP has an administrative distance of 100.

    Incorrect Answers & Explanations: **A**, **B**, and **D**. Answer **A** is incorrect because RIPv1 has an administrative distance of 120. Answer **B** is incorrect because RIPv2 has an administrative distance of 120. Answer **D** is incorrect because OSPF has an administrative distance of 110.

14. You are implementing an OSPF network. One of your network links will be a 56K link. What will be the OSPF cost of this link?

    A. 56

    B. 1785

    C. 48

    D. 560

    Correct Answer & Explanation: **B**. OSPF cost equals link bandwidth, in bps, divided by 10^8.

    Incorrect Answers & Explanations: **A**, **C**, and **D**. Answer **A** is incorrect because OSPF cost equals link bandwidth, in bps, divided by 10^8. Answer **C** is incorrect because OSPF cost equals link bandwidth, in bps, divided by 10^8. Answer **D** is incorrect because OSPF cost equals link bandwidth, in bps, divided by 10^8.

15. Where are EIGRP backup routes stored?

    A. In the backup route table

    B. In the primary routing table

C. In the neighborship table

D. In the topology table

Correct Answer & Explanation: **D**. EIGRP stores its backup routes in the topology table. The topology table stores all the potential routes to a destination.

Incorrect Answers & Explanations: **A**, **B**, and **C**. Answer **A** is incorrect because EIGRP does not keep a separate backup route table. Answer **B** is incorrect because the primary routing table does not store backup routes. It can however store multiple equal cost routes. Answer **C** is incorrect because the neighborship table only stores information about a router' neighbors.

16. You have configured your OSPF topology to use stub areas. What routing information will be sent from the area border router of the stub area to the rest of the routers in the area?

    A. Summarized routes for the networks outside the stub area

    B. Only a default route will be advertised.

    C. Individual routes for all the networks outside the stub area will be advertised.

    D. No routes will be advertised inside the stub area.

    Correct Answer & Explanation: **B**. Only a default route will be advertised by the area border router.

    Incorrect Answers & Explanations: **A**, **C**, and **D**. Answer **A** is incorrect, additional routes will not be sent throughout the stub area. Answer **C** is incorrect because additional routes will not be sent throughout the stub area. Answer **D** is incorrect because routers in the stub area will be sent to one default route.

17. You are implementing an OSPF network. One of your routers has interfaces with the following IP addresses: 192.168.1.1, 192.168.2.1, 172.16.32.1, and 10.3.2.1. What will be the router ID of the router?

    A. 192.168.1.1   **C.** 172.16.32.1

    B. 192.168.2.1   **D.** 10.3.2.1

    Correct Answer & Explanation: **B**. The numerically highest IP address assigned to the router will be the router ID.

    Incorrect Answers & Explanations: **A**, **C**, and **D**. Answer **A** is incorrect because the numerically highest IP address assigned to the router will be the router ID. Answer **C** is incorrect because the numerically highest IP address assigned to the router will be the router ID. Answer **D** is incorrect because the numerically highest IP address assigned to the router will be the router ID.

18. You are designing a very large new network. Some of your networks will use the IPX protocol. Which of the following routing protocols should you use?

    A. RIPv2

    B. IGRP

    C. EIGRP

    D. OSPF

    Correct Answer & Explanation: **C**. EIGRP is one of the protocols recommended for use in large networks. It also supports the use of IPX.

    Incorrect Answers & Explanations: **A**, **B**, and **D**. Answer **A** is incorrect because RIPv2 should not be used in large networks. Answer **B** is incorrect because IGRP does not support IPX. Answer **D** is incorrect because OSPF does not support IPX.

19. How often are RIPv2 routing updates sent?

    A. Every 30 s

    B. Every 60 s

    C. Every 90 s

    D. Only on topology updates

    Correct Answer & Explanation: **A**. RIPv2 updates are sent out every 30 s, just like RIPv1 updates.

    Incorrect Answers & Explanations: **B**, **C**, and **D**. Answer **B** is incorrect because RIPv2 updates are sent out every 30 s. Answer **C** is incorrect because RIPv2 updates are sent out every 30 s. Answer **D** is incorrect because RIPv2 updates are sent out every 30 s.

20. You are implementing an OSPF network. One of your links will have a bandwidth of 1.544 Mbps. What will be the OSPF cost of the link?

    A. 1544

    B. 64

    C. 1785

    D. 640

    Correct Answer & Explanation: **A**. OSPF cost equals link bandwidth, in bps, divided by 10^8.

    Incorrect Answers & Explanations: **B**, **C**, and **D**. Answer **B** is incorrect because OSPF cost equals link bandwidth, in bps, divided by 10^8. Answer **C** is incorrect because OSPF cost equals link bandwidth, in bps, divided by 10^8. Answer **D** is incorrect because OSPF cost equals link bandwidth, in bps, divided by 10^8.

Chapter 6: Implementing RIP, Version 2

1. Which command enables Routing Information Protocol?

   A. *router RIP*

   B. *router RIP 10.0.0.0*

   C. *enable router RIP*

   D. *router RIP enable*

   Correct Answer & Explanation: **A**. You should use the *router RIP* command to enable Routing Information Protocol.

   Incorrect Answers & Explanations: **B**, **C**, **D**. Answer **B** is incorrect, because RIP 2 will not work with autonomous system numbers. Answers **C** and **D** are incorrect, because these commands are not valid.

2. Which of the following describes RIP 2?

   A. It sends multicast updates to 224.0.0.7.

   B. It is a distance vector protocol that uses the hop count as its metric.

   C. It provides clear text and MD5 authentication.

   D. Its default holddown timer is 240 seconds.

   Correct Answers & Explanations: **B**, and **C**. Answer **B** is correct, because RIP uses the hop count as it is metric. Answer **C** is correct, because RIP 2 is able to authenticate route updates by using clear text or MD5 authentication.

   Incorrect Answers & Explanations: **A**, **D**. Answer **A** is incorrect, because RIP 2 will not send to the multicast address 224.0.0.7. Answer **D** is incorrect, because the holddown timer for RIPv2 is 180 seconds.

3. You want to see the routes that only RIP 2 has discovered. Which command should you use?

   A. *show ip protocol*

   B. *show ip interface*

   C. *show ip route*

   D. *show ip route RIP*

   Correct Answer & Explanation: **D**. Answer **D** is correct, because the *show ip route RIP* command displays only the routes learned by RIP.

   Incorrect Answers & Explanations: **A**, **B**, **C**. Answer **A** is incorrect, because the *show ip protocol* command shows the active state of the active routing protocols running on the router. Answer **B** is incorrect, because the *show ip interface* command displays interface details.

Answer **C** is incorrect, because the *show ip route* command shows the routes learned by other routing protocols.

4. Which command displays RIP 2 routing updates when a RIP-enabled router exchanges information with its neighbor?

    A. *show ip route*   **C.** *debug ip RIP*

    B. *show ip protocols*   **D.** *debug ip protocols*

Correct Answer & Explanation: C. Answer **C** is correct, because *debug ip RIP* shows real-time routing information.

Incorrect Answers & Explanations: A, B, D. Answer **A** is incorrect, because *show ip route* displays all routes available in the routing table. Answer **B** is incorrect, because *show ip protocols* displays more information regarding the protocol itself. Answer **D** is incorrect, because *debug ip protocols* does not exist.

5. Which command should you use to verify the new routes learned by your RIP 2-enabled router?

    A. *Router#show ipaddress*

    B. *Router#show ip route*

    C. *Router#show ip interface brief*

    D. *Router#debug ip protocol*

Correct Answer & Explanation: B. Answer **B** is correct, because the *show ip route* command displays new and existing routers from the routing table.

Incorrect Answers & Explanations: A, C, D. Answer **A** is incorrect, because *show ipaddress* displays the IP address of an interface. Answer **C** is incorrect, because *show ip interface brief* displays basic information from an interface. Answer **D** is incorrect, because *debug ip protocol* does not exist.

6. At which time interval does a RIP 2-enabled router send its routing updates by default?

    A. 30 seconds   **C.** 60 seconds

    B. 45 seconds   **D.** 90 seconds

Correct Answer & Explanation: A. Answer **A** is correct. RIP sends its routing table every 30 seconds by default.

Incorrect Answers & Explanations: B, C, D. Answers **B**, **C**, and **D** are incorrect, because these time intervals are too long.

7. Which subnet mask is represented by the /28 notation?

    A. 255.255.255.0   **C.** 255.255.255.224

    B. 255.255.255.220   **D.** 255.255.255.192

Correct Answer & Explanation: B. Answer **B** is correct, because /28 means 28 bits and this is equal to 255.255.255.240.

Incorrect Answers & Explanations: **A, C, D**. Answer **A** is incorrect, because 255.255.255.0 is equal to /24. Answer **C** is incorrect, because 255.255.255.224 is equal to /27. Answer **D** is incorrect, because 255.255.255.192 is equal to /26.

8. What is the CIDR notation for subnet mask 255.255.240.0?

    A. /16   **C.** /20

    B. /24   **D.** /32

Correct Answer & Explanation: C. Answer **C** is correct, because /20 is equal to 255.255.240.0.

Incorrect Answers & Explanations: **A, B, D**. Answer **A** is incorrect, because /16 is equal to 255.255.0.0. Answer **B** is incorrect, because /24 is equal to 255.255.255.0. Answer **D** is incorrect, because /32 is equal to 255.255.255.255.

9. What is the administrative distance for RIP 2?

    A. 90   **C.** 110

    B. 100   **D.** 120

Correct Answer & Explanation: D. Answer **D** is correct. The administrative distance for RIP 2 is 120.

Incorrect Answers & Explanations: **A, B, C**. Answer **A** is incorrect, because 90 is the administrative distance of EIGRP. Answer **B** is incorrect, because 100 is the administrative distance of IGRP. Answer **C** is incorrect, because 110 is the administrative distance of OSPF.

10. Which statements are correct regarding RIP 2?

    A. It has the same maximum hop count as RIP 1.

    B. It uses broadcasts for its routing tables.

    C. It's a classless routing protocol.

    D. It does not send the subnet mask in updates.

Correct Answers & Explanations: **A**, and **C**. Answer **A** is correct, because both RIP 2 and RIP 1 have a maximum hop count of 15. Answer **C** is correct, because RIP 2 does not use default classes to send routing updates.

Incorrect Answers & Explanations: **B**, **D**. Answer **B** is incorrect, because RIP 2 uses multicast for its routing tables. Answer **D** is incorrect, because RIP 2 sends the subnet mask in its updates.

11. Which of the following routes will be used to forward data if the routing table contains entries for static, RIP, IGRP, and OSPF routes?

   A. IGRP route   **C.** RIP route
   B. Static route   **D.** OSPF route

Correct Answer & Explanation: **B**. Answer **B** is correct, because static routes have an administrative distance of 1.

Incorrect Answers & Explanations: **A**, **C**, **D**. Answer **A** is incorrect, because IGRP has an administrative distance of 100. Answer **C** is incorrect, because RIP has an administrative distance of 120. Answer **D** is incorrect, because OSPF has an administrative distance of 110.

12. In the following output, you can see the result of *debug ip rip*. Which of the following statements is true?

```
R1#debug ip RIP
RIP protocol debugging is on
20:40:32: RIP: received v1 update from 192.168.20.5 on
   Serial0
20:40:32: 192.168.30.0 in 1 hops
20:40:32: 192.168.40.0 in 16 hops (inaccessible)
20:40:34: RIP: sending v1 update to 255.255.255.255 via
   Ethernet0 (192.168.10.1)
20:40:34: subnet 192.168.20.0, metric 1
20:40:34: RIP: sending v1 update to 255.255.255.255 via
   Serial0 (192.168.1)
20:40:34: subnet 192.168.20.0, metric 1
```

   A. A ping from R1 to any host on IP subnet 192.168.40.0 would be successful.

   B. A ping to IP address 192.168.20.5 would be successful.

   C. At least two interfaces on R1 are participating in RIP.

   D. The routing sends updates via multicast.

Correct Answers & Explanations: **B**, and **C**. Answer **B** is correct, because a ping to 192.168.20.5 is successful since the network can be reached via Serial0. Answer **C** is correct, because RIP is enabled on the Ethernet and Serial interfaces.

Incorrect Answers & Explanations: **A**, **D**. Answer **A** is incorrect, because network 192.168.40.0 is 16 hops away and is unreachable. Answer **D** is incorrect, because RIP updates are sent via broadcast instead of multicast.

13. Which of the following commands will prevent routes from being out on interface S0, but will not prevent the router from receiving updates?

   A. *Router(config)#int s0*
      Router(config-if)#no routing
   B. *Router(config)#int s0*
      Router(config-if)#passive-interface
   C. *Router(config)#router RIP*
      Router(config-router)#passive-interface s0
   D. *Router(config)#router RIP*
      Router(config-router)#no routing updates

Correct Answer & Explanation: **C**. Answer **C** is correct, because the *passive-interface* command will prevent the router from sending out routing information.

Incorrect Answers & Explanations: **A, B, D**. Answers **A, B, D** are incorrect, because these commands do not exist.

14. The networks connected to R1 have been summarized as a 192.168.176.0/21 route and have been sent to R1. Which two destination addresses will R1 forward?

   A. 192.168.194.166
   B. 192.183.42
   C. 192.168.159.55
   D. 192.168.183.255
   E. 192.168.179.10
   F. 192.168.184.86

Correct Answers & Explanations: **B**, and **E**. Answers **B** and **E** are correct, because these IP addresses fall in the range of network 192.168.176.0 through 192.168.184.0.

Incorrect Answers & Explanations: **A, C, D, F.** Answers **A, C, D,** and **F** are incorrect, because these IP addresses are not in scope.

15. You want to enable RIP 2 to send out routing updates via multicast instead of broadcast addresses. Which command should you use?

    A. *Router(config)#ip RIP-v2 multicast*

    B. *Router(config-if)#ip RIP-v2 multicast*

    C. *Router(config)#no ip RIP v2-broadcast*

    D. *Router(config-if)#no ip RIP v2-broadcast*

    Correct Answer & Explanation: **C.** Answer **C** is correct, because RIP 2 will send routing updates via multicast by default. Only when you specify the *ip RIP v2-broadcast* command will updates be sent via broadcast instead of multicast.

    Incorrect Answers & Explanations: **A, B, D.** Answer **A** is incorrect, because this command does not exist. Answer **B** is incorrect because this command does not exist. Answer **D** is incorrect because you cannot use this command in interface configuration mode.

16. You want to specify a neighboring router on your RIP 2-enabled router. Which command should you use?

    A. *Router(config-router)#neighbor 192.168.10.2*

    B. *Router(config)#neighbor 192.168.10.2*

    C. *Router(config-router)#ip RIP neighbor 192.168.10.2*

    D. *Router(config)#ip RIP neighbor 192.168.10.2*

    Correct Answer & Explanation: **A.** Answer **A** is correct, because you must specify the *neighbor* command in router configuration mode.

    Incorrect Answers & Explanations: **B, C, D.** Answer **B** is incorrect because this command cannot be used in global configuration mode. Answer **C** is incorrect because this command does not exist. Answer **D** is incorrect because this command does not exist.

17. Which command should you use to verify the default RIP 2 update timers?

    A. *Router(config)#show ip RIP timers*

    B. *Router(config-router)#show ip RIP timers*

    C. *Router#show RIP timers*

    D. *Router#show ip protocols*

Correct Answer & Explanation: **D**. Answer **D** is correct. The *show ip protocols* command will display the default RIP 2 update timers.

Incorrect Answers & Explanations: **A**, **B**, **C**. Answers **A**, **B**, and **C** are incorrect, because these commands do not exist.

18. You want to turn off RIP 2 on all your routers. Which command should you use?

    A. *Router(config)#no RIP enable*

    B. *Router(config-if)#no RIP enable*

    C. *Router(config)#no router RIP*

    D. *Router(config-if)#no router RIP*

    Correct Answer & Explanation: **C**. Answer **C** is correct. The *no router RIP* command will disable RIP on the router.

    Incorrect Answers & Explanations: **A**, **B**, **D**. Answer **A** is incorrect because this command does not exist. Answer **B** is incorrect because the command cannot be executed in interface configuration mode. Answer **D** is incorrect because the command cannot be executed in interface configuration mode.

19. You configured your routers with MD5 authentication and you suspect that your RIP 2-enabled routers are receiving updates. You need to verify whether all RIP 2-enabled routers are using the same key chain. Which command should you use?

    A. *Router#show ip protocols*

    B. *Router(config)#show ip protocols*

    C. *Router(config-if)#show ip protocols*

    D. *Router(config)#show ip RIP authentication*

    Correct Answer & Explanation: **A**. Answer **A** is correct. The *show ip protocols* command will display the key chain currently configured on your router.

    Incorrect Answers & Explanations: Answer **B** is incorrect because the command cannot be executed in global configuration mode. Answer **C** is incorrect because this command cannot be executed in interface configuration mode. Answer **D** is incorrect because this command does not exist.

20. You need to verify which RIP version is currently configured on your router. Which command should you use?

A. *Router(config)#show ip protocols*

B. *Router#show ip protocols*

C. *Router(config)#show ip RIP version*

D. *Router#show ip RIP version*

Correct Answer & Explanation: **B**. Answer **B** is correct. The *show ip protocols* command displays the RIP version currently in use.

Incorrect Answers & Explanations: **A**, **C**, **D**. Answer **A** is incorrect because this command displays the state of the active routing protocols. Answers **C**, and **D** are incorrect, because these commands do not exist.

Chapter 7: Implementing the OSPF Protocol

1. As the network administrator of a mid-sized company you have the opportunity to redesign your network from the ground up as part of a datacenter relocation project. One of the things you are currently trying to decide is which protocol you should implement on your routers. You have a mixture of Cisco and Juniper routers in your environment, and you want to be sure that whatever you select will work well on both. Which of the following facts about your environment will lead you to select OSPF as your protocol of choice?

A. You believe you will require a maximum of six hops in your organization.

B. You prefer simplicity in configuration; your staff does not have a lot of time, or an advance skill set in configuring routers.

C. Your environment has many slow and unstable connections.

D. Requirement for VLSM support

Correct Answer & Explanation: **C**. Answer **C** is correct, because RIP will always attempt to take the shortest route to its destination and it has no awareness of the UP/DOWN states of routes. If you have many slow or unstable links, OSPF is optimal since it will be able to determine the status of the links and hence route around the problematic areas when appropriate. RIP will not understand when a particular path becomes unavailable.

Incorrect Answers & Explanations: **A**, **B**, and **D**. Answer **A** is incorrect, because six hops are well within the maximum hop count for RIP. Answer **B** is incorrect, because RIP is a reasonably simple protocol to configure. OSPF requires much more planning before deployment and additional configuration once it is deployed. The administrative overhead associated with OSPF is much greater than with RIP. Answer **D** is incorrect, because RIP V2 supports VLSM.

2. In your environment, you notice that traffic from Miami that is destined for New York is routing from Miami through your routers in Kansas City. The traffic is then leaving Kansas City and heading through Illinois to finally end up in New York. You have connectivity on the network from Miami to Charlotte and then straight on to New York from Charlotte, and you are wondering why the routers are selecting the seemingly longer route. Which of the following Cisco OSPF formulas can be used to calculate an interface's cost to assist you in understanding the chosen route?

   A. 100,000,000 / Bandwidth in bits per second

   B. 100,000,000 / Bandwidth in kilobits per second

   C. 100,000,000 / Bandwidth in megabits per second

   D. There is no formula for OSPF cost; it depends solely on the interface type.

   Correct Answer & Explanation: **A**. Answer **A** is correct, because this is the formula used by Cisco OSPF to calculate link cost. By analyzing the link cost you can determine if the router path is valid.

   Incorrect Answers & Explanations: **B**, **C**, and **D**. Answer **B** is incorrect, because kilobits per second are not utilized by OSPF to calculate cost. Answer **C** is incorrect, because megabits per second are not utilized by OSPF to calculate cost. Answer **D** is incorrect, because cost is not calculated by utilizing interface types.

3. Which of the following is used to calculate the OSPF path cost?

   A. Number of hops

   B. Bandwidth only

   C. Bandwidth and clicks

   D. Bandwidth, reliability, and load

   Correct Answer & Explanation: **B**. Answer **B** is correct, because bandwidth is the only factor in calculating path cost.

   Incorrect Answers & Explanations: **A**, **C**, and **D**. Answer **A** is incorrect, because the number of hops is not considered. Answer **C** is incorrect, because clicks do not exist and are not considered in evaluating path cost, bandwidth is considered. Answer **D** is incorrect because bandwidth is considered but these other two items are not.

4. Your environment is configured with four routers and multiple segments. The first router is the DR for a broadcast segment, and the second router is the BDR. The first router reboots unexpectedly. While the first router is rebooting, the second router becomes the DR. What describes the first router's role when it comes back online?

   A. The first router will start an election when it comes back online to become the DR.

   B. The first router will come back online and become the DR, the second router will be downgraded back to BDR status.

   C. The first router will come back online as a DROTHER.

   D. The first router will come back online as a BDR.

   Correct Answer & Explanation: **C**. Answer **C** is correct, because when the first router comes back online it will come online as a DROTHER. An election will not be held.

   Incorrect Answers & Explanations: **A**, **B**, and **D**. Answer **A** is incorrect, because an election will not be held when the first router comes back online. Answer **B** is incorrect, because a router status only changes with an election, which will not occur from a router rebooting. Answer **D** is incorrect, because a router can only be elected to BDR status, and since an election is not triggered by a router reboot, the first router will not become the BDR in this scenario.

5. Which of the following *must* match between potential OSPF neighbors for an adjacency to form? Select all that apply.

   A. The area number

   B. Authentication method

   C. Interface name

   D. Stub flag setting

   E. Process ID

   F. Administrative password

   G. RID

   Correct Answers & Explanations: **A**, **B**, and **D**. Answers **A**, **B**, and **D** are correct, because these are all items that must match in order for adjacency to form. Other items required for adjacency include Hello Timer Settings and Dead Timer Setting.

Incorrect Answers & Explanations: **C**, **E**, **F**, and **G**. Answer **C** is incorrect, because it is not an item that must match on neighboring routers in order for adjacency to form. Answer **E** is incorrect, because it is not an item that must match on neighboring routers in order for adjacency to form. Answer **F** is incorrect, because it is not an item that must match on neighboring routers in order for adjacency to form. Answer **G** is incorrect, because it is not an item that must match on neighboring routers in order for adjacency to form.

6. You have four routers on your network. One of your routers detects that a neighbor is down. What will this router do with this link-state change information?

   A. It will send an LSA update to 224.0.0.5.

   B. It will send an LSA update to 224.0.0.12.

   C. DROTHERs do not send any kind of link change notifications.

   D. It will send an LSA update to 224.0.0.6.

   Correct Answer & Explanation: **D**. Answer **D** is correct, because a DROTHER will send an LSA update only to the DR and BDR on the segment. It does this by sending the update to 224.0.0.6. The DR will then flood the rest of the network with the update by sending an update out to 224.0.0.5.

   Incorrect Answers & Explanations: **A**, **B**, and **C**. Answer **A** is incorrect, because DROTHER routers will receive updates from the DR on 224.0.0.5. Answer **B** is incorrect, because this address is not used for LSA updates by default. Answer **C** is incorrect, because DROTHER routers will send updates to the DR and BDR, when they detect link-state changes.

7. An OSPF environment can consist of one or more areas. When multiple areas are present, which of the following statements is true?

   A. Internal routers are responsible for routing information redistribution.

   B. ABRs have all interfaces in the same area.

   C. ASBR is responsible for redistribution of routing information in an OSPF network.

   D. Multiple areas cannot be configured in OSPF environments.

Correct Answer & Explanation: C. Answer C is correct, because ASBR routers are routers that are connected to an external system. That system may or may not be an OSPF system, but the ASBR router has the ability to import and propagate routing information between the dissimilar systems.

Incorrect Answers & Explanations: A, B, and D. Answer A is incorrect, because internal routers are only connected to a single area and do not perform routing information redistribution. Answer B is incorrect, because ABRs are connected to multiple areas in an OSPF environment. Answer D is incorrect, because multiple areas are possible and exist primarily in larger OSPF environments.

8. You have not configured a *loopback* interface on your router. What criteria will be used to determine the RID?

    A. The highest IP address from the active interfaces only

    B. You must configure the loopback address to have a RID.

    C. The lowest IP address from the active interfaces only

    D. The highest IP address on all interfaces

Correct Answer & Explanation: A. Answer A is correct, because the loopback address is preferred for the selection of the router ID, but if it is not available, then the highest IP address from active interfaces will be used for the router ID.

Incorrect Answers & Explanations: B, C, and D. Answer B is incorrect, because the loopback address does not have to be configured to have a router ID; however, it is preferred. Answer C is incorrect, because the highest IP address and not the lowest IP address is used. Answer D is incorrect, because the highest IP address on only active interfaces can be selected for the router ID. If interfaces exist in a shutdown state they will not be evaluated when selecting the router ID.

9. You have noticed that support tickets from users reporting network issues in a certain area of your OSPF environment seem to be increasing, and oftentimes they come in from groups of users at the same time. You are trying to determine what exactly is taking place on your routers in order to determine whether or not there is a network-based problem. What could you do to assist with tracking down this issue?

    A. Begin recording neighbor changes with the *ospf log-adjacency-changes* command.

    B. Utilize the *show* command to view the traffic partners and their statistics. Run the *show log-all-neighbors-state* command.

C. Deploy a packet sniffer and analyze the traffic to determine when the network goes down.

D. Utilize *show down* to determine which router is having difficulty.

Correct Answer & Explanation: **A**. Answer **A** is correct, because the *ospf log-adjaency-changes* command will begin logging state changes for all adjacent routers.

Incorrect Answers & Explanations: **A**, **B**, and **D**. Answer **A** is incorrect, because the *ospf log-adjacency-changes* does not exist. Answer **B** is incorrect, because this response is also fictional. Answer **D** is incorrect, because *show down* is not an actual command.

10. How frequently do routers utilizing OSPF send out LSA updates? (Select all that apply.)

    A. When a route changes   **C.** Once a day

    B. Every 10 seconds   **D.** Every 30 minutes

    Correct Answers & Explanations: **A**, and **D**. Answer **A** is correct, because whenever a route has been changed other routers must be made aware of it immediately. Answer **D** is correct because in order to maintain the tables over time, even if changes do not occur the LSA updates are sent out every 30 minutes as a minimum.

    Incorrect Answers & Explanations: **B**, and **C**. Answer **B** is incorrect, because hello packets are sent out every 10 seconds, not LSA updates. Answer **C** is incorrect, because LSA updates occur every 30 minutes if no updates occur.

11. You recently added a new router to your environment and have configured it and put it on your test network. You cannot seem to get traffic from other routers to successfully send packets through the new router. You suspect the wrong authentication type has been enabled. Which of the following commands will allow you to view the configured authentication type?

    A. *show ip ospf*   **C.** *show ip ospf stats*

    B. *show ip ospf encryption*   **D.** *show ospf*

    Correct Answer & Explanation: **A**. Answer **A** is correct, because this command will display information specific to the OSPF configuration, including the authentication type in use.

    Incorrect Answers & Explanations: **B**, **C**, and **D**. Answer **B** is incorrect, because the command doesn't exist. Answer **C** is incorrect, because this command does not exist. Answer **D** is incorrect, because this command is not enough to give you what is required.

12. An election is taking place in your router environment. There are four routers on the segment. How many DRs and BDRs will you end up with, when the election has completed?

    A. 4 DRs and 0 BDRs. The BDRs are only elected after a failure to the DR site.

    B. 2 DRs and 2 BDRs. Each role has a duplicate in case of failure.

    C. 1 DR and 1 BDR. One of each role is elected.

    D. DRs and BDRs are not selected during elections. They are assigned based on interface connectivity.

    Correct Answer & Explanation: C. Answer **C** is correct, because 1 of each role is elected and the BDR will assume the DR duties if the DR happens to become unavailable.

    Incorrect Answers & Explanations: A, **B**, and **D**. Answer **A** is incorrect, because there is only ever 1 DR and 1 BDR per segment. Answer **B** is incorrect, because there is only ever 1 DR and 1 BDR per segment. Answer **D** is incorrect, because the point of an election is to select either the DR or the BDR. Interface values are used to select router ID values.

13. You would like to create a stub area in an attempt to reduce traffic in a problematic portion of your network. Traffic flow is often slow and router performance is poor. Which in the following are characteristics of a stub area? (Choose all that apply.)

    A. Have a default gateway configured

    B. Hold a copy of every area's routing table information

    C. Have a single entry and exit point

    D. Only contain external routes

    Correct Answers & Explanations: A and C. Answer **A** is correct, because typically a stub area has a single point of exit and entry and is therefore configured with a default gateway as opposed to having a routing table to consult for next hop information. Answer **C** is correct, because stub areas typically have a single entry and exit point.

    Incorrect Answers & Explanations: B and D. Answer **B** is incorrect, because stub areas typically are configured to route all traffic out their default gateway. This configuration reduces the overhead requirement on the routers within the sub area. Answer **D** is incorrect, because stub areas do not contain external routes. Their single route typically points to their default gateway.

14. By dividing the network into areas, the routing table that each router has to be aware of can be reduced in size resulting in greater efficiency. What additional process is performed by the routers to further reduce the size of the routing tables?

   A. Path truncation

   B. Route summarization

   C. Efficiency processing

   D. Route reduction

   Correct Answer & Explanation: **B**. Answer **B** is correct, because route summarization is the process performed by the routers to further reduce the routing tables by consolidating multiple routes into a single advertisement.

   Incorrect Answers & Explanations: **A**, **B**, and **D**. Answer **A** is incorrect, because path truncation is fictional. Answer **B** is incorrect, because efficiency processing is fictional. Answer **D** is incorrect, because route reduction is the end state goal, but not the process itself.

15. You currently have three routers and you have to add a new router onto your network to expand to a new building. You would like to set up the router to be sure that it is in working order. After configuring all of the interfaces and getting it plugged up to the network, you configure the OSPF protocol with the plain text password in use on the network. How long will it take for the new router to begin receiving its first hello packets?

   A. From 1 to 2 hours depending on the current network load

   B. A maximum of 10 seconds

   C. You must first reboot the router after configuring OSPF before any hello packets will be received.

   D. A maximum of 100 seconds

   Correct Answer & Explanation: **B**. Answer **B** is correct, because it sends out hello packets every 10 seconds by default. Depending on how long it had been since the last hello packets were sent, it could be anywhere from less than 1 second to 10 seconds for the new router to begin receiving hello packets.

Incorrect Answers & Explanations: **A**, **C**, and **D**. Answer **A** is incorrect, because OSPF packets are transmitted every 10 seconds, not on the hour. Answer **C** is incorrect, because rebooting is not required in order for the router to receive hello packets. Answer **D** is incorrect, because 100 seconds is too long. The default value on a network with more than three nodes is every 10 seconds hello packets are sent.

Chapter 8: Implementing the EIGRP

1. You are interested in the information that EIGRP sends from and receives to your routers, so you've turned on EIGRP debugging on one of your routers. Everything seems to be working fine on the network, but you've been watching the screen for several minutes and nothing is happening. What is the most likely cause of the lack of debug information?

   A. Debug isn't working properly.

   B. EIGRP isn't working properly.

   C. The network isn't working properly.

   D. The network is stable.

   Correct Answer & Explanation: **D**. Because EIGRP only sends incremental updates when something on the network changes, the lack of debug information indicates that nothing is changing on the network. If there were a change to your network, such as a link going down or coming up, then EIGRP would communicate with other routers and you would see debug information.

   Incorrect Answers & Explanations: **A**, **B**, and **C**. Answer **A** is incorrect because there is nothing for debug to display. As soon as there is EIGRP traffic, debug will show it. Answer **B** is incorrect because the network wouldn't be functioning correctly if EIGRP wasn't working. Answer **C** is incorrect because if there was a problem with the network, you would be seeing debug information as EIGRP sent incremental updates to advertise the problem.

2. You are getting ready to bring up EIGRP on your routers. You want all the routers to exchange routing information with each other. What do you need to do during your EIGRP installations on the routers to make this happen?

   A. Configure all the routers with the same AS number.

   B. Configure all the routers with incremental AS numbers (that is, the first router would be AS number 1, the second router would be AS number 2, and so on).

C. Install EIGRP but don't include any AS number.

D. In the EIGRP configurations, list the names of all the routers to exchange information with each other.

Correct Answer & Explanation: **A**. All routers must be configured with the same autonomous system number to exchange routing information with each other.

Incorrect Answers & Explanations: **B**, **C**, and **D**. Answer **B** is incorrect because the routers must all be in the same autonomous system and configuring a different autonomous system on each router tells them not to talk to each other. Answer **C** is incorrect because the *router eigrp* command requires an autonomous system number at the end of the command. Answer **D** is incorrect because there is no option for listing the names of the routers in the configuration. The autonomous system number defines the routers to exchange information.

3. You are in the process of configuring EIGRP on your routers. What would be the correct command to enable EIGRP on each of your routers?

A. (config)# **enable eigrp**   C. (config)# **router eigrp 12**

B. (config)# **router eigrp**   D. (config)# **eigrp no shutdown**

Correct Answer & Explanation: **C**. The command to enable EIGRP is the *router eigrp <AS>* command. The AS number of 12 isn't relevant. As long as all of your routers have the same autonomous system number, it can be any number from 1 through 65,535.

Incorrect Answers & Explanations: **A**, **B**, and **D**. Answer **A** is incorrect because there is no *enable eigrp* command. Answer **B** is incorrect because it is an incomplete command. You must include an AS number in the *router eigrp* command. Answer **D** is incorrect because there is no *eigrp no shutdown* command.

4. As part of the process of troubleshooting problems on your network, you are looking at debug information for EIGRP. You keep seeing the address 224.0.0.10 in the debug information. What does that address mean?

A. It's an address that is assigned to EIGRP processes.

B. It's the broadcast address that EIGRP uses to send updates.

C. It's the address of the router you're running debug on.

D. It's a multicast address EIGRP uses to send updates to neighboring routers.

Correct Answer & Explanation: **D**. The 224.x.x.x addresses are part of the multicasting address space (Class D, identified by 224-239 in the first octet). EIGRP uses 224.0.0.10 to communicate with neighboring EIGRP routers.

Incorrect Answers & Explanations: **A**, **B**, and **C**. Answer **A** is incorrect because EIGRP processes aren't assigned IP addresses. Answer **B** is incorrect because EIGRP uses multicasts to communicate not broadcasts. Answer **C** is incorrect because it isn't a unicast address for a particular device; it is a multicast address that sends traffic to multiple devices.

5. Figure 8.5 is a diagram of your network. You are configuring EIGRP on your network, and you are starting by configuring Router2. You've executed the *router eigrp 100* command to enable EIGRP on the router for AS 100. You are now at the *(config-router)#* prompt. After you finish configuring Router2, you will configure Router1 and Router3 to complete the configuration. What *network* command(s) need to be executed on Router2 so that Router2 will do its part to make sure all network and subnet information for the entire network will be advertised throughout your entire network once all the routers have been configured?

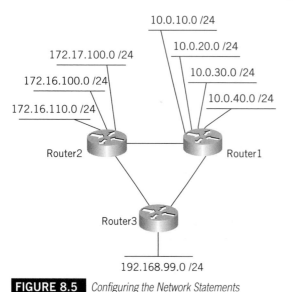

A. *network 10.0.10.0*
   network 10.0.20.0
   network 10.0.30.0
   network 10.0.40.0
   network 192.168.99.0
B. *network 10.0.0.0*
   network 192.168.99.0
C. *network 172.0.0.0*
D. *network 172.16.0.0*
   network 172.17.0.0
E. *network 10.0.0.0*
   network 172.16.0.0
   network 172.17.0.0
   network 192.168.99.0

FIGURE 8.5 *Configuring the Network Statements*

Network diagram labels:
10.0.10.0 /24
172.17.100.0 /24
10.0.20.0 /24
172.16.100.0 /24
10.0.30.0 /24
172.16.110.0 /24
10.0.40.0 /24
Router2
Router1
Router3
192.168.99.0 /24

Correct Answer & Explanation: **D**. When you configure the networks for EIGRP, you use network statements for the classful networks that the router is connected to, that you want to participate in EIGRP. Router2 is connected to the two class B networks in answer **D**. The classful addresses are with all the subnet and host bits turned off, resulting in 0s in the host octets.

Incorrect Answers & Explanations: **A**, **B**, **C**, and **E**. Answers **A** and **B** are incorrect because you must configure the networks that the router is connected to. Both **A** and **B** include the networks that the other routers are connected to. In addition, even if Router2 was connected to the 10 network, answer **A** is not using the classful network address of 10.0.0.0. Answer **C** is incorrect because the 172.0.0.0 network is a completely different network than the 172.16.0.0 and 172.17.0.0 networks that Router2 is connected to. Answer **E** is incorrect because it includes *network* statements for all the networks that all three routers are connected to. Again, Router2 would include network statements only for the networks Router2 is connected to.

6. You just brought up a new router on your network, but it can't see the rest of the network. You configured EIGRP on the new router, but when you check the routing table, you notice that there are no EIGRP routes listed. The other routers were already running EIGRP, and everything was working fine. What is the first thing you should probably check in your EIGRP configuration?

   A. That debug is turned on.

   B. That there isn't a *shutdown* command in the EIGRP configuration.

   C. That the same AS is configured on the new router as what is already on the existing routers.

   D. That you've added the address of the new router into the EIGRP configuration on the other routers.

Correct Answer & Explanation: **C**. Although there are other configuration issues that could be causing your problem, the AS is a really good place to start troubleshooting. If the routers aren't all in the same AS, they won't communicate with each other. It's just too easy to mistype an AS number.

Incorrect Answers & Explanations: **A**, **B**, and **D**. Answer **A** is incorrect because although debug can help you troubleshoot problems, you should always check the EIGRP configuration first. Answer **B** is incorrect because there is no *shutdown* command for EIGRP. Answer **D** is incorrect because you don't configure another router's address for EIGRP. The addresses that are configured are the connected network addresses for the router that you are configuring.

7. You're looking at the information that EIGRP works with in the routing processes it performs. You are executing commands on one of the routers on your network to look at the EIGRP databases. What is the command you would use to look at information about the other routers your router exchanges routing information with?

   A. *show eigrp routers*   **C.** *show eigrp neighbors*
   B. *show ip eigrp neighbors*   **D.** *show ip route*

   Correct Answer & Explanation: **B**. The routers that exchange routing information in EIGRP are neighbors, so the command to look at information about those routers is *show ip eigrp neighbors*.

   Incorrect Answers & Explanations: **A**, **C**, and **D**. Answer **A** is incorrect because there is no *show eigrp routers* command. Answer **C** is incorrect because you have to specify the network layer protocol you want information for. Because EIGRP supports other protocols in addition to IP, the commands are specific to the protocol. Answer **D** is incorrect because the *show ip route* command displays the ip routing table, which is information on destination networks and how packets will be routed for those destination networks.

8. You're looking at the topology table to see information on all possible routes to destination networks. Some of the routes that you see in the topology table are also in the routing table. What are those routes called?

   A. Successors   **C.** Feasible successors
   B. Selected routes   **D.** Feasible distances

   Correct Answer & Explanation: **A**. The best possible route to a destination network is copied into the routing table. That route is called the successor.

   Incorrect Answers & Explanations: **B**, **C**, and **D**. Answer **B** is incorrect because there is no term called selected routes. Answer **C** is incorrect because the feasible successors are the backup routes to the destination networks. The feasible successors are the routes that will get copied to the routing table if the successor fails. Answer

D is incorrect because the feasible distance is part of the distance calculation for determining the best possible route or successor. The feasible distance is the metric of the successor.

9. Some of the routes in the routing table don't appear to be the best routes to you. You're trying to figure out how EIGRP came up with the routes that it put into the routing table, so you are trying to duplicate the router's calculations. What are the two factors EIGRP uses by default to calculate its metrics?

   A. Bandwidth and load
   B. Bandwidth and reliability
   C. Bandwidth and delay
   D. Delay and reliability
   E. Reliability and load

   Correct Answer & Explanation: **C**. By default, the factors included in the calculations to determine the metrics are the smallest bandwidth between the router and the destination network and the cumulative interface delay along the route.

   Incorrect Answers & Explanations: **A**, **B**, **D**, and **E**. Answer **A** is incorrect because load can be configured to be part of the calculation, but it isn't part of it by default. Answer **B** is incorrect because reliability is also a configurable factor but isn't considered by default. Answer **D** is incorrect because reliability isn't a default option although it can be configured to be included in the calculations. Answer **E** is incorrect because reliability and load are the two options that can be configured as part of the calculations but neither is a default option.

10. You are in the process of verifying your EIGRP configurations on your routers. What is the command you would execute to confirm that EIGRP is configured correctly?

    A. *show ip route eigrp*
    B. *show ip eigrp neighbors*
    C. *show ip eigrp topology*
    D. *show ip protocols*

    Correct Answer & Explanation: **D**. The command that shows you the active routing protocol(s) and how they are configured is the *show ip protocols* command.

    Incorrect Answers & Explanations: **A**, **B**, and **C**. Answer **A** is incorrect because the *show ip route eigrp* command displays the EIGRP routes in the IP routing table, which only gives you some information about how EIGRP is configured. Answer **B** is incorrect because *show ip eigrp neighbors* shows you information about the neighboring routers that exchange EIGRP information with your router. Answer **C** is incorrect because the *show ip eigrp topology* command shows you information about all the possible routes to destination networks that your router has received from all neighbors.

11. Figure 8.6 is a diagram of your company network. Packets don't seem to be routing correctly across your network, so you are troubleshooting EIGRP. You've checked the configurations of EIGRP on all the routers, they are all running the same AS, and all the *network* statements are correct to exchange all routing information among all routers. Now you're looking at the configuration for Router1, and you've determined that EIGRP is auto-summarizing routes because the *no auto-summary* command is not listed in the configuration. What network address(es) should Router1 be advertising to the other two routers?

FIGURE 8.6

Verifying Auto-Summarization

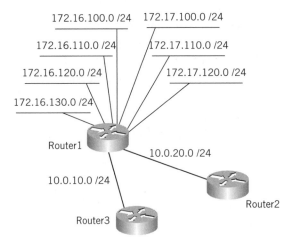

172.16.100.0 /24   172.17.100.0 /24

172.16.110.0 /24   172.17.110.0 /24

172.16.120.0 /24   172.17.120.0 /24

172.16.130.0 /24

Router1

10.0.20.0 /24

10.0.10.0 /24

Router2

Router3

A. 172.16.0.0, 172.17.0.0, and 10.0.0.0

B. 172.0.0.0 and 10.0.0.0

C. 172.16.100.0, 172.16.110.0, 172.16.120.0, 172.16.130.0, 172.17.100.0, 172.17.110.0, and 172.17.120.0

D. 172.16.0.0

Correct Answer & Explanation: **A.** Answer **A** is correct because Router1 will advertise the directly connected networks that were specified in the *network* commands. When EIGRP auto-summarizes, it will auto-summarize to the classful boundary, so it will summarize all the Class B subnets to the classful network addresses (all subnet and host bits turned off). The two subnets that are being used to connect Router1 to Router2 and Router3 will be summarized to the classful Class A network address.

Incorrect Answers & Explanations: **B**, **C**, and **D**. Answer **B** is incorrect because 172.0.0.0 is a different Class B network than what you are using on your network. Answer **C** is incorrect because EIGRP auto-summarizes to the classful boundary which in a Class B address means all zeros in the third and fourth octets. Answer **D** is incorrect because it only includes one of the Class B networks we are using. To make all routers aware of all networks EIGRP has to advertise all networks.

12. Now that you know the benefits of EIGRP, you have decided to implement it on your network. Up to this point, all the routing has been handled with static routes. Your only concern is that one of your routers connects directly to the Internet, and you don't want to advertise routing information about your network out to the Internet. What is the command that you would use to prevent routing information from being advertised to the Internet?

    A. shutdown in interface configuration mode

    B. *passive-interface* in interface configuration mode

    C. *passive-interface <interface>* in router configuration mode

    D. *disable* in interface configuration mode

Correct Answer & Explanation: **C**. The *passive-interface <interface>* command at the *(config-router)#* prompt stops the interface from sending or receiving EIGRP packets.

Incorrect Answers & Explanations: **A**, **B**, and **D**. Answer **A** is incorrect because although shutting down the interface would certainly prevent EIGRP packets from going out to the Internet, it would prevent all other traffic as well, so no one would be able to access the Internet. Answer **B** is incorrect because although *passive-interface* is part of the correct command, it is executed in router configuration mode not interface configuration mode. Answer **D** is incorrect because there is no *disable* command in interface configuration mode.

13. Part of the network that you've inherited at your new job is shown in Figure 8.7. Your new boss wants you to clean up the router configurations as much as possible, and one of the things you've decided to do is configure summary routes on every interface on every router where it makes sense. You need to calculate the summary address and mask to apply to interface FastEthernet0/0 on Router1 in the diagram. What is the address and mask that you should have come up with?

FIGURE 8.7

Calculating a Summary Address and Mask

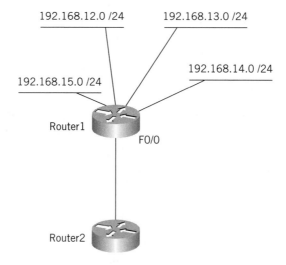

192.168.12.0 /24   192.168.13.0 /24

192.168.14.0 /24

192.168.15.0 /24

Router1

F0/0

Router2

A. 192.168.12.0 255.255.252.0

B. 192.168.0.0 255.255.255.0

C. 192.168.12.0 255.255.255.0

D. 192.168.15.0 255.255.252.0

Correct Answer & Explanation: **A.** To calculate the summary address and mask, you have to determine which bits are the same for all the network addresses you want to summarize. The common bits for the four networks are the first 22 bits. That converts to 192.168.12.0 for the summary address. The mask is created by turning on all those 22 bits and adding them together, which gives us 255.255.252.0.

Incorrect Answers & Explanations: **B**, **C**, and **D**. Answer **B** is incorrect because there is no 192.168.0.0 network anywhere in the diagram. Answer **C** is incorrect because the mask is incorrect. The mask in answer C keeps the four networks separate, Class C networks and doesn't summarize any of them. Answer **D** is incorrect because calculating the common bits results in 12 in the third octet not 15.

14. While cleaning up the configurations on your routers, you are configuring summary routes everywhere it is appropriate. What command do you use to configure a summary route for EIGRP?

   A. *ip summary-address eigrp <summary-address> <mask>* in router configuration mode

   B. *ip summary-address eigrp <AS> <summary-address> <mask>* in *Global Configuration* mode

   C. *ip summary-address eigrp <AS> <summary-address> <mask>* in router configuration mode

   D. *ip summary-address eigrp <AS> <summary-address> <mask>* in interface configuration mode

   Correct Answer & Explanation: **D**. Summary addresses are configured in interface configuration mode and the command to configure a summary route is *ip summary-address eigrp <AS> <summary-address> <mask>*.

   Incorrect Answers & Explanations: **A**, **B**, and **C**. Answer **A** is incorrect because you must include the AS number and the command is executed in interface configuration mode, not router configuration mode. Answer **B** is incorrect because the command is executed in interface configuration mode not *Global Configuration* mode. Answer **C** is incorrect because the command is executed in interface configuration mode not router configuration mode.

15. What is the powerful component of EIGRP that tracks all reported routes, manages successors and feasible successors, and implements loop-free routing?

   A. PDMs   **C.** Hello

   B. DUAL   **D.** MD5

Correct Answer & Explanation: **B**. Diffusing Update Algorithm (DUAL)'s role in EIGRP is to discover routes, keep track of routes, calculate the best paths to destination networks, and route packets in a loop-free manner.

Incorrect Answers & Explanations: **A**, **C**, and **D**. Answer **A** is incorrect because Protocol-Dependent Modules (PDMs) are what makes it possible for EIGRP to support multiple network layer protocols. Answer **C** is incorrect because the Hello packet is something that DUAL uses as a part of what it does, but DUAL is what manages and oversees the routing process. Answer **D** is incorrect because Message Digest 5 (MD5)'s function is to provide authentication so that routers can be sure they are really talking to the router they think they're talking to.

16. You're troubleshooting EIGRP and trying to identify why a particular route isn't showing up in the routing table. Right now you're watching debug information to make sure all the correct packets are being sent and received. To figure out where the problem is occurring, you are verifying each step of the process EIGRP goes through. You see a lot of information about hello packets. What is the hello packet's part of the process?

    A. To send route updates

    B. To ask for route updates

    C. To respond to requests for route updates

    D. Neighbor discover/recovery

Correct Answer & Explanation: **D**. The hello packet is used for neighbor discovery and to check the status of the neighbors periodically.

Incorrect Answers & Explanations: **A**, **B**, and **C**. Answer **A** is incorrect because an update packets sends route updates. Answer **B** is incorrect because the type of packet that asks for route updates is a query packet. Answer **C** is incorrect because the reply packet responds to requests for updates.

17. Security is such an important consideration these days. You are concerned about the possibility of unauthorized or false routing information being sent to your EIGRP routers. What is the technology you would implement to prevent this from happening?

A. MD5 Authentication

B. Summary routes

C. Clear text authentication

D. Passwords

Correct Answer & Explanation: **A**. EIGRP supports MD5 authentication, which will cause the routers to authenticate every packet. With MD5 you configure an authenticating key and a key ID for each sending and receiving router.

Incorrect Answers & Explanations: **B**, **C**, and **D**. Answer **B** is incorrect because summary routes consolidate information for routing tables but don't prevent unauthorized or false routing information. Answer **D** is incorrect because EIGRP doesn't support clear text authentication although some other routing protocols do. Answer **D** is incorrect because it is only a part of the authentication process. MD5 keys are sometimes called passwords.

18. EIGRP isn't working correctly on your network since you brought up a new router. The messages that you're seeing in debug tell you that there's an authentication mismatch. What problem you are experiencing?

A. A neighbor went down.

B. The MD5 keys don't match on the routers that are trying to communicate.

C. The ASes don't match on the routers that are trying to communicate.

D. A *network* statement wasn't typed correctly.

Correct Answer & Explanation: **B**. An authentication mismatch tells you that the keys don't match on the routers trying to communicate.

Incorrect Answers & Explanations: **A**, **C**, and **D**. Answer **A** is incorrect because a neighbor can cause problems with EIGRP communication but it wouldn't result in an authentication mismatch. Answer **C** is incorrect because the routers wouldn't communicate if the ASes don't match but, again, there wouldn't be authentication mismatch messages. Answer **D** is incorrect because an incorrect network statement would prevent routing information about that network from being sent out but wouldn't generate an authentication message.

19. You have gotten several calls from users on one of your remote networks telling you that communicating with the other company networks has gotten extremely slow. In the process of troubleshooting the problem with the network, how would you figure out the path being used to send packets from your network to the remote network?

A. Look at the neighbors with the *show ip neighbors* command.

B. Look at the interfaces with the *show ip interfaces* command.

C. Look at the routing table with the *show ip route* command.

D. Look at your physical network diagram.

Correct Answer & Explanation: **C**. The *show ip route* command will show you all routes currently being used to send traffic to destination networks, including the remote network.

Incorrect Answers & Explanations: **A**, **B**, and **D**. Answer **A** is incorrect because looking at your neighbors will show you the other routers that your router exchanges information but not the current routes. Answer **B** is incorrect because looking at your ip interfaces will allow you to confirm the EIGRP configuration on the interfaces but doesn't display route information. Answer **D** is incorrect because the physical diagram won't show you which path the router is currently using to send the data.

20. You're looking at the information in the IP routing table, and it looks like the route to one of your remote networks is not the best or most efficient route. How can you look at the information on all the EIGRP routes your router knows about to the destination network to see if the router knows about the route you believe is the best one?

A. *show all routes*   **C.** *show all ip routes*

B. *show ip eigrp topology*   **D.** *show ip route eigrp*

Correct Answer & Explanation: **B**. The topology table contains information on all the routes EIGRP knows about.

Incorrect Answers & Explanations: **A**, **C**, and **D**. Answers **A** and **C** are incorrect because there is no *show all routes* or *show all ip routes* commands. Answer **D** is incorrect because this will only display the EIGRP routes that are currently being used, the routes the router has determined are the best routes.

21. You're looking at the information in the IP routing table to determine how packets are being delivered to different destination networks. You've identified the entries beginning with C's as directly connected and the entries beginning with S's as static routes. There are several entries with D's at the front. What type of routes are those?

A. Detoured routes that the router is redirecting

B. Direct routes from point-to-point

C. EIGRP routes

D. RIPv2 routes

Correct Answer & Explanation: **C**. The D stands for DUAL, the algorithm used by EIGRP to discover and maintain routes.

Incorrect Answers & Explanations: **A**, **B**, and **D**. Answers **A** and **B** are incorrect because the routing table doesn't have routes called detoured routes or direct routes. Answer **D** is incorrect because RIP routes are identified with Rs.

22. There seems to be an unusual amount of traffic on your network and you're trying to track down the problem. You're looking at the topology table, and you want to make sure that the routes aren't being recalculated. What are you looking for in the first column of the topology table to see if the routes are recalculating?

A. The R for Recalculate or the N for Not Recalculating

B. The A for Active or the P for Passive

C. An X in the field

D. A blank field

Correct Answer & Explanation: **B**. If the field shows an A for the route, it means the route is being recalculated. A P means it isn't being recalculated.

Incorrect Answers & Explanations: **A**, **C**, and **D**. Answer **A** is incorrect because an R means Reply. Answers **C** and **D** are incorrect because they are not valid values for the field.

23. You have configured summary routes on some of your interfaces, and you want to verify that you've configured them correctly. How could you look at the EIGRP configuration on your interfaces?

A. *show ip eigrp interfaces*   **C.** *show ip eigrp topology*

B. *show ip route*   **D.** *show ip eigrp summary-routes*

Correct Answer & Explanation: **A**. Use *show ip eigrp interfaces* to verify your EIGRP configuration on your interfaces.

Incorrect Answers & Explanations: **B**, **C**, and **D**. Answer **B** is incorrect because it displays active routes not interface configuration information. Answer **C** is incorrect because it displays the topology table of all possible routes, again, not configuration information. Answer **D** is incorrect because it is an invalid command.

24. EIGRP has been running on your network for a few days and you want to see how many and what types of EIGRP packets your router has sent and received. How would you find this information?

    A. Execute the *show ip eigrp* command.

    B. Turn on debugging.

    C. Execute the *show ip eigrp traffic* command.

    D. Execute the *show eigrp statistics* command.

    Correct Answer & Explanation: **C**. The *show ip eigrp traffic* displays statistics EIGRP statistics by packet type.

    Incorrect Answers & Explanations: **A**, **B**, and **D**. Answer **A** is incorrect because it is an incomplete command. Answer **B** is incorrect because debugging allows you to watch particular types of traffic currently crossing the router, not counts of what has already been sent and received. Answer **D** is incorrect because it is an invalid command.

25. Right now your routers are all running IGRP. After hearing about the advanced features in EIGRP, you want to change your network over to EIGRP. The problem is that you have a lot of routers, and although they are all in the same AS, some of them are at remote locations and not set up for remote access. There's just no way it would be possible to get all the routers changed to IGRP all at once. What do you need to do to transition your network to EIGRP more slowly?

    A. Use the same AS on your EIGRP routers as is on your IGRP routers.

    B. It wouldn't work. All the routers would have to be changed to EIGRP at the same time.

    C. Execute the *convert igrp* command on the EIGRP routers as you bring them up.

    D. Configure static routes to route between the EIGRP and IGRP routers.

    Correct Answer & Explanation: **A**. If you configure the EIGRP routers with the same AS as the IGRP routers, EIGRP will do an automatic redistribute and translate between the two protocols. Because EIGRP automatically sets up redistribution for IGRP, you get the benefits of dynamic routing and the ability to take your time with the EIGRP transition.

Incorrect Answers & Explanations: **B**, **C**, and **D**. Answer **B** is incorrect because EIGRP can do an automatic redistribute. Answer **C** is incorrect because that is an invalid command. Answer **D** is incorrect because although you could configure enough static routes to route between your EIGRP and IGRP routers, that would require a great deal more time and effort than configuring EIGRP on all the routers. In addition, configuring static routes defeats the purpose of dynamic routing.

26. You're in the process of transitioning your network from EIGRP to IGRP. So far, you've configured EIGRP on some of your routers and the rest are still running IGRP. You're trying to understand why some of the routes that are in the routing table aren't the same ones that were there before you started bringing up EIGRP on some of the routers. What is the factor that is most likely causing the change?

   A. Administrative distances

   B. Autonomous systems

   C. Something is wrong with your configuration

   D. Network numbers

   Correct Answer & Explanation: **A**. When IGRP and EIGRP are installed in the same autonomous system, EIGRP does an automatic redistribute to communicate between the two. The routes that originate in IGRP are considered to be external routes which have an administrative distance of 170 compared with internal routes with an administrative distance of 90.

   Incorrect Answers & Explanations: **B**, **C**, and **D**. Answer **B** is incorrect because if the IGRP and EIGRP routers are in the same autonomous system, they will communicate with each other. Answer **C** is incorrect because although the possibility of a configuration problem always exists, in this case it appears more likely that the administrative distance is the factor. Answer **D** is incorrect because if the network numbers weren't correct, the information wouldn't be advertised at all.

27. You are looking at debug information and watching the EIGRP packets cross the router. You see information about sequence numbers and retransmits. You know these are part of the function of the EIGRP component that handles reliability. What is this component called?

A. DUAL

B. PDMs

C. RTP

D. AS

Correct Answer & Explanation: **C.** Reliable Transport Protocol handles reliable transmission of packets.

Incorrect Answers & Explanations: **A**, **B**, and **D**. Answer **A** is incorrect because DUAL handles route discovery and management. Some of the DUAL functions use RTP but DUAL's responsibility isn't reliability. Answer **B** is incorrect because Protocol Dependent Modules support multiple network layer protocols. Answer **D** is incorrect because the autonomous system identifies the routers that will exchange information with each other.

28. You are documenting your network, and you need the IP address of the devices with which the router has established an adjacency. You also need to check the queue counts for those routers. What is the command that will allow you to look at this information?

A. *show ip eigrp adjacency*

B. *show ip eigrp interfaces*

C. *show ip eigrp neighbors*

D. *show ip eigrp topology*

Correct Answer & Explanation: **C.** The *show ip eigrp neighbors* command gives you IP address and queue count information for your neighbors.

Incorrect Answers & Explanations: **A**, **B**, and **D**. Answer **A** is incorrect because it is an invalid command. Answer **B** is incorrect because it displays information about your own interfaces. Answer **D** is incorrect because it displays information about all possible routes but not neighbors.

29. While looking at the *show ip eigrp topology* table, you see something at the end of each route that says *FD is* and is followed by a big number. What is it that you are looking at?

A. Administrative distances for the routes

B. Network numbers for the routes

C. Next hop information

D. The metric for the route

Correct Answer & Explanation: **D**. The feasible distance (FD) is the metric that was calculated for the route.

Incorrect Answers & Explanations: **A**, **B**, and **C**. Answer **A** is incorrect because the administrative distance isn't included in the topology table. Answer **B** is incorrect because the network numbers are at the beginning of each line in the second field. Answer **C** is incorrect because the next hop information appears after the word *via* not after FD.

30. While troubleshooting routing problems on your network, you discover that some of the routes in the topology table have an A in the first column for Active, meaning that the routes are being recalculated. As you continue to check the topology table periodically, those routes are often showing Active. You've verified that the routers are okay and there doesn't seem to be any problem other than a very busy network. What is the command that will most likely correct the problem?

    A. *ip hello-interval eigrp 100 15*
    B. *ip hold-time eigrp 100 45*
    C. *debug ip eigrp*
    D. *show ip eigrp*

Correct Answer & Explanation: **B**. Sometimes on a very busy network EIGRP packets don't get to neighboring routers in the expected length of time. This can cause the router to think the route has disappeared and to initiate the recalculation of the route. By increasing the hold time that a router will wait for replies back from those routers, there will be more time for replies to come back from the routers, avoiding unnecessary recalculations. The default is 15 s and the command in answer B changes it to 45 s.

Incorrect Answers & Explanations: **A**, **C**, and **D**. Answer **A** is incorrect because this will reduce how frequently hello packets are sent but doesn't affect how long the router waits for responses. Answer **C** is incorrect because although debug may give you some insight into what the problem is, it doesn't change anything. Answer **D** is incorrect because the *show* commands show you particular information but don't correct problems.

Chapter 9: Access Control Lists

1. Which is the correct syntax for a numbered ACL?
   - **A.** `access-list 14 permit ip 10.1.1.0 0.0.0.255`
   - **B.** `access-list 14 permit tcp 10.1.1.0 0.0.0.255 10.2.2.0 0.0.0.255`
   - **C.** `access-list 101 permit tcp 10.1.1.0 0.0.0.255 10.2.2.0 0.0.0.255`
   - **D.** `access-list 101 permit ip 10.1.1.0 0.0.0.255`

   Correct Answer & Explanation: **C**. Answer **C** is correct because the ACL number 101 defines an extended ACL, which requires a protocol (tcp) and both source and destination addresses in the ACE.

   Incorrect Answers & Explanations: **A**, **B**, and **D**. Answer **A** is incorrect because the protocol keyword "ip" is not used in a standard access list (ACL number = 14). Answer **B** is incorrect because ACL number 14 is for a standard access list and neither protocol nor destination address are used for matching. Answer **D** is incorrect because ACL number 101 defines an extended access list, which requires a destination address (even if it is the keyword "any").

2. Which set of ACEs is mostly likely in the correct order?
   - **A.** `access-list 10 permit host 10.1.1.1`
     `access-list 10 permit 10.0.0.0 0.255.255.255`
     `access-list 10 deny 10.1.1.0 0.0.0.255`
   - **B.** `access-list 10 permit 10.0.0.0 0.255.255.255`
     `access-list 10 deny 10.1.1.0 0.0.0.255`
     `access-list 10 permit host 10.1.1.1`
   - **C.** `access-list 10 permit host 10.1.1.1`
     `access-list 10 deny 10.1.1.0 0.0.0.255`
     `access-list 10 permit 10.0.0.0 0.255.255.255`
   - **D.** `access-list 10 deny 10.1.1.0 0.0.0.255`
     `access-list 10 permit host 10.1.1.1`
     `access-list 10 permit 10.0.0.0 0.255.255.255`

   Correct Answer & Explanation: **C**. Answer **C** is correct because the order of ACEs is from most specific (permit the host 10.1.1.1) to least specific (permit 10.0.0.0/8).

   Incorrect Answers & Explanations: **A**, **B**, and **D**. Answer **A** is incorrect because the final "deny" statement will never match because all packets sourced from 10.1.1.0/24 will be permitted by the middle ACE. Answer **B** is incorrect because all packets will match the first ACE—no packets that are intended to match the other ACEs will make it that far. Answer **D** is incorrect because host 10.1.1.1 is contained within 10.1.1.0/24, so traffic from this host will match the first ACE.

3. Which ACE will correctly match traffic sourced from all the following hosts, and no others—172.16.1.4, 172.16.1.5, 172.16.1.6, and 172.16.1.7
   A. `access-list 2 permit 172.16.1.4 255.255.255.252`
   B. `access-list 2 permit 172.16.1.0 0.0.0.252`
   C. `access-list 2 permit 172.16.1.0 0.0.0.3`
   D. `access-list 2 permit 172.16.1.4 0.0.0.3`

   Correct Answer & Explanation: **D**. The wildcard mask 0.0.0.3 has 1s in the last two bit positions in the fourth octet—which matches four hosts—172.16.1.4-7.

   Incorrect Answers & Explanations: **A**, **B**, and **C**. Answer **A** is incorrect because the administrator probably used a subnet mask instead of a wildcard mask. This wildcard actually matches all except addresses where the fourth octet is 4-7. Answer **B** is incorrect because the wildcard in the ACE matches when the last octet is 5-255. Answer **C** is incorrect because the IP address and wildcard matches 172.16.1.0-3.

4. What is the primary difference between an extended IP ACL and an extended TCP ACL?
   A. An IP ACL can match all IPs, including ICMP, TCP, and UDP. But, it can't match on source or destination port.
   B. An IP ACL allows you to match based on whether the session is established, but TCP ACLs do not.
   C. A TCP ACL does not support source and destination port checking, but the IP ACL does.
   D. An IP ACL can match on DSCP information (TOS or precedence) but TCP ACLs cannot.

   Correct Answer & Explanation: **A**. Answer **A** is correct because all IP can be matched by an IP ACL, but only a TCP or UDP ACL allows you to match on port information.

   Incorrect Answers & Explanations: **B**, **C**, and **D**. Answer **B** is incorrect because an IP ACL can't match on session established—that is only done with a TCP ACL. Answer **C** is incorrect because a TCP does support port checking in an ACE. Answer **D** is incorrect because both IP and TCP ACLs can match based on the QoS values in the IP header.

5. What is the best way to define ACEs to match on an inclusive range of destination TCP ports between 1025 and 1028?

   A. `access-list 101 permit tcp any gt 1025 any`
      `access-list 101 permit tcp any lt 1028 any`
   B. `access-list 101 permit tcp any any gt 1025`
      `access-list 101 permit tcp any any lt 1028`
   C. `access-list 101 permit tcp any any range 1025 1028`
   D. `access-list 101 permit tcp any range 1025 1028 any`

   Correct Answer & Explanation: **C.** Answer **C** is correct because the range command is inclusive (includes 1025 and 1028) and the destination port is defined following the destination address.

   Incorrect Answers & Explanations: **A**, **B**, and **D**. Answer **A** is incorrect because the gt and lt operators do not include the specified port (for example, gt is "greater than" not "greater than or equal to"). Answer **B** is incorrect because of the operators, and also because the source ports are being checked. Answer **D** is incorrect because the source ports are what the ACE is matching on.

6. What are the limitations of numbered ACLs?

   A. There is no way to remove a single ACE and no way to reorder ACEs.

   B. There is no way to remove a single ACE, no way to add an ACE in a specific spot in the ACL, and no way to reorder ACEs.

   C. There is no way to add an ACE, but it is possible to remove a specific ACE.

   D. ACEs in numbered ACLs can be manipulated just as they can in named ACLs.

   Correct Answer & Explanation: **B**. The three limitations given are all correct.

   Incorrect Answers & Explanations: **A**, **C**, and **D**. Answer **A** is incorrect because there is no way to add an ACE in the middle of a numbered ACL. Answer **C** is incorrect because it is not possible to remove a specific ACE. If this is tried, the entire ACL is deleted. Answer **D** is incorrect because numbered ACLs are difficult to manage because of the limitations given.

7. Which of the following TCP ACEs use the correct syntax?

   A. `access-list  101  permit  tcp  10.5.4.0  255.255.255.0 172.16.3.0 eq 23`

   B. `access-list 101 tcp permit 10.5.4.0 0.0.0.255 172.16.3.0 eq 23`

   C. `access-list  101  permit  tcp  10.5.4.0  255.255.255.0 172.16.3.0 0.0.0.3 eq 23`

   D. `access-list 101 tcp permit 10.5.4.0 0.0.0.255 172.16.3.0 0.0.0.3 eq 23`

Correct Answer & Explanation: **C**. The question was asking for correct syntax. It looks as if the subnet mask has been used instead of the wildcard mask, but the syntax is correct and the command will be accepted by the CLI.

Incorrect Answers & Explanations: **A, B**, and **D**. Answer **A** is incorrect because the destination address does not include a wildcard mask or the keyword "host" preceding the IP address. Answer **B** is incorrect also because of the destination address but also because the protocol precedes the action (permit). Answer **D** is incorrect only because the protocol precedes the action.

8. What is the best way to add an ACE to the middle of the list of ACEs in the following named ACL?

```
Router # show ip access-list TEST
Standard IP access list TEST
    10 permit 10.1.1.1
    20 permit 10.1.1.2
    30 permit 10.1.1.3
    40 permit 10.1.1.5
```

   A. Delete the ACL and recreate it with the new ACEs in the proper sequence.

   B. `permit 10.1.1.4`
      `no 40`
      `permit 10.1.1.5`

   C. `35 permit 10.1.1.4`

   D. `40 permit 10.1.1.4`

Correct Answer & Explanation: **C**. Answer **C** is correct because you can use sequence numbers to place an ACE at any location within an ACL.

Incorrect Answers & Explanations: **A, B**, and **D**. Answer **A** is incorrect (even though it would work) because removing the ACL entirely can be very disruptive. Answer **B** is not correct (even though it would work) because removing the final ACE is unnecessary and potentially disruptive. Answer **D** is incorrect because the CLI would not allow a duplicate sequence number.

9. If you have IPX, IP, and DECnet addresses on an interface, how many ACLs can be applied to that interface?
   A. 6
   B. 3
   C. 2
   D. 0

   Correct Answer & Explanation: **A**. The rule for applying ACLs is one ACL per protocol per interface per direction. So you can have inbound ACLs for each protocol and outbound ACLs for each protocol.

   Incorrect Answers & Explanations: **B**, **C**, and **D**. Answer **B** is incorrect—the assumption was probably that you can have one ACL per protocol. Don't forget that each protocol can have an inbound and outbound ACL. Answer **C** is incorrect—the assumption was probably that you can only have an inbound and outbound ACL for a single protocol. Each protocol can have a set of two ACLs—one in and one out. Answer **D** is incorrect because ACLs can be applied to multiprotocol interfaces.

10. You want to apply an ACL named TEST inbound on a FastEthernet interface. Which of the following is the correct way to do this?
    A. `ip access-group test in`
    B. `ip access-group in TEST`
    C. `ip access-class TEST in`
    D. `ip access-group TEST in`

    Correct Answer & Explanation: **D**. Answer **D** is correct because the keyword "in" must appear at the end of the command and the case matches the ACL definition (names are case-sensitive).

    Incorrect Answers & Explanations: **A**, **B**, and **C**. Answer A is not correct because the name does not match—remember that spelling and case must match exactly. Answer **B** is incorrect because the direction keyword "in" must be at the end of the command. The CLI would not accept this. Answer C is incorrect because "access-class" is used only on lines not interfaces.

11. Refer to Figure 9.7. You want to block all read/write SNMP access to the router, except from a single management VLAN. What is the best way to accomplish this?

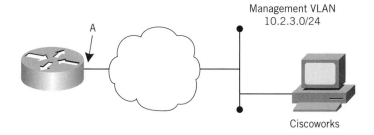

Management VLAN
10.2.3.0/24

A

Ciscoworks

FIGURE 9.7

Using an ACL to Block SNMP Access to the Router

A. Create an extended ACL with the source being the management VLAN and the destination being the router's IP on interface A. The ACL should block destination ports udp/161 and udp/162 and be applied inbound on interface A.

B. Create an extended ACL with the destination being the management VLAN and the source being the router's IP on interface A. The ACL should block destination ports udp/161 and udp/162 and be applied outbound on interface A.

C. Create a standard ACL that only permits traffic from the management VLAN. The ACL should be applied to the router's VTY lines.

D. Create a standard ACL that permits only traffic from the management VLAN. The ACL should be appended to the end of the *snmp-server community* command in the configuration.

Correct Answer & Explanation: **D**. A standard ACL is the right way to configure this since any available router IP could be used for SNMP access. And the only way to block read/write access specifically must be done using the *snmp-server community* command.

Incorrect Answers & Explanations: **A**, **B**, and **C**. Answer **A** is incorrect (even though it would work) because it would block all incoming SNMP, not just the read/write. Answer **B** is incorrect because the source/destination addresses are not correct and an incoming SNMP request would have the destination port be udp/161-162. Answer **C** is incorrect because an ACL configured on a VTY line won't block incoming SNMP.

12. You are building an ACL to control incoming EIGRP routes. You want to permit the summary route 10.2.32.0/20, block any more specific routes, and permit all others. How would you define and apply this ACL?

A.
```
ip access-list standard ACCEPT_SUMMARY
    permit    10.2.32.0
    deny      10.2.32.0 0.0.15.255
    permit    any
router eigrp 1
    distribute-list ACCEPT_SUMMARY in
```

B.
```
ip access-list standard ACCEPT_SUMMARY
    permit    10.2.32.0 255.255.240.0
    deny      10.2.32.0 0.0.15.255
router eigrp 1
    distribute-list ACCEPT_SUMMARY in
```

C.
```
ip access-list standard ACCEPT_SUMMARY
    deny      10.2.32.0 0.0.15.255
    permit    10.2.32.0
    permit    any
router eigrp 1
    distribute-list ACCEPT_SUMMARY in
```

D.
```
ip access-list standard ACCEPT_SUMMARY
    deny      10.2.32.0 0.0.15.255
    permit    10.2.32.0 255.255.240.0
    permit    any
router eigrp 1
    distribute-list ACCEPT_SUMMARY out
```

Correct Answer & Explanation: **A.** The ACL permits the summary (the exact route because there is no specified wildcard mask), then blocks any routes more specific than the summary, and then permits all others.

Incorrect Answers & Explanations: **B**, **C**, and **D**. Answer **B** is incorrect because the wildcard mask is incorrect and will result in not matching the summary. Also, the implicit "deny any" ACE which ends this ACL will block any other routes outside of the summary. Answer **C** is incorrect because the first deny ACE will end up blocking the summary as well as all more specific routes. Answer **D** is incorrect because the deny ACE is first, the wildcard is incorrect in the second ACE, and the direction of the distribute-list is wrong to filter incoming routes.

13. Time-based ACLs are a good way to implement security policy that changes based on time and date. Where does the router get the time it uses to match incoming traffic, and what is the best way to ensure the policy works properly?

A. Time-based ACLs get the time from a NTP server. To ensure this is accurate, NTP should synchronize with a stratum 1 or 2 time-source. Time zone and daylight-savings-time offsets are provided by the NTP server.

B. Time-based ACLs get the time from the router's system clock. To ensure this is accurate, NTP should be used for synchronization. Time zone and daylight-savings-time offsets are provided by NTP, so there is no need to adjust for local time.

C. Time-based ACLs get the time from the router's system clock. To ensure this is accurate, NTP should be used for synchronization and correct time zone and daylight-savings-time values must be configured.

D. Time-based ACLs get the time from an NTP server. To ensure this is accurate, NTP should synchronize with a stratum 1 or 2 timesource, but time zone and daylight-savings-time values must be configured on the router to adjust to local time.

Correct Answer & Explanation: **C**. Answer **C** is correct because time-based ACLs use the system clock. To ensure accuracy, use NTP to synchronize—but time zone and DST must be configured on the router to ensure accurate local time.

Incorrect Answers & Explanations: **A**, **B**, and **D**. Answer **A** is incorrect because time-based ACLs do not get time directly from the NTP server, and NTP does not provide local time zone and DST settings. Answer **B** is incorrect because NTP does not provide local time zone and DST settings. These must be configured on each router to ensure accurate local time. Answer **D** is incorrect because time-based ACLs don't use NTP directly.

14. How does CBAC protect internal hosts?

A. CBAC allows response traffic by evaluating TCP sequence numbers to verify a session is in progress. Only internal hosts can initiate sessions.

B. CBAC evaluates outbound traffic and dynamically prepends ACEs to an inbound ACL to permit response traffic.

C. CBAC evaluates outbound traffic and creates a session host map to allow internal hosts to freely request sessions to external hosts and permit only response traffic flowing in the other direction.

D. CBAC inspects outbound traffic and builds a TCP session table that permits inbound traffic without the need for an ACL.

Correct Answer & Explanation: **B**. Answer **B** is correct because CBAC inspects traffic in one direction and permits response traffic in the other direction by dynamically modifying an inbound ACL. It can operate in other ways, but this is the typical way it is deployed on a border router.

Incorrect Answers & Explanations: **A**, **C**, and **D**. Answer **A** is incorrect because CBAC can inspect more than just TCP and does not track sequence numbers as a way to match request and response traffic. Answer **C** is incorrect because CBAC does not use a host map to identify response traffic. Answer **D** is incorrect because an inbound ACL is required so ACEs can be dynamically added to permit response traffic.

15. How are Dynamic or "Lock and Key" ACLs used?
    A. Dynamic ACLs begin by evaluating packets in software, but as flows are built packets can then be matched by an ASIC in hardware without requiring as many router resources.
    B. Dynamic ACLs provide a way to change an ACL in response to application traffic—like FTP dynamically negotiating ports.
    C. Dynamic ACLs can match not only header fields but also on packet payload by using bit pattern matching, packet length, and so forth.
    D. Dynamic ACLs require a user to connect and authenticate to the router using an application (for example, Telnet) before the ACL permits traffic.

Correct Answer & Explanation: **D**. Dynamic ACLs use extended ACLs and Telnet to authenticate a user prior to opening ports in an ACL.

Incorrect Answers & Explanations: **A**, **B**, and **C**. Answer **A** is incorrect because dynamic ACLs don't change how they are processed based on flow information. Answer **B** is incorrect because dynamic ACLs don't change the ACL based on application traffic. This is a function of CBAC. Answer **C** is incorrect because dynamic ACLs aren't any different from normal extended ACLs—it just does authentication prior to permitting traffic. What is described in the answer is Flexible Packet Matching.

16. You are troubleshooting an ACL using the *show ip access-list* command, but you see the hit counters are not incrementing. What could be wrong and how do you fix it?

   A. On some platforms, hit counters don't increment when the packets are processed in hardware. This can't be "fixed," but you can temporarily disable hardware processing during troubleshooting by using "no ip route-cache" on the interface.

   B. Many older routers don't support ACL hit counters. The command still works but does not provide accurate output.

   C. ACL hit counters depend on a service running on the router. This is enabled by default but can be enabled if it is disabled by using the command *service acl-hitcount*.

   D. The availability of ACL hit counters depend on the IOS feature pack running on the router. The firewall feature packet is required to fully support ACL hit counters.

   Correct Answer & Explanation: **A**. Answer **A** is correct because ACL processing on some hardware (for example, PFCs on Catalyst 6500s) is performed on ASICs, and hit counters don't increment. The *no ip route-cache* can be used temporarily to enable hit counters but should be disabled when you are done troubleshooting.

   Incorrect Answers & Explanations: **B**, **C**, and **D**. Answer **B** is incorrect because hit counters are supported on nearly all routers, and the command should always show accurate output. Answer **C** is incorrect because there is no such service, and hit counters should work without requiring any other software. Answer **D** is incorrect because ACL hit counters work in all feature packets of IOS.

17. Without doing a *show running-config*, what is the best way to determine which ACLs are applied to an interface and in what direction?

   A. Create a testing scenario where you can initiate traffic from both sides of the suspected ACL which will tell you if a certain protocol is allowed. For example, if TCP/23 is allowed, you should be able to create a Telnet session from a PC off one side of the router to the router's far-end IP address.

   B. Use the *show ip access-list detail* command. The output will provide detail about each interface, whether an access list is applied and in which direction.

C. Use the *show ip access-list interface <interface>* command or the *show ip interface <interface>* command. Both will show which ACLs are applied and the direction.

D. Use the *show protocols <interface>* command, which will provide detail about each interface, whether an Access list is applied, and in which direction.

Correct Answer & Explanation: **C.** Either of the commands given in the answer will work. The *show ip access-list interface* command provides hit counters, whereas the other command provides less detail about the ACLs, but much more detail about which features are running on the interface.

Incorrect Answers & Explanations: **A**, **B**, and **D**. Answer **A** is incorrect because testing as described may provide some information about what traffic is permitted but won't be able to tell you which ACLs are applied and in which direction. Answer **B** is incorrect because there is no such keyword "detail" at the end of the *show ip access-list* command. If this were tried, the command would show information about the ACL called "detail." Answer **D** is incorrect because the *show protocols* will only show what protocol addresses (such as an IP or DECnet address) are assigned and does not provide any information about access lists.

18. Refer to Figure 9.8. Katherine is unable to access the Web server. You have a Telnet session with the router and are trying to troubleshoot the problem. You ping the server using the following command and get a successful response. What is the best next step in the troubleshooting process?

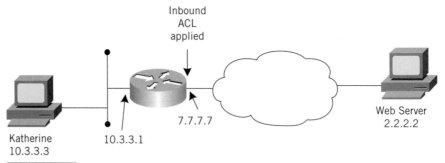

FIGURE 9.8 *Troubleshooting an Internet Connectivity Problem*

```
Router#ping 2.2.2.2
Type escape sequence to abort.
Sending 5, 100-byte ICMP Echos to 2.2.2.2, timeout is 2
   seconds:
!!!!!
Success rate is 100 percent (5/5), round-trip min/avg/max
   = 68/72/84 ms
```

A. Use the IOS extended *PING* command to initiate a ping sourced from the 10.3.3.1 address.

B. Use the IOS *trace* command to determine the path taken through the network to the Web server.

C. Call the Web server administrator and determine if any server-side ACLs are in place.

D. Visit Katherine's PC to determine if a personal firewall may be blocking the traffic.

E. Remove the inbound ACL and retest.

Correct Answer & Explanation: **A**. An extended PING allows an administrator to source an ICMP echo exchange from any local interface. In this case, you know the 7.7.7.7 interface can access the Web server, but not if some ACL may be blocking traffic sourced from the 10.3.3.0 network.

Incorrect Answers & Explanations: **B**, **C**, **D**, and **E**. Answer **B** is incorrect even though trace is a viable test. It is not the best next step. The trace will show you the path, but from the successful ping, you already know that the path taken by the ping is working. Answer **C** is incorrect even though you may eventually need to call the Web server admin. If you can ping the server from the external interface of the router, it is not likely there is an ACL on the server side that would block the user. Answer **D** is not correct but again it may eventually be necessary. If the question had said that *only* Katherine was having the problem, then suspecting the PC would be reasonable. Answer **E** is not correct but may eventually be necessary. Removing the ACL may lead to a serious security breech.

19. Refer to Figure 9.9. You want to create an outbound ACL to limit Elizabeth's access to the Internet. Your policy for this user forbids her to use Telnet (tcp/23) but permits Web surfing (tcp/80) or any other application. Her NATted IP is 7.7.7.8. Which of the following is the correct ACL?

FIGURE 9.9

Configuring ACLs with NAT

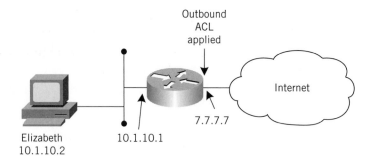

A. access-list 101 deny tcp host 10.1.10.2 any eq 23
   access-list 101 permit tcp host 10.1.10.2 any

B. access-list 101 permit ip host 7.7.7.8 any eq 80
   access-list 101 deny ip host 7.7.7.8 any eq 23

C. access-list 101 deny tcp host 7.7.7.8 any eq 23
   access-list 101 permit ip host 7.7.7.8 any

D. access-list 101 permit ip host 10.1.10.2 any eq 80
   access-list 101 deny ip host 10.1.10.2 any eq 23
   access-list 101 permit ip host 10.1.10.2 any

***Correct Answer & Explanation:* C.** Answer **C** is correct because
the only traffic that needs to be denied is tcp/23, and all other traffic
permitted. Because the outbound ACL is evaluated *after* the NAT
process, you need to specify the NATted IP as the source in the ACL.

***Incorrect Answers & Explanations:* A, B,** and **D**. Answer **A** is incor-
rect because the second ACE permits only tcp traffic—which would
essentially block all non-tcp traffic, including UDP. Also, the source IP
is not correct because NAT has already been performed when the outbound ACL is evaluated. Answer **B** is incorrect because the implicit
"deny any" ACE at the end of the ACL would drop all non-tcp/80
traffic. Answer **D** is incorrect because the source is wrong (based on
the NAT order of operation) and because the first and second ACEs
specify IP instead of TCP, which would block UDP on those ports.

20. You have a Telnet session to a router and you've enabled *debug ip
   packet <access-list-number>* to troubleshoot a problem you're having with an application not working. A *show debug* confirms that the
   debug is active. Yet, no output is seen even though you are convinced
   by looking at the ACL hit counters that traffic is passing that matches
   the ACL in the debug. What could be wrong?

A. You've forgotten that debug output is unavailable over a Telnet session. You need to connect to the router using a console cable.

B. You've forgotten to enable the *terminal monitor* command to echo the debug output to the Telnet session.

C. There is an ACL applied to the VTY interface that is blocking the output of the *debug* command.

D. You've forgotten to enable "logging buffered," which is necessary for the output to be echoed to the Telnet session.

Correct Answer & Explanation: **B**. Answer **B** is correct because the *terminal monitor* command run in *Privileged Exec* mode is required before debug output will be sent to a Telnet session.

Incorrect Answers & Explanations: **A**, **C**, and **D**. Answer **A** is incorrect because debug output is supported over VTY lines. Answer **C** is incorrect because an ACL on the VTY would affect only Telnet access in or out of the router—it has no effect on debug output. Answer **D** is incorrect because buffered logging to the routers log has no effect on debug output to the VTY.

Chapter 10: IPv6

1. You're ready to start the process of transitioning your network to IPv6. You have multiple locations with several hundred computers, printers, and other devices that currently are all configured for IPv4. You aren't sure if all of the applications or devices on your network are IPv6 compatible. What will be the easiest and least disruptive method for you to use to start the transitioning process?

   A. 6to4 tunneling   **C.** Dynamic overlay tunneling

   B. Dual stacking   **D.** IPv4/IPv6 translation

   Correct Answer & Explanation: **B**. Answer **B** is correct as the easiest and least disruptive method of starting the transitioning process is dual stacking. By configuring IPv6 and IPv4 on all of the devices that will support IPv6, those devices will be able to communicate with the IPv4 and IPv6 devices. Both protocols run independently of each other, reducing the likelihood of compatibility issues.

   Incorrect Answers & Explanations: **A**, **C**, **D**. Answer **A** and Answer **C** are incorrect, because both of the tunneling methods involve encapsulating IPv6 packets in IPv4 packets to send the data across an IPv4 network between IPv6 networks. **D** is incorrect because IPv4/IPv6 translation would require packets to cross a router which wouldn't benefit you within your network segments. In addition, none of the IPv4/IPv6 translation methods that have been used in the past are currently being used because they didn't work properly.

2. Your company has transitioned all of its networks to IPv6 addressing. The home office is connected to two satellite offices across the Internet, as shown in Figure 10.11. What tunneling type is your company using?

FIGURE 10.11

Network Diagram for Self-Test Question #2

A. IPv6 VPN

B. Dual stacking

C. 6to4 tunneling

D. 4to6 tunneling

Correct Answer & Explanation: **C**. Answer **C** is correct as the 6to4 tunnel is a transitioning method that was developed to carry IPv6 traffic across intermediary IPv4 networks. It encapsulates the IPv6 packets in IPv4 packets, making the packets look like IPv4.

Incorrect Answers & Explanations: **A**, **B**, **D**. Answer **A** is incorrect because the VPN uses the IPv4 Internet itself as a connection point. Answer **B** is incorrect because dual stacking isn't a tunneling method but, instead, is a method of running both IPv4 and IPv6 on the devices that are dual stacked. Answer **D** is incorrect because we need to carry IPv6 across the IPv4 Internet rather than IPv4 across an IPv6 network.

3. You have started the process of setting up IPv6 on your networks. You are ready to start implementing IPv6 on your routers. What is the command that you would execute on each router to turn on IPv6?

A. *ipv6 enable*

B. *enable ipv6*

C. *mode ipv6*

D. *ipv6 unicast-routing*

Correct Answer & Explanation: **D**. The command to enable IPv6 on the router is *ipv6 unicast-routing*, which is entered at the (config) prompt.

Incorrect Answers & Explanations: **A**, **B**, **C**. Answer **A** is incorrect because it is the command to enable IPv6 on an individual interface, in interface configuration mode. Answer **B** is incorrect because it isn't a valid command. Answer **C** is incorrect because it is part of the command to identify the type of traffic to carry across a 6to4 tunnel. The full command is *tunnel mode ipv6*.

4. You need to set an IPv6 address on an interface on your router. It needs to be an address that can be routed across the Internet. What type of address do you need to assign to the interface?
   A. Link-local address
   B. Unique local address
   C. Multicast address
   D. Global unicast address
   E. Reserved address

Correct Answer & Explanation: **D**. The global unicast address is the public, routable type of address.

Incorrect Answers & Explanations: **A**, **B**, **C**, **E**. Answer **A** is incorrect because link-local addresses are private addresses that are only usable on the link. Answer **B** is incorrect because unique local addresses are also a type of private address and are not intended to be routed beyond a site or group of sites. Answer **C** is incorrect because multicast addresses are sent to a group of devices for special functions. Answer **E** is incorrect because reserved addresses are reserved for use by the IETF and are not available to assign to devices on organizations' networks.

5. You need to assign the address 2001:0db8:0000:0000:0000:eb00: 0000:0002 to an interface on your router. You don't want to type the entire address out. What is the correct shortened expression for the address?
   A. 2001:db8:eb:0:2   **C.** 2001:db8:eb00:0:2
   B. 2001:db8::eb00:2   **D.** 2001:db8:0:eb00:2

Correct Answer & Explanation: **C**. To shorten the address in the question we can eliminate all of the leading zeros and replace the three contiguous fields of all zeros with :: .

Incorrect Answers & Explanations: **A, B, D**. Answer **A** is incorrect because we can't eliminate the trailing zeros in the sixth field. Answer **B** is incorrect because we can only use two colons to replace the three contiguous fields of zeros. Answer **D** is incorrect because we can replace all three fields of contiguous zeros with : so we don't need the zero in the third field.

6. You have a very busy ftp server on your network that serves users in three different buildings. It's no longer able to keep up with the demands on it so you are adding two additional ftp servers to take some of the load off of the existing ftp server. All of the ftp servers will serve up the same files but you want your users to be able to access the ftp server that's closest to them so there is some load balancing taking place. What type of an address do you need to assign to your ftp servers to accomplish this?

   A. Anycast   **C.** Link-local

   B. Multicast   **D.** Loopback

   Correct Answer & Explanation: **A**. An anycast address can be assigned to multiple devices. By assigning the same address to all of the servers with the same files and services the routers will send the packets to the device that's closest.

   Incorrect Answers & Explanations: **B, C, D**. Answer **B** is incorrect because multicast packets are sent to multiple devices at the same time. Answer **C** is incorrect because a link-local address is a regular unicast address for communicating between individual devices within a link. Answer **D** is incorrect because the loopback address is a troubleshooting mechanism, used for internal loopback. Packets sent to a loopback address are looped back to the same location.

7. When you execute the command *debug ipv6 routing* you see information that includes the IPv6 address FE80:0011:22FF:FE37:1234 in the information on your screen. What type of IPv6 address are you looking at?

   A. Global unicast   **C.** Link-local

   B. Loopback   **D.** Multicast

   Correct Answer & Explanation: **C**. The address begins with FE80 which means it is a link-local address.

Incorrect Answers & Explanations: **A, B, D**. Answer **A** is incorrect because global unicast addresses begin with 2000. Answer **B** is incorrect because the loopback address is :1/128. Answer **D** is incorrect because multicast addresses use the address space FF00:/8.

8. You have been given the address 2001:db8:eb00:0:2 to apply to your router. What is the command to assign this address to an interface on your router?

   A. *ip address 2001:db8:eb00:0:2 /64*

   B. *ipv6 address 2001:db8:eb00:0:2 /64*

   C. *configure interface 2001:db8:eb00:0:2 /64*

   D. *configure address 2001:db8:eb00:0:2*

   Correct Answer & Explanation: **B**. The correct command to assign an IPv6 address is *ipv6 address <address> / <prefix>* in interface configuration mode.

   Incorrect Answers & Explanations: **A, C, D**. Answer **A** is incorrect because we have to include the "v6" in our command. This command was the command for assigning an IP address in IPv4. Answer **C** is incorrect because the IPv6 address command is executed within interface configuration mode. Configure interface isn't included in the command. Answer **D** is incorrect because, again, we execute the IPv6 address command from within interface configuration mode and the word configure isn't part of the command.

9. You are verifying the autoconfigured IPv6 address on a host computer on the network. You obtain the MAC address for the device which is 0010:AB23:4567. What is the correct global-unicast interface identifier that was automatically created using the EUI-64 modification?

   A. 0010:ABFF:FE23:4567   **D.** 210.23.256.0

   B. 0210:ABFF:FE23:4567   **E.** 0000:0010:AB23:4567

   C. 0010:AB23:4567

   Correct Answer & Explanation: **B**. The EUI-64 modification involves inserting FFFE into the middle of the address. In addition, if the address is to be a global address, the seventh highest bit is turned on which makes the second hexadecimal digit a 2 (a zero bit in the seventh position indicates the address is to remain local).

Incorrect Answers & Explanations: **A, C, D, E**. Answer **A** is incorrect because it isn't a global address. With the second digit still a zero it means that the address is intended to remain local. Answer **C** is incorrect because it hasn't been modified. Answer **D** is incorrect because it isn't in IPv6 format (not to mention that it doesn't match much of our original MAC address). Answer **E** is incorrect because the MAC address is padded by adding FFFE to the middle of the address, not by adding leading zeros.

10. One of the computers on your network is unable to access the rest of the network. One of the steps in your troubleshooting process is to ping the local host or loopback address. What is the command you use?

   A. ping ipv6 127.0.0.1   **C.** ping ipv6 :1
   B. ping 0.0.0.0   **D.** ping ipv6 0:0

   Correct Answer & Explanation: **C**. The loopback address in IPv6 is ::1 and *ping ipv6* is used to ping an IPv6 address. This command loops the packets back to the source.

   Incorrect Answers & Explanations: **A, B, D**. Answer **A** is incorrect because 127.0.0.1 is the loopback address for IPv4. Answer **B** is incorrect because it is a command for pinging an IPv4 address and 0.0.0.0 isn't a loopback address. Answer **D** is incorrect because 0::0, which could be written as :: indicates an unspecified address.

11. You are going to set up a test network to get an idea how IPv6 works before deploying it on your network. You want to enable IPv6 on your serial interfaces and they need private addresses like the other devices on your test network. Which command would you use to enable IPv6 and have a private address automatically created on the serial interfaces?

   A. *ipv6 enable*   **C.** *ipv6 local address*
   B. *ipv6 enable address*   **D.** *enable unicast-routing*

   Correct Answer & Explanation: **A**. The correct command to enable IPv6 on an interface and cause a link-local (private) address to be generated is *ipv6 enable*, executed in interface configuration mode.

   Incorrect Answers & Explanations: **B, C, D**. Answer **B** is incorrect because address is not a correct addition to the *ipv6 enable* command. By just enabling IPv6 on the interface, it will autoconfigure an address. Answer **C** is incorrect because *ipv6 local address* isn't a valid command. Answer **D** is incorrect because *ipv6 unicast-routing* is the command to enable IPv6 on the router itself. Once IPv6 is enabled on the router, then you have to enable IPv6 on the interfaces by using the *ipv6 enable* command or configuring an IPv6 address on the interface.

12. The company networks have been set up for IPv6. You've installed IPv6 addresses on all of the devices and now you need to be able to route packets between your different networks so everyone can access all of the resources on all of the network devices. What's the next thing you need to do to make this happen?

    A. Give everyone a list of all of the IPv6 addresses.

    B. Set up host tables to map names to the IPv6 addresses.

    C. Create access control lists to give people access.

    D. Enable and configure a Dynamic Routing Protocol.

    Correct Answer & Explanation: **D**. The correct answer is to enable and configure a dynamic routing protocol to exchange information between your networks and build routing tables in the routers.

    Incorrect Answers & Explanations: **A**, **B C**. Answer **A** is incorrect because, until the routers can route packets between the networks, some of the IPv6 addresses won't be reachable. Answer **B** is incorrect for the same reason that Answer **A** is incorrect. Mapping names to IPv6 addresses will be a benefit on the network but first the addresses have to be reachable. Answer **C** is incorrect because Access Control Lists (ACL) filter packets crossing the router. They allow or deny access but the packets have to be able to get to the router with the ACL before they can be filtered and the router needs to know how to find the addresses in the ACL.

13. You've decided to use RIP to dynamically build your routing tables on your routers. What is the command to enable RIP on the routers?

    A. company(config)# *ipv6 router rip process1*

    B. company(config-router)# *enable RIP*

    C. company# *enable rip*

    D. company(config)# *router rip*

    Correct Answer & Explanation: **A**. The *ipv6 router rip process1* command starts a RIP process named *process1* on the router and takes you into (config-router) where RIP can be further configured.

    Incorrect Answers & Explanations: **B**, **C**, **D**. Answer **B** is incorrect because configuration commands are executed in configuration mode and *enable rip* isn't a complete command. Answer **C** is incorrect because the enable command for RIP is *ipv6 rip <tag> enable* which is executed in interface configuration mode. Answer **D** is incorrect because this is the command we use to enable RIP in IPv4.

14. You want to use another, quicker method of bringing up RIP on the router than the *ipv6 router rip <tag>* command executed in global configuration mode. The command is:

    A. company(config)# *router rip process1*

    B. company(config-router)# *enable*

    C. company(config-if)# *ipv6 rip process1 enable*

    D. company(config)# *router ipv6 rip*

    Correct Answer & Explanation: **C.** Executing this command in interface configuration enables RIP on the interface.

    Incorrect Answers & Explanations: **A**, **B**, **D**. Answer **A** is incorrect because the quick way to bring up RIP is to do it directly on the interface. To use this command in global configuration mode, we have to include IPv6—*router ipv6 rip process1* would be the correct command. Answer **B** is incorrect because enable by itself doesn't do anything even within the router configuration mode. Answer **D** is incorrect because the IPv4 command has been changed for IPv6 more than just adding IPv6 to the IPv4 command, *router rip*.

15. RIP doesn't seem to be working correctly on your network so you are looking at RIP debug information to try to identify the problem. You keep seeing the address FF02::/9 in the debug information. What does that address mean?

    A. It's RIPs loopback address.

    B. It's all of the local-link addresses on your network.

    C. It's a multicast address for all RIP routers.

    D. It's a broadcast address that RIP uses to send updates.

    Correct Answer & Explanation: **C.** The FF02::/9 address space is a permanent multicast address space for the group all-RIP-routers. RIP sends updates to this address so that all RIP routers receive the updates.

    Incorrect Answers & Explanations: **A**, **B**, **D**. Answer **A** is incorrect because loopback addresses are ::1/128. Answer **B** is incorrect because link-local addresses start at FE80. Answer **D** is incorrect because IPv6 no longer uses broadcasts, so RIP uses multicasts instead.

16. You have one IPv6 address that you're using on your router. It's assigned to your *Ethernet 0* interface. Now you need to configure IPv6 on your serial interface, but you don't want to use another address. Instead, you'd like the packets sent from the serial interface to use the *Ethernet 0* interface address as their source address. What's the command to configure this on the router?

    A. company(config-if)# *ipv6 enable*

    B. company(config-if)# *ipv6 unicast-routing*

    C. company(config-if)# *ipv6 address copy Ethernet 0*

    D. company(config-if)# *ipv6 unnumbered Ethernet 0*

    Correct Answer & Explanation: **D**. The correct command to enable IPv6 on an interface without an IP address is *ipv6 unnumbered*, and Ethernet 0 at the end of the command tells the router to use the Ethernet 0 interface's address for the source of packets sent from the unnumbered interface.

    Incorrect Answers & Explanations: **A**, **B**, **C**. Answer **A** is incorrect because, even though it is a correct command for enabling IPv6 on an interface, it also causes a link-local address to be generated. Answer **B** is incorrect because this is the command to enable IPv6 in global configuration mode. Each interface has to be configured for IPv6 separately. Answer **C** is incorrect because there is no *address copy* command.

17. The global unicast prefix your company uses is 2001:db8::/64. You need to put an IPv6 address on your *Ethernet 0* interface on your router. You want the router to create an interface identifier from the interface's MAC address. What is the command to configure this on your router?

    A. ip address 2001:db8:: /64

    B. ipv6 address 2001:db8::/64 MAC

    C. ipv6 address 2001:db8::/64 EUI-64

    D. ipv6 address 2001:db8::/64

    E. ip address 2001:db8::/64 MAC

    Correct Answer & Explanation: C. The correct command to assign an IPv6 address is *ipv6 address <address> / <prefix>*. The EUI-64 option at the end of the command tells the router to create the interface identifier from the MAC address.

Incorrect Answers & Explanations: **A**, **B**, **D**, **E**. Answer **A** is incorrect because we have to include the "v6" in our command and it needs the *EUI-64 option* to tell it to create the interface identifier from the MAC. Answer **B** is incorrect because the qualifier to use the MAC address in the interface identifier is EUI-64 not MAC. Answer **D** is incorrect because it doesn't have the EUI-64 option. Answer **E** is incorrect because it is the command to assign an IPv4 address and the MAC option is not valid.

18. All of the devices on your network have been assigned IPv6 addresses and you are testing connectivity across your network. When you type the command *ping ipv6 pc24* from the router you get a reply back from the computer called pc2 instead of the computer called pc24. What is the most likely cause of the problem?

    A. An entry in your host table is incorrect.

    B. RIP obtained incorrect information about where to send the packets.

    C. pc24 is forwarding packets to pc2.

    D. pc24 has an ACL on it.

    Correct Answer & Explanation: **A**. The most likely problem is that you have an entry in your host table that incorrectly maps the name pc24 to the IPv6 address for pc2. If you do an *ipv6 ping* to pc24 the host table will map that name to the IPv6 address listed in the table for pc24 and forward your packets to that address.

    Incorrect Answers & Explanations: **B**, **C**, **D**. Answer **B** is incorrect because RIP keeps track of destination networks not individual devices. Answer **C** is incorrect because packets are sent to the destination IPv6 address in the packet header. Besides, it's unlikely that pc24 has the ability to forward packets somewhere else. Answer **D** is incorrect because an ACL causes the device to block or forward routed packets on routers and firewalls.

19. Now that you have IPv6 set up on your network, you need to set up some ACLs to control access to your devices and particular services on the network. What command could you use to begin configuring an ACL for IPv6?

    A. *ipv6 access-list 4000*

    B. *ipv6 acl*

    C. *ipv6 access-list inbound-list*

    D. *permit any any*

Correct Answer & Explanation: **C**. This command takes you into the ACL configuration mode and begins the process of configuring an access list called *inbound-list*.

Incorrect Answers & Explanations: **A, B, D**. Answer **A** is incorrect because with IPv6 ACL's must be named, not numbered. Answer **B** is incorrect because ACL isn't a valid keyword. Answer **D** is incorrect because you have to access ACL configuration mode before you execute your permit and deny commands.

20. There are three implicit statements at the end of IPv6 ACLs. The last line is an implicit *deny any any* to deny any IPv6 that hasn't been explicitly permitted previously in the list. What do the other two statements permit?

    A. Inbound and outbound e-mail

    B. IPv6 pings and telnet

    C. Multicasts and anycasts

    D. Two ICMP message types for neighbor discovery

    Correct Answer & Explanation: **D**. The implicit permit statements at the end of an ACL are for ICMP neighbor discovery message types nd-na (neighbor advertisements) and nd-ns (neighbor solicitations). Because neighbor discovery is such an important part of how IPv6 works, these neighbor discovery messages are permitted. They are the only types of packets implicitly permitted in an access list.

    Incorrect Answers & Explanations: **A, B, C**. Answers **A, B**, and **C** are all incorrect because we have to explicitly permit E-mail, IPv6 pings, and telnets, and multicasts and anycasts if we are using an ACL.

21. You want to limit access to your router via telnet. You've created an ACL called *stay-out*, permitting only administrators. How do you apply the ACL to control access to the router itself?

    A. The *ipv6 traffic-filter stay-out in* command at the (config-line) prompt

    B. The *ipv6 access-class stay-out in* command at the (config-IPv6-acl) prompt

    C. The *ipv6 access-class stay-out in* command at the (config-line) prompt

    D. The *ipv6 access-group stay-out in* command at the (config-line) prompt

Correct Answer & Explanation: **C**. The *ipv6 access-class stay-out in* command executed in line configuration mode for the virtual terminal (vty) lines is the correct answer. Access-classes are applied when configuring ACLs on lines. The *in* at the end of the command specifies to filter inbound packets against the list.

Incorrect Answers & Explanations: **A, B, D**. Answer **A** is incorrect because the *ipv6 traffic-filter* command is the command to apply an ACL to an interface. Answer **B** is incorrect because the list is created in (config-IPv6-acl) mode but you must be in line configuration mode to apply the list to the vty lines. Answer **D** is incorrect because the *access-group* command is the command used to apply an ACL to an interface in IPv4.

22. You are configuring some new routing options on your routers to route IPv6. You want to make sure all of your networks appear in the routing table and you want to see what types of routes are being used to access the networks. What is the command you would use to get this information?

    A. *show ip route*

    B. *show ipv6 route*

    C. *show ipv6 static*

    D. *ipv6 route*

Correct Answer & Explanation: **B**. The *show ipv6 route* command displays the IPv6 routing table, with all of the types of routes currently being used.

Incorrect Answers & Explanations: **A, C, D**. Answer **A** is incorrect because we have to include the "v6" in our command. This command is the command for displaying the IPv4 routing table. Answer **C** is incorrect because it limits the type of route displayed to only static routes. Answer **D** is incorrect because the command to look at the routing table is a show command.

23. You have been comparing Dynamic Routing Protocols and you are trying to decide if a Distance-Vector or Link-State Routing Protocol is best. You know that Distance-Vector Protocols use distance calculations to obtain routing information. How does a link-state protocol such as OSPF obtain routing information?

    A. The same way a Distance-Vector Protocol does only faster

    B. With link-state advertisements

C. By using fast convergence

D. By querying a DHCP server

Correct Answer & Explanation: **B**. Link-State Protocols send link-state advertisements around the network and use the information to get an overall "picture" of the topology of the network. They use that information to choose the best route.

Incorrect Answers & Explanations: **A, C, D**. Answer **A** is incorrect because Distance-Vector Protocols use distance calculations and Link-State Protocols get an overall picture of the network using the shortest path first algorithm. Answer **C** is incorrect because fast convergence allows the Routing Protocol to maintain information about multiple routes to the same network at the same time, for quick failover. This only comes into play after the link-state advertisements have gathered the information. Answer **D** is incorrect because DHCP servers can provide a number of configuration options to devices but route information isn't one of those options.

24. You're verifying the IPv6 configuration on your router. The first thing you want to check is to make sure IPv6 has been enabled on the router. How would you accomplish this?

A. The *show running-config* command

B. The *show ipv6?* command

C. The *show ip protocols* command

D. The *show ipv6 enable* command

Correct Answer & Explanation: **A**. The *show running-config* command displays your configuration commands that are currently being used by the router. If the *ipv6 unicast-routing* command is in the running-config, IPv6 has been enabled.

Incorrect Answers & Explanations: **B, C, D**. Answer **B** is incorrect because it doesn't tell you if IPv6 has been enabled, it tells you if the IOS includes IPv6 capabilities. If you get an error message when you do the *show ipv6?* command, your version of the IOS doesn't support IPv6. Answer **C** is incorrect because the *show ip protocols* command displays information about routing protocols for IPv4. Answer **D** is incorrect because the *ipv6 enable* command enables IPv6 on a specific interface. There is no *show* command for this.

25. You aren't able to communicate between your router and the other IPv6 devices on your network. You've checked the configurations on the host devices, so now you need to check your IPv6 address configurations on your router. When verifying your IPv6 address configurations, what command will you use?

A. *show ipv6 address*   **C.** *show ipv6 interface*

B. *show ip address*   **D.** *show ipv6 route*

Correct Answer & Explanation: **C.** The *show ipv6 interface* command will show you the IPv6 configuration on the interfaces. You can see both the link-local and global unicast addresses with this command.

Incorrect Answers & Explanations: **A**, **B**, **D**. Answers **A** and **B** are incorrect because there are no *show address* commands in the Cisco IOS. Answer **D** is incorrect because *show ipv6 route* displays the IPv6 routing table but not addresses of the interfaces.

26. While troubleshooting your network and verifying connectivity, you execute the *ipv6 ping* command. When you try to ping some devices you get the exclamation marks (!!!!) that indicate you're getting replies to your pings. But, with other devices, you're getting Us (UUUU). What do the U's mean when you are trying to do an *ipv6* ping?

A. The server timed out waiting for a reply

B. Unknown error

C. Network unreachable

D. No route to host

Correct Answer & Explanation: **D.** The U's when doing *ipv6* pings indicate that there's no route to the host.

Incorrect Answers & Explanations: **A**, **B**, **C**. Answer **A** is incorrect because the periods (....) indicate the server timed out waiting for a reply. Answer **C** is incorrect because the symbol for network unreachable is N's (NNNN).

27. While you're troubleshooting the IPv6 traffic crossing your network you want to look at traffic information for IPv6. You know there are commands that can show you statistics and other information as well as commands you can use to clear existing information and start fresh. How does the *clear ipv6 traffic* command help you?

A. Resets the IPv6 counters   **C.** Drops all IPv6 packets

B. Disables IPv6   **D.** Resets the IPv6 routing table

Correct Answer & Explanation: **A**. The *clear ipv6 traffic* command resets the IPv6 counters so you can start monitoring from zero.

Incorrect Answers & Explanations: **B, C, D**. Answer **B** is incorrect because the command to disable IPv6 is *no ipv6 unicast-routing*. Answer **C** is incorrect because the clear commands don't drop packets. Answer **D** is incorrect because the *clear ipv6 route* is the command that resets the IPv6 routing table.

28. You're interested in the process the routers go through to gather information about other routers and how they are able to communicate with each other. You know neighbor discovery is an important part of how routers discover each other and you want to watch what types of information are exchanged. How can you do this?

    A. *show discovery info*   **C.** *debug ipv6 nd*
    B. *show ipv6 nd*   **D.** *debug ipv6 neighbors*

Correct Answer & Explanation: **C**. The correct answer is the *debug ipv6 nd* command to watch the neighbor discovery packets crossing your router.

Incorrect Answers & Explanations: **A, B, D**. Answer **A** is incorrect because there are no *show discovery* commands. Answer **B** is incorrect because the *show* command displays the neighbor discovery database which could give you more information about what neighbor discovery is doing, but the command is *show ipv6 neighbor*. Answer **D** is incorrect because with debug, we watch the neighbor discovery (nd) information not the neighbors themselves.

29. How would you get rid of the IPv6 routing table so the router can recreate its routing table and start fresh? You want to do this without restarting the router.

    A. *clear ipv6 route**   **C.** *erase ipv6 route*
    B. *clear ipv6 router*   **D.** *no ipv6 route*

Correct Answer & Explanation: **A**. The *clear ipv6 route** command will clear the entries from the routing table and the router will rebuild its table. The * means clear everything. (Note: There will be more CPU utilization while the router is rebuilding its routing table.)

Incorrect Answers & Explanations: **B, C, D**. Answers **B** and **C** are incorrect because these are not valid commands. Answer **D** is incorrect because the *no ipv6 route* command is used to delete individual static routes from the configuration.

30. How would you quickly make sure that all debugging has been turned off?

A. *no debug*

B. *no debug all*

C. *debug off*

D. *no debug ipv6*

Correct Answer & Explanation: **B**. The *no debug all* command stops all possible debugging on the router.

Incorrect Answers & Explanations: **A**, **C**, **D**. Answer **A** is incorrect because it is an incomplete command and only turns off one type of debugging at a time if it is complete. Answer **C** is incorrect because there is no *debug off* command. Answer **D** is incorrect because, again, it isn't a complete command and only turns off one type of IPv6 debugging at a time when it is a complete command.

Chapter 11: Configuring Cisco Switches

1. Which of the following statements regarding hubs are true?

A. They operate at the data link layer.

B. They increase the number of collisions.

C. Layer 2 addresses are used to make forwarding decisions.

D. Signals are distributed through all ports except the source port.

Correct Answers & Explanations: **B**, and **D**. Answer **B** is correct, because a hub increases collisions on your network. When you use hubs on your network, all of them use shared media. Answer **D** is correct, because when a hub sends traffic it does this to all ports except the originating port.

Incorrect Answers & Explanations: **A**, and **C**. Answer **A** is incorrect, because a hub works at the physical layer. Answer **C** is incorrect, because hubs don't work with MAC addresses.

2. Which switching mode creates the most latency and offers the best error detection?

A. Cut-through

B. Store-n-forward

C. Fragment-free

D. Adaptive cut-through

Correct Answer & Explanation: **B**. Answer **B** is correct, because a switch configured with store-n-forward copies the frame into its buffer.

Incorrect Answers & Explanations: **A**, **C**, and **D**. Answers **A**, **C**, and **D** are incorrect, because these methods provide no error detection.

3. Which of the following is used to build a dynamic MAC address table?

A. Source IP address   **C.** Source MAC address

B. Destination IP address   **D.** Destination MAC address

Correct Answer & Explanation: **C.** Answer **C** is correct, because when a switch receives a frame, it first reads the source MAC address and places this entry into the MAC address table.

Incorrect Answers & Explanations: **A**, **B**, and **D**. Answers **A** and **B** are incorrect, because a switch will not work with IP addresses. Answer **D** is incorrect, because if a switch doesn't know the destination MAC address, it will flood the MAC address to all switchports.

4. What does it means when the System LED is amber?

A. The POST is running.

B. The POST has failed.

C. The POST was successful.

D. The switch has experienced a fatal error.

Correct Answer & Explanation: **B.** Answer **B** is correct. If the System LED is amber it means the POST has failed.

Incorrect Answers & Explanations: **A**, **C**, and **D**. Answer **A** is incorrect, because if the POST is running, the System LED is off. Answer **C** is incorrect, because if the POST is successful, the System LED will turn green. Answer **D** is incorrect, because all the switchports are also disabled.

5. How can a switch be configured to prevent unauthorized hosts to access your network?

A. Assign a MAC address to a switchport.

B. Add unused switchports to VLAN 1.

C. Use port-based security to allow only the first host to access the network.

D. Shut down all unused ports.

Correct Answers & Explanations: **A** and **D**. Answer **A** is correct, because when you assign a MAC address to a switchport, only that MAC address can connect. Answer **D** is correct, because if you disable unused switchports, a malicious user cannot use them to connect to your network.

Incorrect Answers & Explanations: **B**, and **C**. Answer **B** is incorrect, because adding unused switchports to VLAN 1 will not prevent unauthorized hosts from connecting to your network. Answer **C** is incorrect, because a malicious user will still be able to connect to your network with his MAC address.

6. Which command do you use to back up the IOS of your switch to a PC?

   A. *Switch#copy tftp flash*   **C.** *Switch(config)#copy tftp flash*
   B. *Switch#copy flash tftp*   **D.** *Switch(config)#copy flash tftp*

   Correct Answer & Explanation: **B**. Answer **B** is correct. This command will back up the IOS from flash to a TFTP server running a PC.

   Incorrect Answers & Explanations: **A**, **C**, and **D**. Answer **A** is incorrect, because this command will copy an IOS image from the PC to your switch. Answers **C** and **D** are incorrect, because you cannot execute these commands from this configuration mode.

7. If a host is powered down, how long will the MAC address in the MAC address table stay on your switch?

   A. 30 seconds   **C.** 600 seconds
   B. 300 seconds   **D.** 120 seconds

   Correct Answer & Explanation: **B**. Answer **B** is correct. A switch keeps the MAC address in the MAC address table for 300 seconds when a host is powered down.

   Incorrect Answers & Explanations: **A**, **C**, and **D**. Answers **A**, **C**, and **D** are incorrect, because a switch does not use these values.

8. Which commands can you use to change from Global Configuration mode to Privileged Exec mode?

   A. Logout   **D.** Quit
   B. Disable   **E.** End
   C. Exit

   Correct Answers & Explanations: **C** and **E**. Answers **C** and **E** are correct. You can use *exit* and *end* to change from Global Configuration mode to Privileged mode.

   Incorrect Answers & Explanations: **A**, **B**, and **D**. Answer **A** is incorrect, because the *logout* command logs you out from the switch. Answer **B** is incorrect, because this command is used to go from

Privileged mode to User Exec mode. Answer **D** is incorrect, because the *quit* command is used to close a connection.

9. You lost the password of your Cisco Catalyst 2950 switch and you need to initiate the password recovery procedure. What do you do?

   A. Rename the Flash file.

   B. Hold down the MODE button during switch startup.

   C. Connect a PC via a console cable, and after startup press Ctrl+Break.

   D. Enter the setup program by deleting the switch configuration file.

   Correct Answer & Explanation: **B**. Answer **B** is correct, because when you press the MODE button during switch startup, you can manually initiate the switch without executing the current configuration file.

   Incorrect Answers & Explanations: **A**, **C**, and **D**. Answer **A** is incorrect, because when you rename the Flash file, your switch will not boot. Answer **C** is incorrect, because at this point, the switch already executed the current configuration file. Answer **D** is incorrect, because when you delete the configuration file, you lose all configuration information of the switch.

10. Which protocol do you use to upgrade an IOS image from a Cisco Catalyst 2950?

    A. HTTP   **C.** Telnet

    B. SNMP   **D.** TFTP

    Correct Answer & Explanation: **D**. Answer **D** is correct, because a switch uses TFTP to copy an IOS image from a TFTP server.

    Incorrect Answers & Explanations: **A**, **B**, and **C**. Answer **A** is incorrect, because HTTP is a protocol used for Web servers. Answer **B** is incorrect, because SNMP is a management protocol. Answer **C** is incorrect, because Telnet is used to manage your switch.

11. You need to connect your PC to the console port of your switch. Which cable do you use?

    A. Crossover cable   **C.** Rollover cable

    B. Straight cable   **D.** Serial cable

    Correct Answer & Explanation: **C**. Answer **C** is correct. You need a rollover cable to connect your PC to the console port of your switch.

Incorrect Answers & Explanations: **A**, **B**, and **D**. Answer **A** is incorrect, because a crossover cable is used to connect a switch to a switch. Answer **B** is incorrect, because a straight cable is used to connect a host to a switch. Answer **D** is incorrect, because a serial cable is used for modem connections.

12. What does port-based security use to allow or deny access to a switchport?

A. Source IP address   **C.** Source MAC address

B. Destination IP address   **D.** Destination MAC address

Correct Answer & Explanation: **C**. Answer **C** is correct, because if a switch is configured with port-based security, the switch will verify whether the source MAC address is configured for port-based security.

Incorrect Answers & Explanations: **A**, **B**, and **D**. Answers **A** and **B** are incorrect, because port-based security will not work with IP addresses. Answer **D** is incorrect, because port-based security works with the MAC address of the host currently connected to that switchport.

13. What are the three modes of port-based security?

A. Restrict   **E.** Protect

B. Stop   **F.** Close

C. Start   **G.** Disable

D. Shutdown

Correct Answers & Explanations: **A**, **D**, and **E**. Answers **A**, **D**, and **E** are correct, because port-based security uses the Restrict, Shutdown, and Protect security modes to protect a switch if a violation occurs.

Incorrect Answers & Explanations: **B**, **C**, **F**, and **G**. Answers **B**, **C**, **F**, and **G** are incorrect, because they are not used in port-based security.

14. Which of the following is a reason why a switch does not add the broadcast address to its MAC address table?

A. A broadcast address will never be the source address of a frame.

B. A broadcast is never forwarded by a switch.

C. Broadcast addresses are not compatible with the switching table.

D. A switch will drop broadcasts to avoid broadcast storms.

Correct Answer & Explanation: **A**. Answer **A** is correct, because a switch builds the MAC address table based on incoming source MAC addresses.

Incorrect Answers & Explanations: **B, C,** and **D**. Answer **B** is incorrect, because a switch forwards a broadcast if the frame must be received by all hosts. Answer **C** is incorrect, because a broadcast address is compatible with the switching table. Answer **D** is incorrect, because a switch forwards broadcasts if there is a need to do that.

15. You need to execute the command *show mac-address-table*. In which mode(s) can you execute this command?

   A. User mode
   D. Setup mode

   B. Enable mode
   E. Interface Configuration mode

   C. Global Configuration mode

Correct Answers & Explanations: **A** and **B**. Answers **A** and **B** are correct, because you can execute the *show mac-address-table* command only from User mode and Enable mode.

Incorrect Answers & Explanations: **C, D,** and **E**. Answers **C, D,** and **E** are incorrect, because you cannot execute the command from these modes.

16. You need to reboot your switch. Which command do you use?

   A. *Switch>reboot*
   C. *Switch(config)#reboot*

   B. *Switch#reboot*
   D. *Switch#reload*

Correct Answer & Explanation: **D**. Answer **D** is correct, because you can restart your switch by using the command *reload*.

Incorrect Answers & Explanations: **A, B,** and **C**. Answers **A, B, C** are incorrect, because these commands are not supported.

17. What type of memory is used to store the configuration of your switch?

   A. ROM
   C. NVRAM

   B. RAM
   D. Flash

Correct Answer & Explanation: **C**. Answer **C** is correct. A switch stores its configuration into NVRAM.

Incorrect Answers & Explanations: **A, B**, and **D**. Answer **A** is incorrect, because ROM is read-only memory and you cannot write information to it. Answer **B** is incorrect, because a switch does not use RAM to store configuration information. Data stored in RAM is deleted when the switch is powered off. Answer **D** is incorrect, because a switch stores the IOS in Flash.

18. What command copies the configuration information from RAM to NVRAM?

    A. *copy running-config tftp*

    B. *copy tftp running-config*

    C. *copy running-config startup-config*

    D. *copy startup-config running config*

    Correct Answer & Explanation: **C**. Answer **C** is correct. The *copy running-config startup-config* command copies configuration information in RAM to NVRAM.

    Incorrect Answers & Explanations: **A, B**, and **D**. Answer **A** is incorrect, because the *copy running-config tftp* command copies the running-config to a TFTP server. Answer **B** is incorrect, because the *copy tftp running-config* command copies the configuration from a TFTP server to the running-config. Answer **D** is incorrect, because the *copy startup-config running config* command copies configuration information from NVRAM to RAM.

19. Which of the following is true about switches and hubs for network connectivity?

    A. Switches increase the number of collision domains.

    B. Hubs increase the number of collision domains.

    C. Switches do not forward broadcasts.

    D. Hubs dedicate more bandwidth per host than switches.

    Correct Answer & Explanation: **A**. Answer **A** is correct, because a switch creates one collision domain per switchport.

    Incorrect Answers & Explanations: **B, C**, and **D**. Answer **B** is incorrect, because when you use a hub, you have one large collision domain. Answer **C** is incorrect, because a switch is able to forward broadcast frames to all switchports. Answer **D** is incorrect, because a hub shares the total amount of bandwidth with the other hosts on the network.

20. What will an Ethernet switch do when it receives a frame and the MAC address of the destination host is in the MAC address table?

   A. The switch will forward the frame to all switchports except the source switchport.

   B. The switch will forward the frame to the specific switchport.

   C. The switch will drop the frame.

   D. The switch will delete the MAC address from the MAC address table.

Correct Answer & Explanation: **B**. Answer **B** is correct. The switch will forward the frame to the specific switchport.

Incorrect Answers & Explanations: **A**, **C**, and **D**. Answer **A** is incorrect, because the MAC address is already in the MAC address table, so there is no need to flood the frame to all switchports. Answer **C** is incorrect, because there is no reason to drop the frame. Answer **D** is incorrect, because the switch will not delete the MAC address from the MAC address table.

Chapter 12: Spanning-Tree Protocol

1. You're using a network protocol analyzer to troubleshoot an application problem for a user. This tool enables you to capture all frames and you are connected to a different port but the same switch as the server. Yet, you are unable to see the application traffic—frames between the application server and user don't appear. What is a potential problem that can cause this?

   A. The CAM table is not updating properly so the switch isn't forwarding traffic to your tool.

   B. The switch has CAM entries for the destination of the traffic so it isn't flooded to the port connected to your analyzer.

   C. Your analyzer isn't transmitting on the network so the switch doesn't know to send traffic to your port.

   D. The server and host aren't sending traffic to the analyzer so this configuration won't work.

Correct Answer & Explanation: **B**. One benefit of Ethernet switching is the ability to forward traffic intelligently—without needing to forward all frames out all ports. Because the application server and the host are communicating together, the switch knows not to send frames toward your tool. In practice, a "monitor" port is used to mirror information sent out one port over to a special port used for analysis.

Incorrect Answers & Explanations: **A**, **C**, and **D**. Answer **A** isn't correct, because the switch can't be expected to send traffic to you since the CAM table has a MAC/port mapping for both the application server and the host. Answer **C** isn't correct, because the switch wouldn't send you the server/host traffic even if your analyzer were known in the MAC table. The switch would only send you traffic that is destined for you (and flooded traffic, broadcasts, and multicasts). Answer **D** isn't correct, because the application traffic flows directly between the server and the host. Even if both server and host were sending different data to your analyzer data, the application traffic would still be sent directly between the server and the host.

2. You have a large switched network with some pretty old switches. The network seems to be operating correctly, but when evaluating network traffic, you notice that a lot of unicast traffic is being flooded to ports that don't contain the destination host. What can cause this?

   A. The STP isn't converging which is causing a loop.

   B. The frames are being sent too quickly and the old switches can't filter the frames that fast.

   C. There are too many hosts and the CAM table of the old switch is being overrun, which causes traffic to flood.

   D. Memory problems on the switch are causing a lack of frame buffers to process the traffic, which causes traffic to flood.

   Correct Answer & Explanation: **C**. The number of available CAM entries depends on the type of switch. Old switches have smaller CAM tables and networks with many hosts can easily overwhelm them. When CAM space is exhausted, traffic sent to destinations not in the CAM table is flooded.

   Incorrect Answers & Explanations: **A**, **B**, and **D**. Answer **A** is incorrect even though a loop does not cause traffic to flood out the wrong ports. If there was a bridge loop, the network would not be operating properly. Answer **B** is incorrect because an overworked switch would tend to drop frames rather than to transmit them out incorrect ports. Answer **D** is wrong for the same reason. Memory exhaustion would cause frame loss, not incorrect forwarding.

3. A frame is forwarded through an Ethernet switch between two ports in the same VLAN. What information changes in the frame as this happens?

A. The source **MAC** address of the frame is changed to the switch **MAC** address.

B. The destination **MAC** address of the frame is changed to the router **MAC** address.

C. The source and destination **MAC** addresses remain the same, but destination IP address is changed to the router IP.

D. There is no change made to the frame.

Correct Answer & Explanation: **D**. Ethernet switches are called "transparent" because no change is made to the frame as it flows between the ports in the same VLAN.

Incorrect Answers & Explanations: **A**, **B**, and **C**. Answer **A** is incorrect, because the source MAC address remains the same when the frame is forwarded at Layer 2. If the frame were routed, the source MAC would be changed by the router. Answer **B** is incorrect because the router MAC would be the destination only for traffic sent directly to the router. Answer **C** is incorrect, because the destination IP address never changes on the path through the network (unless there is Network Address Translation involved).

4. When a bridge loop forms, what stops frames from flowing around the loop indefinitely or proliferating?

A. There is a hop count field in the Ethernet header that is decremented each time a frame is forwarded through a switch.

B. When the frame is received by the router, it is sent toward its destination IP address and stops looping as a result.

C. Breaking the loop (by removing links or turning off hardware) will stop a frame from looping.

D. The routing protocol concept of infinity is breached and the frame is dropped.

Correct Answer & Explanation: **C**. Breaking the loop is the only thing that will stop a frame from looping forever. In certain cases, frames will proliferate and crash the network as a result—which stops the loop too.

Incorrect Answers & Explanations: **A**, **B**, and **D**. Answer **A** is incorrect, because the Ethernet header has no hop count field. Answer **B** is incorrect, because it doesn't matter who the frame is destined for when there is a loop. The frame will continue to loop even after it is received by its destination MAC. Answer **D** is incorrect, because there is no routing protocol that operates at Layer 2 where Ethernet frames are switched.

5. Are bridge loops worse than routing loops, and why?

   A. Yes, because with a routing loop, a frame may loop forever but there is only a single copy of the frame. Frames can proliferate with bridge loops, which can crash the network.

   B. No, routing loops are worse because more router resources are expended by routing a looping frame than switching a looping frame.

   C. Yes, bridge loops are worse because switching is often performed in hardware and so a frame loops much faster being switched than routed.

   D. No, routing loops are worse because they are more difficult to stop. Routing loops require a reboot of network equipment to clear.

   Correct Answer & Explanation: **A**. Bridge loops often cause network crashes because of proliferating frames. Because of switching speed, even a short duration loop can crash a network.

   Incorrect Answers & Explanations: **B**, **C**, and **D**. Answer **B** is incorrect, because routing loops don't proliferate frames. Answer **C** is incorrect, because both switching and routing is performed in hardware—and a single looping frame isn't likely to consume enough resources to crash a network. Answer **D** is incorrect, because routing protocol convergence ensures a loop-free topology. Even if temporary loops form, the routing protocol eventually breaks the loop.

6. You are given the opportunity to build a network for a large new building and have a lot of fiber that can be used to create a very well-connected topology. Is it a good idea to build the switched network so that each switch has four possible paths to the root bridge?

   A. Yes, because more redundancy is always better for important networks.

   B. No, because the STP protocol can only support two redundant paths between switches.

   C. Yes, because STP operates more efficiently as the number of switches and links increases.

   D. No, because STP convergence takes longer as the number of switches and links increases.

Correct Answer & Explanation: **D**. As the number of network devices increases, the STP works harder to create and maintain a loop free topology.

Incorrect Answers & Explanations: **A**, **B**, and **C**. Answer **A** is incorrect because more redundancy is not always preferred. Too much redundancy not only makes STP slower, but also makes the environment more complex to troubleshoot and maintain. Answer **B** is incorrect, because STP can support many redundant paths—but this is not desired. Answer **C** is incorrect, because STP takes more time to converge as the number of switches and links increases.

7. Refer to Figure 12.15. Which switch is the spanning-tree root and how can you tell given the information shown in the figure?

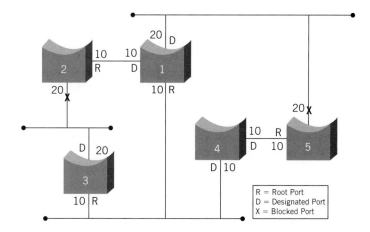

FIGURE 12.15

Example Topology for Questions 7 to 9

A. Switch 1 is the root because it has the highest cumulative port costs.

B. Switch 4 is the root because all its ports are in the *designated* state.

C. Switch 1 is the root because it has the smallest address.

D. Switch 5 is the root because it has the highest address.

Correct Answer & Explanation: **B**. The root of this network does not have the lowest address, so the Bridge Priority must be lower than the other switches. The easiest way to quickly tell the root given this figure is that all ports are designated. The root is the only one in the network that has all *designated* ports.

Incorrect Answers & Explanations: **A**, **C**, and **D**. Answer **A** is incorrect, because the sum of the port costs is not factor in root bridge election. Answer **C** is incorrect, because this switch has a root port. The root bridge does not have any root ports—as crazy as that sounds. Answer **D** is not correct, because the switch with the highest MAC is actually the least likely to be elected root.

8. Refer again to Figure 12.15. Assume that the root port on switch 3 fails and that no proprietary feature is used to speed convergence. How long could it take for 802.1d to converge after this failure, and why?

   A. 35 seconds, because switch 2 would take 20 seconds to recognize the failure (Max Age) and 15 seconds to transition to *forwarding* state.

   B. 30 seconds, because it would take switch 3 up to 15 seconds to recognize the failure and 15 seconds to transition to *forwarding* state.

   C. 50 seconds, because it would take up to 20 seconds for switch 2 to recognize the failure and 30 seconds to transition to *forwarding* state.

   D. 30 seconds, because it would take switch 2 exactly 30 seconds to transition to *forwarding* state.

   Correct Answer & Explanation: **C**. From switch 2's perspective, this is an indirect failure. It would take switch 2 up to 20 seconds (Max Age) to learn about the failure (assuming that *Backbonefast* isn't used) and another 30 seconds to transition from blocking, through listening and learning, to forwarding state.

   Incorrect Answers & Explanations: **A**, **B**, and **D**. Answer **A** is incorrect, because the port must progress through both *listening* and *learning* states and each takes 15 seconds by default. Answer **B** is incorrect because this is a direct failure from switch 3's perspective and that is recognized immediately. Plus, it takes 30 seconds to progress through *listening* and *learning* states. Answer **D** is incorrect, because it can take as long as 20 seconds for an indirect failure to be detected.

9. The root path cost is important to the STP algorithm because it determines the best path from any switch to the root bridge. How is the root path cost calculated?

   A. It is the sum of the port costs for all ports in the path from the root to the receiving switch.

   B. It is the sum of the port costs for all sending ports in the path from the root to the receiving switch.

C. It is the sum of the port costs for all receiving ports in the path from the root to the receiving switch.

D. The root path cost is equal to the port cost of the sending port on the root.

Correct Answer & Explanation: **C.** The root path cost is a sum of port costs, and it is calculated only on the receive ports in the path from root to the final switch.

Incorrect Answers & Explanations: **A**, **B**, and **D**. Answer **A** is incorrect, because the port costs for the sending ports are not added to the root path cost as it is sent from switch to switch. Answer **B** is incorrect for the same reason. Answer **D** is incorrect, because the root path cost is additive—a sum calculated over the entire path. If the switch were directly connected to the root, then the root path cost is equal to the port cost, but it is the receiving port, port cost.

10. The *Rootguard* feature is intended to protect the placement of the root by ensuring that no other switch can take over the root by advertising itself with a better Bridge ID. Where is the *Rootguard* feature configured?

A. *Rootguard* is configured on individual ports that you know don't have a path back to the root.

B. *Rootguard* is configured globally only on the root and backup root bridges.

C. *Rootguard* is configured globally on all switches in the network.

D. *Rootguard* is configured on individual ports that you know have a path back to the root.

Correct Answer & Explanation: **A.** The *Rootguard* command is applied in *interface configuration* mode and applied to edge ports and on switch ports where you know that the root should not be.

Incorrect Answers & Explanations: **B**, **C**, and **D**. Answer **B** is incorrect because *Rootguard* is an interface command. There is a macro "spanning-tree vlan <vlan> root primary | secondary" that is applied to force root placement—but that's not the *Rootguard* feature. Answer **C** is not correct because *Rootguard* is not a global command. Answer **D** is incorrect because the feature should never be applied on root or designated ports.

11. How does the *Portfast* feature eliminate startup problems for some hosts?

A. The *Portfast* feature eliminates startup problems by stopping the switch from sending a TCN Bpdu to the root when a host connects.

B. The *Portfast* feature eliminates startup problems by allowing the switch to transition the port directly to *forwarding* state, which eliminates the 30 second wait for *listening* and *learning* states.

C. The *Portfast* feature eliminates startup problems by dropping the CAM timeout from 5 minutes to 15 seconds when a host connects.

D. The *Portfast* feature eliminates startup problems by disabling the spanning tree on the port.

Correct Answer & Explanation: **B**. Normally when a host connects, the port moves from disabled (not connected) to Listening (discarding for 15 seconds) to Learning (discarding for 15 seconds) and finally to Forwarding. This delay can cause DHCP and other problems for the host.

Incorrect Answers & Explanations: **A**, **C**, and **D**. Answer **A** is incorrect even though *Portfast* does suppress the TCN Bpdu. This helps maintain network stability and does not affect the host startup. Answer **C** is incorrect, because Portfast suppresses the TCN Bpdu, which is what causes the root to drop the CAM timeout. Answer **D** is incorrect because Portfast does not disable spanning tree. In fact, by default if the port receives a Bpdu through a Portfast port, Portfast is automatically disabled and the port is treated like any other port.

12. *Loopguard* and UDLD perform a similar function, but by a different method. How are these functions different and how are they similar?

A. *Loopguard* and UDLD both block loops from forming only over 802.1q trunked ports. *Loopguard* does this by detecting invalid Bpdus and UDLD does this by detecting duplicate frames.

B. *Loopguard* and UDLD both block loops from forming due to unidirectional links. *Loopguard* does this by detecting missing Bpdus and UDLD does this by watching for **MAC** addresses that flap between ports in the CAM table.

   C. *Loopguard* and UDLD both avoid loops from forming only over Etherchannel link bundles. *Loopguard* does this by detecting bundle instability and UDLD does this by watching for Bpdus with invalid source **MAC**s.

   D. *Loopguard* and UDLD both avoid loops from forming due to unidirectional links. *Loopguard* does this by watching for Bpdus that suddenly stop, and UDLD does this by sending special frames to a neighboring switch and expecting a response.

Correct Answer & Explanation: **D**. *Loopguard* and UDLD both detect unidirectional links and shut down ports to avoid loops. *Loopguard* monitors Bpdus on ports and transitions the port to "loop inconsistent" state if the Bpdus disappear. UDLD sends keepalives to neighbor switches and expects a response to prove the link is bidirectional.

Incorrect Answers & Explanations: **A**, **B**, and **C**. Answer **A** is incorrect, because neither protocol is limited to working only over trunks. Answer B is incorrect, because UDLD does not watch for **MAC** flapping. Answer **C** is incorrect, because neither protocol is limited to Etherchannel bundles.

13. What is the main limitation of a CST?

   A. A CST does not support more than a single VLAN.

   B. CST supports multiple VLANs but doesn't operate properly over 802.1q trunk ports.

   C. A CST only supports a single physical topology, which doesn't fully utilize network resources.

   D. CST is not supported only older legacy switches.

Correct Answer & Explanation: **C**. Since it only supports a single physical topology, a CST works well in small environments. However, as the number of VLANs increase, the inability to utilize all links in a redundant network becomes very inefficient.

Incorrect Answers & Explanations: **A**, **B**, and **D**. Answer **A** is incorrect, because a CST can support multiple VLANs, but all must share a single physical topology. Answer **B** is incorrect, because there is nothing that stops a CST from operating properly over trunk ports. Answer **D** is incorrect, because CST is not a protocol, but a type of Spanning-Tree protocol. In fact, original versions of 802.1d (non-PVST) that ran on legacy switches were common spanning trees.

14. Ports in 802.1d that would be placed in *blocking* state have been changed in RSTP. The 802.1w protocol makes these either alternate or backup ports. What is the difference between these ports?

    A. An alternate port has a backup path to the root bridge, but a backup port does not.

    B. Both alternate and backup ports have a path to the root bridge, but the path through the backup port may not be loop-free.

    C. An alternate port has a backup path to the root bridge and can be transitioned immediately to *forwarding* state. A backup port can't guarantee a unique path to the root bridge, because the port is self-looped.

    D. Both alternate and backup ports have a path to the root bridge. The difference involves how the two ports send and receive Bpdus.

    Correct Answer & Explanation: **C**. An alternate port is guaranteed to be loop free and can be transitioned immediately to forwarding state if the root port fails. A backup port receives "better" Bpdus from itself through the port, which means there is no guarantee that a different path (aside from the switch's own root port) to the root exists.

    Incorrect Answers & Explanations: **A**, **B**, and **D**. Answer **A** is incorrect, because the switch doesn't know whether there is a different path to the root through the backup port—it only knows that there is a self-loop. Answer **B** is incorrect, because there is no guarantee that a unique path to the root exists through the backup port. Answer **D** is incorrect, because there may not be a unique path to the root through the backup port.

15. What is the primary reason that a network designer may prefer MST (802.1s) over RSTP (802.1w)?

    A. In networks with many VLANs, RSTP consumes too many resources because each VLAN runs a unique instance of the STP.

    B. Convergence in RSTP is slower than MST, so the 802.1s is preferred in mission critical environments.

    C. The configuration complexity of RSTP make the environment difficult to manage compared to 802.1s.

    D. RSTP doesn't work well in networks that contain a lot of redundancy.

    Correct Answer & Explanation: **A**. With MST, VLANs can be mapped one or more spanning tree instances, which makes the protocol very efficient and flexible for networks with a large number of VLANs.

Incorrect Answers & Explanations: **B**, **C**, and **D**. Answer **B** is incorrect, because convergence speed is not significantly different between the two protocols—scale is the most important difference. Answer **C** is incorrect, because RSTP is actually easier to configure than MST. Answer **D** is incorrect, because both RSTP and MST work fine regardless of the amount of redundancy. However, it is a good design practice to build in enough but not too much redundancy.

16. You want to force a specific switch to be the root of your spanning tree. What is the best way to accomplish this?
    A. Implement the *Rootguard* feature to ensure only your preferred switch can become the root.
    B. Lower the spanning-tree priority of your preferred root to a value lower than any other Bridge Priority.
    C. Use the *Bpdu Guard* feature to block any other switch from advertising itself as a more preferred root.
    D. Select a lower value **MAC** address in the Bridge ID of your preferred root to a value lower than any other bridge address.

    Correct Answer & Explanation: **B**. Setting a low spanning-tree priority is the preferred way to select a root and backup root.

    Incorrect Answers & Explanations: **A**, **C**, and **D**. Answer **A** is incorrect, because the *Rootguard* feature can't be used in this way to rig a root election. Answer **C** is incorrect, because the Bpdu-guard feature would block all Bpdu transmissions if used in this way. Answer **D** is incorrect even though it would work if all bridge priorities are the same. The question asked for the best way and setting the priority is much easier than forcing your preferred root to advertise itself with the lowest **MAC** address.

17. You have been asked to configure STP throughout a network made up of both new and older hardware. Your design goal is to provide for the fastest convergence possible. What is the best approach to this problem?
    A. Run MST (802.1s) throughout the network, because it provides the widest possible support for legacy devices while maintaining fast convergence.
    B. Run 802.1d throughout the network to support interoperability with the older hardware and implement *Backbonefast* to speed convergence.

C. Run RSTP (802.1w) throughout the network, because it provides the widest possible support for legacy devices while maintaining fast convergence.

D. Run RSTP (802.1w) on newer devices and 802.1d on legacy devices. The two protocols are interoperable, but the convergence benefits of RSTP are lost on links to 802.1d switches.

Correct Answer & Explanation: **D**. If legacy devices are placed properly (on the edges of the network), you can maximize convergence speed using RSTP while still maintaining the legacy hardware.

Incorrect Answers & Explanations: **A**, **B**, and **C**. Answer **A** is incorrect, because MST is not supported on legacy hardware. Answer **B** is incorrect, because RSTP provides for faster convergence than an 802.1d network with *Backbonefast*. Answer **C** is incorrect, because RSTP is not supported on legacy hardware.

18. You have configured RSTP throughout a small test lab and you have found that your network does not converge very quickly. What is the most likely cause?

A. The STP timers are not the same on all switches in the network.

B. The links between switches are not configured to be full-duplex.

C. The root bridge is not placed properly.

D. The port costs are not configured correctly.

Correct Answer & Explanation: **B**. RSTP uses the operational duplex of a link to determine if it is a point-to-point link. The sync process of RSTP can only speed convergence on links that are either point-to-point or edge ports.

Incorrect Answers & Explanations: **A**, **C**, and **D**. Answer **A** is incorrect, because the STP timers in RSTP aren't used unless there are legacy switches. Answer **C** could be correct in a really large network, but a small test lab network would not be affected by an improperly placed root bridge. Answer **D** is incorrect because port costs are not relevant to convergence performance.

19. You are troubleshooting a potential bridge loop that caused your network to crash. After rebooting all your switches to get your network back online, you begin your investigation. What is your best source of information about the problem?

A. The *show spanning-tree vlan <vlan> detail* command will provide spanning tree statistics to help isolate a loop.

B. The *show interface* command will show evidence of a loop by showing huge traffic that's been sent on the ports.

    C. The *debug spanning-tree all* command will provide useful information for troubleshooting the loop formation.

    D. Your *syslog* or *snmp* server logs will contain information that can help.

Correct Answer & Explanation: **D**. Since the switches have been rebooted, any *show* command can't provide meaningful counters to troubleshoot a problem. The *syslogs* and *snmp* traps sent by the devices prior to and during loop formation will be the most helpful.

Incorrect Answers & Explanations: **A**, **B**, and **C**. Answer **A** is incorrect, because there are no counters in this command to directly help in troubleshoot loops. Answer **B** is incorrect, because these statistics are cleared after a reboot. Answer **C** is incorrect, because a *debug* command can't help troubleshoot a problem that has already occurred and cleared.

20. Consider Figure 12.16. You want to influence the spanning tree topology to enable servers connected to switches B and C to communicate directly without traffic flowing through the root bridge. Assume all links are of the same speed. How would you modify the port costs to accomplish this?

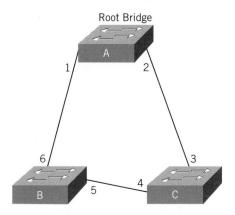

FIGURE 12.16

Example Topology for Question 20

    A. Raise the port cost on port 3.

    B. Raise the port cost on ports 4 and 5

    C. Lower the port cost on ports 4 and 5

    D. Lower the port cost on port 1.

Correct Answer & Explanation: **A**. This is only one of a few ways to accomplish the goal. You could raise or lower the port cost on port 6 or port 3 and achieve the same result.

Incorrect Answers & Explanations: **B**, **C**, and **D**. Answer **B** is incorrect, because any changes to the port costs on the cross connect won't force the root port to port 4 or 5. Answer **C** is incorrect for the same reason. Answer **D** is incorrect, because the root path cost (which controls root port selection) is calculated on receipt and does not include the port cost of the egress port of the sending switch.

Chapter 13: VLANs

1. Your company has an Ethernet network that has been exhibiting signs of being overloaded. Of the four uses for VLANs discussed in this chapter, which one is the most appropriate?
   A. Security
   B. Broadcast domains
   C. Departmental grouping
   D. Segmenting protocols

   Correct Answer & Explanation: **B**. This network has become overloaded and most often this is because of excessive broadcasts on the network. Segmenting broadcast domains will allow the network to be more efficient.

   Incorrect Answers & Explanations: **A**, **C**, and **D**. Answer **A** is incorrect, because security is not the focus of this solution. Answer **C** is incorrect, though departmental grouping might cause a reduction in network traffic, there still may be enough machines that could cause broadcast domain issues. Answer **D** is incorrect, because we have no knowledge from the question that the issues are caused by different protocols that could be controlled by VLANS.

2. Your company has an Ethernet network that has confidential information that must be protected for the HR department. Of the four uses for VLANs discussed in this chapter, which one is the most appropriate?
   A. Security
   B. Broadcast domains
   C. Departmental grouping
   D. Segmenting protocols

   Correct Answer & Explanation: **A**. To secure confidential information so it cannot be intercepted, VLANS are an appropriate way to segment the network.

   Incorrect Answers & Explanations: **B**, **C**, and **D**. Answer **B** is incorrect, this is not a overloaded broadcast situation. Answer **C** is incorrect, though departmental grouping might be an answer, in this case the focus is security. Answer **D** is incorrect, because we have no knowledge from the question that the issues are caused by different protocols that could be controlled by VLANS.

3. Your company has a departmental application that relies on broadcasts as its main transmission mode. Of the four uses for VLANs discussed in this chapter, which one is the most appropriate?

A. Security

B. Broadcast domains

C. Departmental grouping

D. Segmenting protocols

Correct Answer & Explanation: **B**. This network has become overloaded and most often this is because of excessive broadcasts on the network. Segmenting broadcast domains will allow the network to be more efficient.

Incorrect Answers & Explanations: **A**, **C**, and **D**. Answer **A** is incorrect, because security is not the focus of this solution. Answer **C** is incorrect, though departmental grouping might cause a reduction in network traffic, there still may be enough machines that could cause broadcast domain issues. Answer **D** is incorrect, because we have no knowledge from the question that the issues are caused by different protocols that could be controlled by VLANS.

4. Your company has an Ethernet network which you will implement VOIP on. Of the four uses for VLANs discussed in this chapter, which one is the most appropriate?

A. Security

B. Broadcast domains

C. Departmental grouping

D. Segmenting protocols

Correct Answer & Explanation: **D**. Using VLANS to implement a protocol such as that used for VOIP is an extremely effective use of VLANS.

Incorrect Answers & Explanations: **A**, **B**, and **C**. Answer **A** is incorrect, because security is not the focus of this solution. Answer **B** is incorrect, because we are not controlling broadcasts in this situation. Answer **C** is incorrect, there is no departmental issue especially since VOIP is most often implemented network wide.

5. There are a series of different networking devices in your corporate network. VLANs can be created on with of the following devices?

A. HUB

B. Network interface card

C. Wireless access point

D. Switch

Correct Answer & Explanation: **D**. VLANS can only be created on networking switches.

Incorrect Answers & Explanations: **A**, **B**, and **C**. Answer **A** is incorrect, a hub is a device that just repeats the signal and does no intelligent switching. Answer **B** is incorrect, VLANS are not created on wireless access points; there are no VLANS in wireless. Answer **C** is incorrect, though some network cards may be able to use VLANS, they cannot create VLANS.

6. Your network has several departments that are spread over several different floors in a building. HR resides on both the 1st and 3rd floor. Why would we use VLANs in this situation? There are a series of different networking devices in your corporate network.

   A. Departmental grouping
   B. Security
   C. Broadcast domains
   D. Segmenting protocols

Correct Answers & Explanations: **A** and **B**. VLANS can be used to protect the confidential data in human resources as well as providing a departmental grouping for all the users in the HR department.

Incorrect Answers & Explanations: **C** and **D**. Answer **C** is incorrect, the VLANS for above may separate a broadcast domain, but this is not the main focus for the HR department. Answer **D** is incorrect, VLANS are not used in this scenario to segment any protocols for HR.

7. You have been tasked with creating VLANs to solve broadcast issues. You access the switch and go to global configuration mode, what is the correct command for creating VLAN 3?

   A. *Switch#VLAN 3*
   B. *Switch(config-if)#VLAN 3*
   C. *Switch>VLAN 3*
   D. *Switch(config)#VLAN 3*

Correct Answer & Explanation: **D**. This is the proper mode, global configuration mode to create the VLAN.

Incorrect Answers & Explanations: **A**, **B**, and **C**. Answer **A** is incorrect, this is privileged exec mode. Answer **B** is incorrect, this is interface configuration mode. Answer **C** is incorrect, this is user exec mode.

8. You have been tasked with setting the IP address on VLAN. You access the switch, what is the correct command for creating VLAN 3?

   A. *Switch#ip address 10.1.1.1 255.0.0.0*

   B. *Switch(config-if)# ip address 10.1.1.1 255.0.0.0*

   C. *Switch> ip address 10.1.1.1 255.0.0.0*

   D. *Switch(config)# ip address 10.1.1.1 255.0.0.0*

   Correct Answer & Explanation: **B**. This is the proper mode, interface configuration mode.

   Incorrect Answers & Explanations: **A**, **C**, and **D**. Answer **A** is incorrect, this is privileged exec mode. Answer **C** is incorrect, this is user exec mode. Answer **D** is incorrect, this is global configuration mode.

9. You have been tasked with setting the IP address on VLAN. You access the switch, if the VLAN is inactive, what command do you issue to activate the interface?

   A. *Switch(config-if)# activate*   **C.** *Switch(config-if)# turnon*

   B. *Switch(config-if)# reactivate* **D.** *Switch(config-if)# no shutdown*

   Correct Answer & Explanation: **D**. We use the opposite of the shutdown command *No Shutdown* to turn on a VLAN interface.

   Incorrect Answers & Explanations: **A**, **B**, and **C**. Answer **A** is incorrect, there is no such command. Answer **B** is incorrect, there is no such command. Answer **C** is incorrect, there is no such command.

10. You have been tasked with setting up a new VLAN. You are to name this new VLAN HR. What is the correct command for creating setting the name to HR?

    A. *Switch#name HR*   **C.** *Switch(config-vlan)# name HR*

    B. *Switch(config-if)# name HR* **D.** *Switch(config)# name HR*

    Correct Answer & Explanation: **C**. This is the proper mode, VLAN configuration mode.

    Incorrect Answers & Explanations: **A**, **B**, and **D**. Answer **A** is incorrect, this is privileged exec mode. Answer **B** is incorrect, this is interface configuration mode. Answer **D** is incorrect, this is global configuration mode.

11. You have been tasked with setting up a new VLAN, VLAN 6. You are to name this new VLAN Production. What is the correct command for creating this VLAN?

    A. *Switch#vlan 4*

       Switch(config-vlan)# name production

    B. *Switch(config-if)# vlan 4*

       Switch(config-vlan)# name production

    C. *Switch(config-vlan)# vlan 4*

       Switch(config-vlan)# name production

    D. *Switch(config)# vlan 4*

       Switch(config-vlan)# name production

    Correct Answer & Explanation: **D**. This is the proper mode, you start in global configuration mode, and then transition to VLAN configuration mode.

    Incorrect Answers & Explanations: **A**, **B**, and **C**. Answer **A** is incorrect, this is privileged exec mode. Answer **B** is incorrect, this is interface configuration mode. Answer **C** is incorrect, this is VLAN configuration mode.

12. You have been tasked with renaming an existing VLAN. You are to name this new VLAN HR. What is the correct command for creating setting the name to HR?

    A. *Switch(config-vlan)# name HR*

    B. *Switch(config-vlan)# rename HR*

    C. *Switch(config-vlan)# newname HR*

    D. *Switch(config-vlan)# vlan name HR*

    Correct Answer & Explanation: **A**. This is the proper command, the name overrides the previous name for the VLAN.

    Incorrect Answers & Explanations: **B**, **C**, and **D**. Answer **B** is incorrect, there is no such command. Answer **C** is incorrect, this is no such command. Answer **D** is incorrect, there is no such command.

13. You have been tasked with assigning port fa0/1 to VLAN 3. What is the correct command for assigning putting this port into an access mode?

    A. *Switch(config-if)# switchport mode trunk*

    B. *Switch(config-if)# switchport mode access*

    C. *Switch(config-if)# switchport mode VLAN*

    D. *Switch(config-if)# switchport access*

Correct Answer & Explanation: **B**. This is the proper command, this puts the port into access mode.

Incorrect Answers & Explanations: **A**, **C**, and **D**. Answer **A** is incorrect, this puts the port into trunking mode. Answer **C** is incorrect, this is no such command. Answer **D** is incorrect, the command is missing the word mode.

14. You have been tasked assigning port fa0/3 to VLAN 100. What is the correct command for creating setting the name to HR?
    A. *Switch(config-if)# switchport access VLAN 100*
    B. *Switch(config-if)# access VLAN 100*
    C. *Switch(config-if)# switchport 100*
    D. *Switch(config-if)# VLAN 100 add*

Correct Answer & Explanation: **A**. This is the proper command; this command assigns the port to VLAN 100.

Incorrect Answers & Explanations: **B**, **C**, and **D**. Answer **B** is incorrect, you need the switchport command. Answer **C** is incorrect, you need to include the term access and VLAN. Answer **D** is incorrect, there is no such command.

15. You are setting up a network where you will be having different kinds of traffic based on protocol. You should set up what type of VLAN?
    A. static   C. dynamic
    B. traffic   D. switching

Correct Answer & Explanation: **C**. Dynamic VLANS can be setup to assign VLANS based on different types of traffic.

Incorrect Answers & Explanations: **A**, **B**, and **D**. Answer **A** is incorrect, static VLANS are setup using port-based assignment. Answer **B** is incorrect, there is no such type of VLAN. Answer **D** is incorrect, there is no such type of VLAN.

16. You are setting up a network where PCs need to be assigned based on department. These PCs will not be moved, what type of VLAN should you set up?
    A. Dynamic   C. Port-based
    B. Traffic-based D. Protocol-based

Correct Answer & Explanation: **C**. The VLANS should be port-based as the systems will not change often.

Incorrect Answers & Explanations: **A**, **B**, and **D**. Answer **A** is incorrect, you would not need to set up an dynamic VLAN because the machines will not be moving locations. Answer **B** is incorrect, VLANS would not need to be assigned based on traffic. Answer **D** is incorrect, VLANS would not need to be assigned based on protocol.

17. The standard VLANs are stored in a file on our switch. What is that file called?

   A. VLAN.SDR   **C.** VLAN.SWITCH

   B. VLAN   **D.** VLAN.DAT

   Correct Answer & Explanation: **D**. The standard VLANS that have been configured are stored in a file called VLAN.DAT.

   Incorrect Answers & Explanations: **A**, **B**, and **C**. Answer **B** is incorrect, this is not the name of the file. Answer **C** is incorrect, this is not the name of the file. Answer **D** is incorrect, this is not the name of the file.

18. The standard VLANs use only a portion of the total VLANs that are available. From what range do the standard VLANs come from?

   A. 1 to 1,024   **C.** 1 to 100

   B. 1 to 1,005   **D.** 1 to 4,094

   Correct Answer & Explanation: **B**. The standard VLANS stretch from VLAN 1 through VLAN 1,006.

   Incorrect Answers & Explanations: **A**, **C**, and **D**. Answer **A** is incorrect, this is the range for the standard port numbers. Answer **C** is incorrect, this is the range for the standard ACLS. Answer **D** is incorrect, this is the full range of VLAN numbers.

19. VLANs are supported on several different network types on a Cisco Switch. Which one of the following is not supported in standard VLANs?

   A. Ethernet   **C.** FDDI

   B. Arcnet   **D.** Token Ring

   Correct Answer & Explanation: **B**. The ArcNet is a networking standard that is not supported by Cisco VLANS.

   Incorrect Answers & Explanations: **A**, **C**, and **D**. Answer **A** is incorrect, Ethernet is supported. Answer **C** is incorrect, FDDI is supported. Answer **D** is incorrect, Token Ring is supported.

20. Extended VLANs are configurable on Cisco switches but do not have the functionality of standard VLANs. What VLAN numbers represent extended VLANs?

A. 1,000 to 4,094   **C.** 100 to 4,094

B. 1,006 to 4,094   **D.** 1 to 4,094

Correct Answer & Explanation: **B**. Extended VLANS are numbered 1,006–4,094.

Incorrect Answers & Explanations: **A**, **C**, and **D**. Answer **A**, **C** and **D** are incorrect because Cisco only uses 1,006–4,094 for the extended VLAN range.

21. The extended VLANs are stored in a different location than our standard VLANs. Where are extended VLANs stored?

A. Running-config   **C.** Memory

B. Flash   **D.** VLAN.DAT

Correct Answer & Explanation: **A**. Extended VLANS are stored in the Running-Config file.

Incorrect Answers & Explanations: **B**, **C**, and **D**. Answer **B** is incorrect, the Flash does not store VLANS directly. Answer **C** is incorrect, the switch memory does not store VLANS directly. Answer **D** is incorrect, standard VLANS are stored in the VLAN.DAT.

22. The standard VLANs are stored in the VLAN.DAT file. Where does this file reside?

A. Running-config   **C.** Memory

B. Flash   **D.** Hard drive

Correct Answer & Explanation: **B**. The VLAN.DAT is stored in flash.

Incorrect Answers & Explanations: **A**, **C**, and **D**. Answer **A** is incorrect, the Running-Config contains the extended VLANS. Answer **C** is incorrect, the VLAN.DAT has to be stored in a non volatile medium. Answer **D** is incorrect, switches do not contain hard drives normally.

23. To completely clear a switch of all VLAN information, you must erase the startup-config and do what of the following?

A. Clear the whole flash.   **C.** Reset the memory.

B. Erase the Running-Config.   **D.** Delete the Flash:VLAN.DAT.

Correct Answer & Explanation: **D**. The VLAN.DAT must be deleted as well from flash.

Incorrect Answers & Explanations: **A**, **B**, and **C**. Answer **A** is incorrect, clearing the whole flash would clear the IOS as well. Answer **B** is incorrect, the running-config only clears current VLANS and those VLANs will come back after a restart of the switch. Answer **C** is incorrect, there is no way to reset the memory.

24. There are several ways to verify VLAN assignment for the ports on the system. Choose the correct *show* command.

    A. *SHOW VLAN*   **C.** *VLAN SHOW*

    B. *SHOW VLANS*   **D.** *SHOW ALL VLANS*

Correct Answer & Explanation: **A**. *SHOW VLAN* will show you the VLANS and ports that are associated with them.

Incorrect Answers & Explanations: **B**, **C**, and **D**. Answer **B** is incorrect, and it should not be plural. Answer **C** is incorrect, incorrect usage of the command. Answer **D** is incorrect, not a valid command.

25. You would like to view all available VLANs in an abbreviated form. Which show command will allow you to view the VLANs in this form?

    A. *SHOW VLAN*   **C.** *SHOW VLAN 1*

    B. *SHOW VLAN BRIEF*   **D.** *SHOW VLANS*

Correct Answer & Explanation: **B**. *SHOW VLAN BRIEF* will show you the VLANS and ports that are associated with them in an abbreviated form.

Incorrect Answers & Explanations: **A**, **C**, and **D**. Answer **A** is incorrect, it will show the VLANS plus statistics. Answer **C** is incorrect, this will only show the information for VLAN 1. Answer **D** is incorrect, not a valid command.

26. Your company has a homogenous infrastructure made up of only Cisco switches. You wish to use a proprietary Cisco only VLAN protocol, which one would you choose?

    A. 802.1Q   **C.** Interswitch link (ISL)

    B. 802.10   **D.** LANE (LAN emulation)

Correct Answer & Explanation: **C**. This is the Cisco proprietary protocol that is being phased out of newer Cisco switches for VLANS.

Incorrect Answers & Explanations: **A**, **B**, and **D**. Answer **A** is incorrect, 802.1Q is an IEEE standard. Answer **B** is incorrect, this is an IEEE standard for FDDI VLANS. Answer **D** is incorrect, this is the standard for ATM VLANS.

27. Your company has an infrastructure made up of FDDI connections. You wish to use a VLAN protocol to segment the FDDI ring networks, which one would you choose?

    A. 802.1Q

    B. 802.10

    C. Interswitch link

    D. LANE

    Correct Answer & Explanation: **B**. This is the IEEE standard for FDDI VLANS.

    Incorrect Answers & Explanations: **A**, **C**, and **D**. Answer **A** is incorrect, 802.1Q is an IEEE standard. Answer **C** is incorrect, this is a Cisco proprietary standard for VLANS. Answer **D** is incorrect, this is the standard for ATM VLANS.

28. Your company has an infrastructure made up of ATM connections which you want to control via a less complicated VLAN solution. You wish to use a VLAN protocol to segment the ATM networks, which one would you choose?

    A. 802.1Q

    B. 802.10

    C. Interswitch link

    D. LANE

    Correct Answer & Explanation: **D**. This is the standard to control ATM connections for VLANS.

    Incorrect Answers & Explanations: **A**, **B**, and **C**. Answer **A** is incorrect, 802.1Q is an IEEE standard. Answer **B** is incorrect, this is an IEEE standard for FDDI VLANS. Answer **C** is incorrect, this is a Cisco proprietary standard for VLANS.

29. Your company has an infrastructure made up of many different kinds of switching equipment for Ethernet. You wish to use a VLAN protocol to interconnect this equipment, which one would you choose?

    A. 802.1Q

    B. 802.10

    C. Interswitch link

    D. LANE

    Correct Answer & Explanation: **A**. This is the IEEE standard that allows you to use equipment from many different vendors.

Incorrect Answers & Explanations: **B**, **C**, and **D**. Answer **B** is incorrect, this is an IEEE standard for FDDI VLANS. Answer **C** is incorrect, this is a Cisco proprietary standard for VLANS. Answer **D** is incorrect, this is the standard for ATM VLANS.

30. You have implemented VLANs on your network. You wish to make sure that all the ports in your switch are set to access mode. How would you verify that fact?

    A. SHOW FLASH

    B. SHOW VLAN B1

    C. SHOW RUNNING-CONFIG

    D. SHOW VTP STATUS

    Correct Answer & Explanation: C. SHOW RUNNING-CONFIG will show you the configuration mode for each port.

    Incorrect Answers & Explanations: **A**, **B**, and **D**. Answer **A** is incorrect, this will show what is on the flash memory. Answer **B** is incorrect, this will only show the information for VLAN 1. Answer **D** is incorrect, not a valid command.

31. You have recently made changes to the VLANs in your network. You would like to clear all the statistics of VLAN information to get a fresh start. What command would allow you to reset VLAN statistics?

    A. *CLEAR VTP COUNTERS*

    B. *ERASE STARTUP-CONFIG*

    C. *ERASE FLASH*

    D. *ERASE VLAN.DAT*

    Correct Answer & Explanation: **A**. The *CLEAR VTP COUNTERS* command will reset the statistics for VLANS.

    Incorrect Answers & Explanations: **B**, **C**, and **D**. Answer **B** is incorrect, this would erase the startup-config. Answer **C** is incorrect, this would erase flash. Answer **D** is incorrect, not a valid command.

Chapter 14: VLAN Trunking Protocol

1. Your network has a large number of VLANs which must be configured on multiple switches. Which of the following protocols allow you to replicate your VLAN information to the different switches?

    A. 802.1Q

    B. ISL

    C. LANE

    D. Cisco VTP

    Correct Answer & Explanation: D. Cisco VTP is a proprietary protocol for exchanging VLAN information among Cisco switches.

Incorrect Answers & Explanations: **A**, **B**, and **C**. Answer **A** is incorrect, as this is a VLAN tagging protocol for Ethernet networks. Answer **B** is incorrect. This is a Cisco proprietary VLAN tagging protocol for Ethernet networks. Answer **C** is incorrect. This is a VLAN tagging protocol for ATM networks.

2. Your network has a large number of VLANs which must be configured on multiple switches. You wish to replicate this information on your Token Ring network that comprised older Cisco equipment, which version of VTP would you use?

   A. Version 1   **C.** Version 3

   B. Version 2   **D.** Version 4

   Correct Answer & Explanation: **B**. Version 2 supports Token Ring networks. Figure 14.16 shows you how to configure VTP version 2.

```
Switch>enable
Switch#configure terminal
Enter configuration commands, one per line.  End with CNTL/Z.
Switch(config)#vtp version 2
Switch(config)#^Z
%SYS-5-CONFIG_I: Configured from console by console
```

FIGURE 14.16

Enabling VTP Version 2

   Incorrect Answers & Explanations: **A**, **C**, and **D**. Answer **A** is incorrect, version 1 does not support Token Ring networks. Answer **C** is incorrect. This version would support Token Ring but is only available on newer switches. Answer **D** is incorrect. This is no version 4.

3. Your network has a large number of VLANs which must be configured on multiple switches. What mode must the port be put into to accomplish sending multiple VLANs data between switches?

   A. Connected   **C.** Trunk

   B. Access   **D.** STP

   Correct Answer & Explanation: **C**. The port that connects the two switches together to exchange VLAN data is called a trunk port. It can carry multiple VLANS worth of data independently.

   Incorrect Answers & Explanations: **A**, **B**, and **D**. Answer **A** is incorrect. There is no mode called connected. Answer **B** is incorrect. Access mode is when only a single VLANS information is carried. Answer **D** is incorrect. STP is Spanning Tree Protocol and does not have anything to do with VLANS.

4. Your network has a large number of VLANs which must be configured on multiple switches. You wish to replicate this information on your Ethernet network. Which version of VTP would you use?

   A. Version 1

   B. Version 2

   C. Version 3

   D. Version 4

   Correct Answer & Explanation: **A**. Version 1 is recommended unless you have a need for Token Ring or you have newer Cisco Catalyst switches.

   Incorrect Answers & Explanations: **B**, **C**, and **D**. Answer **B** is incorrect, version 2 is not needed for Ethernet networks. Answer **C** is incorrect. This version is only available on newer switches. Answer **D** is incorrect. This is no version 4.

5. Your network has a large number of VLANs which must be configured on multiple switches. You wish to replicate this information on your Ethernet network. You need a focal point to make all changes to the VLAN which is Switch1. What VTP mode would you set Switch1 to?

   A. Server

   B. Client

   C. Transparent

   D. Off

   Correct Answer & Explanation: **A**. VTP mode server replicates its VLAN information to clients.

   Incorrect Answers & Explanations: **B**, **C**, and **D**. Answer **B** is incorrect; clients receive their VLAN information from the server. Answer **C** is incorrect; transparent does not apply VLAN information from server but does forward VTP messages. Answer **D** is incorrect; off uses standalone information for VLANS.

6. Your network has a large number of VLANs which must be configured on multiple switches. You wish to replicate this information on your Ethernet network. Switch2 needs to gain it's VLAN information from Switch1. What VTP mode would you set Switch2 to?

   A. Server

   B. Client

   C. Transparent

   D. Off

Correct Answer & Explanation: **B**. VTP mode client replicates its VLAN information from the server.

Incorrect Answers & Explanations: **A**, **C**, and **D**. Answer **A** is incorrect. Server sends its information to other switches. Answer **C** is incorrect. Transparent does not apply VLAN information from server but does forward VTP messages. Answer **D** is incorrect. Off uses standalone information for VLANS.

7. Your network has a large number of VLANs which must be configured on multiple switches. You wish to replicate this information on your Ethernet network. You have Switch3 that has specialized VLAN information that must not be changed. Switch3 is between Switch1 and Switch2 that need to replicate VLAN information. What VTP mode would you set Switch3 to?

   A. Server
   B. Client
   C. Transparent
   D. Off

Correct Answer & Explanation: **C**. VTP mode transparent forwards VTP messages but does not apply the information to its database.

Incorrect Answers & Explanations: **A**, **B**, and **D**. Answer **A** is incorrect; server sends its information to other switches. Answer **B** is incorrect; clients receive their VLAN information from the server. Answer **D** is incorrect; off uses standalone information for VLANS.

8. Your network has a large number of VLANs which must be configured on multiple switches. You wish to replicate this information on your network. You have Switch4 that does not need to exchange VLAN information with others. What VTP mode would you set Switch4 to?

   A. Server
   B. Client
   C. Transparent
   D. Off

Correct Answer & Explanation: **A**. VTP mode server replicates its VLAN information to clients.

Incorrect Answers & Explanations: **B**, **C**, and **D**. Answer **B** is incorrect. Clients receive their VLAN information from the server. Answer **C** is incorrect. Transparent does not apply VLAN information from server but does forward VTP messages. **D** is incorrect as Off mode uses standalone information for VLANS.

9. Your network has a large number of VLANs which must be configured on multiple switches. You wish to replicate this information
on your network. You have Switch1 that will be the focal point for
VLAN information. What command would you use to set this switch
to this mode?

A. *Vtp mode client*

C. *Vtp mode transparent*

B. *Vtp mode server*

D. *Vtp mode off*

Correct Answer & Explanation: **B.** To set the switch to VTP server,
you use the *vtp mode server* command. In Figure 14.17, you see how
to set the switch to VTP server mode.

FIGURE 14.17

*Setting the Switch to VTP
Server Mode*

```
Switch>enable
Switch#configure terminal
Enter configuration commands, one per line.   End with CNTL/Z.
Switch(config)#vtp mode server
Device mode already VTP SERVER.
Switch(config)#
```

Incorrect Answers & Explanations: **A**, **C**, and **D**. Answer **A** is incorrect; this sets the switch to VTP client. Answer **C** is incorrect; this
sets the switch to VTP transparent. Answer **D** is incorrect; this sets
the switch to not use VTP.

10. Your network has a large number of VLANs which must be configured on multiple switches. You wish to replicate this information on
your network. To group together your VLAN information, you need
to create what?

A. Group

C. Switchblock

B. Vtp group

D. Domain

Correct Answer & Explanation: **D.** To have a VTP infrastructure,
you need to create a management domain.

Incorrect Answers & Explanations: **A**, **B**, and **C**. Answer **A** is
incorrect; a group is not the unit to administer VLANS. Answer **B**
is incorrect; a VTP group is not used to administer VLANS. Answer
C is incorrect; a switchblock is a group of switches but not a unit
of VTP.

11. Your network has a large number of VLANs which must be configured on multiple switches. You wish to replicate this information on your network. You want to create a VTP management domain CORP. What command would you use to create that?

   A. *VTP CORP*

   B. *VLAN VTP CORP*

   C. *VTP DOMAIN CORP*

   D. *VLAN DOMAIN CORP*

   Correct Answer & Explanation: **C**. This command would set the switch to management domain CORP.

   Incorrect Answers & Explanations: **A**, **B**, and **D**. Answer **A** is incorrect. This is not a valid command. Answer **B** is incorrect; this is not a valid command. Answer **D** is incorrect; this is not a valid command.

12. Your network has a large number of VLANs which must be configured on multiple switches. You wish to replicate this information on your network. You want to set a switch to support VTP for Token Ring networks. What command would you use to enable that?

   A. *Version 1*

   B. *Version 2*

   C. *Vtp version 1*

   D. *Vtp version 2*

   Correct Answer & Explanation: **D**. This command would set the switch to VTP version 2 which allows Token Ring VLANS.

   Incorrect Answers & Explanations: **A**, **B**, and **C**. Answer **A** is incorrect. This is not a valid command. Answer **B** is incorrect; this is not a valid command. Answer **C** is incorrect; this sets the switch to VTP version 1 which does not support Token Ring.

13. Your network has a large number of VLANs which must be configured on multiple switches. You wish to replicate this information on your network. You want to set a switch to support VTP for Token Ring networks. You are concerned about security, what command would you use to protect your VLAN information using the password password?

   A. *Password password*

   B. *Vtp password password*

   C. *VLAN password password*

   D. *No vtp password password*

   Correct Answer & Explanation: **B**. This command would set the switch to use VTP password PASSWORD.

Incorrect Answers & Explanations: **A**, **C**, and **D**. Answer **A** is incorrect. This is not a valid command. Answer **B** is incorrect; this is not a valid command. Answer **D** is incorrect; this would remove the password.

14. Your network has a large number of VLANs which must be configured on multiple switches. You wish to replicate this information on your network. You need to change the management domain from CORP1 to CORP2. What command would you use to accomplish this task?

   A. *VTP DOMAIN CORP1 CORP2*

   B. *VTP DOMAIN CORP2 CORP1*

   C. *VTP DOMAIN CHANGE CORP2*

   D. *VTP DOMAIN CORP2*

   Correct Answer & Explanation: **D**. This command would set the switch to use VTP domain to CORP2.

   Incorrect Answers & Explanations: **A**, **B**, and **C**. Answer **A** is incorrect. This is not a valid command. Answer **B** is incorrect; this is not a valid command. Answer **C** is incorrect; this is not a valid command.

15. Your network has a large number of VLANs which must be configured on multiple switches. You wish to replicate this information on your network. You are having problems with a switch and want to remove its VTP password. What command would you use to remove a VTP password?

   A. *No vtp password*   **C.** *No vlan password*

   B. *No password*   **D.** *Vtp password null*

   Correct Answer & Explanation: **A**. This command would set the switch to not use a VTP password.

   Incorrect Answers & Explanations: **B**, **C**, and **D**. Answer **B** is incorrect. This is not a valid command. Answer **B** is incorrect; this is not a valid command. Answer **D** is incorrect; this would set the password to NULL.

16. Your network has a large number of VLANs which must be configured on multiple switches. You wish to see the current state of VTP on the system. What command would you use to show the current VTP configuration?

   A. *Show vtp counters*   **C.** *Show vlan*

   B. *Show vtp status*   **D.** *Show running-config*

Correct Answer & Explanation: **B**. This command would show the current configuration for VTP on the switch.

Incorrect Answers & Explanations: **A**, **C**, and **D**. Answer **A** is incorrect; this would show the current statistics for VTP on the switch. Answer **B** is incorrect; this command shows VLAN and not VTP information. Answer **D** is incorrect; this command shows the running-configuration.

17. Your network has a large number of VLANs which must be configured on multiple switches. You wish to see what errors have occurred with VTP transmissions on the switch. What command would you use to show this statistics current VTP configuration?

    A. *Show vtp counters*   **C.** *Clear vtp counters*
    B. *Show vtp status*   **D.** *Show running-config*

Correct Answer & Explanation: **A**. This command would show the current statistics on the switch including the errors.

Incorrect Answers & Explanations: **B**, **C**, and **D**. Answer **B** is incorrect; this would show the VTP configuration but not statistics. Answer **C** is incorrect; this clears the statistics. Answer **D** is incorrect; this command shows the running-configuration.

18. Your network has a large number of VLANs which must be configured on multiple switches. You wish to see how many errors are occurring, and you want to look at current information. What command would you use to set these statistics to a clean state?

    A. *Show vtp counters*   **C.** *Clear vtp counters*
    B. *Show vtp status*   **D.** *Show running-config*

Correct Answer & Explanation: **C**. This command would clear the current statistics.

Incorrect Answers & Explanations: **A**, **B**, and **D**. Answer **A** is incorrect; this shows the current VTP statistics. Answer **B** is incorrect; this shows the current VTP status. Answer **D** is incorrect; this command shows the running-configuration.

19. Your network has a large number of VLANs which must be configured on multiple switches. You wish to see how many advertisements are occurring. What command would you use to see this information?

    A. *Show vtp counters*   **C.** *Clear vtp counters*
    B. *Show vtp status*   **D.** *Show running-config*

Correct Answer & Explanation: **A**. This command would show the current statistics including how many advertisements.

Incorrect Answers & Explanations: **B**, **C**, and **D**. Answer **B** is incorrect; this shows the current VTP status. Answer **C** is incorrect; this clears the current VTP statistics. Answer **D** is incorrect; this command shows the running-configuration.

20. Your network has a large number of VLANs which must be configured on multiple switches. You are unable to connect to switches that are using a VTP password. What command would you use to see the MD5 digest for a switch?

   A. *Show vtp counters*   **C.** *Clear vtp counters*

   B. *Show vtp status*   **D.** *Show running-config*

Correct Answer & Explanation: **B**. This command includes the MD5 digest.

Incorrect Answers & Explanations: **A**, **C**, and **D**. Answer **A** is incorrect; this does not show the digest. Answer **C** is incorrect; this does not show the MD5 digest. Answer **D** is incorrect; this command does not show the MD5 digest.

21. Your network has a large number of VLANs which must be configured on multiple switches. Some switches do not have ports that are in all the VLANs in the enterprise. What would you enable to keep these switches from having unnecessary broadcast traffic?

   A. VTP server   **C.** VTP pruning

   B. 802.1Q   **D.** VTP transparent

Correct Answer & Explanation: **C**. VTP pruning allows switches that don't have ports in a certain VLAN from receiving unnecessary broadcast traffic.

Incorrect Answers & Explanations: **A**, **B**, and **D**. Answer **A** is incorrect; this is a VTP mode. Answer **B** is incorrect; this is a VLAN Tagging Protocol. Answer **D** is incorrect; this is a VTP mode.

22. Your network has a large number of VLANs which must be configured on multiple switches. Some switches do not have ports that are in all the VLANs in the enterprise. You have enabled VTP pruning on these switches, yet they are still receiving traffic. What must you also do to keep these switches from receiving unnecessary broadcast traffic?

A. Reload the switch.

B. Make the unused VLANs prune eligible.

C. Enable trunking.

D. Set the mode to server.

Correct Answer & Explanation: **B**. VTP pruning allows switches that don't have ports in a certain VLAN from receiving unnecessary broadcast traffic. Not only must it be enabled, but VLANS that are unused must be made prune eligible.

Incorrect Answers & Explanations: **A**, **C**, and **D**. Answer **A** is incorrect; reloading the switch will not solve the problem. Answer **C** is incorrect; trunking is already enabled to route VLAN traffic between switches. Answer **D** is incorrect; this is a VTP mode.

Chapter 15: Cisco WAN Configuration

1. In a typical WAN environment, your router loses connection to the service provider on Frame Relay link. Which of the following would most likely be the cause of the loss of connection?

   A. DCE lost clock rate

   B. DTE lost clock rate

   C. ISDN lost clock rate

   D. PPP lost clock rate

   Correct Answer & Explanation: **A**. Answer **A** is correct; the DCE (remember C for Clock and C for DCE) controls the clock signal for synchronization of the WAN Link.

   Incorrect Answers & Explanations: **B**, **C**, and **D**. Answer **B** is incorrect as the DTE side receives the signal from the DCE. Answer **C** is incorrect as ISDN is a completely different carrier than Frame Relay and does not use the clocking signal. Answer **D** is incorrect as it is an encapsulation format that Frame Relay could be carried over but is not relevant to the DTE/DCE circuit.

2. You are studying the legacy X.25 Protocol for the CCNA exam. What is the name of the X.25 device that connects the router to the X.25 cloud?

   A. Modem

   B. Router

   C. Switch

   D. PAD

   E. Hub

Correct Answer & Explanation: **D**. Answer **D** is correct; the Packet Assembler/Disassembler is the device that is used on the X.25 network.

Incorrect Answers & Explanations: **A**, **B**, **C**, and **E**. Answer **A** is incorrect as a Modem is either connected to the PSTN or the Cable Internet. Answer **B** is incorrect as the Router is a Layer 3 device and used the PAD to connect to the cloud. Answer **C** is incorrect as a Switch is used in the LAN to separate collision domains. Answer **E** is incorrect as Hubs are used in LANs to connect devices to the network.

3. You are setting up a point-to-point connection between your core router to a spoke router at a remote location. What is the appropriate command to set the clock rate on a Cisco router to support a full T1?

   A. *router>clockrate 1536000*

   B. *router#clockrate 1536000*

   C. *router(confiig-line)#clockrate 1536000*

   D. *router(config-if)#clockrate 1536000*

   E. *router(config)#clockrate 1536000*

Correct Answer & Explanation: **D**. Answer **D** is the correct answer; remember the clock rate will be set on a serial interface and the prompt for this is the router(config-if)# for interface configuration mode.

Incorrect Answers & Explanations: **A**, **B**, **C**, and **E**. Answer **A** is incorrect as the prompt shows you are in user exec mode, which is very limited in the commands that can be issued. Answer **B** is incorrect as you are only in privileged exec mode; while it is more powerful than user exec mode you can not make changes to the router. Answer **C** is incorrect as you are in a configuration mode you are in the line configuration mode and are working on the Console or the VTY ports of the router. Answer **E** is incorrect; you are in a config mode but at that level you are only able to change things global to the whole router.

4. You are diagnosing a Frame Relay circuit that has been working for a long time. The circuit is a full T1 from your service provider operating at full speed. You think that the service provider has dropped a piece of the header information. What field in the header would most likely cause this problem?

   A. BECN   **C.** DE

   B. FECN   **D.** DLCI

Correct Answer & Explanation: **D**. The correct answer is **D**; the Data Link Control Identifier is used to address the Frame Circuit and is normally passed automatically from the provider. If this is missing the link will go down.

Incorrect Answers & Explanations: **A**, **B**, and **C**. Answers **A** and **B** are incorrect as the BECN and FECN are used as indicators of congestion on the link and have nothing to do with addressing the circuit. Answer **C** is incorrect as the DE is used to determine if the packet is eligible to be discarded in the event of high load and latency on the circuit.

5. You are a network administrator and you are building a new facility. You have to chose between DSL and cable for your connectivity. Which of the following is the most important factor in determining between DSL and cable?
   A. Number of repeaters between source and destination
   B. Line of sight between source and destination
   C. Distance from the CO
   D. Cost of installation

   Correct Answer & Explanation: **C**. Answer **C** is the correct answer. Remember DSL has a maximum distance from the CO of 18000 ft.

   Incorrect Answers & Explanations: **A**, **B**, and **D**. Answer **A** is incorrect as this is not information that affects your decision as it most likely will not be available to you. Answer **B** is incorrect as Cable and DSL will use underground cable to connect to your facility, and line of sight is more for satellite and wireless broadband. Answer **D** is incorrect; as competition increases the cost of installation of Cable and DSL are nearly the same.

6. You are preparing for your CCNA exam and are studying the WAN terms for the test and the question that is asked is: Which of the following terms means the same as Smart Jack?
   A. Central office (CO)
   B. Customer premise equipment (CPE)
   C. Demarcation point (demarc)
   D. Last Mile
   E. Toll network

   Correct Answer & Explanation: **C**. The correct answer is **C**. Demarcation Point is used interchangeably with Smart Jack. Installers mostly use the term Demarc point, while sales and support call it Smart Jack.

Incorrect Answers & Explanations: **A, B, D,** and **E**. Answer **A** is incorrect as the CO is the place where all the business and residential links for a particular area of the city come together. Answer **B** is incorrect as the CPE is what plugs into the Smart Jack. Answer **D** is incorrect as the Last Mile is the providers connection to the Smart Jack. Answer **E** is incorrect as the Toll Network is the connections between Cos.

7. You are designing a new network connection from your office to a new office. You only need a fractional T1 circuit for this new office. You have decided to purchase three channels of a T1. What would the clock rate be on this link?

A. 1,536,000	**C.** 320,000
B. 192,000	**D.** 64,000

Correct Answer & Explanation: **B**. Answer **B** is correct. Remember the formula 64,000 × number of channels. So in this case, 64,000 × 3 = 192,000.

Incorrect Answers & Explanations: **A, C,** and **D**. Answer **A** is incorrect as 1,536,000 is a full T1. Answer **C** is incorrect as that would be five channels. Answer **D** is incorrect as 64,000 is a single channel.

8. You are in charge of designing the new office and all the networking and communications equipment and circuits for the new office. You have decided to purchase a PBX for the voice communications services. Which of the following services would you order to connect to your PBX?

A. T1	**C.** DSL
B. ISDN – PRI	**D.** Frame Relay

Correct Answer & Explanation: **B**. Answer **B** is correct. ISDN–PRI is similar to T1 but is designed primarily for Voice PBX connectivity. The key differences between PRI and T1 is how the signaling and control is handled. In a T1 you have 24 channels each 64 K and you lose 8 K of each channel for control and signaling. In the PRI you have 24 channels of 64 K and you get 23 64 K channels and lose one for signaling and control. T1 is primarily used for data and Voice Over Internet Protocol (VOIP) where PRIs are for Voice PBX systems.

Incorrect Answers & Explanations: **A**, **C**, and **D**. Answer **A** is incorrect; as we explained above, it is primarily used for Data and VOIP networks. Answer **C** is incorrect as DSL is not designed to handle older analog voice traffic, you would see DSL as a carrier for VOIP and Internet Data. Answer **D** is incorrect as Frame Relay is a data carrier protocol that can be used over a T1, there is a voice protocol called Voice Over Frame Relay that can carry digital voice traffic.

9. You are troubleshooting a T1 connection and the provider has asked you to provide some information about the Frame Relay connection. What command would you use to find the DLCI for the provider?
    A. *router# show frame-relay map*
    B. *router>show frame-relay map*
    C. *router(config)# show frame-relay map*
    D. *router(config-if)# show frame-relay map*
    E. *router(config-line)# show frame-relay map*

    Correct Answer & Explanation: **A**. Answer **A** is correct; the show frame-relay map command is issued in privileged exec mode.

    Incorrect Answers & Explanations: **B**, **C**, **D**, and **E**. Answer **B** is incorrect as the > indicates you are in user exec mode and have limited command functionality. Answer **C** is incorrect as you can not issue show command in global configuration mode. Answer **D** is incorrect as the config-if prompt signifies you are making changes to an interface. Answer **E** is incorrect as the config-line prompt says you are working with the console port or the vty sessions.

10. You are designing a new network for your company. They require 100 percent uptime even in the event of a single link failure. You are told that cost is no object. Which network model would you use to provide this functionality to your company?
    A. Full Mesh
    B. Partial Mesh
    C. Hub and Spoke

    Correct Answer & Explanation: **A**. The correct answer is **A**; if cost is not the major concern and you want full interconnectivity Full Mesh is the solution.

    Incorrect Answers & Explanations: **B** and C. Answer **B** is incorrect as there are links that can go down that could compromise connectivity, it is not as complete as Full Mesh. Answer **C** is incorrect as the Hub and Spoke does not provide redundant connections between links. The primary purpose of the Hub and Spoke is to provide for ease of setup and control of Internet access.

11. You are setting a hub and spoke network and are working on the core router. You want to tell the 3rd serial port on card 0 of the router to use the same IP address as the 1st port of the FastEthernet on card 3. What command would you use?

    A. *router(config)# interface serial 3/3*
       router(config-if)# ip unnumbered fastethernet 3/0
    B. *router(config)# interface serial 3/0*
       router(config-if)# ip unnumbered fastethernet 0/3
    C. *router(config)# interface serial 0/3*
       router(config-if)#ip unnumbered fastethernet 3/0
    D. *router(config)#interface serial 3/0*
       router(config-if) ip unnumbered fastethernet 3/0

    Correct Answer & Explanation: **C**. Answer **C** is correct; remember in the configuration of interfaces it is card number/port number, so for the serial it would be card 0 port 3, and for the fast Ethernet it would be 3/0 as port 0 would be the first.

    Incorrect Answers & Explanations: **A**, **B**, and **D**. Answer **A** is incorrect as it would be card 3 and port 3 which is incorrect, but on the fast Ethernet card 3 is correct and port 0 is correct. Answer **B** is incorrect as it is backwards from our intention. Answer **D** is incorrect as you would be trying to tie the address on serial 3/0 to the same card and port and you will not find mixed ports on a single card.

12. You are studying for your CCNA exam; you are reading the section that talks about default gateways or gateways of last resort. The question is, what character signifies that a static route is the candidate default/gateway of last resort?

    A. S and   **C.** S*
    B. S#   **D.** S@

    Correct Answer & Explanation: **C**. Answer **C** is the correct answer. The * is the candidate default as highlighted in the output below which is the key for the Cisco router:

```
Codes: I  -  IGRP derived, R  -  RIP derived, O  -  OSPF
   derived,
C  -  connected, S  -  static, E  -  EGP derived, B  -  BGP
   derived,
* - candidate default route, IA  -  OSPF inter area route,
i  -  IS-IS derived, ia  -  IS-IS, U  -  per-user static
   route,
o  -  on-demand routing, M  -  mobile, P  -  periodic downloaded
   static route,
D  -  EIGRP, EX  -  EIGRP external, E1  -  OSPF external type
   1 route,
E2  -  OSPF external type 2 route, N1  -  OSPF NSSA external
   type 1 route,
N2  -  OSPF NSSA external type 2 route
```

Incorrect Answers & Explanations: **A**, **B**, and **D**. Answers **A**, **B** and **D** are incorrect as they are not used in the Cisco router routing key.

13. You are setting up a network and your company has chosen to go with the Hub and Spoke topology. You are trying to determine how many routes you have to create on each spoke in a 25-spoke network. What is the number of routes you have to configure on each spoke?

   A. 25   **D.** 10

   B. 12   **E.** 1

   C. 0

   Correct Answer & Explanation: **E**. Answer **E** is correct; the only route you have to set on the spoke is the gateway of last resort; the core router handles routing between offices and passes traffic destined to the Internet out its gateway.

   Incorrect Answers & Explanations: **A**, **B**, **C**, and **D**. Answers **A**, **B**, **C** and **D** are incorrect as the spoke only needs one route set; the core router would need one route for each remote office and 1 for the default gateway so the core would need 26 routes setup.

14. You are working for a large company and are setting up a new router for a branch location. This router is to connect the company to the internet. What command would you type to set the gateway of last resort to send all traffic that does not have an entry in the routing table to pass traffic to the ISP on serial 0?

Correct Answers & Explanation: Correct answer is: ip route 0.0.0.0 0.0.0.0 s0

or ip route 0 0 s0

Either of these commands would be acceptable on the exam. This creates the entry in the routing table that shows as the gateway of last resort and the S* candidate default.

15. You are studying for the CCNA exam and are studying the WAN Configuration section. Match the following technologies with the appropriate layer of the OSI Model.

   A. Router   1 Physical

   B. CSU/DSU   2 Network

   C. Modem   3 Data Link

Correct Answers & Explanations: **A** – 2, **B** – 3, **C** – 1.

Routers are Layer 3 Network Layer Device (as they handle IP traffic)

CSU/DSU are Data Link (as the connect to Frame Relay networks)

Modems are Physical layer as they modulate and demodulate the bits (the 1s and 0s over the analog media)

Chapter 16: Configuring PPP and CHAP

1. You are a Cisco engineer assigned to configure a WAN connection for a company. You are configuring the WAN connection utilizing PPP. When using PPP, it's important to understand the underlying protocols used to facilitate processes such as link setup and, eventually, teardown of the circuit, link, or line. In PPP, which underlying protocol is responsible for establishing and configuring as well as testing, maintaining, and terminating PPP WAN-based connections? (Choose all that apply.)

   A. NCP   **C.** CDP

   B. LCP   **D.** X.25

Correct Answers & Explanations: **A**, **B**. Answer **A** is correct, because NCP is responsible for the configuration supporting network layer protocols. Answer **B** is correct, because LCP's primary responsibility is for a PPP connection. BRI and PRI are not components within PPP.

Incorrect Answers & Explanations: **C**, **D**. Answer **C** is incorrect, because CDP (Cisco Discovery Protocol) is not part of PPP; it's a proprietary Cisco protocol used for Cisco device discovery. Answer **D** is incorrect, because X.25 is a WAN protocol much like PPP, and is not part of PPP.

2. As a network consultant, you are asked to set up a secure way to connect a WAN link utilizing PPP. Which of the following statements regarding PPP authentication protocols is true? (Choose all that apply.)
   A. When CHAP is used over a WAN connection, the username and password are sent by the dialing router without encryption.
   B. When PAP is used over a WAN connection, the username and password are sent by the dialing router with encryption.
   C. When CHAP is used over a WAN connection, the username and password are sent by the dialing router with encryption.
   D. When PAP is used over a WAN connection, the username and password are sent by the dialing router without encryption.

   Correct Answers & Explanations: **C**, **D**. Answers **C** and **D** are correct, because when either CHAP or PAP are used over the WAN connection the username and password are sent by the dialing router with encryption.

   Incorrect Answers & Explanations: **A**, **B**. Answer **A** is incorrect, because CHAP does use encryption. When CHAP is used over a WAN connection, the router receiving the connection sends a challenge which includes a random number that can be input into an MD5 hash algorithm. Answer **B** is incorrect, because PAP does not use encryption. When PAP is used over a WAN connection, the username and password are sent by the dialing router without encryption.

3. Which of the following PPP sublayers is responsible for all of PPP's network layer protocol negotiations?
   A. IPCP
   B. LCP
   C. X.25
   D. NCP

   Correct Answer & Explanation: **D**. Answer **D** is correct, because NCP is responsible for all of PPP's network layer protocol negotiations.

   Incorrect Answers & Explanations: **A**, **B**, **C**. Answer **A** is incorrect, because IPCP is only one protocol within NCP. Although IPCP is IP's NCP, it's not responsible for handling all NCPs, such as

IPX/SPX-based IPXCP. Answer **B** is incorrect, because LCP handles lower-level PPP-based operations, not network layer-based operations. Answer **C** is incorrect, because X.25 is a WAN protocol much like PPP, and it does not use (or have) NCP. NCP is used to negotiate the network layer protocols. Commonly used NCPs are IPCP, IPXCP, ATCP, and CDPCP.

4. What verification command can show the current state of the PPP LCP?

   A. The *debug NCPLCP* command is used to verify the current state of PPP LCP negotiations.

   B. The *test-network* command is used to verify the current state of PPP LCP negotiations.

   C. The *show interface* command is used to verify the current state of PPP LCP negotiations.

   D. The *show network-status* command is used to verify the current state of PPP LCP negotiations.

Correct Answer & Explanation: C. Answer **C** is correct, because issuing the *show interface* command will verify the current state of PPP LCP negotiations. This is important to remember because on the CCNA exam, you may have to find out where PPP is configured on an interface and what that configuration consists of. When you use this command the output shown is that of the state of LCP, including what state it is currently in and what is in use. Some of the configured states are Open, Listen, Ack/Sent, and Term/Sent.

Incorrect Answers & Explanations: **A**, **B**, **D**. Answer **A** is incorrect, because the *debug NCPLCP* command is not a real Cisco command. Only *show interface* will show you the correct output. Answer **B** is incorrect, because the *test-network* command is not a real Cisco command. Only *show interface* will show you the correct output. Answer **D** is incorrect, because the *show network-status* command is not a real Cisco command. Only *show interface* will show you the correct output.

5. As a new Cisco engineer, you are configuring a set of routers using PPP. You need to configure CHAP authentication. What Cisco IOS configuration mode is used when enabling PPP authentication?

A. Interface Configuration mode

B. Global Configuration mode

C. PPP Configuration mode

D. Authentication Configuration mode

E. CHAP Configuration mode

Correct Answer & Explanation: **A**. Answer **A** is correct, because to configure authentication, first you enter Interface Configuration mode and then you enter the command *ppp authentication* and select *chap* or *pap* at the end of the string. You can use either PAP or CHAP depending on your needs.

Incorrect Answers & Explanations: **B**, **C**, **D**, **E**. Answer **B** is incorrect, because although you can enter and configure Global Configuration mode, PPP authentication is not configured there; it is configured only on the interface in which you need it. Answer **C** is incorrect, because there is no such thing as PPP Configuration mode. Answer **D** is incorrect, because there is no such thing as Authentication Configuration mode. Answer **E** is incorrect, because there is no such thing as CHAP Configuration mode.

6. Which of the following best describes the inherent problems of PPP using PAP during the LCP phase?

    A. PAP enables the client to control the authentication attempt.

    B. PAP will send the transmission across the wire unauthenticated.

    C. PAP during the LCP phase will send out Hello packets to find the adjacent router.

    D. PAP will use CHAP for its authentication and the handoff is unsafe.

Correct Answer & Explanation: **A**. Answer **A** is correct, because being the older of the two PPP authentication protocols, PAP has major security flaws, including sending passwords in clear text and allowing the client to choose when it sends the password. MD5 hashing and server control is a function of CHAP.

Incorrect Answers & Explanations: **B**, **C**, **D**. Answer **B** is incorrect, because PAP does not send data across the wire unauthenticated; it sends credentials to be authenticated across the wire in clear text. Answer **C** is incorrect, because no Hello packets are sent out via PPP,

LCP or otherwise. Answer **D** is incorrect, because PAP does not do a handoff to CHAP. PAP is unsafe to use if security is a major concern.

7. You are a network engineer looking to implement security on your network. Your WAN router is connected to two other routers on the other side of the world. You need to secure these three routers correctly. You would like to use a secure function of PPP to authenticate each device. A three-way handshake is preferred over a two-way handshake in terms of authentication methods available. Which PPP authentication protocol uses a three-way handshake and thus is the one you should configure on all of your network routers?

   A. NCP   C. PAP

   B. CHAP   D. LCP

   Correct Answer & Explanation: **B**. Answer **B** is correct, because CHAP uses a three-way handshake. The first shake is a local host requesting authentication. Next, the remote host sends an encrypted response. The local host then compares the information and accepts or rejects the connection attempt.

   Incorrect Answers & Explanations: **A, C, D**. Answer **A** is incorrect, because NCP is not an authentication protocol, but rather a part of PPP which allows for different OSI layer functionality. Answer **C** is incorrect, because PAP uses only a two-way handshake, not a three-way handshake. Answer **D** is incorrect, because LCP is not an authentication protocol, but rather a part of PPP which allows for different OSI layer functionality.

8. You are a network engineer trying to resolve a particularly difficult authentication problem. You are investigating the routers involved and are using debug commands. While troubleshooting, you try to find where authentication failures are taking place within PPP. Which protocol should you analyze to find the source of the issue?

   A. PPPoE

   B. LCP

   C. IPCP

   D. CDPCD

   E. CDP

   Correct Answer & Explanation: **B**. Answer **B** is correct, because LCP is the most important protocol functioning within PPP. LCP is considered the workhorse and is the protocol which negotiates all options related to PPP during the Link Establishment phase. Once Link Dead has passed and Link Establishment takes place, LCP handles authentication between peers.

Incorrect Answers & Explanations: **A**, **C**, **D**, **E**. Answer **A** is incorrect, because PPPoE (PPP over Ethernet) is not relevant to this question, although it is a functional PPP-based protocol. Answer **C** is incorrect, because IPCP is an NCP and NCP handles only upper-layer protocols, whereas LCP handles all options and negotiations at Layer 2 of the OSI model. Answer **D** is incorrect, because CDPCP is also an NCP, which does not handle negotiation of options. Answer **E** is incorrect, because CDP is a separate protocol that is not associated directly with PPP unless it is converted within NCP.

9. You are a Cisco engineer troubleshooting a PPP-based connectivity issue on an IPv6-based network. The routers were taken from an older IPv4 network and were installed on the one you are testing. You check that IPv4 is currently in use on the router and that PPP is configured. You find that you cannot communicate across your network. From the answers given, what is the reason you are not getting your routers to connect?

   A. You need to configure the correct NCP, which is IPv6CP. If you do not configure IPv6 on your routers, they will not be able to communicate over the network.

   B. You need to configure the correct LCP, which is IPv6CP. If you do not configure IPv6 on your routers, they will not be able to communicate over the network.

   C. You need to configure the correct NCP, which is IPv4CP. If you do not configure IPv6 on your routers, they will not be able to communicate over the network.

   D. You need to configure the correct LCP, which is IPNGCP. If you do not configure IPv6 on your routers, they will not be able to communicate over the network.

Correct Answer & Explanation: **A**. Answer **A** is correct, because PPP uses NCP for establishing and configuring different network layer protocols. The NCP phase in the PPP link connection process is used for establishing and configuring different network layer protocols, the most common of which are IP, IPX, and AppleTalk. With the advent of IPv6 (also known as IPng or Next Generation), you should know that PPP's corresponding NCP is called IPv6CP.

Incorrect Answers & Explanations: **B**, **C**, **D**. Answer **B** is incorrect, because LCP is not used, NCP is. Answer **C** is incorrect, because although NCP is used, IPv4CP is an incorrect label for IPCP. IPCP would be the wrong answer as well, since it's an IPv6-based network. Answer **D** is incorrect, because LCP is not used and IPNGCP is not the correct NCP name; it's called IPv6CP.

10. While configuring a network router, you need to find an interface in which to configure PPP for WAN communications among three sepa- rate routers. From the answers given, which interface type can you use to configure PPP? (Select all that apply.)

    A. Synchronous serial   **D.** HSSI

    B. Asynchronous serial   **E.** ISDN

    C. LMI

    Correct Answers & Explanations: **A**, **B**, **D**, **E**. Answers **A**, **B**, **D**, and **E** are correct, because PPP can operate on a variety of DTE and DCE-type interfaces. Most physical interfaces are supported, including ISDN, asynchronous serial, synchronous serial, and HSSI.

    Incorrect Answer & Explanation: **C**. Answer **C** is incorrect, because LMI (Local Management Interface) is a Frame Relay-based protocol used to help traffic flow on dedicated PVCs. Although *interface* is in the name of the protocol, LMI is not a physical interface, but rather a protocol.

11. As a network analyst, you are working on a solution for configuring PPP, and you are connecting one TCP/IP-based network to another TCP/IP-based network. You will need to communicate between both networks using IP. Which of the following statements regard- ing the PPP NCP-based IPCP protocol is true? (Choose all that apply.)

    A. IPCP will pass WINS and DNS information.

    B. IPCP will pass NDS information.

    C. IPCP will handle compression.

    D. You will need to use IPCP for address assignment.

    Correct Answers & Explanations: **A**, **C**, **D**. Answers **A**, **C**, and **D** are correct, because IPCP negotiates options such as compression and IP address assignment and configuration. IPCP can also be used to pass network-based information such as WINS and DNS server assignments.

Incorrect Answer & Explanation: **B**. Answer **B** is incorrect, because NDS (Novell Directory Services) is a Novell-based technology and is not passed along with IPCP information.

12. You are troubleshooting a WAN-based problem for your company. You want to configure an interface protocol that will allow error correction. From the answers given, which protocol listed will *not* provide error-correction features?

    A. SDLC
    B. HDLC
    C. PPP
    D. LAPD

    Correct Answer & Explanation: **B**. Answer **B** is correct, because although all WAN protocols provide error detection, HDLC does not provide error-correction capability. Essentially, HDLC will acknowledge that there is an error but will not perform corrections of any kind.

    Incorrect Answers & Explanations: **A**, **C**, **D**. Answer **A** is incorrect, because SDLC (Synchronous Data Link Control) does offer error-correction features. Answer **C** is incorrect, because PPP does offer error-correction features. Answer **D** is incorrect, because LAPD does offer error-correction features.

13. While solving an issue on a PPP-based connection, you notice that you do not have the correct encapsulation type on a particular interface on a troubled router. If Router A has a serial interface you would like to configure with DDR, what protocol choice given should be configured? (Choose only one answer.)

    A. HDLC
    B. SDLC
    C. X.25
    D. PPP

    Correct Answer & Explanation: **D**. Answer **D** is correct, because PPP can be used for both synchronous and asynchronous interfaces and is the protocol of choice when configuring DDR.

    Incorrect Answers & Explanations: **A**, **B**, **C**. Answer **A** is incorrect, because HDLC cannot be used with DDR. Answer **B** is incorrect, because SDLC cannot be used with DDR. Answer **C** is incorrect, because X.25 is a WAN protocol and is not used in the same aspect as HDLC, SDLC, or PPP.

14. While working as a Cisco engineer, you are assigned to help resolve an ISDN network design issue. You are not sure whether you should use PPP on the B channels. From the list of answers given, which answer provides the correct design for the solution needed?

    A. You should use PPP for the B channels and LAPD for the D channel.

    B. You should use HDLC for the B channels and PPP for the D channel.

    C. You should use CDP for the B channels and LAPD for the D channel.

    D. You should use PPP for the B channels and HDLC for the D channel.

    E. You should use LAPD for the B channels and HDLC for the D channel.

    Correct Answer & Explanation: **A**. Answer **A** is correct, because ISDN was created for the express purpose of enabling voice, video, and data over links. The B channel has a capacity of 64 Kbs and, with two B channels, a combined bandwidth value of 128 Kbs. The B channel is for sending data and uses either the PPP or HDLC encapsulation method. The CCNA exam focuses on the use of PPP for B channel encapsulation, but note that HDLC is valid per the standard. The D channel has a standard capacity of 16 Kbs, but different vendors implement a capacity as high as 64 Kbs. This is unusual, but nevertheless, it does exist. The D channel utilizes LAPD for its protocol and not the PPP or HDLC encapsulation method that is used over B channels.

    Incorrect Answers & Explanations: **B**, **C**, **D**, **E**. Answer **B** is incorrect, because although HDLC could be used on the B channels, PPP cannot be used for the D channel. Answer **C** is incorrect, because CDP cannot be used on the B channels, although LAPD can be used for the D channel. Answer **D** is incorrect, because although PPP could be used on the B channels, HDLC cannot be used for the D channel. Answer **E** is incorrect, because LAPD cannot be used on the B channels and HDLC cannot be used for the D channel.

15. You are a consultant working on a new network rollout. You have three Cisco routers that will be connected together over a WAN. You need to use a protocol on the connected interfaces on each router. From the list of options, which answer clearly defines which protocol is used on Cisco-based hardware by default?

A. PPP

B. HDLC

C. LAPB

D. CDP

E. SLIP

Correct Answer & Explanation: **B**. Answer **B** is correct, because HDLC is used on Cisco hardware interfaces by default. It is also proprietary in nature, much like CDP. The Cisco HDLC frame uses a proprietary "Type" field that usually runs into compatibility issues with third-party vendor equipment and is rarely used outside of Cisco-to-Cisco-connected gear.

Incorrect Answers & Explanations: **A**, **C**, **D**, **E**. Answer **A** is incorrect, because although it would make sense to have PPP used as the default, it is not and PPP would have to be configured on the interfaces instead. PPP encapsulation is usually recommended only for serial links between connected network devices from multiple vendors. Answer **C** is incorrect, because like PPP, LAPB is not configured on a Cisco interface by default. Answer **D** is incorrect, because CDP is also not configured on a Cisco interface by default, it is also not used as a WAN-based encapsulation protocol for transmitting frames. Answer **E** is incorrect, because SLIP (like PPP) is not set by default, and you likely would use PPP instead anyway because SLIP does not support multiprotocol communications.

16. You are a Cisco engineer troubleshooting a connectivity issue between two routers in a new network design. You enter the *debug ppp authentication* command on the Router B router. Based on the graphic in Figure 16.7 and, beneath that, the output received from the router, what's the most likely cause of this connectivity issue?

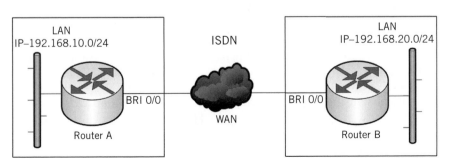

FIGURE 16.7

Debugging an ISDN Link

```
RouterA#debug ppp authentication
01:10:30:  %LINK-3-UPDOWN:  interface  BRI0/0:1,  changed
    state to up
01:10:30: BRI0/0:1 PPP: using dialer call direction
01:10:30: BRI0/0:1 PPP: treating connection as callin
01:10:30: BRI0/0:1 CHAP: O CHALLENGE id 10 len 24 from
    'RouterB'
01:10:30: BRI0/0:1 CHAP: 1 CHALLENGE id 10 len 23 from
    'RouterA'
01:10:30: BRI0/0:1 CHAP: waiting for peer to authenticate
    first
01:10:30: BRI0/0:1 CHAP: 1 RESPONSE id 10 len 24 from
    'RouterA'
01:10:30: BRI0/0:1 CHAP: unable to validate response,
    username RouterB not found
01:10:30: BRI0/0:1 CHAP: O FAILURE id 10 len 27 msg is
    'authentication failure'
01:10:30: BRI0/0:1 %ISDN-6-CONNECT: interface BRI0/0:1,
    is now connected to unknown
01:10:30:  %LINK-3-UPDOWN:  interface  BRI0/0:1,  changed
    state to down
<-output omitted->
```

A. Router A has only PAP configured.

B. The username and password are not properly configured on the Router B router.

C. You cannot connect two BRI interfaces together in this manner without using ISDN B channels.

D. Currently, your ISDN circuit is no longer available and is causing peers to drop authentication.

Correct Answer & Explanation: **B**. Answer **B** is correct, because if you carefully examine the debug generated by the *global debug PPP authentication* command, you will see that Routers A and B can communicate over the WAN link, and when authentication begins there is an issue with Router B's username and password set. Since *username RouterB* shows this fact, all other answers are incorrect.

Incorrect Answers & Explanations: **A**, **C**, **D**. Answer **A** is incorrect, because using CHAP is secure. PAP is less secure than CHAP, and if PAP were used on one end and CHAP on the other, authentication would not take place. Answer **C** is incorrect, because there is nothing wrong with the diagram or the routers' connectivity over the WAN. Also, you cannot use B channels in this fashion. Answer **D** is incorrect, because the ISDN link is up; otherwise, the authentication wouldn't take place. In the debug you can see that authentication is tried, but not successful.

17. You are working on your company's network and you are asked to deploy an authentication scheme that can help provide the most security offered with PPP. Based on the diagram in Figure 16.8, which statement best describes CHAP functionality and why is it more secure than PAP?

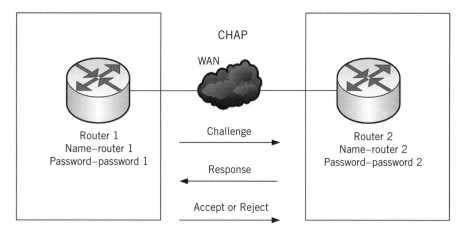

FIGURE 16.8

Viewing CHAP Used on a PPP Link

A. Using CHAP, the challenge and response used are based on the Two-Fish algorithm, thereby adding a layer of security to your authentication scheme.

B. Using CHAP, you will find that no challenge and response are used; rather, a system of key numbers connected in sequence when the receiving router receives them provides a layer of security.

C. You should use PAP for added security; CHAP is secure only if AES encryption and a digital certificate are added.

D. Using CHAP, the challenge and response used are based on the MD5 algorithm, thereby adding a layer of security to your authentication scheme.

Correct Answer & Explanation: **D**. Answer **D** is correct, because when CHAP is used over a WAN connection, the router receiving the connection sends a challenge which includes a random number. The MD5 algorithm is used to create a hash. This random number is input into an MD5 algorithm and will provide an encryption key. This is then used to send authentication information between Routers 1 and 2. Since CHAP uses encryption, it is inherently secure.

Incorrect Answers & Explanations: **A**, **B**, **C**. Answer **A** is incorrect, because although Two-Fish is a 128-bit block cipher that does provide a layer of security, Two-Fish is not used with CHAP, whereas MD5 is. Answer **B** is incorrect, because although a numbering system is used for the challenge and response set, there is no "sequence" of numbers that provide a layer of security. Answer **C** is incorrect, because you do not need a certificate. AES encryption is not used and PAP is absolutely not secure. When PAP is used over a WAN connection, the username and password are sent by the other configured router without using encryption, and all credentials are sent in clear text.

18. You are working on your company's network. When asked to deploy an authentication scheme that can help secure a PPP-based link, you decide to use PAP. Based on the diagram in Figure 16.9, what should you be concerned with when deploying PAP over an unsecured PPP link?

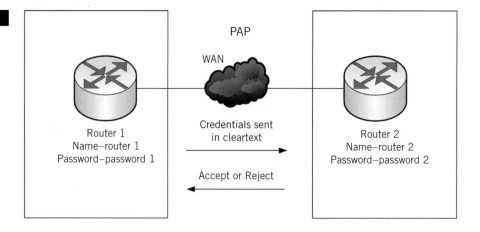

FIGURE 16.9

Viewing PAP Used on a PPP Link

A. The passwords for both Router 1 and Router 2 are easily guessed.

B. Credentials are broadcast to all routers configured on the WAN, instead of to a single peer.

C. Passwords are sent in clear text and can easily be captured by malicious users.

D. Routers 1 and 2 cannot communicate over the WAN link without the use of Frame Relay.

Correct Answer & Explanation: **C**. Answer **C** is correct, because when PAP is used over a WAN connection the username and password are sent by the dialing router without encryption.

Incorrect Answers & Explanations: **A**, **B**, **D**. Answer **A** is incorrect, because although the passwords configured may be easily guessed (or cracked) this has nothing to do with why PAP should or should not be used. The passwords can be changed without issue; the true problem here is that PAP sends any configured credentials in clear text. Answer **B** is incorrect, because PAP (or PPP) does not "broadcast" credentials to all devices connected on a network; a peer system is used. Answer **D** is incorrect, because the medium (or connection method) chosen does not play a part in why PAP would or wouldn't be secure and its inherent problems with security. The WAN connection type is inconsequential to the question itself.

19. You are a consulting engineer working on a WAN issue for a client. The client's systems are antiquated and use SLIP. You have a requirement to upgrade to PPP to support multiprotocol transmissions. What other reasons would you use PPP over SLIP? (Choose all that apply.)
    A. You want to use PPP instead of SLIP as PPP can operate at the transport layer.
    B. You want to use PPP instead of SLIP as SLIP does not function with TCP/IP.
    C. You want to use PPP instead of SLIP as PPP is more stable.
    D. You want to use PPP instead of SLIP as PPP has error-checking features included.

Correct Answers & Explanations: **C**, **D**. Answers **C** and **D** are correct, because PPP works at the data link layer, is more stable than SLIP, and has error-checking features included. Do note that both SLIP and PPP encapsulate datagrams and other network layer protocol information over point-to-point links, and that PPP negotiation consists of three phases: LCP, Authentication, and NCP.

Incorrect Answers & Explanations: **A**, **B**. Answer **A** is incorrect, because PPP does not operate at the transport layer of the OSI model. Answer **B** is incorrect, because SLIP does work with TCP/IP, although this has nothing to do with why you would want to use PPP instead. SLIP would not be used simply because it does not function with any other protocol stack except for TCP/IP.

20. You are a Cisco engineer and you need to configure PPP on a set of routers. PPP can be configured to work at which OSI model layer for Internet access?

A. Data link   **C.** Physical

B. Network   **D.** Application

Correct Answer & Explanation: **A**. Answer **A** is correct, because PPP works at the data link layer. Do not be confused by the words *Internet access*, as this may lead you to believe this is a Layer 3 operation.

Incorrect Answers & Explanations: **B**, **C**, **D**. Answer **B** is incorrect, because PPP functions primarily at the data link layer and works within the network layer, with IPCP as an example. Answer **C** is incorrect, because although physical connections are made via media (e.g., a modem), the physical connection is not where PPP would operate. Answer **D** is incorrect, because PPP functions only at the lower layers of the OSI model.

Index